For Dou

with appreciation

for your assistance and

your continued frienship

Jim Darsh

8/4/90

THE GREAT DETECTIVE PICTURES

by
JAMES ROBERT PARISH
and
MICHAEL R. PITTS

The Scarecrow Press, Inc.
Metuchen, N.J., & London
1990

British Library Cataloguing-in-Publication data available

Library of Congress Cataloging-in-Publication Data
Parish, James Robert.
    The great detective pictures / by James Robert Parish & Michael
R. Pitts.
            p.   cm.
    Includes bibliographical references (p.)
    ISBN 0-8108-2286-5 (alk. paper)
    1. Detective and mystery films—Catalogs.   I. Pitts, Michael R.
    II. Title.
PN1995.9.D4P37   1990
016.79143'655—dc20   90-8551

To the memory of
cinema historian Don Miller
(1928-1982)

CONTENTS

ACKNOWLEDGMENTS

Academy of Motion Picture Arts & Sciences Library

Beverly Hills Public Library

Richard Bojarski

John Cocchi

Howard Davis

Film Favorites (Bob & Charles Smith)

Kim Holston

The Library of Congress: Motion Picture, Broadcasting & Recorded
Sound Division

Doug McClelland

Alvin H. Marill

Jim Meyer

Peter Miglierini

Arleen Schwartz

Gerald F. Vaughn

Dr. Ray White

Editorial Consultant: T. Allan Taylor

INTRODUCTION

When Edgar Allan Poe created the character of Parisian police detective C. August Dupin for his trio of short stories, "Murders in the Rue Morgue" (1841), "Mystery of Marie Roget" (1842) and "The Purloined Letter" (1844), he began, or is credited with beginning, the perennially popular cycle of the fictional detective, a character which has translated well to the other entertainment media: stage, radio, films and television. Ironically, Poe's creation, however, has never been appropriately brought to the screen since the stories in which he appeared have been made into horror movies rather than the detective stories their author intended.

THE GREAT DETECTIVE PICTURES is a continuation of our long-running *The Great . . . Pictures* book series and here we delve into more than 350 feature-length films (plus serials and made-for-television movies) dealing with fictional sleuths and their cinematic adventures. As we have noted before, the word "Great" in the title refers to the specific film genre covered and *not* to all the titles included as we continue to run the gamut from the very best to the very worst, with lots of selections in between. Of course, we cannot include every English-language detective film ever made in one volume, so please let us know if your favorite is missing or you would like us to discuss a specific title. We are happy to incorporate such suggestions into future volumes.

Like most cinema genres, the detective film is not always easy to define. In writing this book we have uncovered a wide variety of screen characters who have ended up as detectives although many of them were hardly professionals. Among the films we have included, all kinds of characters (lawyers, newspaper reporters, criminologists, police detectives) have become detectives for some reason, usually to clear themselves or someone close to them of a crime, in most cases homicide. Naturally we have tried to include mostly films dealing strictly with professional private eyes, but overall we have taken a broad definition of the detective film in making our inclusions.

In writing this book it has been revealing to note how the image

ix

Introduction

of the fictional detective has changed with the passing of time, especially since the fictional sleuth has now been a very popular character for at least a century. Although Edgar Allan Poe started it all, it was probably Sir Arthur Conan Doyle's 1887 novel about Sherlock Holmes, *Study in Scarlet*, which established the continuing popularity of the genre. Holmes, of course, became immensely popular around the world, while in the United States such fictional sleuths as Nick Carter and Craig Kennedy developed their own huge followings. After the turn of the century another type of character appeared, the gentleman thief pursued by a detective. This category came from France in the guise of Raffles and Arsène Lupin. Again, an American counterpart soon emerged in Louis Joseph Vance's Michael Lanyard, The Lone Wolf, who gave up thievery for the right side of the law. Perhaps as much or more so than is true of other film genres, the fictional detective owes his success to literature, which first spawned him before his successful transition to celluloid. The movies were very quick to take advantage of the popularity of detectives, with SHERLOCK HOLMES BAFFLED (circa 1900) being the first of thousands of detective movies to follow.

In 1926 a major trend in the fictional detective took place when Willard Huntington Wright, under the pen name of S. S. Van Dine, created the character of Philo Vance in *The Benson Murder Case*. Vance was a wealthy, erudite gentleman who, like Sherlock Holmes, used his cerebral abilities to solve cases. Henceforth, for a decade or more, sleuths, both in book and on film, were mostly solving cases at remote estates, creepy old houses or at chic weekend parties. Of course, Agatha Christie also had a huge influence on the genre and her Belgian sleuth Hercule Poirot predated Vance by six years, having first appeared in print in 1920 in *The Mysterious Affair at Styles*. Still, Philo Vances' influence on the detective film cannot be overemphasized; most of the Van Dine novels were translated successfully to film, spawning a whole raft of well dressed, highly educated gentleman detectives who solved a wide range of killings, mostly among the well-to-do.

Other fictional detectives emerged and many were translated to movies. Perhaps the most enduring of these was Earl Derr Biggers' Chinese sleuth, Charlie Chan, who had a lengthy film life thanks mainly to his being enacted so expertly by Warner Oland and later by Sidney Toler. Chan also made way for two more Oriental detectives, John P. Marquand's Mr. Moto and Hugh Wiley's Mr. Wong. In addition, the genre bred such continually popular detectives as Ellery Queen; Erle Stanley Gardner's Perry Mason; Chester Gould's cartoon character, Dick Tracy; and from England, Mr. J. G. Reeder, a creation of the master thriller writer, Edgar Wallace, as well as

Introduction

Leslie Charteris' long-enduring adventurer, Simon Templar (better known as The Saint). All of these, and more, had long literary and cinema runs (and often TV series as well). However, other successful literary sleuths, such as Nero Wolfe and Lord Peter Wimsey, for one reason or another, failed to last long on the screen. Probably the best known type of private eye, again with origins in the written word, is the hard-boiled detective, as exemplified in the writings of Dashiell Hammett, Raymond Chandler and scores of others who worked for such pulp magazines as *Black Mask*. Hammett and Chandler were among the very few of the group who managed to win lasting fame, successfully enlarging their gumshoes' daring adventures for full-length novels. While Hammett's *The Maltese Falcon* (1930) has been filmed three times and copied scores more, with the 1941 movie version being considered perhaps the best detective film of all-time, his other works, outside of The Thin Man series and a TV version of *The Dain Curse* (1929), have remained untouched cinematically. Chandler, on the other hand, has had all of his Philip Marlowe novels, except the last one, *Playback* (1958), filmed at least once and several more than once. (For example, *Farewell, My Lovely*, 1940, to date has had three cinema versions.) Naturally, the popularity on film of such hard-boiled private eyes as Sam Spade and Philip Marlowe brought many followers, some from literature like Brett Halliday's [Davis Dresser] Michael Shayne, but most were screen originals who had a solo run on film.

Contrary to this trend was the popular continuing detective film series of the 1930s and 1940s, featuring fictional sleuths who had ongoing motion picture series made about their exploits. Among these were Boston Blackie, Bulldog Drummond, Charlie Chan, The Crime Doctor, The Falcon, The Lone Wolf, Michael Shayne, Mr. Moto, Mr. Wong, Perry Mason, and The Saint. More often than not, these properties catered to their individual stars and were mainly inexpensive screen vehicles for their cinematic personalities: Basil Rathbone and Nigel Bruce *were* Sherlock Holmes and Dr. Watson; Tom Conway *was* The Falcon, Warren William *was* The Lone Wolf, Warner Baxter *was* The Crime Doctor, Richard Dix *was* The Whistler, etc. These series sleuths had a long and profitable run on film, but, like the "B" Western, they were swallowed up by television, which translated some of their adventures to half-hour TV series episodes.

Another interesting aspect of 1930s and 1940s cinema (and fictional) detectives is the number of distaff sleuths. While individual films like MISS PINKERTON (1932) and MR. AND MRS. NORTH (1941) displayed female snoopers, the genre also included several series based around the exploits of women who outsmarted their male counterparts—usually police detectives—in crime solving. Among them were Stuart Palmer's beloved Miss Hildegarde Withers (played to perfection in a trio of RKO features by Edna May Oliver), Mignon G. Eberhart's Nurse Sarah Keate (whose name kept changing from entry to entry), newshound Torchy Blane, and Carolyn Keene's perennial teenager, Nancy Drew. There were a number of one-shot lady detectives too, such as Jane Wyman in PRIVATE DETECTIVE (1939), Stephanie Bachelor in THE UNDERCOVER WOMAN (1946), and Adela Mara in EXPOSED (1947), to name just a few. In addition, Dashiell Hammett's Nick and Nora Charles, from The Thin Man series, resulted in a whole host of husband-and-wife sleuths in screwball murder mysteries such as THERE'S ALWAYS A WOMAN (1938), FAST AND LOOSE (1939) and MR. AND MRS. NORTH (1941). While the female detective seemed to fade from the screen for a time, she came back in the 1960s with Margaret Rutherford as Agatha Christie's eccentric Miss Jane Marple, a character which has since populated a number of posh theatrical and TV features.

Radio and television (as our supplemental listing notes) programmed loads of detective series and in the post-World War II era hard-bitten gumshoes such as Mickey Spillane's Mike Hammer emerged. Nearly forgotten were the debonair Philo Vance and Tom Lawrence (The Falcon) or the calculating Mr. Moto, or even the slightly seedy Philip Marlowe. In Hammer and his ilk was exhibited a tough, hard-nosed type who made law and order on his own terms, turning the weapons of the criminals against themselves for ultimate victory. As court decisions encroached more and more on law enforcement, fictional detectives became even more aggressive in righting wrongs in their own way, using their own form of anarchy to enforce justice. Lew Archer, Tony Rome and Travis McGee are among these later-day operatives, while in the 1960s a hazy combination of detective and super agent evolved in the screen personas of such characters as James Bond, Lemmy Caution and Nick Carter, the latter now revitalized as the secret-agent hero of scores of globe-trotting novel adventures.

With all of these various guises for cinema sleuths since the movies were born, it is interesting to note that real private eyes have rarely been depicted as they are in actuality, either in fiction or on film. Don Miller, in his article "Private Eyes," in the Autumn 1975, issue of *Focus on Film* magazine, noted that one of the most realistic of cinema gumshoes was the one played by Lou Lubin in the 1943 psychological horror film, THE SEVENTH VICTIM. Miller wrote, "Lubin was one Irving August, a seedy, rodent-faced private eye, not a very good one, who gets in over his head investigating a cult of devil worshippers and quickly winds up a corpse propped up unceremoniously on a subway train. Hammett knew (did Chandler?)—but was inclined to romanticize for purposes of fiction—the truism, that on average, private investigators are neither very adventurous nor particularly bright, and when involved with some case of proportions will, more oft often than not, blow it." Here Miller hit the nail on the head, for the detective, that modern-day knight in shining armor, is in reality a part of a basically mundane profession, which has had to be greatly embellished (like the cowboy) for its perennial entertainment value.

Still, fictional detectives have provided countless hours of entertainment as readers, viewers and listeners have traveled down many a darkened path and mean street with them in solving a plethora of crimes. No doubt this audience participation is one of the reasons why the fictional sleuth remains so enduring (along with being a strong individualist) and the detective genre, both in print and on film, appears to have no diminution in sight. Thanks to the medium of television, many old detective feature films were saved from oblivion. And now, thanks to home video, many of these films—some not seen since the dawn of TV—are available again for viewing.

We hope this volume will serve as a useful reference companion for such explorations by fans, either for a viewpoint or two on a film already seen or to whet the appetite for a title yet to be seen. Whatever the use, our opinions on these films are shared for the reader's knowledge and enjoyment and are hardly intended to be the final word on any movie. After all, films are to be enjoyed, no matter what our likes and dislikes as they vary from movie to movie. It is simply our goal to provide detailed information and a discussion of a wide variety of detective movies. We would appreciate additions, corrections, or comments you may have, sent in care of the publisher.

With armchair in place, deerstalker in hand and comfort insured, sit back and relive some of the glorious moments of cinematic detection. "Come, Watson, Come!. . . . The game is afoot. . . ."

James Robert Parish
Michael R. Pitts
December 1988

GREAT DETECTIVE PICTURES

ACCOMPLICE (Producers Releasing Corp., 1946) 66 minutes.
Producer, John K. Teaford; director, Walter Comes; based on
the novel *Simon Lash, Private Detective* by Frank Gruber; screenplay,
Irving Elman, Gruber; art director, Frank Dexter; music, Alexander
Laszlo; assistant director, B. C. Gottlieb; camera, Jockey Feindel;
editor, Robert Jahns.

Richard Arlen (Simon Lash); Veda Ann Borg (Joyce Bonniwell);
Tom Dugan (Eddie Slocum); Michael Branden (Sheriff Rucker);
Marjorie Manners (Evelyn Price); Earle Hodgins (Marshal Jeff
Bailey); Francis Ford (Peter Connors); Edward Earle (Jim Bonniwell);
Herbert Rawlinson (Vincent Springer).

"Racing Wheels . . . Spitting Bullets . . . Flaming Love . . .
Reach New Heights of Thrilling Suspense!" read the poster blurb
for ACCOMPLICE, based on Frank Gruber's 1941 detective thriller *Simon Lash, Private Detective*, with Gruber co-authoring the
scenario with Irving Elman. Unfortunately, a minimal budget and
bland direction greatly hindered the film and no further Simon Lash
films were forthcoming, although Richard Arlen was well-cast as the
glamorless, hard-driving and not overly likable gumshoe—perhaps
a portrait closer to reality than many other celluloid sleuths.

Intellectual private eye Simon Lash (Richard Arlen) is hired by a
beautiful woman (Veda Ann Borg) to locate her wealthy, but
missing, spouse. The trail leads to a desert hideout where the man
apparently committed suicide. However, Lash does not accept this
theory. With the aid of his bumbling handyman (Tom Dugan), Lash
gets to the bottom of the case, proving that the man was murdered,
and brings in the killer. Helping the investigation is bright Sheriff
Rucker (Michael Branden) and hindering is corrupt Marshal Jeff
Bailey (Earle Hodgins).

When it was released *Variety* pegged the programmer as a "dull
whodunit" and retrospective reviewers of ACCOMPLICE have not
been overly kind either. In his article "Private Eyes" (*Focus on Film*,
Autumn, 1975), Don Miller termed it "mediocre," and in *The*

Richard Arlen in ACCOMPLICE (1946).

Detective in Film (1972), William K. Everson labeled the picture "above average" for Producers Releasing Corporation (PRC), but added that it was ". . . concerned more with action than detection and [was] afflicted with an artificially prolonged climactic chase. Lash was a surly and unattractive hero." Worse came from Jon Tuska in *The Detective in Hollywood* (1978): "The wretched acting wasn't helped by the wall-to-wall music track, which only occasionally reflected what was happening on the screen."

THE ADVENTURE OF SHERLOCK HOLMES' SMARTER BROTHER (Twentieth Century-Fox, 1975) Color 91 minutes.
Producer, Richard A. Roth; associate producer, Charles Orme; director/screenplay, Gene Wilder; production designer, Terry Marsh; set decorator, Peter Howitt; costumes, Ruth Myers; music, John Morris; orchestrators, Jonathan Tunick, Morris; choreography, Alan Johnson; assistant director, David Tomblin; stunt coordinator, William Hobbs; sound, Simon Kaye; sound editor, Dino Di Campo; special effects, Roy Whybrow; camera, Gerry Fisher; editor, Jim Clark.

Gene Wilder (Sigerson Holmes); Madeline Kahn (Jenny Hill); Marty Feldman (Sergeant Orville Sacker); Dom DeLuise (Gambetti); Leo McKern (Professor Moriarty); Roy Kinnear (Finney—Moriarty's Aide); John LeMesurier (Lord Redcliff); Douglas Wilmer (Sherlock Holmes); Thorley Walters (Dr. John H. Watson); George Silver (Bruner); Susan Field (Queen Victoria); Nicholas Smith (Hunkston); Tommy Godfrey (Fred); John Hollis (Colonel Von Stulberg); Aubrey Morris (Coach Driver); Joseph Behramannis (Russian); Wolfe Morris (Frenchman); Julian Orchard (Man in Tails); Kenneth Beade (Butler); Michael Crane (Renato); Tony Sympson (Opera Conductor); and: Richard A. Roth.

Following his success as an actor in the outrageous film genre spoofs presented by Mel Brooks in the 1970s, Gene Wilder wrote the story for this frantic Sherlock Holmes send-up, and also made his directorial debut with it. With a supporting cast (Madeline Kahn, Dom DeLuise, Marty Feldman) from the Brooks' stock company, the movie proved to be successful, grossing $9,400,000 in domestic theatrical rentals. Overall, though, this picture is far less amusing than it might have been and about the only elements detective film buffs can appreciate are that Douglas Wilmer and Thorley Walters play their roles as Holmes and Watson straight while Leo McKern is a deliciously hissable Moriarty.

In 1891 London a secret state document has been stolen from Lord Redcliff (John LeMesurier) and Queen Victoria (Susan Field) has requested Sherlock Holmes (Douglas Wilmer) to retrieve it

Douglas Wilmer, Madeline Kahn and Marty Feldman in THE ADVENTURE OF SHERLOCK HOLMES' SMARTER BROTHER (1975).

since the future of Britain rests upon its timely recovery. Holmes suspects Professor Moriarty (Leo McKern) of the theft and enlists the aid of Dr. Watson (Thorley Walters) in an involved scheme in which the two will pretend to leave the country with all of Holmes' current cases being handed over to his jealous younger brother, Sigerson Holmes (Gene Wilder). Holmes and Watson will then work incognito to retrieve the vital document. Sigerson gladly accepts the hand-me-downs, aided by his pal Sergeant Orville Sacker (Marty Feldman) of Scotland Yard's records office who has a very useful photographic memory. One of their new clients is music hall entertainer Jenny Hill (Madeline Kahn) who is being blackmailed by opera singer Gambetti (Dom DeLuise). Sherlock realizes that Jenny's problem is entangled with that of the missing document (since her father turns out to be Lord Redcliff). Holmes and Watson work to solve the mystery while Sigerson (after interrupting a performance of the opera *The Masked Ball*) ends up battling Moriarty in a tower above the River Thames.

"Unlike Billy Wilder's affectionate pastiche [THE PRIVATE LIFE OF SHERLOCK HOLMES, 1970, *q.v.*] this SHERLOCK

HOLMES has little to do with the original: the period sets are unnecessarily cluttered and the appearance of Sherlock and Dr. Watson is a perfunctory addition. . . . Unlike his mentor Mel Brooks, with whom he shares a schoolboy fondness for lavatory jokes, Gene Wilder demonstrates a Chaplinesque tendency to take romance seriously" (John Pym, British *Monthly Film Bulletin*). Hugh James wrote in *Films in Review* magazine (January 1976) that this madcap comedy is "overproduced, overwritten" and "Lovers of Holmes stories will be outraged they will have missed Wilder's point of view; unfortunately, because he has so fuzzed it, the film seems to have none."

THE ADVENTURES OF NICK CARTER (NBC-TV, 2/20/72) Color 78 minutes.

Executive producer, Richard Irving; producer, Stanley Kallis; associate producer, Arthur D. Hilton; director, Paul Krasny; teleplay, Ken Pettus; art director, Henry Bumstead; music, John Andrew Tartaglia; camera, Alric Edens; editor, Robert F. Shugrue.

Robert Conrad (Nick Carter); Shelley Winters (Bess Tucker); Broderick Crawford (Otis Duncan); Neville Brand (Captain Dan Keller); Pernell Roberts (Neal Duncan); Pat O'Brien (Hallelujah Harry); Sean Garrison (Lloyd Deams); Laraine Stephens (Joyce Jordan); Dean Stockwell (Freddy Duncan); Brooke Bundy (Roxy O'Rourke); Jaye P. Morgan (Plush Horse Singer); Sorrell Booke (Dr. Zimmerman); Ned Glass (Maxie); Joe Maross (Archer); Arlene Martel (Flo); Byron Morrow (Sam Bates); Arthur Peterson (Coroner); Booth Colman (Parsons); Warren Parker (Butler); Larry Watson (Desk Sergeant); Leon Lontoc (Desk Clerk); James McCallion (Manager); Charles Davis (Minister); William Benedict (Newsboy); Elizabeth Harrower (Sister Effie); Deidre Hudson (Ivy Duncan).

Fictional detective Nick Carter has been one of the most prolific of literary sleuths, having been the subject of some 1,500 stories and novels, beginning in *The New York Weekly* in 1886 and continuing through various formats and publications into the 1980s. Nick Carter's screen career dates back to 1908 but he had surprisingly few cinema outings in comparison with other detectives, although Walter Pidgeon portrayed a modernized Carter in a trio of modestly-budgeted MGM features: NICK CARTER, MASTER DETECTIVE (1939), *q.v.*, PHANTOM RAIDERS (1940), and SKY MURDER (1940). In the 1960s Eddie Constantine was Nick Carter in two screen adventures in French: NICK CARTER VA TOUT CASSER (1964) and NICK CARTER ET LE TREFLE ROUGE (1965). It was not until 1972 that Nick Carter finally was

portrayed in the sound era as he was originally presented on paper—
as a sleuth in turn-of-the century New York City.

Universal-TV's THE ADVENTURES OF NICK CARTER,
like most TV features, was conceived as a series pilot, but it did not
sell. The plot is set in 1912 Manhattan with detective Nick Carter
(Robert Conrad) trying to avenge the murder of a fellow operative
and finding the case involves the disappearance of the wife of a rich
playboy. The search takes him to nightclub owner Bess Tucker
(Shelley Winters), corrupt robber baron Otis Duncan (Broderick
Crawford) and his son Neal (Pernell Roberts), likable underworld
figure Hallelujah Harry (Pat O'Brien), and crooked police Captain
Dan Keller (Neville Brand).

In *TV Guide to the Movies* (1974), Judith Crist complained,
"There's little more than cheap-jack nostalgia and routine plotting. . . ." In *Movies on TV and Videocassette: 1988-89* (1987), Steven
H. Scheuer summarizes, "Flavor of the era is nicely captured in this
glossy production, but it's familiar gangland stuff."

Fortunately, Nick Carter was reincarnated in the 1960s as a
super secret agent in scores of paperback books which have sold into
the millions of copies.

ADVENTURES OF SHERLOCK HOLMES (1905) 8 minutes.
   Director, J. Stuart Blackston; screenplay Theodore Liebler.
   Maurice Costello (Sherlock Holmes).
   A.k.a.: HELD FOR RANSOM.

THE ADVENTURES OF SHERLOCK HOLMES (Twentieth Cen-
tury-Fox, 1939) 85 minutes.
   Associate producer, Gene Markey; director, Alfred Werker;
based on the play *Sherlock Holmes* by William Gillette; screenplay,
Edwin Blum, William Drake; art directors, Richard Day, Hans
Peters; music director, Cyril J. Mockridge; camera, Leon Shamroy;
editor, Robert Bischoff.
   Basil Rathbone (Sherlock Holmes); Nigel Bruce (Dr. Watson);
Ida Lupino (Ann Brandon); Alan Marshal (Jerrold Hunter); Terry
Kilburn (Billy); George Zucco (Professor Moriarty); Henry Stephenson
(Sir Ronald Ramsgate); E. E. Clive (Inspector Bristol); Arthur Hohl
(Bassick); May Beatty (Mrs. Jameson); Peter Willes (Lloyd Brandon);
Mary Gordon (Mrs. Hudson); Holmes Herbert (Justice); George
Regas (Mateo); Mary Forbes (Lady Conynham); Frank Dawson
(Dawes); William Austin (Stranger); Anthony Kemble Cooper (To-
ny); Denis Green (Sergeant of Guard); Robert Noble (Jury Fore-
man); Neil Fitzgerald (Court Clerk); Leonard Mudie (Barrows); Ivan
Simpson (Gates).

British release title: SHERLOCK HOLMES.
Sherlock Holmes first came to the screen ca. 1900 in the brief
Edison film, SHERLOCK HOLMES BAFFLED. In 1905 Vitagraph
produced an eight-minute one-reeler entitled ADVENTURES OF
SHERLOCK HOLMES, starring early film idol Maurice Costello as
the intrepid Holmes. The plot had the sleuth rescuing a young
woman abducted by a kidnap gang. The title, THE ADVENTURES
OF SHERLOCK HOLMES, was used again by Twentieth Century-
Fox in 1939, but this far more elaborate outing owed its plotline
more to William Gillette's perennial play, *Sherlock Holmes* (1899),
than to the long lost Vitagraph short.

The 1939 edition was a sequel to the immensely popular THE
HOUND OF THE BASKERVILLES (1939), *q.v.*, and it cemented
Basil Rathbone and Nigel Bruce as the public's image as Holmes and
Dr. Watson. Set in gaslight era London, the film opens with Professor Moriarty (George Zucco) acquitted of a murder charge just as
Holmes (Basil Rathbone) arrives with sufficient evidence to hang
him. Freed, Moriarty informs Holmes he will commit the greatest
crime of all time and eliminate the meddlesome detective at the
same time. At his digs at 221B Baker Street, which he shares with
friend and confidant Dr. Watson (Nigel Bruce), Holmes is asked by
old friend Sir Ronald Ramsgate (Henry Stephenson) to be on hand
at the Tower of London when the emerald, "The Star of Delhi,"
arrives because there has been a threat to steal the gem. At the same
time, Holmes accepts the case of pretty Ann Brandon (Ida Lupino),
whose brother Lloyd (Peter Willes) has received a death threat in the
form of a sketch of an albatross hung around a man's neck. It is the
same threat which came to her father a decade before, predicting his
sudden demise. Ann's fiancé, lawyer Jerrold Hunter (Alan Marshal),
resents her consulting Holmes, and when Lloyd is found murdered it
is Jerrold who is accused of the crime. Holmes proves to the local
police inspector (E. E. Clive) that the man is innocent. Despite the
fact that Ann receives a similar death threat, Holmes urges her to
attend a society party and he appears in the guise of an entertainer to
keep a watchful eye on her. Ann, however, has a row with Jerrold
and goes into the garden, where a man disguised as a South American gaucho tries to kill her with a bolas. Holmes extracts from the
would-be gaucho that Moriarty put him up to the crime. Realizing
that Ann was being used by the Professor to get him off the trail of
the Tower of London robbery, Holmes heads there to find that the
Professor has already attempted to steal the Crown Jewels. In a
struggle between the two, Moriarty is hurled by Holmes from the
top of the Tower to his demise in the streets below.

In the *New York Herald-Tribune*, Howard Barnes reports, "Far from seeming old-fashioned, the mystery melodrama takes on heightened effectiveness and rivals any contemporary murder mystery that you are likely to find. . . ." Ron Haydock observes in *Deerstalker! Holmes and Watson on Screen* (1978) that it ". . . certainly rivals THE HOUND for the best Holmes picture ever . . . the picture was in many ways really better than Rathbone's Hound film. For one thing, all the action this time was centered around London and the Baker Street digs, and the story was complete with many amazing Holmes deductions and complex, intriguing problems for him to solve." Haydock appreciated that the film ". . . also presented the masterful villainy of the arch fiend Moriarty, who was extremely well played by George Zucco: appropriately menacing and diabolically insidious; the very epitome of subtle, chortling, plotting evil."

Despite the public success of THE ADVENTURES OF SHERLOCK HOLMES and its predecessor, no further Holmes features followed from Twentieth Century-Fox. It was not until 1942 that Basil Rathbone and Nigel Bruce returned to these screen roles for their Universal series. The duo, however, did continue the parts on radio, beginning in 1939 with "The Adventures of Sherlock Holmes" series; Rathbone stayed with it until 1946 when Tom Conway took over as Holmes, while Nigel Bruce remained as Watson.

AFTER THE THIN MAN (Metro-Goldwyn-Mayer, 1936) 110 minutes.

Producer, Hunt Stromberg; director, W. S. Van Dyke II; story, Dashiell Hammett; screenplay, Frances Goodrich, Albert Hackett; songs: Arthur Freed and Nacio Herb Brown; Bob Wright, Chet Forrest, and Walter Donaldson; music director, Herbert Stothart; art director, Cedric Gibbons; sound, Douglas Shearer; camera, Oliver T. Marsh; editor, Robert J. Kern.

William Powell (Nick Charles); Myrna Loy (Nora Charles); James Stewart (David Graham); Joseph Calleia (Dancer); Elissa Landi (Selma Landis); Jessie Ralph (Aunt Katherine Forrest); Alan Marshal (Robert Landis); Sam Levene (Lieutenant Abrams); Dorothy McNulty [Penny Singleton] (Polly Byrnes); Dorothy Vaughn (Charlotte); Maude Turner Gordon (Helen); Teddy Hart (Floyd Casper); William Law (Lum Kee); William Burress (General); Thomas Pogue (William); George Zucco (Dr. Adolph Kammer); Tom Ricketts (Henry, the Butler); Paul Fix (Phil Byrnes); Joe Caits (Joe); Joe Phillips (Willie); Edith Kingdon (Hattie); John T. Murray (Jerry); John Kelly (Harold); Clarence Kolb (Lucius); Zeffie Tilbury (Lucy); Donald Briggs, Frederic Santley, Jack Norton (Reporters); Baldwin Cooke, Sherry Hall, Jack E. Raymond (Photographers); Ed Dearing (Bill, the San Francisco Policeman); Dick Rush (San Francisco Detective); Monte Vandergrift, Eddie Allen, Jimmy Lucas (Men); Heinie Conklin (Trainsman); Mary Gordon (Rose the Cook); Ben Hall (Butcher Boy); George H. Reed (Porter); John Butler (Racetrack Tout); Vince Barnett (Wrestler's Manager); Ethel Jackson (Girl with Fireman); Arthur Housman (Man Rehearsing Welcoming Speech); Jack Daley (Bartender); Bert Scott (Man at Piano); George Guhl (San Francisco Police Captain); Norman Willis (Fireman); Edith Craig (Girl with Fireman); Kewpie Martin (Boy Friend of Girl Standing on Hands); Bert Lindley (Station Agent); James Blaine (San Francisco Policeman); Guy Usher (Chief of Detectives); Bob Murphy (Arresting Detective); Harry Tyler (Fingers); Bobby Watson (Leader of Late Crowd); Eric Wilton (Peter the Butler); Henry Roquemore (Actor's Agent); Constantine Romanoff (Wrestler); Sam McDaniel (Pullman Porter); Ernie Alexander (Filing Clerk in Morgue); Louis Natheaux (Racetrack Tout); Jonathan Hale (Night City Editor); Jennie Roberts (Girl Who Works with Jerry); Charlie Arnt (Drunk); Harvey Parry (Man Who Stands on Hands); Jesse Graves (Red Cap); Alice H. Smith (Emily); Richard Powell (Surprised Policeman); Cecil Elliott, Phyllis Coghlan (Servants); Frank Otto (Taxi Driver); Jack Adair (Escort of Dizzy Blonde); Irene Coleman, Claire Rochelle, Jean Barr, Jane Tallant (Chorus Girls); Sue Moore (Sexy Blonde); Edith Trivers (Hat Check Girl); George Taylor (Eddie); Lee Phelps (Flop House Proprietor); Chester Gan (Chinese Waiter); Richard Loo (Chinese Headwaiter); Lew Harvey, Jimmy Brewster (Thugs); Harlan Briggs (Burton Forrest); Billy Benedict (Newsboy); Murray Alper (Kid); Charles Trowbridge (Police Examiner); Eadie Adams (Girl).

Nick Charles (William Powell) and his wife Nora (Myrna Loy) come to San Francisco's Nob Hill to celebrate their wedding anniversary with her Aunt Katherine (Jessie Ralph). Among the guests are relative Selma Landis (Elissa Landi), whose two-timing husband Robert (Alan Marshal) is murdered. The police, led by Lieutenant Abrams (Sam Levene), place the wife under arrest. Nick and Nora, however, feel she is innocent and the woman's brother, David Graham (James Stewart), joins them in trying to prove her innocence. Nick comes across a number of people involved in the homicide, including gangster Dancer (Joseph Calleia), corrupt lawyer Floyd Casper (Teddy Hart), Chinese culprit Lum Kee (William Law), and the dead man's girlfriend, Polly Byrnes (Dorothy McNulty [Penny Singleton]). Two more murders occur, including that of Dancer, before Nick puzzles out the situation. He summons all the suspects and points out the killer, thus exonerating Selma. Nora then tells Nick they are expecting a new member in the Charles family.

This polished follow-up to the highly successful THE THIN MAN (1934), *q.v.*, is just as good as its predecessor, with the killer most difficult to spot. Although nearly two hours in running time (making it the longest entries in the series), AFTER THE THIN MAN moves quickly and is highly entertaining, especially in its variety of police and underworld denizens. Frank S. Nugent (*New York Times*) judged it "one of the most urbane comedies of the season" and acknowledged, ". . . Dashiell Hammett's sense of humor has endured, W. S. Van Dyke retains his directorial facility and William Powell and Myrna Loy still persuade us that Mr. and Mrs. Nick Charles are exactly the sort of people we should like to have on our calling list on New Year's Day and for all the rest of the year." To be noted is still youngish Jimmy Stewart in one of his few screen bad guy roles.

This film was followed three years later by ANOTHER THIN MAN, (*q.v.*) and by this time the title refers to the Charles' new son.

AGATHA CHRISTIE'S A CARIBBEAN MYSTERY (CBS-TV, 10/22/83) Color 100 minutes.

Producer, Stan Margulies; director, Robert Michael Lewis; based on the novel by Agatha Christie; teleplay, Sue Grafton, Steven Humphrey; art director, Robert Mackichan; music, Lee Holdridge; camera, Ted Voigtlander; editor, Les Green.

Helen Hayes (Miss Jane Marple); Barnard Hughes (Mr. Rafiel); Jameson Parker (Tim Kendall); Season Hubley (Molly Kendall); Swoosie Kurtz (Ruth Walter); Cassie Yates (Lucky Dyson); Zakes Mokae (Captain Daventry); Beth Howland (Evelyn Hillingdon); Maurice Evans (Major Geoffrey Palgrave); Lynne Moody (Victoria Johnson); George Innes (Edward Hillindon); Brock Peters (Dr. Graham); Mike Preston (Arthur Jackson); Bernard McDonald (Minister); Santos Morales (Miguel); Sam Scarber (Police Sergeant); Cecil Smith (Hotel Guest).

AGATHA CHRISTIE'S DEAD MAN'S FOLLY (CBS-TV, 1/8/ 86) Color 100 minutes.

Producer, Neil Hartley; director, Clive Donner; based on the novel by Agatha Christie; teleplay, Rod Browning; production designer, Brian Ackland-Snow; music, John Addison; camera, Curtis Clark; editor, Donald R. Rode.

Peter Ustinov (Hercule Poirot); Jean Stapleton (Ariadne Oliver); Constance Cummings (Mrs. Folliot); Tim Pigott-Smith (Sir George Stubbs); Jonathan Cecil (Captain Hastings); Kenneth Cranham (Inspector Bland); Susan Woolridge (Amanda Brewis); Christopher Guard (Alec Legge); Jeff Yagher (Eddie South); Nicolette Sheridan

Advertisement for AGATHA CHRISTIE'S DEAD MAN'S FOLLY (1986).

(Hattie Stubbs); Ralph Arliss (Michael Weyman); Caroline Langrishe (Sally Legge); James Gaddas (Young Foreign Man); Jimmy Gardner (Old Meredell); Pippa Hinchley (Marlene Tucker); Marjorie Yates (Mrs. Tucker); Leslie Schofield (Mr. Tucker); Vicky Murdock (Marilyn Tucker); Sandra Dickinson (Marilyn Gate); Alan Parnaby (Crew Man); Simon Cowell-Parker (Forensic Man); Siv Borg (Blond

Hostel Girl); Dorothea Phillips, Fanny Carby, Joanna Dickens (Women); Gerald Hely, Cyril Conway (Men).

AGATHA CHRISTIE'S MURDER IN THREE ACTS (CBS-TV, 9/30/86) Color 100 minutes.

Producer, Paul Waigner; director, Gary Nelson; based on the novel by Agatha Christie; teleplay, Scott Swanton; art director Fernando Ramirez; music, Alf Clausen; camera, Neal Roach; editor, Donald R. Rode.

Peter Ustinov (Hercule Poirot); Tony Curtis (Charles Cartwright); Emma Samms (Jennifer "Egg" Eastman); Jonathan Cecil (Captain Hastings); Fernando Allende (Ricardo Montoya); Pedro Armendariz (Colonel Mateo); Lisa Eichhorn (Cynthia Dayton); Dana Elcar (Dr. Walter Strange); Frances Lee McCain (Miss Milray); Diana Muldaur (Angela Stafford); Marian Mercer (Daisy Eastman); Nicholas Pryor (Freddie Dayton); Concetta Tomei (Janet Crisp); Jacqueline Evans (Mrs. Babbington); Angeles Gonzalez (Housekeeper); Philip Guilmant (Reverend Babbington); Claudia Guzman (Rosa); Rodolfo Hernandez (Miguel); Martin LaSalle (Doctor): Alma Levy (Nurse): Julio Monterde (Manager); Rene Pereyra (Waiter); Jose Chavez Trowe (Watchman).

AGATHA CHRISTIE'S MURDER IS EASY (CBS-TV, 1/2/82) Color 100 minutes.

Executive producer, David L. Wolper; producer, Stan Margulies; director, Claude Whatham; based on the novel *Easy to Kill* by Agatha Christie; teleplay, Carmen Culver; art director, Ian Whittaker; music, Gerald Fried; camera, Brian Tufano; editor, David Newhouse.

Bill Bixby (Luke Williams); Lesley-Anne Down (Bridget Conway); Olivia de Havilland (Honoria Waynflete); Helen Hayes (Lavinia Fullerton); Patrick Allen (Major Horton); Shane Briant (Dr. Thomas); Freddie Jones (Constable Reed); Leigh Lawson (Jimmy Lorrimer); Jonathan Pryce (Mr. Ellsworthy); Ivan Roberts (Vicar); Trevor T. Smith (Rivers); Anthony Valentine (Abbot); Timothy West (Easterfield); Carol MacReady (Mrs. Pierce); Diana Goodman (Rose Humbleby); Gordon Lord (King Edward); Frederick Wolfe (Avery); Patrick Wright (Attendant).

AGATHA CHRISTIE'S MURDER WITH MIRRORS (CBS-TV, 2/20/85) Color 100 minutes.

Executive producer, George Eckstein; producer, Neil Hartley; associate producer, Maria Padilla; director, Dick Lowry; based on the novel by Agatha Christie; teleplay, George Eckstein; art director, Leigh Malone; music, Richard Rodney Bennett; camera, Brian West; editor, Richard Bracken.

Helen Hayes (Miss Jane Marple); Bette Davis (Carrie Louise Serrocold); John Mills (Lewis Serrocold); Leo McKern (Inspector Curry); Liane Langland (Gina Markham); John Laughlin (Wally Markham); Dorothy Tutin (Mildred Strete); Anton Rodgers (Dr. Max Hargrove); Frances De La Tour (Miss Bellaver); John Woodvine (Christian Gilbranson); James Coombes (Steven Restarick); Tim Roth (Edgar Lawson); Christopher Fairbank (Sergeant Lake); Amanda Maynard (Miss Valentine).

AGATHA CHRISTIE'S SPARKLING CYANIDE (CBS-TV, 11/ 5/83) Color 100 minutes.

Producer, Stan Margulies; director, Robert Michael Lewis; based on the novel by Agatha Christie; teleplay, Robert Malcolm Young, Sue Grafton, Steven Humphrey; art director, Robert MacKichan; music, James DiPasquale; camera, Ted Voigtlander; editor, David Saxon.

Anthony Andrews (Tony Browne); Deborah Raffin (Iris Murdoch); Pamela Bellwood (Ruth Lessing); Nancy Marchand (Lucilla Drake); Josef Sommer (George Barton); David Huffman (Stephan Farraday); Christine Belford (Rosemary Barton); June Chadwick (Sandra Farraday); Barrie Ingham (Eric Kidderminster); Harry Morgan (Captain Kemp); Anne Rogers (Viola Kidderminster); Michael Woods (Victor Drake); Shera Danese (Christine Shannon); Ismael Carlo (Medical Examiner); Linda Hoy (Boat Manager); Abby Haman (Cabaret Singer); Juan Fernandez (Bus Boy); Eric Sinclair (Charles).

AGATHA CHRISTIE'S THIRTEEN AT DINNER (CBS-TV, 10/ 19/85) Color 100 minutes.

Producer, Neil Hartley; director, Lou Antonio; based on the novel by Agatha Christie; teleplay, Rod Browning; production designer, Andrew Sanders; music, John Addison; camera, Curtis Clark; editor, David A. Simmons.

Peter Ustinov (Hercule Poirot); Faye Dunaway (Jane Wilkinson [Lady Edgware]/Carlotta Adams); David Suchet (Inspector Japp); Jonathan Cecil (Captain Hastings); Bill Nighy (Ronald Marsh); Diane Keen (Jenny Driver); John Stride (Film Director); Benedict Taylor (Donald Ross); Lee Horsley (Bryan Martin); Allan Cuthbertson (Sir Montague Corner); Glyn Baker (Lord Edgware's Butler); John Barron (Lord George Edgware); Peter Clapham (Mr. Wildburn); Lesley Dunlop (Alice Bennett); Avril Elgar (Miss Carroll); Orianne Grievew (Serious Actress); Russell Keith-Grant (Moxon); Roger Milner (Duke of Merton's Footman); David Neville (Fluttering Young Man); Amanda Pays (Geraldine Marsh); John Quarmsby (Sir Montague's Butler); Geoffrey Rose (Duke of Merton); Pamela

Salem (Mrs. Wildburn); Jean Sincere (Ellis the Maid); Lou Antonio (Movie Producer); David Frost (Himself). Late in 1980 Warner Bros. Television, in association with David L. Wolper/Stan Margulies Productions, announced a production deal with Agatha Christie, Ltd., to make several big-budget television movies for the American small screen based on Miss Christie's works. The features were to be entitled: DESTINATION UNKNOWN, THE MAN IN THE BROWN SUIT, MURDER IS EASY, THE SECRET OF THE CHIMNEYS, and THEY CAME TO BAGHDAD. While seven Christie-derived telefeatures have been aired to date, only one of the above announced entries, MURDER IS EASY, has appeared. It was the premiere installment of this "Agatha Christie Mystery Theatre" series.

MURDER IS EASY, based on the 1939 novel *Easy to Kill*, was telecast on CBS-TV on January 2, 1982, and its ads exclaimed, "Cold-Blooded Murder. Hot-Blooded Love. He plays with rich men's money. She plays with rich men's hearts. Now, one of them is the prime suspect in the deadliest game of all!" The story opens on a train headed for London on which American tourist Luke Williams (Bill Bixby) meets elderly Lavinia Fullerton (Helen Hayes), who confides she is on her way to Scotland Yard to report the murder of three people in her home town of Wychwood. Williams privately scoffs at the dotty old woman's statement but begins to believe her when he sees her run down by a car when she disembarks at London. He goes to the small village to investigate the case on his own and finds that the prime suspects include Lavinia's old friend Honoria Waynflete (Olivia de Havilland) and beautiful Bridget Conway (Lesley-Anne Down), whom he romances. The TV movie won an Emmy Award for its costume design and Judith Crist in *TV Guide* magazine judged it "First-rate Agatha Christie. . . . It's good fun for armchair detectives."

In her review of MURDER IS EASY Judith Crist noted that Helen Hayes "makes us realize she'd be the ultimate [Miss] Marple," and it was that part that the veteran actress portrayed in the second Agatha Christie telefilm outing, A CARIBBEAN MYSTERY, telecast by CBS-TV on October 22, 1983. Filmed in Santa Barbara, California and advertised as "Murder In the Steamy Tropics," the made-for-television production has elderly Miss Jane Marple (Helen Hayes) arriving at a remote Caribbean resort to recover from a bout of pneumonia and there she befriends Major Geoffrey Palgrave (Maurice Evans), who is soon found murdered. Miss Marple deduces that the place is populated by a baker's dozen of suspects, including assorted guests, the near-bankrupt owners, and a strange house doctor (Brock Peters). As usual, the amateur detective pinpoints the killer. *TV Guide* magazine's Judith Crist judged, ". . . [It] is given its elegance not only by Christie's classic style and by Helen Hayes' charming portrait of the writer's elderly maiden sleuth, Miss Marple. It's also marked by a first-rate supporting cast. . . . Hayes, in fine form at 83, is the truest Marple to date. Christie would approve." The TV movie was based on Agatha Christie's 1964 novel, and with Miss Hayes in the lead assignment it offered an interesting contrast to the more earthy, bumbling, yet sincere performance by Dame Margaret Rutherford in the quartet of MGM Miss Marple theatrical features in the mid-1960s.

Following the completion of A CARIBBEAN MYSTERY, the same production crew made a third Agatha Christie TV film, SPARKLING CYANIDE, based on the 1945 novel, also called *Remembered Death*. The locale was switched from the author's native England to Pasadena, California. The plot has British journalist Tony Browne (Anthony Andrews) in California attending a dinner party hosted by wealthy Iris Murdoch (Deborah Raffin). During the evening Iris' sister Rosemary Barton (Christine Belford) and her husband George (Josef Sommer) die from drinking cyanide-laced champagne and Browne aids police Captain Kemp (Harry Morgan) in puzzling out the case and locating the murderer. The production gained an Emmy Award nomination for its costume designs, but in *TV Movies and Video Guide* (1988), Leonard Maltin assessed, "Deadly brew loses some of the Agatha Christie zing in this Americanization of her whodunit. . . . Average."

"Two of America's legendary stars create a lethal combination in Agatha Christie's most mysterious tale of murder ever," insisted the TV advertising for the fourth Christie TV movie, MURDER WITH MIRRORS, from her 1952 book, which CBS-TV telecast on February 20, 1985. Helen Hayes again starred as the intrepid Miss Jane Marple while Bette Davis portrayed her contemporary, Carrie Louise Serrocold, whose stepson Christian (John Woodvine) is murdered by an unknown assailant. Miss Marple comes to visit dear Carrie Louise at her remote country estate and finds the woman in frail health. Her husband, Lewis (John Mills), who tries to rehabilitate delinquent youths, tells Miss Marple that his wife has been secretly poisoned. Several family members are suspects in the case and, after another murder, local Inspector Curry (Leo McKern) investigates. However, it is Miss Marple who establishes the identity of the killer and that the motive was monetary. The movie was filmed at Brocket Hall, a thirteenth-century estate in England's Hertfordshire. While Helen Hayes was again quite good as the plucky and intuitive Miss Marple, Bette Davis was hard to watch in her second-billed role. Miss Davis, who was recovering from the effects of cancer surgery and a stroke, was painfully delicate and visibly ill-at-ease in the feature.

For the fifth Agatha Christie CBS-TV movie outing, THIR-TEEN AT DINNER (telecast October 19, 1985), Hercule Poirot was the "guest detective" and he was portrayed by Peter Ustinov. Ustinov had previously played the moustachioed Belgian in two theatrical features, DEATH ON THE NILE (1978) and MURDER UNDER THE SUN (1982), *qq.v.* This telefilm was based on the 1933 novel which had been filmed previously as LORD EDGWARE DIES (1934), *q.v.* The updated version has Hercule Poirot (Peter Ustinov) appearing on David Frost's (himself) television talk program where he meets actress Jane Wilkinson (Faye Dunaway) who invites him to dinner at her estate. Jane, also known as Lady Edgware, informs Poirot she would kill to obtain a divorce from her husband, Lord Edgware (John Barron). The latter confides to the sleuth he is willing to give her a divorce. Lord Edgware, however, is murdered and Scotland Yard Inspector Japp (David Suchet) wants to arrest Lady Edgeware for the crime. However, Poirot insists that she is innocent. A second murder occurs before the detective (who believes in "order and method") realizes that the crimes have been committed by a clever impersonator of the accused. Judith Crist, in her *TV Guide* magazine review, decided the movie has "special appeal," adding, ". . . it provides the Christie-and-complexity of plot, variety of setting and mix of characters."

On January 8, 1986, CBS-TV telecast DEAD MAN's FOLLY, derived from Agatha Christie's 1956 novel and teaming Hercule Poirot with another Christie character, mystery writer Ariadne Oliver (Jean Stapleton), who many believe closely resembles the famous detective novelist. Ariadne is chosen to set up a "murder hunt" for the elite at an English manor house and she asks Hercule Poirot (Peter Ustinov) to be on hand since she feels uneasy about the situation. Poirot arrives with long-time friend Captain Hastings (Jonathan Cecil) and during the game a murder occurs. Among the suspects are the philandering lord of the manor, Sir George Stubbs (Tim Piggot-Smith), his young wife, Lady Hattie Stubbs (Nicolette Sheridan), her secretary, Miss Brewis (Susan Woolridge), and Sir George's former wife, Mrs. Folliot (Constance Cummings). The movie was filmed on location in England at West Wycombe Park in Buckinghamshire. *TV Guide* magazine's Judith Crist wrote that it ". . . emerges as one of the best of the TV-movies based on Christie's works. . . . The cast is very good indeed as is the case itself and Poirot's lecture on wine is just one of the many incidental pleasures on hand."

Peter Ustinov played vain Hercule Poirot for the fifth time in the September 30, 1986 CBS-TV telecast of MURDER IN THREE ACTS, taken from Agatha Christie's 1934 book. Here Poirot (Peter Ustinov) and faithful compatriot Captain Hastings (Jonathan Cecil) are in Acapulco to attend a number of posh society festivities and they become involved in the solution of a trio of murders. Among the many eccentric suspects are young, beautiful, but not so innocent "Egg" Eastman (Emma Samms); one-time matinee idol Charles Cartwright (Tony Curtis); cheery neurologist Dr. Strange (Dana Elcar); Cartwright's secretary, Miss Milray (Frances Lee McClain); and actress Angela Stafford (Diana Muldaur). Poirot determines eventually who is the poison-using killer. "The solution is as surprising as the production is elegant," judged Judith Crist in *TV Guide* magazine.

The next time Hercule Poirot appeared on screen was in the theatrical release APPOINTMENT WITH DEATH (1988), *q.v.*, which again featured Peter Ustinov in the lead assignment.

ALIAS THE LONE WOLF (Columbia, 1927) 65 minutes.

Producer, Harry Cohn; director, Edward H. Griffith; based on the novel by Louis Joseph Vance; screenplay, Dorothy Howell, Griffith; art director, Robert E. Lee; assistant director, Joe Cook; camera, J. O. Taylor.

Bert Lytell (Michael Lanyard); Lois Wilson (Eve de Montalais); William V. Mong (Whitaker Monk); Ned Sparks (Phinuit); James Mason (Popinot); Paulette Duval (Liane Delorme); Ann Brody (Fifi); Alphonz Ethier (Inspector Crane).

Stage and screen star Bert Lytell first played Louis Joseph Vance's gentleman thief-turned-detective Michael Lanyard (the Lone Wolf) in THE LONE WOLF in 1917. He returned to this dashing characterization for Columbia Pictures in the late 1920s with THE LONE WOLF RETURNS (1926), ALIAS THE LONE WOLF, and THE LONE WOLF'S DAUGHTER (1929). ALIAS THE LONE WOLF was based on Vance's 1921 novel of the same title and the resulting film was "A crook story, well told, agreeably acted and safely presented for the family," according to *Photoplay* magazine.

Wealthy young French lady Eve de Montalais (Lois Wilson) plans to bring her diamonds into the U.S., but finds her shipmates include jewel thieves Liane Delorme (Paulette Duval) and dour Phinuit (Ned Sparks). In New York City Eve hires Michael Lanyard (Bert Lytell) to pass her gems through customs since he is held in high regard for having just thwarted the schemes of crook Popinot (James Mason). At a night spot Liane tells Eve that Lanyard is actually the notorious Lone Wolf and she almost turns her jewels over to customs agent Whitaker Monk (William V. Mong). However, she runs away when she finds out he is a fake as well. Lanyard, meanwhile, is captured by the gang but escapes and takes the jewels through customs and then rounds up the gang members. Eve finds out Lanyard has been working undercover for the Secret Service.

"It has its flaws," insisted Mordaunt Hall (*New York Times*), "but it is well photographed and not at all badly acted. . . . There are some excellent 'shots' on the deck of an ocean greyhound, with crooks and others enjoying romances. Whatever Michael Lanyard is thought to be there is no gainsaying the fact that he is gallant. . . . Bert Lytell lives up to what is asked of him in this picture." *Variety* was more stringent: ". . . it's simple and insipid, loosely directed and more loosely played, with the 'detective situations' at times quite irritating."

Michael Lanyard's past as a thief often overshadows his sleuthing efforts and ALIAS THE LONE WOLF is no exception to this pattern. It would not be until the late 1930s and early 1940s, when Warren William played the part at Columbia Pictures, that the celluloid Michael Lanyard would become a full-fledged, but still slick and sophisticated, sleuth. In ALIAS THE LONE WOLF he is a member of an official government agency, which gives the ex-thief some legitimacy.

ALIBI (United Artists, 1929) 90 minutes.

Presenter, Joseph M. Schenck; producer/director, Roland West; based on the play *Nightstick* by John Griffith Wray, J. C. Nugent, Elaine S. Carrington; screenplay/titles/dialogue, Roland West, C. Gardner Sullivan; art director, William Cameron Menzies; music arranger, Hugo Riesenfeld; choreography, Fanchon; camera, Ray June; editor, Hal Kern.

Chester Morris (Chick Williams/Number 1065); Harry Stubbs (Buck Bachman); Mae Busch (Daisy Thomas); Eleanor Griffith (Joan Manning); Irma Harrison (Toots, the Cabaret Dancer); Regis Toomey (Danny McGann); Al Hill (Brown, a Crook); James Bradbury, Jr. (Blake, a Crook); Elmer Ballard (Soft Malone, the Cab Driver); Kernan Cripps (Trask, the Plainsclothesman); Purnell B. Pratt (Pete Manning, the Police Sergeant); Pat O'Malley (Tommy Glennon, the Detective); De Witt Jennings (O'Brien, the Policeman); Edward Brady (George Stanislaus, David); Edward Jardon, Virginia Fiohri (Singers in Theater).

Taken from the 1927 Broadway play *Nightstick*, ALIBI was more of a gangster melodrama than a sleuthing film, but the pivotal role belongs to a detective who solves the crime. *Photoplay* magazine termed it " . . . an almost flawless talkie. . . . Elegant melodrama."

Hoodlum Chick Williams (Chester Morris) is released from

prison and pretends to go straight through his marriage to Joan Manning (Eleanor Griffith), the daughter of a police sergeant (Purnell B. Pratt). Police detective Danny McGann (Regis Toomey) does not believe Williams' posturing as a reformed crook, and meanwhile the latter puts his gang back together using a nightclub owned by Buck Buchman (Harry Stubbs) as his front. Williams and his confederates rob a fur warehouse and Williams kills a guard. But he has an alibi: he was at the theater with Joan. McGann works to break the alibi and prove Williams' guilt. He is assisted by detective Tommy Glennon (Pat O'Malley) in infiltrating Williams' gang. In the process Glennon is killed. Williams falls to his death when he tries to escape from McGann and loses his footing while jumping between two high buildings.

ALIBI took three months to produce at a cost of some $600,000; the cast rehearsed the film for six weeks before shooting began on this production independently made by filmmaker Roland West for United Artists release. There was even an attempt to keep it from playing gangster-plagued Chicago when the police commissioner there refused to grant it a film permit, but this decision was later overturned in court and the film was released there.

ALIBI, with a $2.00 per ticket admission high, debuted at Times Square's Astor Theater. Mordaunt Hall (*New York Times*) approved of this "audible thriller": "There are realism and genuine thrills in the latest talking crook melodrama. . . . It is by far the best of the gangster films, and the fact that it is equipped with dialogue makes it all the more stirring. It also possesses the qualification of sticking to life, . . . " *Variety* concurred: "Jolt-packed crook melodrama in dialog. Lots of reliable excitement, deluxe production values and general audience satisfaction."

ALIBI (Woolf and Freedman Film Service, 1931) 75 minutes.

Producer, Julius Hagen; director, Leslie Hiscott; based on the novel *The Murder of Roger Ackroyd* by Agatha Christie and the play *Alibi* by Michael Morton; screenplay, H. Fowler Mear; camera, Sydney Blythe.

Austin Trevor (Hercule Poirot); Franklin Dyall (Sir Roger Ackroyd); Elizabeth Allan (Ursula Browne); H. J. Roberts (Dr. Sheppard); John Deverell (Lord Halliford); Ronald Ward (Ralph Ackroyd); Mary Jerrold (Mrs. Ackroyd); Mercia Swinburne (Caryll Sheppard); Harvey Braban (Inspector Davis), and: Diana Beaumont, Clare Greet, Earle Grey.

Agatha Christie published *The Murder of Roger Ackroyd* in 1926 and two years later it was adapted for the stage by Michael Morton as *Alibi* with Charles Laughton receiving critical acclaim as Belgian detective Hercule Poirot. The British studio Twickenham bought the rights to the property and filmed it as ALIBI in 1931 with Austin Trevor in his first of three films as Poirot. The others were BLACK COFFEE (1931) and LORD EDGWARE DIES (1934), *qq.v.*.) The plot has the sleuth at a country home where Roger Ackroyd (Franklin Dyall) supposedly committed suicide. The intrepid Poirot proves the crime was a hoax. *Variety* complained, "Development is cramped, along stage lines, but while suspense values are occasionally good, comedy values are practically non-existent." Michael Tennenbaum in *The New Bedside, Bathtub & Armchair Companion to Agatha Christie* (1986) contends, "[Austin] Trevor, a dapper character actor, was totally wrong for the role, physically. He once suggested that he was cast for his ability to do a French accent." The year after ALIBI was issued, Charles Laughton brought the play to Broadway, co-starring Jane Wyatt. As *Fatal Alibi* it lasted only two dozen performances.

THE ALIBI (Columbia, 1939) 82 minutes.

Director, Pierre Chenal; based on the novel *L'Alibi* by Marcel Archard; adaptor, Jacques Companeez, R. Juttke; music, George Auric, Jacques Dallin; English titles, Clement Douenias.

Erich von Stroheim (Professor Winckler); Louis Jouvet (Inspector Calas); Albert Préjean (Laurent); Jany Holt (Helene); Phillippe Richard (Gordon); Margo Lico (Dany); Florence Marly (The Blonde); Fun-Sen (The Professor's Assistant); Maurice Baquet (Gerard); Roger Blin (Kretz); Bobby Martin and His Orchestra with Thelma Minor (Themselves).

It took two years for the 1937 French film L'ALIBI to reach the United States and, by then, it was heavily pruned to appease the Hollywood censors. Parisian detective Inspector Calas (Louis Jouvet), along with his assistant (Albert Préjean), sets out to solve the case of the illusionist murderer (Erich von Stroheim), the latter being blackmailed by a nightclub thrush (Jany Holt) whom the detectives employ to trap the real killer. While Jouvet received plaudits for his performance, *Variety,* in reviewing this film import (with English language subtitles), noted that " . . . [Albert Préjean] is fairly satisfying but the way he is dragged into the plot merely prolongs the ultimate climax. French writers probably thought he would make the best love interest when there actually was little excuse for it."

THE ALIBI (Republic, 1943) 66 minutes.

Producer, Josef Somlo; director, Brian Desmond Hurst; based

on the novel *L'Alibi* by Marcel Archard; screenplay, Lesley Storm; Jacques Companeez, Justine & Carter; camera, W. McLeod; editor, Alan Jaggs.

Margaret Lockwood (Helene Ardouin); Hugh Sinclair (Inspector Calas); James Mason (Andre Laurent); Raymond Lovell (Professor Winkler); Enid Stamp-Taylor (Dany); Hartley Power (Gordon); Jane Carr (Delia); Rodney Ackland (Kretz); Edana Romney (Winkler's Assistant); Elisabeth Welch (Singer); Olga Lindo (Mlle. Loureau); Muriel George (Madame Bretonnet); George Merritt (Bourdille); Judy Gray (Josette); Philip Leaver (Dodo); Derek Blomfield (Gerard); Claire Wear's Embassy Orchestra (Themselves).

In 1942 L'ALIBI, *supra*, was remade in England as THE ALIBI with Hugh Sinclair and James Mason as the detectives, Margaret Lockwood as the entertainer, and Raymond Lovell as the accused illusionist. In comparing the two versions, *Variety* reported, when the film had its U.S. distribution in March 1943, " . . . Josef Somlo's English production has little more to recommend it. . . director Brian Desmond Hurst has failed to realize its full potentialities and there is an uneven quality about the production as a whole." In

Hugh Sinclair and Margaret Lockwood in THE ALIBI (1943).

retrospect, William K. Everson, in *The Detective in Film* (1972), compared the performances by the actors playing the detectives in both films and concluded that the British actors did so " . . . with considerably less individual style, and with the unmistakable feeling that they were type cast both as to role and as to what 'names' the budget could afford."

THE ALPHABET MURDERS (Metro-Goldwyn-Mayer, 1966) 90 minutes.

Producer, Lawrence P. Bachmann; associate producer, Ben Arbeid; director, Frank Tashlin; based on *The A.B.C. Murders* by Agatha Christie; screenplay, David Pursall, Jack Seddon; art director, Bill Andrews; music/music director, Ron Goodwin; song, Brian Fahey and Norman Newell; assistant director, David Tomblin; recording supervisor, A. W. Watkins; sound, Sash Fisher; sound editor, Bill Creed; camera, Desmond Dickinson; editor, John Victor Smith.

Tony Randall (Inspector Hercule Poirot); Anita Ekberg (Amanda Beatrice Cross); Robert Morley (Major Hastings); Maurice Denham (Inspector Japp); Guy Rolfe (Duncan Doncaster); Sheila Allen (Lady Diane); James Villiers (Franklin); Julian Glover (Don Fortune); Grazina Frame (Betty Barnard); Clive Morton ("X"); Cyril Luckham (Sir Carmichael Clarke); Richard Wattis (Wolf); David Lodge (Sergeant); Patrick Newell (Cracknell); Austin Trevor (Judson); Alison Seebohm (Miss Sparks); Windsor Davies (Dragbot); Sheila Reid (Mrs. Fortune); Margaret Rutherford (Miss Jane Marple); Stringer Davis (Mr. Stringer).

Noted Belgian detective Hercule Poirot (Tony Randall) comes to London to visit his tailor and is trailed by Major Hastings (Robert Morley), a member of British Intelligence who is all too aware of Poirot's penchant for getting involved in crimes. When a clown is killed by a poisoned dart, the body is found next to a copy of the A.B.C. Guide to London. Later, while Poirot and Hastings are at a Turkish bath, voluptuous Amanda Beatrice Cross (Anita Ekberg) breaks in and claims she is a compulsive killer; she then vanishes. Poirot explores the case, which leads him to bowling instructor Betty Barnard (Grazina Frame), who is also killed by a dart. The detective believes the next victim will be Sir Carmichael Clarke (Cyril Luckham). However, when Amanda is cornered by the police and leaps into the Thames, police Inspector Japp (Maurice Denham) insists the case is closed. But, Poirot persists and unveils the killer due to a link to the alphabet.

Based on Agatha Christie's 1936 novel, THE ALPHABET MURDERS languished for two years in pre-production before being filmed, because Miss Christie objected to the script which had been prepared initially for Zero Mostel as Poirot. Austin Trevor, who first played Poirot onscreen in ALIBI (1931), BLACK COFFEE (1931) and LORD EDGWARE DIES (1934), *qq.v.*, was in the cast in the role of Judson. Margaret Rutherford and her real life husband, Stringer Davis, briefly appeared in guest cameos as Miss Jane Marple and Mr. Stringer from the Christie-detective series they were doing at the time for MGM in England.

There were/are few endorsers for this slapstick-like rendering which made the beloved intellectual Poirot into more a clown than a wit. " . . . It goes very wrong—there's no suspense, because we have no idea what's going on, and the spoofy, slapstick embellishments are almost painfully self-conscious. . . . [Randall] mugs too much: he's always doing something, and then when he does something really good, we're too tired of him to react" (Pauline Kael, *5001 Nights at the Movies*, 1984). The poorly-received THE ALPHABET MURDERS quickly vanished from theatrical distribution.

AND THEN THERE WERE NONE (Twentieth Century-Fox, 1945) 97 minutes.

Producer, Harry J. Popkin; director, René Clair; based on the novel and play *10 Little Niggers* by Agatha Christie; adaptor, Dudley Nichols; art director, Ernst Fegte; assistant director, Sam Nelson; sound, Carson F. Jowett; camera, Lucien Androit; editor, Harvey Manger.

Barry Fitzgerald (Judge Quincannon); Walter Huston (Dr. Armstrong); Louis Hayward (Philip Lombard); Roland Young (Blore); June Duprez (Vera Claythorne); Sir C. Aubrey Smith (General Mandrake); Judith Anderson (Emily Brent); Mischa Auer (Prince Nikki Starloff); Richard Hayden (Rogers); Queenie Leonard (Mrs. Rogers); Harry Thurston (Fisherman).

Agatha Christie authored the thriller *10 Little Niggers* in 1939 and when she adapted it to the stage as *And Then There Were None* in 1943, she added a character who does the detection work necessary to solve the mystery. While a private detective appears as one of the characters in all three screen versions of the Christie work, all ten of the protagonists are really sleuths. It is they who attempt to find out why they are called to a remote locate, why they are marked for murder and, most importantly, who is trying to eliminate them— one by one.

The initial screen version of AND THEN THERE WERE NONE is considered the definitive one. Frenchman René Clair directed AND THEN THERE WERE NONE for Twentieth Century-Fox release in 1945. Ten diverse people from all stations in life are brought by boat to mysterious and misty Indian Island off the Cornish coast. They are: an adventurer (Louis Hayward), secretary Vera (June Duprez), a doctor (Walter Huston), a judge (Barry Fitzgerald), retired General Mandrake (C. Aubrey Smith), spinster Emily Brent (Judith Anderson), private detective Blore (Roland Young), a regal playboy named Prince Nikki Starloff (Mischa Auer), and a married domestic couple (Richard Hayden, Queenie Leonard). Once there they are played recordings which tell each how they committed a crime and escaped punishment, with their mysterious benefactor promising to make amends for their non-punishment. One by one, as in the nursery rhyme, the guests meet shocking ends, until only the secretary and the adventurer (who is there by mistake) are left to confront the killer.

From the start, AND THEN THERE WERE NONE was recognized as a superior screen entertainment. "Out of this lethal hocus-pocus, René Clair has produced an exciting film and has directed a splendid cast in it with humor and a light macabre touch" (Bosley Crowther, *New York Times*). Years later the film's classic genre stature was still being questioned. In *Magill's American Film Guide* (1983), William H. Brown, Jr. notes that exiled director Clair " . . . plays [Dudley] Nichols' script for comedy and mystery rather than for the fearful or the bizarre," and that ". . . Clair quietly avoids the gruesome, showing only two deaths on camera, both by poison and both essential to the development of the plot." Finally, Brown perceives that "Clair holds his characters somewhat coldly at a distance. . . . The question of who will die next, and how, quickly becomes more interesting than any of the victims themselves." In *The Detective in Hollywood* (1978), Jon Tuska calls the film a "masterpiece" and adds, ". . . in many ways the only excellent film based on any of Agatha Christie's works. . . ." John Pym (British *Monthly Film Bulletin*) would judge that the enduring appeal of the premise lies " . . . in a neat resolution without the help of a detective and in the irony of [the denouement]. . . ."

TEN LITTLE INDIANS was the second filming of the project, done in Ireland in 1965 by George Pollock, who had directed Margaret Rutherford in her mid-1960s series of "Miss Jane Marple" detective thrillers. As a gimmick (and the film badly needed one) the motion picture was stopped for one minute at the climax to provide filmgoers time to guess for themselves the identity of the murderer. The *New York Times* reported, "Considering the fact that the brilliant source of this whodunit, an Agatha Christie novel, already yielded a dandy movie back in 1940 [*sic*], AND THEN THERE WERE NONE, this second version, in color, is surprisingly palatable. Maybe it's the reliable old plot. . . . There remains enough of the Christie essence, although it doesn't even scrape the other picture, to provide gripping entertainment. And director George Pollock sets a good, fast uncomplicated pace." The plot remains basically the same as the 1945, film with minor alterations: the locale is now the Swiss Alps, with the guest, arriving at their hotel by cable car; the playboy has become an obnoxious pop singer (Fabian); a few of the murders are executed differently; there is a pointless fight between the adventurer (Hugh O'Brian) and the manservant (Mario Andorf); and the blonde secretary (Shirley Eaton) has a steamy sex bout with the debonair adventurer.

Hollywood filmmakers are notorious for not leaving well enough alone in their refilming of movie classics. In this case, a third rendition of Dame Agatha's classic, called TEN LITTLE INDIANS, was brought out in 1975. It was directed by Peter Collinson, had an international cast and was made with international financing. Now the ten guests are summoned by helicopter to the Shah Abbas Hotel in Isfahan in the Iranian desert, where their crimes are proclaimed by the voice of Mr. Owen (Orson Welles). Again minor plot alterations exist: the playboy is still a singer (Charles Aznavour), but now a more amenable one and he sings a few songs; the general (Adolfo Celi) is as inept as he was in the 1945 version; the passion between the secretary (Elke Sommer) and the adventurer (Oliver Reed) is far tamer, and there is a happy ending. The *New York Times* dubbed this mediocre period piece "Global disaster in Iran."

ANGEL HEART (Cannon, 1987) Color 113 minutes.

Executive producers, Mario Kassar, Andrew Vajna; producers, Alan Marshall, Elliott Kastner; associate producer, Robert Dattila; director, Alan Parker; based on the novel *Falling Angel* by William Hjortsberg; screenplay, Parker; production designer, Brian Morris; art directors, Kristi Zea, Armin Ganz; set decorators, Robert J. Franco, Leslie Pope; costumes, Aude Bronson-Howard; makeup, David Forrest; special makeup effects, Robert Laden; stunt coordinator, Harry Madsen; animal trainer, Steve McAulif; music, Trevor Jones; choreography, Louis Falco; sound, Danny Michael, Paul Hulme; sound editor, Eddy Joseph; sound effects, William Trent; camera, Michael Seresin; editor, Gerry Hambling.

Mickey Rourke (Harry Angel); Robert De Niro (Louis Cyphre); Lisa Bonet (Epiphany Proudfoot); Charlotte Rampling (Margaret Krusemark); Stocker Fontelieu (Ethan Krusemark); Brownie McGhee (Toots Sweet); Michael Higgins (Dr. Fowler); Elizabeth Whitcraft (Connie); Eliott Keener (Sterne); Charles Gordone (Spider Simpson); Dann Florek (Winesap); Kathleen Wilhoite (Nurse); George Buck (Izzy); Judith Drake (Izzy's Wife); Gerald L. Orange (Pastor John):

Peggy Severe (Mammy Carter); Pruitt Taylor Vince (Deimos); David Petitjean (Baptism Preacher); Rick Washburn, Neil Newlon (Cajun Heavies); Oakley Dalton (Big Jacket); Yvonne Bywaters (Margaret's Maid); Loys T. Bergeron (Mike); Joshua Frank (Toothless); Karmen Harris (Harlem Mourner); Nicole Burdette (Ellie); Kendell Lupe, Percy Martin (Oyster Cajuns); Viola Dunbar (Concierge); Murray Bandel (Bartender); Jarrett Narcisse (Epiphany's Child); Ernest Watson (Oyster Bar Saxophonist); Rickie Monie (Oyster Bar Pianist); Roselyn Lionheart (Voodoo Musician); Joel Adam, Darrel Beasley, Stephen Beasley, Jerome Reddick (Tap Dancers).

For convenience and proximity of subject matter the detective film and the gangster genre have usually been intermingled over the years so far as plots are concerned. However, few other genres have ever been interpolated into the realm of detective fiction. William Hjortsberg's 1978 novel *Falling Angel* was an exception, combining the detective and horror species. It 1987 it was brought to the screen as ANGEL HEART.

In 1955 Gotham private eye Harry Angel (Mickey Rourke) is hired by a puzzling foreigner, Louis Cyphre (Robert De Niro), to find once famous band singer Johnny Favorite, who disappeared during World War II and who owes Cyphre an unstated debt. Apparently, Angel learns, the singer was brain dead from a war injury, but a doctor (Michael Higgins) informs the gumshoe that he recovered with the aid of Ethan Krusemark (Stocker Fontelieu) and his daughter Margaret (Charlotte Rampling) and then disappeared. The doctor is found murdered and Angel heads to New Orleans where he discovers that Krusemark and his daughter are involved in voodoo. Margaret is murdered and musician Toots Sweet (Browne McGhee) tells Angel that Ethan had a daughter, Epiphany Proudfoot (Lisa Bonet), from an alliance with a voodoo priestess. Epiphany is following in her mother's footsteps but this does not stop him from having an affair with the young woman. Eventually Angel comes to realize the truth: Favorite changed his identity by devouring the heart of a soldier and taking on his face and memories. And then deeper truths become apparent. Angel is Favorite and Cyphre is really the devil come to collect his due. Angel now knows he is the one who committed the killings (including Epiphany's) and he is arrested, realizing he will be executed both on earth and in hell.

When ANGEL HEART was set for release there was a great deal of furor over a provocative ten-second sex scene between TV favorite Lisa Bonet (of "The Bill Cosby Show") and star Mickey Rourke. After the deletion of the controversial footage, the film was given an R instead of an X-rating. (Versions with and without the highly-touted blood-dripping scene are available now on videocassette.) As for the movie itself, Richard Corliss (*Time* magazine) pointed out that director Alan Parker " . . . occasionally tries to pump up his flashback talkathon with chase scenes that distract from the film's mood. But he has located a chic, grim style for the story. Garish ominous colors flash vividly across his monochrome palette." When released in England, Kim Newman (British *Monthly Film Bulletin*) analyzed, "As a *film noir*, ANGEL HEART tends towards the fatalistic and uneventful. . . . There is a fertile common ground between the horror and hard-boiled detective genres . . . but to transfer this cross-breed to the screen requires a film-maker take it seriously rather than striving for extra weightiness. . . ." This baffling, titillating film, which confused some viewers and annoyed others, was not a box-office success. It grossed an unspectacular $17,185,632 in its ten weeks of domestic theatrical distribution. When ANGEL HEART was issued on video by IVE in the spring of 1988, Dennis Hunt (*Los Angeles Times*) concluded, "This is a good film for home video because you can rewind parts of it to ferret out the clues you invariably missed." Of the ANGEL HEART cast, Robert De Niro, as the impeccably dressed and satanic Louis Cyphre, received the most plaudits.

ANOTHER THIN MAN (Metro-Goldwyn-Mayer, 1939) 102 minutes.

Producer, Hunt Stromberg; director, W. S. Van Dyke II; story, Dashiell Hammett; screenplay, Frances Goodrich, Albert Hackett; art director, Cedric Gibbons; music, Edward Ward; sound, Douglas Shearer; camera, Oliver T. Marsh, William Daniels; editor, Frederick Y. Smith.

William Powell (Nick Charles); Myrna Loy (Nora Charles); C. Aubrey Smith (Colonel Burr MacFay); Otto Kruger (Van Slack, the Assistant District Attorney); Nat Pendleton (Lieutenant Guild); Virginia Grey (Lois MacFay); Tom Neal (Freddie Coleman); Muriel Hutchinson (Smitty); Ruth Hussey (Dorothy Waters [Linda Mills]); Sheldon Leonard (Phil Church); Phyllis Gordon (Mrs. Bellam); Don Costello ("Diamond Back" Vogel); Patric Knowles (Dudley Horn); Harry Bellaver ("Creeps" Binder); Abner Biberman (Dum-Dum); Marjorie Main (Mrs. Dolley, the Landlady); Asta (Himself); Horace McMahon (MacFay's Chauffeur); Nell Craig (Maid); William Anthony Poulsen (Nicky, Jr.); Milton Kibbee (Les, the Deputy); Walter Fenner, Thomas Jackson (Detectives); Charles Brokaw, Frank Coletti, Edwin Parker, William Tannen (Troopers); Edward Gargan (Quinn, the Detective); Joseph Dowling, Matty Fain (Thugs); Bert Roach (Cookie, the Drinker); Shemp Howard (Wacky, the Temporary Father); Nellie V. Nichols (Mrs. Wacky); Eddie Gribbon, Ralph

Dunn (Baggage Men); George Guhl (Guard at Gate); Claire Rochelle (Telephone Operator); Winstead "Doodles" Weaver, Paul "Tiny" Newlan (Guards); Roy Barcroft (Slim the Guard); Joe Devlin (Barney, the Bodyguard); Paul E. Burns (Station Agent); Milton Parsons (Medical Examiner); Dick Elliott (Investigator); Jack Gardner (Driver); Nestor Paiva (Cuban Proprietor); Anita Camargo (Hat Check Girl); Gladden James (Fingerprint Man); Charles Sherlock (Police Photographer); John Kelly (Father); Edward Hearn (Detective); Eddie Buzzard (Newsboy); Martin Garralaga (Pedro, the Informant); Alexander D'Arcy (South American); Jack Clifford, Howard Mitchell, William Paga, Lee C. Shumway (Policemen); Stanley Taylor (Taxi Driver); Frank Sully (Pete); Murray Alper (Louie); Frank Moran (Butch); James Guilfoyle (Jake); Richard Calderon (Wacky's Baby); James G. Blaine (Policeman in Charles' Suite); Rosemary Grimes, Blanca Vischer, Sandra Andreva, Tina Menard, Toni LaRue (Cafe Bits); Guy Rett, Alphonse Martel, Alberto Morin (Waiters).

In SON OF FRANKENSTEIN (1939), the title character complains how the villagers refer to his father's unfortunate monster by the name "Frankenstein," thus using a misnomer to describe the creature. Much the same can be said of MGM's glossy The Thin Man movies, especially ANOTHER THIN MAN, since the title refers to Nick and Nora Charles' young son and *not* to the quaint character of the Thin Man from the original 1934 feature film. By now the term "The Thin Man" was associated with Nick Charles and has remained so up to the present time.

ANOTHER THIN MAN was the third of six screen versions of the exploits of droll detective Nick Charles (William Powell). In it he and his equally charming wife Nora (Myrna Loy) and their infant son Nick, Jr. (William Anthony Poulsen) are visiting New York City. They are summoned to the fashionable Long Island estate of weapons manufacturer Colonel Burr MacFay (C. Aubrey Smith). It seems the colonel's former partner, Phil Church (Sheldon Leonard), has threatened to do him in because he feels MacFay was responsible for sending him to prison ten years earlier. Now out of jail, Church predicts the colonel will die and his forecast comes true; then he insists that Nick will also die, but it is Church who is later found shot to death. A number of suspects are gathered at the MacFay estate and eventually Nick leaves strong drink alone long enough to piece together the mystery and solve the homicides.

Dashiell Hammett, who wrote *The Thin Man* (1934), provided the original storyline for this film and Nat Pendleton reprised his role of thick-skulled Lieutenant Guild which he did in the initial 1934 series opener. Since the producing studio was genteel Metro-

Goldwyn-Mayer and the co-stars were debonair William Powell and perfect screen wife Myrna Loy, the mixture was geared more to sophisticated froth than realistic detective work. " . . . This third of the trade-marked Thin Men takes its murders as jauntily as ever, confirms our impression that matrimony need not be too serious a business and provides as light an entertainment as any holiday-amusement seeker is likely to find" (Frank S. Nugent, *New York Times*). But Nugent was also aware that "Some of the bloom is off the rose. A few of the running gags are beginning to show signs of pulling up lame." Director W. S. Van Dyke II did not display the same brisk direction he had with the original THE THIN MAN screen episode.

Next came SHADOW OF THE THIN MAN (1941), *q.v.*

APPOINTMENT WITH DEATH (Cannon, 1988) Color 108 minutes.

Executive producers, Menaham Golan, Yoram Globus; producer/director, Michael Winner; based on the novel by Agatha Christie; screenplay, Anthony Shaffer; production designer, John Blezard; costume designer, John Bloomfield; music, Pino Donaggio; camera, David Gurfinkel; editors, Arnold Crust, Winner.

Peter Ustinov (Hercule Poirot); Lauren Bacall (Lady Westholme); Carrie Fisher (Nadine Boynton); John Gielgud (Colonel Carbury); Piper Laurie (Mrs. Emily Boynton); Hayley Mills (Miss Quinton); Jenny Seagrove (Sarah King); David Soul (Jefferson Cope); John Terlesky (Raymond Boynton); Valerie Richards (Carol Boynton); Nicholas Guest (Lennon Boynton); Amber Bezer (Ginevra Boynton).

Having played impeccably mannered Belgian detective Hercule Poirot in the theatrical films DEATH ON THE NILE (1978) and MURDER UNDER THE SUN (1982) and in the TV movies THIRTEEN AT DINNER (1985), DEAD MAN'S FOLLY (1986) and MURDER IN THREE ACTS (1986), *qq.v.*, Peter Ustinov returned to his alter ego role for the sixth time. The big-screen release, APPOINTMENT WITH DEATH, was based on Agatha Christie's 1938 novel. Despite an intriguing cast and the scenic locales of Israel, the overall results were not good. " . . . The script and characterizations [are] bland, and there simply are not enough murders to sustain the interest of even the most avid Agatha Christie fan. . ." (*Daily Variety*). More severe was *People* magazine's Ralph Novak, "The punch lines are like straight lines, the straight lines like stage directions. . . . When Ustinov solves the murder during the climactic gathering of possible culprits, he doesn't relieve the audience's tension; he puts it out of its misery." Added the reviewer for

Advertisement for APPOINTMENT WITH DEATH (1988).

Movieline magazine, "Even the mugging of Peter Ustinov seems lackluster and ill-timed."

Set in 1937, APPOINTMENT WITH DEATH revolves around nasty and greedy Mrs. Emily Boynton (Piper Laurie), who arranges her rich husband's will so that the rest of his family will be disinherited. Following the annexation of the fortune, this American travels to Europe and the Middle East. Chaperoning Emily are her dominated son Raymond (John Terlesky) and his wife Nadine (Carrie Fisher, who serves as the elder woman's nurse). Along with them are Nadine's coddled daughter Ginevra (Amber Bezer), her dishonest attorney Jefferson Cope (David Soul), who is having an affair with Nadine, and medical student Sarah King (Jenny Seagrove), who has a yen for weak-willed Raymond. Also on the ocean trip are American-born British Parliament member Lady Westholme (Lauren Bacall), her traveling companion Miss Quinton (Hayley Mills), and Belgian detective Hercule Poirot (Peter Ustinov). During an archaeological dig, Emily is found murdered and Poirot, who works in league with the head (John Gielgud) of the British army in Palestine, must name the killer, although most of the travelers have sufficient motive for wanting the woman out of the way permanently.

In analyzing this film, Michael Healy *(Los Angeles Daily News)* judged, "Director Michael Winner . . . seems glad to have a picture in which there is little opportunity for action of any sort. The movie has a relaxed, lackadaisical quality that is indistinguishable from dullness. . . . What jokes there are are wan and not very funny. No one is particularly bad, and no one is particularly good."

APPOINTMENT WITH DEATH grossed a paltry $603,650 in its first week of domestic distribution, quickly disappeared from theatrical release and was soon circulating in its videocassette version.

ARSENE LUPIN (Vitagraph, 1917) 5,000'.

Director, Paul Scardon; based on the play by Maurice LeBlanc, Francis de Croisset.

Earle Williams (Arsène Lupin); Brinsley Shaw (Guerchard); Mr. Leone (Guernay-Martin); Bernard Seigel (Charcolais); Gordon Gray (Anatase); Logan Paul (Firmid); Hugh Wynn (Alfred); Ethel Gray Terry (Sonia); Billie Billings (Germaine); Julia Swayne Gordon (Victorie).

ARSENE LUPIN (Metro-Goldwyn-Mayer, 1932) 64 minutes.

Director, Jack Conway; based on the play by Maurice LeBlanc, Francis de Croisset; adaptor, Carey Wilson; dialogue, Bayard Veiller, Lenore Coffee; sound, Jack Jordon; camera, Oliver T. Marsh; editor, Hugh Wynn.

John Barrymore (Duke of Charmerace [Arsène Lupin]); Lionel Barrymore (Guerchard); Karen Morley (Sonia); John Miljan (Prefect of Police); Tully Marshall (Gourney-Martin); Henry Armetta, George Davis (Sheriff's Men); John Davidson (Butler); James Mack (Laurent); Mary Jane Irving (Marie).

ARSENE LUPIN RETURNS (Metro-Goldwyn-Mayer, 1938) 81 minutes.

Producer, John W. Considine, Jr.; director, George Fitzmaurice; based on the character created by Maurice LeBlanc, Francis de Croisset; story/screenplay, James Kevin McGuiness, Howard Emmett Rogers, George Harmon Coxe; music, Franz Waxman; art director, Cedric Gibbons; sound, Douglas Shearer; camera, George Folsey; editor, Ben Lewis.

Melvyn Douglas (Rene Farrard [Arsène Lupin]); Virginia Bruce (Lorraine de Crissac); Warren William (Steve Emerson); John Halliday (Count de Grissac); Nat Pendleton (Joe Dole); Monty Woolley (Georges Bouchet); E. E. Clive (Alf); George Zucco (Prefect of Police); Rollo Lloyd (Duval); Vladimir Sokoloff (Ivan Pavloff); Ian Wolfe (Le Marchard); Tully Marshall (Monelle); Jonathan Hale (F.B.I. Special Agent); Leonard Penn, Harry Tyler, Chester Clute (Reporters); Jack Norton (Hotel Manager); William Norton Bailey, Mitchell Lewis, Chris Frank (Detectives); Robert Middlemass (Sergeant); Ruth Hart (Phone Girl); Egon Brecher (Vasseur); Otto Fries

(Truck Driver); Priscilla Lawson (Switchboard Operator); William H. Royle (Burly Detective); George Douglas, Jean Perry (Gendarmes); Frank Leigh (English Eddie); Sid D'Albrook (Detective Alois).

The character of Arsène Lupin was the French counterpart of E. W. Hornung's British Raffles or Louis Joseph Vance's Michael Lanyard, the Lone Wolf. All three were master thieves who eluded various detectives and eventually all three converted to the right side of the law—at least on film—and became sophisticated sleuths. Arsène Lupin was created by French newspaper reporter Maurice LeBlanc who wrote a number of books centering on the popular character. The first was *Arsène Lupin, Gentleman Burglar* (1907) and the last was *The Memoirs of Arsène Lupin* (1925). Like Sherlock Holmes, Lupin is a master of disguise and uses a number of aliases; he is also a good-natured rogue with women.

The early Arsène Lupin stories sometimes incorporated Sir Arthur Conan Doyle's Sherlock Holmes as Lupin's protagonist and the initial Lupin entries, a 1910 German Vitascope series of one- and two- reel shorts, ARSENE LUPIN VS. SHERLOCK HOLMES, followed this plot device. Paul Otto was Lupin and Viggo Larsen portrayed Holmes. In the stories the British detective had been called Herlock Sholmes for copyright purposes, but on film Vitascope used the detective's correct monicker. In 1916 the British company, London Films, produced ARSENE LUPIN, starring Gerald Ames in the title role, and the plot finds the master thief being trailed by a Paris police detective (Kenelm Foss). The next year the first American adaptation of ARSENE LUPIN was made by Vitagraph, with Earle Williams as Lupin and co-starring Ethel Grey Terry and Billie Billings. *Variety* lambasted the production, calling it "a joke" and "an insult to the intelligence of a ten-year-old schoolboy." The final American silent Arsène Lupin production was Robertson-Cole's 1920 production of 813, starring Wedgewood Newell as Lupin with Laura La Plante and Wallace Beery. Of this rendition, *Variety* reported it was a "poorly acted and utterly senseless version" which "unless a person is at all acquainted with Lupin's former history, that person may resolve himself from the start into absolute ignorance of what goes on until the finale."

The best known feature film derived from LeBlanc's popular character is MGM's 1932 production of ARSENE LUPIN, which co-starred John and Lionel Barrymore on film for the first time. Here John Barrymore portrays the suave Lupin while Lionel Barrymore is Guerchard, his police detective nemesis. The plot has Lupin carrying out various large thefts right under the nose of the French police and Guerchard being thwarted in each attempt to bring in the master criminal. When Lupin falls in love with beautiful Sonia (Karen Morley), Guerchard uses the young woman to trap his prey; she is on parole from prison and will be sent back there unless she aids in the capture of her lover. Meanwhile, Lupin works out an intricate plot to carry off the Mona Lisa painting from the Louvre museum. Eventually Guerchard captures Lupin, but by now he so admires the gentleman thief that on the way to police headquarters he allows him to escape. After firing a few shots in the vague direction of Lupin, who has jumped into the Seine River and is swimming to safety, the Parisian law enforcer declares Lupin has drowned. Lupin is now free to go away with his beloved Sonia.

The highlight of the 1932 ARSENE LUPIN is the smooth interaction of the Barrymore brothers and they are surrounded by the usual posh MGM production values, solid direction by Jack Conway, and a fine supporting cast. Only the creaky plot detracted from the grade-A proceedings. *Variety* noted, "Perhaps it was good production judgment that dictated the picture's handling, so that it avoided all the clap-trap of the commercial detective-thief chase device to which the Royal Family declined to stoop. At least it addresses itself to a higher class of fans than the lurid type of dime-novel subject."

In 1938 MGM produced a follow-up to ARSENE LUPIN with ARSENE LUPIN RETURNS and William Powell, who had played Philo Vance and Nick Charles on screen, was offered the title role but declined it. Melvyn Douglas, who had had the lead in THE LONE WOLF RETURNS (*q.v.*) three years before at Columbia Pictures, took the part. The new version of the screen detective finds him as a gentleman farmer who raises pigs on his country estate and appears more British than Gallic. He is also adept now at coin and card tricks. Co-starred was Warren William (who portrayed Perry Mason and Philo Vance on film and would himself become the screen's most noted Lone Wolf) in the role of an American detective. The plot concerns (a newly smart-mouthed) Lupin working with brisk Yankee sleuth Steve Emerson (Warren William) in Paris as the two track a jewel thief during which Lupin romances his fiancée (Virginia Bruce). As for Douglas' interpretation of Arsène Lupin, Frank S. Nugent (*New York Times*) confessed, "Melvyn Douglas's Lupin is considerably less and considerably more than M. LeBlanc might have desired. . . . Mr. Douglas may not be the Lupin we used to read about, but he is a nice chap." Of the film itself, Nugent reported, "It is fairer than most in its presentation of clues—the significant ones always excepted—and more fortunate than most in its cast."

By 1944 Universal had acquired rights to the property and

made the glossy programmer ENTER ARSENE LUPIN, directed by Ford Beebe and adapted to the screen by Bertram Millhauser, who had written a number of the studio's Sherlock Holmes pictures. Here the suave Lupin (Charles Korvin) steals Stacie's (Ella Raines) priceless emerald, but becomes entranced by her beauty and returns the cache. When he learns she is about to be murdered by her aunt (Gale Sondergaard) and uncle (Miles Mander) for her inheritance, Lupin tries to protect her and is aided by his usual foe, police detective Ganimard (J. Carrol Naish). As for the impact of Hungarian actor Charles Korvin in the title assignment, *Variety* judged he " . . . isn't much of an actor, but he has the continental ease of manner and attractive face to catch the femme trade."

The next year a Mexican film, Pereda's ARSENIO LUPIN [Arsène Lupin], was issued and the plot has Lupin at odds again with Sherlock Holmes. Thus the gentleman thief ended his screen career as he had begun it in 1910.

ARSENIO LUPIN   *see*   ARSENE LUPIN [essay].

THE BAT (United Artists, 1926) 91 minutes.
Producer/director, Roland West; based on the play by Mary Roberts Rinehart, Avery Hopwood; adaptor, West; screenplay, Julien Josephson; titles, George Marion, Jr.; art director, William Cameron Menzies; camera, Arthur Edeson.
Andre de Beranger (Gideon Bell); Charles W. Herzinger (Man in Black Mask); Emily Fitzroy (Miss Cornelia Van Gorder); Louise Fazenda (Lizzie Allen); Arthur Houseman (Richard Fleming); Robert McKim (Dr. Wells); Jack Pickford (Brooks Bailey); Jewel Carmen (Miss Dale Ogden); Kamiyama Sojin (Billy); Tullio Carminati (Moletti); Eddie Gribbon (Detective Anderson); Lee Shumway (The Unknown).

THE BAT (Allied Artists, 1959) 80 minutes.
Producer, C. J. Tevlin; director, Crane Wilbur; based on the play by Mary Roberts Rinehart, Avery Hopwood; screenplay, Wilbur; art director, David Milton; music director, Louis Forbes; camera, Joseph Biroc; editor, William Austin.
Vincent Price (Dr. Malcolm Wells); Agnes Moorhead (Cornelia Van Gorder); Gavin Gordon (Lieutenant Anderson); John Sutton (Warner); Lenita Lane (Lizzie Allen); Elaine Edwards (Dale Bailey); Daris Hood (Judy Hollender); John Bryant (Mark Fleming); Harvey Stephens (Carter Fleming); Mike Steele (Jack Bailey); Riza Royce (Mrs. Patterson); Robert B. Williams (Detective).

THE BAT WHISPERS (United Artists, 1931) 82 minutes.

Producer/director, Roland West; based on the play *The Bat* by Mary Roberts Rinehart, Avery Hopwood; sound, Oscar E. Lagerstrom; camera: (standard screen footage), Ray June; (wide screen footage), Robert H. Panck; editor, James Smith.

Chester Morris (Detective Anderson); Spencer Charters (The Caretaker); Una Merkel (Dale Van Gorder); William Bakewell (Brook); Gustav Von Seyffertitz (Dr. Venrees); Hugh Huntley (Richard Fleming); Charles Dow Clark (Detective Jones); Ben Bard (The Unknown); Chance Ward (Police Lieutenant); Richard Tucker (Mr. Bell); Wilson Benge (The Butler); DeWitt Jennings (Police Captain); Sidney D'Albrook (Police Sergeant); S. E. Jennings (Man in Black Mask); Grayce Hampton (Cornelia Van Gorder); Maude Eburne (Lissie Allen).

Mary Roberts Rinehart's 1906 novel, *The Circular Staircase,* was filmed in 1915 by Selig and in 1920 Ms. Rinehart and Avery Hopwood adapted the book into a play called *The Bat,* which became one of the most popular mystery plays in the theater.* In 1926 the play was then novelized and that year United Artists distributed the initial film version of the play, which was produced, directed, and adapted by Roland West. (Independent filmmaker West had paid a great deal for the screen rights to this stage hit; far more than D. W. Griffith had been willing to do in 1922 when he sought the property.) *Photoplay* magazine announced of this silent feature, "It's thrilling and it's chilling. Your spine will quiver and your hair will stiffen every moment. See it!" Equally enthusiastic was *Harrison's Reports:* "Few pictures have been released lately that hold the spectator as breathless as does THE BAT, and not only does it hold him breathless but it thrills him and at the same time makes him laugh to his heart's content."

The Bat, an unknown criminal genius announces he will execute a jewel heist but a rival thwarts his plans during the robbery. Both criminals are believed to have come to a remote estate leased by wealthy spinster Cornelia Van Gorder (Emily Fitzroy). At the same time $200,000 has been stolen from a bank, the banker Richard Fleming (Arthur Houseman) has died and his cashier, Brooks Bailey (Jack Pickford), who loves Cornelia's pretty niece, Dale Ogden (Jewel Carmen), has disappeared. Detective Moletti (Tullio Carminati) is sent to unravel the mystery. Hysterical maid

---

The Bat ran for 878 performances on Broadway and starred Effie Ellsler, May Vokes, and Edward Ellis. The January 20, 1953 Broadway revival, starring Lucile Watson, ZaSu Pitts, Shepperd Strudwick, and Harry Bannister, lasted only twenty-three performances.

Lizzie Allen (Louise Fazenda) believes the finger of guilt points to either Dr. Wells (Robert McKim) or the Oriental butler (Kamiyama Sojin). Hoping to find the culprit, Brooks masquerades as the estate's gardener. It turns out that one of the people involved has killed the character he impersonates and this person, who is really The Bat, is captured eventually.

The *New York Times'* Mordaunt Hall reported, "People in the theatre yesterday were distinctly affected by the spine-chilling episodes, and they were relieved by the comedy interludes." *Variety* rated the production as "interesting every minute of the way" and offered a suggestion regarding Italian actor Tullio Carminati (making his American film debut). " . . . His playing as the detective immediately suggests that someone should feature him in a series of detective thrillers, for he suggests the bearing, the urbanity and the lightning mind one usually expects in master criminals."

THE BAT was a huge success, although no prints of it are known to exist today.

When the sound era was ushered in, Roland West remade the project, again directing and adapting the play for the screen, including using much of the original dialogue. Chester Morris, who had starred for West in the highly popular ALIBI (1930), *q.v.*, was hired to play the detective. For this version this character reverts back to the stage surname of Detective Anderson, and not Moletti as in the 1926 film edition. Leading lady Dale (Una Merkel) became Miss Van Gorder's (Grayce Hampton) niece, while the Japanese butler became an American one played by Wilson Benge. The role of the physician became that of an European due to the casting of Gustav von Seyffertitz in the part. The film's plot adheres basically to the original but is highlighted by West's use of eerie shadows and the heightened reality of sound.* As an added gimmick, the film utilizes a wide screen process for some of the panoramic sequences.

Unfortunately THE BAT WHISPERS was buried in the maze of old house murder mysteries then in vogue and failed to recoup its

---

*In *Between Action and Cut: Five American Directors* (1985) Scott MacQueen notes, in his essay on Roland West, "Borrowing from German Expressionism, The Bat is shown as a shadow or silhouette. As the camera dollies up to the bank's skylight to observe a robbery in progress, West's Expressionistic sense of lettering is repeated in the hugely exaggerated, three dimensional B A N K sign atop the building. The Bat's descent by rope from the rooftop is in silhouette, framed by scraggly leafless trees. Flashes of lightning reveal him perched in the treetops—a breathless, high-angle shot from above and behind—wings spread majestically as he swoops down on his unsuspecting victim on the walk below."

heavy production costs. Shot in both 35mm and 65mm versions, the film exists today in truncated versions derived from the former; the 65mm version is thought to be lost.

"When the Bat Flies Someone Dies" was the catchline for the 1959 Allied Artists release, THE BAT, which was adapted by director Crane Wilbur. Here Agnes Moorhead plays Cornelia Van Gorder, a mystery writer who rents a gloomy estate from a banker who has stolen a large sum of money and hidden it in the mansion. A local physician, Dr. Malcolm Wells (Vincent Price), has murdered the banker and comes to the manse seeking the money, but everyone there soon is threatened by a fiend, "The Bat," who murders his victims by cutting their jugular veins. Detective Lieutenant Anderson (Gavin Gordon) is called in to solve the case. *Variety* complained, "What is missing is definition, both of character and incident. The film unspools in nondescript touches, leaving the viewer

Chester Morris and Una Merkel in THE BAT WHISPERS (1931).

to care only little about the victims and, for that matter, about the identity of The Bat himself."

BEHIND THAT CURTAIN (Fox, 1929) 91 minutes.

Presenter, William Fox; director, Irving Cummings; based on the novel by Earl Derr Biggers; screenplay, Sonya Levien, Clarke Silvernail; titles, Wilbur Morse, Jr.; assistant director, Charles Woolstenhulme; sound, George P. Costello; camera, Conrad Wells, Dave Ragin, Vincent Farrar; editor, Alfred De Gaetano.

Warner Baxter (John Beetham); Lois Moran (Eve Mannering); Gilbert Emery (Sir Frederic Bruce); Claude King (Sir George Mannering); Philip Strange (Eric Durand); Boris Karloff (Sudanese Servant); Jamiel Hassen (Habib Hanna); Peter Gawthorne (Scotland Yard Inspector); John Rogers (Alf Pornick); Montague Shaw (Hilary Galt); Finch Smiles (Galt's Clerk); Mercedes De Valaco (Nunah); E. L. Park (Charlie Chan).

Heiress Eve Mannering (Lois Moran) marries Eric Durand (Philip Strange), not realizing he is only after her fortune. When her uncle (Claude King) hires a London barrister named Hilary Galt (Montague Shaw) to investigate Durand's past, the scoundrel kills the investigator. On their honeymoon in India, Eve discovers Durand is after her money and she leaves him to embark on a Sudanese desert expedition with an old family acquaintance, John Beetham (Warner Baxter), an explorer and lecturer. However, fearing she will involve her friend in the sordid mess with Durand, she leaves for San Francisco where she takes a job as an elevator operator. Also arriving in the city is Scotland Yard investigator Sir Frederic Bruce (Gilbert Emery), who is hunting Galt's killer and still suspects Beetham, since a gift (a pair of Chinese slippers) from him was found on the victim. Bruce attends a lecture given by Beetham and there it is revealed that Durand is the true murderer. As the latter attempts to escape, he is killed by Bruce's police associate, Charlie Chan (E. L. Park). Eve can now wed Beetham.

BEHIND THAT CURTAIN was based on Earl Derr Biggers' 1928 novel of the same title, which had also been serialized in The Saturday *Evening Post* . The book had been written as a Charlie Chan adventure but when it was filmed (in both sound and silent versions) the bulk of the sleuthing was shifted to the Scotland Yard inspector; Chan (E. L. Park) makes only a brief, subordinate appearance. Considering the future of the Charlie Chan character on screen, it is ironic that *Variety* should report of BEHIND THAT CURTAIN, "The production hasn't a conspicuously dull moment except in one short sequence in which E. L. Park as Charlie Chan, Bruce's Chinese lieutenant, is forced to recite several Sunday comic strip lines." Also in a brief appearance in BEHIND THAT CURTAIN is Boris Karloff, in his sound film debut, as a Sudanese servant. *Photoplay* magazine dubbed the picture a "Well done but rambling mystery melodrama well acted by Warner Baxter and Lois Moran."

The novel *Behind That Curtain* would be refilmed by Fox in 1932 as CHARLIE CHAN'S CHANCE, the third feature to star Warner Oland as the Chinese sleuth.

BEHIND THE MASK (Monogram, 1946) 67 minutes.

Producer, Joe Kaufman; associate producer, Lou Brock; director, Phil Karlson; based on the radio character "The Shadow" created by Maxwell Grant [Walter B. Gibson]; screenplay, George Callahan; art director, David Milton; set decorator, George Mitchell; assistant director, Arthur Gardner; camera, William A. Sickner; editor, Ace Herman.

Kane Richmond (Lamont Cranston); Barbara Reed (Margo Lane); George Chandler (Shrevvie); Joseph Crehan (Cardona); Pierre Watkin (Weston); Dorothea Kent (Jennie); Joyce Compton (Lulu); Marjorie Hoshelle (Mae Bishop); June Clyde (Edith Merrill); Robert Shayne (Brad Thomas); Lou Crosby (Marty Greane); Edward

Kane Richmond and George Chandler in BEHIND THE MASK (1946).

Gargan (Dixon); Bill Christy (Copy Boy); James Cardwell (Jeff Mann); Nancy Brinckman (Susan); Dewey Robinson (Headwaiter); Marie Harmon (Girl); Ruth Cherrington (Dowager); James Nataro (Reporter).

The popular radio crime-fighting series, "The Shadow" by Maxwell Grant [Walter B. Gibson], ran on the airwaves for two decades from 1936 to 1956 and the Mutual series first starred Orson Welles as Lamont Cranston, who used invisibility to uphold the law. He was abetted by his troubleshooting girl friend, Margo Lane. Bret Morrison, who performed the lead part from 1944 to 1956, is most often associated with "The Shadow" role, although in 1946 Kane Richmond essayed the part in a trio of low-budget entries for Monogram Pictures: THE SHADOW RETURNS, *q.v.*, BEHIND THE MASK, and THE MISSING LADY. According to an article on Richmond in *Screen Thrills Illustrated* magazine (April, 1963), "Fitting the part to a 'T', Kane provided mystery fans with an unforgettable masked performance in the three films."

When blackmailer/newspaper columnist Brad Thomas (Robert Shayne) is murdered mysteriously, playboy Lamont Cranston (Kane Richmond), who is really The Shadow, gets on the case with the aid of his jealous lady friend, Margo Lane (Barbara Reed). Since it is The Shadow who is accused of the crime, Cranston is eager to clear his alter-ego and he goes to a nightclub which he finds is a front for a clip joint operation. He also discovers that a dance hall run by Mae Bishop (Marjorie Hoshelle) is really the base for a bookie sham and that Mae was being blackmailed by Thomas. Finally Lamont finds that the newspaper for which Thomas worked was being utilized as the headquarters for a blackmail racket operated by its city editor (George Chandler). Cranston also unmasks the killer who has been impersonating The Shadow.

Variety, in judging the film, said it had " . . . trouble deciding whether to be comedy or melodrama. . . . Phil Karlson's direction launches the melodrama with a bang to set the scene but isn't as adept at comedy."

The Shadow's most recent screen appearances occurred in INVISIBLE AVENGER (1958) and BOURBON STREET SHADOWS (1962), with Richard Derr playing Lamont Cranston. These cheap entries derived from segments of an unsold TV series produced by Republic Pictures.

THE BENSON MURDER CASE (Paramount, 1930) 65 minutes.

Director, Frank Tuttle; based on the novel by S. S. Van Dine [Willard Huntington Wright]; screenplay, Bartlett Cormack; dialogue director, Perry Ivins; sound, Harold M. McNiff; camera, A. J. Stout; editor, Doris Drought.

William Powell (Philo Vance); Natalie Moorhead (Fanny Del Roy); Eugene Pallette (Sergeant Ernest Heath); Paul Lukas (Adolph Mohler); William Boyd (Harry Gray); E. H. Calvert (District Attorney John F. X. Markham); Richard Tucker (Anthony Benson); May Beatty (Mrs. Paula Banning); Mischa Auer (Albert); Otto Yamaoka (Sam); Charles McMurphy (Burke); Dick Rush (Welch); Perry Ivins (Dealer).

Suave William Powell enacted the role of sophisticated sleuth Philo Vance for the third time* in THE BENSON MURDER CASE, based on S. S. Van Dine's 1926 novel of the same title. It was to be his last Vance movie for three years, until Powell returned to the part for a final time in Warner Bros.' THE KENNEL MURDER CASE (1933), *q.v.* The fact that the scenarists had taken great liberties with the book original did not go unnoticed by astute filmgoers, nor by the critics. ("What Paramount has produced is an original mystery yarn studio-tailored by Bartlett Cormack in a misguided effort to gild the lily," reported *Variety*.) The *New York Times*' Mordaunt Hall was underwhelmed by the production, judging it only "a moderately entertaining affair" and noting that "several of the players appear to be somewhat conscious of the microphone as they speak their lines." As for Powell's assured performance as the upper-crust gumshoe, Hall of the Times acknowledged, "Mr. Powell handles the part of Vance . . . with no little skill" and the reviewer appreciated that "While most of the other characters suspect each other, Mr. Vance, through his keen observation, is never mistaken."

Having betrayed and sold out many of his friends and acquaintances in the Wall Street market, stock broker Anthony Benson (Richard Tucker) retreats to his remote hunting lodge accompanied by Harry Gray (William Boyd), whom he also cheated. Three others follow Benson. They are: Adolph Mohler (Paul Lukas), a forger whose checks are held by Benson; Mohler's lover, Mrs. Paula Banning (May Beatty), a widow who has been fleeced by Benson; and Fanny Del Roy (Natalie Moorhead), an actress who provided her pearls as collateral for Mohler's checks only to have them stolen. Detective Philo Vance (William Powell) and District Attorney John F. X. Markham (E. H. Calvert) visit the lodge and soon afterwards

---

*William Powell had played Philo Vance in THE CANARY MURDER CASE (1929) and THE GREENE MURDER CASE (1929), *qq.v.*, and he as Vance and Pallette (again as Heath) had made guest appearances in the "Detective Sequence" in PARAMOUNT ON PARADE (1930).

Benson is found murdered. Police Sergeant Ernest Heath (Eugene Pallette)* is called into the case, but he cannot figure out who committed the murder. Vance puzzles out the facts by re-enacting the crime and establishes who the actual killer is.

THE BENSON MURDER CASE was released in both sound and silent versions. In addition, a Spanish-language edition of the detective feature, called EL CUERPO DEL LITO [The Corpus Delicti] was shot on the same sets as the Powell picture. Ramon Pereda was Vance, Antonio Moreno played Mohler, Maria Alba was the actress, and Carlos Villarias was Markham.

BERMUDA MYSTERY (Twentieth Century-Fox, 1944) 65 minutes.

Producer, William Girard; director, Benjamin Stoloff; story, John Larkin; screenplay, W. Scott Darling; art directors, James Bassevi, Russell Spencer; set decorators, Thomas Little, Al Orenbach; assistant director, Tom Dudley; music, Arthur Lange; music director, Emil Newman; sound, George Leverett, Harry M. Leonard; special effects, Fred Sersen; camera, Joseph La Shelle; editor, Norman Colbert.

Preston Foster (Steve Carromond); Ann Rutherford (Constance Martin); Charles Butterworth (Dr. Tilford); Helene Reynolds (Angela); Jean Howard (Mrs. Tilford); Richard Lane (Detective Sergeant Donovan); Roland Drew (Mr. Best); John Eldredge (Mr. Brooks); Theodore Von Eltz (Mr. Cooper); Pierre Watkin (Mr. Bond); Jason Robards (Dunham); Kane Richmond (Mr. Martin); Holmes Herbert (Judge).

Six World War I veterans and long-time pals—Dr. Tilford (Charles Butterworth), Best (Roland Drew), Brooks (John Eldredge), Cooper (Theodore Von Eltz), Bond (Pierre Watkin), and Martin (Kane Richmond)—jointly purchase a ten-year annuity with the survivors to collect the benefits on the due date. When that time approaches some of the members begin to die mysteriously and Constance Martin (Ann Rutherford) worries that her uncle, Mr. Martin, was killed by a poisoned cigarette, although the official verdict was heart failure. She hires private investigator Steve Carromond (Preston Foster) to delve into the matter, but he is initially more concerned with his pending marriage to Angela (Helene Reynolds) than with the case. Still, Carromond carries out his assignment and soon begins to feel that Constance is right in her

---

*Much was made of the fact that gruff-voiced, rotund Sergeant Heath in this film showed a marked improvement in numbskull intelligence and a recent schooling in the detection techniques of Sherlock Holmes. He constantly responds to plot advances with "purely elementary," and even growls "My dear Watson" on occasion; all as part of the character's hokum comedy relief requirements.

assumption. In addition, the two fall in love with each other. Receiving little assistance from police Sergeant Donovan (Richard Lane), the duo ferret out the killer and Carromond breaks his engagement with Angela to continue romancing his new client.

Variety termed this "B" unit programmer from Twentieth Century-Fox " . . . a routine whodunit with stock situations and obvious development. Too many characters are rung in as possible villains to make the yarn at all plausible and some weak comedy doesn't help it along." And Bosley Crowther (*New York Times*) queried, "The only mystery about BERMUDA MYSTERY . . . is why do they call it BERMUDA MYSTERY when everything happens in New York?"

THE BIG FIX (Universal, 1978) Color 108 minutes.

Producers, Carl Borack, Richard Dreyfuss; director, Jeremy Paul Kagan; based on the novel by Roger L. Simon; screenplay, Simon; production designer, Robert F. Boyle; art director, Raymond Brandt; set decorator, Mary Ann Biddle; costumes, Edith Head; makeup, Charles Schram, Alan Friedman; music, Bill Conti; assistant directors, Robert Latham Brown, Candace Allen, John C. Andersen, Paul Chavez; stunt co-ordinator, Richard E. Butler; sound, David Ronne; sound editor, John Gosden; sound effects editor, John Stacy; special effects, Jack Faggart; camera, Frank Stanley; editor, Patrick Kennedy; documentary/additional sequences editor, James Symons.

Richard Dreyfuss (Moses Wine); Susan Anspach (Lila); Bonnie Bedelia (Suzanne); John Lithgow (Sam Sebastian); Ofelia Medina (Alora); Nicholas Coster (Spitzler); F. Murray Abraham (Howard Eppis) Fritz Weaver (Oscar Procari, Sr.); Jorge Cervera, Jr. (Jorge); Michael Hershewe (Jacob); Rita Karin (Aunt Sonya); Ron Rifkin (Randy); Larry Bishop (Wilson); Andrew Block (Michael Linker); Sidney Clute (Mr. Johnson); John Cunningham (Miles Hawthorne); Frank Doubleday (Jonah's Partner); Joyce Easton (Woman in Mercedes); Martin Garner (Bittleman); Danny Gellis (Simon); William Glover (Commentator); Kathryn Grody (Wendy Linker); Murray MacLeod (Perry); Ray Martucci, Bob O'Connell, Caskey Swaim (Policemen); Lupe Ontiveros (Maid); Dick Whittington (Newsman); Steven Benedict (Student); Rene Botana (Rene); Harry Caesar (Burke); Billy Cardenas (Chicano); Jane Chastain (Sports Announcer); Willie Dovan (Elderly Servant); Fred Franklyn, Joel Frederick, Margie Gordon, Gregory Prentiss (Reporters); Chester Grimes (Chester); Pat Hustis (Dealer); David Matthau (Volunteer); John Mayo (Dillworthy); Mandy Patinkin (Pool Man); Raphael Simon (Nicholas Eppis); David Rowlands (Jonah); Al Ruban (Detective); Running Deer (Luis Vasquez); June Sanders (Policewoman); Miiko Taka (Saleswoman); Joe Warfield (Worker); James Wing Woo (Harold Pak Chung).

Roger L. Simon's 1973 detective novel featured Moses Wine, a Los Angeles-based industrial investigator, whose days of glory were in the 1960s as a college campus radical. The property was tailored by the author as a screen vehicle for co-producer/star Richard Dreyfuss. Despite production problems, THE BIG FIX was heralded as the start of a new movie detective series. *Variety* pegged Moses Wine as "the 1970's answer to Philip Marlowe, Lew Archer and Sam Spade" and insisted the film was "surefire" as a box-office winner.

Disillusioned Moses Wine (Richard Dreyfuss), divorced from his wife (Bonnie Bedelia) and with custody of their two young sons, meets Lila (Susan Anspach) with whom he shared romance and radical ideals during college days at Berkeley. Lila is working for the middle-of-the-road political campaign of Miles Hawthorne (John Cunningham), who is running for California's governorship. Lila asks Wine to investigate a troublesome situation at campaign headquarters. There organizer Sam Sebastian (John Lithgow) asks Wine to learn why extreme activist Howard Eppis (F. Murray Abraham) is supporting Hawthorne's candidacy, which is sure to discredit Hawthorne with many of his followers. Eppis, Wine learns, is supposedly living in Cuba. The trail points to Oscar Procari, Jr., who has disappeared, and to a Korean named James Wing Woo (Harold Pak Chung) who apparently ordered the damaging leaflets printed, but the latter refuses to talk. When Lila is found murdered, Wine quits the case in disgust. However, he is now the focus of several people's interest and they draw him back into activity on the case. Wealthy Oscar Procari, Sr. (Fritz Weaver) insists that Wine find his vanished son, and the C.I.A. wants to know more about Wine's political associations. Wine discovers that Sebastian's girlfriend is working for Hawthorne's opponent in the gubernatorial race, but Sebastian claims she is a plant to gain information for Hawthorne's cause. Wine locates Eppis, who is living quietly with his wife and children, but when two thugs attempt to kill Eppis, the detective realizes he was set up to lead them to Eppis. Later, Wine prevents Woo from blowing up the freeway in the name of Eppis (which would discredit Hawthorne's campaign). It develops that Sebastian is not who he says he is and that his dictatorial father is behind the scheme, intent on dishonoring radicals in favor of right-wing conservatives.

With all the hoopla surrounding this feature—it was Richard Dreyfuss' first screen appearance since winning an Academy Award for THE GOODBYE GIRL (1977) and much was made of the film's talent being former 1960s political demonstrators—it was a major surprise to many that the picture did such insignificant box-office business. After all, here was a different type of private eye. As Pauline Kael analyzed in *The New Yorker* magazine, "Moses Wine isn't merely the usual cynical, down-at-the-heels private eye; he's warm and Jewish and disillusioned, with two small sons to support from a failed marriage. . . ." But, warned Kael, "This a private eye so full of love it oozes out of him; he's creamy." The reviewer further emphasized the counter-aesthetics of Dreyfuss' self-indulgent performance, "He's so endearing, he acts with such cherubic self-satisfaction, that he should be billed as Richard 'Cuddles' Dreyfuss." Viewers did not respond to his overly ethnic and maudlin professional snoop who spends more time reminiscing over his lost youth and ideals than in dealing practically with day-to-day survival. The gimmick of the single father traipsing around the by-ways and barrios of Los Angeles with his Aunt Sonya (Rita Karin) and two small boys in tow, wore thin very quickly. Tom Milne (British *Monthly Film Bulletin*) summed up the critical opinion: "Disappointingly, the final sequences, increasingly flashy and mechanical (complete with cute coda), turn into routine TV thriller stuff."

Needless to say, plans to film Simon's other Moses Wine novels, including Peking Duck (1979), never materialized.

THE BIG SLEEP (Warner Bros., 1946) 114 minutes.

Producer/director, Howard Hawks; based on the novel by Raymond Chandler; screenplay, William Faulkner, Leigh Brackett, Jules Furthman; music, Max Steiner; orchestrator, Simon Burcharoff; assistant director, Robert Vreeland; art director, Carl Jules Weyl; set decorator, Fred M. MacLean; gowns, Leah Rhodes; sound, Robert B. Lee; special effects, E. Roy Davidson, Warren E. Lynch, William McGann, Robert Burks, William Van Enger; camera, Sid Hickox; editor, Christian Nyby.

Humphrey Bogart (Philip Marlowe); Lauren Bacall (Vivian Sternwood Rutledge); John Ridgely (Eddie Mars); Martha Vickers (Carmen Sternwood); Dorothy Malone (Bookshop Proprietress); Peggy Knudsen (Mrs. Eddie Mars): Regis Toomey (Bernie Ohls); Charles Waldron (General Sternwood); Charles D. Brown (Norris); Bob Steele (Canino); Elisha Cook, Jr. (Harry Jones); Louis Jean Heydt (Joe Brody); Sonia Darrin (Agnes); James Flavin (Captain Cronjager); Thomas Jackson (District Attorney Wilde); Dan Wallace (Caroll Lundgren); Theodore Von Eltz (Arthur Gwynn Geiger); Joy Barlowe (Taxicab Driver); Tom Fadden (Sidney); Ben Welden (Pete); Trevor Bardette (Art Huck); Joseph Crehan (Medical Examiner); Emmett Vogan (Ed).

THE BIG SLEEP (United Artists, 1978) Color 99 minutes.

Producers, Elliott Kastner, Michael Winner; associate producer, Bernard Williams; director, Winner; based on the novel by Raymond Chandler; screenplay, Winner; production designer, Harry Pottle; art director, John Graysmark; costumes, Ron Beck; makeup, Richard Mills; music, Jerry Fielding; song, Lynsey de Paul; assistant director, Michael Dryhurst; sound, Brian Marshall; sound editors, Russ Hill, Mike Le Mare, John Pouyner; camera, Robert Paynter; editor, Freddie Wilson.

Robert Mitchum (Philip Marlowe); Sarah Miles (Charlotte Sternwood Regan); Richard Boone (Lash Canino); Candy Clark (Camilla Sternwood); Joan Collins (Agnes Lozelle); Edward Fox (Joe Brody); John Mills (Inspector Jim Carson); James Stewart (General Guy de Brisai Sternwood); Oliver Reed (Eddie Mars); Harry Andrews (Butler Norris); Colin Blakely (Harry Jones); Richard Todd (Commander Barker); Diana Quick (Mona Grant); James Donald (Inspector Gregory); John Justin (Arthur Gwynn Geiger); Simon Turner (Karl Lundgren); Martin Potter (Owen Taylor); David Savile (Rusty Regan); Dudley Sutton (Lanny); Don Henderson (Lou); Nik Forster (Croupier); Joe Ritchie (Taxi Driver); Patrick Durkin (Reg); Derek Deadman (Customer in Bookstore); Mike Lewin (Detective Waring); David Jackson (Inspector Willis); David Millett (Detective); Clifford Earl (Police Doctor); Michael Segal (Barman); Norman Lumsden (Lord Smethurst); Judy Buxton (Receptionist at the Cheval Club).

Raymond Chandler's first novel, *The Big Sleep* (which refers to death), was published in 1939 and featured rugged private eye Philip Marlowe dipping in and out of the underside of the sinister and seedy parts of Los Angeles. Following Dick Powell's onscreen success as detective Marlowe in another Chandler property—RKO's MURDER, MY SWEET (1944), *q.v.,*—*The Big Sleep* was purchased by Warner Bros. and Humphrey Bogart was cast as Marlowe. Chandler's initial Marlowe detective novel is an intriguing but highly complicated mystery which heavily relies on its feel for the Los Angeles of its day and its raft of corrupt characters; Marlowe himself being just a cut above the rest of the shady lot. The 1946 film's best attribute is that it was shot in the period in which the novel took place, although due to contemporary censorship codes many of the racy subplots were eliminated or only hinted at in the resultant scenario. Nevertheless, the movie captures beautifully the flavor of Chandler's work and it is grandly cast, especially in its supporting roles, such as Bob Steele's cold-blooded killer Canino, Martha Vickers as nymphomaniac Carmen Sternwood, and Louis Jean Heydt as the grasping Joe Brody.

Private eye Philip Marlowe (Humphrey Bogart) is hired by dying General Sternwood (Charles Waldron) to put a stop to blackmailer Arthur Gwynn Geiger (Theodore Von Eltz), who has taken nude photos of his younger daughter Carmen (Martha Vickers) and is peddling them to the highest bidder. Geiger, however, is murdered by the family chauffeur, who has been romancing Carmen. The chauffeur also is later found dead. Meanwhile the photos come into the possession of Joe Brody (Louis Jean Heydt), the boyfriend of Agnes (Sonia Darrin), Geiger's Hollywood bookstore employee. Brody attempts to sell the photos to Vivian Sternwood (Lauren Bacall), Carmen's older sister, who thinks her father has hired Marlowe to find the missing Shawn Regan. Brody, however, is murdered by Caroll Lundgren (Dan Wallace), the boyfriend of Geiger, since Lundgren thought it was Brody who had murdered Geiger. Marlowe brings in Lundgren and turns him over to police Captain Bernie Ohls (Regis Toomey). Vivian now wants Marlowe to drop the case since the photos have been recovered. However, Marlowe discover a connection with gambler Eddie Mars (John Ridgely), Geiger's landlord, who apparently knows something about

Lauren Bacall, Paul Webber and Humphrey Bogart in THE BIG SLEEP (1946).

Vivian, and whose wife (Peggy Kundsen), it is rumored, has run off with Regan. After Marlowe prevents Vivian from being robbed outside Mars' gambling boat he meets Harry Jones (Elisha Cook, Jr.), Agnes' new squeeze, who says he can take him directly to Eddie's wife. At his office building Marlowe, however, witnesses Jones' murder by Canino (Bob Steele), Mars' hired gun. Agnes then instructs Marlowe to go to a garage owned by Art Huck (Trevor Bardette); there he is captured by Canino and finds Mrs. Mars is there as well as Vivian. The latter sets Marlowe free and when Canino returns, the gumshoe kills him in a fight. Marlowe then takes Vivian and makes an appointment with Mars to meet at Geiger's home. Mars brings his thugs with him and leaves them outside to ambush Marlowe. However, the detective is already in the house with Vivian and he announces to Mars that Mars is behind all the crimes. Regan was killed by crazy Carmen when he refused her advances and to protect her sister, Vivian got Mars to spread the rumor that Regan had run away with wife, whom he then kept hidden. In return he blackmailed Vivian and ordered Canino to kill Jones when the later learned of Mrs. Mars' whereabouts; Mars also ordered Marlowe killed. Since he knows Marlowe has no proof, Mars admits to this and the detective forces him outside where the gangster is killed by his own men. Marlowe summons Ohls and his men.

Variety reported, "THE BIG SLEEP follows the Raymond Chandler formula. Mix one private eye, hard-skilled and honest, with a police blotter full of murder and mayhem, chiselers, treacherous females, gunfire, assault and battery, sordid motives and sexual by-play. . . . Rumors around Hollywood had it that THE BIG SLEEP needed a lot of patching via retakes and cutting, but it comes off as first-rate melodrama." The film, which was completed in January 1945 but not generally released until August 1946, did go through much re-writing (for example the killer was changed from Carmen in the novel to Mars in the film) and the character of Vivian was toned down greatly for the feature version.

The resultant film was a big commercial hit. It did not seem to matter that many moviegoers (like readers of the original novel) were confused by the too intricately tangled plot. The screen teaming of Bogart and Bacall* was at its box-office peak, and viewers

---

*Bogart and Bacall, who married on May 21, 1945, had already appeared together in producer/director Howard Hawks' TO HAVE AND HAVE NOT (1944), with a screenplay written by William Faulkner and Jules Furthman. Hawks, Faulkner, Furthman (and added scenarist Leigh Brackett) would be responsible for THE BIG SLEEP. Earlier in 1946 Bogart and Bacall were seen in guest cameo assignments in the Dennis Morgan-Jack Carson comedy, TWO GUYS FROM MILWAUKEE.

responded enthusiastically to the romantic sparks that flowed between the cynical gumshoe, who is still more of an optimist, and his wealthy lady love, Vivian. James Agee *(The Nation* magazine) concluded, "THE BIG SLEEP is a violent, smoky cocktail shaken together from most of the printable misdemeanors and some that aren't. . . . Humphrey Bogart and several proficient minor players keep anchoring it to some sufficient kind of reality. The picture is often brutal and sometimes sinister. . . ."

With THE BIG SLEEP Humphrey Bogart consolidated the celluloid image of the typical movie gumshoe, complete with trench coat, cigarette dangling from his lip, and lots of tough talk. In *Film Noir: An Encyclopedic Reference to the American Style* (1979), James Paris, Julie Kirgo, and Alain Silver examine the complex Philip Marlowe character in their essay on THE BIG SLEEP: "Both the novel Marlowe and the film Marlowe are outsiders. . . . They seem to search in the world for fleeting glimpses of compassion, of simple human feeling; but they are unwilling to be the first to betray such feelings in themselves. In fact, both Marlowes guard their private ground . . . tenaciously. . . . Both versions of Marlowe possess a fairly explicit sense of, if not morality per se, at least right conduct."

It was in the mid-1970s that the Philip Marlowe character had a resurgence of popularity when Eliot Kastner produced FAREWELL MY LOVELY (1975), *q.v.* with Robert Mitchum as the detective. Three years later Kastner teamed with director Michael Winner to do a remake of THE BIG SLEEP, with Winner himself adapting Chandler's classic novel. Marc Sigloff judged in *The Films of the Seventies* (1984) that it was ". . . a disastrous remake. . . . All the elements that made the first such a success were completely ignored in the sequel. Mitchum nicely repeats his role as Marlowe, but nothing else seems to work, from its contemporary London setting to its poor script." F. Maurice Speed was more accepting in *Film Review 1979-80* (1979); he reported, "Far below the original but if you can temporarily forget that (or are unable to make such comparison) it is nevertheless a pretty entertaining thriller."

The 1978 version of THE BIG SLEEP has two major detriments, both of which occurred in order to reduce production budget costs. The film's locale is switched from Los Angeles to London and its time frame is the present rather than the late 1930s. Otherwise this film is a more faithful adaptation of the Chandler work, so faithful, in fact, that flashbacks within flashbacks are necessary to explain its complicated plot. Also, the evaporation of screen censorship provides a greater opportunity to delve into the more unsavory aspects of the case and nudity is also used: Candy Clark as nympho Camilla (instead of Carmen as in the novel and the first film)

Sternwood bares her assets on more than one occasion and near the finale of the film Sarah Miles as Charlotte (instead of Vivian) Sternwood shows up in a see-through blouse.

As noted, Robert Mitchum (despite being too old and too stocky for the character) is again top notch as the veteran detective, who, the script tells us, came to England during World War II and remained. The rest of the casting of this generally underrated melodrama is uniformly good, although Richard Boone's Canino is nowhere near as chilling as Bob Steele's portrayal in the 1946 edition. James Stewart provides an offbeat cameo as the dying General Sternwood, who is coming face to face with the "big sleep" and intends to have his affairs settled by Marlowe before his demise.

THE BISHOP MURDER CASE (Metro-Goldwyn-Mayer, 1930) 91 minutes.

Directors, Nick Grinde, David Burton; based on the novel by S. S. Van Dine; adaptor/screenplay/dialogue, Lenore J. Coffee; titles, Fred Niblo, Jr.; art director, Cedric Gibbons; wardrobe, Henrietta Frazer; sound, G. A. Burns; camera, Roy Overbaugh; editor, William Le Vanway.

Basil Rathbone (Philo Vance); Leila Hyams (Belle Dillard); Roland Young (Sigurd Arnesson); Alec B. Francis (Professor Bertrand Dillard); George F. Marion (Adolph Drukker); Zelda Sears (Mrs. Otto Drukker); Bodil Rosing (Greta Menzel); Carroll Nye (John F. Sprigg); Charles Quartermaine (John Pardee); James Donlan (Sergeant Ernest Heath); Sidney Bracey (Robin Pyne); Clarence Geldert (District Attorney John F. X. Markham); Delmer Daves (Raymond Sperling); Nellie Bly Baker (Beedle).

William Powell played Philo Vance in two 1929 Paramount entries: THE CANARY MURDER CASE and THE GREENE MURDER CASE, *qq.v.*, and, early in 1930, MGM, eager to cash in on the rival studio's success, issued the first of a trio of its own Vance detective films. The first was based on S. S. Van Dine's 1929 novel, THE BISHOP MURDER CASE and starred Basil Rathbone as Vance.

On the archery range at the home of Professor Bertrand Dillard (Alec B. Francis), the body of Robin Pyne (Sidney Bracey) is found with an arrow in his chest. Amateur sleuth Philo Vance (Basil Rathbone) is also a guest and he takes over the investigation of the case in league with police Sergeant Ernest Heath (James Donlan) and District Attorney J. F. X. Markham (Clarence Geldert). The dead man's best friend, John Sprigg (Carroll Nye), vows revenge and he finds out that invalid Adolph Drukker (George F. Marion), a hunchback, witnessed the murder. However, he too is killed. The chief suspect appears to be Sigurd Arnesson (Roland Young), who had wanted to use scientific methods to solve the original murder. By now Vance realizes the killer has been fashioning his homicides around Mother Goose rhymes and he forces the killer's hand. The madman, who had lusted after his own niece (Leila Hyams), takes poison.

Although THE BISHOP MURDER CASE, issued in both sound and silent versions, had all the ingredients of which good mysteries are made, it was a slow-moving affair (a common problem with MGM products of that time). Still the film had "plenty of thrills" (*Variety*) and urbane and angular Basil Rathbone made a good Philo Vance as the *New York Times* noted: "Mr. Rathbone vies easily with William Powell as an interpreter of Philo Vance. So far as to which of the two is preferable in the role is a matter to be decided by the imaginative Mr. Van Dine."

It would be five years before MGM next offered the public a Philo Vance entertainment. In the meantime, the premier screen Vance, William Powell, had become MGM contract star (and was busy with a new detective series, The Thin Man) and Basil Rathbone had gone on to play an assortment of prime villains in the studio's major productions. Later, he was to emerge in his most famous role—as Sherlock Holmes—on film, radio, TV, stage, and recordings. So THE CASINO MURDER CASE (1935), *q.v.*, starred Paul Lukas and THE GARDEN MURDER CASE (1936), *q.v.*, featured Edmund Lowe.

THE BLACK BIRD (Columbia, 1975) Color 98 minutes.

Executive producer, George Segal; producers, Michael Levee, Lou Lombardo; director, David Giler; story, Don M. Mankiewicz, Gordon Cotler; screenplay, Giler; production designer, Harry Horner; set decorator, Darrell Silvera; music, Jerry Fielding; assistant director, Art Levinson; sound, Jack Solomon; camera, Phil Lathrop; editors, Margaret Booth, Walter Thompson, Lombardo.

George Segal (Sam Spade, Jr.); Stephane Audran (Anna Kemidon); Lionel Stander (Andrew Jackson Immelman); Lee Patrick (Effie Perine); Elisha Cook, Jr. (Wilmer); Felix Silla (Litvak); Signe Hasso (Dr. Crippen); John Abbott (DuQuai); Connie Kreski (Decoy Girl); Titus Napoleon, Harry Kenoi (Hawaiian Thugs); Howard Jeffrey (Kerkorian); Richard B. Shull (Prizer); Ken Swofford (McGregor).

Following the box-office success of THE MALTESE FALCON (1941), *q.v.*, Warner Bros. planned to team director John Huston again with Humphrey Bogart, Mary Astor, Sydney Greenstreet, and Peter Lorre for a sequel called THE FURTHER ADVENTURES

George Segal and Lee Patrick in THE BLACK BIRD (1975).

OF THE MALTESE FALCON. Unfortunately, the project was never realized. Long after the 1941 feature had become a cult classic, writer/director David Giler concocted THE BLACK BIRD in 1975, with star George Segal functioning as executive producer for this whimsical venture for Ray Stark's production unit at Columbia Pictures. It was shot in Los Angeles and not San Francisco, the locale of the film. About the only real interest engendered by this complicated spoof on Dashiell Hammett's beloved characters was that Lee Patrick and Elisha Cook, Jr. reprised their roles from the Huston milestone.

Sam Spade, Jr. (George Segal) operates his late father's detective agency in a sleazy section of San Francisco, with the now embittered (and much overweight) Effie Perine (Lee Patrick) staying on as his secretary. Caspar Gutman is found dead in the lobby of the building where Spade has his office and the detective learns that the fat man was still looking for the elusive and priceless Maltese Falcon statue. Mysterious beauty Anna Kemidon (Stephane Audran) enlists

Spade's aid in finding the relic and he is assisted by an unwanted bodyguard, Andrew Jackson Immelman (Lionel Stander). Also on the trail of the valuable bird is Litvak (Felix Silla), an evil dwarf who dispatches Gutman's former gunman Wilmer (Elisha Cook, Jr.) when the latter sets up a meeting with Spade. Spade realizes it was Litvak who also murdered Gutman, so he joins forces and soon falls in love with Anna. Spade obtains the Falcon finally but not before nearly getting double-crossed and almost killed.

THE BLACK BIRD rightfully did little box-office business. As George Larkin wrote in *Films in Review* magazine (February, 1976), filmmaker Giler ". . . sees the story of the falcon as mod black zany comedy, succeeding part of the time. . . . It all adds up to a mishmash which will infuriate the Hammett purists, and mildly entertain some filmgoers."

THE BLACK CAMEL (Fox, 1931) 71 minutes.

Director, Hamilton MacFadden; based on the novel by Earl Derr Biggers; screenplay, Hugh Strange, Barry Conners, Philip Klein; dialogue, Conners, Klein; sound, W. W. Lindsay, Jr.; camera, Joseph August, Dan Clark; editor, Al De Gaetano.

Warner Oland (Charlie Chan); Sally Eilers (Julie O'Neil); Bela Lugosi (Tarneverro); Dorothy Revier (Shelah Fane); Victor Varconi (Robert Fyfe); Robert Young (Jimmy Bradshaw); Marjorie White (Rita Ballou); Richard Tucker (Wilkie Ballou); J. M. Kerrigan (Thomas MacMaster); Mary Gordon (Mrs. MacMaster); C. Henry Gordon (Van Horn); Violet Dunn (Anna); William Post, Jr. (Alan Jaynes); Dwight Frye (Jessop); Murray Kinnell (Smith); Otto Yamaoka (Kashimo); Rita Roselle (Luana); Robert Homans (Chief of Police); Louise Mackintosh (Housekeeper).

THE BLACK CAMEL, taken from Earl Derr Biggers' 1929 novel, is the only Charlie Chan film to be made on location outside Hollywood, in this case in Honolulu, where the lure of the tropical islands was nicely captured by cinematographers Joseph August and Dan Clark. *Variety* noted, "Cleverly directed . . . there's enough plot development to switch anyone's convictions." The film's title derives from the old proverb, "Death is the black camel that kneels unbid at every gate." At the time of its release THE BLACK CAMEL gained extra box-office mileage from the fact that it co-starred Hungarian Bela Lugosi, fresh from his screen triumph in Universal's DRACULA (1931).

A movie company has come to Honolulu to make a picture and the star is Shelah Fane (Dorothy Revier), who intends to marry Alan Jaynes (William Post, Jr.). However, first she must consult the mystic Tarneverro (Bela Lugosi), whom she deeply trusts. Mean-

Violet Dunn, Warner Oland, and Bela Lugosi in THE BLACK CAMEL (1931).

while press agent Jimmy Bradshaw (Robert Young) is romancing Julie O'Neil (Sally Eilers), who travels with Shelah and Shelah's maid Anna (Violet Dunn) and butler Jessop (Dwight Frye), who is in love with Anna. Local police Inspector Charlie Chan (Warner Oland), with little help from bumbling assistant Kashimo (Otto Yamaoka), is still investigating the murder of Hollywood star Danny Mayo three years before. Shelah tells Tarneverro that she had been in Mayo's last picture, that she was in his home the night he died and that she witnessed the killing. Later Jaynes threatens Tarneverro over Shelah's decision not to marry him, but Chan intercedes. That evening Shelah is found murdered in the pavilion of her beach house and Chan pursues the assorted suspects. They include house guests Rita (Marjorie White) and Wilkie Ballou (Richard Tucker) and Van Horn (C. Henry Gordon), performers in her film, and her ex-husband Robert Fyfe (Victor Varconi), who was seen leaving the beach house that evening. Then beachcomber Smith (Murray Kinnell) is shot after being outside the pavilion and he accuses Fyfe of the shooting. Chan learns that Tarneverro is Danny Mayo's brother and he insists that Shelah told him she had killed the film actor because the latter was already married and could not wed her. Chan confronts the suspects at Shelah's home and draws out the killer.

The Charlie Chan films are known for the title character's constant use of aphorisms and THE BLACK CAMEL is no exception. The Chinese sleuth intones such phrases of wisdom as: "Wages of stupidity is hunt for new job," "Always harder to keep older secret than egg to bounce on sidewalk," "Alibi have habit of disappearing like hole in water," and "Sometimes wisest man mistake bumble bee for blackbird." In his second appearance as Charlie Chan, Swedish actor Warner Oland was well received. He ". . . gives to the picture a good and even performance," decided the *New York Times* which approved that "He follows clues to their ends, retains his bland manner while the lights go out and knives rattle about his head. . . ."

In *The Detective in Hollywood* (1978), Jon Tuska notes a similarity between this film's plot and an actual Hollywood scandal: "In making Shelah the murderer of the celebrated actor in the book, changed to a director in the photoplay (an even stronger analogy with William Desmond Taylor's murder), both Biggers and the Fox screenwriters were hinting at a solution to the real-life crime which was then whispered all over Hollywood: silent screen comedienne Mabel Norman had murdered Taylor in a lover's quarrel." It should be noted, however, than in the finished Charlie Chan film the murdered man, Danny Mayo, is an actor, not a director.

THE BLACK CAMEL would be remade in 1941 by Twentieth Century-Fox as CHARLIE CHAN IN RIO, *q.v.*

BLACK COFFEE (Woolf and Freedman Film Service, 1931) 78 minutes.

Producer, Julius Hagen; director, Leslie Hiscott; based on the play by Agatha Christie; screenplay, Brock Williams, H. Fowler Mear.

Austin Trevor (Hercule Poirot); Adrianne Allen (Lucia Amory); Richard Cooper (Captain Hastings); Elizabeth Allan (Barbara Amory); C. V. France (Sir Claude Amory); Philip Strange (Richard Amory); Dino Galvani (Dr. Carelli); Michael Shepley (Raynor); Melville Cooper (Inspector Japp); Marie Wright (Miss Amory); and: Harold Meade, S. A. Cookson, Leila Page.

Agatha Christie wrote the stage play *Black Coffee* in 1930 and it was produced in London late in the year with Francis L. Sullivan as the cultivated Belgian sleuth, Hercule Poirot. In 1931 Twickenham filmed the play with Austin Trevor, who had already played Poirot in

ALIBI (1931), again enacting the part of the crime-solver. The novelization of *Black Coffee* would appear in 1934.

Sir Claude Emory (C. V. France) has developed the formula for a powerful new weapon but he fears it may be stolen. He requests Belgian detective Hercule Poirot (Austin Trevor) and his long-standing friend Captain Hastings (Richard Cooper) to come to his country estate. However, before they arrive Amory is murdered. Also staying at the house are the murdered man's son, Richard (Philip Strange), and his wife Lucia (Adrianne Allen), his niece Barbara (Elizabeth Allan) and his maiden sister (Marie Wright), as well as his secretary, Raynor (Michael Shepley), and the visiting Dr. Carelli (Dino Galvani). Following the murder, Poirot and investigating officer Inspector Japp (Melville Cooper) discover that Amory's formula and private papers have been stolen and deduce that he was eliminated with poisoned coffee. Poirot allows the murderer to believe he too has succumbed to the tainted drink as he listens to the culprit's premature and very incriminating confession.

In British Sound Films: The Studio Years 1928-59 (1984), David Shipman summarized of BLACK COFFEE, "As usual, Poirot triumphs, but critical reaction was mixed." *Variety* judged it the "Sort of film which is never less than interesting, but never much more so. . . ." Michael Tennenbaum opined in *The New Bedside, Bathtub & Armchair Companion to Agatha Christie* (1986), "This film suffered from being stage-bound, and Trevor's portrayal was completely overshadowed by the true-to-Christie characterizations of Poirot by Charles Laughton and Francis Sullivan on stage."

Austin Trevor would interpret the role of the colorful criminal investigator once again in 1934 in LORD EDGWARE DIES, *q.v.*

THE BLACK DOLL (Universal, 1938) 66 minutes.

Producer, Irving Starr; director, Otis Garrett; based on the novel by William Edward Hayes; adaptor, Harold Buckley; art director, Ralph Berger; set decorator, Emil Kuri; gowns, Vera West; music director, Charles Previn; sound, Charles Carroll; camera, Stanley Cortez, Ira Morgan; editor, Maurice Wright.

Nan Grey (Marion Rood); Donald Woods (Nick Halstead); Edgar Kennedy (Sheriff Renick); William Lundigan (Rex Leland); C. Henry Gordon (Nelson Rood); John Wray (Walling); Doris Lloyd (Mrs. Laura Leland); Holmes Herbert (Dr. Giddings); Addison Richards (Mallison); Inez Palange (Rosita); Syd Saylor (Red); Arthur Hoyt (Coroner); Fred Malatesta (Estaban).

An atmospheric "B" film based on William Edward Hayes' 1936 novel, THE BLACK DOLL was produced as part of Universal's ongoing "Crime Club" movie series. Set in a spooky, remote house on a stormy night, the film is filled with red herrings and supported by a fair mystery plot. The proceedings are greatly lightened (or burdened, depending on your viewpoint) by Edgar Kennedy's work as the bumbling sheriff who is at odds with private eye Nick Halstead (Donald Woods), whom the sheriff refers to as a "pussy footer." It is, of course, the detective who solves the case by pointing out the murderer.

Wealthy Nelson Rood (C. Henry Gordon) tells his playboy nephew Rex Leland (William Lundigan) to straighten up or go to jail after the latter forges a check. When Leland's overprotective mother Laura (Doris Lloyd) asks Rood for money to cover her son's debts, he refuses and they quarrel. A black doll—a sign of death—is left on Rood's desk and he calls ex-partners Mallison (Addison Richardson) and Walling (John Wray) to come and stay the night. He confronts them with the doll but they feign no knowledge of it. Rood also orders detective Nick Halstead (Donald Woods) off his property when he finds him with his pretty daughter Marion (Nan Grey). That night Rood is murdered by a knife in the back and a black doll is left beside him. Sheriff Renick (Edgar Kennedy) and his dense deputy, Red (Syd Saylor), arrive to question the suspects, who also include butler Estaban (Fred Malatesta) and his wife, maid Rosita (Inez Palange). The coroner (Arthur Hoyt) comes with Renick and later Dr. Giddings (Holmes Herbert) appears and soon Mallison is found strangled to death. Walling admits to Renick and Halstead that he and Mallison had once been partnered with Rood in a Mexican mine property and that Rood had killed the fourth partner, Knox Burrows—who is Marion's real father—and feared they would tell. The man insists Burrows has returned for revenge. Later, Dr Giddings tells Halstead that he and Laura plan to wed, something Rood had strongly opposed. When someone throws a doll at Marion, Estaban comes to her rescue and is shot. The suspects are summoned to the kitchen and as Halstead prepares a late dinner ("I may be a rotten detective, but I'm a very good potato fryer," he insists), he reviews the case, eliminating suspects and singling out the killer. The latter tries to escape but is captured.

In its unpretentious way, THE BLACK DOLL is diverting entertainment, thanks particularly to an ingratiating performance by Donald Woods (who had appeared as Perry Mason in a Warner Bros. programmer a few years earlier). B. R. Crisler (*New York Times*) took the occasion to tease the movie genre when he wrote in his THE BLACK DOLL review, "If we were members of the Crime Club . . . we'd blackball any mystery story . . . unless the murder or murders were committed by (1) the amateur detective himself; (2) the ingenue—and don't think ingenues are so innocent! (3) the comic relief, including even Edgar Kennedy, or (4) the author, who, in most murder stories, we think, is really the guiltiest party. Moreover, we'd keep our murders psychologically clean by insisting that they be motiveless. . . ."

BLACK MAGIC (Monogram, 1944) 67 minutes.

Producer, Philip N. Krasne, James S. Burkett; director, Phil Rosen, based on the character created by Earl Derr Biggers; story/ screenplay, George Callahan; art director, David Milton; music, Alexander Laszlo; music director, David Chudnow; assistant director, Richard L'Estrange; sound, Max Hutchinson; camera, Arthur Martinelli; editor, John Link.

Sidney Toler (Charlie Chan); Mantan Moreland (Birmingham Brown); Frances Chan (Frances Chan); Joseph Crehan (Captain Matthews); Jacqueline DeWit (Justine Bonner); Ralph Peters (Rafferty); Helen Beverley (Norma Duncan); Frank Jaquet (Paul Hamlin); Dick Gordon (Bonner); Charles Jordan (Tom Starkey); Claudia Dell (Vera Starkey); Geraldine Wall (Harriet Green); Harry Depp (Charles Edwards); Edward Earle (Dawson).

Birmingham Brown (Mantan Moreland) takes a job as a butler in the home of Justine Bonner (Jacqueline DeWit), who operates a spiritualist racket which she uses to blackmail her clients. Frances Chan (herself), the daughter of the famous detective Charlie Chan (Sidney Toler), who is Birmingham's former employer, is present at a seance where a man is murdered. Police Captain Matthews (Joseph Crehan) threatens to hold Frances as an accessory unless Chan agrees to solve the caper. Thus the unwilling Charlie Chan comes to the mysterious house and uncovers the fake racket, prevents another intended homicide, and brings the culprit (one of Justine's customers) to justice.

Also called CHARLIE CHAN IN BLACK MAGIC, the film is an eerie affair, especially in the seance segments, although the old house set employed in the feature was seen in many, many other Monogram films. Particularly interesting are the scenes showing Chan uncovering the various devices used by the fake medium to carry out her scam. The murder weapon is ingenious: the killer uses bullets made from frozen blood which are kept in a refrigerated cigar case. The missiles melt after impact, thus removing any traces of a weapon.

For once a Charlie Chan picture had a distaff Chan offspring involved in the case instead of Chan's usual number one, two or three son providing interfering help. Frances Chan made a most comely addition, not only to the Chan household but also to this fairly well executed mystery programmer.

When United Artists released its Orson Welles' feature, BLACK MAGIC, in 1949, this Charlie Chan film's title was altered to MEETING AT MIDNIGHT for reissues. It is the only Chan film so far in the public domain and as such is a popular video-cassette item.

BLACKMAIL (Wardour, 1929) 96 minutes.

Producer, John Maxwell; director, Alfred Hitchcock; based on the play by Charles Bennett; screenplay, Bennett, Benn W. Levy, Garnett Weston, Hitchcock; camera, Jack Cox.

Anny Ondra (Alice White);* John Longden (Frank Webber); Donald Calthrop (Tracy); Cyril Ritchard (The Artist); Sara Allgood (Mrs. White); Charles Paton (Mr. White); Harvey Braban (Inspector);** Phyllis Monkman (Gossip); Hannah Jones (Landlady); Percy Parsons (Crook); Johnny Butt (Sergeant).

Alfred Hitchcock's first sound thriller, BLACKMAIL, went into production as a silent feature but with the acceptance of sound as a commercial reality, partially re-shot and issued as a talkie, the second such British feature. (The first was Edgar Wallace's THE CLUE OF THE NEW PIN, 1929, also a mystery). John Baxter wrote of BLACKMAIL in *Cinema in Britain* (1973), "For its time it is an astonishing tour-de-force, particularly in its use of subjective sound. Moments such as the doorbell which swells into a knell of doom in the girl's ears, or the neighbour's idle chatter dwindling into an indistinguishable murmur until only the word 'knife' is heard, climaxed by the father's demand for the bread-knife, are quoted to this day as examples of Hitchcock's virtuosity in so new a medium. . . . In general, however, the film is a fairly commonplace suspense story, deprived for boxoffice reasons of the ironic ending Hitchcock wanted."

Pretty Alice White (Anny Ondra, and the voice of Joan Barry in one of the sound era's first examples of voice substitution) is sexually attacked by an artist (Cyril Ritchard) and the young woman is forced to kill him. The police detective assigned to find the killer is actually Alice's fiancé, Frank Webber (John Longden), and he finds one of her gloves at the scene of the crime. The other glove is located by Tracy (Donald Calthrop), who attempts to blackmail her. Webber, however, believes that Tracy is the killer and corners him at the British Museum. Alice finally confesses to the crime but she is freed because the killing is judged as self-defense.

In the original script the "heroine" is arrested for the crime at

---

*Dialogue spoken by Joan Barry.

**Played by Sam Livesey in the silent version.

the end of the film, but a happier finale was shot for the final release print. Co-star John Longden later became familiar to American audiences for his role as the superintendent in the British series "The Man from Interpol," shown in the U.S. in 1960 on NBC-TV.

For the record, director Alfred Hitchcock can be spotted early in BLACKMAIL as a train passenger being annoyed by a youngster.

BLACKMAIL (Republic, 1947) Color 67 minutes.

Associate producer, William J. O'Sullivan; director, Lesley Selander; story, Robert Leslie Bellem; screenplay, Roy K. Cole; additional dialogue, Albert DeMond; art director, Frank Arrigo; set decorators, John McCarthy, Jr., James Redd; music director, Mort Glickman; assistant director, Al Wood; sound, Herbert Norsch; camera, Reggie Lanning; editor, Tony Martinelli.

William Marshall (Dan Turner); Adele Mara (Sylvia Duane); Ricardo Cortez (Ziggy Cranston); Grant Withers (Inspector Donaldson); Stephanie Bachelor (Carla); Richard Fraser (Antoine); Roy Barcroft (Spice Kelloway); George J. Lewis (Blue Chip Winslow); Gregory Gay (Jervis); Tristram Coffin (Pinky); Eva Novak (Mamie); Bud Wolfe (Gomez).

Near the bottom-of-the-barrel of pulp fiction lies the work of Robert Leslie Bellem, who churned out scores of stories for unsophisticated publications. Most of them were centered around his Hollywood gumshoe Dan Turner, a strange mixture of Philip Marlowe and Dick Tracy. In 1947 Republic attempted to bring Dan Turner to the screen in BLACKMAIL, but the results were not fortuitous. As Don Miller notes in "Private Eyes" (*Focus on Film* magazine, Autumn 1975), "Roy Cole and Albert DeMond retained Bellem's grammatical style to the essence. . . . [But] in a casting coup of nightmarish proportions, Turner was played by William Marshall, a blond cherub with the manner of a milk-fed country boy. . . . Marshall delivering the calloused dialogue was like Hemingway read by Li'l Abner. Fortunately, in the Republic scheme of things, [Lesley] Selander directed it as a slight plot interlude sandwiched in among several bruising fisticuffs sessions, with Marshall looking okay in that department. It was when he ceased punching and commenced talking that the mind boggled."

Hollywood private investigator Dan Turner (William Marshall) is offered $50,000 by wealthy gambler Ziggy Cranston (Ricardo Cortez) to protect him from blackmailer Antoine (Richard Fraser), but Turner refuses the case until his fee is tripled. He immediately finds himself embroiled in several murders and fist fights, and at odds with harassing police Inspector Donaldson (Grant Withers) over the case. Turner pinpoints Cranston's lady love, Sylvia Duane

(Adele Mara), as being in cahoots with Antoine, and after that he brings forth the murderer.

While BLACKMAIL may have had an inappropriate leading man and "dull talk keep[s] interest at a minimum" (*Variety*), the movie does feature two beautiful actresses whom Republic starred as screen sleuths themselves: Stephanie Bachelor as THE UNDER-COVER WOMAN (1946) and Adele Mara in EXPOSED (1947), *qq.v.*

THE BLUE DAHLIA (Paramount, 1946) 96 minutes.

Producer, George Marshall; associate producer, John Houseman; director, Marshall; story/screenplay, Raymond Chandler; art directors, Hans Dreier, Walter Tyler; set decorators, Sam Comer, Jimmy Walters; assistant director, C. C. Coleman; music director, Victor Young; sound, Gene Merritt; process camera, Farciot Edouart; camera, Lionel Lindon; editor, Arthur Schmidt.

Alan Ladd (Johnny Morrison); Veronica Lake (Joyce Harwood); William Bendix (Buzz Wanchek); Howard da Silva (Eddie Harwood); Doris Dowling (Helen Morrison); Tom Powers (Captain Hendrickson); Hugh Beaumont (George Copeland); Howard Freeman (Corelli); Don Costello (Leo); Will Wright ("Dad" Newell); Frank Faylen (The Man); Walter Sande (Heath); Vera Marshe (Blonde); Mae Busch (Jenny the Maid); Gloria Williams (Assistant Maid); Harry Hayden (Mr. Hughes the Assistant Hotel Manager); George Barton (Cab Driver); Harry Barris (Bellhop); Paul Gustine (Doorman); Roberta Jonay (Girl Hotel Clerk); Milton Kibbee (Night Hotel Clerk); Dick Winslow (Piano Player at Party); Anthony Caruso (Marine Corporal); Matt McHugh (Bartender); Arthur Loft (The Wolf); Stan Johnson (Naval Officer); Ernie Adams (Joe—Man in Coveralls); Henry Vroom (Master Sergeant); Harry Tyler (Clerk in Bus Station); Jack Clifford (Plainclothesman); George Sorel (Paul, the Captain of Waiters); James Millican, Albert Ruiz (Photographers); Charles A. Hughes (Lieutenant Lloyd); Leon Lombardo (Mexican Bellhop); Nina Borget (Mexican Waitress); Douglas Carter (Bus Driver); Ed Randolph (Cop); Bea Allen (News Clerk); Perc Launders (Hotel Clerk); Jimmy Dundee (Driver of Gangster Car); Tom Dillon (Prowl Car Cop); Dick Elliott (Motor Court Owner); Clark Eggleston (Elevator Operator); George Carleton (Clerk at DeAnza Hotel); Jack Gargan (Cab Driver); Lawrence Young (Clerk); Franklin Parker (Police Stenographer); Noel Neill, Mavis Murray (Hat Check Girls); Brooke Evans, Carmen Clifford, Lucy Knock, Beverly Thompson; Audrey Westphal, Audrey Korn, Jerry James, Charles Mayon, William Meader (Cocktail Party Guests).

Raymond Chandler, the creator of the distinctive Philip Marlowe character, wrote the script for this taut *film noir* melodrama from his own unfinished novel. It was a rush assignment, as Paramount required a new film for contract star Alan Ladd before he went into military service (in World War II). Chandler completed the project for associate producer John Houseman and producer/director George Marshall in a few weeks' time (although the feature went into production before his script was finished) and it netted Chandler an Academy Award nomination.*

War hero Johnny Morrison (Alan Ladd) returns home to Los Angeles to find his wife (Doris Dowling) drunk and in the arms of another man (Tom Powers) during a wild party in their apartment. Morrison breaks up the party but has trouble with an elderly house detective (Will Wright). Morrison leaves his wife when she confesses that their son died as a result of her drunken neglect. With two wartime buddies, shellshock victim Buzz Wanchek (William Bendix) and George Copeland (Hugh Beaumont), Morrison sets out to make a new life for himself. However, when his estranged wife is found murdered he is a prime suspect. Also implicated in the case is Joyce (Veronica Lake), the wife of nightclub owner Eddie Harwood (Howard da Silva), who had been the late woman's lover. Joyce not only believes in Morrison's innocence but the two fall in love. Hiding out from the law, Morrison, the girl, and his friends attempt to find the culprit. Morrison accumulates the evidence necessary to force a confession from the murderer, proving that Wanchek, who suffers from blackouts and amnesia, is innocent.

This was the sixth of seven joint screen appearances by Alan Ladd and Veronica Lake, and for many it is the pinnacle of their 1940s film teaming. The film contrasts beautifully the impassive but tough Ladd and the brazenly coy Lake, both of them handsome, blond figures. No little credit goes to the film's amazing ambiance, which ranges from the tacky Cavendish Hotel apartments in Hollywood to the Blue Dahlia Club on Sunset Strip, to a rundown Los Angeles hotel for transients. Not to be forgotten is the admirable car interior scene on the rainy night when Joyce picks up hitchhiking Morrison on the Cahuenga Pass and drives him to Malibu. Their terse yet emotion-charged exchanges, with the rain beating down, the windshield wipers pulsating back and forth, and the car humming along the wet road, are full of sexual tension.

The irony of THE BLUE DAHLIA is that it focuses on a

The Blue Dahlia: A Screenplay (1976) reprints John Houseman's telling *Harper Magazine* (August 1965) recollections of the chaotic filming of THE BLUE DAHLIA. According to Houseman, during most of the days that Chandler wrote his excellent scenario, he was inebriated. THE BLUE DAHLIA was filmed in March-May 1945, but not released until April 1946.

returning war hero who must hide from the society he fought to protect and who must become a detective to prove his own innocence of a crime he did not commit. There is further irony in the portrayal of the elderly house detective (Will Wright), who is actually a voyeuristic blackmailer. Within such twists of fate are the crux of good detective stories, with people caught in webs of happenstance and scrambling for survival while trapped by their emotions and abetted by their cynicism. As James Agee enthused in *The Nation* magazine, "The picture is as neatly stylized and synchronized, and as uninterested in moral excitement, as a good ballet; it knows its own weight and size perfectly and carries them gracefully and without self-importance. . . . It crawls with American types; and their mannerisms and affectations, and their chief preoccupations—blackmail and what's-in-it-for-me. . . ."

BLUE, WHITE AND PERFECT (Twentieth Century-Fox, 1941) 74 Minutes.

Producer, Sol M. Wurtzel; director, Herbert I. Leeds; based on the character created by Brett Halliday [Davis Dresser] and the story "Diamonds of Death" by Borden Chase; screenplay, Samuel G. Engel; camera, Glen MacWilliams; editor, Alfred Day.

Lloyd Nolan (Michael Shayne); Mary Beth Hughes (Merle Garland); Helene Reynolds (Helen Shaw); George Reeves (Juan Arturo O'Hara); Steve Geray (Vanderhoefen); Henry Victor (Hagerman); Curt Bois (Nappy); Marie Blake (Ethel); Emmett Vogan (Charlie); Mae Marsh (Mrs. Toby); Frank Orth (Mr. Toby); Ivan Lebedeff (Alexis Fournier); Wade Boteler (Judge); Charles Trowbridge (Captain Brown); Edward Earle (Richards); Cliff Clark (Inspector); Arthur Loft (Captain McCordy); Charles Williams (Printer); Ann Doran (Miss Hoffman).

The fourth of seven entries in producer Sol M. Wurtzel's Michael Shayne budget detective series at Twentieth Century-Fox, starring Lloyd Nolan in the title role. BLUE, WHITE AND PERFECT is an updated reworking of Borden Chase's 1934 story, "Diamonds of Death." A fast affair, the movie interpolates the theme of industrial espionage into its plot and the various story ingredients ". . . have a topical and breezy air about them which should make pic a definite program pleaser. . . . [It] travels at a good pace" (*Film Daily*).

When best girl Merle Garland (Mary Beth Hughes) tires of his detective work and impulsively decides to wed a Russian (Ivan Lebedeff), gumshoe Michael Shayne (Lloyd Nolan) informs the local police inspector (Cliff Clark) that the man is a fake. Merle then agrees to marry Shayne if he will give up being a professional sleuth

Lloyd Nolan and George Reeves in BLUE, WHITE AND PERFECT (1941).

and take a "normal" job. He obtains employment as an airplane factory riveter but the job is merely a cover for his real activity—working as a government detective to stop a smuggling operation which is stealing synthetic diamonds used for industrial work in Hawaii and selling them to the Japanese. The trail leads Shayne aboard a ship bound for Hawaii and there he corrals the crooks as well as enemy spies.

Being released within weeks after the Japanese surprise attack on Pearl Harbor, BLUE, WHITE AND PERFECT benefitted from being so timely. Then too, it is buoyed by Lloyd Nolan's breezy interpretation of the devil-may-care detective. With seeming effortlessness, he seems to be the quintessential private eye, always ready with a wise crack, a solid right to the villain's jaw, and a fine appreciation for feminine pulchritude, the dollar, and (now that World War II had reached the U.S.) a sense of patriotism.

BOMBAY MAIL (Universal, 1934) 66 minutes.
Director, Edwin L. Marin; story, L. G. Blochman; screenplay, Tom Reed, Blochman; camera, Charles Stumar.

Edmund Lowe (Inspector Dyke); Shirley Grey (Beatrice Jones); Onslow Stevens (John Hawley); Ralph Forbes (William Luke-Patson); John Davidson (Xavier); Hedda Hopper (Lady Daniels); Tom Moore (Civil Surgeon); John Wray (Martini); Ferdinand Gottschalk (Sir Anthony Daniels); Gary Owen (Cuthbert Neal); Huntley Gordon (Burgess); Herbert Corthell (Edward Breeze); Walter Armitage (Maharajah of Zungore); Jameson Thomas (Captain Gerald Worthing); Georges Renavent (Toxicologist); Brandon Hurst (Pundit Chundra).

Murder on a train has been a popular motif in detective fiction for over half a century, as reflected by such diverse features as TERROR BY NIGHT (1946) and MURDER ON THE ORIENT EXPRESS (1975), *qq.v.*, both top notch exponents of this sub-genre of mystery movies. Another very fine example is BOMBAY MAIL, starring Edmund Lowe, who enjoyed one of the most extensive careers on film as a sleuth although he never headlined any particular series. Among his many screen outings as a debonair detective were MR. DYNAMITE (1935), THE GREAT HOTEL MURDER (1935), and THE GARDEN MURDER CASE (1936), *qq.v.*. In the early days of television he headlined the series "Your Witness" (DuMont, 1949-50) and "Front Page Detective" (DuMont, 1951-53).

On the train from Bombay to Calcutta the Governor of Bengal (Ferdinand Gottschalk) is poisoned and Scotland Yard detective Inspector Dyke (Edmund Lowe) is placed in charge of the investigation. Among the suspects are two young lovers, Beatrice Jones (Shirley Grey) and John Hawley (Onslow Stevens); the dead man's widow (Hedda Hopper); his secretaries, William Luke-Patson (Ralph Forbes) and Captain Gerald Worthing (Jameson Thomas); a French toxicologist (Georges Renavent); corrupt Xavier (John Davidson), and home rule agitator Pundit Chundra (Brandon Hurst). Just as Dyke begins the investigation, another passenger, the Maharajah of Zungore (Walter Armitage), is killed by a gunshot, leaving the detective with two murders to solve before the fast moving Bombay Mail arrives at its destination.

"Universal's version of the train murder mystery genre sticks pretty closely to the pattern set down by its predecessors, but it mixes a colorful set of characters and maintains a moderately absorbing pace" (*Variety*).

BORN TO KILL (RKO, 1947) 93 minutes.

Executive producer, Sid Rogell; producer, Herman Schlom; director, Robert Wise; based on the novel *Deadlier Than the Male* by James Gunn; screenplay, Eve Green, Richard Macaulay; music, Paul Sawtell; music director, C. Bakaleinikoff; dialogue director, Anthony Jowitt; art directors, Albert S. D'Agostino, Walter E. Keller;

set decorators, Darrell Silvera, John Sturtevant; sound, Robert H. Guhl, Roy Granville; special effects, Russell A. Cully; assistant director, Sam Ruman; camera, Robert de Grasse; editor, Lee Millbrook.

Lawrence Tierney (Sam Wild); Claire Trevor (Helen Trent); Walter Slezak (Arnett); Philip Terry (Fred Grover); Audrey Long (Georgia Staples); Elisha Cook, Jr. (Marty Waterman); Isabel Jewell (Laury Palmer); Esther Howard (Mrs. Kraft); Kathryn Card (Grace); Tony Barrett (Danny); Grandon Rhodes (Inspector Wilson); Sayre Dearing, Joe Dixon, Sam Lufkin, Sammy Shack (Crap Dealers); Ruth Brennan (Sally); Tom Noonan (Bellboy); Al Murphy (Cab Driver); Phil Warren (Chauffeur); Ben Frommer (Delivery Boy); Netta Packer (Mrs. Perth); Lee Frederick (Desk Clerk); Demetrius Alexis (Maitre d'); Martha Hyer, Ellen Corby (Maids); Jean Fenwick (Margaret Macy); Reverend Neal Dodd (Clergyman); Napoleon Whiting (Porter); Perc Launders (Detective Bryson); Jason Robards, Sr. (Conductor); Beatrice Maude (Cook); Stanley Stone (Train Conductor).

If ever there was a *film noir* detective film in which the spiraling fates force anti-social characters together with devastating results it is BORN TO KILL, based on the 1942 novel *Deadlier Than the Male* by James Gunn. While the plot may be too contrived and the direction unsure, a lot can be forgiven for the inspired casting of Lawrence Tierney (star of DILLINGER, 1945), Claire Trevor (who excelled at hard-bitten screen dames), and Walter Slezak (a specialist at odious cinema skunks)

In Reno, psychotic Sam Wild (Lawrence Tierney), a former rancher and boxer, kills an ex-girlfriend (Isabel Jewell) and her new boyfriend. He flees, being protected by his pal Marty Waterman (Elisha Cook, Jr.). The bodies are found in Mrs. Kraft's (Esther Howard) boarding house by tenant Helen Trent (Claire Trevor). However, she does not notify the police because, just having gotten a divorce, she is in a rush to return to San Francisco and her new groom-to-be. On the train to the Bay city, Helen and Wild meet, but she refuses his advances because she is engaged to wed affluent Fred Grover (Philip Terry). When Wild cannot have Helen, he romances her wealthy step-sister, Georgia Staples (Audrey Long), whom he marries. Meanwhile Mrs. Kraft employs oily, fat detective Arnett (Walter Slezak) to locate her daughter's killer. The shady investigator traces the crime to Wild but offers to sell the proof to Waterman. The latter attempts to murder Mrs. Kraft to help his friend, but Wild, wrongly convinced that Waterman is having an affair with Helen, arrives on the scene and kills Waterman. Later, Helen pressures Mrs. Kraft to drop the case and then, in the midst of a fracas with Georgia, she urges Wild to shoot her step-sister. The police arrive and, when Wild learns it was Helen who summoned them, he shoots her and in turn is killed by the police.

A film filled with such despicable characters was bound—in the 1940s, to earn the enmity of critics. Bosley Crowther (*New York Times*) lashed out, ". . . the whole atmosphere and detail of corruption is so indulgently displayed that it looks as though the aim of the producers was to include as much as possible within the limits of the Production Code." Walter Slezak, who made a specialty of screen villainy (ONCE UPON A HONEYMOON, 1942, CORNERED, 1945, etc.) provides a sharp characterization of a slimy private investigator who eagerly sells out his client for the right (or any) price. It is a notion infrequently depicted in the cinema. Reported *Variety* of this gumshoe, "Walter Slezak, shady private detective, is in keeping with unsavory mood of principals as developed by Robert Wise's direction." As for the film itself, the trade paper pointed out, "Not too much suspense develops as he [Slezak] tracks down [Lawrence] Tierney, which is one of the factors that keeps film from top classification."

British release title: LADY OF DECEIT.

THE BRASHER DOUBLOON (Twentieth Century-Fox, 1947) 72 minutes.

Producer, Robert Bassler; director, John Brahm; based on the novel by Raymond Chandler; adaptor, Leonard Praskins; screenplay, Dorothy Hannah; art directors, James Basevi, Richard Irvine; set decorators, Thomas Little, Frank E. Hughes; costumes, Eleanor Behm; makeup, Ben Nye; music, David Buttolph; music director, Alfred Newman; orchestrator, Maurice de Packh; assistant director, Hal Herman; sound, Eugene Grossman, Harry M. Leonard; special effects, Fred Sersen; camera, Lloyd Ahern; editor, Harry Reynolds.

George Montgomery (Philip Marlowe); Nancy Guild (Merle Davis); Conrad Janis (Leslie Murdock); Roy Roberts (Lieutenant Breeze); Fritz Kortner (Vannier); Florence Bates (Mrs. Elizabeth Murdock); Marvin Miller (Blair); Houseley Stevenson (Morningstar); Bob Adler (Sergeant Spangler); Jack Conrad (George Anson); Alfred Linder (Eddie Prue); Jack Overman (Manager); Jack Stoney (Mike); Ray Spiker (Figaro); Paul Maxey (Coroner); Reed Hadley (Dr. Moss); Edward Gargan (Truck Driver); Ben Erway (Shaw).

In 1942 Twentieth Century-Fox acquired the screen rights to Raymond Chandler's Philip Marlowe detective novel, *The High Window* (1942), and filmed it as TIME TO KILL (1942), *q.v.* However, the lead character of Marlowe became Davis Dresser's Michael Shayne and it was the last of the studio's film series about that sleuth to star Lloyd Nolan. Following the success of Dick Powell as Marlowe in RKO's MURDER, MY SWEET (1944) and Humphrey Bogart in the same detective role in Warner Bros.' THE BIG SLEEP (1946), *qq.v.*, Fox decided to remake *The High Window* as THE BRASHER DOUBLOON (one of the novel's working titles). Contract leading man George Montgomery was cast as Philip Marlowe. In a career study of the film's director, John Brahm, Jack Edmund Nolan (*Films in Review* magazine, January 1966) judged the picture "The least violent, moodiest, and perhaps finest, U.S. private-eye film." There are many viewers who disagree with this judgment.

Private investigator Philip Marlowe (George Montgomery) is hired by eccentric Mrs. Elizabeth Murdock (Florence Bates) to trace the whereabouts of a rare Dutch coin, the Brasher Doubloon, missing from her valuable collection. She claims she knows who took the coin but refuses to divulge the information to Marlowe. He will not take the case until he is persuaded by the woman's secretary/companion, Merle Davis (Nancy Guild), who fears being touched by men. Marlowe is visited by Eddie Prue (Alfred Linder), a gunman working for club owner Blair (Marvin Miller), but the gumshoe refuses to see the man's boss. Instead he consults with rare coin dealer Morningstar (Houseley Stevenson), who knows the history of the Doubloon and says that someone recently tried to sell it to him. Marlowe, after overhearing Morningstar call George Anson (Jack Conrad), goes to interview the man, but finds him murdered. From the crime scene he obtains a baggage claim check before policemen Breeze (Roy Roberts) and Spangler (Bob Adler) arrive. Redeeming the claim ticket, Marlowe now has the coin and returns to Morningstar, but finds that he too has been silenced with a gun which belongs to Merle. Marlowe receives a telegram from Merle advising him that he is now off the case. Mrs. Murdock's son Leslie (Conrad Janis) appears at Marlowe's office, insists he took the coin to pay a gambling debt, and explains that Merle is mentally ill since seeing his father, who was her employer, fall from a high window to his death seven years prior. Venal Rudolph Vannier (Fritz Kortner), a freelance photographer, tries to steal the coin from Marlowe but fails. Later, Merle tells Marlowe that her late employer had made physical advances and in fighting him off she had caused his fall. She also advises Marlowe that Vannier made a newsreel film of the death and that she must have the coin because he is blackmailing her. Blair's thugs forcibly take Marlowe to the gangster's club to learn the whereabouts of the Doubloon, but the detective escapes. At Vannier's home Marlowe finds the photographer dead and a distraught Merle insists she did not do it. After finding the newsreel footage, Marlowe convinces the police and the suspects to congregate at his office, where he screens the footage. It plainly reveals who pushed the victim out of the high window and from that he deduces who murdered Vannier. With the guilty party arrested, Marlowe is now free to romance Merle.

Perhaps the weakest aspect in the adaptation of Chandler's complex story of greed and twisted mentalities to the screen is the tampering with the character of Merle Davis. No doubt due to the censorship of the time this young woman's phobia about being touched by men is greatly minimized and vanishes rather patly and quickly (like many other plot points) once Marlowe has kissed her. The novel had no such quick solution and her mental problems, though somewhat eased, are not wrapped up at the book's finale. As for handsome (and bland) George Montgomery as the tough detective. ". . . [He] just looks too respectable and intelligent and lacks the ruggedness and borderline honesty of the Marlowes created by Dick Powell in MURDER MY SWEET and Humphrey Bogart in THE BIG SLEEP" (Thomas M. Pryor, *New York Times*). "More than any other Marlowe film, THE BRASHER DOUBLOON most completely violates the spirit of Chandler, especially in the area of characterizations," wrote Stephen Pendo in *Raymond Chandler on Screen* (1976). He added, however, "Florence Bates gives an excellent performance as Mrs. Murdock. Her Murdock has all the pent-up hatred and total disregard for everyone but her son Chandler instilled in the character. She stands out as the perfect Chandler villainess: an over-possessive rich woman far more evil than the blackmailer with whom she deals."

British release title: THE HIGH WINDOW.

BULLDOG DRUMMOND (Astra-National, 1922) 6,000'.

Producer, Maurits Binger; director, Oscar Apfel; based on the play by Sapper [Herman Cyril McNeile] and Gerald Du Maurier; screenplay, C. B. Doxat-Pratt.

Carlyle Blackwell (Captain Hugh Drummond); Evelyn Greeley (Phyllis Benton); Dorothy Fane (Irma Peterson); Warwick Ward (Dr. Lakington); Horace de Vere (Carl Peterson); Gerald Dean (Algy Longworth); Harry Bogarth (Sparring Partner); William Browning (James Handley).

BULLDOG DRUMMOND (United Artists, 1929) 90 minutes.

Presenter, Samuel Goldwyn; producer/director, F. Richard Jones; based on the play by Sapper [Herman Cyril McNeile] and Gerald Du Maurier; screenplay, Wallace Smith, Sidney Howard; continuity, Smith; dialogue, Howard; art director, William Cameron

Menzies; song, Jack Yellen and Harry Akst; associate director, A. Leslie Pearce; assistant director, Paul Jones; camera, George Barnes, Gregg Toland; editors, Viola Lawrence, Frank Lawrence.

Ronald Colman (Bulldog Drummond); Joan Bennett (Phyllis Benton); Lilyan Tashman (Erma); Montagu Love (Peterson); Lawrence Grant (Dr. Lakington); Wilson Benge (Danny); Claude Allister (Algy Longworth); Adolph Milar (Marcovitch); Charles Sellon (Travers); Tetsu Komai (Chong); Donald Novis (Singer); Gertrude Short (Barmaid); Tom Ricketts (Colonel).

Herman Cyril McNeile (1888-1937), who used the pen name "Sapper," first wrote *Bulldog Drummond* in 1920, and in the next seventeen years produced eleven more Drummond novels. Gerald T. Fairlie later used the non-de-plume of Sapper for another seven Drummond adventures from 1939 to 1954. *In The Detective in Film* (1972), William K. Everson described Bulldog Drummond: "As his rank and the date (1920) suggest, he was a World War I veteran. He was also something of a Fascist and a thug, looking for an outlet for violence and finding it in a kind of moralistic crusade against crime. He was in his own way a forerunner of America's Mike Hammer. . . ."

Sapper's initial novel was popular enough to be adapted to the stage in 1921, with Sir Gerald du Maurier as Hugh "Bulldog" Drummond; A. E. Mathews played the part on Broadway and H. B. Warner headed a U.S. touring company in the thriller. In 1922 Astra-National, a British company, brought BULLDOG DRUMMOND to the screen in the guise of matinee idol Carlyle Blackwell, the American actor who would later portray Sherlock Holmes in the 1929 German version of DER HUND VON BASKERVILLES [The Hound of the Baskervilles]. Although *Photoplay* magazine termed the British feature (shot in Holland), "Dime novel thrills with a dime-stagey hero," the film was a rather faithful adaptation of the book and Blackwell, unlike many of his successors, looked the role of Drummond. (*Variety* enthused of the actor, "From first to last he never loses his grip, and whether he is fighting, bluffing or making love, his characterization lives.") In 1925, Astra-National produced a second Drummond feature, BULLDOG DRUMMOND'S THIRD ROUND, based on the Sapper novel, *The Third Round* (1924). Jack Buchanan appeared as a most debonair Drummond who employs a variety of disguises to capture a gang of foreign criminals who have abducted a scientist in order to learn his secret for producing synthetic diamonds.

In 1929 Samuel Goldwyn produced an elaborate remake of the initial novel, but this BULLDOG DRUMMOND presented a title character unlike that depicted in the book; Drummond became suave and sophisticated instead of tough and surly with the tenacity of a bulldog. Tired of life in England after the excitement of the World War, wealthy Hugh "Bulldog" Drummond (Ronald Colman) advertises in the hope of some type of adventure, to the chagrin of his fun-loving pal Algy Longworth (Claude Allister). He receives several replies but the most intriguing comes in the form of beautiful Phyllis Benton (Joan Bennett), who asks Drummond's assistance in extricating her uncle, wealthy Mr. Travers (Charles Sellon). She claims he is being held prisoner in a nursing home by the wicked Dr. Lakington (Lawrence Grant) and his associates, Peterson (Montagu Love) and Erma (Lilyan Tashman). She insists that the doctor is torturing her uncle in an attempt to force him to sign over his fortune. Drummond takes the case and it leads him into a series of adventures in the British hinterlands, where he attempts to rescue the drugged Travers. He succeeds only in having Phyllis abducted by Lakington, who plans to molest her. Drummond and Longworth obtain her rescue. Drummond kills Lakington in a confrontation, but allows Peterson and Erma to escape. He and Phyllis plan to wed.

BULLDOG DRUMMOND was Ronald Colman's first sound feature. For his performance herein (along with CONDEMNED) he was nominated for an Academy Award. Everson wrote in *The Detective in Film,* "Colman's flawless diction, his beautiful timing, and the sense of fun he brought to the role not only dominated the film, but influenced the tongue-in-cheek playing of the rest of the cast." Contemporary reviewers were also enthusiastic about the feature. Photoplay magazine judged it "a corking melodrama—and Ronald Colman gives the best talkie performance to date. . . . Goldwyn took a lot of pains with the film. It is intelligently and tastefully done. The sounding is highly expert." The *New York Times* opined, "It is the happiest and most enjoyable entertainment of its kind that has so far reached the screen. This latest combination of voices and shadows has been produced with remarkable savoir faire. . . ."

In 1930 Fox produced another Drummond film, TEMPLE TOWER, *q.v.*, with Kenneth MacKenna as the intrepid adventurer, and in 1934, Ronald Colman returned as the gentleman sleuth in BULLDOG DRUMMOND STRIKES BACK for Twentieth Century/United Artists. Here Drummond is on the trail of an Oriental fur smuggler (Warner Oland). The *New York World-Telegram* reported, "The picture is full of quite effortless nonsense and is highly entertaining throughout." Even more than in his first portrayal, Colman's Drummond here is an effervescent adventurer, fearless and inventive in any sort of peril. As he tells sidekick Algy Longworth (Charles Butterworth) in the midst of potential calamity, "Think of it, Algy! Alone. . . . Unarmed. . . . Surrounded by villains. . . . Locked in a cellar. . . . From that to complete mastery of the situation in ten minutes. *If* we can do that, we'll be magnificent." The British, not to be left out of the picture, turned out two (modest) Bulldog Drummond entries: THE RETURN OF BULLDOG DRUMMOND (1934), with Ralph Richardson as the now married Hugh Drummond, taken from Sapper's 1922 novel, *The Black Gang;* and BULLDOG JACK (1935), a comedy about a young man (Jack Hulbert) on the trail of jewel thieves after the real Drummond (Atholl Fleming) is supposedly injured. In an about face, Ralph Richardson was cast as the villain in the latter film.

BULLDOG DRUMMOND'S PERIL (Paramount, 1938) 66 minutes.

Associate producer, Stuart Walker; director, James Hogan; based on the novel *The Third Round* (1924) by Sapper [Herman Cyril McNeile]; screenplay, Stuart Palmer; art directors, Hans Drier, Robert Odell; music director, Boris Morros; camera, Harry Fishbeck; editor, Edward Dmytryk.

John Barrymore (Colonel Nielson); John Howard (Hugh Drummond); Louise Campbell (Phyllis Clavering); Reginald Denny (Algy Longworth); E. E. Clive (Tenny); Porter Hall (Dr. Botulian); Elizabeth Patterson (Aunt Blanche); Nydia Westman (Gwen Longworth); Michael Brooke (Anthony Greer); Halliwell Hobbes (Profesor Bernard Goodman); Matthew Boulton (Sir Raymond Blantyre); Zeffie Tilbury (Mrs. Weevens); David Clyde (Constable McThane); Clyde Cook (Constable Sacker); Austin Fairman (Roberts); Gregory Gaye (Raoul); Pat X. Kerry, Dave Thursby (Expressmen); Torben Meyer (Hoffman).

Mystery writer Stuart Palmer, who created the character of spinster school teacher detective Hildegarde Withers, wrote the screenplay for this "Bulldog Drummond" series outing, basing it on Sapper's third Drummond novel, *The Third Round* (1924). The character had successfully been brought to the screen in both the silent and sound eras and in 1937 Paramount had launched a series of assembly line "B" pictures adventures with Britisher Ray Milland* as Bulldog Drummond. After one appearance Milland was elevated to "A" movies and American John Howard** took over the role for seven budget outings churned out between 1937 and 1939. The

---

Variety warned, "Ray Milland's performance as the almost legendary Drummond is smooth to a degree, but might suffer from comparison with the more suave Ronald Colman."

**Variety* reported that John Howard as the intrepid Drummond ". . . resembles and essays a Gable manner and speech, but it doesn't impress. He has a tough role wherein he follows a well remembered and tip-top performer."

crux of each formula episode was not high danger and adventure but the detective's near-and-final marriage to perennial girlfriend Phyllis Clavering. Reginald Denny played Drummond's loyal pal Algy Longworth in this pleasant but undemanding series, while E. E. Clive was Tenny. For the first trio of John Howard installments John Barrymore was top-billed as Colonel Nielson of Scotland Yard (replacing Sir Guy Standing, who had been in the Milland entry). This part went to H. B. Warner for the final four films. BULLDOG DRUMMOND'S PERIL was Barrymore's final series outing and it also introduced Elizabeth Patterson as Aunt Blanche, a part she repeated in two more chapters, BULLDOG DRUMMOND'S SECRET POLICE and BULLDOG DRUMMOND'S BRIDE, both 1939.

Bulldog Drummond (John Howard) is almost at the altar, ready to wed patient fiancée Phyllis Clavering (Louise Campbell), who is given a synthetic diamond as a wedding present by Gwen Longworth (Nydia Westman). The formula for the fake stone is stolen and Drummond postpones his nuptials to recover it, only to find that two gangs are after it also. One is led by a corrupt diamond merchant (Porter Hall) who wants to destroy it to save his trade, while the other faction wants to utilize the formula to pass off fake stones as real ones. Drummond is assisted by Scotland Yard's Colonel Nielson (John Barrymore). With the gangs captured and the formula recovered, Drummond and Phyllis head back to the altar.

B. R. Crisler (*New York Times*) acknowledged, ". . . The Bulldog Drummond formula continues to enjoy a modest but periodical success."

BUSMAN'S HOLIDAY see HAUNTED HONEYMOON.

CAMPUS SLEUTH (Monogram, 1948) 57 minutes.

Producer, Will Jason; associate producer, Maurice Duke; director, Jason; story, Max Wilson, Hal Collins; screenplay, Collins; art director, David Milton; music director, Edward J. Kay; songs: Freddie Stewart; Jason; Jason and Sid Robin; Bobby Sherwood; Tony Beaulieu; camera, Mack Stengler; editor, William Austin.

Freddie Stewart (Freddie Trimball); June Preisser (Dodie Rogers); Warren Mills (Lee Watson); Noel Neill (Betty Rogers); Donald MacBride (Inspector Watson); Monte Collins (Dean McKinley); Stan Rose (Winkler); Bobby Sherwood (Bobby Davis); Billy Snyder (Ronnie Wallace); William Norton Bailey (Coroner); Charles Campbell (Dunkel); Paul Bryar (Houser); George Eldredge (Officer Edwards); Dottye D. Brown (Telegraph Girl); Harry Taylor (Husband); Margaret Bert (Wife); Lane Chandler (Police Officer); Joey Preston (Joey); Mildred Jorman (Little Miss Cornshucks); Jimmy

Grisson (Boy in Wagon); George Fields (Band Boy); and: Bobby Sherwood's Orchestra with Gerri Gallian.

Between 1946 and 1948 Maurice Duke served as associate producer for Monogram Pictures' Teen-Agers series, starring Freddie Stewart and June Preisser, the musical comedies dealing with vagaries and adventures of campus life. The budget films, which had variations on the standard premise, featured a number of noted bandleaders (e.g., Charlie Barnett, Jimmy Dorsey, Spade Cooley, Freddie Slack, Eddie Heywood, Abe Lyman, Russ Morgan, Gene Krupa, and Jan Savitt). CAMPUS SLEUTH employed a detective motif along with Bobby Sherwood's orchestra.

Dunkel (Charles Campbell), a photographer for the San Juan Junior College campus magazine, is found murdered by student Lee Watson (Warren Mills) during a campus performance by Bobby Davis (Bobby Sherwood) and his band. Watson tells his father, police Inspector Watson (Donald MacBride) and his pal Freddie Trimball (Freddie Stewart). In the interim, janitor Winkler (Stan Rose) hides Dunkel's body in a harp case. When the corpse cannot be located Inspector Watson accuses his impressionable son of reading too many mystery stories. The body is found by Trimball and his girl friend Dodie Rogers (June Preisser) and by Lee and his girl, Betty Rogers (Noel Neill). Winkler then admits to the police that he hid the body, fearing arrest for the crime since he is an ex-convict. Trimball investigates and uncovers that Dunkel is a jewel thief who was scheduled to meet someone on campus the night of the killing. Inspector Watson goes along with a ruse that Winkler can identify the killer by his voice and they trap the murderer and his henchman who were acting as fences for the deceased.

More enjoyable than the reviewers acknowledged ("the results are just adequate," claimed *Variety*), CAMPUS SLEUTH contains six songs in addition to its more than passable whodunit gambit. Star Freddie Stewart composed the song "Baby You Can Count on Me" while the film's producer/director Will Jason provided "What Happened?" and co-wrote "Neither Could I" with Sid Robin. Tony Beaulieu provided "Jungle Rhythm," and bandleader Bobby Sherwood wrote "Sherwood's Forest" and "Jump for Joey," which his band performed in the feature, the penultimate entry in the Teen-Agers series.

THE "CANARY" MURDER CASE (Paramount, 1929) 81 minutes.

Director, Malcolm St. Clair; based on the novel by S. S. Van Dine [Willard Huntington Wright]; adaptors, Florence Ryerson, Albert S. Le Vino; dialogue, Van Dine; titles, Herman J. Mankiewicz; camera, Harry Fischbeck; editor, William Shea.

William Powell (Philo Vance); James Hall (Jimmy Spotswoode); Louise Brooks (Margaret O'Dell);* Jean Arthur (Alyce La Fosse); Gustav von Seyffertitz (Dr. Ambrose Lindquist); Charles Lane (Charles Spotswoode); Eugene Pallette (Sergeant Ernest Heath); Lawrence Grant (Charles Cleaver); Ned Sparks (Tony Skeel); Louis John Bartels (Louis Mannix); E. H. Calvert (District Attorney John F. X. Markham); Oscar Smith (Stuttering Hallboy); and: George Y. Harvey, Tim Adair.

The character of Philo Vance, as created by Willard Huntington Wright (1888-1939)** under the name S. S. Van Dine, changed the whole scope of detective fiction, both in literature and the cinema. Vance was a sophisticated sleuth and his solving of crimes in drawing rooms and on society weekends in the country gave murder and its participants an elegant air, a condition which would hold its grip on the detective drama until the 1940s despite the far more realistic (but still often fantasy world) writings of the likes of Dashiell Hammett, Raymond Chandler and various other *Black Mask* magazine contributors. Wright had been an author of basically unsuccessful highbrow literary works, including two books on art criticism. It was not until ill health forced him into light reading that he became fascinated with detective fiction and fashioned his initial Philo Vance adventure, *The Benson Murder Case*, in 1926. His second Vance novel, *The "Canary" Murder Case*, was issued in 1927 and became the first Philo Vance feature film when Paramount filmed it late in 1928 in both sound and silent versions.

THE "CANARY" MURDER CASE tells of a promiscuous stage star, Margaret O'Dell (Louise Brooks; voice of Margaret Livingston), who blackmails the various men she beds. Known as "The Canary," Margaret is found strangled to death in her apartment. Burglar Tony Skeel (Ned Sparks), her ex-husband, has witnessed the crime by looking through a closet keyhole. The suspects include a quartet of prominent men whom Margaret has known intimately: Dr. Ambrose Lindquist (Gustav von Seyffertitz), whose love for the woman nearly drove him mad; politician Charles Cleaver (Lawrence Grant), whose reputation would be ruined if his affair with the dead woman became known; obese Louis Mannix

---

*Dialogue spoken by Margaret Livingston.

**In *Detectionary* (1977), edited by Otto Penzler, Chris Steinbrunner, and Marvin Lachman, it is stated that Willard Huntinton Wright ". . . was much like Vance. Wright, too, was a poseur and a dilettante, dabbling in art, music and criticism. He lived in an expensive penthouse, was fond of costly clothes and food, and collected art. . . . He wrote [his novels] . . . under a pseudonym because he feared ostracism if his friends discovered he was the author."

(Louis John Bartels), who fears his wife might find about his affair with "The Canary"; and Jimmy Spotswoode (James Hall), the scion of wealthy Charles Spotswoode (Charles Lane). Margaret had been attempting to coerce Jimmy into marrying her. His father asks the aid of amateur detective and friend Philo Vance (William Powell) in solving the case since Jimmy has been arrested for the crime and police Sergeant Ernest Heath (Eugene Pallette) and District Attorney Markham (E. H. Calvert) feel he is guilty. When Tony Skeel is also murdered, Vance deduces the murderer's identity and names him during a climactic card game.

Photoplay magazine termed the whodunit a "logical and well-constructed mystery story" and felt polished William Powell was "perfectly swell as the detective." Indeed, debonair Powell, who had been making a specialty of villains in the late silent era, would become the prime debonair screen performer of 1930s and 1940s Hollywood, specializing as the cosmopolitan amateur sleuth (in particular the Philo Vance and the Thin Man series). As *Variety* described the new series lead, "It's a picture wherein the principal character, Philo Vance (Powell), detective, doesn't look at a dame without a professional motive. He's strictly a crime solver, but he troups so well that no one, man or woman, will escape being fascinated." Mordaunt Hall (*New York Times*) emphasized that THE "CANARY" MURDER CASE ". . . dismisses certain happenings with alarming haste, obviously to avoid the spectators having a chance to suspect the person who is guilty," but agreed that "It is indeed a far more compelling and satisfactory tale of its type than has so far been translated to the screen."

THE "CANARY" MURDER CASE had started as a silent production late in 1928 but was turned into a talkie. By that time, however, Louise Brooks had finished her scenes and had gone to Europe to star in G. W. Pabst's PANDORA'S BOX and her voice was dubbed (all too obviously) by another actress, Margaret Livingston. In addition, this film added a love interest (Jean Arthur) for the accused man, and the finale has the killer being hit by a speeding train. The movie also employs the gimmick of asking the audience at the finale not to reveal the identity of "the Canary's" killer.

Jon Tuska commented in *The Detective in Hollywood* (1978), "The cinematic Philo Vance was nothing like his literary counterpart. The exaggerated British accent, the posturing, the erudition was replaced by Powell's rather clipped, precise movements and mannerisms of speech. Eugene Pallette, cast as Sergeant Heath, took so well to the role that for many moviegoers he became inextricably associated with the part even when other studios sought to recast the role. Director Malcolm St. Clair achieves an exquisite Expressionist poetry as he has the incomparably beautiful [Louise] Brooks swing out over her theatre audience, the camera focusing from the rafters on the distressed countenances of her blackmail victims watching her in lecherous awe from below."

S. S. Van Dine produced a dozen Philo Vance novels and, to date, seventeen feature films have been made about the dapper sleuth, the second being THE BENSON MURDER CASE (*q.v.*) in 1930.

THE CARIBBEAN MYSTERY (Twentieth Century-Fox, 1945) 65 minutes.

Producer, William Girard; director, Robert Webb; based on the novel *Murder in Trinidad* by John W. Vandercook; screenplay, W. Scott Darling; camera, Clyde De Vinna; editor, John McCafferty.

James Dunn (Mr. Smith); Sheila Ryan (Mrs. Jean Gilbert); Edward Ryan (Gerald McCracken); Jackie Paley (Linda Lane); Reed Hadley (Rene Marcel); Roy Roberts (Captain Van den Bark); Richard Shaw (Captain Bowman Hall); Daral Hudson (Hartshorn); William Forrest (Colonel Lane); Roy Gordon (McCracken, Sr.); and: Katherine Connors, Robert Filmer, Lucien Littlefield, Lai Chand Mehra, Virginia Walker.

See: MURDER IN TRINIDAD [essay].

THE CASE OF JONATHAN DREW *see* THE LODGER (1926).

THE CASE OF THE BLACK CAT (Warner Bros., 1936) 65 minutes.

Associate producer, Bryan Foy; director, William McGann; based on the novel *The Case of the Caretaker's Cat* by Erle Stanley Gardner; screenplay, F. Hugh Herbert; camera, Allen G. Siegler; editor, Frank Magee.

Ricardo Cortez (Perry Mason); June Travis (Della Street); Jane Bryan (Wilma Laxter); Craig Reynolds (Frank Oafley); Carlyle Moore, Jr. (Douglas Keene); Gordon [Bill] Elliott (Sam Laxter); Nedda Harrigan (Louise DeVoe); Garry Owen (Paul Drake); Harry Davenport (Peter Laxter); George Rosener (Ashton); Gordon Hart (Dr. Jacobs); Clarence Wilson (Shuster); Guy Usher (Burger); Lottie Williams (Mrs. Pixley); Harry Hayden (Rev. Stillwell); Milton Kibbee (Brandon); John Sheehan (Sergeant Holcomb).

THE CASE OF THE CURIOUS BRIDE (First National, 1935) 80 minutes.

Associate producer, Harry Joe Brown; director, Michael Curtiz; based on the novel by Erle Stanley Gardner; adaptor, Tom Reed;

Nedda Harrigan and Ricardo Cortez in THE CASE OF THE BLACK CAT (1936).

additional dialogue, Brown Holmes; music, Bernhard Kaun; art directors, Carl Jules Weyl, Anton Grot; gowns, Orry-Kelly; assistant director, Jack Sullivan; sound, Dolph Thomas; special effects, Fred Jackman, Fred Jackman, Jr.; camera, Dave Abel; editor, Terry Morse.

Warren William (Perry Mason); Margaret Lindsay (Rhoda Montaine); Donald Woods (Carl Montaine); Claire Dodd (Della Street); Allen Jenkins (Spudsy); Barton MacLane (John Lucas); Phillip Reed (Dr. Claude Millsap); Winifred Shaw (Doris Pender); Warren Hymer (Oscar Pender); Olin Howland (Coroner); Henry Kolker (Stacey, the State's Attorney); Charles Richman (Montaine, Sr.); Thomas Jackson (Toots Howard); Errol Flynn (Gregory Moxley); Mayo Methot (Florabelle); James Donlon (Fritz, the Detective); George Humbert (Luigi); Hector Sarno (Greek Proprietor); Antonio Filauri (Pierre); Mary Green (Girl); Bruce Mitchell, Frank G. Fanning (Detectives); Paul Hurst (Fibo); Milton Kibbee (Reporter); Tom Wilson (Cab Starter); Nick Copeland (Cab Driver); Olive Jones (Telephone Operator); Ky Robinson (Cop); Frank Bull (Broadcaster); George Guhl (Typist).

THE CASE OF THE HOWLING DOG (Warner Bros., 1934) 75 minutes.

Producer, Sam Bischoff; director, Alan Crosland; based on the novel by Erle Stanley Gardner; screenplay, Ben Markson; art director, John Hughes; dialogue director, Arthur Grenville Collins; camera, William Rees.

Warren William (Perry Mason); Mary Astor (Bessie Foley); Helen Trenholme (Della Street); Allen Jenkins (Sergeant Holcomb); Grant Mitchell (Claude Drumm); Dorothy Tree (Lucy Benton); Helen Lowell (Elizabeth Walker); Gordon Westcott (Arthur Cartwright); Harry Tyler (Sam Martin); Arthur Aylesworth (Bill Pemberton); Russell Hicks (Clinton Foley); Frank Reicher (Dr. Cooper); Addison Richards (Judge Markham); James Burtis (George Dobbs); Eddie Shubert (Ed Wheeler); Harry Seymour (Donald Clark).

THE CASE OF THE LUCKY LEGS (Warner Bros., 1935) 76 minutes.

Associate producer, Henry Blanke; director, Archie L. Mayo; based on the novel by Erle Stanley Gardner; adaptor, Brown Holmes, Ben Markson, Jerry Chodorov; music director, Leo F. Forbstein; art director, Hugh Reticker; camera, Tony Gaudio; editor, James Gibson.

Warren William (Perry Mason); Genevieve Tobin (Della Street); Patricia Ellis (Margie Clune); Lyle Talbot (Dr. Doray); Allen Jenkins (Spudsy); Barton MacLane (Bissonette); Peggy Shannon (Thelma Bell); Porter Hall (Bradbury); Anita Kerry (Eva Lamont); Craig Reynolds (Frank Patton); Henry O'Neill (Manchester); Charles Wilson (Ricker); Joseph Crehan (Johnson); Olin Howland (Doctor); Mary Treen (Mrs. Soudsy); Joseph Downing (Sanborne).

THE CASE OF THE MISSING BLONDE see LADY IN THE MORGUE.

THE CASE OF THE STUTTERING BISHOP (Warner Bros., 1937) 70 minutes.

Associate producer, Bryan Foy; director, William Clemens; based on the novel by Erle Stanley Gardner; adaptor, Don Ryan, Kenneth Gamet; camera, Rex Wimpy; editor, Jack Saper.

Donald Woods (Perry Mason); Ann Dvorak (Della Street); Anne Nagel (Janice Alma Brownley); Linda Perry (Janice Seaton); Craig Reynolds (Gordon Baxter); Gordon Oliver (Philip Brownley); Joseph Crehan (Paul Drake); Helen MacKellar (Stella Kenwood); Edward McWade (Bishop Mallory); Tom Kennedy (Jim Magooney); Mira McKinney (Ida Gilbert); Frank Faylen (Charles Downs); Douglas Wood (Ronald C. Brownley); Veda Ann Borg (Gladys); George

Lloyd (Peter Sacks); Selmer Jackson (Victor Stockton); Gordon Hart (Judge Knox); Charles Wilson (Hamilton Burger); Eddie Chandler (Detective); Jack Richardson (Taxi Driver).

THE CASE OF THE VELVET CLAWS (Warner Bros., 1936) 63 minutes.

Producer, Henry Blanke; director, William Clemens; based on the novel by Erle Stanley Gardner; adaptor, Tom Reed; art director, Esdras Hartley; camera, Sid Hickox; editor, Jack Saper.

Warren William (Perry Mason); Claire Dodd (Della Street); Winifred Shaw (Eva Belter); Gordon [Bill] Elliott (Carl Griffin); Joseph King (George C. Belter); Addison Richards (Frank Locke); Eddie Acuff (Spudsy Drake); Olin Howland (Wilbur Stran); Kenneth Harlan (Peter Milner); Dick Purcell (Crandal); Ruth Robinson (Mrs. Velte); Paula Stone (Norma Velte); Robert Middlemass (Sergeant Hoffman); Stuart Holmes (Digley); Carol Hughes (Esther Linton).

Erle Stanley Gardner wrote more than seventy Perry Mason novels. In 1934 Warner Bros. bought the rights to seven Mason works and initiated a series of Perry Mason movies with Warren William as the attorney/detective. William, however, played the part in his usual debonair, glib fashion, in contrast to the more adventurous type Gardner depicted in his books.* Also, a more romantic mood prevailed between Mason and secretary Della Street than in the books. Still the Warners' Perry Mason movies, which descended into slick budget installments, proved popular, although Gardner detested them and refused to sell Hollywood the rights to any more of his books.

Warner Bros. inaugurated the Perry Mason series with THE CASE OF THE HOWLING DOG, which was published in 1934, the same year the film was produced. Here Los Angeles-based lawyer Perry Mason (Warren William) accepts the case of Bessie Foley (Mary Astor) who is accused of killing her husband. Although Mason at first believes in her guilt he does his best to prove her innocence. Thanks to circumstances involving a mad watchdog, the

---

*In *Detectionary* (1977), editors Otto Penzler, Chris Steinbrunner, and Marvin Lachman note that according to the literary originals, "Mason is a big man with long legs, broad shoulders and a rugged face. He has thick, wavy hair, an unlined face and he speaks in a well-modulated voice. He has little or no time for sports or exercise, yet he seems to be in good condition and acquits himself well in a fight. . . . The earliest Mason novels (1933-36) were masterpieces of hardboiled pulp realism combined with staggeringly complex plotting. About 1937, under the influence of the slick magazines, the Mason tales became smoother, had more 'love interest,' but were as complex and fast-paced as ever. . . . No Mason novel has ever gone out of print in this country."

perspicacious investigator shows that Bessie did not commit the crime and reveals the true culprit of the three murders. Mason is aided by resourceful secretary Della Street (Helen Trenholme) and police Sergeant Holcomb (Allen Jenkins), with the evidence being presented to the courtroom jury. The *New York Times* (Frank S. Nugent) endorsed the film as a ". . . well-knit story, swiftly paced, dramatically punctuated and, above all, honest with its audience." The *Times* described the detective character as ". . . a criminal attorney whose indifference to legal ethics is exceeded only by his good luck—or is it his sleuthing ability?—in discovering the culprits." As for angular Warren William, the *Times* decided he ". . . gives an easy performance. He is infinitely better suited to the part than he was to that of Philo Vance in THE DRAGON MURDER CASE [1934, *q.v.*], where he was stumbling over William Powell's footprints."* *Variety* was appreciative that "Warners tried an interesting [if unsuccessful because it was overdone] experiment in this film by casting the types in an unobvious manner. . . . the district attorney doesn't look like a district attorney and the judge looks more like a racketeer than the last word legally. . . . Even the dumb dick, Allen Jenkins, is tamed down. And too much so." As for the new series' future, the trade paper estimated, it "ought to be good for three or four more pictures." In retrospect, Clive Hirschhorn wrote in *The Warner Bros. Story* (1979), "Eschewing the usual touches of melodramatic hokum so germane to the genre, the film . . . was underpinned by an intelligent, if somewhat wordy screenplay . . . which Alan Crosland's direction did wonders to keep fluid. The film was also characterized by the complete absence of background music save on one isolated occasion when the title number from DAMES blared forth from a radio."

The next entry in the series, THE CASE OF THE CURIOUS BRIDE (1935), was even better. It was directed in fine style by Michael Curtiz and was based on Gardner's 1934 novel of the same title. Perry Mason's (Warren William) old friend Rhoda Montaine (Margaret Lindsay) consults the criminal lawyer about the embarrassing return of her first husband, Gregory Moxley (Errol Flynn), whom she thought was dead, and his threats against her new husband, heir Carl Montaine (Donald Woods). Mason finds Moxley dead, with Rhoda's keys beside him. With the aid of secretary Della Street (Claire Dodd) and pal Spudsy (Allen Jenkins), Mason must prove Rhoda innocent despite the opinions of the police and the

---

*William Powell had starred in 1933 in Warner Bros.' Philo Vance adventure, THE KENNEL MURDER CASE, *q.v.*, which, like THE CASE OF THE HOWLING DOG, had featured Mary Astor as the heroine.

district attorney's office. Finally he gathers all the suspects at a cocktail party and re-enacts the crime. He pinpoints the killer. *Variety* evaluated the film as "Good whodunit entertainment." The picture contains interesting casting notes: Errol Flynn made his American film debut as the corpse, while Donald Woods, who portrays the second husband and one of the suspects, later was cast as Mason in THE CASE OF THE STUTTERING BISHOP (1937), the last Warner Bros./Mason movie. Regarding THE CASE OF THE CURIOUS BRIDE, Tony Thomas, Rudy Behlmer and Clifford McCarty wrote in *The Films of Errol Flynn* (1969), "A good cut above most B pictures of the time, and following in the tradition of THE THIN MAN the year before, it combined mystery, humor, sleuthing, and clever legal quirks, and managed to lace a fairly interesting plot with crisp dialogue and swift pacing. The book's lengthy courtroom scenes were eliminated, and comic relief was added."

Another 1934 Gardner novel, *The Case of the Lucky Legs*, became the third Perry Mason film entry in 1935. Unfortunately, it was a comedown from the previous two installments; Mason (Warren William) appears distracted (almost tipsy?) too much of the time and there is little chemistry in his relationship with supposedly spunky Della Street (Genevieve Tobin). The plot, which opts for too much humor, has Mason hired by a man (Porter Hall) to look into the murder of the promoter of fixed beauty contests who has stolen the prize money. Again Spudsy (Allen Jenkins) comes along to help solve the case. Still, the *New York Times* thought it "A gay, swift, and impertinent excursion into the sombre matter of murder."

Warren William's final appearance as Perry Mason came with THE CASE OF THE VELVET CLAWS, which Warners issued in the summer of 1936, the film being based on the 1933 Gardner novel of the same title. The picture opens with Perry Mason (Warren William) and Della Street (Claire Dodd) getting married, with the new bride making her husband promise to give up sleuthing (a maxim of 1930s screwball detective comedies/murder mysteries). But their honeymoon is interrupted by a comely young woman (Wini Shaw) with a gun who insists that she has murdered her husband. Mason doubts this and sets out to prove her innocence. He does and pins the crime properly on a relative of the murder victim. He and Della resume their honeymoon. The *New York Times* found it to be a "Felonious photoplay."

Warren William departed Warner Bros. to freelance and was replaced in the Mason series by former silent film idol Ricardo Cortez, who continued the Mason character as a very refined, well-bred sleuth. The detective series had now become part of Bryan

Foy's budget unit at the studio. The film, THE CASE OF THE BLACK CAT, was derived from the 1934 Gardner novel *The Case of the Caretaker's Cat*, and was issued late in 1936, with William McGann replacing director Alan Crosland, who had been killed in a car crash. This case has Mason (Ricardo Cortez) defending a young woman (Jane Bryan) who is charged with slaying her infirm grandfather (Harry Davenport) after he leaves her out of his will because she married a man (Craig Reynolds) he did not like. Della Street (June Travis)—here shown *not* married to Mason—aids in the caper, while the opposition is led by prosecutor Hamilton Burger (Guy Usher). In *The Detective in Hollywood* (1978), Jon Tuska reports, "At least the picture ended with a courtroom scene, even if it was poorly staged, with Mason providing the court with a reconstruction of the crime by means of flashbacks."

The final Warners/Perry Mason movie, THE CASE OF THE STUTTERING BISHOP, was distributed in the early summer of 1937 and *Variety* found it "Slow going." Based on the 1936 novel of the same title, the film has Mason (now played by Donald Woods) and Della Street (Ann Dvorak, once a premier dramatic actress at the studio) involved in a case in which a stammering Australian clergyman (Edward McWade) requests that Mason aid a woman who has been framed for a crime by her father-in-law. The father-in-law, however, is murdered and a bogus granddaughter is brought in for the collection of his tidy estate. Mason puzzles out the clues and brings it to a conclusion. In *The Detective in Film* (1972), William K. Everson evaluated it ". . . the weakest of the group, though with a fascinatingly complicated plot. Unfortunately, Donald Woods was too youthful and too much of an eager beaver to suggest Mason's courtroom experience."

Although THE CASE OF THE STUTTERING BISHOP proved to be the final Perry Mason adventure for Warner Bros., the studio still owned screen rights to *The Case of the Dangerous Dowager* (1937) and, after negotiating with Erle Stanley Gardner, Warners filmed the property as a May Robson vehicle entitled GRANNY GET YOUR GUN (1940), but with the character of Perry Mason deleted from the script.

Probably more satisfying to Perry Mason readers was the 1940s radio series, "Perry Mason," which debuted in 1943 on CBS and ran each weekday (in a soap opera format) for fifteen minutes. Bartlett Robinson played Mason and the role was later handled by Santos Ortega, Donald Briggs and John Larkin.

The most realistic portrayal of Perry Mason came on television when burly Raymond Burr enacted the role on "Perry Mason," which ran for 245 episodes between 1957 and 1966. Also featured on the one-hour program produced by Gail Patrick Jackson were Barbara Hale as Della Street, William Hopper as investigator Paul Drake, Ray Collins as police Lieutenant Tragg, and William Talman as prosecutor Hamilton Burger. After Collins' death, Wesley Lau and Richard Anderson played the leading policemen. For most of the series Kenneth MacDonald portrayed the trial judge and George E. Stone was the court clerk. The series was highlighted by well-written scripts and fine guest casts (including one installment with Bette Davis substituting as a visiting lawyer). In the final 1966 episode Erle Stanley Gardner portrayed the presiding judge.

In 1973-74 CBS-TV briefly revived the format with "The New Adventures of Perry Mason," starring Monte Markham in the title role, supported by Sharon Acker (Della Street), Dane Clark (Lieutenant Tragg), Harry Guardino (Hamilton Burger); Albert Stratton (Paul Drake), and Brett Sommers (Gertrude Lade). The series had only a five-month network run.

Beginning late in 1985, a far heavier Raymond Burr reappeared in his trademark role of Perry Mason for PERRY MASON RE-TURNS, *q.v.*, which was followed by several more Mason TV movies, all of them extremely successful in the ratings.

THE CASINO MURDER CASE (Metro-Goldwyn-Mayer, 1935) 85 minutes.

Producer, Lucien Hubbard; director, Edwin L. Marin; based on the novel by S. S. Van Dine [Willard Huntington Wright]; screenplay, Florence Ryerson, Edgar Allan Woolf; camera, Charles Clarke; editor, Conrad A. Nervig.

Paul Lukas (Philo Vance); Rosalind Russell (Doris Reed); Alison Skipworth (Mrs. Llewellyn); Donald Cook (Lynn Llewellyn); Arthur Byron (Richard Kincaid); Ted Healy (Sergeant Ernest Heath); Eric Blore (Currie); Isabel Jewell (Amelia); Louise Fazenda (Becky); Leslie Fenton (Dr. Kane); Louise Henry (Virginia Llewellyn); Purnell Pratt (Inspector John F. X. Markham); Leo G. Carroll (Smith); Charles Sellon (Dr. Doremus); William Demarest (Auctioneer); Grace Hayle (Fat Lady); Ernie Adams (Husband of Fat Lady); Milton Kibbee, Tom Herbert (Reporters); Keye Luke (Taki); Edna Bennett (Nurse).

Philo Vance (Paul Lukas) receives a letter from Lynn Llewellyn (Donald Cook) who fears he will be murdered if he gambles that night in the casino owned by his uncle, Richard Kincaid (Arthur Byron). On the same day, Vance outbids the man's aunt, Mrs. Llewellyn (Alison Skipworth), on a piece of worthless sculpture at an auction and finds himself attracted to her pretty secretary, Doris Reed (Rosalind Russell). Vance learns that Lynn's wife Virginia

(Louise Henry) wants a divorce so she can return to the stage. Soon the young woman is murdered and Mrs. Llewellyn apparently commits suicide, although Vance quickly deduces she too has been killed (despite having left a suicide note). Making a test to discern that the murders were accomplished by a poison which deteriorates the brain cells, Vance allows the killer to corner him and shoot him with blanks, thus giving the law the right to kill the unbalanced murderer in self-defense.

Based on S.S. Van Dine's 1934 novel, the film was MGM's attempt to carry on the popular Philo Vance movie series with continental Paul Lukas replacing William Powell as the dapper Vance, since Powell was then doing Metro's The Thin Man movies. The production also attempts to make a screen team of Lukas and Rosalind Russell, here in her first major film role, like William Powell and Myrna Loy in THE THIN MAN (1934), *q.v.* None of it works very well, however, since Hungarian Paul Lukas, although looking much the way Van Dine had described Vance in his books, had a heavy accent which was greatly at odds with previous screen Vances.

It is interesting to note that this film does include an actual scientific experiment, the "Vitali Test," to determine if atrophine was the poison used by the killer. In initial release prints, the liquid in the test tube was photographed in Technicolor. THE CASINO MURDER CASE was the second of three Philo Vance offerings produced by MGM, preceded by THE BISHOP MURDER CASE (1930), *q.v.*, with Basil Rathbone, and followed by THE GARDEN MURDER CASE (1936), *q.v.*, with Edmund Lowe.

CASTLE IN THE DESERT (Twentieth Century-Fox, 1942) 62 minutes.

Producer, Ralph Dietrich; director, Harry Lachman; based on the character created by Earl Derr Biggers; screenplay, John Larkin; music director, Emil Newman; camera, Virgil Miller; editor, John Brady.

Sidney Toler (Charlie Chan); Arleen Whelan (Brenda Hartford); Richard Derr (Carl Dethridge); Douglass Dumbrille (Manderley); Henry Daniell (Watson King); Edmund MacDonald (Walter Hartford); [Victor] Sen Yung (Jimmy Chan); Lenita Lane (Lucy Manderley); Ethel Griffies (Madame Saturnia); Milton Parsons (Fletcher); Steven Geray (Dr. Retling); Lucien Littlefield (Professor Gleason); Paul Kruger (Bodyguard); George Chandler (Bus Driver); Oliver Prickett (Wigley the Hotel Manager).

After a dozen years, the Twentieth Century-Fox Charlie Chan series came to a conclusion with its twenty-seventh entry, CASTLE

IN THE DESERT, which has a setting similar to Earl Derr Biggers' novel, *The Chinese Parrot* (1926). Opinions on the feature were diverse. *Variety*, at the time of its release, judged it "A very mild murder mystery without clear-cut reasons for action." On the other hand, in retrospect, Leonard Maltin wrote in his article "Charlie Chan" (*Film Fan Monthly* magazine, April 1968) that it was ". . . an ingenious mystery with an especially good cast. . . ."

Wealthy but facially scarred Manderley (Douglass Dumbrille) and his wife Lucy (Lenita Lane), have built a mansion in the Mojave Desert, many miles from the nearest town. Charlie Chan (Sidney Toler) and number two son Jimmy ([Victor] Sen Yung) are invited to spend a formal weekend at the place. Among the other guests are Brenda Hartford (Arleen Whelan), Carl Dethridge (Richard Derr), the sinister Watson King (Henry Daniell), medium Madame Saturnia (Ethel Griffies), Professor Gleason (Lucien Littlefield), and a physician, Dr. Retling (Steven Geray). When one of the guests is apparently poisoned, Chan must ferret out the killer as the house is now completely cut off from civilization.

CASTLE IN THE DESERT is one of the most eerie films in the entire CHARLIE CHAN film canon, due mainly to the exotic locale, which was originally used as Baskerville Hall in THE HOUND OF THE BASKERVILLES (1938), *q.v.* Ethel Griffies is especially effective as the spiritualist who predicts murder, and the castle, with its medieval look and a torture dungeon, adds flavor to the brief (62 minutes) proceedings. The murder weapon (i.e., the poison) used in the storyline is also ingenious: as it is concocted from a plant which causes the heartbeat to cease for short periods.

When budget unit producer Sol M. Wurtzel dropped the commercially diminished Chan series, star Sidney Toler brought the screen rights to the Chan character from Earl Derr Biggers' widow. Two years later he returned to the screen as the Oriental sleuth at Monogram Pictures, where he starred in eleven more Chan features before his death in 1947.

CHANDLER (Metro-Goldwyn-Mayer, 1971) Color 85 minutes.

Producer, Michael S. Laughlin; director/story, Paul Magwood; screenplay, John Sacret Young; music, George Romanis; art director, Lawrence G. Paull; assistant director, Robert Dijoux; stunt coordinator, Erik Cord; camera, Alan Stensvold; editors, Richard Harris, William B. Gulick.

Warren Oates (Chandler); Leslie Caron (Katherine); Alex Dreier (Carmady); Gloria Grahame (Selma); Lal Baum (Thug); Mitchell Ryan (Chuck) and: Gordon Pinsent, Charles McGraw, Scatman Crothers, Royal Dano.

In what was intended to be a homage to detective genre writer Raymond Chandler, this film baptized the title sleuth Chandler. However, the resulting film is nothing more than a "Mediocre crime film. Scenery great, plot unclear" (*Variety*). Usually associated with screen gangsters and Western bad men, Warren Oates here essays the title role of the snooper, but to little avail, as he and the rest of the uncomfortable cast are swept away by a foggy script.

Bored with his job as a security guard Chandler (Warren Oates) returns to his old profession as a private investigator and is hired to guard Katherine (Leslie Caron), a state's witness, in a trial against several underworld figures. Unknown to Chandler, the mob plans to use him as the patsy when the woman is murdered. However, the detective and his charge fall in love and when they learn the truth, they flee the hoodlums, receiving little assistance from the government that is supposedly committed to protect them.

Not only is the film confusing concerning the relationships among Chandler, the witness, the government, and the hoodlums, but it is further muddled by dramatics involving the racketeering kingpin (Gordon Pinsent). The government is allegedly out to crucify him, but he is double-crossed and murdered by two allies (Alex Drier, Mitchell Ryan). Further distractions arise from the in-and-out cameo appearance by such well known players as Gloria Grahame, Charles McGraw, Scatman Crothers, and Royal Dano.

In "Private Eyes" (*Focus on Film* magazine, Autumn 1975), Don Miller rates the film a "Pastiche" and adds, ". . . the producers claim the film was spoiled by studio butchery, but the question remains as to what if anything was there in the first place."

CHARLIE CHAN AND THE CURSE OF THE DRAGON QUEEN
(United Artists, 1981) Color 102 minutes.

Executive producers, Michael Leone, Alan Belkin; producer, Jerry Sherlock; director, Clive Donner; story, Sherlock; screenplay, Stan Burns, David Axelrod; production designer, Joel Schiller; set designers, Joseph G. Pacelli, E. C. Chen; set decorators, Anne D. McCulley, Sam Jones; costumes, Jocelyn Rickards, David McGough, Robert Newman; makeup, Charles Schram, Fred Williams; music, Patrick Williams; orchestrators, Herbert Spencer, Arthur Morton; dance co-ordinator, Jill Okura; assistant directors, Richard Luke Rothschild, Rafael Elortegui, Pamela Eilerson, Jon Pare, Doug Metzger; stunt co-ordinator, Richard Washington; sound, Bruce Bisenz, Victor Goode; sound effects editor, Ray Alba, Bert Schoenfeld; special effects, Gene Griggs, Mike Wood, Sam Price; camera, Paul Lohmann; second unit camera, El Koons; editors, Walt Hannemann, Phil Tucker.

Peter Ustinov (Charlie Chan); Lee Grant (Mrs. Lupowitz); Angie Dickinson (Dragon Queen); Richard Hatch (Lee Chan, Jr.); Brian Keith (Police Chief); Roddy McDowall (Gillespie); Rachel Roberts (Mrs. Dangers); Michelle Pfeiffer (Cordelia); Paul Ryan (Masten); Johnny Sekka (Stefan); Bennett Ohta (Hawaiian Chief of Police); David Hirokane (Lee Chan, Sr.); Karlene Crockett (Brenda Lupowitz); Michael Fairman (Bernard Lupowitz); James Ray (Haynes); Momo Yashima (Dr. Yu Sing); Kael Blackwood, Jerry Loo (Medical Assistants); Laurence Cohen, Robin Hoff, Kathie Kei, James Bacon (Reporters at Clinic); Frank Michael Liu (Homicide Detectives); John Hugh, George Chiang, David Chow (Shopkeepers); Alison Hong (Maysie Ling); Dewi Yee (TV Interviewer); Joe Bellan, Garrick Huey (Reporters at Pier); Duane Tucker (Cocktail Waiter); Don Parker (Hotel Manager); John Fox, Kenneth Snell, Nicholas Gunn, Don Murray (Pimps); Peter Michas (Chauffeur to Dragon Queen); Larry Duran (Man Getting Traffic Ticket); Chuck Hayward, Bear Hudkins, Rock Walker (Hansom Drivers); Henry Kingi, Faith Minton, Peter Stader, Mike Vendrell (Tourists); *Classic Chan Film episode*: Molly Roden (Lady Rodeworthy); Pavla Ustinov (Cherie); Trevor Hook (Colonel Blass); Paul Sanderson (Mr. Finnegan).

Charlie Chan's return to the screen in 1981 was met with pickets as Chinese Americans protested the fact that a Britisher, Peter Ustinov, not someone of their own race, was cast as Chan. Ironically none of the other players who had performed the screen role were Chinese, Swede Warner Oland and American Sidney Toler being most noted in the assignment. No matter, the film was not worth the trouble. It was a "weak return" (*Variety*) and Ustinov (un)intentionally made a mockery of the part, as the same trade paper observed: ". . . Ustinov adds absolutely nothing original to the role, concentrating for the most part on his squint."

Suspended perilously somewhere between comedy and detection, the overblown film is filled with outlandish characters and the tiresome byplay between Chan and his clumsy Chinese-Jewish grandson Lee Chan, Jr. (Richard Hatch), as well as that with the young man's pretty fiancee (Michelle Pfeiffer). While solving the crime has always been the strong suit of the Chan films, this one almost completely ignores that aspect to focus on its exotic characters, including the Dragon Queen (Angie Dickinson), a hot-headed police chief (Brian Keith), a nasty, handicapped butler (Roddy McDowall), and several red herrings played by Lee Grant, Rachel Roberts, et al. The so-called "storyline" has Chan attempting to solve a series of dastardly murders perpetrated by the Dragon Queen. But the best the veteran detector can advise his confederates is: "When faced with the obvious, look elsewhere," and "Experience good school, but sometimes fees high."

The film's one potential highlight occurs in a chase scene which detours into a movie theater where the killer is confused by the real-life Charlie Chan pursuing him and the celluloid figure engaged in one of his romps on the silver screen. But even this segment is played for the obvious and misses its mark.

CHARLIE CHAN AND THE DRAGON QUEEN, which was novelized in 1981 by Michael Avallone, is a prime example of Hollywood's tampering with tried and true characters, imbuing them with modern comic ineptitudes, resulting in a travesty of the character and plain bad screen fare.

CHARLIE CHAN AT ALCATRAZ see DARK ALIBI [essay].

CHARLIE CHAN AT MONTE CARLO (Twentieth Century-Fox, 1937) 71 minutes.

Producer, Sol M. Wurtzel; associate producer, John Stone; director, Eugene Forde; based on the character created by Earl Derr Biggers; story, Robert Ellis, Helen Logan; screenplay, Charles Belden, Jerry Cady; art directors, Bernard Herzbrun, Haldane Douglas; music director, Samuel Kaylin; camera, Daniel B. Clark; editor, Nick De Maggio.

Warner Oland (Charlie Chan); Keye Luke (Lee Chan); Virginia Field (Evelyn Grey); Sidney Blackmer (Victor Karnoff); Harold Huber (Inspector Jules Joubert); Kay Linaker (Joan Karnoff); Robert Kent (Gordon Chase); Edward Raquello (Paul Savarin); George Lynn (Al Rogers); Louis Mercier (Taxi Driver); George Davis (Pepite); John Bleifer (Ludwig the Chauffeur); Georges Renavent (Renault); George Sorrel (Gendarme).

CHARLIE CHAN AT MONTE CARLO was Warner Oland's final appearance as Charlie Chan; he played the role in fifteen previous Chan features from 1931 onwards and died following the completion of this outing. This proved to be a complicated but rather unengaging mystery. The film is hindered by a running gag about a broken-down taxicab and by devoting far too much footage to the overzealous French police inspector, Jules Joubert (Harold Huber).

Charlie Chan (Warner Oland) and son Lee (Keye Luke) are in Monte Carlo as the guests of Police Inspector Jules Joubert (Harold Huber). When they leave for Paris, where Lee is to exhibit a painting, their taxi breaks down on the road to Nice and, while walking, they find a car with a dead man inside. The police arrive and promptly arrest them, but Joubert negotiates their release. Chan learns that the dead man was Renault (Georges Renavent), a courier for Victor Karnoff (Sidney Blackmer) and that he was carrying one million dollars in bonds which were stolen. Later the car's chauffeur (John Bleifer) is also found murdered near the scene. A vehicle at the scene of the crime belongs to Evelyn Grey (Virginia Field), but she denies knowledge of the affair, although she later admits she was there and that she had left fearing involvement. She claims she was advised to do so by her boyfriend Paul Savarin (Edward Raquello), Karnoff's business rival. Chan learns from Karnoff that only he, his wife Joan (Kay Linaker), his secretary Gordon Chase (Robert Kent) and the chauffeur knew of the bond shipment. Chase, Joan's brother, has been romancing Evelyn but she and Savarin have been using him to get information about Karnoff's dealings. When bartender Al Rogers (George Lynn), who had some of Karnoff's bonds, is found murdered, Chan confronts Joan and she admits that she was once married to Rogers, that he had been blackmailing her and that she had given him the bonds. At Karnoff's home Chan reveals the murderer, who had previously robbed Karnoff to get money to keep Evelyn and then had committed the murders to cover up his crime. In trying to escape, the guilty party is hit and killed by a passing automobile. Charlie and Lee start out for Nice in the same cab, only to have it break down once again.

Although in ill health during the filming of CHARLIE CHAN AT MONTE CARLO, Warner Oland then began CHARLIE CHAN AT THE FIGHTS but died of pneumonia (August 5, 1938) after completing only a few scenes. The movie was salvaged as a Mr. Moto vehicle called MR. MOTO'S GAMBLE (1938), with Keye Luke continuing his role of Lee Chan, here a student of criminologist Moto. After testing several actors, including Noah Beery and Leo G. Carroll, the role of Charlie Chan went to Sidney Toler, who made a very impressive debut in the part in CHARLIE CHAN IN HONOLULU (1938), *q.v.*

CHARLIE CHAN AT THE CIRCUS (Twentieth Century-Fox, 1936) 72 minutes.

Producer, Sol M. Wurtzel; associate producer, John Stone; director, Harry Lachman; based on the character created by Earl Derr Biggers; screenplay, Robert Ellis, Helen Logan; art director, Duncan Cramer; music director, Samuel Kaylin; camera, Daniel B. Clark; editor, Alex Troffey.

Warner Oland (Charlie Chan); Keye Luke (Lee Chan); George and Olive Brasno (Tim and Tiny); Francis Ford (John Gaines); Maxine Reiner (Marie Norman); John McGuire (Hal Blake); Shirley Deane (Louise Norman); Paul Stanton (Joe Kinney); J. Carrol Naish

(Tom Holt); Boothe Howard (Dan Farrell); Drue Leyton (Nellie Farrell); Wade Boteler (Lieutenant Macy); Shia Jung (Su Toy); Franklyn Farnum (Mike the Ticket Taker); John Dilson (Doctor).

The eleventh Charlie Chan feature in the Fox series with Warner Oland, and the second of a quartet of pictures released in 1936, CHARLIE CHAN AT THE CIRCUS is a flavorful, atmospheric thriller with a hard-to-spot killer and plenty of action. The circus backdrop adds zest to the proceedings, with an ape on the rampage, son Lee romancing a pretty Chinese contortionist (Shia Jung), and an attempt on Charlie's life with a cobra. The feature is loaded with Chan's wise sayings: "One grain of luck sometimes worth more than whole rice field of wisdom," "Much evil can enter through small space," "Man who seeks trouble never find it far off," "Frightened bird often difficult to catch," "Far away water no good for nearby fire," "Silent witness sometimes speak loudest," "Mind like parachute—only function when open," and "Enemy who misses mark like serpent who must coil to strike again."

Charlie Chan (Warner Oland) takes his family to the circus where he has an appointment with co-owner Joe Kinney (Paul Stanton). He finds the man dead in his locked circus wagon. Chan unearths that Kinney had many enemies, including his partner John Gaines (Francis Ford); animal trainer Hal Blake (John McGuire), who is in love with Louise Norman (Shirley Deane), the sister of Kinney's fiancée, aerialist Marie Norman (Maxine Reiner); and wardrobe mistress Nellie Farrell (Drue Leyton) and her brother Dan (Boothe Howard). When Caesar the ape is let out of his cage he attacks Chan but is stopped by Hindu snake charmer Tom Holt (J. Carrol Naish). The police investigate the death of Kinney. Lieutenant Macy (Wade Boteler) believes the ape is guilty of the crime, but when he threatens to close down the circus, midget Tiny (Olive Brasno) appeals to Chan for help since she and her husband Tim (George Brasno) are afraid of losing their jobs. Charlie and son Lee (Keye Luke) agree to accompany Macy as the circus moves to its next engagement. That night a cobra is let loose in Chan's train compartment, but Lee arrives in time to kill it. It is alleged that Kinney and Nellie were secretly married, and she demands her share of the show. However, Marie insists Nellie is lying, but while performing her trapeze act Marie is shot and badly hurt. Emergency surgery is performed on Marie at the circus grounds. Caesar is free and attempts to stop the operation, but the ape is shot. It develops that it is one of the circus workers in an ape suit; the man having killed Kinney who was blackmailing him.

The *New York Times* (B. R. Cristler) thought it fitting to provide a few statistics. " . . . The humble detective . . . now has twelve children, which averages a child and a fraction for every picture. And since any artistic property as long-lived as the Chan series must sooner or later run up against the phenomenon of human growth, if not of decay, the latest picture faces the issue bravely by taking the whole Chan family partially, and the eldest son, Lee Chan (Keye Luke) wholly, as a detective-apprentice into the plot." The *Times* reporter concluded, ". . . Any Chan picture is bound to be an essentially hack job at this late date, regardless of highlights. Eleven pictures will take it out of anybody."

CHARLIE CHAN AT THE FIGHTS   *see*   CHARLIE CHAN AT MONTE CARLO [essay].

CHARLIE CHAN AT THE OLYMPICS (Twentieth Century-Fox, 1937) 71 minutes.

Producer, Sol M. Wurtzel; associate producer, John Stone; director, H. Bruce Humberstone; based on the character created by Earl Derr Biggers; story, Paul Burger; adaptors, Robert Ellis, Helen Logan; music director, Samuel Kaylin; camera, Daniel B. Clark; editor, Fred Allen.

Warner Oland (Charlie Chan); Katherine de Mille (Yvonne Roland); Pauline Moore (Betty Adams); Allan Lane (Richard Masters); Keye Luke (Lee Chan); C. Henry Gordon (Arthur Hughes); John Eldredge (Cartwright); Layne Tom, Jr. (Charlie Chan, Jr.); Jonathan Hale (Hopkins); Morgan Wallace (Honorable Charles Zaraka); Fredrik Vogeding (Captain Strasset); Andrew Tombes (Police Chief Scott); Howard Hickman (Dr. Burton); Selmer Jackson (Navy Commander); Don Brodie (Radio Announcer); George Chandler (Ship's Radio Operator); Emmett Vogan (Ship's Officer); Minerva Urecal (Olympic Matron).

In an effort to keep the property viable, topicality became a strong suit of the Charlie Chan pictures in the mid-1930s. CHARLIE CHAN AT THE OLYMPICS is a good example, since it not only utilized footage of the *Hindenberg* for its air ship sequences but its plot is built around the 1936 Berlin Olympic Games and the film interweaves documentary footage from that sports event. A subplot of this whodunit has Lee Chan (Keye Luke) as a member of the U.S. swimming team competing at the Olympics and winning a gold medal at the finale. The movie also offers Layne Tom, Jr. as the sleuth's number two son, Charlie Chan, Jr.

After a foreign agent steals a robot pilot device and kills an aviator in Hawaii, Charlie Chan (Warner Oland) is charged with retrieving the vital invention and bringing in the killer. To do so he flies to Berlin in a dirigible. His number one son Lee (Keye Luke) is a member of the American Olympic swimming team participating in the German competition. In Berlin another murder occurs over the valuable device, with Chan trapping the murderer.

The *New York Times* (John T. McManus) criticized that this film ". . . has a lugubrious quality that overhangs it like a pall. . . . As a murder mystery, the film gets a bit out of hand. . . there is an apparent necessity for accenting the activities of an airline, and that, together, with the efforts of the script writers to outwit an audience that is becoming extremely perceptive about mysteries, creates a little too much of a maze." On the other hand, William K. Everson notes in *The Detective in Film* (1972), "CHARLIE CHAN AT THE OLYMPICS was livelier than most in its period, and the interpolation of newsreel footage of the games, with neat back projection and the use of some of Fox's standing sets, created an effective illusion that the film might have been shot there."

CHARLIE CHAN AT THE OPERA (Twentieth Century-Fox, 1936) 66 minutes.

Producer, Sol M. Wurtzel; associate producer, John Stone; director, H. Bruce Humberstone; based on the character created by Earl Derr Biggers; story, Bess Meredyth; screenplay, Scott Darling. Charles Belden; libretto, William Kernell; opera music, Oscar Levant; orchestrator, Charles Maxwell; music director, Samuel Kaylin; camera, Lucien Andriot; editor, Alex Troffey.

Warner Oland (Charlie Chan); Boris Karloff (Gravelle); Keye Luke (Lee Chan); Charlotte Henry (Mlle. Kitty); Thomas Beck (Phil Childers); Margaret Irving (Mme. Lilli Rochelle); Gregory Gaye (Enrico Barelli); Nedda Harrigan (Mme. Lucretia Barelli); Frank Conroy (Mr. Whitely); Guy Usher (Inspector Regan); William Demarest (Sergeant Kelly); Maurice Cass (Mr. Arnold); Tom McGuire (Morris); Fred Kelsey (Cop); Selmer Jackson, Emmett Vogan (Newspaper Wire Photo Technicians); Benson Fong (Opera Extra).

Thought to have died in a theatrical fire, once famous opera singer Gravelle (Boris Karloff) is an inmate in a mental institution. He happens to see a picture of his diva wife Lilli Rochelle (Margaret Irving), which prompts him to escape. Charlie Chan (Warner Oland) is on the crazy man's trail and he and son Lee (Keye Luke) visit the theater where Mme. Rochelle is to perform in an opera. Unknown to them, Gravelle has taken sanctuary in the theater and has contacted Lucretia Barelli (Nedda Harrington), whose husband Enrico (Gregory Gaye) has been romancing Lilli. Enrico Barelli, the lead singer in the company's production of *Carnival*, receives a threatening letter and several cast members insist there is a phantom-like figure stalking the wings of the theater in the Mephistopheles costume Enrico wears in the opera. It seems that Gravelle has regained his memory and recalls that Lilli and Enrico had once tried to kill him by trapping him in a long-ago theatrical fire. During the opera that night both Lilli and Enrico are stabbed to death and Chan captures Gravelle, whom police Inspector Regan (Guy Usher) and the especially dumb Sergeant Kelly (William Demarest) believe is the murderer. Chan is not convinced, however, and asks that the opera be staged again in hopes of ambushing the killer. Anita agrees to sing Lilli's part and Gravelle performs Enrico's baritone role. During the performance Gravelle is shot as Chan captures the real executioner. Gravelle recovers and his daughter Kitty (Charlotte Henry) and her boyfriend Phil Childers (Thomas Beck) visit him in the hospital.

"Warner Oland vs Boris Karloff" read the promotional copy title card for CHARLIE CHAN AT THE OPERA, a very well put-together entry in the Charlie Chan series which is reminiscent of the classic horror story, Gaston Leroux's *The Phantom of the Opera*. The *New York Times* (Thomas M. Pryor) reported that this ". . . is by far the best of the recent crop of Chan pictures. . . . . Warner Oland, the perennial, who has just signed for ten more Chan pictures, performs the title role with his customary dexterity." As for the detecting methods of the super sleuth, the *Times* observed, "Mr. Chan tackles this latest assignment in his usual leisurely but thoroughgoing fashion, a style of sleuthing which unfortunately necessitates allowing a few more people, in this case a prima donna and her admirer, to be murdered practically under his nose before he unmasks the culprit."

For this well-mounted feature William Kernell and Oscar Levant composed a special opera, and Denis Gifford in his book *Karloff: The Man, The Monster, The Movies* (1973) claims that Karloff did his own singing in the picture and was not, as most sources claim, dubbed. Not only is the film eerie, but it has a classy look about it due to director H. Bruce Humberstone's resourceful use of standing sets from Fox's CAFE METROPOLE (1937).

CHARLIE CHAN AT THE RACE TRACK (Twentieth Century-Fox, 1936) 70 minutes.

Producer, Sol M. Wurtzel; associate producer, John Stone; director, H. Bruce Humberstone; based on the character created by Earl Derr Biggers; story, Lou Breslow, Saul Elkins; adaptor, Robert Ellis, Helen Logan, Edward T. Lowe; music director, Samuel Kaylin; camera, Harry Jackson; editor, Nick De Maggio.

Warner Oland (Charlie Chan); Keye Luke (Lee Chan); Helen Wood (Alice Fenton); Thomas Beck (Bruce Rogers); Alan Dinehart (George Chester); Gavin Muir (Bagley); Gloria Roy (Catherine

Chester); Jonathan Hale (Warren Fenton); G. P. Huntley, Jr. (Denny Barton); George Irving (Major Kent); Frank Coghlan, Jr. (Eddie Brill); Frankie Darro ("Tip" Collins); John Rogers (Mooney); John H. Allen ("Streamline" Jones); Harry Jans (Al Meers); Robert Warwick (Chief of Police); Jack Mulhall (Purser); Paul Fix (Gangster); Charles Williams (Reporter); Sidney Bracey (Steward).

Detectives and racing have been combined in several entertaining films, including the Sherlock Holmes British feature, SILVER BLAZE (MURDER AT THE BASKERVILLES) (1937); the Hildegarde Withers mystery, MURDER ON A BRIDLE PATH (1936); and the Nick and Nora Charles outing, SHADOW OF THE THIN MAN (1941), *qq.v.* Charlie Chan also become involved in the sport in CHARLIE CHAN AT THE RACE TRACK, the third of four 1936 Chan releases and the first of four films in the programmer series to be directed by H. Bruce Humberstone. The racing sequences were shot on location at the Santa Anita Race Track.

"Suspicion is the father of truth," Charles Chan (Warner Oland) intones in this adventure in which his friend, racehorse owner Major Kent (George Irving), is found murdered on a steamship. It appears he was trampled to death by the prize stallion Avalanche. Charlie Chan and son Lee (Keye Luke) board the vessel in Honolulu and remain aboard until it docks in California. There gangsters switch horses, hoping to make a fortune off the disguised Avalanche at the Santa Anita Handicap. Chan uncovers their nefarious doings but the hoodlums kidnap Chan and Lee. However, the two escape and at the race track Chan switches the horses back, and Avalanche wins the event. The Chinese sleuth corrals the hoodlums and exposes his friend's murderer.

The *New York Times* (John T. McManus) opined, ". . . The film follows Hollywood's latest adaptation from Greek tragedy, dictated for all we know by the Hays office of having its murders done offstage somewhere. You may have noticed that the clutching hand has been a cinematic archaism, that no longer do daggers descend from crannies in haunted walls and that the death rattle has unaccountably been replaced in pictures by the radio newsflash and the newspaper headline." The *Times'* reviewer teased, "Mr. Chan's son, Lee (Keye Luke), is a willing, if inept, aide, and it does seem a bit unfair of Mr. Chan not to give the boy credit for a good try. As it is, Lee comes dashing in with a hot clue after Mr. Chan has knotted all the loose ends and delivered the whole criminal kaboodle over to the police." (At which point Charlie tells his earnest son, "Too late. Save for next case, please.")

It was during the filming of CHARLIE CHAN AT THE RACE TRACK that star Warner Oland embarked on another of his drinking binges and disappeared. Director Humberstone had extras comb the Santa Anita track looking for the actor and finally found him passed out in a restaurant.

CHARLIE CHAN AT THE WAX MUSEUM (Twentieth Century-Fox, 1940) 63 minutes.

Producer, Sol M. Wurtzel; associate producers, Walter Morosco, Ralph Dietrich; director, Lynn Shores; based on the character created by Earl Derr Biggers; screenplay, John Larkin; art directors, Richard Day, Lewis Creber; music, Emil Newman; camera, Virgil Miller; editor, James B. Clark.

Sidney Toler (Charlie Chan); Victor Sen Yung (Jimmy Chan); C. Henry Gordon (Dr. Cream); Marc Lawrence (Steve McBirney); Joan Valerie (Lily Latimer); Marguerite Chapman (Mary Bolton); Ted Osborn (Tom Agnew); Michael Visaroff (Dr. Otto von Brom); Hilda Vaughn (Mrs. Rocke); Charles Wagenheim (Willie Fern);

Sidney Toler, Marguerite Chapman, Ted Osborn and Joan Valerie in CHARLIE CHAN AT THE WAX MUSEUM (1940).

Archie Twitchell (Carter Lane); Edward Marr (Grenock); Joe King (Inspector Matthews); Harold Goodwin (Edwards); Charles Trowbridge (Judge); Stanley Blystone (Court Attendant); Emmett Vogan (District Attorney); Jimmy Conlin (Barker).

One of the most atmospheric and bizarre episodes in the Charlie Chan film series is CHARLIE CHAN AT THE WAX MUSEUM, which is set in an old wax museum on a stormy night, with all the proper trimmings for such a murder mystery excursion, including forbidding wax figures of Jack the Ripper and Bluebeard, trap doors and a hidden room, shadowy figures, creaking doors and a determined murderer with a bandaged face. In *Saturday Afternoon at the Bijou* (1973), David Zinman endorsed the picture: "It gets our ballot because of its suspense and eerie setting and a storyline that keeps you guessing as to who is dead, who is alive and who is a dummy." However, at the time it was issued, *Variety*, surfeited by too many such installments, dismissed the well-constructed programmer with, "It's all flimsy, muddled, absurd and never for an instant believable. But frequently it's preposterous enough to be amusing."

After escaping from prison, hoodlum Steve McBirney (Marc Lawrence) seeks sanctuary in a wax museum operated by Dr. Cream (C. Henry Gordon), who features lifelike wax figures of infamous criminals. The doctor is a plastic surgeon specializing in operating on gangsters, providing them with new faces. Cream operates on McBirney, who wants to get even with Charlie Chan (Sidney Toler) for having sent him to jail. A weekly Crime League radio broadcast originates from the museum and Dr. Cream asks Chan to be a panelist discussing the case of executed murderer Joe Rocke. McBirney wires the chair Chan is to use, intending to electrocute the Chinese sleuth. Other panelists include newspaperwoman Mary Bolton (Marguerite Chapman), Dr. Otto von Brom (Michael Visaroff), a noted criminologist, the program's director, Tom Agnew (Ted Osborn), and Dr. Cream. Secreted in the museum are Joe Rocke's widow (Hilda Vaughn) and McBirney. During the show Chan states that he believes Rocke was falsely convicted and executed and that the crime was actually committed by Butcher Dagan, a well-known hoodlum. The lights go out and when they come back on, von Brom is dead, having accidentally sat in the chair reserved for Chan. Chan, however, deduces that the man, whose evidence had sent Rocke to the electric chair, was really disposed of with a poisoned dart. Agnew immediately cuts off the broadcast. After finding Dr. Cream's operating theater, Chan deduces that Dagan was given a new face by the surgeon and had killed von Brom because he knew his identity. McBirney too is found dead by a poisoned dart and Mrs. Rocke is captured, but she claims she did not kill the man and that she has come to the broadcast to beg von Brom to reopen her husband's case. Local police Inspector Matthews (Joe King) is about to arrest Mrs. Rocke for the killings but Chan gathers everyone together in the museum, including number two son Jimmy (Victor Sen Yung) who has accompanied his dad to the broadcast. Chan demonstrates how the poisoned dart was used to kill the victims. When he shoots a dart into one of the wax figures it suddenly comes to life; Dagan has been hiding there. The killer, one of the people present during the broadcast but in the fresh guise provided by Dr. Cream, begs for an antidote and confesses to the crimes before Chan admits that the dart does not contain poison.

CHARLIE CHAN AT TREASURE ISLAND (Twentieth Century-Fox, 1939) 72 minutes.

Producer, Sol M. Wurtzel; associate producer, Edward Kaufman; director, Norman Foster; based on the character created by Earl Derr Biggers; story/screenplay, John Larkin; camera, Virgil Miller; editor, Norman Colbert.

Sidney Toler (Charlie Chan); Cesar Romero (Rhadini); Pauline Moore (Eve); Victor Sen Yung (Jimmy Chan); Douglas Fowley (Pete Lewis); June Gale (Myra Rhadini); Douglass Dumbrille (Thomas Gregory); Sally Blane (Stella Essex); Billie Seward (Bessie Sibley); Wally Vernon (Elmer Kelner); Donald MacBride (Chief J. J. Kilvaine); Charles Halton (Redley); Trevor Bardette (Abdul); Louis Jean Heydt (Paul Essex); Gerald Mohr (Dr. Zodiac); John Elliott (Doctor).

The twenty-second film in the enduring Charlie Chan series and the third to star Sidney Toler in the title role, CHARLIE CHAN AT TREASURE ISLAND is also one of the best entries in the long-running series. *Variety* reported that the ". . . solution is secondary to the story unwinding through a maze of weird and spooky episodes."

When a writer friend of detective Charlie Chan (Sidney Toler) commits suicide aboard a clipper ship heading from San Francisco, the Chinese sleuth investigates, and clues lead him to Treasure Island, an amusement exhibit at the San Francisco Fair. He finds that a mysterious mystic, Dr. Zodiac (Gerald Mohr), may be involved. Chan is aided in the investigation by local police chief Kilvaine (Donald MacBride) and crime fighting newspaper reporter Pete Lewis (Douglas Fowley) as well as by Chan's well-meaning but bumbling Number Two son, Jimmy (Victor Sen Yung). They determine that Zodiac has been using hypnotism to inveigle secrets out of the wealthy and then blackmail them. To stop the crook, Chan enlists the aid of Rhadini (Cesar Romero), the star attraction at Treasure Island. The mystery deepens when the man thought to be Zodiac is found dead and is revealed to be his assistant masquerading as Zodiac to cover his real identity. Chan unmasks the murderer on stage while Rhadini conducts his magic show.

While most devotees of the Chan series consider this feature to be top notch, William K. Everson complains about the picture in *The Detective in Film* (1972), "CHARLIE CHAN AT TREASURE ISLAND has one of the most ingenious plots of all, and one of the cleverest concealments of the villain; yet a typical plot contrivance knocked the supports out from under the carefully constructed box of tricks, and tipped off the 'surprise' revelation of the killer's identity somewhat ahead of schedule." On the other hand, Leonard Maltin decided in his article "Charlie Chan" in *Film Fan Monthly* magazine (April 1968), "Undoubtedly Toler's best film was CHARLIE CHAN ON [*sic*] TREASURE ISLAND, with a large cast and a terrific plot; again, the killer was well disguised."

CHARLIE CHAN CARRIES ON (Fox, 1931) 76 minutes.

Director, Hamilton MacFadden; based on the novel by Earl Derr Biggers; screenplay/dialogue, Philip Klein, Barry Connors; settings, Joe Wright; sound, George P. Costello; camera, George Schneidermann; editor, Al De Gaetano.

Warner Oland (Charlie Chan); John Garrick (Mark Kenaway); Marguerite Churchill (Pamela Potter); Warren Hymer (Max Minchin); Marjorie White (Sadie Minchin); C. Henry Gordon (John Ross); William Holden (Patrick Tait); George Brent (Captain Ronald Keane); Peter Gawthorne (Inspector Duff); John T. Murray (Dr. Lofton); John Swor (Elmer Benbow); Goodee Montgomery (Mrs. Benbow); Jason Robards (Walter Honeywood); Lumsden Hare (Inspector Hanley); Zellie Tillbury (Mrs. Luce); Betty Francisco (Sybil Conway); Harry Beresford (Kent); John Rogers (Martin); J. G. Davis (Eben).

Taken from Earl Derr Biggers' 1930 novel of the same title (the fifth of six Charlie Chan novels by Biggers), CHARLIE CHAN CARRIES ON was Fox Pictures' initial entry in its Chan series starring Swedish-born Warner Oland, although in 1929 the studio had released BEHIND THAT CURTAIN, *q.v.*, in which the Oriental character had been reduced to a small part played by E. L. Park. Oland was beautifully cast in the role of Charlie Chan.* He grew to

---

*In Detectionary, editors Otto Penzler, Chris Steinbrunner, and Marvin Lachman describe the inestimable Chan as "..quite fat but walks with light, graceful steps. His cheeks are as round as a baby's, his skin is ivory, his amber eyes are slanted, and his black hair is close-cropped. Charlie, his wife and eleven honorable children live on Honolulu's Punchbowl Hill. . . . His dress is Americanized but his speech retains many Oriental patterns."

Variety wrote of Warner Oland in CHARLIE CHAN CARRIES ON, "Warner

love the character and, in turn, to be loved by the movie-going public who considered him and Chan inseparable. Oland often created the many aphorisms Chan employed in his detective capers and it is said that in his later years, when he was drinking heavily, his own speech reflected his great empathy for the Charlie Chan role. The *New York Times* dubbed his initial Chan outing "amusing and suspenseful" and it led to the production of forty-four more Chan theatrical features in the next eighteen years, clearly making Charlie Chan one of the most durable of celluloid sleuths.

A man is killed mysteriously in a London hotel and Scotland Yard Inspector Duff (Peter Gawthorne) traces the killer to a luxury liner presently on a world cruise under the command of Captain Ronald Keane (George Brent). Another murder occurs on board the ship and, when the vessel reaches Honolulu, police detective Charlie Chan (Warner Oland) is assigned to the homicides. When he consults Duff, the inspector too is killed and Chan joins the cruise as it steams to San Francisco. Aboard are his friend Mark Kenaway (John Garrick), who is romancing pretty Pamela Potter (Marguerite Churchill), the granddaughter of the first man killed; one-time bootlegger, the wise-cracking Max Minchin (Warren Hymer), and his shopping-addicted wife Sadie (Marjorie White); and several wealthy passengers, including John Ross (C. Henry Gordon), Patrick Tait (William Holden), and Walter Honeywood (Jason Robards). Piecing together the various clues Chan deduces who the killer is. It develops that he is a man seeking revenge on another of the passengers for having seduced his wife long ago.

"Only a brave mouse will make its nest in a cat's ear," "Only a very sly man can shoot off a cannon quietly," and "He who feeds the chicken deserves the egg" are but a few of the many Chan sayings which pepper the picture's dialogue and helped to endear Charlie Chan and Warner Oland to the public. Sadly, prints of this initial Oland-Chan screen collaboration no longer exist.

CHARLIE CHAN IN EGYPT (Fox, 1935) 72 minutes.

Associate producer, Edward T. Lowe; director, Louis King; based on the character created by Earl Derr Biggers; screenplay, Robert Ellis, Helen Logan; music arranger/conductor, Samuel Kaylin; art director, William Darling; sound, E. H. Hansen; camera, Daniel B. Clark; editor, Alfred De Gaetano.

Warner Oland (Charlie Chan); Pat Paterson (Carol Arnold); Thomas Beck (Tom Evans); Rita Cansino [Rita Hayworth] (Nayda);

Oland takes his Oriental character swell although a bit lethargic. That may be due to the picture pace which lacks some punch that maybe could have been stuck in."

Stepin Fetchit (Snowshoes); Jameson Thomas (Dr. Anton Racine); Frank Conroy (Professor Thurston); Nigel de Brulier (Edfu Ahmad); James Eagles (Barry Arnold); Paul Porcasi (Fouad Soueida); Arthur Stone (Dragoman); Frank Reicher (Dr. Jaipur); George Irving (Professor Arnold); Anita Brown (Snowshoes' Friend); John Davidson (Daoud Atrash the Chemist); Gloria Roy (Bit); John George (Dwarf Egyptian Helper).

The eighth feature in Fox's very successful Charlie Chan series, CHARLIE CHAN IN EGYPT is considered by many to be Warner Oland's best film in the sixteen offerings in which he portrayed the Oriental sleuth. The movie is rife with horror trappings, including a curse for opening an ancient Egyptian tomb, the supposedly living statue of a god of vengeance and a murderer masquerading as that vengeful idol, along with the ghostly atmosphere of the tomb. Finally there are the comedy antics of Stepin Fetchit, here cast as Snowshoes, a houseboy who claims to be descended from the ancient Egyptians.

Charlie Chan (Warner Oland) is sent by the French Archaeological Society to Egypt to find out why artifacts from the tomb of the high priest Ameti have been appearing in private collections and rival museums in Europe. He encounters Carol Arnold (Pat Paterson) and her fiancée Tom Evans (Thomas Beck), who works with the expedition at Ameti's tomb which is led by her uncle, Professor Thurston (Frank Conroy), in the absence of her father, Professor Arnold (George Irving). Carol is worried because her father has been gone for a month searching for another excavation site. Chan examines the artifacts from the Ameti explorations and suggests to Thurston that Ameti's coffin be x-rayed. They find that the body inside has a bullet lodged near the heart and when the coffin is opened the corpse proves to be that of Professor Arnold. Thurston admits to Chan that he was the one who sold some of the lesser items from the Ameti expedition to pay for his brother's work, since the French Archaeological Society had withdrawn its financial support and local Dr. Anton Racine (Jameson Thomas) was owed money by Arnold because he had helped to continue their work. Chan also discovers that the dead man's son, Barry Arnold (James Eagles), had been crippled by a falling wall at the tomb site and that Tom Evans had argued with the professor over the interpretation of hieroglyphics in the Ameti tomb, but had been rehired by Thurston after Arnold had fired him. That night Chan, Evans, and Snowshoes visit the Ameti tomb and an attempt is made on the detective's life. Local police chief Fouad Soueida (Paul Porcasi) enters the case and later Barry Arnold is found dead after hinting that he knew who killed his father. Egyptian houseman Edfu Ahmad (Nigel de Brulier) is suspected of the crimes and runs away, while back at the tomb Chan, Evans, and Snowshoes locate a secret passage. In a hidden room Evans finds an even larger cache of Egyptian treasures but is shot after recognizing his would-be assailant. Evans is treated by a local physician (Frank Reicher) and Chan deduces that the killer committed the crimes to keep the Ameti treasure a secret. When the murderer attempts to eliminate Evans for good, he is captured by Chan.

Variety endorsed, "Combines a suavely sustained concept of drama, another surehanded interpretation of the central role by Warner Oland and effective interplay of background color." Andre Sennwald (*New York Times*) judged that it was "a lively and entertaining if somewhat minor mystery work," while *Photoplay* magazine enthused, "Grand atmosphere and unique settings plus some hilarious comedy with Stepin Fetchit puts this one way up in the Charlie Chan series. Oland is A-1."

As had come to be expected, CHARLIE CHAN IN EGYPT is loaded with Chan's pig-English philosophizing: "Inconspicuous molehill sometimes more important than conspicuous mountain," "Admitting failure like drinking bitter tea," "Cannot believe piece of hard stone can cause evil unless dropped on foot," "Theory like mist on eyeglasses, obscures facts," "Waiting for tomorrow wastes of today," "Cannot read words in new book until pages cut," and "Hasty conclusion easy to make like hole in water."

It should be noted that this film provided future screen star Rita Hayworth, here billed as Rita Cansino, with one of her first sizeable screen assignments. She appears as the comely native servant, Nayda, who is somewhat of a red herring due to her actions, but is proved to be a loyal family retainer.

CHARLIE CHAN IN HONOLULU (Twentieth Century-Fox, 1938) 67 minutes.

Producer, Sol M. Wurtzel; associate producer, John Stone; director, H. Bruce Humberstone; based on the character created by Earl Derr Biggers; screenplay, Charles Belden; art directors, Richard Day, Haldane Douglas; music director, Samuel Kaylin; camera, Charles Clarke; editor, Nick De Maggio.

Sidney Toler (Charlie Chan); Phyllis Brooks (Judy Hayes); Victor Sen Yung (Jimmy Chan); Eddie Collins (Al Hogan); John King (Randolph); Claire Dodd (Mrs. Carol Wayne); George Zucco (Dr. Cardigan); Robert Barrat (Captain Johnson); Marc Lawrence (Johnny McCoy); Richard Lane (Joe Arnold); Layne Tom, Jr. (Tommy Chan); Philip Ahn (Wing Fo); Paul Harvey (Inspector Rawlins); Dick Alexander (Sailor); James Flavin (Police Dispatcher).

Claire Dodd, John King and Sidney Toler in CHARLIE CHAN IN HONOLULU (1938).

Warner Oland died in the summer of 1938 at the age of fifty-seven, on the eve of appearing in CHARLIE CHAN AT THE FIGHTS, and producer Sol M. Wurtzel revamped the script to utilize already shot footage for an entry in Twentieth Century-Fox's Mr. Moto series, MR. MOTO'S GAMBLE, in which Keye Luke continued his role of Lee Chan, Charlie's number one son. Missouri-born character actor Sidney Toler was chosen to replace Oland in the Chan features and his initial appearance was in CHARLIE CHAN IN HONOLULU, a top-notch affair. It was an excellent debut showcase for Toler and he remained with the role until the Fox series concluded in 1942. Then he played Chan again at Monogram Pictures from 1944 until his death in 1947. In *Close Up: The Contract Director* (1976), Jon Tuska calls this initial outing ". . . the finest Chan film that Sidney Toler made."

Charlie Chan (Sidney Toler) is about to become a grandfather and is anxiously awaiting the news of the impending birth with his son-in-law Wing Foo (Philip Ahn) when number two son Jimmy (Victor Sen Yung) receives word that a murder has been committed aboard a U.S.-bound tramp steamer anchored in Honolulu harbor. Jimmy decides to solve the case himself and he and younger brother Tommy (Layne Tom, Jr.) go to the site with Jimmy masquerading as his father. Jimmy badly bungles the assignment and his father arrives to assume control of the investigation. He finds the boat full of likely suspects: pretty Judy Hayes (Phyllis Brooks); animal trainer Al Hogan (Eddie Collins) and his pet lion; Randolph (John King), the dead man's widow, Mrs. Carol Wayne (Claire Dodd); Dr. Cardigan (George Zucco), a criminologist who keeps a live brain in his cabin; Captain Johnson (Robert Barrat); and gangster Johnny McCoy (Marc Lawrence), who is being brought to prison by lawman Joe Arnold (Richard Lane). Chan ascertains that the murdered man was attempting to sneak money out of China to avoid a divorce settlement, but soon Mrs. Wayne too is murdered. Charlie then concludes that Arnold is a bogus lawman and that he and cohort McCoy eliminated the real law enforcer. Chan ensnares the killer, who is arrested just as Chan receives the tidings that he has a new grandson.

Variety heralded, "Adventures of Charlie Chan get off to a fresh start with Sidney Toler handling the title role in most capable fashion. His Chan has more poise and lightness, and is less theatric than previously. . . . [It] measures up to mark set by previous releases of the series, and will prove a good programmer. . . ." Frank S. Nugent (*New York Times*) observed, "Mr. Toler has been as respectful of Mr. Oland's interpretation as Scriptwriter Charles Belden has been of Mr. Biggers' durable hero. He has copied the round Panama hat, the dab of whisker beneath the lower lip, the oriental mustache." Of the film itself, he concluded, it ". . . is practically a letter-perfect duplicate of all the other Chan films—beginning with the body on the floor and ending with Charlie saying 'thank you so much' to the snarling killer. It is the usual, red-herring scented, passably diverting mystery film."

CHARLIE CHAN IN LONDON (Fox, 1934) 79 minutes.

Associate producer, John Stone; director, Eugene Forde; based on the character created by Earl Derr Biggers; screenplay, Philip MacDonald; art director, Duncan Cramer; music director, Samuel Kaylin; camera, L. W. O'Connell.

Warner Oland (Charlie Chan); Drue Leyton (Pamela Gray); Douglas Walton (Paul Gray); Alan Mowbray (Geoffrey Richmond); Mona Barrie (Lady Mary Bristol); Raymond [Ray] Milland (Neil Howard); George Barraud (Major Jardine); Paul England (Bunny Fothergill); Madge Bellamy (Becky Fothergill); Walter Johnson (Jerry Garton); Murray Kinnell (Phillips); E. E. Clive (Detective Sergeant Thacker); Elsa Buchanan (Alice Rooney); Reginald Sheffield (Flight Commander King); Perry Ivins (Kemp); John Rogers (Lake); Helena Grant (Secretary); Montague Shaw (Doctor); Phyllis Coughlan (Nurse); Margaret Mann (Housemaid); David Torrence (Sir Lionel

Bashford); Claude King (RAF Commandant); Ann Doran (Young Woman).

Thanks to an abundance of stock footage and the technology of rear projection, Charlie Chan and his entourage were able to globe-trot frequently in their celluloid adventures, adding exotic settings and novelty to the formula whodunits. CHARLIE CHAN IN LONDON is the sixth film in Fox's Charlie Chan series and the first not based directly on an Earl Derr Biggers novel. It is a fetching murder mystery with a most involved plot and the crime motive eluding the Chinese investigator until well on in the proceedings. The film includes a bit of racism, a Cockney maid referring to Chan as a "creepin', murderin', foreign man." The picture also contains several sage Chan sayings, including: "Thoughts are like noble animal, undirected they run away causing awful smashup," "Case like inside of radio—many connections but not always related," and "If you want wild bird to sing do not put him in cage."

Charlie Chan (Warner Oland) is about to depart London when Pamela Gray (Drue Leyton) and her fiancée, barrister Neil Howard (Raymond [Ray] Milland), come to see him. Pamela's brother Paul (Douglas Walton) has been sentenced to hang for the murder of a romantic rival, Hamilton, an RAF flight officer. Pamela breaks her engagement to Howard when he admits to Chan that he actually believes Paul, whom he defended in court, is guilty of the crime. Chan takes the case although he has only sixty-five hours to solve it before Gray is hanged. The Chinese detective heads for the country home of Geoffrey Richmond (Alan Mowbray) in Retfordshire, where the murder took place in the estate stables. The detective questions those who were at the estate when the killing occurred and unearths that tipsy Bunny Fothergill (Paul England), Major Jardine (George Barraud)—who has taken over Paul's post as Geoffrey's hunt secretary, and Jerry Garton (Walter Johnson)—who has been romancing Geoffrey's fiancée Lady Mary Bristol (Mona Barrie, had heard Gray and Hamilton quarreling violently. It was Fothergill and Jardine who discovered the corpse. Chan has the crime re-enacted and questions tableman Lake (John Rogers), who is found dead the next day, local police detective Sergeant Thacker (E. E. Clive) believing Lake's death is suicide. However, Chan substantiates that the man was murdered. Believing that Lake was blackmailing Hamilton's real killer, Chan imparts this information to Pamela who informs her brother that Chan is seeking to prove his innocence. That night an attempt is made on the detective's life with an air gun and Lady Mary sees the assailant. The next day Chan visits the local RAF airfield where he hears that Hamilton has invented a device for silencing planes. Returning to the estate he is given a note from Lady

Mary asking to see him, but she has already gone on a fox hunt and when he and Neil trace her, she has been badly injured as a result of her horse falling. Back at the main house, Chan announces that Lady Mary's fall was no accident and that Hamilton had been murdered for his aircraft silencer plans. That evening Charlie locates the plans and Hamilton's killer shoots him, but his gun is loaded with blanks and Chan subdues him. The murderer is really a foreign agent masquerading as a British nobleman in order to capture the important blueprints. Paul is released from prison and Pamela and Neil resume their engagement. The freed man insists that the humble Charlie Chan is "the greatest detective in the world."

CHARLIE CHAN IN PANAMA (Twentieth Century-Fox, 1940) 67 minutes.

Producer, Sol M. Wurtzel; associate producer, John Stone; director, Norman Foster; based on the character created by Earl Derr Biggers; screenplay, John Larkin, Lester Ziffren; music director, Samuel Kaylin; camera, Virgil Miller; editor, Fred Allen.

Sidney Toler (Charlie Chan); Jean Rogers (Kathi Lenesch); Lionel Atwill (Cliveden Compton); Mary Nash (Miss Jennie Finch); Victor Sen Yung (Jimmy Chan); Kane Richmond (Richard Cabot); Chris-Pin Martin (Lieutenant Montero); Lionel Royce (Dr. Rudolph Grosser); Helen Ericson (Stewardess); Jack La Rue (Manolo); Edwin Stanley (Governor Webster); Don Douglas (Captain Lewis); Frank Puglia (Achmed Halide); Addison Richards (Godley); Edward Keane (Dr. Fredericks); Lane Chandler (Officer); Eddie Acuff (Suspicious Sailor); Ed Gargan (Plant Worker); Jimmy Aubrey (Drunken Sailor); Alberto Morin (Desk Clerk).

In CHARLIE CHAN IN THE CITY OF DARKNESS (1939), *q.v.*, the Chinese investigator had his initial major confrontation with foreign spies and that plot motif is continued in the far better CHARLIE CHAN IN PANAMA, the twenty-first Chan feature at Fox and the fifth feature with Sidney Toler in the key assignment. Well written and fast moving, with a murderer who is not easily spotted, the film nicely merges the detective and the topical espionage genres into solid entertainment. *Variety* printed, "This latest Chan whodunit is a real chiller and ranks high among the many turned out." That trade paper also commented on Sidney Toler's portrayal of Chan: "Toler dominates every scene once he's introduced. . . . He is tremendously effectual in the well-conceived climax. . . ."

The government asks Charlie Chan (Sidney Toler) to investigate a murder in the Panama Canal Zone and he and number two son Jimmy (Victor Sen Yung) fly there. The elder Chan works incognito as the owner of a hat store while aiding the local authorities, led by Lieutenant Montero (Chris-Pin Martin), in the case. Among the colorful suspects are Kathi Lenesch (Jean Rogers), a Czechoslovakian refugee show girl working at a local cabaret; British mystery novelist Cliveden Compton (Lionel Atwill); handsome American mining engineer Richard Cabot (Kane Richmond), who falls in love with Kathi; nightclub proprietor Manolo (Jack La Rue), who is blackmailing Kathi who, in addition, lacks a passport; crooked Achmed Halide (Frank Puglia), who operates a tobacco shop; and physician Dr. Rudolph Grosser (Lionel Royce). Supporting Chan's investigation is maiden school teacher Jennie Finch (Mary Nash) from Chicago, who is in the Canal Zone on a tour. Chan learns that Ryner, a notorious German spy, is the killer and is behind a scheme to blow up the Canal as the American fleet is passing through its waters. In a remote graveyard, Chan gathers the suspects and unmasks the Nazi killer.

The first of a quartet of 1940 Chan movies, this programmer was a timely one, with its plot revolving around an attempted Axis destruction of the Panama Canal and the then U.S. territory being infiltrated by enemy spies determined to cripple the vital waterway. The denouement at the graveyard is especially well staged, with the murderer vainly trying to do in Charlie before being ensnared in the lawman's net. Charlie Chan would again battle fifth columnists in MURDER OVER NEW YORK, *q.v.*, the last of the four 1940 series releases.

CHARLIE CHAN IN PARIS (Fox, 1935) 70 minutes.

Associate producer, John Stone; director, Lewis Seiler; based on the character created by Earl Derr Biggers; screenplay, Edward T. Lowe, Stuart Anthony; art directors, Duncan Cramer, Albert Hogsett; music director, Samuel Kaylin; camera, Ernest Palmer.

Warner Oland (Charlie Chan); Mary Brian (Yvette Lamartine); Thomas Beck (Victor Descartes); Erik Rhodes (Max Corday); John Miljan (Albert Dufresno); Ruth Peterson (Renee); Murray Kinnell (Henri Latouche); Minor Watson (Renard); John Qualen (Concierge); Keye Luke (Lee Chan); Henry Kolker (M. Lamartine); Dorothy Appleby (Nardi); Harry Cording (Gendarme); Perry Ivins (Bedell).

Charlie Chan (Warner Oland) arrives in Paris and calls dancer Nardi (Dorothy Appleby); she tells him she has information to give him that evening after her performance. Charlie visits Victor Descartes (Thomas Beck), the son of an old friend and a clerk in the bank of Lamartine (Henry Kolker) whose daughter Yvette (Mary Brian) is Descartes' fiancée. Chan meets Yvette as well as Descartes' friends, tipsy artist Max Corday (Erik Rhodes) and his girlfriend Renee

(Ruth Peterson). They all go to Nardi's show but the dancer is murdered at the finale. At Nardi's apartment Chan locates her diary, which incriminates banker Albert Dufresno (John Miljan), who has had heavy gambling losses. As he leaves the hotel an attempt is made on Chan's life, and back at his own rooms he finds number one son Lee (Keye Luke) who is in Europe on a buying trip for his employer. Lee insists on helping his father with the case. When Lamartine and Dufresno are told that London investors are claiming to have been sold forged bonds issued by Lamartine's bank, they deny knowing of the forgery and agreed to aid Chan. Later, Dufresno attempts to blackmail Yvette because they once had a love affair and he has an incriminating letter she wrote to him. That night Yvette comes to Dufresno's apartment to claim the letters and he is murdered by an assailant, the crippled Max Xavier. Yvette, however, is blamed for the crime and is arrested by police Inspector Renard (Minor Watson), an old ally of Chan's. Also at the scene are Corday and Renee and Dufresno's bank associate, Henri Latouche (Murray Kinnell). Lee tails Xavier and finds that he uses a car belonging to Corday, but the latter denies any knowledge of it. Charlie and Lee stop him from leaving Paris and find that he is carrying forged bonds and is Dufresno's killer, but *not* Nardi's murderer. Descartes asks Chan's assistance in proving Yvette's innocence. Near Xavier's lodgings they uncover a room used to make the forged bonds. Xavier is captured and Lee brings Renard and his policemen. They unmask Xavier as one of the bank officials. He and Corday were in cahoots in the forgery scheme, with both men using the bogus Xavier disguise. With the case now closed, Renaud frees Yvette.

Following CHARLIE CHAN IN LONDON, *q.v.*, the Chinese investigator traveled to France in this fairly engrossing episode, this being the seventh entry to headline Warner Oland. It was also the first to feature Keye Luke as number one son Lee Chan, a part he would perform in seven more films prior to Oland's death in 1938. He also played Lee Chan in MR. MOTO'S GAMBLE (1938) and resumed the part in the last two Monogram-Chan features, THE FEATHERED SERPENT (1948) and THE SKY DRAGON (1949), qq.v.

CHARLIE CHAN IN RENO (Twentieth Century-Fox, 1939) 70 minutes.

Producer, Sol M. Wurtzel; associate producer, John Stone; director, Norman Foster; based on the character created by Earl Derr Biggers and the story "Death Makes a Decree" by Philip Wylie; screenplay, Frances Hyland, Albert Ray, Robert E. Kent; art directors, Richard Day, David Hall; set decorator, Thomas Little; music director, Samuel Kaylin; camera, Virgil Miller; editor, Fred Allen.

Sidney Toler (Charlie Chan); Ricardo Cortez (Dr. Ainsley); Phyllis Brooks (Vivian Wells); Slim Summerville (Sheriff Tombstone Fletcher); Kane Richmond (Curtis Whitman); Victor Sen Yung (James Chan); Pauline Moore (Mary Whitman); Eddie Collins (Cab Driver); Kay Linaker (Mrs. Russell); Louise Henry (Jeanne Bently); Robert Lowery (Wally Burke); Charles D. Brown (Chief of Police King); Iris Wong (Choy Wong); Morgan Conway (George Bently); Hamilton MacFadden (Night Clerk); Fred Kelsey (Police Desk Clerk).

Sidney Toler made his series debut in CHARLIE CHAN IN HONOLULU (1938), *q.v.*, and this solid opener for him was followed by one of the best in the group, CHARLIE CHAN IN RENO. It is a superior mystery enhanced by a solid cast of red herrings and the use of a spooky ghost town for added effect. There is fine comedy relief by Slim Summerville as a bumbling hick sheriff and by Eddie Collins as a nervous driver. Toler, however, is the show as Chan and his finely etched portrayal of the crime solver would be the pinnacle of his lengthy show business career. He would continue as Chan until his death in 1947. This film was one of the few Chan features not to be based on either an Earl Derr Biggers novel or an original screenplay. It was taken from Philip Wylie's story, "Death Makes a Decree"

Mary Whitman (Pauline Moore) has come to Reno to divorce her husband Curtis (Kane Richmond). He wants to marry socialite Jeanne Bently (Louise Henry) who dumps her boyfriend, Wally Burke (Robert Lowery), for him. At Mrs. Russell's (Kay Linaker) hotel Jeanne causes a scene with both Mary and Burke, and Mrs. Russell orders her to leave. A little later Jeanne's personal maid, Choy Wong (Iris Wong), finds Mary leaning over the body of her employer, who was stabbed to death. The local police charge Mary with the homicide and Curtis Whitman goes to Honolulu to ask the aid of long-standing friend Charlie Chan (Sidney Toler) in proving her innocence. Chan accepts and goes to Reno where police Chief King (Charles D. Brown) and local Sheriff Tombstone Fletcher (Slim Summerville) are in charge of the case. King gives Chan a free hand in the matter, much to Fletcher's chagrin. In a police lineup, Chan recognizes his number two son Jimmy (Victor Sen Yung), who has lost his car and clothes to hitchhikers, and Jimmy joins his father on the caper. Charlie asks that Mary be placed in her husband's custody since the murder weapon has not been found. He and Jimmy move into the victim's hotel room and find that pages from her scrapbook have been torn out. Chan questions the others at the hotel, including resident physician Dr. Ainsley (Ricardo Cortez) and his hotel hostess girlfriend, Vivian Wells (Phyllis Brooks). Charlie learns that Jeanne had visited a nearby ghost town the day before she died, and that night he has the hotel driver (Eddie Collins) take him there. He is attacked by a mysterious man, but survives the assault and finds a mining engineer's kit belonging to George Bently (Morgan Conway), the murdered woman's estranged husband. Although Jimmy has placed bogus scissors in the suspects' rooms, the real pair used to kill Mrs. Bently is found in Mary's room and Tombstone Fletcher wants her indicted for the crime. From police records Chan learns that Jeanne was once married to a man who died mysteriously, that the man's ex-wife was Mrs. Russell, and that his death certificate had been signed by Dr. Ainsley. When someone tries to strangle Mrs. Russell, Chan orders all the suspects to return to the murder room wearing the same clothes they wore on the night of the homicide. Tombstone arrives with Bently, whom the police have located. Chan reveals the reasons each of the suspects had for killing Mrs. Bently. He explains that Dr. Ainsley was blackmailing the dead woman because he knew she murdered her first husband. Then he exposes the killer who murdered Jeanne over jealousy. Ainsley too is arrested for trying to kill Mrs. Russell, while Mary and Curtis Whitman are reconciled.

Again CHARLIE CHAN IN RENO boasts a number of sage proverbs by the sleuth, including: "Man yet to be born who can tell what woman will or will not do," "Words cannot cook rice," "Tombstone often engraved with words of wisdom," "Lovely company turn lowly sandwich into rich banquet," "When searching for needle in haystack, haystack only sensible location," and "Sometimes necessary to strike innocent to trap guilty."

CHARLIE CHAN IN RIO (Twentieth Century-Fox, 1941) 60 minutes.

Producer, Sol M. Wurtzel; director, Harry Lachman; based on the novel *The Black Camel* by Earl Derr Biggers; screenplay, Samuel G. Engel, Lester Ziffren; sets, Thomas Little; song, Mack Gordon and Harry Warren; music director, Emil Newman; art director, Richard Day; camera, Joseph P. MacDonald; editor, Alexander Troffey.

Sidney Toler (Charlie Chan); Mary Beth Hughes (Joan Reynolds); Cobina Wright, Jr. (Grace Ellis); Ted North (Clark Denton); Victor Jory (Alfredo Marana); Harold Huber (Chief Souto); Victor Sen Yung (Jimmy Chan); Richard Derr (Ken Reynolds); Jacqueline Dalya (Lola Dean); Kay Linaker (Helen Ashby); Truman Bradley (Paul Wagner); Hamilton MacFadden (Bill Kellogg); Leslie Denison

(Rice); Iris Wong (Lili); Eugene Borden (Armando); Ann Codee (Margo).

Charlie Chan (Sidney Toler) visits Rio with number two son Jimmy (Victor Sen Yung) to arrest cabaret star Lola Dean (Jacqueline Dalya) for murdering Manuel Cardoza in Honolulu several years before. Chan is working directly with Rio police chief Souto (Harold Huber) and plans to carry out the arrest at the woman's home, although all three of them come to the club where she works to see her perform. Meanwhile, Lola agrees to wed wealthy Clark Denton (Ted North), who is craved by socialite Grace Ellis (Cobina Wright, Jr.), while beautiful Joan Reynolds (Mary Beth Hughes) believes her husband Ken (Richard Derr) is after Lola. After her performance Lola visits mystic Marana (Victor Jory) and he places her in a comatose state in which she confesses to Cardoza's murder, with Marana recording the confession. Lola has had her secretary, Helen Ashby (Kay Linaker), invite several people, including Grace, the Reynolds and Bill Kellogg (Hamilton MacFadden), to a party to celebrate her engagement to Clark. Not long after she arrives home,

Victor Jory, Truman Bradley, Victor Sen Yung and Sidney Toler in CHARLIE CHAN IN RIO (1941).

Chan, Jimmy and Chief Souto appear to arrest the hostess. But they find her murdered in her bedroom and the jewels stolen from her safe. Tipsy Joan accuses Grace of the crime and the police bring Marana and Lola's suitor, Paul Wagner (Truman Bradley), to the house. Wagner informs Chan that Lola was his ex-wife and that he had visited her briefly that night, attempting a reconciliation. The butler, Rice (Leslie Denison), confirms that he showed Wagner out of the house on Lola's orders. Marana plays the record of Lola's murder confession and admits to Chan that he is the brother of the murdered Cardoza. When Rice attempts to leave the house with the jewels, Jimmy and the police stop him, but when the butler starts to name the killer, he too is murdered. Using Marana's method of getting the truth from a patient, Charlie Chan sets a trap for the killer, who is revealed to be Cardoza's wife. After the case is closed and Jimmy is ready to romance pretty house maid Lili Wong (Iris Wong), he learns he is about to be drafted into military service.

The penultimate entry in the Twentieth Century-Fox Charlie Chan series, CHARLIE CHAN IN RIO is a remake of THE BLACK CAMEL (1931), *q.v.*, based on Earl Derr Biggers' 1929 novel. It is the last Chan film to be based on a Biggers' work. In addition to the mystery plot the film offers a nightclub samba production dance number and the character of Lola Dean singing the popular Mack Gordon-Harry Warren tune, "They Met in Rio." Quite a bit of screen time is devoted to the character of Jimmy Chan and his overzealous explanations of always foolish theories, his romancing of the pretty Chinese domestic and, while in a hypnotic trance, his confession to his "Pop" about denting Charlie's car and earning a poor mathematics grade at college.

This feature provides the usual quota of Chan aphorisms, such as: "Sweet wine often turn nice woman sour," "Biggest mistakes in history made by people who didn't think," "Until murderer found, suspect everybody!" "Slippery man sometimes slip in own oil," "To one who kill, life can suddenly become most precious," and "Fruits of labor sometimes very bitter."

CHARLIE CHAN IN SHANGHAI (Fox, 1935) 70 minutes.

Associate producer, John Stone; director, James Tinling; based on the character created by Earl Derr Biggers; adaptor, Gerald Fairlie; screenplay, Edward T. Lowe; art directors, Duncan Cramer, Lewis Creber; music director, Samuel Kaylin; camera, Barney McGill; editor, Nick De Maggio.

Warner Oland (Charlie Chan); Irene Hervey (Diana Woodland); Charles Locher [Jon Hall] (Philip Nash); Russell Hicks (James Andrews); Keye Luke (Lee Chan); Halliwell Hobbes (Chief of

Police, Colonel Watkins); Frederik Vogeding (Burke); Neil Fitzgerald (Dakin); Max Wagner (Taxi Driver); David Torrence (Sir Stanley Woodland); Pat O'Malley (Belden); Harry Strang (Chauffeur).

Directly following the atmospheric CHARLIE CHAN IN EGYPT (1935), *q.v.*, Warner Oland headlined the rather mundane CHARLIE CHAN IN SHANGHAI, his ninth appearance in the detective property. Keye Luke, who had played number one son Lee Chan in CHARLIE CHAN IN PARIS (1935), *q.v.*, but who had only been mentioned in the EGYPT installment, was back in his recurring role, and except for the next release, CHARLIE CHAN'S SECRET (1936), *q.v.*, would remain with the adventures until Oland's demise in 1938.

Unfortunately CHARLIE CHAN IN SHANGHAI is a slow moving, talky situation mystery with the real culprit too easy to spot. To enliven it, the film has the running gag of Lee, Number One son, always on the phone trying to romance a local girl, and in a cafe sequence, there is even a dance number.

Charlie Chan (Warner Oland) and son Lee (Keye Luke) are in Shanghai where the elder Chan is honored by the Chamber of Commerce. He has been invited to China by his good friend Scotland Yard Inspector Sir Stanley Woodland (David Torrence), who is killed during the dinner by a gun secreted in a box containing a scroll honoring Chan. The box has been in the possession of the man's secretary, Philip Nash (Charles Lochner [Jon Hall]), who is in love with Diana Woodland (Irene Hervey), Sir Stanley's niece. Just before dying, Sir Stanley told Charlie he had important information to impart to him, and the next day Chan learns from Diana that her late uncle's library has been burglarized. A bogus note is sent to Chan and a chauffeur (Harry Strang) takes him to a strange destination where Chan is held prisoner by one Ivan Marloff. After his father leaves, Lee receives a call from Colonel Watkins (Halliwell Hobbes), the city's chief of police, and Lee follows the car taking his father, since Watkins advises him he did not send a note asking Charlie to meet him. The cab driver (Max Wagner) transporting Lee is also in cahoots with Marloff and the two Chans end up temporarily as prisoners in the man's house, but they escape. FBI agent James Andrews (Russell Hicks) arrives to see Sir Stanley and, after hearing about the man's death, tells Chan that the three of them were scheduled to work together to smash an opium smuggling operation headquartered in Shanghai. Chan deduces that the ringleader is Marloff. When another attempt is made on Charlie's life, Watkins arrests Nash, since his thumb print is found on the firearm which was fired at Charlie. Nash is placed in police custody but Diana smuggles a gun to him which leads to his escape. Later, Andrews summons

Chan to his hotel room, where he has captured the kidnapping chauffeur. He forces the man to reveal that Marloff has his headquarters at a cafe. At the night spot Nash is found incognito as a sailor but the crooked taxi driver spots him. Nash is abducted, but again escapes. In the basement of the waterfront cafe Chan and Andrews locate the drug stash. Marloff and his henchmen are captured in a shootout with the police. Charlie unmasks the real head of the opium ring.

As for number one's son prowess, Frank S. Nugent (*New York Times*) decided, "Lee Chan is a trifle weak on the Chinese proverbs and is always a few steps behind his father in drawing deductions, but he makes up for that by being handy with his fists and by playing an amiable Chinese Dr. Watson to an equally amiable—and equally Chinese—Sherlock Holmes." As for the heavy-lidded Oriental detective, the Times added, "Nor should you, if you ever have seen Chan at work, be astonished to discover that Mr. Chan, in the last five minutes of the picture, shows that he knew who was guilty all along, but merely wanted to give the chap enough rope to hang half of China."

As for those edifying Chan words of wisdom, "Motive like many strings tied in knots—end may be in sight but hard to unravel," "Silence best answer when uncertain," "Distance no hindrance to fond thoughts," "Dreams like good liar—distort fact," "Spider does not spin web for single fly," and "Only foolish dog follow fleeing bird."

CHARLIE CHAN IN THE CITY OF DARKNESS (Twentieth Century-Fox, 1939) 75 minutes.

Producer, Sol M. Wurtzel; associate producer, John Stone; director, Herbert I. Leeds; based on the character created by Earl Derr Biggers and the play by Gina Kaus and Ladislaus Fodor; screenplay, Robert Ellis, Helen Logan; camera, Virgil Miller; editor, Harry Reynolds.

Sidney Toler (Charlie Chan); Lynn Bari (Marie Dubon); Richard Clarke (Tony Madero); Harold Huber (Inspector Marcel); Pedro de Cordoba (Antoine); Dorothy Tree (Charlotte Ronnell); C. Henry Gordon (Prefect of Police); Douglass Dumbrille (Petroff); Noel Madison (Belescu); Leo J. Carroll (Louis Santelle); Lon Chaney, Jr. (Pierre); Louis Mercier (Max); George Davis (Alex); Barbara Leonard (Lola); Adrienne d'Ambricourt (Landlady); Frederik Vogeding (Captain); Alphonse Martel, Eugene Borden (Gendarmes).

Like most celluloid sleuths, Charlie Chan often combatted spies and enemy agents in the World War II period, and this type of plot action was used first in CHARLIE CHAN IN THE CITY OF

DARKNESS, also known as CITY OF DARKNESS. The film opens with the detective in Paris, where he had earlier combatted criminal elements in CHARLIE CHAN IN PARIS (1934), *q.v.* This picture was the fourth to star Sidney Toler as Chan and was the poorest of all his Twentieth Century-Fox Chan installments. It is, in fact, one of the most vapid of all the Chan entries. ". . . [The] plot is stereotyped to the core," reported the *New York World-Telegram,* while *Variety* concurred that the feature ". . . is decidedly weak in story factors, and slow in proceeding through to the eventual finish. It's one of the weakest in the 'Chan' series."

Charlie Chan (Sidney Toler) is in Paris on the eve of the Munich Conference, with the city under a blanket of darkness in case war planes should attack. The detective is about to book passage out of the country when a murder takes place and Paris police Inspector Marcel (Harold Huber) asks Chan to aid him in the investigation. It develops that the victim was a spy involved in attempting to maneuver a large arms shipment out of France and into an enemy port. Marcel sets out to round up all the known fifth columnists working in the city while Chan uncovers the fact that Louis Santelle (Leo G. Carroll) and his assistant Pierre (Lon Chaney, Jr.) are the heads of the spy ring responsible for the killing.

Following this film, CHARLIE CHAN continued to combat spies in far superior offerings such as CHARLIE CHAN IN PANAMA (1940) and MURDER OVER NEW YORK (1940), *qq.v.* When the series was moved to Monogram pictures in 1944 he continued the good fight in such outings as CHARLIE CHAN IN THE SECRET SERVICE (1944), THE JADE MASK (1945), and THE SCARLET CLUE (1945), *qq.v.*, all superior to CHARLIE CHAN IN THE CITY OF DARKNESS.

CHARLIE CHAN IN THE SECRET SERVICE (Monogram, 1944) 65 minutes.

Producers, Philip N. Krasne, James S. Burkett; director, Phil Rosen; based on the character created by Earl Derr Biggers; screenplay, George Calllahan; art director, David Milton; set decorator, Al Greenwood; music director, Karl Hajos; assistant director, George Moskov; sound, Glen Glenn; camera, Ira Morgan; editor, Marty Cohen.

Sidney Toler (Charlie Chan); Gwen Kenyon (Inez); Mantan Moreland (Birmingham Brown); Marianne Quon (Iris Chan); Arthur Loft (Jones); Lelah Tyler (Mrs. Winters); Benson Fong (Tommy Chan); Gene Stutenroth [Roth] (Vega); Eddie Chandler (Lewis); George Lessey (Slade); George Lewis (Paul); Muni Seroff (Peter); and: Barry Bernard, Dave Clark, Sarah Edwards, Gene Oliver.

Twentieth Century-Fox dropped its long-running Charlie Chan series after CASTLE IN THE DESERT (1942), *q.v.*, believing there was no more mileage to be gained from the overexposed property. However, Sidney Toler, who had portrayed Chan since 1938, acquired the screen rights to the character. In 1944 he made a deal with Monogram Pictures to again portray the Oriental crime stopper, and he did so in eleven programmers before his death in 1947 at the age of 72. His only non-Chan appearance during this final Monogram period was the Fred Allen-Jack Benny comedy, IT'S IN THE BAG (1945), for United Artists.

A Washington, D.C. scientist, who is working on a new explosive torpedo device for the military, is murdered in his home and Charlie Chan (Sidney Toler), now working for the U.S. government in the war effort, is called in to investigate the killing. Against his orders Chan's daughter Iris (Marianne Quon) and son Tommy (Benson Fong) follow and attempt to help him with the case. At the dead man's house Chan finds several people, including socialite Mrs. Winters (Lelah Tyler) and her chauffeur, Birmingham Brown (Mantan Moreland), pretty Inez (Gwen Kenyon), and the mysterious Von Vega (Gene Stutenroth [Roth]). While Chan is unraveling the clues, three attempts are made on his life, and after suspect Von Vega is murdered, the detective has a man arrested for the killings. But this action is merely a ruse to capture the real killer, who is a Nazi agent. At the finale overly loquacious and superstitious Birmingham agrees to become Chan's chauffeur.

While ensuing Monogram entries in the Chan series greatly improved, this initial item is often used to measure the entire output from the poverty row production company. In *The Detective in Film* (1972), William K. Everson labels it "a tedious and talkative film with a dreary musical score," while Jon Tuska in *The Detective in Hollywood* (1978) complains, "Toler was if anything even more aged. He shuffled through most of his scenes. . . . The biggest problem was Monogram Pictures. The company's writers had no sense of story; no production standards were combined with the cheapest possible sets; and Phil Rosen, a veteran of the lowest grade pictures, directed. Monogram always had that amazing facility of making a bad picture worse just because it was Monogram."

CHARLIE CHAN ON BROADWAY (Twentieth Century-Fox, 1937) 68 minutes.

Producer, Sol M. Wurtzel; associate producer, John Stone; director, Eugene Forde; based on the character created by Earl Derr

Biggers; story, Art Arthur, Robert Ellis, Helen Logan; screenplay, Charles Belden, Jerry Cady; music director, Samuel Kaylin; camera, Harry Jackson; editor, Al De Gaetano.

Warner Oland (Charlie Chan); Keye Luke (Lee Chan); Joan Marsh (Joan Wendall); J. Edward Bromberg (Murdock); Douglas Fowley (Johnny Burke); Harold Huber (Inspector Nelson); Donald Woods (Speed Patten); Louise Henry (Billie Bronson); Joan Woodbury (Marie Collins); Leon Ames (Buzz Moran); Marc Lawrence (Thomas Mitchell); Tashia Mori (Ling Tse); Charles Williams (Meeker); Eugene Borden (Louie); Creighton Hale (Reporter); Jack Dougherty (Policeman); Lon Chaney, Jr. (Desk Man); James Flavin (Cop); Edwin Stanley (Police Lab Technician).

Warner Oland had portrayed Charlie Chan nonstop since 1931 and this feature marked his fifteenth appearance. It was his next-to-last one before his death in mid 1938. CHARLIE CHAN ON BROADWAY was an appealing series' installment which benefits from an "early fast tempo" (*Variety*) in its narrative of the Chinese sleuth in Gotham. It involved a case of murder, a stolen diary, and a massive swindle.

Charlie Chan (Warner Oland) and number one son Lee (Keye Luke) arrive in New York City and are welcomed by Inspector Nelson (Harold Huber), since the elder Chan is to be honored at a police testimonial dinner. A young woman, gangster's moll Billie Bronson (Louise Henry), is murdered and Chan and Nelson investigate. They are aided by newspaper reporters Speed Patten (Donald Woods) and Johnny Burke (Douglas Fowley) and by pert freelance photographer Marie Collins (Joan Woodbury). The range of suspects includes the reporters' leathery editor, Murdock (J. Edward Bromberg), and dapper gangster Buzz Moran (Leon Ames). Eventually Chan deduces that the case is tied to a graft swindle and the perpetrator is revealed to be one of his associates on the case.

CHARLIE CHAN ON BROADWAY enjoys several engaging plot twists, the most notable being son Lee Chan being charged with the murder and on a more humorous note, Nelson having the police band play "Chinatown, My Chinatown" when Charlie arrives in the Big Apple. Sharing almost as much footage with Warner Oland as Chan is Harold Huber as the fast-talking, glib Nelson. The producers evidently liked Huber's screen work because he returned in the series as a French police inspector in the film, CHARLIE CHAN AT MONTE CARLO (1937), as well as in the later CHARLIE CHAN IN THE CITY OF DARKNESS (1939), *q.v.* Huber also portrayed a Spanish-speaking police inspector in CHARLIE CHAN IN RIO (1941), *q.v.*

CHARLIE CHAN'S CHANCE   *see*   BEHIND THAT CURTAIN [essay].

CHARLIE CHAN'S COURAGE (Fox, 1934) 70 minutes.
Associate producer, John Stone; director, George Hadden; based on the novel *The Chinese Parrot* by Earl Derr Biggers; screenplay, Seton I. Miller; music director, Samuel Kaylin; camera, Hal Mohr.
Warner Oland (Charlie Chan); Drue Leyton (Paula Graham); Donald Woods (Bob Crawford); Paul Harvey (J. P. Madden/Jerry Delaney); Murray Kinnell (Martin Thorne); Harvey Clark (Professor Gamble); Jerry Jerome (Maydorf); Si Jenks (Will Holley) Jack Carter (Victor Jordan); James Wang (Wong); Reginald Mason (Mr. Crawford); Virginia Hammond (Mrs. Jordan); De Witt Jennings (Constable Brackett); Francis Ford (Hewitt).
The fifth Fox feature to star Warner Oland as Charlie Chan, CHARLIE CHAN'S COURAGE was a solid remake of Earl Derr Biggers' novel *The Chinese Parrot* (1926), which had been filmed in the silent era by Universal in 1927 under that title, *q.v.* Neither the silent nor the remake are known to have extant prints. The talking remake was the first of fourteen Chan features on which John Stone served as producer. The *New York Times* referred to the feature as ". . . a good baffler, with Mr. Oland keeping faith with his public." The storyline of this film remains fairly close to the novel original, as did the initial screen version.
Wealthy J. P. Madden (Paul Harvey) purchases a $300,000 pearl necklace from a woman he once loved. Honolulu police detective Charlie Chan (Warner Oland), who was once a houseboy for the woman, agrees to transport the jewelry to Madden's remote desert mansion. He is aided in this endeavor by young Bob Crawford (Donald Woods). Chan and Bob realize they are being trailed and Crawford goes to the ranch first. There he meets pert Paula Graham (Drue Layton), really the daughter of the seller. An old servant Wong (James Wang) has been killed, as has Madden's pet, a Chinese parrot. Chan arrives incognito as the replacement servant and secretes the necklace, realizing that gangsters are hunting for the pearls. He soon realizes that hoodlum Jerry Delaney (Paul Harvey) and his henchman Maydorf (Jerry Jerome) have abducted the real Madden and Delaney has taken his place. Chan rounds up the guilty parties, turns the necklace over to the real Madden and sees Crawford and Paul fall in love.
Like most Chan movies, CHARLIE CHAN'S COURAGE is sprinkled with Chan aphorisms. Among them are: "Hen squats with caution on thin egg," "Anxious man hurries too fast—often stubs big

toe," "Large sugar bowl tempts many flies," and "Hunting needle in haystack requires only careful inspection of hay."

CHARLIE CHAN'S MURDER CRUISE (Twentieth Century-Fox, 1940) 70 minutes.

Producer, Sol M. Wurtzel; associate producer, John Stone; director, Eugene Ford; based on the novel *Charlie Chan Carries On* by Earl Derr Biggers; screenplay, Robertson White, Lester Ziffren; art directors, Richard Day, Chester Gore; music director, Samuel Kaylin; camera, Virgil Miller; editor, Harry Reynolds.

Sidney Toler (Charlie Chan); Marjorie Weaver (Paula Drake); Lionel Atwill (Dr. Suderman); Victor Sen Yung (Jimmy Chan); Robert Lowery (Dick Kenyon); Don Beddoe (James Ross); Leo G. Carroll (Professor Gordon); Cora Witherspoon (Susie Watson); Kay Linnaker (Mrs. Pendleton); Harlan Briggs (Coroner); Charles Middleton (Jeremiah Walters); Claire Du Brey (Mrs. Walters); Leonard Mudie (Walter Pendleton); James Burke (Wilkie); Richard Keene (Buttons); Layne Tom, Jr. (Willie Chan); Montague Shaw (Inspector Duff); Harry Strang (Guard); Walter Miller (Officer); Wade Boteler (Police Chief); Emmett Vogan (Hotel Manager); Cliff Clark (Lieutenant Wilson); John Dilson (Police Doctor).

In Honolulu Scotland Yard Inspector Duff (Montague Shaw) asks Charlie Chan (Sidney Toler) to help in capturing a murderer who is a member of a world cruise before it winds up in San Francisco. Duff, however, is strangled to death in Chan's office. Later, Charlie and number two son Jimmy (Victor Sen Yung) join the cruise, which is supervised by Dr. Suderman (Lionel Atwill). Among the other passengers are socialite Susie Watson (Cora Witherspoon) and her secretary, Paula Drake (Marjorie Weaver). The latter is being romanced by Dick Kenyon (Robert Lowery), the nephew of another passenger who is found murdered after trading cabins with Walter Pendleton (Leonard Mudie). Other voyagers include rich Ross (Don Beddoe), who is romancing Susie, archaeologist Professor Gordon (Leo G. Carroll); and the pious Mr. Jeremiah Walters (Charles Middleton) and his wife (Claire Du Brey). The latter tells Chan that Kenyon had argued violently with his uncle before the elder man was killed. Aboard ship Pendleton receives a small bag containing thirty pieces of silver, the same item left next to the murdered man and also the same amount of money sent to Pendleton's wife five years before just as an attempt was made on her life. That night Suderman gives a shipboard party for his guests. Pendleton is found murdered in his cabin. Since photographs were taken at the social gathering, Chan intends to develop them, but he is knocked out and the negatives are stolen. Jimmy gives chase to the assailant, who is dressed as a beggar, and the man is shot and killed. It turns out to be Ross. When the vessel reaches San Francisco all the cruise party members attend an inquest at the city morgue. Charlie brings in Mrs. Pendleton (Kay Linaker), who reveals she was once married to a man named Jim Eberhardt, whom she found out to be a crook. In fact, it was her testimony which sent him to prison. He vowed revenge and is the shipboard killer. Charlie explains that Ross was his accomplice. When Mrs. Pendleton is left alone deliberately, Eberhardt tries to kill her and is captured by Chan.

The twenty-second film in the Charlie Chan canon at Twentieth Century-Fox and the sixth entry to star Sidney Toler, CHARLIE CHAN'S MURDER CRUISE is a remake of the initial series entry, CHARLIE CHAN CARRIES ON (1931), being based on the 1930 novel of the same title. *Variety* referred to it as " . . . a fair enough mystery meller. . . . Both the direction and camera work are up to the Chan series average." Besides featuring number two son Jimmy Chan, the movie also presented family member, number seven son Willie Chan, played by Layne Tom Jr. who, in CHARLIE CHAN IN HONOLULU (1939), *q.v.*, had played Charlie's offspring Tommy.

For the aficionado of Oriental maxims (Charlie Chan style), the film contains: "Truth like oil—will in time rise to surface," "To speak without thinking is to shoot without aiming," "Only knowledge of horse races is empty pocketbook," "Better a father loses his son than a detective his memory," and "In darkness sometimes difficult to distinguish hawk from vulture."

CHARLIE CHAN'S SECRET (Twentieth Century-Fox, 1936) 72 minutes.

Producer, Sol M. Wurtzel; associate producer, John Stone; director, Gordon Wiles; based on the character created by Earl Derr Biggers; story/screenplay, Robert Ellis, Helen Logan, in collaboration with Joseph Hoffman; music director, Samuel Kaylin; camera, Rudolph Mate; editor, Nick De Maggio.

Warner Oland (Charlie Chan); Rosina Lawrence (Alice Lowell); Charles Quigley (Dick Williams); Henrietta Crosman (Henrietta Lowell); Edward Trevor (Fred Gage); Astrid Allwyn (Janice Gage); Herbert Mundin (Baxter); Jonathan Hale (Warren T. Phelps); Egon Brecher (Ulrich); Gloria Roy (Carlotta); Ivan Miller (Morton); Arthur Edmund Carew (Professor Bowan); William Norton Bailey (Harris); Jerry Miley (Allan Coleby); James T. Mack (Fingerprint Man); Francis Ford (Boat Captain); Landers Stevens (Coroner).

The tenth Charlie Chan feature with Warner Oland in the role, CHARLIE CHAN'S SECRET was the first such film to be issued by the newly-formed Twentieth Century-Fox. Like its predecessor,

CHARLIE CHAN IN EGYPT (1935), *q.v.*, this episode is an exotic affair. Even more than the earlier film it emphasizes horror and the occult. Afterwards, the series, both at Fox and Monogram, would employ horror trappings to add zest to the plotlines, often with good results.

Set in a remote fog-enshrouded San Francisco estate, this mystery tells of a long-lost heir to the Lowell fortune who arrives at the home only to be murdered. Charlie Chan (Warner Oland) is called in to investigate and finds the household dominated by Henrietta Lowell (Henrietta Crossman) along with a group of likely suspects. When a seance is staged to recall the murder victim, Chan exposes the fakery of the medium and ferrets out the homicidal criminal.

The *New York Times* commented, "The mystery in itself is an almost exclusively mechanical affair, leaning heavily upon a camera with a restricted range of vision that notes only a murderous hand, a knife flying through the air or quivering in a panel, the face of a clock—a method which makes for superficial and rapidly paced dramatic effects without being quite fair to the customers."

A highlight of this feature is Rudolph Mate's cinematography which adds an ominous quality to the proceedings and highlights such activities as the seances with their apparitions, the spooky mansion with its secret panels and passages, a baffling caretaker and the shooting from a nearby church tower.

CHARLIE McCARTHY, DETECTIVE (Universal, 1939) 78 minutes.

Producer, Frank Tuttle; associate producer, Jerry Sackheim; director, Tuttle; story, Robertson White, Darrell Ware; screenplay, Edward Ediscu, Harold Shurnate, Richard Mack; songs: Sam Lerner and Ben Oakland, Eddie Cherkose and Jacques Press; assistant directors, Fred Frank, Ralph Cedar; camera, George Robinson; editor, Bernard Burton.

Edgar Bergen (Himself); Charlie McCarthy (Himself); Mortimer Snerd (Himself); Robert Cummings (Scotty Hamilton); Constance Moore (Sheila Stuart); John Sutton (Bill Banning); Louis Calhern (Arthur Aldrich); Edgar Kennedy (Inspector Dailey); Samuel S. Hinds (Count Aldrich); Harold Huber (Tony Garcia); Warren Hymer (Dutch); Ray Turner (Harrison "Gravy" Randolph).

It is ironic that ventriloquist Edgar Bergen received a Special Academy Award (a wooden Oscar) in 1937 for "his outstanding comedy creation," Charlie McCarthy, although he and Charlie did not make their film debut until THE GOLDWYN FOLLIES (1938). Ventriloquists had not fared well on the screen before that; Erich

Robert Cummings, Constance Moore, Charlie McCarthy and Edgar Bergen in CHARLIE McCARTHY, DETECTIVE (1939).

von Stroheim played one (dubbed) in THE GREAT GABBO (1930), but it was not until Max Terhune proved popular with his ventriloquist's doll, Elmer Sneezewood, in Republic Pictures' "The Three Mesquiteers" Western, series that Bergen attempted a screen appearance. Earlier he had caused a sensation on Rudy Vallee's radio show and then became the star of his own Saturday night radio variety program, "The Chase and Sanborn Hour," which ran on NBC from 1936 to 1954. W. C. Fields was Charlie's radio nemesis and Fields and Bergen (and Charlie) headlined the very funny YOU CAN'T CHEAT AN HONEST MAN for Universal in 1939. Bergen and McCarthy and his other dummy, Mortimer Snerd, went it alone in CHARLIE McCARTHY, DETECTIVE late that year.

"In CHARLIE McCARTHY, DETECTIVE ... the mighty woodman gets the discredit for being a sleuth, which he isn't; for solving a murder, which he doesn't, and for making some very poor jokes which, after all, he can't help. . . . The people who put this one

together must have done it with an egg-beater, for every ingredient—including cheese—is mixed into it without discrimination"
(Bosley Crowther, *New York Times*).

Edgar Bergen and Charlie McCarthy (themselves) are the star
attractions at a big Gotham nightclub and are invited to entertain at a
party at the home of magazine publisher Arthur Aldrich (Louis
Calhern). Aldrich is in cahoots with gangster Tony Garcia (Harold
Huber) who gets rid of anyone whom the publisher does not like.
During the party Aldrich is murdered and Bergen and McCarthy
(with an occasional assist from Mortimer Snerd) take it upon themselves to solve the case despite the bumblings of police Inspector
Dailey (Edgar Kennedy). They also try to cement the budding
romance between Scotty Hamilton (Robert Cummings) and Sheila
Stuart (Constance Moore). Bergen eventually pieces together the
clues which lead to the gangsters and killer being captured.

This picture just helped to prove what an abiding fascination the
American public had (and still has) with the gumshoe profession. It
was fair game for anyone to enter the near-mystical private eye ranks
to accomplish the great fantasy of taking the law into one's own
hands and outwitting the police in bringing felons to justice. Nevertheless, filmgoers (and critics) had limits to their artistic acceptance
level. *Variety* complained that the film suffers from an "inadequate
script and inept direction" and that "Charlie's monologues with
Bergen are naturally the high spots of the picture, but aside from
those appearances yarn is a trite and poorly done cops-and-robbers
theme, which, in its attempts to be serious, becomes laughable."

THE CHEAP DETECTIVE (Columbia, 1978) Color 92 minutes.

Producer, Ray Stark; associate producer, Margaret Booth;
director, Robert Moore; screenplay, Neil Simon; production designer, Robert Luthardt; art director, Phillip Bennett; set decorator,
Charles Pierce; costumes, Theoni V. Aldredge; makeup, Charles
Scharm, Joe Di Bella; music, Patrick Williams; music supervisor,
Stewart Levine; orchestrators, Herbert Spencer, Billy May; assistant
directors, John C. Chulay, Steve H. Perry; sound, Al Overton;
sound editor, Gene Eliot; special effects, Augie Lohman; camera,
John A. Alonzo; editors, Sidney Levin, Michael A. Stevenson.

Peter Falk (Lou Peckinpaugh); Ann-Margret (Jezebel Dezire);
Eileen Brennan (Betty DeBoop); Sid Caesar (Ezra Dezire); Stockard
Channing (Bess Duffy); James Coco (Marcel); Dom DeLuise (Pepe
Damascus); Louise Fletcher (Marlene DuChard); John Houseman
(Jasper Blubber); Madeline Kahn (Mrs. Montenegro); Fernando
Lamas (Paul DuChard); Marsha Mason (Georgia Merkle); Phil
Silvers (Hoppy); Abe Vigoda (Sergeant Rizzuto); Paul Williams

(Clockwise bottom left): Marsha Mason, Madeline Kahn, Louise Fletcher, Stockard Channing, Eileen Brennan, Ann-Margret and Peter Falk in THE CHEAP DETECTIVE (1978).

(Boy); Nicol Williamson (Colonel Schlissel); Emory Bass (Butler); Carmine Caridi (Sergeant Crossett); Scatman Crothers (Tinker); David Ogden Stiers (Captain); Vic Tayback (Lieutenant DiMaggio); Carole Wells (Hatcheck Girl); John Calvin (Qvicker); Barry Michlin (Bandleader); Jonathan Banks (Cabbie), Lew Gallo (Cop); Lee McLaughlin (Fat Man); Zale Kessler, Jerry Ziman (Couriers); Wally Berns (Floyd Merkle); Bella Bruck (Scrub Woman); Henry Sutton (Desk Clerk); Maurice Marks (Doorman); Joe Ross (Michel); Dean Perry, George Rondo, Ronald L. Schwary (Cab Drivers); Louis H. Kelly, Charles A. Bastin (Croupiers); Armando Gonzalez (Bartender); Gary L. Dyer, Steven Fisher (Men in Crusades Bar); Lee Menning, Laurie Hagen, Nancy Warren (Elegant Ladies): Nancy Marlowe Coyne, Lynn Griffis (Ladies of the Night); Paula Friel, Sheila Sisco, Lauren Simon (Military Wives); Cindy Land (Navy Wife); Tina Ritt (Army Wife); David Mathau (Military Man); Gary Alexander, Michele Bernath (Dancers); George F. Simmons (Reporter); Joree Sirlanni (Cigarette Girl); Cornell Chulay (German Singer).

Peter Falk was exceedingly popular in the title role of "Columbo"

(NBC-TV, 1971-78) as the slow-talking, trenchcoat-wearing police detective. He reenacted the part, with a Humphrey Bogart imitation, in the all-star MURDER BY DEATH (1976), *q.v.* Two years later the production team (producer Ray Stark, director Robert Moore and scenarist Neil Simon) reunited to produce this heavily tongue-in-cheek parody, which is a too often labored send-up of the Bogart *films noir* of the 1940s. It grossed nearly $20,000,000 in domestic theatrical rentals at the box-office, largely on the basis of its big name cast and scenarist, not for its inspired wit or burlesque of THE MALTESE FALCON (1941 version in particular), CASABLANCA (1942), and TO HAVE AND HAVE NOT (1944), *qq.v.*

In 1939 San Francisco, rather careless private eye Lou Peckinpaugh (Peter Falk) is accused of murdering his partner (Wally Berns) for the man's wife, Georgia (Marsha Mason). The incompetent police Lieutenant DiMaggio (Vic Tayback) thinks Peckinpaugh is guilty but cannot prove it and the detective decides he must solve the case himself to clear his good name. Meanwhile Lou is approached by slinky Mrs. Montenegro (Madeline Kahn) who wants him to aid her in finding a priceless treasure—twelve diamond eggs—which are also sought by dapper crooks Jasper Blubber (John Houseman) and Pepe Damascus (Dom DeLuise) and the former's gunman, Boy (Paul Williams). Also arriving on the scene is Peckinpaugh's former lover, Marlene DuChard (Louise Fletcher) and her husband Paul (Fernando Lamas), who desire passage to Oakland where Marcel (James Coco) wants to open a Free French restaurant. Pianist Tinker (Scatman Crothers) then reminds Lou of his affair with Marlene by continually playing *their* song, "Jeepers Creepers." To further complicate matters, Cincinnati Nazi Colonel Schissel (Nicol Williamson) is on the trail of the Free French patriots, while cafe singer Betty DeBoop (Eileen Brennan) falls for Peckinpaugh. While all this is transpiring, another client, beautiful Jezebel Dezire (Ann-Margret) becomes involved with the main case at hand when she tells her aged husband Ezra (Sid Caesar) that he holds the secret to the entire mystery. Finally it is solved by Peckinpaugh's loyal secretary, Bess Duffy (Stockard Channing).

"Like MURDER BY DEATH . . . the weakness of THE CHEAP DETECTIVE lies in the overall structure of the plot: parody on this scale is not Simon's forte; what he excels at is the creation of jigsaw puzzle comedies where half the audience's pleasure is derived from an easily assimilated admiration of his skill in making the pieces fit together. . . . [That this film] lacks something of Simon's customary freshness can perhaps be attributed to the fact that in recent years the shade of Humphrey Bogart has been conjured just a few times too many" (John Pym, British *Monthly Film Bulletin*).

CHEATERS AT PLAY (Fox, 1932) 58 minutes.

Director, Hamilton MacFadden; based on the novel *The Lone Wolf's Son* by Louis Joseph Vance; screenplay, M. S. Boylan; assistant director, Jasper Blystone; sound, Joseph Aiken; camera, Ernest Palmer; editor; Irene Morra.

Thomas Meighan (Michael Lanyard); Charlotte Greenwood (Mrs. Crozier); William Bakewell (Maurice Perry); Ralph Morgan (Freddie Isquith); Barbara Weeks (Fenno Crozier); Linda Watkins (Tess Boyce); William Pawley (Wally); Olin Howland (Secretary); James Kirkwood (Detective Crane); Dewey Robinson (Strong Arm Algy); Anders Van Haden (Captain).

Sandwiched between Columbia's last of the lone wolf (1930), *q.v.*, with Bert Lytell, and THE LONE WOLF RETURNS (1935), *q.v.*, with Melvyn Douglas, is a Fox low-budget item called CHEATERS AT PLAY, a Lone Wolf adventure based on Joseph Louis Vance's 1932 novel, *The Lone Wolf's Son.* The film's chief interest today is the fact that Michael Lanyard is portrayed by Thomas Meighan, the famous silent film star, who was coming to the end of his long cinema career. Otherwise, the picture is a slow moving, tired, and old-fashioned effort with surprisingly lifeless direction by Hamilton MacFadden, who had helmed a trio of Fox's earliest and finest Charlie Chan features: CHARLIE CHAN CARRIES ON (1931) and THE BLACK CAMEL (1931), *qq.v.*, and CHARLIE CHAN'S GREATEST CASE in 1933.

One-time jewel thief Michael Lanyard (Thomas Meighan), who has reformed, is on an ocean voyage from Southampton, England to New York City and has made an agreement with Detective Crane (James Kirkwood) that he have a free hand in locating $375,000 worth of stolen pearls which have been smuggled aboard ship by pseudo-society dame Mrs. Crozier (Charlotte Greenwood). Also after the pearls are crook Wally (William Pawley), his girlfriend, Tess Boyce (Linda Watkins), and young Maurice Perry (William Bakewell), who is romancing pretty Fenno Crozier (Barbara Weeks), the society gal's niece. While the thieves attempt to steal the jewels, Lanyard comes to the realization that Maurice is the son he did not know he had. Thus, while thwarting the machinations of the robbers, he sets his offspring onto the right track.

Variety branded the film "Sophomoric and familiar crook stuff. . . . It is replete with incongruities and elementary matters of a calibre associated with the serial genera of a decade ago. . . ."

CHINATOWN (Paramount, 1974) Color 131 minutes.

Producer, Robert Evans; associate producer, C. O. Erickson; director, Roman Polanski; screenplay, Robert Towne; music, Jerry

Goldsmith; costumes, Anthea Sylbert; production designer, Richard Sylbert; art director, W. Stewart Campbell; set decorator, Ruby Levitt; camera, John A. Alonzo; editor, Sam O'Steen.

Jack Nicholson (J. J. "Jake" Gittes); Faye Dunaway (Evelyn Mulwray); John Huston (Noah Cross); Perry Lopez (Escobar); John Hillerman (Yelburton); Darrell Zwerling (Hollis Mulwray); Diane Ladd (Ida Sessions); Roy Jenson (Mulvihill); Roman Polanski (Man with Knife); Dick Bakalyan (Loach); Joe Mantell (Walsh); Bruce Glover (Duffy); Nandu Hinds (Sophie); James O'Reare (Lawyer); James Hong (Evelyn's Butler); Beulah Quo (Maid); Jerry Fujikawa (Gardener); Belinda Palmer (Katherine); Roy Roberts (Mayor Bagby); Noble Willingham, Elliott Montgomery (Councilmen); Rance Howard (Irate Farmer); George Justin (Barber); Doc Erickson (Customer); Fritzi Burr (Mulwray's Secretary); Charles Knapp (Mortician); Claudio Martiniz (Boy on Horseback); Frederico Roberto (Cross's Butler); Allan Warnick (Clerk); Burt Young (Curly); Elizabeth Harding (Curly's Wife); John Rogers (Mr. Palmer); Cecil Elliott (Emma Dill); Paul Jenkins, Lee DeBroux, Bob Golden (Policemen); John Holland, Jesse Vint, Jim Burke, Denny Arnold (Farmers in the Valley).

Made on a budget of slightly over $3,000,000, CHINATOWN grossed more than $12,000,000 in domestic film rentals and received several Academy Award nominations: Best Picture, Best Actor (Jack Nicholson), Best Director. Robert Towne's script was awarded the Oscar for Best Screenplay. The cynical—even pessimistic—film, with its complicated plot and beautiful recreation of the California of the 1930s, is considered to be one of the best detective films of all time. "It's a 1930s private-eye movie that doesn't depend on nostalgia or camp for its effect, but works because of the enduring strength of the genre itself. . . . It accepts its conventions and categories at face value and doesn't make them the object of satire or filter them through a modern sensibility, as Robert Altman did with THE LONG GOODBYE [*q.v.*]. Here's a private-eye movie in which all the traditions, romantic as they seem, are left intact. . . . At its center, of course, is the eye himself: J. J. Gittes, moderately prosperous as a result of adultery investigations. . . . He . . . possesses the two indispensable qualities necessary for any traditional private eye. He is deeply cynical about human nature, and he has a personal code and sticks to it" *Roger Ebert's Movie Home Companion, 1989* (1988).

A retired Los Angeles policeman once assigned to the no-action Chinatown beat, J. J. "Jake" Gittes (Jack Nicholson) now runs a divorce case detective agency with associates Walsh (Joe Mantell) and Duffy (Bruce Glover). Gittes is hired by a young woman (Diane

Jack Nicholson and Faye Dunaway in CHINATOWN (1974).

Ladd) claiming to be Evelyn Mulwray, who wants him to obtain evidence against her husband, Los Angeles water commissioner Hollis Mulwray (Darrell Zwerling). He is also hired by tycoon Noah Cross (John Huston) to locate his missing daughter, (Faye Dunaway) and small granddaughter. When he finds the water commissioner's mistress, Gittes will actually have located Cross' daughter and when he begins to realize the truth he is attacked by two thugs (Roy Jenson, Roman Polanski), one of whom (Polanski) slits his nose with a knife, ordering him off the case. Finally, Gittes finds the woman he is seeking and realizes why Cross wanted her found. The case revolves around Cross having parlayed an extensive swindle in which water purchased for the city of Los Angeles will be used to irrigate his newly acquired farmland, and the child he is seeking is really the result of his incestuous relationship with his daughter. Gittes, who has a brief flirtation with the real Evelyn, tries to protect her but when he and his men arrive in Chinatown to spirit her away, they are arrested, Evelyn is murdered by her father's thugs, and Cross takes the child away.

In *The Films of the Seventies* (1984), Marc Sigoloff ranks CHINATOWN as "The finest achievement in the detective genre to date. . . . J.J. Gittes is a classic screen detective and CHINATOWN proves that it is unnecessary to continually exhume the detectives of the past." *Variety* ranked it "an outstanding picture" and added, "Richard Sylbert's production design is magnificent. . . . Sylbert's production design hasn't missed a trick in recreating the period. And the most gratifying aspect is that the audience is never insulted by overemphasis on period. There's absolutely no offensive showoff of the nostalgia; the clothes, cars, houses, etc., are simply part of the scenes."

Don Miller analyzed it in "Private Eyes" (*Focus on Film* magazine, Autumn 1975); "What gives the film a permanency, an enduring value, is its re-creation of the Los Angeles of 1937, not only for nostalgia's sake but as an important part of the plot. Perhaps a clue to the relative failure of recent private-eye stories is that they often seemed to belong to another age, even though they would be tricked up with modernities. By placing the genre in the past and making that past a part of the story, Towne and Polanski elevated the private-eye yarn to a genuine work of art." Jon Tuska opined in *The Detective in Hollywood* (1978), "The picture is told from the first person, with the camera, not through narration. The camera sees very little that Nicholson doesn't see. The viewer comes to know the truth no more quickly than Nicholson does. And the truth, in contradiction to those philosophers who once imputed it with the mystical ability to make us free, is discovered to do nothing at all.

The truth is unimportant. More than ever, it is a simple case of the inexorable fact that when someone wins someone has to lose."

Because of CHINATOWN's enormous popularity,* there has long been talk of a sequel to the picture, but it has yet to come to reality.

THE CHINESE CAT (Monogram, 1944) 65 minutes.

Producers, Philip N. Krasne, James S. Burkett; director, Phil Rosen; based on the character created by Earl Derr Biggers; story/screenplay, George Callahan; art director, David Milton; set decorator, Tommy Thompson; sound, Tom Lambert; camera, Ira Morgan; editor, Fred Allen.

Sidney Toler (Charlie Chan); Benson Fong (Tommy Chan); Mantan Moreland (Birmingham Brown); Weldon Heyburn (Harvey Dennis); Joan Woodbury (Leah Manning); Ian Keith (Dr. Paul Recknick); Sam Flint (Tom Manning); Cy Kendall (Deacon); Anthony Warde (Catlen); Dewey Robinson (Salos); John Davidson (Carl/Kurt); Betty Blythe (Mrs. Manning); George Chandler (Taxi Dispatcher); Jack Norton (Hotel Desk Clerk); I. Stanford Jolley (Henchman).

The second of four 1944 Charlie Chan releases, THE CHINESE CAT was also the second Chan entry to be issued after the series and star Sidney Toler began filming at Monogram. The film is an improvement over the earlier CHARLIE CHAN IN THE SECRET SERVICE (1944), *q.v.*, in that it is briskly paced and well written with an engrossing plotline. Especially well done are the eerie sequences in a ghost-filled house. By now Birmingham Brown (Mantan Moreland), soon to be Charlie's chauffeur, had become a permanent fixture in the Charlie Chan celluloid exercises.

Wealthy Thomas Manning (Sam Flint) is found murdered in his locked study by his wife, socialite Mrs. Manning (Betty Blythe) and her daughter Leah (Joan Woodbury). The police are baffled by the case and when the District Attorney drops the matter Leah seeks out Charlie Chan (Sidney Toler). However, she mistakes his number three son Tommy (Benson Fong) for his father. Once the mix-up is settled she hires Chan to investigate her stepfather's murder. He agrees, although he has only forty-eight hours to solve it as he has pressing government business to complete. Leah informs Chan that noted criminologist Dr. Paul Recknick (Ian Keith) has written a book about the crime which alleges that her mother did the deed and that police detective Harvey Dennis (Weldon Heyburn) has covered

---

*In a 1977 survey conducted by the American Film Institute, CHINATOWN emerged as one of the fifty most popular Hollywood films ever.

up the matter because he is in love with Leah. Chan suspects that Manning's ex-partner may have committed the murder but the man is found dead at a funhouse. The sleuth deduces that the two men had stolen a gem worth a great deal of money and that Manning had hidden it in the statue of a Chinese cat. Furthermore, the ex-partner had killed Manning for it, but then had been killed himself by a gang which also wanted the gem. Charlie and Tommy enlist the aid of cab driver Birmingham Brown (Mantan Moreland) and the trio go to the funhouse where Charlie and Tommy are captured while the gang pursues Brown. Charlie and Tommy escape and bring in reinforcements and the crooks are apprehended.

THE CHINESE PARROT (Universal, 1927) 65 minutes.

Presenter, Carl Laemmle; director, Paul Leni; based on the novel *The Chinese Parrot* by Earl Derr Biggers; adaptor/screenplay, J. Grubb Alexander; titles, Walter Anthony; camera, Ben Kline.

Marian Nixon (Sally Phillimore); Florence Turner (Sally Phillimore Sr.); Hobart Bosworth (Philip Madden/Jerry Delaney); Edward Burns (Robert Eden); Albert Conti (Martin Thorne); Kamiyama Sojin (Charlie Chan); Fred Esmelton (Alexander Eden); Ed Kennedy (Maydorf); George Kuwa (Louie Wong); Slim Summerville, Dan Mason (Prospectors); Anna May Wong (Nautch Dancer); Etta Lee (Gambling Den Habitué); Jack Trent (Jordan).

Charlie Chan came into his own toward the finale of Earl Derr Biggers' first novel about the Chinese sleuth, *The House Without a Key* (1925), which Pathé filmed as a serial in 1926, *q.v.*, nearly eliminating the Chan role. George Kuwa, who played Chan in that cliffhanger, was also in the cast of the second Chan film, THE CHINESE PARROT, in 1927, but the role of the detective went to Japanese actor Kamiyama Sojin. Kuwa was also Japanese. *The Chinese Parrot* (1926), Biggers' second Chan novel, must rank with *The Black Camel* (1929) as the two best literary works about the Honolulu-based detective. German Paul Leni, who had scored a sensation with his first American film, THE CAT AND THE CANARY in 1925, directed THE CHINESE PARROT. *Photoplay* magazine noted, "The mystery is well-sustained and the Oriental backgrounds are interesting." *Variety* was more direct, "A very good Universal program of the thrilling mystery stuff. . . but as a story or a thriller or a mystery, it's terrible applesauce." Unfortunately, no prints of this film are known to exist today.

In financial difficulties, Sally Phillimore (Florence Turner) needs to sell a pearl necklace given to her by her father and she entrusts it to detective Charlie Chan (Kamiyama Sojin) for safekeeping. Two decades before, Sally, the daughter of a rich Hawaiian planter, was given the pearls by the man she loved, Philip Madden (Hobart Bosworth). However, she bowed to her father's wishes and married Phillimore and Madden declared that he would some day buy her back with the pearls. To her surprise Madden is one of the bidders for the necklace and he agrees to purchase them if her daughter, also named Sally (Marian Nixon), will bring them to his mansion in the desert. She arrives at the house with Robert Eden (Edward Burns), a jeweler's son, and the jewels are stolen. Chan masquerades as a servant in the house and the only witness to the theft, Madden's Chinese parrot, provides the clue Chan requires to wrap up the case. It seems that gangster Jerry Delaney (Hobart Bosworth) abducted Madden and attempted to steal the necklace.

THE CHINESE PARROT was remade by Fox in 1934 as CHARLIE CHAN'S COURAGE, *q.v.*, its fourth Chan series film with Warner Oland in the title role.

To be noted in the film is Anna May Wong as an exotic dancer who is murdered early on in a dispute over the pearls.

THE CHINESE RING (Monogram, 1947) 68 minutes.

Producer, James S. Burkett; director, William Beaudine; based on the character created by Earl Derr Biggers; screenplay, W. Scott Darling; music, Edward J. Kay; camera, William Sickner; editor, Ace Herman.

Roland Winters (Charlie Chan); Mantan Moreland (Birmingham Brown); Warren Douglas (Sergeant Bill Davidson); Victor Sen Yung (Tommy Chan); Louise Currie (Peggy Cartwright); Philip Ahn (Captain Kong); Byron Foulger (Armstrong); Thayer Roberts (Captain Kelso); Jean Wong (Princess Mei Ling); Chabing (Lilly Mae); Paul Bryar (Sergeant); George L. Spaulding (Dr. Hickey); Charmienne Harker (Stenographer); Thornton Edwards (Hotel Clerk); Lee Tung Foo (Butler); Richard Wang (Hamishin); Spencer Chan (Chinese Officer); Kenneth Chuck (Chinese Boy).

Sidney Toler, who had portrayed Charlie Chan on-screen since 1938, died on February 12, 1947, and Monogram Pictures brought in forty-three-year-old Boston, Massachusetts-born Roland Winters to take over the part, one he would play in a half-dozen features in the next two years. His initial Chan appearance was in THE CHINESE RING and the film's advertising carried the blurb, "Meet The New 'Chan'! Fascinating! Mysterious!" The promotional copy further announced, "Murder Meets its Master! Chan clashes with the slayer of a beautiful Chinese princess in his weirdest mystery-thriller!"

Chinese Princess Mei Ling (Jean Wong) comes to the San Francisco home of detective Charlie Chan (Roland Winters) asking for help, but before she can consult the sleuth she is murdered with an air rifle. Before dying she writes the words "Captain K" on paper. House-man Birmingham Brown (Mantan Moreland) and Chan's number two son Tommy (Victor Sen Yung) make vain attempts to help Chan with the case, as does police Sergeant Bill Davidson (Warren Douglas), who tries to keep his overly inquisitive lady love, newspaper reporter Peggy Cartwright (Louise Currie), from finding out too much about the case. The trail leads Chan to Captain Kong (Philip Ahn) and Captain Kelso (Thayer Roberts), who were in partnership with the late princess in purchasing war planes for her warlord brother's Chinese rebellion. Aboard a docked ship Chan traces the killer and is captured. However, with the aid of Brown and Tommy he escapes and exposes the murderer.

A remake of MR. WONG IN CHINATOWN (1938), starring Boris Karloff, THE CHINESE RING (produced as THE RED HORNET) was also a reworking of scripter W. Scott Darling's MURDER AT MIDNIGHT (1931) *q.v.* The film was hardly a good debut vehicle for Roland Winters as the new Chan since it tended to be on the dull side. Critics, however, responded favorably to Winters in the characterization: ". . . Famed oriental detective [is] well portrayed by Roland Winters" (*Variety*). "Roland Winters proves an able successor to the oriental sleuthing role" (*New York Daily News*).

THE CIRCUS QUEEN MURDER (Columbia, 1933) 63 minutes.

Director, Roy William Neill; based on the novel *About the Murder of the Circus Queen* by Anthony Abbot [Fulton Oursler]; screenplay, Jo Swerling; sound, Edward Bernds; camera, Joseph August; editor, Richard Cahoon.

Adolphe Menjou (Thatcher Colt); Greta Nissen (Josie La Tour); Ruthelma Stevens (Kelly); Dwight Frye (Flandrin); Donald Cook (Sebastian); Harry Holman (Dugan); George Rosener (Rainey).

See: NIGHT CLUB LADY [essay].

COCAINE AND BLUE EYES (NBC-TV, 1/2/83) Color 100 minutes.

Executive producer, O. J. Simpson; producer, Dan Mark; director, E. W. Swackhamer; based on the novel by Fred Zackel; teleplay, Kendall J. Blair; art directors, Ross Bellah, William L. Campbell; set decorators, Audrey Basdell Goddard, Jim Duffy; costume designers, Grady Hunt, Christina Smith; music, Morton Stevens; music editor, Erma Levin; assistant director, Mack Bing; sound, Richard Rague; sound editor, Joseph Melody; camera, Richard C. Glouner; editor, George B. Hively.

O. J. Simpson (Michael Brennen); Cliff Gorman (Rikki Anatole);

Candy Clark (Ruthann Gideon); Eugene Roche (Sergeant Khoury); Maureen Anderman (Lillian Anatole); Cindy Pickett (Catherine); Tracy Reed (Chris Brennen); Leonardo Cimino (Orestes Anatole); Van Nessa L. Clarke (Maid); Keye Luke (Tana Ng); Irene Ferris (Blue Eyes [Dani Anatole]); John Spencer (Joey Crawford); Evan Ki (Davy Huey); Ted LePlat (Alex Simons); Belita Moreno (Waitress); Dick Balduzzi (Barkeep); Stephen Toblowsky (TV Clerk); Haunani Minn (Receptionist); Bumper Robinson (Brennen's Son); Micah Morton (Brennen's Daughter); Jessica Biscardi (Mexican Nurse); Nigel Butland (Arnold); Stephen Burks (Doc); Beach Dickerson (Bartender); Marc Silver (Morgue Clerk); Sam Vicenzio (Hotel Clerk).

This was a pilot for an unsold teleseries produced by and starring ex-professional football player O. J. Simpson. It would have revived the plot premise of a black detective, as featured in television's earlier short-lived series, "Shaft" (1973), with Richard Roundtree, and "Tenefly" (1973) with James McEachin. *Daily Variety* judged, "Weak, by-the-numbers murder story never creates a stir."

"He's a detective who takes life as it comes. One beautiful risk at a time," announced the ads for this TV film. San Francisco private eye Michael Brennen (O. J. Simpson) becomes enmeshed in a drug-smuggling scam while hunting for the attractive girlfriend, named Blue Eyes (Irene Ferris), of a dead client. The path leads him to a politically powerful family in the fish cannery business headed by patriarch Orestes Anatole (Leonardo Cimino) and his double-dealing son Rikki (Cliff Gorman). It develops that the elderly Tana Ng (Keye Luke) is a drug-dealing cohort of Rikki's and that the latter was intending to leave his wife/distant cousin (Maureen Anderman) and scamper off to Mexico with his relative (the dead Blue Eyes).

This botched detective caper is full of clichés. There are large portions of stale Mickey Spillane private eye narration ("They say insight is 20-20 . . . "), lots of hard-boiled chatter ("I don't like my place being broken into. I don't like being threatened and I don't like being considered a fool"), and too much "useful" shop talk ("when you take a man down with a gun, you stick it in his ear"). There are in-jokes about football great O. J. Simpson's on-screen character not knowing anything about football or the San Francisco 49ers. There are recurring racial slurs to continually remind the audience that this lead character is someone different—a black detective. The one pleasant ingredient of this misfire is comely Tracy Reed as the detective's ex-wife and the mother of their two children.

CONFESSIONS OF BOSTON BLACKIE (Columbia, 1941) 65 minutes.

Producer, William Berke; director, Edward Dmytryk; based on the character created by Jack Boyle; story/screenplay, Paul Yawitz; music director, Morris W. Stoloff; camera, Philip Tannura; editor, Gene Milford.

Chester Morris (Boston Blackie); Harriet Hilliard (Diane Parrish); Richard Lane (Inspector Farraday); George F. Stone (The Runt); Lloyd Corrigan (Arthur Manleder); Joan Woodbury (Mona); Walter Sande (Detective Mathews); Ralph Theodore (Buchanan); Kenneth MacDonald (Caulder); Walter Soderling (Erle Allison); Billy Benedict (Ice Cream Man); Mike Pat Donovan (Cop); Jack Clifford ((Motorcycle Cop); Eddie Laughton (Express Man); Jack O'Malley (Taxi Driver); Al Hill (Police Desk Sergeant); Ralph Dunn (Officer McCarthy); Harry Hollingsworth (Plainclothesman); Budd Fine (Express Man's Helper); Martin Spellman (Jimmy Parrish); Harry Bailey, Dorothy Curtis, Betty Mack (Bidders): Bill Lally (Sergeant Dennis); Julius Tannen (Dr. Crane); Eddie Kane (Auctioneer); Herbert Clifton (Albert, the Butler); Jessie Arnold, Lorna Dunn, Gwen Kenyon (Nurses); Harry Depp (Mr. Bigsby); Stanley Brown (Interne); Eddie Fetherstone (Taxi Driver).

Over twenty feature films were made around reformed crook Boston Blackie, the character created by Jack Boyle in his novel *Boston Blackie* (1919). The best known of these minor detective outings were the fifteen Columbia budget features in which Chester Morris enacted the hard-boiled role from 1941 to 1949; he also did the part on radio. MEET BOSTON BLACKIE (1941) opened the adventures and it was followed late the same year by CONFESSIONS OF BOSTON BLACKIE, which Jon Tuska in *The Detective in Hollywood* (1978) terms "the best film in the series."

At a Gotham art auction Diane Parrish (Harriet Hilliard) spots a phony statue of Augustus Caesar; she owns the original and wants to sell it to raise money for her tubercular younger brother. Boston Blackie (Chester Morris) is also at the auction and when Diane tries to expose the crooks peddling the fake statue, they shoot her, with Blackie attempting to shoot her assailant. Meanwhile, fraudulent sculptor Erle Allison (Walter Soderling) is killed in the melee. Inspector Farraday (Richard Lane) thinks fast-dealing Blackie may be behind the bogus art object and arrests him. Blackie also gets into trouble with his girlfriend Mona (Joan Woodbury), who insists he is sweet on Diane since he came to her rescue. When another member of the art dodge is found dead, Blackie is suspected and he and his colorful pal Runt (George E. Stone) enlist the aid of addled, wealthy art dealer Arthur Manleder (Lloyd Corrigan) in tracking the villains.

Variety reported the dualer to be ". . . a compact, deftly paced murder meller, embellished with light comedy touches. . . . With Chester Morris in the title role it represents the type of celluloid thriller which finds a ready audience. . . ." In retrospect, Doug McClelland judged, in *The Golden Age of 'B' Movies* (1978), "CONFESSIONS OF BOSTON BLACKIE was not art, but its headlong pace and sense of its own ridiculousness could give some of today's filmmakers a lesson. There was no 'Method' involved in this madness. After all, in a 65-minute movie could hapless ice-cream vendor Billy Benedict, stiff after being locked in his freezer by Chester Morris, have time to ponder how it actually *felt* to be a human popsicle?"

CONFESSIONS OF BOSTON BLACKIE cast George F. Stone in the sidekick role of Runt, a part he would play for all the remaining films except the last, BOSTON BLACKIE'S CHINESE VENTURE (1949). Lloyd Corrigan would remain as upper-crust Arthur Manleder for several more entries. Finally, Richard Lane, who had played the harassing Farraday in the initial entry, would be a plot fixture for the duration of the series, always there to assume that Blackie is guilty of the crime at hand and the last to admit that the breezy ex-thief has used his ingenuity to solve the caper.

CONVICTED (Artclass, 1931) 63 minutes.

Producer, Alfred T. Mannnon; director, Christy Cabanne; story, Ed Barry; screenplay, Jo Van Ronkel, Barry Barringer; dialogue, Arthur Hoerl; assistant director, Wilbur McGaugh; sound, L. E. Tope; camera, Sidney Hickox; editors, Thomas Persons, Don Lindberg.

Aileen Pringle (Claire Norville); Jameson Thomas (Bruce Allen); Harry Meyers (Sturgeon); Dorothy Christy (Constance Forbes); Richard Tucker (Tony Blair); Wilfred Lucas (Captain Hammond); Niles Welch (Roy Fenton); John Vosburg (Dr. Dayton); Jack Mower (Henderson).

Criminologist Bruce Allen (Jameson Thomas) is on an ocean voyage. Other passengers include Broadway producer Tony Blair (Richard Tucker), who has suffered huge stock market losses; actress Claire Norville (Aileen Pringle), who starred in Blair's show, *Spring Blossoms,* and who rejects his unwanted romantic attentions; Blair's girlfriend, Constance Forbes (Dorothy Christy), and her cohort Henderson (Jack Mower); and crooked gambler Roy Fenton (Niles Welch) and his tipsy pal Sturgeon (Harry Meyers). After Allen intercedes when Blair attempts to force himself on Claire, Blair plays poker with Fenton, Sturgeon, Henderson and Dayton (John Vosburg), the ship's radio operator. Following the game Blair, who has suffered heavy betting debts, accuses both Fenton and Henderson of cheating and both vow revenge. Later Claire comes to Blair's cabin to return a gift and tells him to leave her alone once and for all. The next morning Blair is found murdered in his cabin and the ship's captain (Wilfred Lucas) asks Allen to conduct the investigation. Allen brings all the suspects into Blair's cabin. This group includes the gamblers and Claire, along with Constance, whom Blair had tried to dismiss romantically. The detective is able to parse through the clues and name the killer and the motive.

This early Weiss Brothers talkie is hampered by a poorly recorded soundtrack and stiff, formalized acting from the leading players. Only Harry Meyers in his usual drunk portrayal provides much relief from the stage-bound histrionics. On the other hand, the film boasts a solid plot and director Christy Cabanne keeps it moving along; the killer is extremely difficult to spot. As with many films of this vintage, the detective is *not* actually involved in that profession but is rather a criminologist/newspaperman who is drafted on the spot to explore the murder case.

CORPSE IN THE MORGUE   *see*   LADY IN THE MORGUE.

CRIME BY NIGHT (Warner Bros., 1944) 72 minutes.

Producer/director, William Clemens; based on the novel *Forty Whacks* by Geoffrey Homes [Daniel Mainwaring]; screenplay, Richard Wells, Joel Malone; art director, Charles Novi; set decorators, Julie Heron, Casey Roberts; dialogue director, Harry Seymour; assistant director, Don Page; sound, Robert B. Lee; special effects, Lawrence Butler, Edwin Linden; camera, Henry Sharpe; editor, Doug Gold.

Jane Wyman (Robbie Vance); Jerome Cowan (Sam Campbell); Faye Emerson (Ann Marlow); Charles Lang (Paul Goff); Eleanor Parker (Irene Carr); Stuart Crawford (Larry Borden); Cy Kendall (Sheriff Ambers); Charles Wilson (District Attorney Hyatt); Juanita Stark (Telephone Operator); Creighton Hale (Grayson); George Guhl (Dick Blake); Hank Mann (Desk Clerk); Bill Kennedy (Attendant); Dick Rich (Chauffeur); Fred Kelsey (Dad Martin); Bud Messinger (Bellboy); Jack Cheatham, Eddie Parker, Jack Stoney, Frank Mayo (Deputies); Jack Mower (Tenant); Roy Brant (Roy the Waiter).

While on vacation at a lakeside resort with his secretary, Robbie Vance (Jane Wyman), private detective Sam Campbell (Jerome Cowan) becomes embroiled in an axe-murder case. At first he is hired to look into the matter of a child's custody but soon he learns that an inventor has been murdered and that the victim, a well-to-do

Charles C. Wilson, Jane Wyman, Eleanor Parker, Cy Kendall and Jerome Cowan in CRIME BY NIGHT (1944).

industrialist/publisher, had been engaged in classified government war work. Among the suspects is Larry Borden (Stuart Crawford) whose career as a pianist had ended prematurely when the victim, his ex-father-in-law, had chopped off his hand with an axe. Other suspects include two young women: Ann Marlow (Faye Emerson), who had previously managed Borden and now represents Paul Goff (Charles Lang), and Irene Carr (Eleanor Parker), daughter of the late industrialist and Borden's former wife. After Campbell fools the guilty party into attempting to kill Dad Martin (Fred Kelsey)—who is actually blind and could not have witnessed the crime—Campbell solves the caper. The guilty party is actually an operative for an international spy ring and is after the inventor's defense project. With Robbie's aid, Campbell solves the mystery, with minor assists from the blustering local sheriff (Cy Kendall).

CRIME BY NIGHT was based on Geoffrey Homes' [Daniel Mainwaring] novel *Forty Whacks* (1943) but the film has too little to do with Homes' original. *Variety* reported the film as ". . . a frankly unpretentious 'B'. . . . [It] is filled with talk and tends toward boredom. Supposedly a mystery picture, anyone should be able to pick out the murderer in short order. . . . Film lacks suspense. Settings are ordinary. . . ." But, as Doug McClelland writes in *The Golden Age of 'B' Movies* (1978), "Warner Brothers' CRIME BY NIGHT was spun out with a little more élan than most of the studio's 'B's, but the main reason it rates attention today is because it featured three budding contract actresses: Jane Wyman, Eleanor Parker, and Faye Emerson."

It should be noted that co-stars Jane Wyman and Jerome Cowan were not new to sleuthing roles. Wyman had the leads as the female private eye in TORCHY PLAYS WITH DYNAMITE and PRIVATE DETECTIVE, both 1939 Warner Bros. dual-billers, while Cowan played Miles Archer in the 1941 classic version of THE MALTESE FALCON, *q.v.*, and followed CRIME BY NIGHT with FIND THE BLACKMAILER (1944), *q.v.*, also with Faye Emerson.

CRIME DOCTOR (Columbia, 1943) 66 minutes.

Producer, Ralph Cohn; director, Michael Gordon; based on the radio program "Crime Doctor" by Max Marcin; story, Graham Baker, Louis Lantz; adaptor, Jerome Odlum; music, Lee Zahler; camera, James S. Brown; editor, Dwight Caldwell.

Warner Baxter (Dr. Robert Ordway [Phil Moran]); Margaret Lindsay (Grace Fielding); John Litel (Three Fingers); Ray Collins (Dr. Carey); Harold Huber (Joe); Don Costello (Nick); Leon Ames (Captain Wheeler); Constance Worth (Betty); Dorothy Tree (Pearl); Vi Athene (Myrtle).

Max Marcin's popular radio program, "The Crime Doctor," debuted on CBS radio in 1940, with Ray Collins starring as Dr. Robert Ordway, and had a long run, the lead role being played in later years by a succession of actors: House Jameson, Everett Sloane, and John McIntire. In 1943 Columbia Pictures purchased the screen rights to the Martin creation and initiated a film series based on the radio show, with Warner Baxter (just a few short years ago a major studio leading man) as Ordway; running for six years, the series spawned ten rather engaging programmers.

The first series film was CRIME DOCTOR and in it gangster Phil Moran (Warner Baxter) executes a $200,000 robbery. Gang members turn on him for their share and he is knocked unconscious, losing his memory. At a hospital Dr. Carey (Ray Collins) helps the man start a new life and he takes the name Robert Ordway. He studies medicine, majoring in psychiatry, and becomes involved in criminal rehabilitation. With the aid of parole officer Grace Fielding (Margaret Lindsay) he reforms a hardened criminal (Leon Ames) and is appointed to the state parole board. There a former gangland

John Litel and Warner Baxter in CRIME DOCTOR (1943).

associate, Three Fingers (John Litel), recognizes Ordway and tries to blackmail him into revealing the hiding place of the loot from the robbery which took place fifteen years prior. Hit on the head again, Ordway regains his memory and is forced to stand trial for his past deed. He is given a suspended sentence and is thus able to continue his professional career.

"Mr. Baxter contributes a conscientious and engrossing performance," said the *New York Times*. Screen veteran Baxter lent a quiet dignity to the role of Robert Ordway. Here is a detective film in which the sleuth is actually investigating his own past as well as bringing criminals to justice. In the following features in the series the Crime Doctor would do more normal detective work, although a couple in the series, SHADOWS IN THE NIGHT (1944) and CRIME DOCTOR'S COURAGE (1945), qualify as horror movies.

THE CRIME NOBODY SAW (Paramount, 1937) 60 minutes.

Director, Charles Barton; based on the play *Danger, Men*

Working by Ellery Queen [Frederic Dannay, Manfred B. Lee] and Lowell Brentano; adaptor, Bertram Millhauser; camera, Harry Fischbeck; editor, James Smith.

Lew Ayres (Nicholas Carter); Ruth Coleman (Kay Mallory); Benny Baker (Horace Smith); Eugene Pallette (Babe); Colin Tapley (Dr. Brooks); Howard C. Hickman (Robert Mallory); Vivienne Osborne (Suzanne Duval); Robert Emmett O'Connor (Burke); Jed Prouty (William Underhill); Hattie McDaniel (Ambrosia); Ferdinand Gottschalk (John Atherton).

Danger, Men Working, a play written by Ellery Queen [Frederic Dannay, Manfred B. Lee] and Lowell Brentano, failed to reach Broadway. However, Paramount purchased the film rights and brought it to the screen with Bertram Millhauser as adapter and Charles Barton as director. In the midst of production the studio front office decided the film was too leisurely-paced and ordered the tempo to be speeded up; the result was that a rather easy-paced mystery suddenly became hectic in its action, making it not always comprehensible to viewing audiences. Nevertheless, the film is

Lew Ayres, Jed Prouty, Ruth Coleman and Howard C. Hickman in THE CRIME NOBODY SAW (1937).

quite entertaining, due largely to ingratiating performances by Lew Ayres, Benny Baker, and Eugene Pallette as detective playwrights and Hattie McDaniel in a very amusing screen assignment as Ambrosia the hotel maid.

Theater producer John Atherton (Ferdinand Gottschalk) hands over $500 to fledgling playwrights Nicholas Carter (Lew Ayres), Horace Smith (Benny Baker) and Babe (Eugene Pallette) for an unseen production centering around a murder. The three writers do not have a script. They sequester themselves in an apartment to complete the project, and a drunk with an unsavory past walks in and soon passes out. The three decide to use this ploy for their play and they call upon individuals the man has blackmailed and accuse them of murdering the lush. Suddenly, the drunk turns up dead, and then the corpse disappears. To solve the case and avoid arrest themselves, the trio question several suspects, including Kay Mallory (Ruth Coleman) and her father Robert (Howard C. Hickman), before solving the caper with the aid of house maid Ambrosia (Hattie McDaniel). Based on what they have solved in real life, the three complete their murder mystery play.

Variety carped, "Story is . . . static, action never moving out of adjoining apartments except for three momentary shots of negligible value."

THE CRIMSON KEY (Twentieth Century-Fox, 1947) 76 minutes.

Producer, Sol M. Wurtzel; associate producer, Howard Sheehan; director, Eugene Ford; story/screenplay, Irving Elman; art director, Eddie Imazu; set decorator, Al Greenwood; music, Dale Butts; music director, Morton Scott; assistant director, Paul Wurtzel; sound, Buddy Meyers; camera, Benjamin Kline; editor, Frank Baldridge.

Kent Taylor (Larry Morgan); Doris Dowling (Mrs. Loring); Dennis Hoey (Steven Loring); Iran Triesault (Peter Vandaman); Arthur Space (Fitzroy); Vera Marshe (Dizzy); Edwin Rand (Jeffrey Regan); Bernadene Hayes (Mrs. Swann); Victoria Horne (Miss Phillips); Doug Evans (Dr. Swann); Ann Doran (Parris Wood); Victor Sen Yung (Wing); Chester Clute (Hotel Clerk); Ralf Harolde (Gunman); Milton Parsons (Dr. Harlow); Jimmy Magill (Detective Sergeant); Marletta Canty (Petunia); Stanley Mann (Night Clerk).

Private investigator Larry Morgan (Kent Taylor) is employed by a woman (Bernadene Hayes) to study the nighttime activities of her physician husband (Douglas Evans). But almost as soon as Morgan signs onto the case both his client and her spouse are murdered. The local police warn Morgan to drop the case but he continues his

Doris Dowling and Kent Taylor in THE CRIMSON KEY (1947).

inquiry and ends up being beaten up twice before the clues lead him to wealthy Mrs. Loring (Doris Dowling), an alcoholic who was being treated by the murdered doctor. The law suspects Steven Loring (Dennis Hoey), the woman's husband, of the killings but the detective has a hunch that Steven is innocent, and instead captures the actual killer.

Unlike most celluloid detectives, THE CRIMSON KEY has a sleuth who was based on an original screen story, this time by Irving Elman. Kent Taylor was especially good as the private eye, a career assignment he would play on television in "Boston Blackie" (Syndicated, 1951-53).

Don Miller commented in "Private Eyes" (*Focus on Film* magazine, Autumn 1975), "The dialogue was better than usually heard in Grade-B product, but that's about all there was to the picture, with the lack of physical action dragging the already over-length footage further."

CRISS CROSS   *see*   P.J.

THE CROOKED CIRCLE (World-Wide, 1932) 70 minutes.

Producer, William Sistrom; director, H. Bruce Humberstone; screenplay, Ralph Spence; additional dialogue, Tim Whelan; art director, Paul Roe Crawley; music, Val Burton; sound, William Fox; camera, Robert B. Kurrle; editor, Doane Harrison.

Ben Lyon (Brand Osborne); ZaSu Pitts (Nora); James Gleason (Patrolman Crimmer); Irene Purcel (Thelma); C. Henry Gordon (Yoganda); Raymond Hatton (Harmon); Roscoe Karns (Harry); Berton Churchill (Colonel Wolters); Spencer Charters (Kinny); Robert Frazer (The Stranger); Ethel Clayton (Yvonne); Frank Reicher (Rankin); Christian Rub (Dan); and: Paul Panzer, Tom Kennedy.

A mysterious organization called the Crooked Circle is upset by the activities of a group of amateur detectives known as The Sphinx Club. One of the members of the latter clique, Brand Osborne (Ben Lyon), resigns because of pressure from his fiancée, Thelma (Irene Purcel). The group selects a new member, the Hindu Yoganda (C. Henry Gordon), who claims something evil is about to happen. The Sphinx Club bunch go to the home of Colonel Wolters (Berton Churchill) and find that his housekeeper Nora (ZaSu Pitts), is fearful that something dreadful will happen. Soon, her boss disappears. When Thelma also vanishes, the police, led by Patrolman Crimmer (James Gleason), are called into the case and Crimmer locates a hidden room behind a bookcase and finds Wolters' corpse. Brand arrives, only to be confronted by a mysterious man and then be knocked out by butler Rankin (Frank Reicher), the leader of the Crooked Circle. Brand is convinced that Yoganda is the culprit behind the happenings but Yoganda leads the Sphinx Club to a secret room where Thelma and the Crooked Circle members are found. The group is captured and Yoganda reveals that he is a Secret agent, as is Thelma. It develops that the Colonel was in a trance in order to protect him from the Crooked Circle. Brand and Thelma remain engaged, and policeman Crimmer is credited with solving the case even though he has no understanding of it.

"Everything From Spooks to Nuts!!!! Something happens to somebody every minute and when the crazy clock strikes thirteen—The Lid is Off!" read the poster for THE CROOKED CIRCLE. This flavorful old house murder mystery is by Ralph Spence, the author of the popular play, *The Gorilla* (1925). Nicely directed by H. Bruce Humberstone, with a fine blend of comedy and mystery, THE CROOKED CIRCLE proved to be a successful venture for independent production outfit World-Wide Pictures. George E. Turner and Michael H. Price note in *Forgotten Horrors* (1979), "The CROOKED CIRCLE defies classification: it opens with weird horror, then becomes a crook melodrama, develops into light comedy, and then returns to mystery. Somehow, it works."

CROSS-EXAMINATION (Weiss Bros.-Artclass, 1932) 74 minutes.

Director, Richard Thorpe; story/dialogue, Arthur Hoerl; sound, Mack Dalgleish; assistant director, Melville Shyer; camera, A. Anderson; editor, Holbrook Todd.

H. B. Warner (Gerald Waring); Sally Blane (Grace Varney); Natalie Moorhead (Inez Wells); Edmund Breese (Dwight Simpson); William V. Mong (Emory Wells); Donald Dillaway (David Wells); Sarah Padden (Mary Stevens); Wilfred Lucas (Judge Hollister); Niles Welch (Warren Slade); Nita Cavalier (Etta Billings); and: Margaret Fealy, Alexander Pollard, B. Wayne LaMont, Frank Clark, John Webb Dillon, Lee Phelps.

This poverty row offering benefits not only from Richard Thorpe's smooth direction, Arthur Hoerl's literate script, and H. B. Warner's outstanding work in the lead role, but also from its unique plot gimmick. It presents a defense attorney becoming a detective to obtain necessary information to keep his client from being executed for a crime he did not commit. CROSS-EXAMINATION predates the first Erle Stanley Gardner "Perry Mason" novel by one year.

David Wells (Donald Dillaway) is in love with Grace Varney (Sally Blane) and the two want to marry but Wells' overbearing millionaire father Emory Wells (William V. Mong) forbids the alliance. He and his son have a heated argument. Later, the father is founded murdered in his home; David Wells is accused of the crime and stands trial. His defense attorney, Gerald Waring (H. B. Warner), does his best to extricate the defendant from the charges, but the case presented by the prosecutor, Dwight Simpson (Edmund Breese), is just too strong. The jury brings in a guilty verdict and Wells is sentenced to die. Convinced that the young man is innocent, Waring begins digging further into the case on his own and gains a confession from Emory's housekeeper, Mary Stevens (Sara Padden). On her death bed she admits that she and Wells Sr. were once lovers and that David was their offspring. The cruel Emory Wells kept her on as a servant but never admitted his true parentage to David. When she saw the way Emory was treating their son she killed him in anger. David is freed and he and Grace plan to wed.

"While wordy and to some extent routine in its forensic calisthenics, there is sufficient entertainment allure wrapped up in the trial drama. . ." (*Variety*). The *New York Times* (Andre Sennwald) admitted that the film "has the virtue of suspense" and agreed, "There is a certain fascination about looking at the same scene through the eyes of different characters, and the director uses this device rather effectively."

THE DAIN CURSE (CBS-TV, 5/22-24/78) Color 312 minutes.
    Executive producer, Bob Markell; producer, Martin Poll; associate producers, William Craver, Sonny Grosso; director, E. W. Swackhamer; based on the novel by Dashiell Hammett; teleplay, Robert W. Lenski; art directors, John Robert Lloyd, Gene Rudolph; music, Charles Gorss; camera, Andrew Laszlo; editor, Murray Solomon.
    James Coburn (Hamilton Nash); Hector Elizondo (Ben Feeney); Jason Miller (Owen Fitzstephan); Jean Simmons (Aaronia Haldorn); Paul Stewart (The Old Man): Beatrice Straight (Alice Drain Leggett); Nancy Addison (Gabrielle Leggett); Tom Bower (Sergeant O'Gar); David Canary (Jack Santos); Beeson Carroll (Marshall Cotton); Martin Cassidy (Eric Collinson); Brian Davies (Tom Vernon); Roni Dengel (Daisy Cotton); Paul Harding (Mr. Leggett); Karen Ludwig (Maria Grosso); Malachy McCourt (Mickey); Brent Spinder (Tom Fink): Ronald Weyand (Judge Cochran); Hattie Winston (Minnie Hershey); Roland Winters (Hubert Collinson); Ellis Rabb (Joseph Haldorn); and: William Andrews, Eric Brown, Jasper Cade, Leora Dana, Jasper McNally, Nicholas Wyman.
    Dashiell Hammett's 1929 novel *The Dain Curse* (also serialized in *Black Mask* magazine) involves the character of the Continental Op, who also figured in *Red Harvest,* published the same year. Although Hammett became well known cinematically for THE MALTESE FALCON, *q.v.* and the Nick and Nora Charles/Thin Man series, *q.v.*, his earlier works were never filmed because they were considered too intricate in their plotting and too raw moralistically for the screen. It was not until 1978 that *The Dain Curse* was filmed, and then as a a three-part TV movie for CBS. James Coburn, who had enjoyed big screen popularity, returned to TV for the first time in fourteen years to play the Op, here dubbed Hamilton Nash. The result was a movie ". . . so loaded with plot twists that Hamilton Nash remarks, 'So what the hell is going on?' But Robert Lenski's witty script captures the story's gritty milieu, and sets superbly evoke the '20s" (*TV Guide* magazine).
    "From the creator of 'The Maltese Falcon,' 'Sam Spade, and 'The Thin Man.' A pulse-pounding six-hour mystery drama for television. Three nights of incredible suspense. Starting tonight. America's favorite indoor sport will be untangling the riddle of the sinister family curse that destroyed all enmeshed in its spell," announced the advertisement for the high-budgeted and well-mounted THE DAIN CURSE.

Private investigator Hamilton Nash (James Coburn) is looking into the minor theft of eight low-grade diamonds and cannot figure out why such a major burglary was staged for such small pickings. The trail leads him to an older couple (Paul Harding, Beatrice Straight) and their neurotic daughter Gabrielle (Nancy Addison), who claims the family is cursed. Four deaths have resulted from the robbery and there are numerous suspects, including members of a religious cult. Gabrielle marries Eric Collinson (Martin Cassidy) and his sudden death takes Nash to a small town. The detective realizes that the young woman is addicted to morphine and under the control of a madman.

THE DAIN CURSE was awarded the Mystery Writers of America Edgar Award as the Best TV show of 1978, the first Edgar given, while Beatrice Straight received an Emmy nomination for her work in the telefilm, as did director E. W. Swackhammer.

A much condensed 118-minute video cassette version of THE DAIN CURSE is available.

DANGER ISLAND   *see*   MR. MOTO IN DANGER ISLAND.

DANGEROUS FEMALE   *see*   THE MALTESE FALCON (1931).

DANGEROUS MONEY (Monogram, 1946) 66 minutes.

Producer, James S. Burkett; director, Terry Morse; based on the character created by Earl Derr Biggers; screenplay, Miriam Kissinger; music director, Edward J. Kay; assistant director, Wesley Barry; sound, Tom Lambert; camera, William Sickner; supervising editor, Richard Currier; editor, William Austin.

Sidney Toler (Charlie Chan); Victor Sen Yung (Jimmy Chan); Willie Best (Chattanooga Brown); Joseph Crehan (Captain Black); Dick Elliott (P. T. Burke); Elaine Lange (Cynthia Martin); Amira Moustafa (Laura Erickson); Gloria Warren (Rona Simmonds); Joe Allen, Jr. (George Brace); Rick Vallin (Tao Erickson); Bruce Edwards (Harold Mayfair); Emmett Vogan (Professor Martin); John Harmon (Freddie Kirk); Alan Douglas (Mrs. Whiple); Leslie Denison (Reverend Whiple); Dudley Dickerson (Big Ben); Tristram Coffin (Scott Pearson); Rito Punay (Pete); Selmer Jackson (Ship's Doctor).

On a passenger liner bound for Samoa, Charlie Chan (Sidney Toler), who is traveling with son Jimmy (Victor Sen Yung) and chauffeur Chattanooga Brown (Willie Best), meets detective Scott Pearson (Tristram Coffin), who is allegedly guarding art treasures which are being transported to the island. When Pearson is murdered, the ship's captain, Black (Joseph Crehan), asks Chan to investigate the situation. Chan finds a number of the passengers had the motive and opportunity for killing Pearson, although each of them claims an alibi. He also discovers that Pearson was really a Treasury Department agent who was investigating the smuggling of currency stolen when the Japanese invaded the Philippines during World War II. When the ship docks at Samoa, Chan locates the jungle hideout of the gang responsible for the murder and the smuggling and, with the police, brings them to justice.

DANGEROUS MONEY was the third and final 1946 Charlie Chan-Monogram release and Sidney Toler's next-to-last Chan appearance, as he died early in 1947 after making THE TRAP, *q.v.* "The Riddle of the 'Knives of Death'!. . . One of Chan's Most Terrifying Cases!" exclaimed the poster advertising for this feature which had nearly all of its action either aboard ship (courtesy of flimsy soundstage sets) or in (equally tacky studio) jungle settings on the Pacific isle.

The Charlie Chan-Monogram films are often compared unfavorably to their (Twentieth Century-) Fox counterparts, as in Leonard Maltin's article, "Charlie Chan" in *Film Fan Monthly* magazine (April 1968): "An example of some of Monogram's ineptitude can be seen by comparing a similar scene in CHARLIE CHAN AT THE WAX MUSEUM (Fox, 1940 [*q.v.*] and DANGEROUS MONEY. . . . In the former, Tommy Chan is peeking into a room where his Pop is making a phone call; the lights are quite dim. Suddenly a knife is thrown from the other doorway—it reaches its mark in Charlie's back. Tommy runs excitedly into the room, crying, when the lights go on and Charlie steps out from behind the door. It seems he has positioned a wax dummy of himself at the telephone to lure the killer. Now compare this exciting sequence with the one in DANGEROUS MONEY, in which the audience sees Chan place a makeshift dummy at the desk and hide in the corner. When the knife hits the decoy there is no reaction at all, since we already know it is phony."

DARK ALIBI (Monogram, 1946) 61 minutes.

Producer, James S. Burkett; director, Phil Karlson; based on the character created by Earl Derr Biggers; screenplay, George Callahan; art director, David Milton; assistant director, Theodore "Doc" Jones; sound, Tom Lambert; camera, William A. Sickner; editor, Ace Herman.

Sidney Toler (Charlie Chan); Benson Fong (Tommy Chan); Mantan Moreland (Birmingham Brown); Teala Loring (June Harley); George Holmes (Hugh Kenzie); Edward Earle (Thomas Harley); Ben Carter (Ben Brown); Joyce Compton (Emily Evans); Janet Shaw (Miss Petrie); Edna Holland (Mrs. Foss); John Eldredge (Morgan);

William Ruhl (Thompson); Milton Parsons (Johnson); Ray Walker (Dancer); Russell Hicks (Warden Cameron); Anthony Warde (Slade); Tim Ryan (Foggy); Frank Marlowe (Barker); George Eldredge (Brand).

Charlie Chan (Sidney Toler) is engaged by June Harley (Teala Loring) to obtain evidence to prove that her father, Thomas Harley (Edward Earle), is innocent of a murder conviction which will result in his execution in nine days. Harley's fingerprints were found at the scene of a bank robbery in which a guard was killed. Although he protested his innocence he was convicted of the crimes and sentenced to death. Chan feels Harley is blameless and he visits the rooming house where the man lived and questions several of the residents. This questioning leads him to confer with a man in prison and there an attempt is made on the Oriental's life, convincing him he is on the right trail. Chan learns that Miss Petrie (Janet Shaw), a resident of the rooming house, is married to convict Jimmy Slade (Anthony Warde) and that the prisoner is a fingerprint expert. When Miss Petrie is found murdered at the theatrical warehouse where Harley claims he was kept prisoner at the time of the robbery/murder, Chan deduces that a fingerprint transfer operation has been used to falsely convict Harley. After Slade and bookkeeper Johnson (Milton Parsons) are also eliminated, Chan apprehends the killer.

"The Master of Mystery Exposes a Genius of a Crime!" intoned the poster art for DARK ALIBI, which was filmed with the working titles of FATAL FINGERPRINTS and CHARLIE CHAN AT ALCATRAZ. Further advertising noted, "Chan Solves the Case of the Fatal Fingerprints! The Screen's Ace Sleuth Invades a Death House For his Most Amazing Adventure."

The first of a trio of 1946 Monogram Chan features, DARK ALIBI is nicely paced by director Phil Karlson. Comedy relief is supplied in large dollops by wide-eyed chauffeur Birmingham Brown (Mantan Moreland), a master of double-talk and overreaction. In this episode, Birmingham interacts with brother Ben Brown (Ben Carter), a convict in this outing, leading to their performing several comedy routines (which they had done on stage). It was a repeat of their interaction in THE SCARLET CLUE (1945), *q.v.*

THE DARK CORNER (Twentieth Century-Fox, 1946) 99 minutes.

Producer, Fred Kohlmar; director, Henry Hathaway; based on the story by Lee Rosten; screenplay, Jay Dratler, Bernard Schoenfeld; art directors, James Basevi, Leland Fuller; set decorators, Thomas Little, Paul S. Fox; makeup, Ben Nye; costumes, Kay Nelson; music, Cyril Mockridge; music director, Emil Newman; orchestrator, Maurice de Packh; choreography, Eddie Heywood; assistant director,

Bill Eckhardt; sound, W. D. Flick, Harry M. Leonard; special camera effects, Fred Sersen; camera, Joe McDonald; editor, J. Watson Webb.

Lucille Ball (Kathleen); Clifton Webb (Hardy Cathcart); William Bendix (White Suit); Mark Stevens (Bradford Galt); Kurt Kreuger (Tony Jardine); Cathy Downs (Mari Cathcart); Reed Hadley (Lieutenant Frank Reeves); Constance Collier (Mrs. Kingsley); Molly Lamont (Lucy Wilding); Forbes Murray (Mr. Bryson); Regina Wallace (Mrs. Bryson); John Goldsworthy (Butler); Charles Wagenheim (Foss); Minerva Urecal (Mother); Raisa (Daughter); Matt McHugh (Milkman); Hope Landin (Scrubwoman); Gisela Verbisek (Mrs. Schwartz); Vincent Graeff (Newsboy); Frieda Stoll (Frau Keller); Thomas Martin (Major Domo); Mary Field (Cashier); Ellen Corby (Maid); Eloise Hardt (Saleswoman); Steve Olsen (Barker); Thomas Louden (Elderly Man); Eugene Gomez (Practical Sign Painter); Lee Phelps, Charles Tannes (Cab Drivers); Colleen Alpaugh (Little Girl); Alice Fleming, Isabel Randolph (Women); John Elliott, Pietro Sosso, Peter Cusanelli (Men); Lynn Whitney (Stenographer); Charles Cane, John Russell, Ralph Dunn, Donald MacBride, Tommy Monroe, John Kelly (Policemen); Eddie Heywood and His Orchestra (Themselves).

THE DARK CORNER is a resourceful *film noir* detective melodrama of the mid-1940s, but one which has been obscured because its veteran director, Henry Hathaway, followed it with far better known crime films: KISS OF DEATH (1947) and CALL NORTHSIDE 777 (1948). Furthermore, this gritty motion picture co-starred waspish Clifton Webb, fresh from his triumphant screen return in LAURA (1945), and the similarity of the two roles caused THE DARK CORNER to pale unjustly in the light of the popularity of LAURA.

Wealthy New York City art dealer Hardy Cathcart (Clifton Webb) plans to murder Tony Jardine (Kurt Kreuger), the lover of his gorgeous young wife Mari (Cathy Downs). The acerbic socialite further plans to place the blame on innocent private detective Bradford Galt (Mark Stevens), who once worked with Jardine and, in fact, went to San Quentin prison after being framed for a crime by Jardine. Wily Cathcart sends his loyal thug henchman, White Suit (William Bendix), to keep on the detective's trail and the tough sleuth cannot figure out why he is being tailed. When Jardine is murdered, carefully planted evidence points to Galt as the murderer. He is bewildered by the situation, especially after his one clue—White Suit—is found dead, pushed from the window of a high-rise building. (As the detective admits, "I feel all dead inside. I'm backed up in a dark corner and I don't know who's hitting me.") But his clear-headed, acid-tongued secretary, Kathleen (Lucille Ball), who adores him, helps to solve the case and place the blame where it very much belongs. At the finale, Cathcart is confronted by his now very much aware wife Mari.

Robert Ottoson remarked in *A Reference Guide to the American Film Noir 1940-1958* (1981), "Often compared with LAURA, THE DARK CORNER is not only a much more entertaining and less static film, but is also the more representative film noir. . . . THE DARK CORNER is one of the best examples of the postwar detective film noir, with some tough, laconic, slang-ridden dialogue, mainly spoken by Stevens and Bendix. . . . Stevens is so effective in his role as a man who is trapped by circumstances over which he has no knowledge or control, that it seems somewhat surprising that he was not used to similar effect in other films noir."

Thomas M. Pryor (*New York Times*) enthused, "Theirs [the three scriptors] is a trick doublecross, but they have worked in that surprise with cunning and logic, so that the scattered story elements all fall together like so many pieces in a well-ordered jigsaw puzzle. The action, and there is plenty of it, is violent and explosive, starting with a going-over Galt gives a mysterious toughie who has been shadowing him." On the other hand, *Variety* suggested, "Better editing job, clipping about 20 minutes of the running time, would have aided considerably. . . . Stymied by an overabundance of dialog, however, the tempo gradually subsides and moves slowly to a so-so climax that misses because of the preceding draggy quality."

THE DARK CORNER proved once again that a detective's life is far from glamorous, fraught with dangers, and that the rewards—when they come—are often not worth the risks to body and soul.

THE DARK HOUR (Chesterfield, 1936) 64 minutes.

Producer, George R. Batcheller; director, Charles Lamont; based on the novel *The Last Trap* by Sinclair Gluck; adaptor, Ewart Adamson; art director, Edward C. Jewell; camera, M. A. Andersen; editor, Roland Reed.

Ray Walker (Jim Landis); Irene Ware (Elsa Carson); Berton Churchill (Paul Bernard); Hedda Hopper (Mrs. Tallman); Hobart Bosworth (Charles Carson); E. E. Clive (Foot); William V. Mong (Henry Carson); Aggie Herring (Mrs. Dubbin); Katherine Sheldon (Helen Smith); Rose Allen (Mrs. Murphy); Miki Morita (Chong); John St. Polis (Dr. Munro); Fred Kelsey (Watson); Harold Goodwin (Blake); Lloyd Whitlock (Dr. Bruce); Harry Strang (Policeman).

Old house murder mysteries with a detective solving the crime(s) were a popular motion picture staple in the 1930s and many a minor studio churned out these eerie (and inexpensive to produce) efforts.

Chesterfield Pictures majored in them and these films helped to keep the company profitable for most of the Depression. THE DARK HOUR, based on Sinclair Gluck's 1928 novel *The Last Trap*, is a typical example of a solid Chesterfield murder mystery programmer. In relation to its cost and goals it was well-written, acted, directed and photographed. In short, it contained all the necessary elements to create a flavorful, if modest, whodunit.

Attractive Elsa Carson (Irene Ware) fears for her uncles, Henry Carson (William V. Mong) and Charles Carson (Hobart Bosworth), and goes to detective Jim Landis (Ray Walker) for help. He is aided in the investigation by retired sleuth Paul Bernard (Berton Churchill). That night Henry orders Landis out of his mansion but, later, Henry is found dead and the house is brim full with suspects. Among the possible culprits are: Mrs. Tallman (Hedda Hopper), Henry's sister-in-law; boarder Blake (Harold Goodwin); mysterious butler Foot (E. E. Clive); Oriental servant Chong (Miki Morita); family doctor Munro (John St. Polis), and three women: Mrs. Dubbins (Aggie Herring), Helen Smith (Katherine Sheldon), and Mrs. Murphy (Rose Allen). Landis has fallen in love with Elsa but feels that her aunt, Mrs. Tallman, is the guilty party; Bernard thinks Foot is culpable, but the butler is also killed. Police detective Watson (Fred Kelsey) cannot fathom the case and later Charles, found disguised as a woman, is charged with killing his brother to gain control of the estate. Elsa admits seeing a woman she thought to be her aunt near the body following the murder. Landis, however, unearths that Henry was killed by gas and that it was manufactured in Blake's laboratory. Evidence even points to Bernard before the true murderer is uncovered.

DARKER THAN AMBER (National General, 1970) Color 97 minutes.

Producers, Walter Seltzer, Jack Reeves; director, Robert Clouse; based on the novel by John D. MacDonald; screenplay, Ed Waters; music, John Parker; art director, Jack Collis; set decorator, Don Ivey; assistant director, Ted Swanson; makeup, Guy Del Russo, Marie Del Russo; sound, Howard Warren, Dale Armstrong; camera, Frank Phillips; editor, Fred Chulack.

Rod Taylor (Travis McGee); Suzy Kendall (Vangie Bellmer/ Merrimay Lane); Theodore Bikel (Meyer); Jane Russell (Alabama Tigress); James Booth (Burk); Janet MacLachlan (Noreen); William Smith (Terry); Ahna Capri (Del); Robert Phillips (Griff); Chris Robinson (Roy); Jack Nagle (Farnsworth); Sherry Faber (Nina); James H. Frysinger (Dewey Powell); Oswaldo Calvo (Manuel); Jeff Gillen (Morgue Attendant); Judy Wallace (Ginny); Harry Wood

William Smith in DARKER THAN AMBER (1970).

(Judson); Michael De Beausset (Dr. Fairbanks); Marcy Knight (Landlady); Warren Bauer, Wayne Bauer (Roy's Companions); Don Schoff (Steward).

Fans of hardboiled detectives enjoy John D. MacDonald's (1916-1987) fictional gumshoe Travis McGee,* who had exciting adventures in sixteen books, but only one of these, DARKER THAN AMBER (1966) has been transformed into a theatrical release.**

---

*In *Detectionary* (1977), editors Otto Penzler, Chris Steinbrunner, and Marvin Lachman describe MacDonald's detective hero thusly: "Boat bum, lover, and philosopher, disgusted and saddened by all but a handful of people, Travis McGee is deeply concerned with whether or not honest relationships are possible. . . . He makes his living by recovering stolen property and keeping half the proceeds. Living on his Florida-based boat, the Busted Flush, and assisted by his maverick economist friend, Meyer. . . ."

**Warner Bros.-TV produced TRAVIS McGEE (5/18/83), *q.v.*, with laid-back Sam Elliott in the pivotal role, based on John D. MacDonald's *The Empty Copper Sky* (1978) and featuring Gene Evans as his reliable pal Meyer. The lackluster item was a pilot for a projected series which never developed.

While fishing near the Florida Keys with his economist pal Meyer (Theodore Bikel), beefy private eye Travis McGee (Rod Taylor) witnesses the attempted murder of a young woman who is thrown from a bridge with an iron boot attached to her foot. The two men rescue her and take her aboard McGee's houseboat, "The Busted Flush," but they only find out her name, Vangie Bellmer (Suzy Kendall). Later, one of the girl's attackers, Terry (William Smith), murders Meyer when he fails to tell him Vangie's whereabouts. When the houseboat docks in Fort Lauderdale at the Bahia Mar Yacht Basin, Vangie goes to her apartment where Terry and Griff (Robert Phillips), the other assailant, murder her. McGee identifies her body in the morgue where she has been taken as a hit-and-run victim. The gumshoe starts investigating her past. At her apartment he finds Griff who forces McGee, at gunpoint, to a deserted beach. But in a fight Griff is killed. From a maid (Janet MacLachlan), McGee learns that Vangie was a close friend of Del (Ahna Capri) and that the two were hookers who were used to lure rich men aboard cruise boats so that Terry and Griff could rob and kill them. McGee finds Del in Nassau and the woman agrees to help him gain retribution for Vangie's death. They receive an assist from Vangie's lookalike, underwater ballerina Merrimay Lane (Suzy Kendall), in trapping Terry. When an iron boot is found in his bathtub, the enraged Terry murders Del but later sees Merrimay waving to him at a dock and goes insane, convinced that the girl is Vangie. After Terry is arrested and committed to an insane asylum, loner McGee rejects Merrimay's advances.

While stocky Rod Taylor is properly tough and surly as the cynical Travis McGee, many moviegoers got the most pleasure from this film by watching Jane Russell's flashy cameo as the Alabama Tiger. After the lukewarm audience reaction to DARKER THAN AMBER, plans to film several of the John D. MacDonald's Travis McGee series were abandoned.

DEAD MEN DON'T WEAR PLAID (Universal, 1982) Color 88 minutes.

Producers, David V. Picker, William E. McEuen; associate producer, Richard F. McWhorter; director Carl Reiner; screenplay, Reiner, George Gipe, Steve Martin; production designer, John DeCuir; set designer, Sig Tingloff; set decorator, Richard Goodard; makeup, Ric Sagliani, Tom Case; costumes, Ron Archer, Michele Dittrick; music, Miklos Rozsa; music director, Lee Holdridge; music editor, Else Blangsted; song, Rozsa and Steve Goodman; assistant

Steve Martin and Rachel Ward in DEAD MEN DON'T WEAR PLAID (1982).

directors, Newton Arnold, Mitchell Bock; sound, Bud Alper; supervising sound editor, James L. Klinger; special effects, Glen Robinson; camera, Michael Chapman; editor, Bud Molin.

Steve Martin (Rigby Reardon); Rachel Ward (Juliet Forrest); Carl Reiner (Field Marshal Von Kluck); Reni Santoni (Carlos Rodriguez); George Gaynes (Dr. Forrest); Frank McCarthy (Waiter); Adrian Ricard (Mildred); Charles Picerni, Gene Labell, George Sawaya (Hoods); Britt Nilsson (Puppy Secretary); Jean Beaudine (Duty Secretary); John "Easton" Stuart, Ronald Spivey, Bob Hevelone, Dieter Curt, Phil Kearns, Kent Deigaard, Eugene Brezany, Brad Baird (German Henchmen).

This simple-minded feature, which extensively incorporates footage from vintage films (out of context) to fill out its slim plot, is concerned with the adventures of a ten dollar a day hard-boiled private eye and his case involving a sultry client. Made as a vehicle for the dubious comedy talents of Steve Martin, the picture is tiresome indeed after the novelty of the star interacting with the old footage becomes mundane. In fact, scenes from seventeen features* (many starring Humphrey Bogart) are interpolated into the proceedings, giving Steve Martin the opportunity to "act opposite" such cinema greats as Bette Davis, James Cagney, Ava Gardner, Kirk Douglas, Joan Crawford, Veronica Lake, Edward G. Robinson, Lana Turner, Ingrid Bergman, Edward Arnold, Fred MacMurray, and Vincent Price. In one scene the new celluloid sleuth consults Philip Marlowe (Humphrey Bogart in the THE BIG SLEEP, 1946, *q.v.*) about the case.

Two-bit Los Angeles gumshoe Rigby Reardon (Steve Martin), a man who constantly washes his firearm with soap and water, is hired by radiant Juliet Forrest (Rachel Ward) to locate her father's killer. The search leads them to South America, where they become enmeshed with dictator Carlos Rodriguez (Reni Santoni) and Nazi Field Marshal Von Kluck (Carl Reiner). The later has a mad scheme to overwhelm America by detonating cheese bombs designed by Juliet's late father. Reardon saves the day—or nearly, with only one bomb exploding, and that in Terre Haute, Indiana.

" . . . The film simply hiccups from one star appearance to the next. Logic is probably the last thing one should look for in the circumstances, but even consistency is lacking . . . the level of humour in the framing sections rarely rises above the most basic sort of undergraduate skit" (Tom Milne, British *Monthly Film Bulletin*). What causes even more shock for the audience is to have these *film noir* classics constantly juxtaposed with the infantile new material.

On the other hand, the film does have three definite assets: Rachel Ward is a knockout as the sultry leading lady, Miklos Rozsa's music score would have done any 1940s melodrama proud, and the Edith Head costumes beautifully capture the feel of the period. In fact, the film is dedicated to Ms. Head (1907-1981), as it was her last movie.

DEAD MEN TELL (Twentieth Century-Fox, 1941) 61 minutes.

Producers, Walter Morosco, Ralph Dietrich; director, Harry Lachman; based on the character created by Earl Derr Biggers; screenplay, John Larkin; sets, Thomas Little; music director, Emil Newman; camera, Charles Clarke; Harry Reynolds.

---

*Film extracts are used from: THE BIG SLEEP (1946), THE BRIBE (1949), DARK PASSAGE (1947), DECEPTION (1946), DOUBLE INDEMNITY (1944), THE GLASS KEY (1942), HUMORESQUE (1946), I WALK ALONE (1948), IN A LONELY PLACE (1950), JOHNNY EAGER (1942), THE KILLERS (1946), THE LOST WEEKEND (1945), NOTORIOUS (1946), THE POSTMAN ALWAYS RINGS TWICE (1946), SUSPICION (1941), THIS GUN FOR HIRE (1942), WHITE HEAT (1949).

Sidney Toler (Charlie Chan); Sheila Ryan (Kate Ransome); Robert Weldon (Steve Daniels); Victor Sen Yung (Jimmy Chan); Don Douglas (Jed Thomasson); Katharine [Kay] Aldridge (Laura Thursday); Paul McGrath (Charles Thursday); George Reeves (Bill Lydig); Truman Bradley (Captain Kane); Ethel Griffies (Miss Patricia Nodbury); Lenita Lane (Dr. Anne Bonney); Milton Parsons (Gene La Farge); Stanley Andrews (Inspector Bessie).

The twenty-fifth entry in the enduring Charlie Chan series, DEAD MEN TELL was the third from the last installment in the group produced at Twentieth Century-Fox. It was the ninth series episode to feature Sidney Toler in the title role. The movie contains "ghostly thrills" (*Boxoffice* magazine) in its account of murder aboard a phantom ship. It is darkly atmospheric, with weird music. There is a peg-legged murderer with a hooked hand, allegedly the ghost of a long dead pirate whose treasure map was the basis for a cruise to a remote isle. For comedy relief there is Charlie's number two son, Jimmy Chan (Victor Sen Yung), who falls into the harbor at least four times during the film's one-hour running time. For intellectual balance there are a number of the detective's sage sayings, such as, "Man has learned much who learns how to die," "Swallow much but digest little," and "Man with eye to keyhole betray excessive curiosity."

Elderly Patricia Nodbury (Ethel Griffies) and press agent Steve Daniels (Robert Weldon) devise a treasure hunt worth $60,000,000 to a remote island. They are waiting aboard the ship *Suva Star*, which has been used by Captain Kane (Truman Bradley) as a pirate museum, for the members of the cruise party. Jimmy Chan (Victor Sen Yung) attempts to sneak on board to join the trip and his father, Charlie Chan (Sidney Toler), comes looking for him and meets Miss Nodbury. She tells Chan of her fears that the treasure map, which came from her pirate grandfather, Black Hook, will be stolen. For this reasons she has divided it into four parts and given three of them to other voyagers. Among the passengers are: secretary Kate Ransome (Sheila Ryan), whom Daniels is romancing; newspaperman Bill Lydig (George Reeves), who is writing a feature story on the trip; rare coin dealer Jed Thomasson (Don Douglas); newlyweds Charles (Paul McGrath), a movie star in disguise, and Laura Thursday (Katharine [Kay] Aldridge); and psychiatrist Dr. Anne Bonney (Lenita Lane) and her patient, Gene La Farge (Milton Parsons). Miss Nodbury is found dead in her cabin and Chan deduces that she has been frightened to death by one of the passengers dressed as Black Hook and that her fragment of the map has been stolen. The Thursdays try to disembark and Lydig attempts to waylay Jimmy Chan, who has been dispatched for the police. Chan requests the passengers with the map pieces to turn them over to him, and two do so; but these papers are later stolen. Jimmy finds the Black Hook disguise in Daniels' cabin and a part of the map belonging to La Farge is located in the press agent's coat pocket. When Kate discovers that Lydig is an escaped convict, he tries to silence her, but it is he who gets murdered. Chan confronts Captain Kane, who has not yet met his passengers, and Kane relates that years before he and another man were after Black Hook's treasure and that his partner left him to die on the remote island. Kane says he now wants revenge. Police Inspector Bessie (Stanley Andrews) comes aboard and arrests Daniels for the murders. However, Chan sets a trap for the real killer. He is aided in the capture by Captain Kane and the police.

By now the formula of these Chan-ian exercises were wearing thin and the *New York Times* (Theodore Strauss) carped, "While the cast plays 'Map, map, who's got the map?' a garrulous parrot screams out clues, sullen faces peer over deck rails, the murderer stalks the deck in the costume of a dead pirate, a psychogenic gentleman gambols about the decks and Charlie Chan never gets a scratch. Most of the proceedings, however, have precious little connection with the plot, which, to our mind, isn't cricket."

DEAD RECKONING (Columbia, 1947) 100 minutes.

Producer, Sidney Biddell; director, John Cromwell; story, Gerald Adams, Biddell; adaptor, Allen Rivkin; screenplay, Oliver H. P. Garrett, Steve Fisher; art directors, Stephen Goosson, Rudolph Sternad; set decorator, Louis Diage; costumes, Jean Louis; makeup, Clay Campbell; music, Marlin Skiles; song, Allan Roberts and Doris Fisher; music director, Morris W. Stoloff; assistant director, Seymour Friedman; sound, Jack Goodrich; camera, Leo Tover; editor, Gene Havlick.

Humphrey Bogart (Rip Murdock); Lizabeth Scott (Coral Chandler); Morris Carnovsky (Martinelli); Charles Cane (Lieutenant Kincaid); William Prince (Johnny Drake); Marvin Miller (Krause); Wallace Ford; (McGee); James Bell (Father Logan); George Chandler (Louis Ord); William Forrest (Lieutenant Colonel Simpson); Ruby Dandridge (Hyacinth); Lillian Wells (Pretty Girl); Charles Jordan (Mike, the Bartender); Robert Scott (Band Leader); Lillian Bronson (Mrs. Putnam); Maynard Holmes (Desk Clerk); William Lawrence (Stewart); Dudley Dickerson, Jesse Graves (Waiters); Syd Saylor (Morgue Attendant); George Eldredge (Policeman); Chester Clute (Martin); Joseph Crehan (General Steele); Gary Owen (Reporter); Alvin Hammer (Photographer); Pat Lane (General's Aide); Frank Wilcox (Desk Clerk); Matthew "Stymie" Beard, Hugh Hooker (Bellboys); Matty Fain (Ed); John Bohn, Joe Gilbert, Sayre Dearing (Croupiers); Harry Denny, Kay Garrett, Dick Gordon (Dealers);

Sam Finn, Jack Santoro (Rakers); Ray Teal (Motorcycle Policeman); Grady Sutton (Maitre d'Hotel); Wilton Graff (Surgeon); Paul Bradley (Man); Isabel Withers (Nurse); Byron Foulger (Night Attendant); Alyce Goering (Woman).

Paratroopers Rip Murdock (Humphrey Bogart) and Johnny Drake (William Prince) are on their way to Washington, D.C. when Drake disappears and is found murdered. Murdock turns detective and learns that Drake had been accused of murdering Coral Chandler's (Lizabeth Scott) husband in a dispute over her affections, and that the chief witness against him at the inquest was Louis Ord (George Chandler), a waiter at a gaming nightclub owned by Martinelli (Morris Carnovsky). At the club, trying to find Ord, Rip also meets Coral and the two fall in love, although the young woman is loyal to Drake's memory and says she will aid Murdock in finding the killer. When Ord is murdered, Murdock believes Martinelli did the deed and, rifling through the man's papers, he is caught by the club owner's brutish henchman, Krause (Marvin Miller), and is badly beaten. Escaping, Murdock accuses Coral of her husband's death. She admits it but insists that it was self-defense. She adds that Drake took the blame to protect her. She also tells Murdock that Martinelli knows the truth, holds the murder weapon and is blackmailing her. Murdock, still in love with Coral and believing her story, goes after the gun. When Martinelli attempts to escape, Coral kills him. As they drive away Murdock accuses Coral of mistaking Martinelli for him. She demands the incriminating gun, and when he refuses, she shoots him. Their car crashes. Coral dies from her injuries but Murdock survives to clear Drake's name.

Whenever a cynical good guy meets a *femme fatale* in a *film noir,* the dire results for their mutual health are predictable. Here Rip Murdock, the soldier-turned-detective (Humphrey Bogart), is caught up in a morass and finds himself being hunted by an animal. He soon finds out the great irony of war: that life on the homefront can be even more dangerous than what one can experience in combat. He is fatally attracted to alluring, deadly club vocalist Coral Chandler (Lizabeth Scott), an amoral creature "owned" by the mobster (Morris Carnovsky). As happens to any sleuth who loses his objectivity and starts believing suspects because he wants to—has to—he is in deep trouble.

" . . . They [the scriptwriters] have provided the star with some of the best all-around dialogue he has had in a long time. And he gets off a mean mouthful in this picture, having long stretches to fill in developments as an off-screen voice. . . . For those with a taste for rough stuff DEAD RECKONING is almost certain to satisfy" (Thomas M. Pryor, *New York Times*).

Deep-voiced, impassive Lizabeth Scott, often overshadowed by more sultry, more popular Lauren Bacall, was a replacement for Bacall in this picture which co-starred Bacall's then husband, Humphrey Bogart.

DEADLIER THAN THE MALE (Universal, 1967) Color 98 minutes.

Producer, Betty E. Box; director, Ralph Thomas; based on the characters created by Herbert Cyril "Sapper" McNeile; story, Jimmy Sangster; screenplay, Sangster, David Osborn, Liz Charles-Williams; art directors, Alex Vetchinsky, Ted Clements; set dresser, Helen Thomas; music/music director, Malcolm Lockyer; song, John Franz and Scott Engel; assistant directors, Simon Relph, Giorgio Gentili, Allan James, Patrick O'Brien; costumes, Cynthia Tingey, Yvonne Caffin; makeup, Geoffrey Rodway, John Wilcox; sound, Dudley Messenger, Gordon K. McCallum; sound editor, Don Sharpe; special effects, Kit West, Pat Moore; camera, Ernest Steward; editor, Alfred Roome; assistant editors, Jack Gardner, Rita Burgess.

Richard Johnson (Hugh "Bulldog" Drummond); Elke Sommer (Irma Eckman); Sylva Koscina (Penelope); Nigel Green (Carl Petersen); Suzanna Leigh (Grace); Steve Carlson (Robert Drummond); Virginia North (Brenda); Justine Lord (Miss Ashenden); Leonard Rossiter (Bridgenorth); Laurence Naismith (Sir John Bledlow); Zia Mohyeddin (King Fedra); Lee Montague (Boxer); Milton Reid (Chang) Yasuko Nagazumi (Mitsouko); Didi Sydow (Anna); George Pastell (Carloggio); Dervis Ward (Keller); John Stone (Wyngarde); and: William Mervyn.

The popularity of James Bond and other assorted secret agents was responsible for the screen return of H. C. "Sapper" McNeile's venerable character, Bulldog Drummond, now in the guise of a Lloyd's of London troubleshooter. *Variety* termed the feature an "okay murder meller" but cautioned that "abundant sex and sadism may offend some audiences." *Movies on Video* (1983) opined, "A British attempt to update the old 'Bulldog Drummond' character by making him an imitation James Bond. Imitation is right—from the chess-playing villain bent on world domination to the shapely spies dancing around in bikinis. . . . Drummond himself is played by Richard Johnson, who was presumably chosen for his resemblance to Sean Connery."

When two oil company executives are murdered, Lloyd's of London dispatches investigator Hugh "Bulldog" Drummond (Richard Johnson) and he finds out that the killings were carried out by Irma Eckman (Elke Sommer) and her associate Penelope (Sylva Koscina).They are employees of Carl Petersen (Nigel Green), who heads an operation involved in crooked business deals. A tape is given to Drummond by the servant of one of the dead men but he cannot decipher it, and twice he is set up for murder. At a mideast oil company meeting, Drummond hears Irma offering the oil rights to a small Arab country, but an executive demands the death of its ruler King Fedra (Zia Mohyeddin), a college student who is a friend of Drummond's nephew Robert (Steve Carlson). When Robert arrives to visit his uncle, he is tortured by Penelope. Drummond then believes Fedra will be killed and he joins the young king and Robert on a Mediterranean cruise. At an old castle Drummond finds Irma, Penelope and other hit women employed by Petersen. Bulldog outwits them and brings about their death in an exploding boat.

The economy-minded DEADLIER THAN THE MALE did sufficiently well at the box-office so that a sequel, SOME GIRLS DO (1969), was released, with Richard Johnson again playing the dashing, elegant Bulldog Drummond. This "light programmer" (*Variety*) finds the detective at odds with a madman-genius (James Villiers), his assistant Helga (Daliah Lavi), and a beautiful, amorous robot. The new installment was not successful. Needless to say both Drummond entries with Richard Johnson in the lead role were a far cry from those cosmopolitan Bulldog Drummond pictures of yore starring Ronald Colman, or even the quickie Paramount budget entries in the latter 1930s featuring Ray Milland and later, John Howard.

DEADLY ILLUSION (Cinetel, 1987) Color 90 minutes.

Executive producers, Michael Shapiro, Rodney Sheldon; producer, Irwin Meyer; associate producer, Steve Mirkovich; directors, William Tannen, Larry Cohen; screenplay, Cohen; art directors, Mariana Zivkow, Ruth Lounsbury; music, Patrick Gleeson; song, Carol Connors and Gleeson; music editor, Doug Lackey; assistant directors, Michael Tedross, Chris Gerrity; stunt coordinator, Peter Hook; sound editors, R. J. Palmee, F. Hudson Miller; sound, Jonathan D. Evans; sound effects/foley editor, Kelly Tartan; special effects, Wilfred Caban; camera, Daniel Pearl; editors, Steve Merkovich, Ronald G. Spang.

Billy Dee Williams (Hamberger); Vanity (Rina); Morgan Fairchild (Jane Malloy/Sharon Burton); John Beck (Alex Burton); Joe Cortese (Paul Lefferts); Michael Wilding, Jr. (Costillian); Dennis Hallahan (Burton Imposter); Jenny Cornualle (Gloria Reed); Allison Woodward (Nancy Costillian); Joe Spinnel (Crazy Man in Gun Bureau); Harriet Rogers (Mrs. Bains); George Oros (Levante); Charles Malcolm (Assistant District Attorney); Thom Curley (Wexler); Richard Triggs (Toll Booth Attendant); Joe Cirillo (Cop in Gun Bureau); Julie Gordon, Mary Kaplan (Receptionists); Debbie Dickinson (Woman on Phone); Michael Emil (Medical Examiner); Don Torres (Man at Ball Park); John Woehrle, Jim Kane, Jack McLaughlin, John Means (Boardroom Executives); Clint Bowers, David Holbrook, Everett Quinton (Clerks); Nick Smith (Security Guard); Al Cerrillo (Helicopter Pilot); Kathryn Leigh-Davis (*Mademoiselle* Magazine Reporter).

Reckless Gotham private eye Hamberger (Billy Dee Williams) has lost his firearms license. He works on a shoestring budget along with his luscious girlfriend cabbie (Vanity), operating from a cafeteria. A wealthy man (Dennis Hallahan) offers the gumshoe a hefty fee to kill his beautiful wife (Morgan Fairchild). However, instead of carrying out his assignment, the free-wheeling detective has sex with the woman and then informs her of the murder plot. That night Hamberger's policeman pal (Joe Cortese) arrives at his apartment to arrest him for killing his client's wife. When they go to identify the body it is not the same woman. The cop gives the detective two days to solve the caper. Hamberger, realizing he was set up by the real husband (John Beck) and the phony wife (Morgan Fairchild), sets out to find them and clear himself, the quest taking him through a chic but deadly fashion show, a skyscraper shoot-out with a hovering helicopter, and gunplay at Shea Stadium. Despite the odds, Hamberger solves the case.

Made on a minimal budget with scriptwriter Larry Cohen being replaced as director part way through production by William Tannen, DEADLY ILLUSION relies a great deal on the charisma of Billy Dee Williams, the beauty of Vanity, and the versatility of actress Morgan Fairchild (in dual roles) to carry the nonsensical proceedings. The few bursts of dramatic violence do not compensate for the unconvincing premise or for the haphazard production values. "DEADLY ILLUSION is a twisty little private-eye thriller—an obvious homage to Dashiell Hammett, Raymond Chandler, Mickey Spillane and company—and it plays most of the way with serpentine tongue firmly in hard-boiled cheek. . . . This is an enervated thriller with a lean budget—which means minimal car-chase carnage. . ." (Michael Wilmington, *Los Angeles Times*).

Had this film been made fifteen years earlier, during the height of the black exploitation film craze, the black detective (Billy Dee Williams) would have been involved in capers concerning his own race and a lot of the story conflict would have been between the rebellious blacks and the antagonistic whites.

DEATH ON THE NILE (Paramount, 1978) Color 140 minutes.

Producers, John Brabourne, Richard Goodwin; associate producer, Norton Knatchbull; director, John Guillermin; based on the book by Agatha Christie; screenplay, Anthony Shaffer; production designer, Peter Murton; art directors, Brian and Terry Ackland; costumes, Anthony Powell; music, Nino Rota; assistant director, Chris Carreras; camera, Jack Cardiff; editor, Malcolm Cooke.

Peter Ustinov (Hercule Poirot); Jane Birkin (Louise Bourget); Lois Chiles (Linnet Ridgeway); Bette Davis (Mrs. Van Schuyler); Mia Farrow (Jacqueline de Bellefort); Jon Finch (Mr. Ferguson); Angela Lansbury (Salome Otterboume); Olivia Hussey (Rosalie Otterbourne); I. S. Johar (Manager of the Karnak); George Kennedy (Andrew Pennington); Simon MacCorkindale (Simon Doyle); David Niven (Colonel Rice); Maggie Smith (Miss Bowers); Jack Warden (Dr. Bessner); Harry Andrews (Barnstaple); Sam Wanamaker (Rockford).

Producers John Brabourne and Richard Goodwin, following the success of MURDER ON THE ORIENT EXPRESS (1975), *q.v.*, filmed Agatha Christie's 1937 book *Death on the Nile* as "Agatha Christie's Second Great Hercule Poirot Mystery." Most of the movie was shot on seven weeks of location in Egypt, with a month done on a steamer on the Nile River between Aswan and Cairo, and other locations such as the ruins at Aswan, Abu Simbel and Luxor, and near the pyramids and the Sphinx. The result was an overlong, but leisurely and pictorially impressive photoplay which—thanks to its name cast—grossed $8,800,000 in domestic theatrical rentals.

Hercule Poirot (Peter Ustinov), the Belgian detective, is on holiday in Egypt enjoying the company of Rosalie Otterbourne (Olivia Hussey), the daughter of racy novelist Salome Otterbourne (Angela Lansbury), who is also on the cruise. Other passengers include: wealthy dowager Mrs. Van Schuyler (Bette Davis); rich Linnet Ridgeway (Lois Chiles) and her new husband Simon Doyle (Simon MacCorkindale); Colonel Rice (David Niven); Andrew Pennington (George Kennedy), Linnet's American trustee; and Jacqueline de Bellefort (Mia Farrow), Linnet's one-time best friend and Doyle's former fiancée. On the Nile cruise Linnet asks Poirot's assistance in getting Jacqueline to stop stalking her and her husband, but he fails to convince the determined young woman to leave the couple alone. At Abu Simbel, Simon saves Linnet from being killed by a falling boulder and, later, on the boat, Jacqueline shoots Doyle, but it is only a flesh wound. The next day Poirot is informed that Linnet has been murdered but that Jacqueline had an alibi: she had been sedated before the crime was committed and a nurse (Maggie Smith) has been with her through the night. Poirot feels obligated to solve the crime and he learns that the other passengers have strong motives for wanting Linnet dead. By piecing together several odd clues he deduces who is the murderer.

DEATH ON THE NILE (1978).

With its all-star cast and posh production values (the film won an Academy Award for Best Costume Design), DEATH ON THE NILE is an engaging detective entry, but its chief weakness is Peter Ustinov's portrayal of Poirot, which is hardly like the fussy little man of the original Agatha Christie novels. Obviously, however, his performance caught the fancy of film viewers—or at least film producers—because Ustinov was back as Poirot in two more theatrical features, MURDER UNDER THE SUN (1982) and APPOINTMENT WITH MURDER (1988), *qq.v.*, and in a trio of glossy telefeatures: THIRTEEN AT DINNER (1985), DEAD MAN'S FOLLY (1986), and MURDER IN THREE ACTS (1986), *qq.v.*

THE DETECTIVE   *see*   FATHER BROWN.

DETECTIVE KITTY O'DAY (Monogram, 1944) 61 minutes.
     Producer, Lindsley Parsons; director, William Beaudine; story, Victor Hammond; screenplay, Tim Ryan, Hammond; art director, David Milton; music director, Edward J. Kay; assistant director, William Strohbach; sound, Tom Lambert; camera, Ira Morgan; editor, Richard Currier.
     Jean Parker (Kitty O'Day); Peter Cookson (Johnny Jones); Tim Ryan (Inspector Miles); Veda Ann Borg (Georgia Wentworth);

Edward Gargan (Mike Storm); Douglas Fowley (Anton Downs); Edward Earle (Oliver Wentworth); Herbert Heyes (Jeffers); Pat Gleason (Cab Driver); Olaf Hytten (Charles).

Female sleuths had been much in vogue in the 1930s, with film series centered around Hildegarde Withers, Nurse Sarah Keate, and Torchy Blane. There were also solo efforts in motion pictures like PRIVATE DETECTIVE (1939), *q.v.*, but by the 1940s the popularity of the hard-boiled male gumshoe had pretty much pushed aside films about distaff detectives. (Women were now relegated generally to being the super private eye's overzealous wife or secretary.) An exception to this was Monogram's DETECTIVE KITTY O'DAY in which the title character becomes a shamus to save herself and her lover from a murder charge. Don Miller noted of this programmer in *B Movies* (1973), "William Beaudine, knocking 'em out on the assembly line, piloted DETECTIVE KITTY O'DAY through in a great hurry. It showed evidence of rush, with dummies substituting for bodies fallen from closets, with no effort to cover the ruse; shaky wear-spotted sets. . . . The plot gimmick of a girl sleuth snooping-where-uninvited was old in the silent days. But Beaudine was seasoned enough to know how to get a laugh, and he had valuable help in this respect. Tim Ryan, a vaude veteran of the Tim and Irene days, now doubling as a performer and script writer for Monogram, played the part of the harrassed cop and collaborated on the screenplay."

"Help! Help! Murder! . . . and You're the Victim! 'Cause You'll Die With Laffter. . . . When you Watch This Female Hawkshaw In Action!" read the ads for DETECTIVE KITTY O'DAY. The premise has Kitty (Jean Parker) and boyfriend Johnny Jones (Peter Cookson) working for an individual (Douglas Fowley) who is really a fence for stolen bonds and securities. In addition, he is in cahoots with dishonest attorney Jeffers (Herbert Heyes) and is also entangled with the wife (Veda Ann Borg) of Oliver Wentworth (Edward Earle), and then there is Jeffers' butler (Olaf Hytten). One night Kitty finds her boss murdered and police Inspector Miles (Tim Ryan) and his assistant Mike Storm (Ed Gargan) are convinced that Kitty and Jones are the prime suspects. Kitty becomes a detective to prove their innocence, and she and Jones take on various disguises, including that of a maid and porter. When they uncover yet another homicide, they talk with Jeffers and learn to their peril that he is seriously involved in the crimes. Jeffers abducts the pair and demands $100,000 in bonds he had accused Jones of stealing. A cab driver (Pat Gleason), who witnessed the kidnapping, phones the police and Miles and his men arrest the guilty party, who has killed his partners because they wanted a bigger share of the stolen funds.

Peter Cookson and Jean Parker in DETECTIVE KITTY O'DAY (1944).

It turns out that Jones had hidden the negotiable bonds to keep them safe.

This modest film was successful enough to generate a sequel, ADVENTURES OF KITTY O'DAY, early in 1945. Here Kitty (Jean Parker) is a switchboard operator in a major hotel where three murders and a number of robberies occur. She and her boyfriend Johnny Jones (Peter Cookson) attempt to solve the mysteries. Again Tim Ryan co-wrote the script and portrayed Inspector Miles. In March 1945, the third and final adventure was issued. FASHION MODEL (made with the working title of THE MODEL MURDERS) now cast Marjorie Weaver as model Peggy Rooney. She sets out to clear stock boy/boyfriend Jimmy (Robert Lowery) who is accused of killing a model. As with the prior low-budget installments, Tim Ryan co-wrote the scenario and played the determined chief police officer, with William Beaudine directing.

THE DEVIL'S MASK (Columbia, 1946) 66 minutes.

Producer, Wallace MacDonald; director, Henry Levin; based on the radio series "I Love a Mystery" created by Carlton E. Morse;

screenplay, Charles O'Neal; additional dialogue, Dwight Babcock; art director, Robert Peterson; set decorator, George Montgomery; music director, Mischa Bakaleinikoff; assistant director, Carl Hiecke; sound, George Cooper; camera, Henry Freulich; editor, Jerome Thomas.

Jim Bannon (Jack Packard); Barton Yarborough (Doc Long); Anita Louise (Janet Mitchell); Michael Duane (Rex Kennedy); Mona Barrie (Eve Mitchell); Paul E. Burns (Leon Hartman); Frank Wilcox (Professor Arthur Logan); Ludwig Donath (Dr. Karger); Edward Earle (E. R. Willard); John Elliott (The Butler); Richard Hale (Raymond Halliday); Thomas Jackson (Captain Quinn); Frank Mayo (Quentin Mitchell).

A shrunken head is found in the wreckage of a transport plane and the police discover that the Cordova Museum has an exhibit of shrunken heads from the Jivaro tribe of South America. These were collected by vanished explorer Quentin Mitchell (Frank Mayo), but now are missing. Mitchell's attractive second wife, Eve (Mona Barrie), hires Jack Packard (Jim Bannon) and Doc Long (Barton Yarborough) to protect her from expected violence from her stepdaughter, Janet (Anita Louise), who blames the woman for her father's disappearance. Janet, meanwhile, hires private eye Rex Kennedy (Michael Duane) to trail Eve, and Janet takes Kennedy with her to meet with a friend of her father, taxidermist Leon Hartman (Paul E. Burns). Janet tells Hartman that she is sure her stepmother is having an affair with Professor Arthur Logan (Frank Wilcox). That night an attempt is made on Logan's life with a poisoned dart from a Jivaro blowgun. Kennedy is suspected of the crime but footprints outside the scene match those of the missing explorer. Packard and Doc Long learn that one of the shrunken heads at the museum actually belongs to a white man and when Kennedy goes to Hartman to force a confession, Janet arrives to accuse Kennedy of blackmail. Kennedy attempts to call the police but the real villain cuts the wires and admits he executed Quentin. Kennedy is then murdered and Janet and Packard escape, saved at the last minute by a pet leopard who turns on his violent master.

"Love . . . in a weird atmosphere of hate! Mystery . . . in an eerie museum of terror!. . . . Adventure . . . in a thrill-a-minute chiller! The jungle curse of the South American Jivaro Indians haunts a lovely young girl, shocks a hard-boiled detective, drives a scientist insane," read the advertising for this melodrama. This film was one of three Columbia features based on Carlton E. Morse's popular radio series, "I Love a Mystery." This horror-tinged detective programmer was the middle entry, preceded by I LOVE A MYSTERY (1945), *q.v.*, and followed by THE UNKNOWN (1946).

DICK TRACY (Republic, 1937) fifteen chapters.

Associate producer, J. Laurence Wickland; directors, Ray Taylor, Alan James; based on the cartoon strip character created by Chester Gould; screenplay, Barry Shipman, Winston Miller; music, Harry Grey; camera, William Nobles, Edgar Lyons.

Ralph Byrd (Dick Tracy); Kay Hughes (Gwen); Smiley Burnette (Mike McGurk); Lee Van Atta (Junior); John Piccori (Dr. Moloch); Carleton Young (Gordon Tracy—After); Fred Hamilton (Steve); Francis X. Bushman (Chief Anderson); John Dilson (Brewster); Richard Beach (Gordon Tracy—Before); Wedgewood Nowell (Clayton); Theodore Lorch (Paterno); Edwin Stanley (Odette); Harrison Greene (Cloggerstein); Herbert Weber (Martino); Buddy Roosevelt (Burke); George DeNormand (Flynn); Byron K. Foulger (Korvitch); Oscar and Elmer (Themselves).

Chapters: 1) The Spider Strikes; 2) The Bridge of Terror; 3) The Fur Pirates; 4) Death Rides the Sky; 5) Brother Against Brother; 6) Dangerous Waters; 7) The Ghost Town Mystery; 8) Battle in the Clouds; 9) The Stratosphere Adventure; 10) The Gold Ship; 11) Harbor Pursuit; 12) The Trail of the Spider; 13) The Fire Trap; 14) The Devil in White; 15) Brothers United.

Police detective Dick Tracy was created in 1931 by cartoonist Chester Gould and the strip quickly became one of the most popular newspaper features in the country. As a result Republic Pictures bought the screen rights to the Gould character and in a stroke of casting genius selected Ralph Byrd as Tracy, a part which would be associated with him for the remainder of his performing career. "Dick Tracy proved to be the most popular detective to appear in a movie serial," Jim Harmon and Donald F. Glut concluded in *The Great Movie Serials* (1972).

Thanks to the success of the initial cliffhanger, Republic starred Byrd in three more Tracy chapterplays, DICK TRACY RETURNS (1938), DICK TRACY'S G-MEN (1939), and DICK TRACY VS. CRIME, INC. (1941). Harmon and Glut further commented on the success of the Gould character, "The *Dick Tracy* strip was unique. The villains were bizarre monstrosities, far surpassing the usual caricatures. They were unbelievable creatures that could not possibly have existed anywhere on this planet, even in the wildest freak show. There was a flat, two-dimensional feel about the strip, which lent even more unreality to *Dick Tracy*. But Gould offset this unbelievably by introducing such authentic crime-stopping techniques and well-conceived plotting and characterization that *Dick Tracy* was accepted as a new and totally serious newspaper serial."

The mysterious Lame One leads the Spider gang and police detective Dick Tracy (Ralph Byrd), along with pal Mike McGurk

(Smiley Burnette), adopted son Junior (Lee Van Atta) and girlfriend Gwen (Kay Hughes), are opposed to his criminal activities. One of the Lame One's associates, Dr. Moloch (John Piccori), performs an operation on Dick's brother Gordon (Richard Beach), turning him into a mindless slave (Carleton Young) who carries out the dastardly orders of the master criminal. Police Chief Anderson (Francis X. Bushman) orders Tracy to stop the Lame One, who uses a ray gun aboard his aircraft, the Flying Wing, to wreak havoc and disrupt police department work. Finally comprehending what the Lame One and Moloch have done to his brother, Tracy corners the master criminal, bringing about his destruction and rounding up his gang.

DICK TRACY'S DILEMMA (RKO, 1947) 60 minutes.
    Producer, Herman Schlom; director, John Rawlins; based on the cartoon strip character created by Chester Gould; screenplay, Robert Stephen Brode; art directors, Albert S. D'Agostino, Lucius O. Croyton; set decorator, Darrell Silvera; music, Paul Sawtel; music director, C. Bakaleinikoff; assistant director, Grayson Rogers; sound, Jean L. Speak, Terry Kellum; camera, Frank Redman; editor, Marvin Colt.
    Ralph Byrd (Dick Tracy); Lyle Latell (Pat Patton); Kay Christoper (Tess Truehart); Jack Lambert (The Claw); Ian Keith (Vitamin Flintheart); Bernadene Hayes (Longshot Lillie); Jimmy Conlin (Sightless); William H. Davidson (Peter Premium); Tony Barrett (Sam); Richard Powers (Fred); Harry Strang (Night Watchman); Tom London (Cop in Squad Car); Jason Robards, Sr. (Watchman); Harry Harvey (Donovan the Cop); Sean McClory (Cop); Al Bridge (Police Detective); William Gould (Police Technician).
    Ralph Byrd is synonymous with the fictional character of Dick Tracy, a part he portrayed enthusiastically and convincingly in a quartet of Republic serials, two RKO features and an ABC-TV half-hour weekly series (1950-51) before his untimely death of a heart attack in 1952 at the age of forty-three. In 1945 RKO launched its "Dick Tracy" budget feature series with character actor Morgan Conway in the lead, but after the first two entries—DICK TRACY (1945) and DICK TRACY VERSUS CUEBALL (1946)—he failed to click and was replaced by Byrd, who completed the series with DICK TRACY'S DILEMMA and DICK TRACY MEETS GRUESOME (1947). Unfortunately, RKO did not provide Byrd's return to the Dick Tracy movie series with sufficient budget trappings.
    When a night watchman is murdered at a warehouse, police detective Dick Tracy (Ralph Byrd) and allies Tess Truehart (Kay Christopher), Vitamin Flintheart (Ian Keith), and Pat Patton (Lyle Latell) focus on the case. Tracy learns that the murder was commit-

ted by a crafty gang of fur thieves involved in an insurance scam. Their chief weapon is a deformed madman called The Claw (Jack Lambert) who uses a claw-like hand as his murder weapon. With the aid of Longhsot Lillie (Bernadene Hayes) and pencil peddler Sightless (Jimmy Conlin), Tracy corners the gang. In a showdown The Claw is dispatched when his weapon comes into contact with electrical wires.

Thanks to Ralph Byrd's typecasting as the square-jawed Tracy, a good script and the frightful villain, The Claw, DICK TRACY'S DILEMMA emerged as a flavorful screen adaptation of the Chester Gould property.

THE DOCKS OF NEW ORLEANS (Monogram, 1948) 67 minutes.

Producer, James Burkett; director, Derwin Abrahams; based on the character created by Earl Derr Biggers; screenplay. W. Scott Darling; set decorator, Ken Schwartz; music, Edward J. Kay; assistant director, Theodore "Doc" Jones; sound, Tom Lambert; camera, William Sickner; editor, Ace Herman.

Roland Winters (Charlie Chan); Victor Sen Yung (Tommy Chan); Mantan Moreland (Birmingham Brown); John Gallaudet (Captain McNally); Virginia Dale (Rene Blanchard); Boyd Irwin (Lafontaine); Carol Forman (Nita Aguirre); Howard Negley (Pereaux); Douglas Fowley (Grock); Emmett Vogan (Henri Castanero); Harry Hayden (Swendstrom); Rory Mallinson (Thompson); Stanley Andrews (Theodore Von Scherbe); George J. Lewis (Dansiger); Dian Fauntelle (Mrs. Swendstrom); Ferris Taylor (Dr. Double); Harwood Jones (Mobile); Eric Wilton (Butler); Forrest Matthews (Detective); Wally Walker (Chauffeur); Harry Steers (Doctor); Paul Conrad (D.A. Man); Frank Stephens (Sergeant); Fred Miller (Armed Guard).

THE DOCKS OF NEW ORLEANS was Roland Winter's second of six efforts as Charlie Chan and, like his initial venture, THE CHINESE RING (*q.v.*) the year before, it was a remake of a Mr. Wong feature, this time MR. WONG, DETECTIVE (1938), *q.v.* It was, however, a marked improvement over THE CHINESE RING, for it boasted a complicated plot and an inventive climax to hold audience attention. (*Variety* did complain of the "mediocre acting" by the supporting cast.) Like all Chan adventures DOCKS OF NEW ORLEANS is dotted with the philosophical wisdom of the Oriental truth seeker, including "Death is one appointment we must all keep." The poster art for this latest whodunit exclaimed, "Probing Into Peril! The ace of detectives digs into a mystery of hidden death!"

New Orleans chemical company owner Lafontaine (Boyd Ir-

Roland Winters, Douglas Fowley, Howard Negley and Carol Forman in THE DOCKS OF NEW ORLEANS (1948).

win) consults Charlie Chan (Roland Winters) concerning an attempt on his life. As he leaves the San Francisco detective's home an unsuccessful effort is made to kidnap him. In case he should die, the man's partners—Henri Castanaro (Emmett Vogan) and Theodore Von Scherbe (Stanley Andrews)—demand that he sign an agreement giving them full interest in the trio's current project, although Lafontaine's niece Rene Blanchard (Virginia Dale) owns a quarter interest in the chemical company. Later Lafontaine is found murdered in his office and Chan shows that the cause was poison gas. At a party Castanaro receives a death threat and is killed before the law can arrive. The inventor of the poison gas, Pereaux (Howard Negley), accuses Von Scherbe of the murder, but the latter is also dispatched with the gas. At Chan's home son Tommy Chan (Victor Sen Yung) and chauffeur Birmingham Brown (Mantan Moreland) are captured by the killer and his cohorts, Nita Aguirre (Carol Forman) and Grock (Douglas Fowley). The three of them want the formula to sell to the highest bidder. Chan, with the assistance of police Captain McNally (John Gallaudet) and his men, nab the criminals.

DOUBLE INDEMNITY (Paramount, 1944) 107 minutes.

Producer, Joseph Sistrom; director, Billy Wilder; based on the novella in the book *Three of a Kind* by James M. Cain; screenplay, Wilder, Raymond Chandler; art directors, Hans Dreier, Hal Pereira; set decorator, Bertram Granger; costumes, Edith Head; music, Miklos Rozsa; assistant director, C. C. Coleman Jr.; sound, Stanley Cooley; process camera, Farciot Edouart; camera, John F. Seitz; editor, Doane Harrison.

Fred MacMurray (Walter Neff); Barbara Stanwyck (Phyllis Dietrichson); Edward G. Robinson (Barton Keyes); Porter Hall (Mr. Jackson); Jean Heather (Lola Dietrichson); Tom Powers (Mr. Dietrichson); Byron Barr (Nino Zachette); Richard Gaines (Mr. Norton) Fortunio Bonanova (Sam Gorlopis); John Philliber (Joe Pete); George Magrill (Bit); Bess Flowers (Norton's Secretary); Kernan Cripps (Redcap); Oscar Smith (Pullman Porter); Betty Farrington (Nettie, the Maid); Edmund Cobb (Train Conductor); Floyd Schackelford, James Adamson (Pullman Porters); Sam McDaniel (Garage Attendant); Judith Gibson (Pacific All-Risk Telephone Operator); Clarence Muse (Black Man); Miriam Franklin (Keyes' Secretary); *Deleted Execution Scene:* Alan Bridge (Execution Chamber Guard); Edward Hearn (Warden's Secretary); George Anderson (Warden); Boyd Irwin, George Melford (Doctors); William O'Leary (Chaplain); Lee Shumway (Door Guard).

DOUBLE INDEMNITY (ABC-TV, 10/13/73) Color 100 minutes.

Executive producer, David Victor; producer, Robert F. O'Neill; based on the novella in the book *Three of a Kind* by James M. Cain and the screenplay by Billy Wilder, Raymond Chandler; teleplay, Steven Bochco; music, Billy Goldenberg; art director, Joseph M. Alves, Jr; camera, Haskell Boggs; editor, Edward A. Biery.

Richard Crenna (Walter Neff); Lee J. Cobb (Barton Keyes); Samantha Eggar (Phyllis Dietrichson); Robert Webber (Edward Norton); Arch Johnson (Dietrichson); Kathleen Cody (Lola Dietrichson); John Fiedler (Jackson); John Elerick (Donald Franklin); Gene Dynarski (Sam Bonventura); Joan Pringle (Neff's Secretary); Ken Renard (Porter) Arnold Turner (Redcap); Rand Brooks (Conductor); Joyce Cunning (Norton's Secretary); Tom Curtis (Charlie); John Furlong (George).

Raymond Chandler and James M. Cain, distinguished authors of diverse materials, are two of the best remembered and most enduringly popular writers from the 1940s. Chandler collaborated with director Billy Wilder on the screenplay for DOUBLE INDEMNITY, which was taken from Cain's novella in the book *Three of a Kind,* 1944. The result was one of the 1940s' most memorable melodramas, a gritty *film noir* of passion, deceit and murder which is remarkable for the offbeat casting of its three leads: usually wholesome Barbara Stanwyck as the blonde (wigged) evil seductress who wears an anklet and skin-tight sweaters; Fred MacMurray, usually a light comedian, as the insurance man driven to murder by passion and greed; and pugnacious gangster star Edward G. Robinson as the methodical insurance detective who dogs everyone's footsteps until he brings the case to a close.

Essentially honest insurance salesman Walter Neff (Fred MacMurray) wants to sell a life insurance policy to businessman Dietrichson (Tom Powers), who is in the oil business. During the policy sale he meets the customer's younger wife, Phyllis (Barbara Stanwyck), and the two develop a lustful attraction for one another (or so it seems). Neff has sold the man a $50,000 life insurance contract with a double indemnity clause which will pay his survivor(s) double the face amount of the policy in case of accidental death. Phyllis persuades Neff that the *only* way they can marry and be happy is to eliminate her husband. Neff conceives a scheme to murder him while he is on a business trip. Neff carries out the murder of Dietrichson on a train and it appears that the man died accidentally. All goes well until Barton Keyes (Edward G. Robinson), an investigator for the same company for which Neff works, is

Fred MacMurray and Barbara Stanwyck in DOUBLE INDEMNITY (1944).

assigned to the case and begins to believe that Dietrichson's death was not accidental. When Neff finally realizes that Phyllis only wanted the $100,000 from the life insurance, he plans to shoot her. In the struggle the two shoot one another and Phyllis dies. Neff relates their plot to Keyes before himself succumbing to his wounds.*

"Anyone who has read Chandler's novels and short stories recognizes the great ear he had for flip and mordant dialogue. Because of its brilliant script, fine characterizations, noir aesthetics and its sense of time and place, DOUBLE INDEMNITY has become one of the cornerstone films in any retrospective screening of films noir." (Robert Ottoson, *A Reference Guide to the American Film Noir: 1940-1958,* 1981). For Bosley Crowther (*New York Times*) it is the unrelenting insurance investigator who is the cornerstone of DOUBLE INDEMNITY. "With a bitter brand of humor and irritability, he creates a formidable guy. As a matter of fact, Mr. Robinson is the only one you care two hoots for in the film. The rest are just neatly carved pieces in a variably intriguing crime game." Pauline Kael, reassessing the film in *The New Yorker* magazine, decided that Barton Keyes, the conscientious man driven beyond duty to find the truth and put together the puzzle pieces no matter what, is the movie's cornerstone. "Edward G. Robinson handles his sympathetic role with an easy mastery that gives the film some realistic underpinnings. It needs them, because despite the fine use of realistic sets—a cheerless middle-class home, a supermarket, offices—Chandler's dialogue is in his heightened laconic mode, and the narration (Walter Neff tells the story) is often so gaudy and terse that it seems an emblem of '40s hardboiled attitudes. This defect may be integral to the film's taut structure."

In 1949 Gloria Swanson played Phyllis Dietrichson in the William Spear-directed radio adaptation of the Cain story on CBS' "The Philip Morris Playhouse."

A television remake of DOUBLE INDEMNITY was telecast on ABC-TV in the fall of 1973. This Universal production was adapted to TV by Steven Bochco (later of "Hill Street Blues" and "LA Law" series fame) from the Billy Wilder-Raymond Chandler film script. Here Samantha Eggar is the destructive Phyllis, Richard Crenna is Walter Neff, and Lee J. Cobb is Keyes, here shown to be Neff's boss. Although a glossy and well-made telefeature, the production has none of the grit, allure, or overall entertainment value of its big-screen counterpart. Judith Crist noted in *TV Guide to the Movies* (1974), "This quickie version is far from a classic, but a

---

*Originally the film included a scene of Walter Neff going to the gas chamber, but it was deleted from the release print.

good plot endures." In *Movies on TV* (1987), Steven H. Scheuer acknowledges, "This remake . . . hasn't the old oomph, but James Cain's clever story will hold one's interest." Regarding Samantha Eggar's work as Phyllis, the same reviewer cracked, ". . . she somehow doesn't seem worth the big risks."

THE DRAGON MURDER CASE (First National, 1934) 68 minutes.

Director, H. Bruce Humberstone; based on the novel by S. S. Van Dine [Willard Huntington Wright]; adaptor, Rian James; screenplay, F. Hugh Herbert, Robert Lee; dialogue director, Daniel Reed; camera, Tony Gaudio; editor, Terry Morse.

Warren William (Philo Vance); Margaret Lindsay (Bernice); Lyle Talbot (Leland); Eugene Pallette (Sergeant Ernest Heath); Robert McWade (District Attorney John F. X. Markham); Helen Lowell (Mrs. Matilda Stamm); Dorothy Tree (Ruby); Robert Barratt (Rudolph Stamm); George E. Stone (Tatum); George Meeker (Montague Stamm); Robert Warwick (Dr. Halliday); William B. Davidson (Greef); Etienne Girardot (Doremus); Charles Wilson (Hennessey).

S. S. Van Dine's 1933 novel was the basis for this popular installment in the Philo Vance series, the second of three Warner Bros. Vance pictures. It was preceded by THE KENNEL MURDER CASE (1933), *q.v.* and followed by CALLING PHILO VANCE (1940), with James Stephenson. Warren William, who had played Perry Mason in several Warners features and who would be The Lone Wolf at Columbia Pictures, was cast as Vance, replacing William Powell, who had finished his part in the series with THE KENNEL MURDER CASE and by now had defected to contract stardom at Metro-Goldwyn-Mayer. Four actors from the KENNEL film, however, retained their recurring roles in this entry: bulky Eugene Pallette as Sergeant Heath, Robert McWade as District Attorney Markham, Etienne Girardot as medical examiner Doremus, and Charles Wilson as detective Hennessey.

Outside the Stamm mansion is a large and deep pool where, legend claims, a huge dragon dwells and the vicious reptile is said to control the destinies of the family members. During a swimming outing at the estate, Montague Stamm (George Meeker) disappears in the pool and his demented, elderly aunt, Mrs. Matilda Stamm (Helen Lowell) claims that the monster killed him. Later, his badly clawed corpse is found encased in ice, and detective Philo Vance (Warren William) aids Sergeant Heath (Eugene Pallette) and District Attorney Markham (Robert McWade) in the investigation. The chief suspect is Rudolph Stamm (Robert Barratt), who was not present when Montague died, but Vance proves that a relative—at the poolside—committed the murder.

Budgeted at slightly over $300,000, THE DRAGON MUR-DER CASE is almost as much a horror film as a mystery with its haunting dragon pool, almost endless aquatic interiors of the Stamm mansion, the hysterical shrieks of the old lady, and the shadowy figure of the "dragon" murderer. Ray Cabana, Jr. in his article, "Murder, Mythology and Mother Goose" in *Kaleidoscope* magazine (Volume 2, Number 3, 1967), notes that director H. Bruce Humberstone ". . . managed to instill some memorable moments into the production. . . ." However, in its day, contemporary reviewers were more critical. *Variety* complained that the film is "a poorly paced detective yarn with several incredible sequences," and the *New York Times* (Mordaunt Hall) observed, ". . . The denouement is scarcely satisfactory, for it is not quite clear how Mr. Vance reaches his conclusions." The reviewer added, "Several persons, as is the case in most murder mysteries, behave as though they were the slayers. Why they act so suspiciously is somewhat vague, but they succeed in deceiving the audience, which, after all, is the main idea." As for the star of this offering, the *Times* decided, "Evidently it takes experience to play the role of Philo Vance, for Mr. William, while he does fair work, is not as easy and smooth in the role as was Mr. Powell."

DRESSED TO KILL (Twentieth Century-Fox, 1941) 75 minutes.

Producer, Sol M. Wurtzel; director, Eugene Forde; based on the character created by Brett Halliday [Davis Dresser] and the novel *The Dead Take No Bows* by Richard Burke; screenplay, Stanley Rauh, Manning O'Connor; camera, Glen McWilliams; editor, Fred Allen.

Lloyd Nolan (Michael Shayne); Mary Beth Hughes (Joanne La Marr); Sheila Ryan (Connie Earle); William Demarest (Inspector Pierson); Ben Carter (Rusty); Virginia Brissac (Emily); Erwin Kaiser (Otto Kuhn); Henry Daniell (Julian Davis); Dick Rich (Al); Milton Parsons (Max Allaron); Charles Arnt (Hal Brennon); Charles Trowbridge (David Earle); Hamilton MacFadden (Reporter); May Beatty (Phyllis Lathrop); Charles Wilson (Editor); Mantan Moreland (Sam).

The title DRESSED TO KILL has been used at least three times for theatrical feature films, the first two occasions for detective programmers, and the third in 1980 for Brian De Palma's elaborate excursion into the realm of erotic brutality. The 1941 feature is a Michael Shayne series opus while the 1946 film, *infra,* is the twelfth and last feature in Universal's Sherlock Holmes series starring Basil Rathbone and Nigel Bruce.

The 1941 film is based on Richard Burke's novel *The Dead Take*

No Bows (1941), which featured detective Quinny Hite and was altered to fit the continuing on-camera adventures of private investigator Michael Shayne. It is the third such case in producer Sol M. Wurtzel's Michael Shayne adventures at Twentieth Century-Fox. The feature opens with glib detective Michael Shayne (Lloyd Nolan) and fiancée Joanne La Marr (Mary Beth Hughes) leaving the marriage license bureau. Suddenly he hears a shot fired in the lobby of a nearby theatre. Shayne finds an elderly theatrical producer has been murdered and that the man had had two young girlfriends. The police, led by thick-headed Inspector Pierson (William Demarest), get on the case, but it is Shayne who brings in the killer. However, he loses the disgusted Joanne in the process.

Because such films as DRESSED TO KILL were churned out for diversion, not as art, filmgoers and reviewers demanded only plenty of action, flip chatter, and a whodunit that merely taxed the brain a bit to decipher. A. H. Weiler (*New York Times*) conceded, ". . . if it is not too tense, it is, at least, pleasantly laced with breezy, idiomatic chatter." As for the denouement, the *Times* reported, "If the mystery addicts detect a dearth of sliding panels and flying dirks in this offering, they, however, are also likely to solve this problem long before Mike Shayne."

DRESSED TO KILL (Universal, 1946) 72 minutes.

Executive producer, Howard Benedict; producer/director, Roy William Neill; based on the story by Sir Arthur Conan Dole; adaptor, Frank Gruber; screenplay, Leonard Lee; art directors, Jack Otterson, Marvin Obzine; set decorators, Russell A. Gausman, Edward R. Robinson; music director, Milton Rosen; song, Jack Brooks; assistant director, Melville Shyer; sound, Bernard D. Brown; camera, Maury Gertsman; editor, Saul A. Goodkind.

Basil Rathbone (Sherlock Holmes); Nigel Bruce (Dr. John H. Watson); Patricia Morison (Hilda Courtney); Edmond Breon (Gilbert Emery); Frederick Worlock (Colonel Cavanaugh); Carl Harbourd (Inspector Hoskins); Patricia Cameron (Evelyn Clifford); Tom P. Dillon (Detective Thompson); Harry Cording (Hamid); Topsy Glyn (Kilgour Child); Mary Gordon (Mrs. Hudson); Ian Wolfe (Man); Lillian Bronson (Tourist).

Universal's 1946 Sherlock Holmes picture begins at Dartmoor Prison where a prisoner is shown making music boxes. These are then sold at a London auction, with Colonel Cavanaugh (Frederick Worlock) failing to buy them. Gilbert Emory (Edmond Breon), a friend of Dr. Watson (Nigel Bruce), visits 221B Baker Street and tells Holmes (Basil Rathbone) and Watson how one of the music boxes was stolen from his home. That night Emory is looking

Basil Rathbone and Patricia Morison in DRESSED TO KILL (1946).

forward eagerly to a visit from lovely Hilda Courtney (Patricia Morison). However, when she arrives her henchman Hamid (Harry Cording) murders him. Holmes soon realizes that the quest for Emory's other music box was at the root of his death and, through underworld connections, Holmes learns that the combined tunes in the music boxes provide the means of finding the hiding place of stolen Bank of England five-pound-note engraving plates. Hilda leaves a clue which draws Holmes to her, and he is captured and left to die from carbon monoxide fumes in a locked garage. He manages to escape and back at Baker Street finds Hilda has been there and has stolen the music box he had hidden in his rooms. Through a statement from Dr. Watson, Holmes deduces the crooks' hiding place is the home of Dr. Samuel Johnson, and there Holmes and the police capture Hilda and her accomplices, Colonel Cavanaugh and Hamid. Both Holmes and Watson give each other full credit for solving the mystery.

Critics and viewers alike were decidedly mixed about DRESSED TO KILL. The *New York Herald-Tribune* offered, "Recommend highly to mystery fans," while the *New York Times* decided, "Heightened mystery is added by the fact that the title has nothing to do with the story. . . ." Suspense-wise, this installment was not up to the standards of the better entries in the series.

Basil Rathbone, tired of being typecast, left the Sherlock Holmes series after DRESSED TO KILL and also departed the popular Holmes radio program. However, unable to escape the role which had made him so famous, he portrayed Holmes again on television in the early 1950s and did the role briefly on Broadway in 1953 for three performances. He also would read several of the Sherlock Holmes stories for Audio Book and Caedmon Records.

THE DROWNING POOL (Warner Bros, 1975) Color 108 minutes.

Producers, Lawrence Turman, David Foster; associate producer, Howard W. Koch, Jr.; director, Stuart Rosenberg; based on the novel by Ross MacDonald [Kenneth Millar]; screenplay, Tracy Keenan Wynn, Lorenzo Semple, Jr., Walter Hill; assistant directors, Lee Rafner. Koch, Jr.; production designer, Paul Sylbert; art director, Ed O'Donovan; set decorator, Phil Abramson; wardrobe, Donald Brooks; music, Michael Small, Charles Fox; sound, Arthur Piantadosi, Les Fresholtz, Dick Tyler, Larry Jost; camera, Gordon Willis; editor, John Howard.

Paul Newman (Lew Harper); Joanne Woodward (Iris Devereaux); Tony Franciosa (Detective Broussard); Murray Hamilton (Kilbourne); Gail Strickland (Mavis Kilbourne); Melanie Griffith (Schuyler Devereaux); Linda Hayes (Gretchen); Richard Jaeckel (Detective Franks); Paul Koslo (Candy); Andy Robinson (Pat Reavis); Coral Browne (Olivia Devereaux); Richard Derr (James Devereaux); Helena Kallianiotes (Elaine Reaves); Leigh French (Redhead); Cecil Elliott (Motel Switchboard Operator); Peter Dassinger (Peter); Joe Canutt (Glo).

Paul Newman had the title role in the very successful detective melodrama, HARPER (1966), *q.v.*, and repeated it in this feature based on Ross MacDonald's 1950 novel. The gumshoe in MacDonald's works was named Lew Archer but Newman insisted that the surname be changed to Harper, so again he was cynical Lew Harper in THE DROWNING POOL*. *Variety* labeled the film "stylish, im-

---

*When THE DROWNING POOL was in pre-production, producers Lawrence Turman and David Foster were not sure whether the project should be a sequel to HARPER or whether to call the detective "Dave Ryan." Said Foster, "Sequels rarely fare well, so we decided to go with a brand new name, while still retaining the Archer/Harper characterization. . . . A few weeks into preproduction, we realized that it was foolish to make this change, since both reviewers and audiences would recognize the private eye as Harper anyway. Warners had taken a poll of moviegoers which determined that there was a strong memory retention with the public of Newman as

Paul Newman and Tony Franciosa in THE DROWNING POOL (1975).

probable, entertaining, superficial, well cast, and totally synthetic."
It summarized, "Production credits are all strong, and it's a pleasure
to watch the film, play smartly through its 108 minutes. But it all
adds up to zero."

Los Angeles private eye Lew Harper (Paul Newman) is called to
the Louisiana bayous by former girlfriend Iris Devereaux (Joanne
Woodward). She is being blackmailed by her homosexual husband
James (Richard Derr) because of a supposed romantic interlude
which she insists did not occur. Harper learns that Iris's mother-in-
law, Olivia Devereaux (Coral Browne), owns tidal lands which have
a fortune in oil beneath them and that corrupt oil baron Kilbourne
(Murray Hamilton) will go to any lengths to get the valuable

Harper." Also, according to Foster, the switch in locale for THE DROWNING
POOL came from Joanne Woodward, who asked early in pre-production, "Why do
all private-eye movies have to take place in California?" It was the actress who
suggested the New Orleans locale.

property which Olivia refuses to sell. When Olivia is murdered the chief suspect is ex-chauffeur Pat Reavis (Andy Robinson) and Harper uses Pat's sister Elaine (Helen Kallianiotes) to help him fit the pieces together. Also involved are Iris's nasty, nymphomaniac daughter Schuyler (Melanie Griffith), gangster Candy (Paul Koslo), prostitute Gretchen (Linda Haynes), Kilbourne's wife Mavis (Gail Strickland) and crooked police Detective Broussard (Tony Franciosa)—who was once Iris's lover—and his sadistic cohort, Detective Franks (Richard Jaeckel). There is also a frenzied quest for a little black book which holds the key to the case.

Arthur Knight (*The Hollywood Reporter*) assessed, "THE DROWN-ING POOL is one of those studio-prized packages that would seem to have every element for a sure-fire success firmly in place—every element, that is, except flair, imagination and daring."

For the record, the film's title refers to a hydrotherapy room in an abandoned mental hospital where the climactic scenes are set.

ELLERY QUEEN: DON'T LOOK BEHIND YOU (NBC-TV, 11/19/71) Color 100 minutes.

Executive producer, Edward J. Montagne; producer, Leonard J. Ackerman; director, Barry Shear; based on the novel *Cat of Many Tales* by Ellery Queen [Frederic Dannay, Manfred B. Lee]; teleplay, Ted Leighton; art director, Alexander A. Mayer; music, Jerry Fielding; camera, William Margulies; editor, Sam E. Waxman.

Peter Lawford (Ellery Queen); Harry Morgan (Inspector Richard Queen); E. G. Marshall (Dr. Cazalis); Skye Aubrey (Christy); Stefanie Powers (Celeste); Coleen Gray (Mrs Cazalis); Morgan Sterne (Police Commissioner); Bill Zuckert (Sergeant Velie); Bob Hastings (Hal Hunter); Than Wyenn (Registrar); Buddy Lester (Policeman); Bill Lucking (Lieutenant Summers); Pat Delany (Miss Price).

ELLERY QUEEN: TOO MANY SUSPECTS (NBC-TV, 3/23/75) Color 78 minutes.

Producers, Richard Levinson, William Link; director, David Greene; based on the novel *The Fourth Side of the Triangle* by Ellery Queen [Frederic Dannay, Manfred B. Lee]; teleplay, Levinson, Link; music, Elmer Bernstein; art director, George C. Webb; camera, Howard R. Schwartz; editor, Douglas Stewart.

Jim Hutton (Ellery Queen); David Wayne (Inspector Richard Queen); Ray Milland (Carson McKell); Kim Hunter (Marion McKell); Monte Markham (Tom McKell); John Hillerman (Simon Brimmer);

John Larch (District Attorney); Tim O'Connor (Ben Waterson); Nancy Mehta (Monica Gray); Warren Berlinger (Eddie Carter); Harry Von Zell (Announcer); Gail Strickland (Gail Stevens); Tom Reese (Sergeant Velie); Vic Mohica (Ramon); Dwan Smith (Cora Edwards); James Lydon (Radio Actor); John Finnegan (Matthew Thomas Cleary); Rosanna Huffman (Penny); and: Basil Hoffman, Ross Elliott.

The character of Ellery Queen was far more successful on television than in the movies. The Frederic Dannay-Manfred Lee character* first came to the small screen in its infancy in the live DuMont network series, "The Adventures of Ellery Queen," with John Hart as the sleuth in the fall of 1950. The show ran until late in 1951 when it switched to ABC-TV, where it ran for a year with Lee Bowman cast as Queen. Florenz Ames played Inspector Richard Queen, Ellery's policeman father, on both networks. In 1954, Hugh Marlowe, who had played Queen on radio, took over the role for a syndicated series which became known as "Murder Is My Business" in 1956. Early in 1959 the property became known as "Ellery Queen" and Lee Philips assumed the title part, while the character of Inspector Queen was deleted from the program.

In 1971 NBC-TV attempted to resurrect Ellery Queen, whose name was still being used for a popular monthly detective short story magazine, with the TV movie ELLERY QUEEN: DON'T LOOK BEHIND YOU. It was telecast November 19, 1971 as the pilot for a projected series which did not sell. Its chief hindrance was the casting of Peter Lawford as a *British* Ellery, although no fault could be found with Harry Morgan as the irascible Inspector Queen, here shown to be Ellery's American uncle. Filmed on location in New York City, the plot has the city's police baffled by a strangler whose victims' ages decrease with each crime. The female targets are disposed of with a pink cord, the men with blue cords. The telefeature was drawn out and static; it was based on the 1949 Queen novel, *Cat of Many Tails*. *TV Movies and Video Guide* (1988) found the film to be an "Entertaining, easily forgettable murder mystery. . . . . " Judith Crist in *TV Guide to the Movies* (1974) noted, ". . . It takes twice as long as it should on tediously plotted course."

Four years later NBC-TV again revived the character with another TV movie, ELLERY QUEEN, which was aired on March

---

*In *Detectionary* editors Otto Penzler, Chris Steinbrunner, and Marvin Lachman describe the detective thusly: "In his early years, Ellery Queen was a supercilious aristocrat who condescendingly assisted his long-suffering father. . . . Young Ellery was a sartorial cliché, dressed in tweeds, wearing pince-nez, and carrying a walking stick. Tall and slender. . . . Later in his career, he dropped both the arrogance and the affected eyeglasses. He acquired a sense of humor. . . ."

23, 1975. This time, however, the network had a success and the movie proved to be a good springboard for the "Ellery Queen" TV series which followed: it ran on the network for the 1975-76 season. The telefeature has Ellery Queen (Jim Hutton) and his father, Inspector Queen (David Wayne), on the trail of the murderer of a fashion designer, the mistress of a wealthy man. The movie was based on the Queen novel, *The Fourth Side of the Triangle* (1965) and was adapted by the team of Richard Levinson and William Link who devised "Columbo" and later "Murder, She Wrote." Judith Crist in *TV Guide* magazine praised the film for being "Stylishly done in late-40s fashion," while *TV Movies and Video Guide* (1988) judged it an "entertaining, light-hearted period detective movie" and Alvin H. Marill in *Movies Made for Television* (1987) appreciated it as "an atmospheric whodunit."

Even better than the TV film, which was also known as TOO MANY SUSPECTS, was the "Ellery Queen" TV series in which Hutton and Wayne continued their roles. Adding to the fun was John Hillerman as brittle, all-knowing radio sleuth, Simon Brimmer. The program, which nicely captured the feel of the Queen works, boasted a bevy of top guest stars, quality scripts, and high production values. But it failed to make sufficient headway in viewer ratings and was cancelled after one season.

EMIL UND DIE DETEKTIVE [Emil and the Detective] (UFA, 1931) 75 minutes.

Production supervisor, Guenther Stapenhorst; director, Gerhard Lamprocht; based on the novel by Erich Kastner; adaptor, Billy Wilder; sound, Hermann Firtzching; camera, Werner Brandes.

Fritz Rasp (The Baron); Rolf Wenkhaus (Emil); Kaethe Haack (Mrs. Tischbein); Olga Engl (Grandmother); Inge Landgut (Pony Huetchen); Hans Schaufuss (Gustav the Hoop); Hans Richeter (Flying Stag); Hans Lochr (Dienstag); Ernst-Eberhard Reling (Gerald).

EMIL AND THE DETECTIVES (Buena Vista, 1964) Color 99 minutes.

Presenter, Walt Disney; associate producer, Peter V. Herald; director, Peter Tewksbury; based on the novel *Emil und die Detektive* by Erich Kastner; screenplay, A. J. Carothers; art directors, Werner Schlichting, Isabella Schlicting; costumes, Leo Bei, Josef Wanke; makeup, Jupp Paschke, Joachim Schmalor; music, Heinz Schreiter; assistant director, Brigitte Liphardt; sound, Bernard Reicherts; camera, Gunter Senfleben; editors, Thomas Stanford, Cotton Warburton.

Walter Slezak (The Baron); Bryan Russell (Emil); Roger Mobley (Gustav); Heinz Schubert (Grundeis); Peter Ehrlich (Muller); Cindy

Cassell (Pony); Elsa Wagner (Nana); Wolfgang Volz (Stucke); Eva-Ingeborg Scholtz (Frau Tischbein); Franz Nicklisch (Desk Sergeant); Brian Richardson (Professor); David Petrychka (Dienstag); Robert Swann (Hermann); Ann Noland (Frieda); Ronnie Johnson (Rudolf); Rick Johnson (Hans); Paul Glawion (Traffic Policeman); Gerhard Retschy (Officer Kiessling); Viktor Hospach (Proprietor of Newsstand); Konrad Thoms (Waiter); Egon Vogel (Dispatcher); Gert Wiedenhofen (Policeman); Georg Rebentisch (Bus Driver); Rolf Rolphs (Butler); Roswitha Habedank (Parlor Maid).

Erich Kastner's novel *Emil und die Detektive* (1929) has been the basis for six(!) theatrical films of the same title, the initial picturization being the 1931 German feature, EMIL UND DIE DETEKTIVE, directed by Gerhart Lamprecht (who later became a film historian) and with a screenplay by Billy Wilder (who gained great fame as a Hollywood scenarist/director/producer). The novel was not published in the United States until two years after the film's release. Walt Disney remade EMIL AND THE DETECTIVES in 1964 and in both films the detectives are a gang of youths who aid a peer in tracking down the thief who stole the boy's money.

EMIL UND DIE DETEKTIVE tells of a young boy, Emil (Rolf Wenkhaus), whose mother sends him from their small home town on a train to Berlin with money for his grandmother. En route a thief, the Baron (Fritz Rasp) steals the envelope containing the money. When the train reaches Berlin Emil begins to systematically trail the thief. Along the way he enlists the assistance of a group of street children. Locating the hotel where the thief is staying, the youngsters establish their headquarters in a vacant lot across the street and one of the boys begins intercepting the man's telephone calls. The local police finally become involved in the case and when the children corner the crook, the law discovers he is a wanted criminal. The youths receive a reward for their efforts.

When the German-language feature opened in New York in December 1931, *Variety* reported, "It's a smart comedy of smart kids well directed, acted and photographed. It's not only modern, it's logical." In *Caligari to Hitler* (1947), Siegfried Kraucauer termed the film "charming and very successful" and noted the use of light and darkness to exemplify good and evil in the feature. "Light once and for all defeats darkness in that magnificent sequence in which the thief is eventually cornered. Under a radiant morning sun, which seems to scoff at his eerie blackness, this Pied Piper in reverse tries in vain to escape the ever-increasing crowd of children who pursue and besiege him."

With its universal theme of honest youths joining together to defeat a thieving adult, *Emil und die Detektive* was a natural property to be remade in a variety of countries. It was produced in England by Gaumont-British in 1935 as the sticky EMIL AND THE DETECTIVES with John Williams as Emil and George Hayes as "the man." (In the U.S., this picture was titled EMIL.) In 1954 another German version of the film, this time in color, starred Kurt Meisel, Peter Finkbeiner, and Margaret Haagan. There was a Japanese movie production of the novel in 1956 and a Brazilian screen adaptation of the book in 1958. In 1964 Peter Tewksbury remade the charming story as EMIL AND THE DETECTIVES, with lensing in West Germany. Plotwise the feature is quite close to the 1931 picture although here the main crook (Walter Slezak) has two comrades and the trio are called "The Three Shrinks." Also a subplot has them planning to tunnel into a bank to carry off a big heist. Bryan Russell plays Emil who, this time, is robbed on a bus not a train. While *Variety* termed the film an "amusing cops-and-robbers tale" it was essentially a drab remake of the 1931 near-classic. Leonard Maltin assessed in *The Disney Films* (1973) that ". . . .this dreary film comes as a severe disappointment. . . . The film moves at a snail's pace, crawling along for ninety-nine minutes, far too much time to spend on such a basic story. . . . It has the raw material for a good movie, but in the end what kills it is the sluggish pace and needlessly padded script." About the technicolor film's only asset, outside its European location settings, is Walter Slezak's performance as the high-living chief crook.

ENEMY AGENTS MEET ELLERY QUEEN (Columbia, 1942) 64 minutes.

Producer, Ralph Cohn; associate producer, Rudolph Flothow; director, James Hogan; based on characters created by Ellery Queen [Frederic Dannay, Manfred B. Lee]; screenplay, Erle Taylor; additional dialogue, Arthur Strawn; music, Lee Zahler; camera, James S. Brown; editor, Dwight Caldwell.

William Gargan (Ellery Queen); Margaret Lindsay (Nikki Porter); Charley Grapewin (Inspector Richard Queen); Gale Sondergaard (Mrs. Van Dorn); Gilbert Roland (Paul Gillette); Sig Ruman (Heinrich); James Burke (Sergeant Velie); Ernest Dorian (Morse); Felix Basch (Helm); Minor Watson (Commodore Lang); John Hamilton (Commissioner Bracken); James Seay (Sergeant Stevens); Louis Donath (Reece); Dick Wessel (Sailor).

Late in the summer of 1942, ENEMY AGENTS MEET ELLERY QUEEN was unleashed as a bottom-half dual-biller. It proved to be the last of seven Ellery Queen features Larry Darmour produced at Columbia Pictures, where low-costing production series were a

Margaret Lindsay and William Gargan in ENEMY AGENTS MEET ELLERY QUEEN (1942).

specialty. Ralph Bellamy starred in the first four entries and then was replaced by William Gargan in the final three;* Margaret Lindsay was helpful secretary Nikki Porter in all the films and Charley Grapewin was wise Inspector Queen. The series, as a whole, was a vapid one, never even attaining the level of mindless breeziness of the Chester Morris/Boston Blackie detective series at the same studio, and this final installment proved to be the least effective of the lot. *Variety* tabbed it as "weak" but noted it brought the property to a close with "a rousing slugfest between some sailors and marines and a gang of Nazi spies. It's a slam-bang brawl and provides

---

*Ralph Bellamy and William Gargan, both excellent actors, walked through their screen roles as Ellery Queen. They did much better as television detectives. Bellamy starred as private eye Mike Barnett in "Man Against Crime" (1949-54) while William Gargan scored in the lead as "Martin Kane, Private Eye" (1949-51) and later in "The New Adventures of Martin Kane" (1957).

virtually the only life to a feeble washup of what had become a tired series."

Allied agent Paul Gillette (Gilbert Roland) had been smuggling diamonds from the Netherlands to the United States by way of Egypt. When he is murdered both the Nazis and the Americans are after the gems, which have been secreted in a mummy case as a part of a display of Egyptian artifacts. Detective Ellery Queen (William Gargan) is hired to escort the relics to the U.S., not knowing that the diamonds are hidden in the case. When the Nazis make an appearance, Ellery and his father, Inspector Queen (Charley Grapewin), along with Ellery's pert girlfriend/secretary Nikki Porter (Margaret Lindsay), become completely involved in the case. It leads them to such diverse spots as an art gallery, a jewelry shop, an athletic club, and a cemetery before the trio are captured by villains, with the military coming to their timely rescue.

ENTER ARSENE LUPIN (Universal, 1944) 72 minutes.

Producer/director, Ford Beebe; based on characters created by Maurice LeBlanc, Frank de Croissent; screenplay, Bertram Millhauser; art directors, John B. Goodman, Abraham Grossman; music/music director, Milton Rosen; camera, Hal Mohr; editor, Saul A. Goodkind.

Charles Korvin (Arsène Lupin); Ella Raines (Stacie); J. Carrol Naish (Ganimard); George Dolenz (Dubose); Gale Sondergaard (Bessie Seagrave); Miles Mander (Charles Seagrave); Leyland Hodgson (Constable Ryder); Tom Pilkington (Pollett); Lillian Bronson (Wheeler); Holmes Herbert (Jobson); Charles Latorre (Inspector Cogwell); Gerald Hamer (Doc Marling); Ed Cooper (Cartwright); Art Foster (Superintendent); Clyde Kenny (Beckwith); Alphonse Martell (Conductor).

See: ARSENE LUPIN (1932) [essay].

EVIL UNDER THE SUN (Universal, 1982) Color 117 minutes.

Producers, John Brabourne, Richard Goodwin; associate producer, Michael-John Knatchbull; director, Guy Hamilton; based on the novel by Agatha Christie; screenplay, Anthony Schaffer; production designer, Elliott Scott; art director, Alan Cassie; set decorator, Peter Howitt; costumes, Anthony Powell; makeup, Jill Carpenter; music, Cole Porter; assistant director, Derek Cracknell; sound, John Mitchell, Bill Rowe, John Richards; sound editor, Nicholas Stevenson; camera, Christopher Challis; editor, Richard Marden.

Peter Ustinov (Hercule Poirot); Colin Blakely (Sir Horace Blatt); Jane Birkin (Christine Redfern); Nicholas Clay (Patrick Redfern [Patrick Ruber]); Maggie Smith (Daphne Castle); Roddy

McDowall (Rex Brewster); Sylvia Miles (Myra Gardener); James
Mason (Odell Gardener); Denis Quilley (Kenneth Marshall); Diana
Rigg (Arlena Marshall); Emily Hone (Linda Marshall); John Alderson
(Police Sergeant); Paul Antrim (Police Inspector); Cyril Conway
(Police Surgeon); Barbara Hicks (Flewitt's Secretary); Richard Vernon
(Flewitt); Robert Dorning (Concierge); Dimitri Andreas (Gino).

Guy Hamilton directed the overlooked Agatha Christie murder mystery, THE MIRROR CRACK'D (1980), *q.v.*, with Angela
Lansbury as Miss Jane Marple and two years later he helmed one of
Miss Christie's Hercule Poirot mysteries, EVIL UNDER THE
SUN, in which Peter Ustinov, who had portrayed the Belgian
detective in DEATH ON THE NILE (1978), *q.v.*, played Poirot
again. Regarding the opulent new production, Michael Tennenbaum
notes in *The New Bedside, Bathtub & Armchair Companion to Agatha
Christie* (1986) that ". . . the real actors' pleasant sojourn in sunny
Majorca was occasionally interrupted by the fact they were to make a
movie. James Mason recalled this time as the most relaxed experience of his long career. His laid-back attitude seems to have infected
the entire production and the critics were unanimous in mentioning
the garish period costumes and Cole Porter sound track over the
slow-moving plot and direction."

In 1938 Belgian detective Hercule Poirot (Peter Ustinov) is
vacationing on the beautiful Adriatic island of Tyrrheian at an
elegant resort owned by former actress Daphne Castle (Maggie
Smith). Among the guests are: retired, self-centered Broadway star
Arlena Marshall (Diana Rigg), her husband Kenneth (Denis Quilley)
and her dour step-daughter Linda (Emily Hone); an unhappy young
married couple (Jane Birkin, Nicholas Clay); a social climbing older
couple who produce plays (James Mason, Sylvia Miles); a British
dignitary (Colin Blakely); and the high-strung Hollywood fan
magazine writer Rex Brewster (Roddy McDowall). The nasty Arlena
causes trouble for many of her fellow guests, including flaunting her
love affairs before her husband, being rude and nasty to Linda, and
going back on a promise to the bitchy Brewster to let him publish a
book on her life. Daphne also has a grudge against her because the
star cheated her out of a stage success. When Arlene is found
murdered on the beach, Poirot sets out to solve the case, in which
most of the isle's inhabitants have a motive for the strangulation and
all have alibis.

Audience response to this adaptation of Agatha Christie's 1941
novel was not positive. As Al Clark reflected in *The Film Year Book
1983* (1983), this fourth John Bradbourne-Richard Goodwin production of a Christie novel ". . . reveals a formula in such an ad-
vanced state of decay that it is virtually pleading to be put out of its

rickety and protracted misery. With an amalgam of Cole Porter tunes to knock up the nostalgia count, and a leadenly overstated Anthony Shaffer screenplay, a bunch of all-star clothes horses amble through some backdated notion of [Noel] Cowardish wit by exchanging a dutiful succession of contrived epigrams. By the time it finally happens, the murder of the bitch Broadway star is almost a relief. By the time Poirot reveals who did it—years later, it feels—nobody cares."

On the other hand, the formula, as before, appealed to Roger Ebert. In his *Movie Home Companion 1989* (1988) he decided, "I can observe, however, that one of the delights of the movies made from Agatha Christie novels is their almost complete lack of passion: they substitute wit and style. Nobody really cares who gets bumped off, and nobody really misses the departed. What's important is that all the right clues be distributed, so that Poirot and the audience can pick them up, mull them over, and discover the culprit." Regarding this film's crime solver Ebert enthused, ". . . Peter Ustinov creates a wonderful mixture of the mentally polished and physically maladroit. He has a bit of business involving a dip in the sea that is so perfectly timed and acted it tells us everything we ever wanted to know about Poirot's appetite for exercise. He is so expansive, so beaming, so superior, in the opening scenes that he remains spiritually present throughout the film, even when he's not on screen."

Despite its "name" cast and heavy production values, EVIL UNDER THE SUN grossed only $4,000,000 in domestic film rentals. Nevertheless, Peter Ustinov continued to play Hercule Poirot in a series of made-for-TV movies such as THIRTEEN AT DINNER (1985) and DEAD MAN'S FOLLY (1986), *qq.v.*, and the disastrous theatrical release failure, APPOINTMENT WITH DEATH (1988), *q.v.*

THE EX-MRS. BRADFORD (RKO, 1936) 87 minutes.

Associate producer Edward Kaufman; director, Stephen Roberts; story, James Edward Grant; screenplay, Anthony Veiller; music director, Roy Webb; camera, J. Roy Hunt; editor, Arthur Roberts.

William Powell (Dr. Lawrence Bradford); Jean Arthur (Paula Bradford); James Gleason (Inspector Corrigan); Eric Blore (Stokes); Robert Armstrong (Nick Martel); Lila Lee (Miss Prentiss); Grant Mitchell (Mr. Summers); Erin O'Brien-Moore (Mrs. Summers); Ralph Morgan (Mr. Hutchins); Lucile Gleason (Mrs. Hutchins); Frank M. Thomas (Salsbury); Frank Reicher (Henry Strand); Charles Richman (Turf Club President); John Sheehan (Murphy); Paul Fix (Lou Pender); Johnny Arthur (Frankenstein Process Server); Spencer

Charters (Coroner); James Donlan (Cabby); Dorothy Granger (Receptionist); Stanley Blystone (Police Radio Operator); Syd Saylor (Detective); Rollo Lloyd (Landlord); Charles McMurphy (Cop); Sam Hayes (Race Announcer); Edward McWade (Minister—on Film); John Dilson (Analyst).

Following the success of STAR OF MIDNIGHT (1935), *q.v.*, an imitator of THE THIN MAN (1934), *q.v.*, RKO signed the debonair star, William Powell, of that pair of comedy-mysteries to do still a third such feature, THE EX-MRS. BRADFORD. Like STAR OF MIDNIGHT it was directed by Stephen Roberts; its author Anthony Veiller had co-scripted the 1935 RKO release. Jean Arthur, as the title character, adds much to the proceedings as the dizzy, nervous, always-jumping-to-conclusions ex-wife who draws her surgeon former husband into several murders while the two of them drink endlessly, hardly drawing a sober breath during the whole pell-mell proceedings.

Surgeon Dr. Lawrence Bradford (William Powell) takes his ex-wife Paula (Jean Arthur), a very nervous and prolific crime novel writer, to the horse races. While there a jockey dies, and Paula has a hunch it is murder. Bradford "takes over" the investigation of the case and after two more murders occur, baffled police Inspector Corrigan (James Gleason) believes the good doctor is the villain. To save himself, Bradford sets out to solve the mystery, which by now includes two additional homicides. The surgeon is hampered by the good intentions of his pesky ex-wife, but he finally unravels the clues. He and the battling Paula plan to rewed.

In the *New York Times*, Frank S. Nugent wrote, "Of all the attempted copies of the justly celebrated William Powell-Myrna Loy comedy (THE THIN MAN), THE EX-MRS. BRADFORD comes closest to approximating its gaiety, impudence and ability to entertain. . . . While the mystery story has been worked out ingeniously, it is not the race track murders or their solution that keeps the picture spinning, but the amusing by-play among Mr. Powell, Miss Arthur and that constant source of delight, Eric Blore, the butler. They are as pleasant a comic trio we have found this year. . . . One of the year's top-flight comedies."

In retrospect, Ted Sennett extolled in *Lunatics and Lovers* (1973), "William Powell and Jean Arthur deliver their flippant lines in high style, especially in a dinner scene at which Paula serves gelatin in a variety of forms. (She is testing a clue, rather than indulging in culinary experiments.) 'The ex-Bradfords at home,' she sighs, but he is determined to stay aloof. 'We're on the verge of getting sentimental,' he warns her—in vain."

EXPOSED (Republic, 1947) 59 minutes.

Producer, William J. O'Sullivan; director, George Blair; story, Charles Moran; screenplay, Royal K. Cole, Moran; music, Ernest Gold; camera, William Bradford; editor, Irving M. Schoenberg.

Adele Mara (Belinda Prentice); Robert Scott (William Foreman, III); Adrian Booth (Judith); Robert Armstrong (Inspector Prentice); William Haade (Iggy Broty); Bob Steele (Chicago); Harry Shannon (Severance); Charles Evans (Jonathan Lowell); Joyce Compton (Emmy); Russell Hicks (Colonel Bentry); Paul E. Burns (Professor Ordson); Colin Campbell (Dr. Richard); Edward Gargan (Big Mac); Mary Gordon (Miss Keets); Patricia Knox (Waitress).

Pretty private detective Belinda Prentice (Adele Mara) is hired by Colonel Bentry (Russell Hicks) to investigate the activities of his stepson, William Foreman III (Robert Scott), but when Belinda visits the man's apartment for information she finds the colonel has been murdered. Aided by the Colonel's assistant, Iggy Broty (William Haade), Belinda investigates the crime, as do the police, headed

Adele Mara and Robert Scott in EXPOSED (1947).

by Inspector Prentice (Robert Armstrong), Belinda's father. When a gunman named Chicago (Bob Steele) is found to be a part of the proceedings, Belinda traces backwards to find his employer as the cause of the mayhem.

EXPOSED is yet another 1940s effort to develop a detective tale around the character of an engaging female sleuth. Earlier attempts had included Jane Wyman in PRIVATE DETECTIVE (1939), *q.v.*, and a trio of pictures focused around Monogram's "Detective Kitty O'Day" in the mid-1940s. Running less than one hour, this compact film was definitely a double-bill item, but not an uninteresting one. On the plus side are a fine support cast, especially Robert Armstrong as the crime solver's cop father and Bob Steele as the hired gunsel, a part he had performed to perfection the year before in THE BIG SLEEP, *q.v.*

Variety rated EXPOSED "OK entertainment" and added that star Adele Mara "continues to show cinema promise." On the other hand, Don Miller opined in "Private Eyes" (*Focus on Film* magazine, Autumn 1975), "Another attempt by the studio [Republic] to develop a feminine private eye was doomed to failure . . . although Royal Cole together with Charles Moran did dish up some breezy dialogue for Moran's creation, Belinda Prentice. . . . Unhappily, their efforts were negated by the presence of Adele Mara in the role, misreading practically every line."

EYES IN THE NIGHT (Metro-Goldwyn-Mayer, 1942) 90 minutes.

Producer, Jack Chertok; director, Fred Zinnemann; based on the novel *Odor of Violets* by Baynard Kendrick; screenplay, Guy Trosper; art director, Cedric Gibbons; camera, Robert Planck, Charles Lawton; editor, Ralph Winters.

Edward Arnold (Captain Duncan Maclain); Ann Harding (Norma Lawry); Donna Reed (Barbara Lawry); Katherine Emery (Cheli Scott); Horace [Stephen] McNally (Gabriel Hoffman); Allen Jenkins (Marty); Stanley C. Ridges (Hansen); Reginald Denny (Stephen Lawry); John Emery (Paul Gerente); Rosemary De Camp (Vera Hoffman); Erik Rolf (Boyd); Barry Nelson (Busch); Reginald Sheffield (Victor); Steven Geray (Anderson); Mantan Moreland (Allistair); Friday (The Dog); Milburn Stone (Pete); Frances Rafferty (Girl); Edward Kilroy (Pilot); John Butler (Driver); William Nye (Hugo); Cliff Danielson Fred Walburn, Robert Winkler, Walter Tetley (Boys); Frank Thomas (Police Lieutenant); Marie Windsor (Bit).

Edward Arnold had a solid reputation as a screen sleuth after appearing in films like MURDER IN THE BLUE ROOM (1933), REMEMBER LAST NIGHT? (1935), and MEET NERO WOLFE (1935), *qq.v.*, and he further enhanced his screen profession by playing Baynard Kendrick's blind sleuth Duncan Maclain in two well-made programmers for MGM in the 1940s: EYES IN THE NIGHT (1942) and THE HIDDEN EYE (1945).

EYES IN THE NIGHT, based on Kendrick's novel *Odor of Violets* (1942) has blind detective Duncan Maclain (Edward Arnold)* being hired by his friend, patrician Norma Lawry (Ann Harding), to investigate stock company actor Paul Gerente (John Emery). Gerente is involved with her demanding stepdaughter Barbara (Donna Reed) and, also may be trying to steal an invention from her husband Stephen (Reginald Denny). With the aid of his associate, Marty (Allen Jenkins), and his seeing-eye German shepherd dog Friday (himself), the detective proves the crimes were perpetrated by a member of a gang of Axis spies. The espionage agents capture Maclain but he escapes thanks to Friday's intervention.

The film was directed by Fred Zinnemann who had previously handled GRAND CENTRAL MURDER (1942), *q.v.* Don Miller evaluated in *B Movies* (1973), "As a mystery thriller, EYES IN THE NIGHT held interest from the beginning to the end, which was action-paced in a way not customarily provided by the rather staid MGM scripting department. Zinnemann paced the last quarter of the film in near-serial fashion. . . . Too, the sequences dealing with the sightless sleuth and his method of working held a fascination of its own." As the *New York Times* (Theodore Strauss) explained, "A blind man walking through a darkened room into which a murderer may stalk at any moment is a highly suggestive situation. . . . And when, about to be shot in the basement, the detective smashes the light and calls to his would-be killer: 'Now you're in my world—darkness!' it is hokum, certainly, but the audience is at the edge of the chairs."

It was three years before another adventure of the blind crime-stopper reached the screen in the summer of 1945. THE HIDDEN EYES was based only on the Kendrick characters. Here sightless detective Duncan Maclain (Edward Arnold) attempts to solve three murders in which the fragrance of an Oriental perfume is evident. The sleuth, however, understands this is merely a cover-up as he strives to locate the killer while working to prove that the main suspect, Barry Gifford (Paul Langton), is innocent. Maclain locates

---

*In *Detectionary* (1977), edited by Otto Penzler, Chris Steinbrunner, and Marvin Lachman, Captain Duncan Maclain is described as "Young, wealthy and handsome" and having received his handicap in World War I while an intelligence officer. "Maclain has cultivated the ability to shoot at sounds. His chief recreations are reading his collection of Braille books, listening to his Capehart, and assembling giant jigsaw puzzles." The other four Duncan Maclain novels are *Blind Man's Buff* (1943), *Death Knell* (1945), *Out of Control* (1945), and *Reservations for Death* (1957).

the guilty party and engages him in a fight. He wins because of his special training in overcoming his handicap. "Whodunit factors fail to develop much suspense as directed by Richard Whorf, and interest goes mainly to the dog, Friday, who acts as the seeing eye for the yarn's blind detective" (*Variety*). The *New York Times* (Thomas M. Pryor) agreed, "Most of the time the characters just stand around talking, and what they have to say is not very enlightening. . . . This one won't stump the armchair sleuths, but as we mentioned before, it is a simple old-fashioned mystery exercise. For that, a mild hooray."

This was the end of the road onscreen for Duncan Maclain but in 1971-72 James Franciscus would star in "Longstreet," a teleseries dealing with a New Orleans insurance company investigator who is blinded. With the aid of his German shepherd guide dog and an electronic cane he continues his case-solving career.

THE FALCON AND THE CO-EDS (RKO, 1943) 67 minutes.

Producer, Maurice Geraghty; director William Clemens; based on the character creator by Michael Arlen [Diran Kuyumjian]; story, Ardel Wray; screenplay, Wray, Gerald Geraghty; art director, Albert D. Agostino; music director, C. Bakaleinikoff; camera, Roy Hunt; editor, Theron Warth.

Tom Conway (Tom Lawrence, the Falcon); Jean Brooks (Vicky Gaines); Rita Corday (Marguerita Serena); Amelita Ward (Jane Harris); Isabel Jewell (Mary Phoebus); George Givot (Dr. Anatole Graelich); Cliff Clark (Inspector Timothy Donovan); Ed Gargan (Bates); Barbara Brown (Miss Keyes); Juanita Alvarez, Ruth Alvarez, Nancy McCollum (The Ughs); Patti Brill (Beanie Smith); Olin Howlin (Goodwilie); Ian Wolfe (Eustace L. Harley); Dorothy Maloney [Malone], Julia Hopkins, Dorothy Kelly (Co-eds); Margaret Landry (Sarey Ann); Carole Gallagher (Elsie); Barbara Lyn (Mildred); Mary Halsey (Telephone Operator); Perc Launders (Garage Man); Elaine Riley (Ellen); Dorothy Christy (Maya Harris); Anne O'Neal (Miss Hicks); Ruth Cherrington (Dowager); and: Rosemary LaPlanche, Barbara Coleman, Daun Kennedy.

After making three films based on Michael Arlen's [Diran Kuyumjian] character the Falcon, George Sanders wanted out of the role. Hoping to keep him for one more such film, RKO teamed him with his brother, Tom Conway, for THE FALCON'S BROTHER (1942), which the studio estimated would conclude the popular series. Instead Conway's performance caught the public's fancy and he went on to star in nine additional Falcon pictures at the studio. Of the ten Falcon adventures Tom Conway made, THE FALCON AND THE CO-EDS is the best with its *film noir* motif at a remote

Nancy McCullum, George Givot, Juanita Alvarez, Jean Brooks, Tom Conway and Ruth Alvarez in THE FALCON AND THE CO-EDS (1943).

girls' school at the seaside and C. Bakaleinikoff's haunting background music. The movie contains a moody, brooding feeling not that often associated with "B" detective features.

Co-ed Jane Harris (Amelita Ward) calls the police and asks for the phone number of her mother's friend, Tom Lawrence, the Falcon (Tom Conway), in connection with the murder of one of her teachers, Professor Alex Jameson, at Bluecliff Seminary. The gullible Sergeant Bates (Edward Gargan) gives her Lawrence's number and his boss, Inspector Timothy Donovan (Cliff Clark), immediately starts to stalk the Falcon. Meanwhile, Lawrence arrives at Bluecliff and informs the head mistress, Miss Keyes (Barbara Brown), that he is an insurance investigator looking into Jameson's death because of a large insurance policy. He meets Professor Anatole Graelich (George Givot), who shared a cottage with Jameson and signed his death report as a heart attack. Lawrence also becomes acquainted with Vicky Gaines (Jean Brooks), the drama coach, who was loved by both Jameson and Graelich. Jane tells the Falcon that another student, Marguerita (Rita Corday), is psychic and had predicted

Jameson's demise. Later, in talking with undertaker Eustace L. Harley (Ian Wolfe), the Falcon is led to believe that Jameson may have committed suicide. Graelich later admits that Miss Keyes ordered him to forge the death report to avoid unfavorable publicity. Soon Miss Keyes is found dead, killed with a sword. Her will reveals that she has left the school to Vicky, which leads Donovan to believe that Vicky and her lover, Graelich are the wrongdoers. But the Falcon points out that he lacks necessary proof. Donovan orders Marguerita arrested (she was found near Miss Keyes' corpse) and thinking herself insane, the hysterical girl rushes to the bluff to throw herself over the cliff. The Falcon arrives in time to find the distraught girl being taunted by the actual murderess. The latter loses her footing and falls to her death.

The *New York Daily News* (Wanda Hale) ranked this film "the most amusing and baffling of the series," while *Variety* endorsed it as a "lively and neatly-concocted whodunit. . . ."

Studying this entry from the perspective of distance, Doug McClelland championed in *The Golden Age of "B" Movies* (1978), "One of the niceties of the Falcon series was its sense of humor, never sprightlier than in THE FALCON AND THE CO-EDS. Early in the film, when Conway alighted from the bus . . . undertaker Ian Wolfe, standing in front of his establishment asked, 'Can I help you?' Responded Conway, checking the setup, 'Not just yet.' Later on, student Amelita Ward told the debonair Conway that Corday had predicted another murder and she feared for his safety because Corday said it would be 'some elderly person.'"

Few films of the 1940s, or of today, have provided such a backdrop of attractive females. The idea of the woman-chasing Falcon loose in a girls' school gave this picture its own special appeal. Among the students was future Academy Award winner Dorothy Maloney [Malone]. And not to be overlooked was the predictable but exemplary comedy relief provided by Edward Gargan as the dense Bates, always the bane of his short-tempered boss, Inspector Donovan.

FAREWELL, MY LOVELY (Avco-Embassy, 1975) Color 97 minutes.

Executive producers, Elliott Kastner, Jerry Bick; producers, George Pappas, Jerry Bruckheimer; director, Dick Richards; based on the novel by Raymond Chandler; screenplay, David Zelag Goodman; assistant directors, Henry Lange, David Sonsa; production designer, Dean Tavoularis; art director, Angelo Graham; set decorator, Bob Nelson; costumes, Tony Scarano, Sandy Berke; makeup, Frank Westmore; music, David Shire; songs: Jule Styne, Ned Miller Chester Cohn, and Bennie Krueger; Styne and Sammy

Cahn; music editor, Ralph James Hall; assistant directors, Henry Langer, Jr., David O. Sosna; sound, Tom Verton, Dick Portman; sound effects, Bill Phillips; special effects, Chuck Gaspar; camera, John Alonzo; editors, Walter Thompson, Joel Cox.

Robert Mitchum (Philip Marlowe); Charlotte Rampling (Mrs. Grayle [Velma]); John Ireland (Detective Lieutenant Nulty); Sylvia Miles (Mrs. Jessie Florian); Jack O'Halloran (Moose Malloy); Anthony Zerbe (Burnette); Harry Dean Stanton (Billy Rolfe); Jim Thompson (Judge Wilson Grayle); John O'Leary (Lindsay Marriott); Kate Murtagh (Frances Amthor); Walter McGinn (Tommy Ray); Jimmy Archer (Georgie); Joe Spinell (Nick); Sylvester Stallone (Kelly/Jonnie); Burt Gilliam (Cowboy); Ted Gehring (Roy); Logan Ramsey (Commissioner); Margie Hall (Woman); Jack Bernardi (Louis Levine); Ben Ohta (Patron in Pool Hall); Jerry Fujikawa (Fence); Richard Kennedy, John O'Neill, Mark Allen (Detectives); Andrew Harris (Mulatto Child); Napoleon Whiting (Hotel Clerk); John Eames (Butler) Rainbeaux [Cheryl] Smith (Doris); Stu Gilliam, Roosevelt Pratt (Men); Bill Gentry (Hood); Cory Shiozaki (Waiter); Noelle Worth (Girl); Wally Berns (Father); Lola Mason (Mother); Joan Shawlee (Woman in Ballroom); Edra Gale (Singer); Karen Gaston (Prostitute).

Raymond Chandler's second Philip Marlowe novel, *Farewell, My Lovely* (1940) first came to the screen in 1942 in the guise of THE FALCON TAKES OVER, with George Sanders as series character The Falcon replacing the Marlowe persona. Two years later appeared the definitive Dick Powell version, MURDER, MY SWEET, *q.v.* Following the fiasco of picturizing Raymond Chandler's THE LONG GOODBYE (1973), *q.v.*, producers Elliott Kastner and Jerry Bick made a third version of *Farewell, My Lovely*. Their ambition was to create a more reverent Philip Marlowe movie which would capture the flavor of the original work but still adapt it to current audience tastes. The result was a highly successful detective motion picture.

In Los Angeles in 1941 detective Philip Marlowe (Robert Mitchum) meets with his pal, police Lieutenant Nulty (John Ireland), in a rundown hotel to explain his involvement in several recent murder cases. Marlowe spells out how it all started with a job he had finding a runaway teenage girl. In the process he was hired by gigantic ex-convict Moose Malloy (Jack O'Halloran) to locate his long-lost lady love Velma. Marlowe is strong-armed into the case by Moose and at an all-black bar called Florian's, where Velma once worked when it was a white joint, Malloy ends up killing the bar owner. Marlowe questions the widow of the one-time owner of the place, a drunk slut named Jessie Florian (Sylvia Miles). She claims not to know Velma's whereabouts but sends him to one-time musician Tommy Ray (Walter McGinn), who gives Marlowe a photograph of Velma. He soon realizes it is a fake. Marlowe is hired by Lindsay Marriott (John O'Leary) to be a bodyguard when O'Leary pays a ransom for the return of a stolen jade necklace. Marlowe is knocked out at the rendezvous and wakes up to find his client murdered. Finding out that the necklace belonged to elderly Judge Wilson Grayle (Jim Thompson), Marlowe is confused when he learns from the judge that it is *not* missing from his collection. He also flirts with young Mrs. Grayle (Charlotte Rampling), who hires him to find Marriott's murderer. Back at his office Marlowe is knocked unconscious and awakens to find himself in a whorehouse run by notorious and politically powerful Frances Amthor (Kate Murtagh), a tough babe who demands to know Malloy's whereabouts—and now! His inability to cooperate results in his being beaten, dosed with drugs, and left to die. He recovers to escape from the brothel when Frances is shot down by her bouncer (Sylvester Stallone). At a party given by Mrs. Grayle he meets gambler Laird Burnette (Anthony Zerbe), who also wants him to find Malloy. After surviving a near fatal ambush, Marlowe finds Jessie Florian dead. At Burnette's offshore gambling yacht Burnette insists he never heard of Velma, but another visitor makes herself known and Malloy at last confronts the much sought after woman. It develops that Velma had been a hooker who later married well and her husband had been unaware of her sordid past. More killings occur before Nulty and his policemen arrive on the scene to wrap up the caper.

Robert Mitchum's memorable performance as the world-weary Philip Marlowe and the production's beautiful recreation of the Los Angeles of the early 1940s are the two prime assets of the sterling FAREWELL, MY LOVELY. Alvin H. Marill in *Films in Review* magazine (October 1975) notes that director Dick Richards " . . . captured the atmosphere; Mitchum captured everything else." Stephen Pendo in *Raymond Chandler on Screen* (1976) analyzed, "FAREWELL, MY LOVELY stands out as the excellent 'Marlowe' film. Its few faults are far outweighed by its many virtues, and it certainly comes close to realizing Richards' goal of creating 'the basic classic detective movie.'" The film does have two major character changes from the novel: the role of Ann Riordan was deleted and the character of mystic Jules Amthor became madam Frances Amthor in the movie. "The use of prostitution, vice, and corruption which was only hinted at in the earlier films is developed with a vengeance in FAREWELL, MY LOVELY; much of this atmosphere can be credited to an interest in simulating the aura of the film noir. A strong feeling of homage is present not only in the period settings but also in the situations and relationships developed in FAREWELL, MY LOVELY" (Carl F. Macek, *Magill's American Film Guide*, 1982).

Robert Mitchum would again play Philip Marlowe—with far less artistic and financial success—in a remake of THE BIG SLEEP (1978), *q.v.*

FAST AND FURIOUS (Metro-Goldwyn-Mayer, 1939) 70 minutes.

Producer, Frederick Stephani; director, Busby Berkeley; screenplay, Harry Kurnitz; music, Daniele Amfitheatrof; camera, Ray June; editor, Elmo Vernon.

Franchot Tone (Joel Sloane); Ann Sothern (Garda Sloane); Ruth Hussey (Lily Cole); Lee Bowman (Mike Stevens); Allyn Joslyn (Ted Bentley); John Miljan (Eric Bartell); Bernard Nedell (Ed Connors); Mary Beth Hughes (Jerry Lawrence); Cliff Clark (Sam Travers); James Burke (Clancy); Frank Orth (Captain Burke); Margaret Roach (Emmy Lou); Gladys Blake (Miss Brooklyn); Granville Bates (Chief Miller).

FAST AND LOOSE (Metro-Goldwyn-Mayer, 1939) 80 minutes.

Producer, Frederick Stephani; director, Edwin L. Marin; story/ screenplay, Harry Kurnitz; camera, George Folsey; editor, Elmo Vernon.

Robert Montgomery (Joel Sloane); Rosalind Russell (Garda Sloane); Reginald Owen (Vincent Charlton); Ralph Morgan (Nicholas Torrent); Etienne Girardot (Christopher Oates); Alan Dinehart (Dave Hillard); Jo Ann Sayers (Christina Torrent); Joan Marsh (Bobby Neville); Anthony Allan [John Hubbard] (Phil Sergeant); Tom Collins (Gerald Torrent); Sidney Blackmer (Lucky Nolan); Ian Wolfe (Wilkes); and: Mary Forbes, Leonard Carey.

FAST COMPANY (Metro-Goldwyn-Mayer, 1938) 73 minutes.

Producer, Frederick Stephani; director, Edward Buzzell; story, Marco Page, Harry Kurnitz; screenplay, Page, Kurnitz, Harold Tashis; art director, Cedric Gibbons; music, Dr. William Axt; camera, Clyde Devinna; editor, Frederick Y. Smith.

Melvyn Douglas (Joel Sloane); Florence Rice (Garda Sloane); Claire Dodd (Julia Thorne); John Shepperd [Shepperd Strudwick] (Ned Morgan); Louis Calhern (Elias Z. Bannerman); Nat Pendleton (Paul Torison); Douglass Dumbrille (Arnold Stamper); Mary Howard (Leah Brockler); George Zucco (Otto Brockler); Minor Watson (Steve Langner); Donald Douglas (Lieutenant James Flanner); Dwight Frye (Sidney Wheeler); Thurston Hall (District Attorney MacMillan); Horace McMahon (Danny Scolado); Roger Converse (Assist-

Above: Inna Gest, Anne Borglum, Lois Lindsay, Ann Sothern, Muriel Barr, Harold Minjir, Gladys Blake (3rd from right) and Yvonne DuVal (far right) in FAST AND FURIOUS (1939).

Below: Melvyn Douglas and Florence Rice in FAST COMPANY (1938).

ant District Attorney Byers); Natalie Garson (Mildred); Henry Sylvester (Auctioneer); Edward Hearn (Policeman); James B. Carson (Safe Expert); Ronnie Rondell (Taxi Driver); Jack Foss (Attendant); Barbara Bedford (Secretary).

U.S. TV title: THE RARE BOOK MURDERS.

In an obvious effort to capitalize on the commercial popularity from the then in vogue husband-and-wife detective capers produced by various studios, including MGM who had started it all with Nick and Nora Charles in THE THIN MAN (1934), *q.v.*, Metro-Goldwyn-Mayer launched a new skein of features around the characters of book collector sleuths Joel and Garda Sloane. Three "A" productions resulted, *each* with a new cast of leads (which showed that the property and genre itself were the truly important ingredients), but *all* with the usual studio gloss and polish. What resulted was a trio of fast-paced, light and entertaining murder mysteries. In each entry, the ambitious and enthusiastic leads follow all the requisites of this celluloid genre: they are amateur detectives (which makes it easy for filmgoers to empathize); they are relatively well-to-do, which allows them the luxury of devoting time to crime-probing (and also affords moviegoers a glimpse into the high life); they are attractive to the eye and ear; and they have the intellectual/cultural breeding to make them both smart enough to piece together the clues to solve the mystery, and silly enough to ignore the obvious dangers that lurk behind every door.

FAST COMPANY (called THE RARE BOOK MURDERS on TV) opened the series with rare book dealers Joel (Melvyn Douglas) and Garda Sloane (Florence Rice), in deference to the wishes of the local police investigator (Donald Douglas), investigating the murder of fellow book dealer Otto Brockler (George Zucco). (He has been clubbed to death with a bookend.) The chief suspect is Ned Morgan (John Shepperd [Shepperd Strudwick]), a former employee of Brockler's who is in love with the man's daughter, Leah (Mary Howard). The Sloanes' investigation, however, turns up three other suspects, Elias Z. Bannerman (Louis Calhern), Julia Thorne (Claire Dodd), and Sidney Wheeler (Dwight Frye), before they conclude the complicated case (during the course of which Joel Sloane is shot in the backside). Irene Thirer (*New York Post*) judged this series debut film a "swift and mystifying and thoroughly entertaining comedy-drama." As for the newest additions to the ranks of non-armchair detectives, Frank S. Nugent (*New York Times*) reported, "Melvyn Douglas, who is playing light comedy detectives this season, tackles the problem with proper nonchalance and the assistance of Florence Rice as a most compatible helpmate. They get cutely squiffed together, and Mr. Douglas deduces a deduction. . . .

In a word, Mr. Douglas's methods are not strictly according to Holmes, but he gets results. Not the least of them is the creation of a brash and amusing detective story of the light-hearted, or THIN MAN, school." *Variety* appreciated the novelty of the leads' daytime careers: "There is freshness in the background of book auctions and dusty tomes, and something new in a glimpse behind the scenes which reveals the 'doctoring of phoney volumes to give them the appearance of age." But the trade paper reprimanded, "More of this phase of the story and less of the conventional district attorney's office activities would have given the film some distinction from routine."

FAST COMPANY, a July 1938 release, was followed in March 1939 by FAST AND LOOSE, with another set of MGM contract stars—Robert Montgomery and Rosalind Russell—appearing as the energetic Sloanes. Here the duo is drawn into the mystery of the disappearance of a rare Shakespearian manuscript from the collection of wealthy Nicholas Torrent (Ralph Morgan). Joel Sloane is working as an investigator for the insurance company which holds the policy on the priceless books. Two murders ensue (and once again Joel is shot in the derrière) before Joel and Garda break the enigma. *Variety* explained, "Surprise situations continually crop up to further complicate matters for Montgomery when he figures his solution is fool-proof. Action speeds along at such fast pace that little time is allowed for detailed direction of suspicion against individuals involved. . . . Interest is generated more in the antics and adventures of Montgomery than in the whodunits at hand, but that seems to be the intent of the picture from the start." Since the play was the thing (and not which expert farceurs parlayed the dialogue), this continuation of the series met with critical endorsement. The *New York Times* (Frank S. Nugent) applauded the "sense of humor, a facile style, genial performances and just enough puzzlement to keep us from suspecting the least suspicious member of the cast."

What proved to be the final film in the series, FAST AND FURIOUS was issued in the fall of 1939, and here Franchot Tone and Ann Sothern were cast as the newest interpreters of the husband-and-wife sleuths. The direction was by Busby Berkeley, who might have seemed out of place in handling a mystery film, but he supervised the chore well and the oceanside setting allowed him the opportunity to stage a well-thought-out bathing beauty pageant.

Rare book dealer Joel Sloane (Franchot Tone) and wife Garda (Ann Sothern) are at a resort city where Joel and his pal Ted Bentley (Allyn Joslyn), a newspaperman, are to judge a bathing beauty contest, much to Garda's chagrin. They are interrupted by a murder, however, and Bentley is the likely suspect, leaving the Sloanes to extricate him from the mess by investigating the crime themselves. Before long another murder occurs and the overcurious duo is almost dispatched when the killer tries to drop an elevator on them. That MGM had lost interest in this series property was indicated by the ranking status of the latest lead players assigned to the property. ". . . Unashamedly a budget lightweight but pleasantly entertaining throughout," reported *Variety*. Moreover, the plot gimmick of mixing rare books and murder was wearing thin. ". . . Metro seems to be stretching an original idea to infinity," argued Bosley Crowther in the *New York Times*.

THE FAT MAN (Universal, 1951) 77 1/2 minutes.

Producer, Aubrey Schenck; director, William Castle; based on the radio series created by Dashiell Hammett; story, Leonard Lee; screenplay, Harry Essex, Lee; art directors, Bernard Herzbrun, Richard H. Riedel; music director, Joseph Gershenson; camera, Irving Glassberg; editor, Edward Curtiss.

J. Scott Smart (Brad Runyan); Julie London (Pat Boyd); Rock Hudson (Roy Clark); Clinton Sundberg (Bill Norton); Jayne Meadows (Jane Adams); John Russell (Gene Gordon); Jerome Cowan (Detective Stark); Emmett Kelly (Ed Deets); Lucille Barkley (Lola Gordon); Teddy Hart (Shifty); Robert Osterloh (Chuck Fletcher); Harry Lewis (Happy Stevens); Marvin Kaplan (Pinkie); Ken Niles (Dr. Bromley); Ed Max (Murray); Bob Roark (Tony); Mary Young (Saleswoman); Tristram Coffin (Missing Persons Officer); Peter Brocco (Clerk); Tom Keene (Mac); Shimen Ruskin (Louie); Harry Tyler (Landlord); Robert Jordan (Bellhop); Gertrude Graner (Mother); Guy Wilkerson (Justice of the Peace); George Wallace (Carl); Cheerio Meredith (Scrubwoman); Art Lind, Everett Hart, Abe Goldstein (Clowns); Jack Chefe (Chef); Eric Alden (Guard).

Dashiell Hammett's character Caspar Gutman, The Fat Man, was a villain in *The Maltese Falcon* (1930), but when he was transferred to ABC radio in 1945 on the series "The Fat Man," he became private investigator Brad Runyan, and was played to perfection by J. Scott Smart, who also looked the part. In 1951 Universal made a screen version of THE FAT MAN and Smart did the part on the big screen, the film also providing future stars Rock Hudson, Julie London, and John Russell with substantial roles, in addition to the appearance of famous circus clown Emmett Kelly in a dramatic assignment. *Variety*, however, found the William Castle-directed feature too "loosely contrived" and a "talky mystery melodrama."

Jane Adams (Jayne Meadows), the widow of a California dentist, hires private eye Brad Runyan (J. Scott Smart) to look into the death of her husband, who died while attending a Manhattan con-

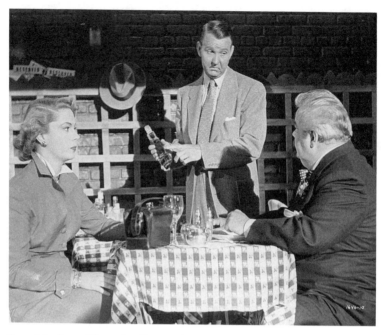

Jayne Meadows, Clinton Sundberg and J. Scott Smart in THE FAT MAN (1951).

vention. She does not believe he committed suicide as the authorities claim. The case later takes Runyan to California where a gangster, Roy Clark (Rock Hudson), has been murdered. He discovers that the victim was done in by several cohorts arguing over the proceeds from a heist they committed. After yet another murder, the Fat Man points out the murderer, a man who wants all the loot for his own purposes.

It is intriguing to note that while the title of the radio series and the film were based on a Dashiell Hammett villain, it was one of the detective heroes—the Continental Op—who provides most of the characteristics of the Fat Man's persona. Regarding the transfer of the character to film, Don Miller concluded in "Private Eyes" (*Focus on Film* magazine, Autumn 1975), "The results were curiously flat and lifeless, with Smart failing to catch the appeal that made his radio program popular." (Another factor was that using one's imagination while listening to a radio program would prove to be far more stimulating than viewing a literal translation brought to the screen, where economies often demand creative limitations.) Jon Tuska opined in *The Detective in Hollywood* (1978), "But neither film nor radio series did justice to the Op. He may well be Hammett's finest creation, a man who in fiction remains nameless because Hammett had known dozens like him. He is a hero because he does not succumb to either greed or vanity." In the 1970s William Conrad played a similar character in the teleseries "Cannon" (CBS-TV, 1971-76) and in the telefeature CANNON (1971) and THE RETURN OF FRANK CANNON (1980), *q.v.*

FATAL FINGERPRINTS *see* DARK ALIBI [essay].

THE FATAL HOUR (Monogram, 1940) 67 minutes.

Producer, William T. Lackey; director, William Nigh; based on the character created by Hugh Riley; screenplay, W. Scott Darling, Joseph West; camera, Harry Neumann; editor, Russell Schoengarth.

Boris Karloff (James Lee Wong); Grant Withers (Captain Street); Marjorie Reynolds (Robbie Logan); Charles Trowbridge (Forbes); John Hamilton (Belden); Craig Reynolds (Francis Belden); Jack Kennedy (Mike); Lita Cheveret (Tanya Serova); Frank Puglia (Hardway); I. Stanford Jolley (Soapy); Jason Robards (Griswold); Pauline Drake (Bessie).

Detective Dan O'Grady, the best friend of police Captain Street (Grant Withers), is found murdered and Street requests private eye James Lee Wong (Boris Karloff) to delve into the matter. O'Grady had been working on a jewel smuggling operation and Wong learns that several gems found in his office came from Francis Belden's (Craig Reynolds) jewelry shop. Newspaper reporter Robbie Logan (Marjorie Reynolds), Street's fiancée, alerts Wong that O'Grady was last seen in the nightclub run by former hoodlum Hardway (Frank Puglia). Wong determines that Hardway and Belden (John Hamilton), Francis' father, were partners in the smuggling racket but had a disagreement when Francis fell in love with Tanya Serova (Lita Cheveret), an entertainer in Hardway's club. Wong and Street interrogate Belden's lawyer, Forbes (Charles Trowbridge), and later Francis finds Tanya murdered. It turns out that the time when the young woman was heard screaming and the time Francis found her were different; Wong discovers that the radio in the victim's hotel apartment had a remote control switch and that her screams had been recorded earlier to throw off the investigation of her homicide. With this information, Wong traces the killer.

THE FATAL HOUR was the fourth of five series films in which Boris Karloff enacted Hugh Wiley's perceptive Oriental sleuth, James Lee Wong, Monogram's counterpart to Twentieth Century-Fox's popular Charlie Chan and Mr. Moto features. Unfortunately the poverty row studio churned out the entries with too much haste and too little budget. *Variety* complained, "A routine mystery, none too well produced, which has as its principal saving grace, the suave Boris Karloff. . . . Its failure to impress is largely due to the elemental plot and inconsistencies. . . ." On the other hand, when the economy production was released in Great Britain as MR. WONG AT HEADQUARTERS, that country's more indulgent *Kinematograph Weekly* judged, "The story quickly gets into its stride, and tension is never relaxed until it arrives at its original, thrilling and entirely plausible climax."

FATHER BROWN (Columbia, 1954) 91 minutes.

Producers, Paul Finder Moss, Vivian A. Cox; director, Robert Hamer; based on the story "Blue Cross" by G. K. Chesterton; screenplay, Thelma Schnee, Hamer; music, Georges Auric; camera, Harry Waxman; editor, Gordon Hales.

Alec Guinness (Father Brown); Joan Greenwood (Lady Warren); Peter Finch (Flambeau); Cecil Parker (Bishop); Bernard Lee (Inspector Valentine); Sidney James (Parkinson); Gerard Oury (Inspector Dubois); Ernest Thesiger (Vicomte); Ernest Clark (Secretary); Austin Trevor (Herald); Noel Howlett (Auctioneer); Marne Maitland (Maharajah); John Salew (Station Sergeant); John Horsley (Inspector Wilkins); Lance Maraschal (Texan).

A.k.a. THE DETECTIVE; FATHER BROWN, DETECTIVE.

FATHER BROWN, DETECTIVE (Paramount, 1935) 67 minutes.

Producer, Bayard Veiller; director, Edward Segwick; based on the story "Blue Cross" by G. K. Chesterton; screenplay, Henry Myers, C. Gardner Sullivan; camera, Theodor Sparkhul; editor, James Smith.

Walter Connolly (Father Brown); Paul Lukas (Flambeau); Gertrude Michael (Evelyn Fischer); Robert Loraine (Inspector Valentine); Halliwell Hobbes (Sir Leopold Fischer); Una O'Connor (Mrs. Biggs); E. E. Clive (Sergeant).

Gilbert Keith Chesterton's Roman Catholic priest sleuth, Father Brown,* was not a conventional detective; the Essex, England clergyman was more interested in bringing criminals into the ways of

---

*In *Detectionary* (1977), editors Otto Penzler, Chris Steinbrunner, and Marvin Lachman describe the methodical Father Brown as "gentle, commonplace" and "inconspicuously short." They add, "However, despite these outward gaucheries, Father Brown possesses a sharp, subtle, sensitive mind. His unusual method of detection ignores the standard practice of collecting clues and making deductions. Instead, he employs his understanding of human nature and tries to think like a criminal." Thus, for this amateur sleuth, ". . . problems of crime are not problems of law so much as they are problems of character."

the righteous instead of into the hands of the law. The character first appeared in the compilation, *Innocence of Father Brown* in 1911, which included the story "Blue Cross" which provided the basis for both Father Brown movies. Ellery Queen considered Father Brown, along with Sherlock Holmes and C. Auguste Dupin, to be one of the three all-time greatest fictional detectives.

Father Brown (Walter Connolly) is the trustee of a diamond cross which master criminal Flambeau (Paul Lukas) intends to steal. At a gaming house Flambeau encounters beautiful Evelyn Fischer (Gertrude Michael) and manages to sneak her out of the place just as the police—led by Inspector Valentine (Robert Loraine)—raid the establishment. The criminal keeps an eye on the young woman as he plans on how to steal from her father, Sir Leopold Fischer (Halliwell Hobbes). He uses Evelyn as a go-between when he pilfers the diamond cross. After Flambeau grabs the cross and compromises Evelyn by being found in her bedroom, Father Brown attempts to spiritually rehabilitate the criminal, although Valentine scoffs at the notion. With the police fast on his trail, Flambeau makes his escape. He eventually returns with the cross and gives it to Father Brown, announcing his plans to reform!

Although *Variety* acknowledged that this Paramount production is "clean and wholesome" the reviewer also stated, ". . . It is not forceful enough as a drama to offer more than supporting value for a program." Connolly was appreciated for his solid performance (in contrast to Paul Lukas' stolid acting), but there was just not enough juice to the venture to make it a likely candidate for continuation. Prior to enacting the role of the priest/detective in this film, Walter Connolly performed as Charlie Chan on the NBC Blue network in 1933 (while his brother-in-law, William Harrigan, played Chan on Broadway the same year in *Keeper of the Keys*). Following FATHER BROWN, DETECTIVE, the rotund Connolly appeared as the detective Nero Wolfe in LEAGUE OF FRIGHTENED MEN (1937), *q.v.*, at Columbia Pictures.

The second Father Brown film was made in Britain in 1954 as FATHER BROWN and is also known as FATHER BROWN, DETECTIVE. It was issued in the U.S. as THE DETECTIVE in 1955 by Columbia. Here Father Brown (Alec Guinness) is dispatched to Rome to guard a holy relic, a valuable cross, which is to be used in a holy Congress. Crook Flambeau (Peter Finch), who uses many disguises, eludes the watchful priest and steals the relic. Wanting its return. Father Brown devises a plan to use a valuable chess set owned by Lady Warren (Joan Greenwood) as bait to catch Flambeau. Again the thief steals his quest and makes a getaway, but the priest doggedly stays on the crook's trail and traces him to a

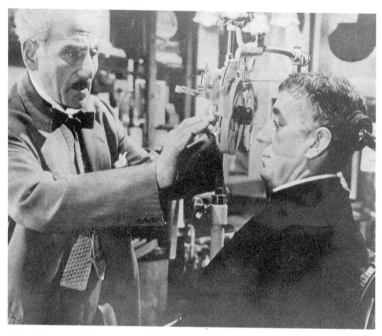

Alec Guinness (right) in FATHER BROWN, DETECTIVE (1954).

Burgundy chateau where he recovers both the cross and the chess set as well as saving Flambeau's besmirched soul.

Ivan Butler commented in *Cinema in Britain* (1973), "Though physically the exact opposite of Chesterton's runcible priest-detective, Guinness is so captivating in the part that this matters little. The emphasis is on detection rather than deduction from character as in the stories, but this does not seem to matter either. . . . The religious element is played down to a degree, but Father Brown does have a few sharp points to make from the pulpit." In *British Sound Films: The Studio Years 1929-1959* (1984), David Quinlan ranks this feature as an "Engaging, stylish, gently humorous piece." Bosley Crowther (*New York Times*) admitted, "Inevitably one feels oneself waiting for the pious priest to do something awry, to let a glint of wicked mischief flash from behind his clerical garb. One expects Mr. Guinness to be sardonic, to slip a little satire into his role. One waits in vain for him to show the slightest impudence in this film."

In addition to the two films, Chesterton's famous literary creation was the subject of a radio series, "The Adventures of Father Brown," in 1945, with Karl Swenson as the priest. In 1974 Kenneth

More played the part in the British ATV Television series, "Father Brown," and in 1986-87 Bernard Cornwell had the title in a PBS-TV series imported from England.

FEAR (Monogram, 1946) 67 minutes.

Producer, Lindsley Parsons; director, Alfred Zeisler; screenplay, Zeisler, Dennis Cooper; art director, Dave Milton; set decorators, Charles Thompson, Vin Taylor; special effects, Bob Clark; camera, Jackson Rose; editor, Ace Herman.

Warren William (Captain Burke); Anne Gwynne (Eileen); Peter Cookson (Larry Crain); James Cardwell (Ben); Nestor Paiva (Schaefer); Francis Pierlot (Morton Stanley); William Moss (Al); Almira Sessions (Mrs. Williams); Darren McGavin (Chuck); Henry Clay (Steve); Ernie Adams (Painter); Johnny Strong (John); Charles Calvert (Doc); Fairfax Burger (Magician); Cedric Stevens (Man); Bubbles Hecht (Woman); Lee "Lasses" White (Janitor); Ken Broeker (Uniformed Officer); Carl Leviness (Tailor); Dewey Robinson (Bartender); Brick Sullivan (Policeman); Jack Richardson, Winnie Nard, Phyllis Ayres, Hy Jason (Pedestrians); Chester Conklin (Switchman).

"FEAR is a solid fistful of entertainment that packs a wallop way out of its class," *Variety* wrote of this programmer which was basically a modern version of Fyodor Dostoevski's 1866 novel, *Crime and Punishment*, which Josef von Sternberg had made for Columbia Pictures in 1935 and which was remade—among other versions—in France in 1956 and again in America in 1959. FEAR, despite its low-budget origins, is a fine retelling (with a twist) of the classic tale of murder and retribution and an unrelenting pursuit to capture the criminal.

Medical student Larry Crain (Peter Cookson), who loves beautiful Eileen (Anne Gwynne), is deeply in debt to grasping pawnbroker Morton Stanley (Francis Pierlot). Needing money too badly, Crain visits the loan shark but is rebuffed. In a fit of anger he murders the shopkeeper and steals the man's money. Police detective Captain Burke (Warren William) is assigned to the case and soon realizes that Crain must be the killer. However, he lacks the necessary evidence to arrest him. The law enforcer begins to put pressure on the young man's conscience, hoping to get him to confess his crime. Hounded day and night by Burke, the killer confesses to the murder, only to awaken and discover it all a terrible dream.

Dapper Warren William, who had played a long line of cinema sleuths such as Perry Mason, Philo Vance, and The Lone Wolf, was exceptionally adept as the police detective. His resourceful performance gave dimension to the movie. FEAR's greatest weakness, however, was its finale which insisted on a happy ending (thus the dream ploy) rather than the downbeat finale of the classic novel. Regarding this device, *Variety* pointed out that it ". . . rebounds as a ruinous mechanism that unsprings audience tension and leaves them feeling cheated."

THE FEATHERED SERPENT (Monogram, 1948) 68 minutes.

Producer, James S. Burkett; director, William Beaudine; based on the character created by Earl Derr Biggers; story/screenplay, Oliver Drake; additional dialogue, Hal Collins; art director, David Milton; set decorator, Ray Boltz; makeup, Webb Overlander; music director, Edward J. Kay; assistant director, William Callihan; sound, Tom Lambert; camera, William Sickner; editor, Ace Herman.

Roland Winters (Charlie Chan); Keye Luke (Lee Chan); Victor Sen Yung (Tommy Chan); Mantan Moreland (Birmingham Brown); Robert Livingston (John Stanley); Martin Garralaga (Pedro); Nils Asther (Professor Paul Evans); Carol Forman (Sonia Cabot); Beverly Jons (Joan Farnsworth); George J. Lewis (Captain Juan Lopez); Leslie Dennison (Professor Farnsworth); Jay Silverheels (Diego); and: Juan Duvan, Frank Leyva, Milton Ross, Fred Cordova, Erville Alderson, Charles Stevens.

The penultimate Charlie Chan/Monogram series film, THE FEATHERED SERPENT, was written by Oliver Drake, who reworked the plot from his 1937 The Three Mesquiteers series Western for Republic Pictures, THE RIDERS OF THE WHISTLING SKULL. By an interesting coincidence, one of the stars of that sagebrusher, Robert Livingston, was cast as the chief villain in the Chan opus. The detective feature also boasts a very strong cast and is the *only* feature in which Keye Luke and Victor Sen Yung, the two best known performers to portray Charlie Chan's celluloid offsprings, appear together in the same Chan adventure. While all this was a plus, THE FEATHERED SERPENT is, nevertheless, a dull, overly talky production with poorly executed night outdoor scenes and careless production values. (E.g., in one scene, a fly lands on actor Roland Winters' hand and the sequence was not reshot.)

"Whoever Enters This Tomb MUST DIE!" read the poster blurbs for this picture, adding, "SEE: Ancient Ruins! Pagan Gods! Aztec Treasure!" and "Chan defies the ancient curse of the death-god 'Kul-Kul-Can' . . . in his strangest murder man-hunt!" Detective Charlie Chan (Roland Winters) is asked to look into the mysterious disappearance of Professor Scott (Erville Alderson), who has disappeared in the Mexican jungles while searching for a lost Aztec treasure. Chan joins an expedition which includes his sons Lee (Keye Luke) and Tommy (Victor Sen Yung) and chauffeur Birmingham Brown (Mantan Moreland). In additon, there are John Stanley (Robert Livingston), Professor Paul Evans (Nils Asther), Professor Farnsworth (Leslie Dennison) and his daughter Joan (Beverly Jons), and exotic Sonia Cabot (Carol Forman). Chan is aided by police Captain Juan Lopez (George J. Lewis). The locals claim that the Aztec death god Kul-Kul-Can is responsible for the series of deaths plaguing the area and Chan's sons uncover underground ruins which house the lost Aztec treasure. Chan finally proves that one of the party, who has succumbed to greed for the treasure, is the villain.

FIND THE BLACKMAILER (Warner Bros., 1943) 55 minutes.

Associate producer, William Jacobs; director, D. Ross Lederman; based on the story "Blackmail with Feathers" by G. T. Fleming-Roberts; screenplay, Robert E, Kent; art director, Charles Novi; set decorator, Clarence Steesen; assistant director, Wilbur McGaugh; sound, Robert B. Lee; camera, James Van Trees; editor, harold McLernon.

Jerome Cowan (D. L. Trees); Faye Emerson (Mona Vance); Gene Lockhart (John M. Rhodes); Marjorie Hoselle (Pandora Pies); Robert Kent (Harper); Wade Boteler (Detective Cramer); John Harmon (Ray Hicky); Bradley Pace (Farrell); Lou Lubin (Olen); Ralph Peters (Coleman).

After portraying private eye Miles Archer in the 1941 remake of THE MALTESE FALCON, *q.v.*, polished performer Jerome Cowan grabbed the lead in two "B" efforts from Warner Bros., and in both he appeared as a shamus. While in CRIME BY NIGHT (1944), *q.v.*, he took second billing to Jane Wyman, FIND THE BLACKMAILER found him with top billing and again appearing with Faye Emerson (of CRIME BY NIGHT).

Political hopeful John M. Rhodes (Gene Lockhart) is being blackmailed by an ex-convict through the use of a talking crow. The mayoral candidate hires private eye D. L. Trees (Jerome Cowan) to hunt the blackmailer before he ruins his client's chances for public office. The gumshoe locates the crook but the latter is murdered and the detective, with the aid of lovely Mona Vance (Faye Emerson) and Rhodes, must determine who is behind the homicide. The needed clue is concealed by the crow.

While *Variety* passed off the film as a "quickie 'B' whodunit of minor program calibre," it acknowledged that Jerome Cowan ". . . slips out of his usual heavy roles to handle spot of the breezy and inpecunious dick." Regarding Cowan's work as the detective, Don Miller recorded in *B Movies* (1973) that ". . . Cowan kept the movie on its feet and moving ahead. His natural cynical demeanor coupled with a tremendous amount of acting ability gave some credence to the plot about the search for a talking blackbird that might turn into a stool pigeon."

FLETCH (Universal, 1985) Color 98 minutes.

Producers, Alan Greisman, Peter Douglas; associate producer, Gordon A. Webb; director, Michael Ritchie; based on the novel by Gregory McDonald; screenplay, Andrew Bergman; production designer, Boris Leven; art director, Todd Hallowell; set designer, Louis Mann; set decorator, Marvin March; costume designer, Gloria Gresham; makeup, Ken Chase; music, Harold Faltermeyer; songs, Faltermeyer and Franie Golde; Dan Hartman and Charlie Midnight; stunt coordinator, Dean Jeffries; second unit director, Peter Norman; assistant director, Wolfgang Glattes, Larry Rapaport; sound, Jim Alexander, Paul Miller; supervising sound editor, Ronald A. Jacobs; sound editors, Robert Shoup, Karen Spangenberg; camera, Fred Schuler; second unit camera, Gary Kibbe; editor, Richard A. Harris.

Chevy Chase (Irwin Maurice "Fletch" Fletcher); Joe Don Baker (Chief Karlin); Dana Wheeler-Nicholson (Gail Stanwyck); Richard Libertini (Frank Walker); Tim Matheson (Alan Stanwyck); M. Emmet Walsh (Dr. Dolan); George Wendt (Fat Sam); Kenneth Mars (Stanton Boyd); Geena Davis (Larry); Bill Henderson (Speaker); William Traylor (Mr. Underhill); George Wyner (Gillet); Tony Long, James Avery (Detectives); Larry Flash Jenkins (Gummy); Ralph Seymour (Creasy); Reid Cruickshanks (Sergeant); Bruce French (Pathologist); Burton Gilliam (Bud); David Harper (Teenager); Alison Laplaca (Pan American Airlines Clerk); Joe Prami (Watchman); William Sanderson (Swarthout); Penny Santon (Velma Stanwyck); Robert Sorrells (Marvin Stanwyck); Beau Starr (Willy); Nico DeSilva (Waiter); Peggy Doyle (Identification Nurse); Rick Garcia (Waiter); Grace Gaynor (Mrs. Underhill); Freeman King, Roger Ammann (Cops); Loraine Shields (Records Nurse); Bill Sorrell, Henry "Hank" Blecker (Surfer Cops); Arnold Turner, Darren Dublin (Reporters); Merv Maruama (Chinese Busboy); Kareem Abdul-Jabbar, Chick Hearn (Themselves); Irene Olga Lopez (Maid).

Los Angeles newspaper investigative reporter Irwin "Fletch" Fletcher (Chevy Chase), who uses a variety of disguises to carry out his assignments, is working on a story about drug smuggling on the beach when aircraft company vice president Alan Stanwyck (Tim Matheson) offers him $50,000 to kill him. The man claims he is dying of bone cancer. Fletch gets hold of the man's medical records and learns he is lying. He meets Stanwyck's pretty wife Gail (Dana Wheeler-Nicholson) and is extremely attracted to her. Meanwhile, police Chief Karlin (Joe Don Baker) has Fletch busted on a heroin

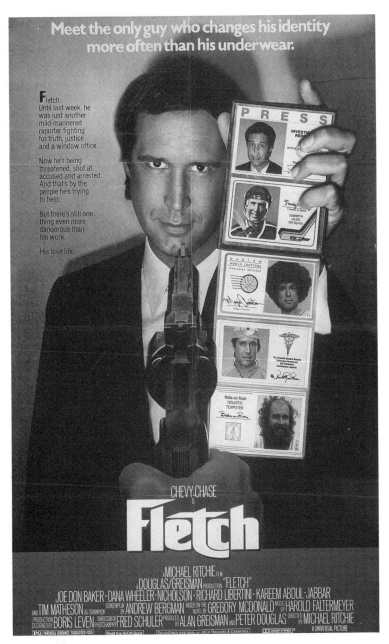

Advertisement for **FLETCH** (1985).

possession charge and threatens to kill him unless he gets off the drug story, claiming his interference will destroy the plans his division has for rounding up the drug pushers. Because he finds out Gail has converted $3,000,000 in stock from her father's aircraft company to buy a ranch in Utah, Fletch goes there and learns that the sale was bogus; the land cost only $3,000. After spying on a meeting between Stanwyck and Karlin, Fletch is chased by the police, but escapes. He learns that Stanwyck plans to go to Rio accompanied by a woman named Sally Cavanaugh. Fletch visits Stanwyck's parents (Penny Santon, Robert Sorrells), pretending to be an insurance agent, and is told that Alan and Sally have been married for eight years, which makes Stanwyck a bigamist. Fletch tells Gail the truth and then confronts beach drug pushers Gummy (Larry Flash Jenkins) and Fat Sam (George Wendt) with the fact that they have been working for Karlin, who had been using Stanwyck to fly drugs to Los Angeles from South America. Both stooges agree to turn state's evidence against Karlin. That night Fletch confronts Stanwyck at his home. With Gail there he tells the man he know the full story about how he plans to take Gail's three million dollars and head to Rio with Sally. Karlin arrives and the doublecrosses ricochet, with Gail saving the occasion and Fletch with a tennis racket, leaving the erstwhile detective to head off to Rio with Gail.

For years there had been talk of transforming Gregory McDonald's popular literary creation* to film, but the author resisted the notion for a long time. The results which reached the screen were less than distinguished, merely creating another unmemorable screen comedy for "Saturday Night Live" alumnus Chevy Chase. "What is more than tedious—in fact somewhat unnerving—about FLETCH is the ineptness with which this has been geared as a vehicle for Chevy Chase. He is somewhat unprepossessing as a comedian to begin with; perhaps because he is physically *too* prepossessing. . . . That he looks like a star in the Rock Hudson rather than Woody Allen mould also tends to nullify his occasional sallies into disguise, while the script seems to be working desperately but aimlessly to define Fletch's comic style, mainly through a puerile strain of movie in-jokiness" (Richard Combs, British *Monthly Film Bulletin*). In analyzing why this newest screen detective lacked the spark of authenticity or attractiveness, Roger Ebert pinpointed in his *Movie Home Companion 1989* (1988), "He projects such an inflexible

---

*To date, Gregory McDonald has written the following Irwin "Fletch" Fletcher novels: *Fletch* (1974), *Confess, Fletch* (1976), *Fletch's Fortune* (1978), *Fletch and the Widow Bradley* (1981), *Fletch's Moxie* (1982), *Fletch and the Man Who* (1983), *Carioca Fletch* (1984), *Fletch Won* (1985), *Fletch, Too* (1986), *The Fletch Chronicle* (1987) [compilation].

mask of cool detachment, of ironic running commentary, that we're prevented from identifying with him. If he thinks this is all just a little too silly for words, what are we to think? If we're more involved in the action than he is, does that make us chumps?"

Obviously the critical perception of the moviegoing public of the mid-1980s was different from that of the above critics. This comedy, which cost an estimated $15,000,000 to produce, grossed $24,5000,000 in domestic film rentals, leading to Chevy Chase starring in FLETCH II filmed during the summer of 1988 for Universal release.

FOLLOW THAT WOMAN (Paramount, 1945) 70 minutes.

Producers, William Pine, William Thomas; associate producer, Maxwell Shane; director, Lew Landers; story, Ben Perry; screenplay, Winston Miller, Maxwell Shane; art director, F. Paul Sylos; set decorator, Glenn Thompson; music, Alexander Laszlo; assistant director, Nat Merman; sound, Joseph I. Kane; camera, Fred Jackman; editor, Henry Adams.

William Gargan (Sam Boone); Nancy Kelly (Nancy Boone); Ed Gargan (Butch); Regis Toomey (Barney Manners); Don Costello (Nick); Byron Barr (John Evans); Pierre Watkin (Mr. Henderson); Audrey Young (Marge).

William Gargan played Ellery Queen in a trio of 1942 action films for Columbia Pictures and the next year appeared as a sleuth in NO PLACE FOR A LADY, *q.v.* In FOLLOW THAT WOMAN, he is again a gumshoe but the bulk of the detection work is accomplished by Nancy Kelly as his loyal spouse and by Ed Gargan as his partner. *Variety* judged it an ". . . inexpensive whodunit, which leans on the lighter side to keep it rolling. . . . Wandering plot is the chief weakness. . . . The Pine-Thomas unit has given it nice production for its type of film."

Private detective Sam Boone (William Gargan) is inducted into the army just as he in the midst of tracking down a murderer. When he leaves for the service, his spouse Nancy (Nancy Kelly) decides to carry on his work with the assist of his partner Butch (Ed Gargan). The two land in all sorts of trouble and Boone is forced to request a seven-day leave to extricate them from the mess and wrap up the case.

While William Gargan was an old sure hand at sleuthing and handled the role ably, Nancy Kelly was far more at ease in dramatic assignments rather than in this brand of dizzy comedy. On the other hand, Ed Gargan, Bill's real-life brother, was always a pleasure in his typical dumb guy role, here as Butch.

FORTY NAUGHTY GIRLS (RKO, 1937) 63 minutes.

Producer, William Sistrom; director, Edward Cline; based on the story "The Riddle of the 40 Naughty Girls" by Stuart Palmer; screenplay, John Grey; art director, Van Nest Polglase; music director, Roy Webb; camera, Russell Metty; editor, John Lockert.

James Gleason (Inspector Oscar Piper); ZaSu Pitts (Hildegarde Martha Withers); Marjorie Lord (June Preston); George Shelley (Bert); Joan Woodbury (Rita Marlowe); Frank M. Thomas (Jeff); Tom Kennedy (Casey); Alan Edwards (Ricky Rickman); Alden Chase (Tommy Washburn); Edward Marr (Windy Bennett); Ada Leonard, Barbara Pepper (Showgirls).

Backstage at Ricky Rickman's (Alan Edwards) posh Broadway musical, a gun is stolen from the trunk of prop man Jeff (Frank M. Thomas). Later, press agent Windy Bennett (Edward Marr) is overheard by Jeff blackmailing the star/playwright Tommy Washburn (Alden Chase). Bennett is also involved with star Rita Marlowe (Joan Woodbury), Rickman's fiancée. He also makes a pass at starlet June Preston (Marjorie Lord) but is knocked down by her leading man/boyfriend Bert (George Shelley). Miss Hildegarde Withers (ZaSu Pitts) and Inspector Oscar Piper (James Gleason) come to enjoy the show and Bennett is found murdered in Bert's dressing room. Piper investigates, being a friend of Rickman, but tells Miss Withers *not* to snoop in this case. Piper accuses June of the crime but she denies it and Washburn insists he heard Bert threaten to kill Bennett over her. Nitrate tests reveal that neither June nor Bert fired the murder weapon, and Piper is knocked out examining Bennett's office. Coming to, he discovers that Bennett was blackmailing Washburn because the latter had taken a play written by another—a man who was killed in an accident—and sold it to Rickman as his own creation. Piper then deduces that Washburn committed the murder but as he goes to arrest him, he finds the man dead, the victim of a supposed blank fired by Rita from a gun as part of the play. Piper then concludes that prop man Jeff is to blame since he loaded the gun, but it is quickly demonstrated that the calibre of bullet which killed Tommy was not the kind used in the prop weapon. Rita also reveals that Jeff is her father. Piper and his assistant, Casey (Tom Kennedy), find the murder weapon discarded in the theater basement and Miss Withers locates a letter which helps her to reveal the true killer.

The sixth and last RKO film in the Hildegarde Withers series, and the second to star ZaSu Pitts (the first was 1936's THE PLOT THICKENS, *q.v.*), FORTY NAUGHTY GIRLS is a sad finale to a once excellent property. This installment is slow moving and not engaging. The killer is too easy to spot and star ZaSu Pitts is too distracting as a fluttery, clumsy Miss Withers. Only Tom Kennedy as the dumb cop assistant provides needed comedy relief among the general tedium. The film's prime significance was that it was the first Hollywood feature to incorporate the newly employed nitrate test to determine if a suspect had recently fired a gun.

FRIDAY THE RABBI SLEPT LATE *see* LANIGAN'S RABBI.

THE GARDEN MURDER CASE (Metro-Goldwyn-Mayer, 1936) 62 minutes.

Producers, Lucien Hubbard, Ned Marin; director, Edwin L. Marin; based on the novel by S. S. Van Dine [Willard Huntington Wright]; screenplay, Bertram Millhauser; camera, Charles Clark; editor, Ben Lewis.

Edmund Lowe (Philo Vance); Virginia Bruce (Zalia Graem); Benita Hume (Nurse Beeton); Nat Pendleton (Sergeant Ernest

H. B. Warner, Virginia Bruce, Gene Lockhart, Edmund Lowe, Kent Smith and Benita Hume in THE GARDEN MURDER CASE (1936).

Heath); H. B. Warner (Major Fenwicke-Ralston); Grant Mitchell (Inspector John F. X. Markham); Henry B. Walthall (Dr. Garden); Charles Trowbridge (Inspector Colby); Douglas Watson (Floyd Garden); Gene Lockhart (Lowe Hammle); Kent Smith (Woode Swift); Frieda Inescort (Mrs. Fenwicke-Ralston); Jessie Ralph (Mrs. Hammle); Etienne Girardot (Medical Examiner Doremus); William Austin (Sneed); Rosalind Ivan (Japson).

MGM made its third and final Philo Vance film* with THE GARDEN MURDER CASE based on S. S. Van Dine's 1935 novel. Edmund Lowe, who played a long string of detectives in films and who was by now past his box-office prime, was nicely cast as Philo Vance, although moviegoers were becoming disenchanted with the rapid succession of screen Vances, a new one almost every picture. In this caper the detective is allowed a romantic interest in Virginia Bruce. The only "regular" to appear from past Vance installments was Etienne Girardot as Medical Examiner Doremus, a role she had performed in Warner Bros.' THE KENNEL MURDER CASE (1933) and THE DRAGON MURDER CASE (1934), qq.v.

Distinguished detective Philo Vance (Edmund Lowe) is called into a penthouse garden shooting by his high society friends. The case takes on a new twist when three of the people involved are also killed: Mrs. Fenwicke-Ralston (Frieda Inescort) is pushed off the top of a bus, Floyd Garden (Douglas Watson) falls to his death from a horse at a steeplechase, and philanderer Lowe Hammle (Gene Lockhart) is found murdered in his library. Faltering Sergeant Ernest Heath (Nat Pendleton) is in charge of the murder investigation but District Attorney John F. X. Markham (Grant Mitchell) has more faith in Vance. The chief suspects include Nurse Beeton (Benita Hume) and Major Fenwicke-Ralston (H. B. Warner), and Vance finds romance with pretty society lady Zalia Graem (Virginia Bruce). One of the suspects is a fakir who tries to hypnotize Vance and make him jump from a high ledge, he fails and is captured by the detective.

This adaptation of a Van Dine work took far more liberties with the original than usual; additional murders being added to the plot, as well as a more dominating romantic relationship for the detective. (At the fadeout he and the heroine are kissing.) *Variety* hastened to add, "It isn't the fault of the players or the director that the filmization of Philo Vance's further exploits does not move as fast as the novel did between covers. Bertram Milhauser's screenplay,

---

*The earlier two Metro-Goldwyn-Mayer films based on the detective Philo Vance were: THE BISHOP MURDER CASE (1930) and THE CASINO MURDER CASE (1935), qq.v.

which changed about everything of the book except its title, is the slower-upper."

On the other hand, in retrospect, Ray Cabana, Jr. stated in "Murder, Mythology and Mother Goose" (*Kaleidoscope* magazine, Vol. 2. No. 3 1967), "Though only 62 minutes in length, the film is wonderfully atmospheric and the murders especially gripping, with the unknown killer being able to perpetrate death when nowhere near the scene of his crimes, and with the selected victims *knowing that they're going to die!* "

It should be noted that the climax of THE GARDEN MURDER CASE, with Vance on the high ledge, predates a similar thrill sequence in the popular Sherlock Holmes-Universal feature, THE WOMAN IN GREEN, *q.v.*, by nine years.

THE GAY FALCON (RKO, 1941) 67 minutes.

Producer, Howard Benedict; director, Irving Reis; based on the story by Michael Arlen [Diran Kuyumjian]; screenplay, Lynn Root, Frank Fenton; music, Paul Sawtell; art director, Van Nest Polglase; camera, Nicholas Musuraca; editor, George Crone.

George Sanders (Gay Lawrence, The Falcon); Wendy Barrie (Helen Reed); Allen Jenkins (Jonathan C. "Goldy" Locke); Anne Hunter (Elinor); Gladys Cooper (Maxine); Edward Brophy (Detective Bates); Arthur Shields (Captain Waldeck); Damian O'Flynn (Weber); Turhan Bey (Retanu); Eddie Dunn (Grimes); Lucile Gleason (Mrs. Gardiner); Willie Fung (Jerry); Hans Conreid (Herman); Jimmy Conlin (Bartender); Walter Soderling (Morgue Attendant); Robert Smith (Cop at Morgue); Lee Bonnell, Virginia Vale (Bits); Bobby Barber (Waiter); Paul Norby (Cigar Clerk); Mickey Phillips (Newsboy); Frank O'Connor (Cop); Lew Kelly (Jailer); Polly Bailey (Landlady); James Baline (Cop in Hallway); Joey Ray (Orchestra Leader).

Between 1939 and 1941 George Sanders played Simon Templar, The Saint, in five RKO Radio programmers about the Leslie Charteris character. He grew tired of these assembly-line films and the studio switched him over to its new The Falcon series, the character allegedly being based on Michael Arlen's [Diran Kuyumjian] 1940 short story, "The Gay Falcon." Actually the title character in the story was a tough Sam Spade-like operative, but in the movies Sanders continued to play him as he had Templar, as a suave sophisticate. Don Miller noted in *B Movies* (1973), "Director Irving Reis did what he could and the net result wasn't too bad, but the adventurous atmosphere of The Saint series was missing. And Sanders, tired of his 'B' Robin Hood roles, wanted out from the start."

Wall Street stockbroker Gay Lawrence (George Sanders), alias The Falcon, is asked by pretty social secretary Helen Reed (Wendy Barrie) to attend a society party given by Maxine (Gladys Cooper), her wealthy employer. Helen fears an attempt will be made to steal the woman's priceless jewels. During the party one of the guests, Mrs. Gardiner (Lucile Gleason), gives The Falcon her diamond ring by mistake and later is found murdered. Policemen Waldeck (Arthur Shields) and thick-headed Bates (Edward Brophy) feel Jonathan C. "Goldy" Locke (Allen Jenkins), an ex-safecracker and The Falcon's buddy, is guilty of the crime. Lawrence proves his friend's innocence by unmasking the real killer at the same time that he becomes engaged to lovely socialite Elinor (Anne Hunter). Before their romance develops too far, however, another pretty girl comes onto the scene and asks The Falcon's aid in a new case.

Following a tried and true formula the new series met with acceptance. "Fable of THE FALCON, amateur detective and lady's man, follows the accepted pattern for such whodunits. . . . It's done with a light, THIN MANnish touch" (*Variety*). George Sanders made three more Falcon films: A DATE WITH THE FALCON (1941), THE FALCON TAKES OVER (1942),* and THE FALCON'S BROTHER (1942), which co-starred Sanders' brother Tom Conway as Tom Lawrence, the brother of The Falcon. When Gay Lawrence is killed by spies in this feature, his brother carries on for nine more installments, Tom Conway having breathed new life into the series.

GENIUS AT WORK   *see*   SUPER SLEUTH [essay].

THE GHOST TALKS (Fox, 1929) 61 minutes.

Presenter, William Fox; director, Lewis Seiler; based on the play *Badges* by Max Marcin, Edward Hammond; screenplay, Frederick Hazlitt Brennan; dialogue, Harlan Thompson, Brennan; assistant director, J. Edmund Grainger; sound, Joseph Aiken; camera, George Meehan; editor, Ralph Dietrich.

Helen Twelvetrees (Miriam Holt); Charles Eaton (Franklyn Green); Stepin Fetchit (Christopher Lee); Carmel Myers (Marie Haley); Earle Foxe (Heimie Heimrath); Henry Sedley (Joe Talles); Joe Brown (Peter Accardi); Clifford Dempsey (John Keegan); Baby Mack (Isobel Lee); Arnold Lucy (Julius Bowser); Bess Flowers (Sylvia); Dorothy McGowan (Miss Eva); Mickey Bennett (Bellboy).

---

*THE FALCON TAKES OVER is the initial screen adaptation of Raymond Chandler's novel, *Farewell, My Lovely* (1940), in which his private eye Philip Marlowe becomes The Falcon.

When one thinks of the detective film the stereotypes of the hardboiled gumshoe (Sam Spade, Philip Marlowe) or the cerebral sleuth (Sherlock Holmes, Hercule Poirot) come frequently to mind. It should be remembered, however, that in the 1920s, especially in the early days of sound, the detective film was also closely linked to the horror feature. Many whodunits were enshrouded with ghostly doings, sinister old houses, dark passage ways, and hand-clutching-cloak figures. One such outing is the now nearly forgotten THE GHOST TALKS, a Fox feature which offered all these trappings but which also took many comical pokes at the genre. It was Fox's second feature length, all talking production.

Taken from Max Marcin (the creator of The Crime Doctor character) and Edward Hammond's 1924 play *Badges,* the film concerns hotel night clerk Franklyn Green (Charles Eaton) who hopes to become a detective. He is taking a course on the subject from a correspondence school, and is the overzealous sort who wears a Sherlock Holmes-style double cap and chaws on a calabash pipe. Pretty, but not-so-bright, Miriam Holt (Helen Twelvetrees) arrives at the hotel and Green learns that the lisping miss is after a million dollars in bonds stolen from her late uncle. When four crooks, also after the bonds, follow Miriam to the hotel, Green mistakes two of them for government agents working for the postal inspector. The case takes the group to a mysterious house where the crooks set up bogus ghostly apparitions to scare Green away. The ruse eventually fails. He turns up the securities, apprehends the crooks, and turns them over to the law. For his efforts, Green wins Miriam's love.

Photoplay magazine termed the film a "talkie farce" with "plenty of laughs." Much of the "comedy" was derived from the shuffling shenanigans of Stepin Fetchit, here playing a character named "Christopher Lee"!

THE GIRL HUNTERS (Colorama/Zodiak International, 1963) 103 minutes.

Producer, Robert Fellows; associate producer, Charles Reynolds; director, Roy Rowland; based on the novel by Mickey Spillane; screenplay, Spillane, Rowland, Fellows; art director, Tony Inglis; music/music director, Philip Green; assistant director, George Pollard; wardrobe supervisor, Rene Coke; makeup, Sydney Turner; fight art, Douglas Robinson; sound, Gerry Turner, Hugh Strain, Fred Turtle; sound editor, Jim Roddan; camera, Kenneth Talbot; editor, Sidney Stone.

Mickey Spillane (Mike Hammer); Shirley Eaton (Laura Knapp); Lloyd Nolan (Art Rickerby); Hy Gardner (Himself); Scott Peters

(Captain Pat Chambers); Guy Kingsley Poynter (Dr. Larry Snyder); James Dyrenforth (Bayliss Henry); Charles Farrell (Joe Grissi); Kim Tracy (Nurse); Benny Lee (Nat Drutman); Murray Kash (Richie Cole); Bill Nagy (Georgie); Clive Endersby (Duck-Duck); Richard Montez (Skinny Guy): Larry Cross (Red Markham); Tony Arpino (Cab Driver); Hal Galili (Bouncer); Nelly Hanham (Landlady); Bob Gallico (Dr. Leo Daniels); Michael Brennan, Howard Greene, Grant Holden (Policemen); Francis Napier (Detective); Larry Taylor ("The Dragon").

Mickey Spillane has been turning out novels about his tough detective Mike Hammer (who uses his fists and gut hunches more than intellectual deduction and charm) since 1950 and is one of the most recognized of mystery writers, his activities ranging from acting to TV talk show appearances and beer commercials. In RING OF FEAR (1954) he portrayed himself solving a murder case, the first detective fiction writer to portray himself on screen. In 1963 he went one better by playing his own Mike Hammer in THE GIRL HUNTERS, based on his 1963 novel and filmed in Great Britain.*

When his secretary/lover Velda disappears, private eye Mike Hammer (Mickey Spillane) turns to the bottle and becomes a lush who finally ends in the Gotham gutters, from which he is rescued by an old pal, city police Captain Pat Chambers (Scott Peters). It seems that a dying sailor, Cole (Murray Kash), will only talk to Hammer and the police need to learn what he knows since the weapon with which he was shot was the same one used to assassinate a senator years earlier. Hammer agrees to interrogate Cole and he confides that he and the senator were targets of a communist spy ring led by The Dragon. The detective, however, ends up in a drunk tank before he can relay this information. Finally he does share what he learned after Art Rickerby (Lloyd Nolan), a federal agent, alerts him that Cole was a U.S. spy. Hammer agrees to bring in the killer and is aided by newsman Hy Gardner (Himself), who directs him to Laura Knapp (Shirley Eaton), the senator's sexy widow. When several people are killed, Hammer believes Laura is involved with the spy ring and has a hunch that Velda may be alive and their prisoner. He

---

*Previous screen Mike Hammers were: Biff Elliott (I, THE JURY, 1953), Ralph Meeker (KISS ME DEADLY, 1955) and Robert Bray (MY GUN IS QUICK, 1957), *qq.v.* On television Darren McGavin played the violent sleuth from 1957-59; later Kevin Dobson appeared as the rugged gumshoe in the telefeature MICKEY SPILLANE'S MARGIN FOR MURDER (1981) and Stacy Keach appeared as the tough private eye in three made-for-television movies: MICKEY SPILLANE's MIKE HAMMER: MURDER ME, MURDER YOU (1983), MICKEY SPILLANE'S MIKE HAMMER: MORE THAN MURDER (1984), and THE RETURN OF MICKEY SPILLANE'S MIKE HAMMER (1986), *qq.v.*, as well as in the on-again, off-again 1984-86 video teleseries.

traces the espionage agents to a remote chicken farm where he tortures The Dragon to death by nailing his hands to the floor. When Laura arrives, Hammer accuses her of aiding the spies in killing her husband. When she aims a shotgun at Hammer and pulls the trigger it explodes and kills her; the gumshoe had rigged the weapon to backfire.

In *The Detective in Film* (1972), William K. Everson called THE GIRL HUNTERS "a pleasant surprise," and added, "Not only was it an enjoyable return to the Marlowe-brand of mystery (with a sexy femme fatale villainess coming to a spectacular end), but Mickey Spillane himself, playing Hammer, was quite effective. In addition, the film was a fascinating (and successful) exercise in illusion: apart from a few establishing shots of New York, the whole film was made in England, yet the intercutting of those few authentic shots were matched with made-up British sets, plus the use of familiar American faces gave the film the wholly convincing veneer of an American-made film."

GIRL MISSING (Warner Bros., 1933) 69 minutes.

Director, Robert Florey; suggested by the screenplay by S. S. Van Dine [Willard Huntington Wright]; story/adaptor, Carl Errickson, Don Mullay; dialogue director, Ben Markson; camera, Arthur Todd; editor, Ralph Dawson.

Ben Lyon (Henry Gibson); Glenda Farrell (Kay Curtis); Mary Brian (June Dale); Peggy Shannon (Daisy); Lyle Talbot (Raymond Fox); Guy Kibbee (Kenneth Van Dusen); Harold Huber (Jim Hendricks); Ferdinand Gottschalk (Alvin Bradford); Helen Ware (Mrs. Bradford); and: Fred Kelsey, Mike Marita.

S. S. Van Dine [Willard Huntington Wright], the creator of Philo Vance, wrote a screenplay called THE BLUE MOON MURDER CASE to star Walter Huston; the project was never filmed but scripters Carl Errickson and Don Mullay used it as the basis for GIRL MISSING. The sluggish results pleased no one. "About the last 30 minutes are almost totally devoid of movement," observed *Variety*, adding, "Too much script faith placed in the wise-cracking showgirl."

Two chorines, fast-talking Kay Curtis (Glenda Farrell) and lady-like June Dale (Mary Brian), are stuck with a big hotel bill when their plans to use June as the bait to pressure a Palm Beach vacation from a rich man fails. He leaves town when June will not share his affections. One of their co-workers, Daisy (Peggy Shannon), and her boyfriend (Lyle Talbot) come up with a scheme to blackmail rich Henry Gibson (Ben Lyon) by having Daisy persuade him to marry her. On the night of the wedding Daisy disappears and her new husband offers a reward for tracing her. Kay and June, needing to rectify their negative cash flow, set out to solve the mystery. But along the way June falls in love with Gibson. The girls locate the missing gal and collect the reward. Gibson plans a quick divorce so he and June can wed.

GIRL MISSING, although implausible in plot, does boast a pleasing cast, highlighted by Glenda Farrell in her sharp-tongued showgirl interpretation, the type of part which would lead to her playing the lead in the Torchy Blane detective series later in the decade at Warner Bros.

THE GLASS KEY (Paramount, 1935) 80 minutes.

Producer, E. Lloyd Sheldon; director, Frank Tuttle; based on the novel by Dashiell Hammett; screenplay, Kathryn Scola, Kubec Glasmon, Harry Ruskin; camera, Henry Sharp; editor, Hugh Bennett.

George Raft (Ed Beaumont); Edward Arnold (Paul Madvig); Claire Dodd (Janet Henry); Rosalind Keith (Opal Madvig); Charles Richman (Senator Henry); Robert Gleckler (Shad O'Rory); Guinn "Big Boy" Williams (Jeff); Ray Milland (Taylor Henry); Tammany Young (Clarkie); Harry Tyler (Henry Sloss); Charles C. Wilson (Farr); Emma Dunn (Mom); Matt McHugh (Puggy); Patrick Moriarty (Mulrooney); Mack Gray (Duke); Frank Marlowe (Walter Ivans); Herbert Evans (Senator's Butler); George H. Reed (Black Serving Man); Percy Morris (Bartender); Irving Bacon (Waiter); Ann Sheridan (Nurse); Henry Roquemore (Rinkle); Frank O'Connor (McLaughlin); Michael Mark (Swartz); Del Cambre (Reporter); Veda Buckland (Landlady); George Ernst (Boy).

THE GLASS KEY (Paramount, 1942) 85 minutes.

Associate producer, Fred Kohlmar; director, Stuart Heisler; based on the novel by Dashiell Hammett; screenplay, Jonathan Latimer; art directors, Hans Dreier, Haldane Douglas; music, Victor Young; sound, Hugo Grenzbach, Don Johnson; camera, Theodor Sparkhl; editor, Archie Marshek.

Brian Donlevy (Paul Madvig); Veronica Lake (Janet Henry); Alan Ladd (Ed Beaumont); Bonita Granville (Opal Madvig); Richard Denning (Taylor Henry); Joseph Calleia (Nick Varna); William Bendix (Jeff); Frances Gifford (Nurse); Donald MacBride (Farr); Margaret Hayes (Eloise Mathews); Moroni Olsen (Ralph Henry); Eddie Marr (Rusty); Arthur Loft (Clyde Matthews); George Meader (Claude Tuttle); Pat O'Malley, Ed Peil, Sr., James Millican (Politicians); Edmund Cobb, Frank Bruno, Jack Luden, Jack Gardner, Joe McGuinn, Frank Hagney (Reporters); John W. DeNoria (Groggins); Jack Mulhall (Lynch); Joseph King (Fisher); Al Hill (Bum); Freddie

Walburn (Kid); Conrad Binyon (Stubby); Vernon Dent (Bartender); Stanley Price, Kenneth Chryst (Men in Barroom); Dane Clark (Henry Sloss); Norma Varden (Dowager); Frank Elliott, George Cowl (Butlers in Henry Home); Arthur Hull, Tom O'Grady, Jack Fowler (Guests at Henry Dinner); Tom Fadden (Waiter); William Wagner (Butler); Charles Sullivan (Taxi Driver); Francis Sayles (Seedy-Looking Man); George Turner (Doctor); Tom Dugan (Jeep); William Benedict (Sturdy); Lillian Randolph (Entertainer at Basement Club).

Dashiell Hammett's 1931 novel *The Glass Key* has been twice adapted to the screen, both times by Paramount Pictures, which bought the property following the success of Hammett's other screen-adapted works, *The Maltese Falcon* (1930) and *The Thin Man* (1934). The title refers to underworld jargon for an invitation, although one without sincerity.

The initial screen rendition came in 1935 under Frank Tuttle's steady direction. Rising politician Paul Madvig (Edward Arnold) and his taciturn henchman Ed Beaumont (George Raft) aid Senator Henry (Charles Richman) in his re-election bid. Beaumont rebels against the assignment but goes along with his boss, who suddenly becomes honest and helps close up the gaming establishment run by gangster Shad O'Rory (Robert Gleckler). In revenge, O'Rory has Madvig framed for the murder of Taylor Henry (Ray Milland), the senator's son who was romantically involved with Madvig's daughter Opal (Rosalind Keith). Ed Beaumont turns detective to free his employer, who has been arrested for the homicide. In delving into O'Rory's underworld empire Beaumont is badly beaten up by the racketeer's drunk thug Jeff (Guinn "Big Boy" Williams). However, Ed manages to turn the sadistic Jeff against O'Rory and the latter is killed as Beaumont gains the needed proof to clear Madvig.

". . . Just when we were beginning to fear that the imitators of THE THIN MAN were becomingly overly jocose on the subject of assassination, Mr. Hammett comes along with proof that murder isn't necessarily funny" (Andre Sennwald, *New York Times*). The *Times* described this screen version as "A salty tale of violence and secret murder" and praised it for being "excellently produced." On the other hand, *Variety* pointed out, "Too much has gone into the narrative that are up the alley of inconsistency" and "Three romances are knitted into the murder mystery, but, in the main, the romantic aspects of the picture don't impress." Nevertheless, the film was successfully received by the public and the film helped to solidify George Raft's popularity in tough guy roles.

If the 1935 version of THE GLASS KEY had seemed rough and tough to audiences of the day, such was certainly the case with the rougher and tougher 1942 version, made as a vehicle for the screen team of Alan Ladd and Veronica Lake, who had scored together effectively the year before in THIS GUN FOR HIRE. Here Ladd took over the Ed Beaumont role while Brian Donlevy was Madvig, and William Bendix was now the sadistic, distraught Jeff. Jonathan Latimer, the creator of the character of fictional sleuth Bill Crane, who came to the screen in a trio of films including THE LADY IN THE MORGUE (1938), *q.v.*, re-adapted the Hammett novel to the screen and it remained fairly close to the 1935 version in plot.* However, in this outing the feminine lead, as played by diminutive Veronica Lake, is not Madvig's daughter but the offspring of a rival politician and is lusted after by both Madvig and Beaumont. Joseph Calleia is the gangster Nick Varna, out to entrap Madvig, and using the perverted Jeff to carry out his carnage.

With viewing attendance at a new high (everyone wanted to forget the real-life carnage of World War II), a glossy star production like THE GLASS KEY was guaranteed box-office success. Nevertheless, the critics found flaws. ". . . It sags under the endless complexity of Mr. Hammett's plot. All too often it paralyzes the adaptor by the necessity for exposition, and at those points the sleight of hand fails and the characters become no more than puppets in a bizarre pattern" (Theodore Strauss, *New York Times*).

Regarding the 1942 version, Robert Ottoson wrote in *A Reference Guide to the Film Noir: 1940-1958* (1981), "THE GLASS KEY depicts the world of the criminal, ignoring for the most part the legal authorities. This in turn leads into the sort of violence and brutality usually associated with the film noir, which certainly makes it a precursor to the more morbid films of the mid- and late forties. Much of the violence here is performed by Bendix, who bounces Alan Ladd around like a rubber ball. . . . The film contains numerous other examples of the new-found brutality of forties films." Veronica Lake, in her autobiography *Veronica* (1971), describes THE GLASS KEY from her special perspective. "Hammett fans hated our version of their favorite author's classic. Others never liked the original version with George Raft and felt we'd accomplished an improvement on the story. Either way, it all came off for me as a humdrum affair. . . ."

---

*In *Film Noir: An Encyclopedic Reference to the American Style*, (1979), Robert Porfirio notes that the 1942 version "lacks the powerful ending of the original novel. . . . Beaumont's character in the film is considerably more amoral than in the novel. . . . Although Beaumont's masochism is deemphasized from the novel by eliminating his suicide attempt and alcoholism, there exists a brutal, almost symbiotic link between the two men [Beaumont and the vulgar, brutal Jeff]."

THE GOLDEN EYE (Monogram, 1948) 69 minutes.

Producer, James S. Burkett; director, William Beaumont; based on the character created by Earl Derr Biggers; screenplay, W. Scott Darling; music director, Edward J. Kay; art director, Dave Milton; set decorator, Raymond Boltz, Jr.; makeup, Webb Overlander; assistant director, Wesley Barry; sound, John Kean, Frank Hansen; camera, William Sickner; editor, Ace Herman.

Roland Winters (Charlie Chan); Wanda McKay (Evelyn Manning); Mantan Moreland (Birmingham Brown); Victor Sen Yung (Tommy Chan); Tim Ryan (Lieutenant Ruark); Bruce Kellogg (Bartlett); Ralph Dunn (Driscoll); Forrest Taylor (Manning); Evelyn Brent (Teresa the Nursing Sister); Lois Austin (Mrs. Driscoll); Lee "Lasses" White (Pete); Edmund Cobb (Miner); and: Herman Cantor, Lee Tung Foo, Richard Loo, John Merton, George L. Spaulding, Tom Tyler, Bill Walker, Barbara Jean Wong.

Towards the end of the Charlie Chan series at Monogram in the late 1940s, a few of the installments took on western settings, actually becoming modern day Westerns with mystery backgrounds. THE GOLDEN EYE and THE FEATHERED SERPENT, *q.v.*, both benefitted from this change of pace although the first film is definitely the more engaging of the two. In fact, it bears a minor resemblance to the lost 1927 Chan silent feature, THE CHINESE PARROT, *q.v.*

Mine owner Manning (Forrest Taylor) has sent for his friend Charlie Chan (Roland Winters) who comes to his Arizona dude ranch with son Tommy (Victor Sen Yung) and chauffeur Birmingham Brown (Mantan Moreland), presumably on a vacation. Once there Chan learns from Manning's daughter Evelyn (Wanda McKay) that her father has fallen down a mine shaft and has been badly injured. He is unconscious and his face is bandaged and he is being cared for by Sister Teresa (Evelyn Brent). Also at the dude ranch is police Lieutenant Ruark (Tim Ryan) who is pretending to be a guest and a jovial drunk. He tells Chan he is there to learn why Manning's mine has become so productive suddenly and he is also studying Manning's alleged injury. Pete (Lee "Lasses" White), an old-time miner, is murdered after stumbling onto an important secret, and from this Chan deduces that smugglers have been bringing in gold ore from Mexico and claiming it is from Manning's mine to avoid import charges. The detective also realizes that Manning is actually dead and someone is masquerading in his stead, with the fake nun in league with them. Chan unmasks the killer behind the operation.

Also called THE MYSTERY OF THE GOLDEN EYE (the title refers to the name of the mine), this third from the last Charlie Chan feature is solid entertainment, with its atmospheric, spooky sequences and the juxtaposition of the Oriental sleuth and the "old" West, a felicitous mixture.

The creative poster blurb for this film announced, "Chan Seeks the Sinister Secret of a 'Murder Mine' Worth Millions! Death lurks at every step . . . as your oriental super-sleuth stalks a desperate killer—below the surface of the earth!"

THE GRACIE ALLEN MURDER CASE (Paramount, 1939) 74 minutes.

Producer, George Arthur; director, Alfred E. Green; based on the novel by S. S. Van Dine [Willard Huntington Wright]; screenplay, Nat Perrin; song, Matty Malneck and Frank Loesser; assistant director, Russell Mathews; art directors, Hans Dreier, Earl Hedrick; camera, Charles Long; editor, Paul Weatherwax.

Gracie Allen (Herself); Warren William (Philo Vance); Ellen Drew (Ann Wilson); Kent Taylor (Bill Brown); Jed Prouty (Uncle Ambrose); Jerome Cowan (Daniel Mirche); H. B. Warner (Richard Lawrence); William Demarest (Sergeant Ernest Heath); Judith Barrett (Dixie Del Marr); Donald MacBride (District Attorney John F. X. Markham); Lee Moore (Benny "The Buzzard" Nelson); Horace MacMahon (Gus); Richard Denning (Fred); Al Shaw, Sam Lee (Thugs); Irving Bacon (Clerk).

In 1939 Paramount Pictures had the deliciously zany notion of ordering a script for a comedy-mystery combining the talents of Philo Vance and Gracie Allen. Vance's creator, S. S. Van Dine [Willard Huntington Wright], devised a story called THE GRACIE ALLEN MURDER CASE which was published as a novel under that title. By the time the work reached the screen, however, a number of plot changes had occurred, the most notable being the elimination of George Burns' character—he had been Gracie's boyfriend in the book—and the denigration of the Vance character into little more than a stooge for Gracie Allen. (In the film she constantly refers to Vance as "Fido.") Warren William, who had played Philo Vance in the fine THE DRAGON MURDER CASE (1934), *q.v.*, here plays a rather world-weary and softer, albeit more callous Vance—but then again, having to deal nonstop with the daffiness of Gracie Allen's non-sequitur logic would be enough to turn around anyone's personality.

While employed at a perfume factory, Gracie Allen (herself) meets Bill Brown (Kent Taylor) who is in love with Ann Wilson (Ellen Drew). A notorious gangster, Benny "The Buzzard" Nelson (Lee Moore), escapes from prison and Gracie, while having dinner at a night club, finds his body in an office. Brown is blamed for the murder because his cigarette case is found beside the corpse. Gracie hires famous detective Philo Vance (Warren William) to prove Brown's innocence but the sleuth is irritated by Gracie's perpetual meddling in the case. When nightclub singer Dixie Del Marr (Judith Barrett) is also murdered, Vance believes that the club owner, Daniel Mirche (Jerome Cowan), and his corrupt mouthpiece, Richard Lawrence (H. B. Warner), are the culprits. Police Sergeant Ernest Heath (William Demarest) and District Attorney Markham (Donald MacBride), however, arrest Vance himself for the latter killing. A wild motorcycle ride through heavy traffic awaits Gracie and, afterwards, Vance uses Mirche to help him trap the real killer. Just as he is about to smoke a poisoned cigarette, Gracie conks Vance on the head to save his life.

Following her successful escapades with crime in THE GRACIE ALLEN MURDER CASE, Gracie next appeared (again sans George Burns) in MR. AND MRS. NORTH (1941), *q.v.*, another comedy whodunit. When *The Gracie Allen Murder Case* was reprinted in 1950 its title was altered to *The Smell of Murder.*

GRAND CENTRAL MURDER (Metro-Goldwyn-Mayer, 1942) 72 minutes.

Producer, B. F. Zeldman; director, S. Sylvan Simon; based on the novel by Sue MacVeigh; screenplay, Peter Ruric; art director, Cedric Gibbons; music, David Snell; camera, George Folsey; editor Conrad A. Nervig.

Van Heflin (Rocky Custer); Patricia Dane (Mida King); Cecilia Parker (Constance Furness); Virginia Grey (Sue Custer); Samuel S. Hinds (Roger Furness); Sam Levene (Inspector Gunther); Connie Gilchrist (Pearl Delroy); Mark Daniels (David V. Henderson); Horace [Stephen] McNally (Turk); Tom Conway (Frankie Ciro); Betty Wells (Baby Delroy); George Lynn (Paul Rinehart); Roman Bohnen (Ramon); Millard Mitchell (Arthur Doolin).

Sue MacVeigh's 1939 novel, *Grand Central Murder,* involved a husband-wife sleuthing team solving a murder, à la The Thin Man and Mr. and Mrs. North. When MGM, the studio responsible for filming the two above-mentioned teams, brought it to the screen in 1942 it had undergone a facelift by scriptor Peter Ruric. He replaced the married detectives team with a hard-boiled private eye named Rocky Custer, although Custer does have some help from his wife Sue. Van Heflin was cast as Rocky and the film greatly benefitted from his having just won a Best Supporting Actor Academy Award for JOHNNY EAGER (1941).

Nasty actress Mida King (Patricia Dane) is found murdered in her train car in the Grand Central yards. Private eye Rocky Custer (Van Heflin), with some unwanted assistance from spouse Sue

Samuel S. Hinds, Cecilia Parker, Mark Daniels and Sam Levene in GRAND
CENTRAL MURDER (1942).

(Virginia Grey), vies with police Inspector Gunther (Sam Levene) in
deducing the identity of the killer. The suspects, who relate their
stories/alibis in flashbacks, include: Constance Furness (Cecilia
Parker) and her father, Roger (Samuel S. Hinds), Pearl Delroy
(Connie Gilchrist), Frankie Ciro (Tom Conway), and Turk (Horace
[Stephen] McNally). There are ten suspects in all and when a vital
clue is uncovered after all of them have been questioned, Rocky
brings forth the killer.

In "Private Eyes" (*Focus on Film* magazine, August 1975), Don
Miller decided that Van Heflin " . . . carried off his undemanding
assignment with aplomb, [S. Sylvan] Simon's direction was in tune,
and Ruric's script, after a confused and confusing beginning was on
target." Bosley Crowther (*New York Times*) commented, "Armchair
detectives who delight in spotting clues and following verbal deductions toward a tedious solution of a crime should find considerable
pleasure in GRAND CENTRAL MURDER. . . ." He added, however, "It's no great shakes of a picture. . . ." Regarding the numerous
flashbacks used to propel the story, *Variety* noted, "It is an involved
and intricate manner of relating what took place, but it all pieces

together at the end, due in large part, no doubt, to the direction of S. Sylvan Simon, who never takes the happenings too seriously."

THE GREAT HOSPITAL MYSTERY (Twentieth Century-Fox, 1937) 58 minutes.

Associate producer, John Stone; director, James Tinling; based on the story "Dead Yesterday" by Mignon C. Eberhart; screenplay, Bess Meredyth, William Conselman, Jerry Cady; music director, Samuel Kaylin; camera, Harry Jackson; editor, Nick DeMaggio.

Sally Blane (Nurse Ann Smith); Thomas Beck (Dr. David McKerry) Jane Darwell (Miss Keats); Sig Rumann (Dr. Triggert); Joan Davis (Nurse Flossie Duff); Wade Boteler (Detective Lieutenant Mattoon); William Demarest (Mr. Beatty); George Walcott (Allen Tracy); Howard Philips (Tom Kirby); Ruth Peterson (Desk Nurse); Carl Faulkner, Frank C. Fanning (Policemen); Margaret Brayton (Chart Room Nurse); Lona Andrew (Miss White); Tom Mahoney (Bank Guard).

See: WHILE THE PATIENT SLEPT [essay].

THE GREAT HOTEL MURDER (Fox, 1935) 70 minutes.

Director, Eugene Forde; based on the story "Recipe for Murder" by Vincent Starrett; screenplay, Arthur Kober; music, Samuel Kaylin; camera, Ernest Palmer.

Edmund Lowe (Roger Blackwood); Victor McLaglen (Andy McCabe); Rosemary Ames (Elinor Blake); Mary Carlisle (Olive Temple); Henry O'Neill (Mr. Harvey); C. Henry Gordon (Dr. Temple); William Janney (Harry Prentice); Charles C. Wilson (Anthony Wilson); John Wray ("Feets" Moore).

Edmund Lowe and Victor McLaglen proved to be one of the screen's most durable teams following the success of WHAT PRICE GLORY? in 1926, in which they immortalized the roles of two battling soldiers, Quirt and Flagg. After that they teamed for a long line of successful follow-ups and spinoffs: THE COCKEYED WORLD (1929), WOMEN OF ALL NATIONS (1931), GUILTY AS HELL (1932), HOT PEPPER (1933), UNDER PRESSURE (1935), and CALL OUT THE MARINES (1942), in addition to the well-executed murder mystery, THE GREAT HOTEL MURDER. This picture offers Lowe as a debonair criminologist and McLaglen as his bumbling law enforcement nemesis, and the two make the most of the proceedings, based on Vincent Starrett's story, "Recipe for Murder."

At a doctor's convention at a big city hotel, a man dies mysteriously and the house detective, Andy McCabe (Victor McLaglen), thinks it is suicide. Also registered at the hotel is crime novelist/

criminologist Roger Blackwood (Edmund Lowe) and he suspects foul play in the death, although McCabe scoffs at this theory. Blackwood continues his clue gathering and uncovers a number of suspects. At one point, the jealous McCabe even arrests Blackwood for the crime. Finally the evidence points to Dr. Temple (C. Henry Gordon), but Blackwood proves the dead man was poisoned by a drug addict who was in love with the murdered man's wife.

Andre Sennwald (*New York Times*) reacted positively: "This time Mr. Lowe's friendly rival, Victor McLaglen, is the hulking house detective who regards the higher ratiocinative processes of the novelist with vast contempt and triumphantly accuses all the wrong people. In their present collaboration Messrs. Lowe and McLaglen are helped in their work by the omission of the usual rivalry over the ingenue, which has been detrimental to their recent pictures. Here they battle amiably for the honor of capturing the slayer and manage to be reasonably humorous in a good average specimen of the detective film."

THE GREEN GHOST   *see*   THE UNHOLY NIGHT [essay].

THE GREENE MURDER CASE (Paramount, 1929) 68 minutes.

Director, Frank Tuttle; based on the novel by S. S. Van Dine [Willard Huntington Wright]; screenplay, Louise Long; dialogue, Bartlett Cormack; titles, Richard H. Digges, Jr.; camera, Henry Gerrard; editor, Verna Willis.

William Powell (Philo Vance); Florence Eldridge (Sibella Greene); Ullrich Haput (Dr. Von Blon); Jean Arthur (Ada Greene); Eugene Pallette (Sergeant Ernest Heath); E. H. Calvert (District Attorney John F. X. Markham); Gertrude Norman (Mrs. Tobias Greene); Lowell Drew (Chester Greene); Morgan Farley (Rex Greene); Brandon Hurst (Sproot); Augusta Burmeister (Mrs. Mannheim); Marcia Harris (Hemmings); Mildred Golden (Barton); Mrs. Wilfred Buckland (Nurse for Mrs. Greene); Helena Phillips (Police Nurse for Mrs. Greene); Shep Camp (Medical Examiner); Charles E. Evans (Lawyer Canon).

When wealthy and eccentric Chester Greene (Lowell Drew) is murdered mysteriously, police Sergeant Ernest Heath (Eugene Pallette) and District Attorney John F. X. Markham (E. H. Calvert) are baffled by the case and summon amateur detective Philo Vance (William Powell). Vance finds the Greene mansion ruled over by bed-ridden Mrs. Tobias Greene (Gertrude Norman) and the entire family held together by hatred and a strange will. Two additional members of the Greene clan are eliminated and Vance finally realizes the identity of the killer as the next victim, Sibella Greene

(Florence Eldridge), narrowly escapes death when the killer plunges into a nearby frigid river.

Based on S. S. Van Dine's [Willard Huntington Wright] 1927 novel, THE GREENE MURDER CASE was Paramount's second Philo Vance film (after THE "CANARY" MURDER CASE, 1929, *q.v.*), with William Powell again playing the title assignment and Eugene Pallette and E. H. Calvert repeating their roles as the police sergeant and district attorney. The film opens with a mysterious figure stalking the snow-enshrouded grounds of the Greene mansion and it retains this eerie flavor throughout the course of its plot, continuing a popular fad in old house murder mysteries which had begun in 1927 with THE CAT AND THE CANARY. In fact, THE GREENE MURDER CASE itself was kidded the next year in MGM's THE LAUREL AND HARDY MURDER CASE.

Photoplay magazine call this fall release—offered in sound and silent versions—"Another fine Van Dine murder mystery film, with Bill Powell an elegant *Philo Vance.*" Regarding the world-famous detective character, Mordaunt Hall (*New York Times*) commented, "Philo Vance permits the audience to hear snatches of his deductions, but never enough to help in the solution of the murder mystery before Mr. Vance gives the full details. . . . It might be said that he was born under a lucky star, for it is quite obvious that Mr. Van Dine or somebody guides his mind and his movements."

By today's standards, THE GREENE MURDER CASE seems sluggish and obvious, but in its day its mixture of murder, detection, comedy relief, and overall "sophistication" was well regarded.

GUILTY BYSTANDER (Film Classics, 1950) 92 minutes.

Producers, Edmund L. Dorfmann, Rex Carlton; co-producer, Joseph Lerner; associate producer, Peter Mayer; director, Lerner; based on the novel by Wade Miller; screenplay, Don Ettlinger; art director, Leo Kerz; makeup, Ira Senz; music, Dimitri Tiomkin; assistant director, James DiGangi; sound, James Shields; camera, Gerald Hirschfeld; editor, Geraldine Lerner.

Zachary Scott (Max Thursday); Faye Emerson (Georgia); Mary Boland (Smitty); Sam Levene (Captain Tonetti); J. Edward Bromberg (Varkas); Kay Medford (Angel); Jed Prouty (Dr. Elder); Harry Landers (Bert); Dennis Harrison (Mace); Elliot Sullivan (Stitch); Garney Wilson (Harvey); Ray Julian (Johnny).

Filmed entirely in New York City, " . . . the slow, sultry, steaming sadism that is usually standard to this type of film is rather effectively accomplished," wrote the *New York Times* (Bosley Crowther), of this engrossing melodrama. Issued by the independent Film Classics, the economy production teamed Zachary Scott and Faye Emerson for the fifth time, the duo having made four features together at Warner Bros. as contract players in the 1940s.

Max Thursday (Zachary Scott) is a drunken former policeman whose only employment is as a house detective in Smitty's (Mary Boland) rundown Bridgeport Hotel. Georgia (Faye Emerson), his ex-wife, tells him his son and her brother have both disappeared. This brings Thursday out of his lethargy and he traces the missing pair to Dr. Elder (Jed Prouty) who has been murdered. Thursday is the chief suspect in the homicide, but Georgia provides him with an alibi and Homicide Bureau chief Tonetti (Sam Levene) lets him go. The kidnap trail leads the detective to a gangster known as "Saint Paul," who heads a diamond smuggling racket. Thursday, however, meets opposition from hoodlum Varkas (J. Edward Bromberg), an ally of the kingpin. Nevertheless, he gets cooperation from hooker Angel (Kay Medford) before solving the case, rescuing his son and former brother-in-law and redeeming his self respect.

Following in the wake of such realistic melodramas as THE NAKED CITY (1948), this film had " . . . an oddly disturbing slow-beat rhythm and plenty of sleazy atmosphere" (*New York Times*). Don Miller in "Private Eyes" (*Focus on Film* magazine, Autumn 1975) stated, "New York-made films were a rarity then and the shabby settings added realism to the tale. Scott gave one of his more restrained performances and Dimitri Tiomkin composed a background score that ably dressed the narrative." Robert Ottoson wrote in *A Reference Guide to the American Film Noir: 1940-1958* (1981), "Scott's odyssey takes him to areas of New York City that most other films eschew. . . . GUILTY BYSTANDER captures the noir aesthetic of these seldom-seen areas, as it shoots night-for-night scenes among low-life bars, waterfront hotels, warehouses, police stations, and subways." The cynical world of GUILTY BYSTAND-ER is filled with losers, but one of them—the alcoholic Max Thursday—emerges a victor, even if he fails to shake his need for booze or ever to rise above his bottom-of-the-barrel ranking in the world of detectives.

GUMSHOE (Columbia, 1971) Color 88 minutes.

Producer, Michael Medwin; associate producer, Davie Barber; director, Stephen Frears; screenplay, Neville Smith; music, Andrew Lloyd Webber; lyrics, Tim Rice; production designer, Michael Seymour; costumes, Daphne Dare; assistant director, Ted Sturgis; camera, Chris Menges; editor, Charles Rees.

Albert Finney (Eddie Ginley); Billie Whitelaw (Ellen); Frank Finlay (William); Janice Rule (Mrs. Blankerscoon); Carolyn Seymour (Alison); Fulton Mackay (Straker); George Innes (Bookshop Proprietor); George Silver (De Fries); Billy Dean (Tommy); Wendy Richard (Anne Scott); Maureen Lipman (Naomi); Neville Smith (Arthur); Oscar James (Azinge); Joey Kenyon (Joey) Bert King (Mal); Chris Cunningham (Clifford); Ken Jones (Labor Exchange Clerk); Tom Kempinski (Psychiatrist); Harry Hutchinson (Klepto-maniac); Ernie Mack and the Saturated Seven, Jason Kane, The Jacksons, Vicki Day, Scott Christian (Club Artists).

Bored with life and forever dreaming about becoming another Sam Spade, Liverpool nightclub emcee and bingo caller Eddie Ginley (Albert Finney), on his thirty-first birthday, takes out a newspaper advertisement asking for detective work. Soon he finds himself with several cases and enmeshed with killings, dope, African gun-running, and an independence movement in an African nation. Another private eye hopeful, Straker (Fulton Mackay), helps Ginley and both are usually in over their heads as they play out in real life their Walter Mitty fantasies.

GUMSHOE is a creative British production, but one which tends to elicit either bravos or thumbs down. *Variety* labeled it " . . . an affectionately nostalgic and amusing tribute to the movie-fiction private-eye genre of yesteryear. . . . [Albert] Finney is brilliant as the key figure and fiction heros with just the right dose of tightlipped panache or—to bridge a plot gap—soliloquizing by quoting chapter and verse from his favorite authors or, again, tipping his hat to them with a look or a gesture." F. Maurice Speed in *Film Review 1972-73* (1972) judged, "Fast, confusing, amusing and tightly directed send-up of the Bogartish detective films of the 1940s. . . ." Amy Verdon reported in *Films in Review* magazine (February 1972), "Eddie is well played by Albert Finney but the shift from Eddie's dream world to harsh reality is not successfully achieved by Stephen Frears, who makes his directorial debut in GUMSHOE. One is never sure whether a particular scene is meant as satire or is to be taken straight, and never certain about what the film is trying to say." Further on the negative reaction side is William K. Everson (*The Detective in Film,* 1972), "Perhaps no film more sums up the detective film's current loss of identity than the British GUMSHOE of 1971. Part SECRET LIFE OF WALTER MITTY, part imitation THE MALTESE FALCON, and part satire, it winds up as a 'whole' nothing." Marc Sigoloff dismissed the film in *The Films of the Seventies* (1984): " . . . The film completely misses its target, and the English setting is entirely wrong for such an American subject."

One of the definite problems of GUMSHOE, over which there was no dispute, was that the Midland accents were very difficult to decipher.

HAMMETT (Warner Bros., 1982) Color 94 minutes.

Executive producer, Francis Ford Coppola; producers, Fred Roos, Ronald Colby, Don Guest; associate producer, Mona Skager; director, Wim Wenders; based on the novel by Joe Gores; adaptor, Thomas Pope; screenplay, Ross Thomas, Dennis O'Flaherty; production designers, Dean Tavoularis, Eugene Lee; art directors, Angelo Graham, Leon Erickson; assistant director, David Valdez, Daniel Attias; costumes, Ruth Morley; music, John Barry; camera, Philip Lathrop, Joseph Biroc; editors, Barry Malkin, Marc Laub, Robert Q. Vovcett, Randy Roberts.

Frederic Forrest (Hammett); Peter Boyle (Jimmy Ryan); Marilu Henner (Kit Conger/Sue Alabama); Roy Kinnear (English Eddie); Elisha Cook (Eli); Lydia Lei (Crystal Ling); R. G. Armstrong (Lieutenant O'Mara); Richard Bradford (Detective Bradford); Michael Chow (Fong); David Patrick Kelly (Punk); Sylvia Sidney (Donaldina); Jack Nance (Gary); Elmer L. Kline (Doc Fallon); Royal Dano (Pops); Samuel Fuller (Old Man); Lloyd Kino (Barber); Fox Harris (News Vendor); Rose Wood (Laundress); Liz Roberson (Lady in Library); Jean Francois Ferreol (Sailor); Alison Hong, Patricia Kong (Young Girls); Lisa Lu (Donaldina's Assistant); Andrew Winner (Guard); Kenji Shibuya (Bouncer); James Quinn (Guard).

Dashiell Hammett (1894-1961) was the author of books and stories about such fictional detectives as Sam Spade. Nick and Nora Charles, Ned Beaumont, and the Continental Op. He is considered the father of the hard-boiled detective genre and his works have taken on a cult status in recent years. Adapted from detective novelist Joe Gores' book (1975), HAMMETT was produced by Francis Ford Coppola and directed by new wave West German filmmaker Wim Wenders, who had earlier done THE AMERICAN FRIEND (1977). While a tribute to Dashiell Hammett and his work, this film emerged as a contrived and complicated affair whose saving grace is having the title character associating with assorted people who would later become the characters in his writings. Like the similarly structured AGATHA (1979), which dealt with episodes in the life of Agatha Christie, HAMMETT is more enticing as a concept than a reality.

In 1928, suffering from tuberculosis, Dashiell Hammett (Frederic Forrest) has given up working as a detective, ekes out a living writing short stories for pulp magazines and has just finished the manuscript for a novel. Jimmy Ryan (Peter Boyle), his former boss at the Pinkerton Agency, asks him to help with a case in which a Chinese prostitute, Crystal Ling (Lydia Lei), has disappeared. Several of the city's most influential men want her found because of what she knows about them. The quest takes Hammett to San Francisco's

Chinatown where he becomes involved with thugs and several murders before realizing that the missing hooker holds pornographic pictures of the city's top politicos. Finding the girl, Hammett hides her in his apartment, where she survives a murder attempt; meanwhile, he becomes the go-between for the girl and one million dollars in blackmail money to be paid to her. Ryan, however, has been bought by the big monied men and attempts to maneuver the cash for himself. This all leads to more murders before the finale. With the case solved, Hammett returns to writing detective stories.

Variety analyzed of this box-office failure, "[It has been] overpolished by too many script rewrites, perhaps emasculated by massive footage scraps and belated re-shoots, project (all shot on interiors) emerges a rather suffocating film taking place in a rickety 'Chinatown'. . . . Frederic Forrest looks like Hammett, talks like Humphrey Bogart and is acceptable in this context—though he lacks a more riveting presence." *People* magazine, which approved of the film, said that "the surprises and quadruple-crosses are snappily handled," and added, "Hammett himself, who eventually all but forsook writing to serve as Lillian Hellman's mentor, probably had little in common with the character created by Forrest—though his stories certainly did."

HARPER (Warner Bros., 1966) Color 121 minutes.

Producers, Jerry Gershwin, Elliott Kastner; director, Jack Smight; based on the novel *The Moving Target* by Ross MacDonald [Kenneth Millar]; screenplay, William Goldman; art directors, Alfred Sweeney, Russell Menzer; set decorator, Claude Carpenter; music, Johnny Mandell; song, Andre and Dory Previn; assistant director, James H. Brown, Phil Ball; wardrobe, Sally Edwards, William Smith; makeup, Otis Malcolm, Gary Liddiard; dialogue supervisor, Bert Steinberger; sound, Stanley Jones; camera, Conrad Hall; editors, Stefan Arnsten, Don Hoskinson.

Paul Newman (Lew Harper); Lauren Bacall (Mrs. Elaine Sampson); Julie Harris (Betty Fraley); Arthur Hill (Albert Graves); Janet Leigh (Susan Harper); Pamela Tiffin (Miranda Sampson); Robert Wagner (Alan Taggert); Robert Webber (Dwight Troy); Shelley Winters (Fay Estabrook); Harold Gould (Sheriff Spanner); Roy Jenson (Puddler); Strother Martin (Claude); Martin West (Deputy); Jacqueline DeWit (Mrs. Kronberg); Eugene Iglesias (Felix); Richard Carlyle (Fred Platt; China Lee (Bunny Dancer).

Ross MacDonald (1915-1983), pseudonym for Kenneth Millar, authored some twenty books centered around his cynical, resourceful private eye, Lew Archer. But when the first of them, *The Moving Target* (1949), was brought to the screen in 1966, star Paul Newman

Julie Harris and Paul Newman in HARPER (1966).

had enough box-office clout to have his wish fulfilled that the character of Lew Archer be redubbed Lew Harper. Newman's reasoning was that he had been successful playing screen characters whose name began with "H" (e.g., THE HUSTLER, HUD) and he was not about to make a change. Thus the film became HARPER.*

It was no coincidence that Lauren Bacall, who had co-starred with Humphrey Bogart in THE BIG SLEEP (1946), *q.v.,* should be cast in this feature, for the filmmakers did everything possible to make this new production a contemporary variation of that success-ful earlier film. Many of the critics would label Newman the "new" Bogart for his characterization.

Private detective Lew Harper (Paul Newman) is being sued for divorce by his wife Susan (Janet Leigh) and obviously needing money, accepts a case on the advice of an old friend, lawyer Albert Graves (Arthur Hill). He goes to the estate of missing millionaire Sampson and there meets his embittered, crippled wife Elaine (Lauren Bacall), Sampson's daughter, Miranda (Pamela Tiffin), and private pilot Alan Taggert (Robert Wagner). Going through Sampson's hotel suite he finds a photograph of former movie actress Fay Estabrook (Shelley Winters) and soon locates the now overweight drunk. At her apartment he takes a call on her phone and goes to see drug-using piano bar singer Betty Fraley (Julie Harris), but is beaten up for his troubles. This leads him to a religious cult led by Claude (Strother Martin), who was given a mountain retreat by Sampson. When Elaine receives a ransom note, Harper leaves the money at the appointed place. It is picked up by Betty and Harper follows her to her room, where she is beaten up by Fay's husband, Dwight Troy (Robert Webber), who, the detective learns, operates a Mexican border alien smuggling racket with Claude. Harper is forced to kill Troy and makes Betty take him to the abandoned tanker where Sampson is being held prisoner. Once there he meets Graves and they find the millionaire murdered. Betty is killed attempting to escape in a speeding car. On the way back to Sampson's mansion, the actual culprit confesses to Harper and tries to shoot him, but cannot bring himself to commit the crime. When all is over, it is Harper and

---

*An alternative (or additonal) rationale for the detective character's name change was that novelist Ross MacDonald was intending at that time that the Archer character be used as the basis for a potential TV series. On May 6, 1974, NBC-TV aired a 100-minute telefeature entitled THE UNDERGROUND MAN, based on Ross MacDonald's 1971 novel. It starred a miscast Peter Graves as Lew Archer, in a cast which included Sharon Farrell, Celeste Holm, Judith Anderson, Jim Hutton, and Vera Miles. On January 30, 1975 NBC-TV debuted an "Archer" series with Brian Keith now featured in the title role as the Melrose, California-based private eye and John P. Ryan as Lieutenant Barney Brighton. The hour program lasted for seven episodes.

not the slow-thinking sheriff (Harold Gould) who has solved the case.

The critics were of mixed feelings about HARPER, with the *New York Times* deciding, "The action is swift and the mystery fetching in this handsomely made color film. But eventually it seems a bit too obvious, imitative, old-fashioned and, worst of all, stale." The public did not agree, for HARPER grossed $6,000,000 in domestic film rentals.

With the favorable commercial returns on HARPER, Filmways Productions obtained screen rights to *The Chill* (1964), another of the Lew Archer novels. It was announced that Newman would star and Jack Smight would (again) direct in this follow-up. But a suitable script was never created and the project was dropped. A few years later producers Lawrence Turman and David Foster acquired the film rights to another Archer detective novel, *The Drowning Pool* (1950), which moved its location from the environs of Los Angeles to the Louisiana swamps. THE DROWNING POOL (1975), *q.v.*, was far less successful than its predecessor and no more Lew Harper theatrical releases were forthcoming.

THE HATBOX MYSTERY (Screen Guild, 1947) 44 minutes.

Producer, Carl Hittleman; director, Lambert Hillyer; story, Maury Nunes, Hittleman; screenplay, Don Martin, Hittleman; music, David Chudnow; camera, Jim Brown; editor, Arthur Brown.

Tom Neal (Russ Ashton); Pamela Blake (Susan); Allen Jenkins (Harvard); Virginia Sale (Veronica); Ed Keane (District Attorney); Leonard Penn (Stevens); William Ruhl (Flint); Zonn Murray (Joe); Olga Andre (Mrs. Moreland).

Featurettes, films running only 40-50 minutes in length, were long a part of the movie tradition, but somehow they never quite found favor with movie audiences. For example, in the early 1940s producer Hal Roach introduced a movie series (mostly comedies) called "Streamliners," with abbreviated running times. In 1943, after two years, Roach ceased producing them as they were not successful. In 1946 Screen Guild again tried to mount a number of these theatrical fillers with a quartet of Royal Canadian Mounted Police features starring Russell Hayden. Among the assorted other featurettes Screen Guild produced was THE HATBOX MYSTERY. Under veteran Lambert Hillyer's strong direction, the featurette proved to be an interesting genre addition as well as another in the then-popular *film noir* type of motion picture. Not only does the movie have a strong plot, it also has a different kind of opening with the performers introducing themselves, in character, to the audience.

"Like a Jack-In-The-Hatbox ... Murder jumped out and claimed its victim!" read the advertising for this release. The plot focuses on private eye Russ Ashton (Tom Neal) and his beautiful but overly curious secretary Susan (Pamela Blake). Ashton is a none-too-successful gumshoe because, each time he gets a case, something goes awry, usually thanks to Susan's help. When Ashton is out of town, a man attempts to hire the sleuth to gain needed evidence to divorce his two-timing wife. Susan, feeling it is an easy task, agrees to do the work for her boss and the man gives her a hatbox which is supposed to hide a concealed camera with which she will take the incriminating photos the man needs. Susan locates the woman but when she attempts to take the picture, the camera turns out to be a hidden gun and the woman is killed. In addition, the deceased turns out to be a wealthy society lady and *not* the man's wife. Ashton returns in time to solve the case, bring in the real culprit and exonerate Susan.

Tom Neal, Allen Jenkins, and Pamela Blake repeated their roles in another Screen Guild featurette directed by Lambert Hillyer, THE CASE OF THE BABY SITTER, in 1947. Here Russ (Tom Neal) and Harvard (Allen Jenkins) are hired to guard a baby. However, in reality the parents are jewel thieves and what the men are guarding is actually the gems they have stolen. Another gang tries to steal the jewels and they almost kill Susan (Pamela Blake) before Russ brings in both sets of lawbreakers. The artistic results were not good, however, since the film seemed " . . . like an elongated short subject but without the usual production care given to the briefies. Pic has been crudely assembled with deficient lighting, inferior camera work, and bare setting framing a weak screenplay" (*Variety*).

HAUNTED HONEYMOON (Metro-Goldwyn-Mayer, 1940) 83 minutes.

Associate producer, Harold Huth; director, Arthur B. Woods; based on the play *Busman's Holiday* by Dorothy L. Sayers and the play by Sayers, Muriel St. Claire Byrne; camera, Freddie Young; editor, Al Barnes.

Robert Montgomery (Lord Peter Wimsey); Constance Cummings (Harriet Vane); Leslie Banks (Inspector Kirk); Sir Seymour Hicks (Bunter); Robert Newton (Frank Crutchley); Googie Withers (Polly); Frank Pettingell (Puffett); Joan Kemp-Welch (Aggie Twitterton); Aubrey Mallalieu (Reverend Simon Goodacre); James Carney (Constable Sellon); Roy Emerton (Noakes); Louise Hampton (Mrs. Ruddle); Eliot Makeham (Simpson); Reginald Purdell (MacBride).

In 1939 Robert Montgomery and Maureen O'Sullivan jour-

neyed to England to make HAUNTED HONEYMOON, taken
from Dorothy L. Sayer's play *Busman's Holiday*, which had a successful run on the London stage during the 1936-37 season before being
novelized in 1937. Troubles plagued the film production from the
start, mainly due to England becoming involved in World War II
with Germany. Miss O'Sullivan returned home and was replaced by
London-based actress Constance Cummings. The director, Arthur
Woods, was an RAF pilot and could only work on the project when
given official permission. Moreover, the Germans threatened to
bomb the studio where the picture was made because of its recent
anti-Nazi release, THE LION HAS WINGS (1939). When the
MGM feature was issued in the United States, Bosley Crowther
pouted in the *New York Times*, "Imagine Englishmen trifling with
such stuff as a musty mystery film while Norway was being invaded
and the Low Countries overrun."

In temporary retirement, gentleman detective Lord Peter Wimsey
(Robert Montgomery) and his new bride, mystery writer Harriet
Vane (Constance Cummings), head for a honeymoon on a remote
moor, only to find a corpse in their cottage. Thick-headed Scotland
Yard Inspector Kirk (Leslie Banks) is called into the case but cannot
fathom who among the many suspects might be guilty: the butler
Bunter (Sir Seymour Hicks), suspicious caretaker Frank Crutchley
(Robert Newton), the deceased's niece, Aggie Twitterton (Joan
Kemp-Welch), Reverend Simon Goodacre (Aubrey Mallalieu),
who was found with the murder weapon, hard-drinking maid Mrs.
Ruddle (Louise Hampton), or Constable Sellon (James Carney),
who was seen at the cottage the night of the murder. With little aid
from the law, Lord Peter and Harriet pinpoint the killer and
continue with their nuptials.

Despite his feelings about the untimeliness of this production,
Bosley Crowther did note, "Seldom has there been a film so
pleasantly conducive to browsing as this leisurely bookish detective
fable of murder in Devonshire; not of late has there been one so
steeped in the genteel tradition of British crime literature."

Lord Peter Wimsey first came to the screen in 1935 in the
British feature film, THE SILENT PASSENGER, with Peter Hadden
as the sleuth, but Wimsey is best known for the BBC-TV serial with
Ian Carmichael in the 1970s and Edward Petherbridge in the
1980s.*

---

*The general consensus is that Ian Carmichael, while good, was not really an authentic
Lord Peter Wimsey. He was too very, very British and not upper class enough.
Edward Petherbridge is considered to be more authentic and the BBC series with him
does have better production values in terms of appropriate atmosphere, although the
episodes drag a bit.

British release title: BUSMAN'S HOLIDAY.

HELD FOR RANSOM *see* ADVENTURES OF SHERLOCK HOLMES (1905).

THE HIDDEN CORPSE *see* STRANGERS OF THE EVENING.

THE HIDDEN EYE (Metro-Goldwyn-Mayer, 1945) 70 minutes.

Producer, Robert Sisk; director, Richard Whorf; based on characters created by Baynard Kendrick; story, George Harmon Coxe; screenplay, Coxe, Harry Ruskin; art directors, Cedric Gibbons, Preston Ames; music, David Snell; camera, Lester White; editor, George Hively.

Edward Arnold (Captain Duncan Maclain); Frances Rafferty (Jean Hampton); Ray Collins (Phillip Treadway); Paul Langton (Harry Gifford); William "Bill" Phillips (Marty Corbett); Thomas Jackson (Inspector Delaney); Morris Ankrum (Ferris); Robert Lewis (Stormvig); Frances Pierlot (Kossnovsky); Sandra Rodgers (Helen Roberts); Theodore Newton (Gibbs the Chauffeur); Jack Lambert (Louie); Ray Largay (Arthur Hampton); Leigh Whipper (Alistair);

William "Bill" Phillips and Audrey Totter in THE HIDDEN EYE (1945).

Byron Foulger (Burton Lorrison); Lee Phelps (Polasky); Eddie Acuff (Whitey); Bob Pepper (Sergeant Kramer); Russell Hicks (Rodney Hampton); Friday (The Dog); and: Audrey Totter.
See: EYES IN THE NIGHT [essay].

THE HIGH WINDOW   *see*   THE BRASHER DOUBLOON.

HILDEGARDE WITHERS   *see*   A VERY MISSING PERSON [essay].

HOT SPOT   *see*   I WAKE UP SCREAMING.

THE HOUND OF THE BASKERVILLES (Robertson-Cole, 1922) 5,500'.
Director, Maurice Elvey; based on the novel by Sir Arthur Conan Doyle; screenplay, William J. Elliott, Dorothy Westlake.
Eille Norwood (Sherlock Holmes); Betty Campbell (Beryl Stapleton); Rex McDougall (Sir Henry Baskerville); Lewis Gilbert (John Stapleton); Hubert Willis (Dr. Watson); Robert English (Dr. Mortimer); Fred Raynham (Barrymore); Miss Walker (Mrs. Barrymore); Mme d'Esterre (Mrs. Hudson); Robert Vallis (The Convict).
Released in England by Stoll in 1921.

THE HOUND OF THE BASKERVILLES (First Division, 1932) 60 minutes.
Producer, Michael Balcon; director, V. Gareth Gundrey; based on the novel by Sir Arthur Conan Doyle; screenplay, Edgar Wallace, Gundrey; camera, Bernard Knowles; editor, Ian Dalrymple.
John Stuart (Sir Henry Baskerville); Robert Rendel (Sherlock Holmes); Reginald Bach (Stapleton); Heather Angel (Beryl Stapleton); Wilfred Shine (Dr. Mortimer); Frederick Lloyd (Dr. Watson); Sam Livesey (Sir Hugo Baskerville); Henry Hallett (Barrymore); Sybil Jane (Mrs. Barrymore); Elizabeth Vaughn (Laura Lyons); Leonard Hayes (Cartwright); Henry Hallett (Barrymore); Champion Egmund of Send (The Hound of the Baskervilles).
Made by Gainsborough Pictures for Gaumont and released in England in 1931 at 75 minutes.

THE HOUND OF THE BASKERVILLES (Twentieth Century-Fox, 1939) 80 minutes.
Producer, Gene Markey; director, Sidney Lanfield; based on the novel by Sir Arthur Conan Doyle; screenplay, Ernest Pascal; art director, Thomas Little; music director, Cyril J. Mockridge; cos-

tumes, Gwen Wakeley; sound, W. D. Flech, Roger Heman; camera, Peverell Marley; editor Robert Simpson.

Richard Greene (Sir Henry Baskerville); Basil Rathbone (Sherlock Holmes); Wendy Barrie (Beryl Stapleton); Nigel Bruce (Dr. Watson); Lionel Atwill (Dr. Mortimer); John Carradine (Barryman); Barlowe Borland (Frankland); Beryl Mercer (Mrs. Mortimer); Morton Lowry (Stapleton); Ralph Forbes (Sir Hugo); E. E. Clive (Gabby); Eily Malyon (Mrs. Barryman); Nigel De Brulier (Convict); Mary Gordon (Mrs. Hudson); Peter Willes (Roderick); Ian MacLaren (Sir Charles); John Burton (Bruce); Dennis Green (Jon); Evan Thomas (Edwin).

THE HOUND OF THE BASKERVILLES (United Artists, 1959) Color 87 minutes.

Executive producer, Michael Carreras; producer, Anthony Hinds; director, Terence Fisher; based on the novel by Sir Arthur Conan Doyle; screenplay, Peter Bryan; camera, Jack Asher; editor, James Needs.

Peter Cushing (Sherlock Holmes); Andre Morell (Dr. John H. Watson); Christopher Lee (Sir Henry Baskerville); Marla Landi (Cecile Stapleton); David Oxley (Sir Hugo Baskerville); Miles Malleson (Bishop Frankland); Francis de Wolff (Dr. Mortimer); Ewen Solon (Stapleton); John Le Mesurier (Barrymore); Sam Kydd (Perkins); Helen Goss (Mrs. Barrymore); Judi Moyens (Servant Girl); Dave Birks (Servant); Michael Mulcaster (Selden); Michael Hawkins (Lord Caphill); Ian Hewitson (Lord Kingsblood); and: Elizabeth Dott.

THE HOUND OF THE BASKERVILLES (ABC-TV, 2/12/72) Color 78 minutes.

Executive producer, Richard Irving; producer, Stanley Kallis; associate producer, Arthur O. Hilton; director, Barry Crane; based on the novel by Sir Arthur Conan Doyle; teleplay Robert E. Thompson; art director, Howard E. Johnson; camera, Harry L. Wolf; supervising editor Richard Belding; editor, Bill Mosher.

Stewart Granger (Sherlock Holmes); Bernard Fox (Dr. John H. Watson); William Shatner (George Stapleton); Anthony Zerbe (Dr. John Mortimer); Sally Ann Howes (Laura Frankland); John Williams (Arthur Frankland); Ian Ireland (Sir Henry Baskerville); Jane Merrow (Beryl Stapleton); Alan Callou (Inspector Lestrade); Brendon Dilon (John Barrymore); Arline Anderson (Eliza Barrymore); Billy Bowles (Billy Cartwright); Chuck Hicks (Seldon); Karen Kondan (Mrs. Mortimer); Liam Dunn (Messenger); Michael St. Clair (Constable); Barry Bernard (Manager); Constance Cavendish (Eel Monger);

Arthur Malet (Higgins); Elaine Church (Maid Servant); Jenifer Shaw (Peasant Girl); Terence Pushman (Chestnut Salesman); Eric Brotherson (Porter).

THE HOUND OF THE BASKERVILLES (Hemdale International/Atlantic, 1980) Color 84 minutes.

Executive producers, Michael White, Andrew Braunsberg; producer, John Goldstone; associate producer, Tim Hampton; director, Paul Morrissey; based on the novel by Sir Arthur Conan Doyle; screenplay, Peter Cook, Dudley Moore, Morrissey; music, Moore; production designer, Roy Smith; costumes, Charles Knode; camera, Dick Bush, John Wilcox; editors, Richard Marden, Glenn Hyde.

Peter Cook (Sherlock Holmes); Dudley Moore (Dr. John H. Watson/Mrs. Holmes/Mr. Spiggot); Denholm Elliott (Stapleton); Joan Greenwood (Beryl Stapleton); Terry-Thomas (Dr. Mortimer); Max Wall (Mr. Barrymore); Irene Handl (Mrs. Barrymore); Kenneth Williams (Sir Henry Baskerville); Hugh Griffith (Frankland); Dana Gillespie (Mary); Roy Kinnear (Seldon); Prunella Scales (Glynis); Penelope Keith (Massage Parlor Receptionist); Spike Milligan (Baskerville Police Force); Jessie Matthews (Bit).

THE HOUND OF THE BASKERVILLES (Weintraub, 1983) Color 100 minutes.

Producer, Otto Plaschkes; director, Douglas Hickox; based on the novel by Sir Arthur Conan Dole; screenplay, Charles Pogue; music, Michael J. Lewis; production designer, Michael Stringer; costumes, Julie Harris; makeup, Tom Smith, John Webber; special effects, Alan Whibley; camera, Ronnie Taylor; editor, Malcolm Cooke.

Ian Richardson (Sherlock Holmes); Donald Churchill (Dr. John H. Watson); Martin Shaw (Sir Henry Baskerville); Nicholas Clay (Jack Stapleton); Denholm Elliott (Dr. Mortimer); Brian Blessed (Geoffrey Lyons); Ronald Lacy (Inspector Lestrade); and: Eleanor Bron, Edward Judd, Glynis Barber.

"Without question the most famous of all Sherlock Holmes stories is the one about THE HOUND OF THE BASKERVILLES, that phantom devil dog of the West country of Devonshire whose curse of violent death had for centuries fallen upon the Baskerville family during those dark hours of the night when the powers of evil are exalted. A classic of mystery and horror, it seems, certain, in fact, that if Conan Doyle had never written another Sherlock Holmes adventure the names of both Conan Doyle and Sherlock would be world renowned for this one alone," wrote Ron Haydock in *Deerstalker! Holmes and Watson on Film* (1978).

The above description by film historian Roy Haydock admirably sums up the impact Doyle's 1901 novel has had on both detective fiction and the cinema. Naturally, such a popular fictional vehicle for Holmes would be filmed and, to date, there have been multiple screen adaptations of the work, plus radio and TV adaptations. THE HOUND OF THE BASKERVILLES is without doubt one of the most durable of all detective stories.

THE HOUND OF THE BASKERVILLES was first filmed* in 1914 by the German Vitascope Pictures as DER HUND VON BASKERVILLE, with Alwin Neuss as Holmes, although Dr. Watson was not incorporated into the script. Slightly changing the Doyle original, the film, nevertheless was quite successful and led to a sequel, a newly written feature called THE ISOLATED HOUSE (1917), with Neuss again portraying Holmes. In 1921 Eille Norwood, who was Holmes in forty-five two-reelers for the British Stoll Films between 1921 and 1923, played the great detective in a feature version of THE HOUND OF THE BASKERVILLES, also for Stoll. In *Holmes of the Movies* (1976), David Stuart Davies complained of this rendition, "THE HOUND OF THE BASKERVILLES of all films needs mood more than it needs logic or action and mood is one thing this version consistently lacks. . . . The result is a stodgy and lack-luster production. There is however one touch of showmanship: the hound was tinted or handpainted with a luminous glow, so that its infrequent appearances do carry a token shock value."

The final silent version of the popular Doyle work came from Germany and the 1929 version of DER HUND VON BASKERVILLE was again adapted and directed by Richard Oswald, who had done the same with the 1914 initial HOUND. Here Holmes was played by one-time American matinee idol Carlyle Blackwell, who had been Bulldog Drummond in the silent film of the same title (*q.v.*) in 1923. Of this German production *Variety* reported that it " . . . suits itself excellently to the pictures and should have a success on the continent." The film, however, was made as a silent when talkies were coming into vogue and it passed by quickly.

A British company, Gainsborough Pictures, produced the first sound era rendition of THE HOUND OF THE BASKERVILLES in 1931, with dialogue by the noted mystery writer Edgar Wallace. Robert Rendel played Holmes and while the film again stayed fairly close to the literary source it was not particularly popular. In *The*

---

*There was a 1909 Danish film entitled DEN GRAA DAME which was an adaptation of this Doyle work, *but* here the Hound became the specter of a woman.

Films of Sherlock Holmes (1978) Chris Steinbrunner and Norman Michaels judge the film " . . . a flawed but interesting Holmesian film. . . . Alas this version of THE HOUND OF THE BASKER-VILLES is among the 'lost films': only sections are known to survive, and the soundtrack, the one element in those early-talkie days which made the film memorable, is completely lost." The next version of the tale came in 1937, again from Germany, but this DER HUND VON BASKERVILLE is completely lost; no prints are known to survive. Produced and directed by Karl Lamac, the film starred Bruno Guttner as Sherlock Holmes and featured Fritz Rasp as the butler. In the 1929 German silent, Rasp had played Stapleton.

The definitive film version of the Doyle work came in 1939 with Darryl F. Zanuck's production of THE HOUND OF THE BASKERVILLES, which offered the first magical teaming of Basil Rathbone and Nigel Bruce as Holmes and Watson. The two fast became the supreme players of the super sleuth and his loyal associate. Set in 1889, the film has Sherlock Holmes (Basil Rathbone) agreeing to take the case of Sir Henry Baskerville (Richard Greene), who has just returned to England from Canada to take possession of his inheritance, Baskerville Hall, which is located in the desolate area of Dartmoor in Devonshire. Dr. James Mortimer (Lionel Atwill) has told Holmes of the curse on the male heirs of the Baskerville family and that many of the locals felt Henry's father had been murdered. Mortimer relates how the curse goes back to 1650 when Sir Hugo Baskerville (Ralph Forbes) had abducted a local maiden for amoral purposes, and the girl had escaped, only to be tracked to the moors by Sir Hugo and his drunken friends. The girl was found dead and Sir Hugo was also found with his throat torn out by a huge, ghost-like hound whose howls had been heard on the moors ever since.

When Sir Henry arrives in London attempts are made on his life and Holmes and Dr. Watson (Nigel Bruce) accompany him to Baskerville Hall where they are greeted by the butler Barryman [the butler was called Barrymore in the novel and the name change was made in the new film version to avoid conflict with the acting Barrymore family] (John Carradine) and his wife (Eily Malyon). Barryman is later seen by Watson, apparently signaling someone on the moors. The next day Sir Henry sets out to look over his property and on the moors meets naturalist John Stapleton (Morton Lowry) and his sister Beryl (Wendy Barrie). A romance develops between Baskerville and the pretty young woman. Holmes returns to London, leaving Watson to watch over the situation. However, Watson soon finds out that Holmes is actually secreted on the moors. When a man is killed there, it turns out to be the one to whom Barryman was signaling, his brother-in-law, who is an escaped convict. The deceased was wearing old clothes belonging to Baskerville and was attacked by a huge dog because the clothes carried Baskerville's scent. Holmes tells Baskerville that because the case is completed, he and Watson are now returning to London—or so they claim. That evening, after dining with the Stapletons Baskerville walks home across the moor. He is attacked by a huge hound. Holmes and Watson appear on the scene and Holmes wounds the animal, which runs away. Baskerville and Watson return to the Hall while Holmes finds an old cemetery and climbs into an open grave. Later the cover above is closed over him and locked. Holmes manages to escape, returns to Baskerville Hall and confronts the killer. The latter draws a gun and runs away. Trying to escape the police Holmes has left along the way, the murderer falls into the Grimpen Mire and is sucked under. It develops that the killer was an illegitimate offspring of the Baskerville line and was attempting to kill off all the clan in order to make a claim on the estate. The case ended, the weary Holmes asks Watson for the needle to soothe his weary soul with drugs.

The *New York Times* enthused about the well-produced film: "It's fairly good fun and like old times to be seeing Sherlock again. . . ." *Variety* felt, "[Basil] Rathbone gives a most effective characterization of Sherlock Holmes, which will be relished by mystery lovers." Ron Haydock wrote in *Deerstalker! Holmes and Watson on Screen* (1978), "Set completely in period, the picture was diabolically menacing, more so than any other Holmes film, past or present. It was powerfully cloaked with a consistently oppressive atmosphere of deep brooding and Gothic foreboding all the way from Baker Street in the opening reels to Dartmoor and Baskerville Hall later on, then finally to the classic finale that saw Holmes and Watson out on the fog-shrouded moors of Grimpen Mire stalking the legendary Hound with pistol, lantern and stealth." William K. Everson opined in *The Detective in Hollywood* (1972), "The best of the many versions of THE HOUND OF THE BASKERVILLES, it remains an impressive, handsomely mounted and certainly 'respectful' treatment of Doyle, even if a little too measured in its pacing and never quite makes the most of its excitement potential. . . . [It] also suffered from a surprising lack of background music." Despite minor drawbacks the film is one of the most entertaining detective features ever produced, deftly interpolating plot, mood and atmosphere into an exceedingly satisfying film, highlighted by Basil Rathbone's brilliant interpretation of the Baker Street detective.

Basil Rathbone and Nigel Bruce were to become typecast as Holmes and Watson after making a sequel to the HOUND, THE

ADVENTURES OF SHERLOCK HOLMES, *q.v.*, also for Twentieth Century-Fox. The year 1939 also saw them begin a seven-year stint on radio as the famous Doyle characters in the weekly thirty-minute Mutual Network program, "The Adventures of Sherlock Holmes." The duo did over 200 broadcasts in the series and among them was the 1942 six-episode serialization of "The Hound of the Baskervilles." Mary Gordon, who played Mrs. Hudson in the Twentieth Century-Fox and Universal Holmes films with Rathbone and Bruce, also recreated her landlady's role for the radio series.

In 1957 Noel Johnson performed a reading of "The Hound of the Baskervilles" on BBC Radio in London, and two years later the British Hammer Films produced a color version of the Doyle property with Peter Cushing as Holmes and Andre Morrell as ever-present Dr. Watson. The studio, who had had great success in teaming Cushing and Christopher Lee in horror films, cast Lee in this film as Sir Henry Baskerville. The Hammer version differs from the Fox one in that the story behind the curse, set in 1974, is told as the prologue to the actual detective story, which is set at the turn of the century. Otherwise the film is a sincere and well-staged remake of the Doyle work and Hammer's THE HOUND OF THE BASKERVILLES stands on its own as one of the best screen renderings of the subject. Allen Eyles, Robert Adkinson and Nicholas Fry noted in *The House of Horror* (1973) that the Doyle work " . . . provided Hammer with a classic story that had some horrific elements the company was well placed to put over with panache." Reviewers were especially taken with Peter Cushing's interpretation of the complex Holmes. *Newsweek* magazine judged that Cushing "seems likely to strike many oldsters as the best Sherlock Holmes yet," while *Film Daily* noted, "Peter Cushing gives a tantalizing performance," and *Variety* offered, " . . . it is difficult to fault the performance of Peter Cushing, who looks, talks and behaves precisely the way approved by the Sherlock Holmes Society. . . ."

To the delight of Holmes fans, Peter Cushing would remain, on and off, associated with the part and in 1968 he returned to the role in fifteen BBC-TV programs in its "Sherlock Holmes" series, with Nigel Stock appearing as Watson. One of the episodes would be a two-part production of "The Hound of the Baskervilles." In the 1970s Cushing was offered the part of Holmes in a Broadway play, but rejected it. In 1984, however, he again played Holmes in the motion picture MASK OF DEATH, *q.v.* Nigel Stock returned to "The Hound of the Baskervilles" in 1969 when, as Watson, he read the novel to radio listeners in a fifteen-episode rendering of the work for the BBC. A 1968 Italian TV production of THE HOUND OF THE BASKERVILLES starred Nando Gazzolo. In 1971 there was a Swedish radio adaptation of the Doyle novel and the same year also saw a British staging of "The Hound of the Baskervilles."

American television next claimed the popular work when Universal produced a telefeature of THE HOUND OF THE BASKERVILLES casting a silver-haired Stewart Granger as a stalwart Holmes and Bernard Fox as a bumbling Watson in what was a pilot for an unsold Holmes teleseries. One can find little fault with Granger's energetic interpretation of the great detective, but the film itself " . . . failed to generate much interest or suspense above and beyond what the viewer nostalgically brought to the home set. . . . HOUND came in on tippytoes where it should have been taking giant steps" (*Variety*). Some tacky sets, such as the moors and Grimpen Mire, failed to generate the needed eerie quality to evoke the required atmosphere for the mystery motif.

As vapid as the 1972 Universal production was, it was a near-classic compared to the 1978 British burlesque of the Doyle novel in the script by Peter Cook, Dudley Moore, and Paul Morrissey (who also directed) for THE HOUND OF THE BASKERVILLES. Apparently the trio tried to poke fun at the HOUND, as Mel Brooks had done in Hollywood with assorted film genres, but the results were disastrous. Peter Cook played Holmes, while Dudley Moore was Watson, Holmes' mother, and a character called Spiggot. In addition, the production wasted former musical comedy star Jessie Matthews in a bit role. It was altogether a thoroughly limp and dreary production. Needless to say it got minimal release and when issued in the U.S. (in 1980) it was cut by six minutes and several sequences were reshuffled, making the production even more confused than before. When it opened in San Francisco, Peter Stack (*San Francisco Chronicle*) labeled his review, "HOUND OF THE BASKERVILLES a Real Dog." He went on to explain, "It's not that we want everything to be High-Brow in our spoofs, it's just that we want such things as a five-minute sight gag with a dog peeing in Doctor Watson's face (and later in his soup) to stop at once, and return to kindergarten."

Fortunately a much finer version of THE HOUND OF THE BASKERVILLES arrived in 1983 from England, the second and last Holmes film from Mapleton Films, which previously produced THE SIGN OF FOUR, *q.v.* As in that film Ian Richardson provides an interesting interpretation of Holmes and the "narrative pace and a skillfully evoked air of mystery ensure good entertainment values" (*Variety*). The film provides a straight rendering of the Doyle novel and does so admirably. *Variety* noted, "Numerous clues and false trails set against an atmospheric backdrop will keep audiences not already in the know guessing throughout. The hound itself is intriguingly evoked and there's romantic interest as usual provided by Doctor Watson." Unfortunately this well-hued adaptation received scant theatrical release and in the U.S. was seen primarily on cable television.

The most recent screen version of *The Hound of the Baskervilles* came in the 1984, seventy-minute production, SHERLOCK HOLMES AND THE BASKERVILLE CURSE, with Peter O'Toole providing the voice of Holmes.

THE HOUSE OF FEAR (Universal, 1939) 65 minutes.

Producer, Edmund Grainger; director, Joe May; based on the novel *Backstage Phantom* by Wadsworth Camp and the story and play *The Last Warning* by Thomas F. Fallon; screenplay, Peter Milne; costumes, Vera West; camera, Milton Krasner; editor, Frank Gross.

William Gargan (Arthur McHugh); Irene Hervey (Alice Tabor); Dorothy Arnold (Gloria DeVere); Alan Dinehart (Joseph Morton); Harvey Stephens (Richard Pierce); Walter Woolf King (Carleton); Robert Coote (Robert Morton); El Brendel (Jeff); Tom Dugan (Mike); Jan Duggan (Sarah Henderson); Donald Douglas (John Woodford); Harry Hayden (Coroner); Emory Parnell, William Gould (Policemen); Charles E. Wilson (Police Chief); Milton Kibbee (Telephone Repair Man); and: Ben Lewis, Stanley Hughes, Raymond Parker.

THE HOUSE OF FEAR (Universal, 1945) 69 minutes.

Producer/director, Roy William Neill; based on the story "The Adventures of the Five Orange Pips" by Sir Arthur Conan Doyle; screenplay, Roy Chanslor; music director, Paul Sawtell; art directors, John B. Goodman, Eugene Lowrie; camera, Virgil Miller; editor, Saul Goodkind.

Basil Rathbone (Sherlock Holmes); Nigel Bruce (Dr. John H. Watson); Aubrey Mather (Bruce Alastair); Dennis Hoey (Inspector Lestrade); Paul Cavanagh (Simon Merrivale); Holmes Herbert (Alan Cosgrave); Harry Cording (John Simpson); Sally Shepherd (Mrs. Monteith); Gavin Muir (Chalmers); Florette Hillier (Alison MacGregory); David Clyde (Alex MacGregory); Wilson Benge (Guy Davies); Leslie Denison (Sergeant Bleeker); Alec Craig (Angus); Dick Alexander (King).

THE HOUSE OF FEAR derived from Wadsworth Camp's 1916 novel and was a remake of the classic Paul Leni-directed screen thriller, THE LAST WARNING, which Universal issued early in 1929 with talking sequences, sound effects, and a music score. That film, which starred Laura La Plante, Montague Love, Roy D'Arcy, John Boles and Margaret Livingston, was a comedy thriller in the vein of Leni's THE CAT AND THE CANARY (1928). Apparently lost to the ages, the film's title was used in 1935 for a play by Thomas F. Fallon, which was based on the Camp novel. To complicate the lineage further, THE LAST WARNING title was used in 1938 by Universal for one of the mysteries in its "Crime Club" series (see LADY IN THE MORGUE).

In 1939 prolific Universal Pictures remade the Leni film using the release title of THE HOUSE OF FEAR. It tells of actor John Woodford (Donald Douglas) dying on stage while performing in a play of his authorship. His body disappears and the police are baffled. A year later theatrical producer Arthur McHugh (William Gargan) leases the theater from owners Joseph Morton (Alan Dinehart) and brother Bobby (Robert Coote) and plans to restage the Woodford play with the original cast. He signs leading lady Alice Tabor (Irene Hervey) and leading man Richard Pierce (Harvey Stephens), the latter having had an argument with Woodford, on the day he died, over his unwanted attentions to Alice, whom Pierce loves. The cast, which includes golddigging newcomer Gloria DeVere (Dorothy Arnold), who immediately romances Bobby, begins getting notes in Woodford's handwriting warning them not to stage the play. McHugh and Pierce remain in the theater overnight and McHugh shoots at a specter and ends by nicking Pierce. They locate a secret panel between Woodford's dressing room and that of Alice, whom they find there. McHugh tells them he is really a detective working undercover to solve Woodford's murder. At a rehearsal Carleton (Walter Woolf King), who is playing Woodford's role, is murdered with poison and Pierce takes over his assignment. On opening night the killer attempts to do in Pierce by placing poison in a hidden glass vial in the microphone Pierce is using in the show, but McHugh stops the play and the guilty party is captured. It turns out that the culprit had committed the homicide because he had forged Woodford's name to a check and was part of a land speculation deal which involved the real estate the theater inhabited. Gloria reveals that she is really Mrs. McHugh, and Alice and Pierce are free to marry.

While a fast paced and attention-holding entry, THE HOUSE OF FEAR lacks the spooky, shadowlike quality of the original, and is a pale remake of the Leni classic. Perhaps the highlight of the film is the opening sequence in which the drama performed, including Woodford's demise, is shown to be part of a stage play—an old ploy, but nonetheless effective here.

In 1945 Universal reused the title THE HOUSE OF FEAR for its eighth entry in its Sherlock Holmes series. The feature proved to be one of the most engaging in the ongoing adventures, bolstered by its unique plot and setting in a remote, windswept Scottish castle where a rash of bizarre murders occur. The film is based on Sir Arthur Conan Doyle's short story, "The Adventures of the Five Orange Pips," and even though greatly embellished by scripter Roy Chanslor, it is a highly satisfying mystery thriller.

Chalmers (Gavin Muir), an insurance company representative, comes to Sherlock Holmes (Basil Rathbone) with a baffling case. The seven members of a club of middle-aged single men called "The Good Comrades" have moved to a West Scotland castle called Drearcliff and two of the members have died after receiving envelopes containing orange pips. Since all the club members are heavily insured with his company, Chalmers asks Holmes to look into the puzzlement. When Holmes finds out that Dr. Simon Merrivale (Paul Cavanagh), who was once implicated in the murder of a young girl, is one of the Good Comrades, Holmes accepts the case and he and Dr. Watson (Nigel Bruce) travel to Drearcliff and stay at the local inn. When another member dies in a fire, Holmes comes to the castle and meets its owner, club member Bruce Alastair (Aubrey Mather), as well as housekeeper Mrs. Monteith (Sally Shepherd), who has delivered the envelopes containing the orange pips after finding them at the manor door. The good comrades begin to fear for their lives and suspect each other of the crimes. Holmes and Watson agree to protect them but after another murder, Scotland Yard Inspector Lestrade (Dennis Hoey) is brought into the case. When Merrivale is eliminated by a falling rock, Lestrade arrests Alastair for the crimes and Watson disappears. Holmes, with the aid of Alastair, finds an old smugglers' cave beneath the manor. There he and the police find Watson a prisoner and solve the baffling case of greed which attempted to make Alastair the fall guy.

David Stuart Davies wrote in *Holmes of the Movies* (1976) that THE HOUSE OF FEAR was ". . . one of the neatest and most effective of the Universal Holmes mysteries. Throughout, the special effects department was kept busy with providing howling winds, thunder and lightning, which added to the dimly lit interiors, give the film a suitably mysterious and sinister mood."

THE HOUSE OF SECRETS (Chesterfield, 1929) 60 minutes.

Director, Edmund Lawrence; based on the novel by Sydney Horler; screenplay, Sidney Hall, Adeline Leitzbach; camera, George Webber, Irving Browning, George Peters, Lester Lang; editor, Selma Rosenbloom.

Marcia Manning (Margery Gordon); Joseph Striker (Barry Wilding); Elmer Grandin (Dr. Gordon); Herbert Warren (Joe Blake); Francis M. Verdi (Sir Hubert Harcourt); Richard Stevenson (Bill);

Harry M. Southard (Wharton); Edward Rosemond (Wu Chang); Walter Ringham (Home Secretary Forbes).

THE HOUSE OF SECRETS (Chesterfield, 1936) 70 minutes.
Producer, George R. Batcheller; director, Roland D. Reed; based on the novel and play by Sydney Horler; screenplay, John W. Krafft; music director, Abe Meyer; camera, M. A. Anderson; editor, Dan Milner.
Leslie Fenton (Barry Wilding); Muriel Evans (Julie Fenmore); Noel Madison (Dan Wharton); Sidney Blackmer (Tom Starr); Morgan Wallace (Dr. Kenmore); Holmes Herbert (Sir Bertram Evans); Ian MacLaren (Commissioner Cross); Jameson Thomas (Coventry); Matty Fain (Jumpy); Syd Saylor (Ed); George Rosener (Hector Munson); Rita Carlyle (Mrs. Shippam); Tom Ricketts (Peters); Matty Kemp (Man on Ship); R. Lancaster (British Policeman); Ramsey Hill (Police Inspector); David Thursby (Gregory).

At the beginning of the sound era and at the end of its trail, Chesterfield Motion Pictures Corporation produced two versions of the 1926 Sydney Horler novel, *The House of Secrets*. One of the first sound-on-film productions (in deference to the current popular sound on disc), the 1929 version was one of the few Chesterfield productions to be filmed in New York City instead of Hollywood. Both adaptations were produced by George R. Batcheller.

In the 1929 film, footloose American Barry Wilding (Joseph Striker) comes to London, where he has inherited an estate which he must not sell according to the terms of the will. He goes to the manse and finds it occupied by Margery Gordon (Marcia Manning), a mysterious young lady he met earlier on the ocean liner coming to England. She is with her father (Francis M. Verdi) and Margaret asks Wilding to allow her to live there with her father for six months. He goes to the Home Secretary (Walter Ringham) for aid but is rejected and ends being attacked by two gangsters (Harry M. Southard, Richard Stevenson). At last Wilding learns the truth: the woman's father is a scientist who has had a breakdown while working on a secret gas formula for the British government. As for the gangsters, they are after a treasure allegedly hidden on the estate hundreds of years before. The hoodlums imprison Wilding, Margery and her father, but the old man regains his senses as the Home Secretary arrives with his men for the rescue. Wilding and Margery plan to marry. *Variety* carped, "The more intelligent the mind, the greater the suffering HOUSE OF SECRETS inflicts, not only upon the performers, who wouldn't rate very high in a backwoods revival of Unk Tom's hut, but on the listeners too."

The equally low-budget 1936 remake stayed fairly close to the original, although it introduced the character of American detective Tom Starr (Sidney Blackmer), who tries to assist his pal, Barry Wilding (Leslie Fenton). Muriel Evans is the leading lady and Noel Madison, in a stereotypical role, is top-notch as the chief gangster. At the finale Wilding locates the treasure as he and the girl plan to marry and settle at the estate. "A guest at 'The House of Secrets' . . . an adventurer finds plenty of excitement when Death plays host," read the poster for this remake which Don Miller (*B Movies*, 1972) termed "an unmysterious mystery."

THE HOUSE WITHOUT A KEY (Pathe, 1926) ten chapters.
    Director, Spencer Gordon Bennet; based on the novel by Earl Derr Biggers; screenplay, Frank Leon Smith; camera, Edward Snyder.
    Allene Ray (Carlotta); Walter Miller (John Quincy Winterslip); George Kuwa (Charlie Chan); Frank Lackteen (The Crook); and: Charles West, John Webb Dillon, Natalie Warfield, William N. Bailey.
    Chapters: 1) The Spite Fence; 2) The Mystery Box; 3) The Missing Numeral; 4) Suspicion; 5) The Death Buoy; 6) Sinister Shadows; 7) The Mystery Man; 8) The Spotted Menace; 9) The Wrist Watch; 10) The Culprit.

Earl Derr Biggers' first adventure with Charlie Chan was serialized in the *Saturday Evening Post* in 1925 and was then novelized as *The House without a Key*. The character of Chinese detective Charlie Chan, a member of the Honolulu police force, did not emerge until late in the work but his impact was so great that Biggers wrote five more Chan adventures, thus creating one of the most popular of fictional sleuths. Pathé purchased the rights to the initial Chan opus for a ten-chapter serial and it was adapted to the screen by Frank Leon Smith. However, on celluloid Chan became a relatively minor figure as the detecting was carried out in conventional terms by chapterplay hero Walter Miller. Unfortunately no prints of THE HOUSE WITHOUT A KEY are known to exist today.
    The narrative is set in Hawaii where the elderly Winterslip brothers live in hatred of one another. The wealthier sibling, Dan Winterslip allegedly committed a crime two decades before and is hated for it by his brother Amos. Dan is murdered and the evidence concerning his past crime is supposed to be in a treasure chest. The man's nephew, John Quincy Winterslip (Walter Miller), is given the job of destroying it. The chest is stolen and the young man, who loves a young lady named Carlotta (Allene Ray)—Amos's partner's daughter—attempts to retrieve it. A crook (Frank Lackteen) also tries to obtain the chest but, with the help of local police detective

Walter Miller, Frank Lackteen, Allene Ray and George Kuwa in THE HOUSE WITHOUT A KEY (1926).

Charlie Chan (George Kuwa), John Quincy gains control of the chest. He clears his uncle's name and wins Carlotta's love.

In *Continued Next Week* (1964), Kalton C. Lahue writes, "It was another fine effort by the cast and Spencer Bennet, but the chest did not take the place of a strong character of mystery in sustaining interest." The property would be remade as a feature film in 1933 by Fox and would be called CHARLIE CHAN'S GREATEST CASE, with Warner Oland as Chan, but it too has not been preserved for future viewing.

DER HUND VON BASKERVILLE (Erda Film, 1929) 000 minutes.

Director, Richard Oswald; based on the novel *The Hound of the Baskervilles* by Sir Arthur Conan Doyle; adaptor, Oswald; screenplay, Herbert Jutke, George Klarens; camera, Frederik Fuglsang.

Carlyle Blackwell (Sherlock Holmes); George Seroff (Dr. Watson); Alexander Murski (Sir Hugo Baskerville); Betty Bird (Beryl

Stapleton); Fritz Rasp (Stapleton); Alma Taylor (Mrs. Barrymore); and: Erich Ponto, Valy Arnheim, Carla Bartheel, Jaro Furth, Robert Garrison.

See: THE HOUND OF THE BASKERVILLES [essay].

I LOVE A MYSTERY (Columbia, 1945) 69 minutes.

Producer, Wallace MacDonald; director, Henry Levin; based on the radio series created by Carlton E. Morse; screenplay, Charles O'Neal; art director, George Brooks; assistant director, Ray Nazarro; sound, Edward Bernds; camera, Burnett Guffey; editor, Aaron Stell.

Jim Bannon (Jack Packard); Nina Foch (Ellen Monk); George Macready (Jefferson Monk); Barton Yarborough (Doc Long); Carole Mathews (Jean Anderson); Lester Matthews (Justin Reeves); Gregory Gay (Dr. Han); Leo Mostovoy (Vovaritch); Frank O'Connor (Ralph Anderson); Isabel Withers (Miss Osgood); Joseph Crehan (Captain Quinn).

I LOVE A MYSTERY (NBC-TV, 2/27/73) Color 100 minutes.

Producer, Frank Price; director, Leslie Stevens; based on the radio series created by Carlton E. Morse; teleplay, Stevens; music, Oliver Nelson; art director, John J. Lloyd; costumes, Burton Miller; camera, Ray Rennahan; editor, Robert F. Shugrue.

Ida Lupino (Randy Cheyne); Les Crane (Jack Packard); David Hartman (Doc Long); Hagan Beggs (Reggie York); Jack Weston (Job Cheyne); Don Knotts (Alexander Archer); Terry-Thomas (Gordon Elliott); Melodie Johnson (Charity); Karen Jensen (Faith); Deanna Lund (Hope); Andre Philippe (Andre); Francine York (Telegram Girl); and: Peter Mamakos, Lewis Charles.

Carleton E. Morse's popular radio series, "I Love a Mystery," ran from 1939 to 1951 and was briefly revived in 1954. Columbia Pictures attempted to make a series centered around the show, just as Universal had done with "Inner Sanctum." Radio series stars Jim Bannon and Barton Yarborough were brought to Hollywood to repeat their roles on screen. However, the "I Love a Mystery" skein lasted for only three movie entries.

The initial excursion, I LOVE A MYSTERY, was issued early in 1945 and it has detectives Jack Packard (Jim Bannon) and Doc Long (Barton Yarborough) looking into a case in which a man, Jefferson Monk (George Macready), is offered $10,000 for his head by a secret Oriental society which wants it to replace that of their ancient founder. Monk fears for his life and his young wife, Ellen (Nina Foch), tries to help the detectives get to the bottom of the case, but three murders ensue. A baffling young woman (Carole Mathews) is also involved. The crime-solvers finally piece together the clues,

Jim Bannon in I LOVE A MYSTERY (1945).

proving that greed and a potential $2,000,000 estate are the prime motives.

Variety intoned, "Incongruous at times, I LOVE A MYSTERY, nevertheless, is a fairly suspenseful low-budget chiller. . . ." Don Miller observed in *B Movies* (1973), "[George] Macready's performance and some clever scripting by Charles O'Neal produced better than average results, although the series apparently never quite caught on and only a couple more were made." The follow-up properties were: THE DEVIL'S MASK, *q.v.* and THE UNKNOWN, both released in 1946.

In 1967 Universal/NBC-TV produced an early telefeature, I LOVE A MYSTERY, as a pilot for a proposed TV series based on the Carleton E. Morse radio program. The result was a film so bad that it was not aired until 1973 and the potential serial never

260 I, the Jury

materialized. Written and directed by Leslie Stevens, the made-for-television misfire has private detectives Jack Packard (Les Crane), Doc Long (David Hartman), and Reggie York (Hagan Beggs) hired by an insurance company to locate a vanished insuree with a $12,000,000 life insurance policy. The trio locate the individual at the remote island castle of brilliant scientist Randy Cheyne (Ida Lupino), who immediately plans to mate them with her three daughters—Faith (Karen Jensen), Hope (Deanna Lund) and Charity (Melodie Johnson)—to produce perfect offspring, after the male trio are changed into perfect specimens. Eventually the detectives thwart the dangerous woman. Judith Crist in *TV Guide* magazine rated the telefilm ". . . less than satisfying. . . attempted camp which is a bit too cutesy-poo for now." *TV Movies and Video Guide* (1988) found it to be a "Depressing attempt at adventure-comedy in spoof of old-time radio series. . . . Waste of good cast. . . . Below average." Jim Meyer (*Miami Herald*) summed it up as "utter bilge."

I, THE JURY (United Artists, 1953) 87 minutes.

Producer, Victor Saville; director, Harry Essex; based on the novel by Mickey Spillane; screenplay, Essex; music, Franz Waxman; camera, John Alton; editor, Frederick Y. Smith.

Biff Elliott (Mike Hammer); Preston Foster (Captain Pat Chambers); Peggie Castle (Charlotte Manning); Margaret Sheridan (Velda); Alan Reed (George Kalecki); Frances Osborne (Myrna); Robert Cunningham (Hal Kines); Elisha Cook, Jr. (Bobo); Paul Dubow (Marty); Mary Anderson (Eileen Vickers); Tani Seitz (Mary Bellamy); Dran Seitz (Esther Bellamy); Robert Swanger (Jack Williams); John Qualen (Dr. Vickers).

I, THE JURY (Twentieth Century-Fox, 1982) Color 111 minutes.

Executive producers, Michael Leone, Andrew T. Pfeffer; producer, Robert Solo; associate producer, Martin Hornstein; director, Richard T. Heffron; based on the novel by Mickey Spillane; screenplay, Larry Cohen; music, Bill Conti; production designer, Robert Gundlach; costumes, Celia Bryant; second unit director/stunts, Don Pike; assistant directors, Jerry Shapiro, Henry Bronchtein; sound, Kim Ornitz; special makeup effects, Carl Fullerton; camera, Andrew Lazlo; second unit camera, Peter Passas; editor, Garth Craven.

Armand Assante (Mike Hammer); Barbara Carrera (Dr. Charlotte Bennett); Alan King (Charles Kalecki); Laurene Lando (Velda); Geoffrey Lewis (Joe); Paul Sorvino (Detective Chambers); Judson Scott (Kenricks); Barry Snider (Romero); Julia Barr (Norma); Jessica James (Hilda); Frederick Downs (Jack); Mary Margaret Amato (Myrna); F. J. O'Neill (Goodwin); William Schilling (Lundee); Rob-

Biff Elliot (right) in I, THE JURY (1953).

ert Sevra (Breslin); Don Pike (Evans); Timothy Myers (Blake); Lee
Anne Harris, Lynette Harris (Twins); Larry Pine (Movie Director);
Joe Farago (Assistant Director); Alan Dellay (Cameraman); Jack
Davidson (Eric Clavel); Loring Pickering (Soap Opera Actor); Corrinne
Bohrer (Soap Opera Actress).

Mickey Spillane's tough private detective, Mike Hammer*
made his literary debut in 1947 in *I, the Jury* and since then more
than a dozen Hammer adventures have appeared, four of which have
been filmed and one remade. I, THE JURY was the first of a trio of
Hammer films brought to the screen in the 1950s by producer
Victor Saville. None of them was critically popular and they grossed
less than $1,000,000 each at the box-office. William K. Everson

---

*In *Detectionary* (1977), edited by Otto Penzler, Chris Steinbrunner and Marvin
Lachman, Mickey Spillane's alter ego detective character is described as ". . . tough
and vulgar, a wise guy who uses vulgarity and crudities more than necessary. . . . He
wears a stereotyped tan trench coat and a hat drawn low on his forehead, and always
carries a .38 revolver in the speed rig at his side."

described the fictional Hammer in *The Detective in Film* (1972): "Hammer was very much a product of the McCarthy era. The earlier private eyes were sometimes not too bright, their basic assets dogged persistence and a strange kind of integrity, a pride in their work, and a responsibility to their clients. Hammer had no such integrity, and few scruples. . . . A latter-day but less exaggerated Captain America, he started where Marlowe and Spade left off; occasionally, they bent the law a little; he took it boldly in both hands and defiantly broke it, the end apparently justifying the means."

I, THE JURY was released in 1953 with Harry Essex adapting Spillane's initial novel to the screen and making his directorial debut as well. "Several miscalculations vitiated the ambitious plans and doomed I, THE JURY. . . . The inexperienced guidance (by Essex) caused the narrative to wobble precariously, and scenes of expected punch never quite mustered enough. Nor did the 3-D process add anything. In addition, an actor named Biff Elliott, chosen to play Hammer, was tough enough in a barrel-chested way, but rather sweaty and soft where the granite was most needed. Hammer on film wasn't much of a detective either" (Don Miller, "Private Eyes," *Focus on Film* magazine, Autumn 1975).

When his wartime buddy, who lost an arm saving his life, is murdered brutally, private detective Mike Hammer (Biff Elliott) vows revenge and sets out to find the killer without the aid of the law, led by Captain Pat Chambers (Preston Foster). The unnerving quest brings him into contact with a series of underworld types, and he meets beautiful psychiatrist Charlotte Manning (Peggie Castle), who turns out to be too heavily involved in the caper. When he confronts her she tries to seduce him and he shoots her in the stomach.

Robert Ottoson details in *A Reference Guide to the American Film Noir: 1940-58* (1981), "In I, THE JURY the chief interest is the photography of John Alton. Some aficionados of the film have been known to turn down the sound on their television sets so they may concentrate on Alton's imagery, which was originally shot in 3-D. . . . Because of the censorship that filmmakers imposed upon themselves in the fifties much of the sex in Spillane's novel is deleted in the film version of I, THE JURY."

In 1982, I, THE JURY was remade as an American/Canadian co-production, with Larry Cohen (who was replaced as director on the production by Richard T. Heffron) adapting the Spillane work to the screen in its second outing. By now film censorship as such was non-existent and the film uses the full measure of sex and violence (and added nudity) from the original work. Another big change came in the villains. In the 1950s Hammer fought Communists; in the

1982 rendition the villain is the Central Intelligence Agency (CIA); another example of the leftward turn of Hollywood since the late 1960s. Plotwise Hammer (Armand Assante) is still on the trail of the killer of his buddy and along the way meets a bevy of beautiful women and much violence. *The Film Yearbook 1982* (1983) reported that the film ". . . is punctuated with numerous grisly deaths, a surfeit of random sadism and the full complement of miscellaneous unpleasantness, which it details with ostentatious relish. It's the comic-strip update with added gore, the traditional tale of revenge fencing for prominence with the CIA references and the sex clinic jokes. . . . It is not without its redeeming factors, however: pace, occasional wit and self-parody on overtime."

I WAKE UP SCREAMING (Twentieth Century-Fox, 1941) 80 minutes.

Producer, Milton Sperling; director, H. Bruce Humberstone; based on the novel by Steve Fisher; screenplay, Dwight Taylor; art directors, Richard Day, Nathan Juran; set decorator, Thomas Little; costumes, Gwen Wakeling; makeup, Guy Pearce; music, Cyril J. Mockridge; song, Harold Barlow and Lewis Harris; assistant director, Ad Schaumer; camera, Edward Cronjager; editor, Robert Simpson.

Betty Grable (Jill Lynn); Victor Mature (Frankie Christopher [Botticelli]); Carole Landis (Vicky Lynn); Laird Cregar (Ed Cornell); William Gargan (Jerry McDonald); Alan Mowbray (Robin Ray); Allyn Joslyn (Larry Evans); Elisha Cook, Jr. (Harry Williams); Morris Ankrum (Assistant District Attorney); May Beatty (Mrs. Handel); Cyril Ring, Chick Chandler, Basil Walker, Bob Cornell (Reporters); Stanley Clements (Newsboy); Tim Ryan, Wade Boteler, Eddie Dunn, Phillip Morris, James Flavin, Dick Rich (Detectives); Stanley Blystone (Cop); Cecil Weston (Police Matron); Brooks Benedict (Extra); Forbes Murray (Mr. Handel); Harry Seymour (Bartender); Edward McWade, Paul Weigel (Old Men); Pat McKee (Newsman); Albert Pollet (Waiter); Dorothy Dearing (Girl at Table).

Originally called HOT SPOT, this feature is based on a Steve Fisher script which was novelized as *I Wake Up Screaming* in 1941 to coincide with the issuance of the picture. Originally the movie had a downbeat ending, but producer Darryl F. Zanuck demanded director H. Bruce Humberstone end the film with (musical comedy) star Betty Grable singing a song. When this ending proved unsatisfactory and out of keeping with the tone of the rest of the melodrama, Humberstone came up with the classic finale in which the killer commits suicide. Despite its popularity with the public (who at this juncture ran to any film featuring Miss Grable), the *New York Times* complained, "the plot is nothing of any consequence."

Movie star Vicky Lynn (Carole Landis) has been murdered and the two chief suspects are her sister, nightclub singer Jill Lynn (Betty Grable), and the sports promoter/film publicist, Frankie Christopher (Victor Mature), who brought Vicky to stardom. He was aided in the endeavor by one-time actor Robin Ray (Alan Mowbray) and gossip columnist Larry Evans (Allyn Joslyn). Jill and Christopher are questioned by police detective Ed Cornell* (Laird Cregar) and his partner Jerry McDonald (William Gargan). Christopher tells the law how he discovered the one-time waitress and aided her climb to movie success. Cornell has a hunch that Christopher is the killer and hounds him relentlessly, although later he admits that he knows the man is innocent. To save his own life Christopher must prove his innocence. Finally, he learns that Vicky's neighbor, elevator operator Harry Williams (Elisha Cook, Jr.), has an overwhelming love for the late actress and that his room is filled with photographs of her. Christopher traps Williams in his room and the squirrely little man confesses not only to the crime but that Cornell, who also has an obsessive attachment for the dead woman, told him to keep quiet so that Christopher would pay the price for the murder. Cornell is caught in his own web and takes poison and dies rather than be arrested by his superiors.

In *A Reference Guide to the American Film Noir: 1940-58* (1981), Robert Ottoson stated that the film ". . . contains one of the earliest examples of the psychopathic film noir cop, in Laird Cregar's portrayal of detective Ed Cornell." Jon Tuska notes in *The Detective in Hollywood* (1978), "Humberstone in direction develops the parallel plot ingredients of learning more and more about Landis through flashbacks while keeping the viewer in suspense as to the identity of the murderer. Mature, like the central character in any noir picture, is a man imprisoned by circumstances." *In Film Noir: An Encyclopedic Reference to the American Style* (1979), Meredith Brody and Alain Silver report, "Part of the original novel's interest, by hard-boiled pump writer Steve Fisher, is its insider's view of Hollywood; but Zanuck had tabooed 'Hollywood' pictures and forced the film makers to switch the story's location to New York City with its atmospheric haunts of nightclubs, ritzy apartments, police stations, and movie theaters."

British release title: HOT SPOT.

THE INNER CIRCLE (Republic, 1946) 57 minutes.

Producer, William J. O'Sullivan; director, Phil Ford; based on the radio script by Leonard St. Clair, Lawrence Taylor; screenplay,

---

*Character Ed Cornell's surname is a tribute to thriller writer Cornell Woolrich.

Dorrell and Stuart E. McGowan; art director, Fred A. Ritter; set decorators, John McCarthy, Jr., George Milo; music director, Mort Glickman; assistant director, Virgil Hart; sound, William E. Clark; camera, Reggie Lanning; editor, Tony Martinelli.

Adele Mara (Gerry Travis); Warren Douglas (Johnny Strange); William Frawley (Chief Webb); Ricardo Cortez (Duke York); Virginia Christine (Rhoda Roberts); Ken Niles (Radio Announcer); Will Wright (Henry Hoggs); Dorothy Adams (Mrs. Wilson); Martha Montgomery (Anne Travis); and: Edward Gargan, Fred Graham, Eddie Parker, Bob Wilke.

When a vicious scandal monger/radio news commentator is murdered, private eye Johnny Strange (Warren Douglas) finds that he is the chief suspect. With the assistance of his comely secretary, Gerry Travis (Adele Mara), he sets out to clear himself. Police chief Webb (William Frawley) believes he is guilty and in the process of proving his innocence Strange gets into several scrapes with the law. In addition, he comes up against nightclub owner Duke York (Ricardo Cortez) and his gangsters. Finally Strange assembles the suspects in the case at the radio station where the murdered man broadcast. There he finds that Gerry's young sister (Martha Montgomery) is implicated in the case, having been involved with the murdered heel. Strange now ferrets out the murderer.

Variety decided that the film ". . . hasn't much to recommend it. Even whodunit addicts will turn a quizzical eyebrow at the tangled, illogical and crudely put-together story . . . slipshod scenario, pedestrian direction, and a total lack of marquee power. . . ."

Unlike most detective films of this vintage, which derived either from novels or original screen stories, THE INNER CIRCLE was based on a radio script. The year after its release, co-star Adele Mara became a detective herself in another Republic private eye mini-melodrama, EXPOSED, *q.v.* Warren Douglas, who plays gumshoe Johnny Strange in this outing, also portrayed other screen sleuths, such as the police detective in THE CHINESE RING (1947), *q.v.*

INSIDE STORY (Twentieth Century-Fox, 1939) 61 minutes.

Producer, Sol M. Wurtzel; associate producer, Howard J. Green; director, Ricardo Cortez; based on the story "A Very Practical Joke" by Ben Ames Williams; screenplay, Jerry Cady; art directors, Bernard Herzbrun, Albert Hogsett; music director, Samuel Kaylin; camera, Virgil Miller; editors, Jack Murray, Norman Colbert.

Michael Whalen (Barney Callahan); Jean Rogers (June White); Chick Chandler (Snapper Doolan); Douglas Fowley (Gus Brawley); John King (Paul Randall); Jane Darwell (Aunt Mary Perkins); June

Gale (Eunice); Spencer Charters (Uncle Ben Perkins); Theodore Von Eltz (Whitey); Cliff Clark (Collins); Charles D. Brown (J. B. Douglas); Charles Lane (District Attorney); Jan Duggan (Flora); Louise Carter (Dora); Bert Roach (Hopkins).

See: TIME OUT FOR MURDER [essay].

INTERNATIONAL CRIME (Grand National, 1937) 64 minutes.

Producers, Max Alexander, Arthur Alexander; director, Charles Lamont; based on the short story "The Fox Hound" by Maxwell Grant; screenplay Jack Nattleford; art director, Ralph Berger; music director, Dr. Edward Killeyni; camera, Marcel Le Picard; editor, Charles Henkel.

Rod La Rocque (Lamont Cranston/The Shadow); Astrid Allwyn (Phoebe Lane); Thomas Jackson (Commissioner Weston); Oscar O'Shea (Heath); William Von Brinken (Flotow); William Pawley (Honest John); Walter Bonn (Stefan); William Moore (Burke); Lew Hearn (Moe Shrevnitz); and: Jack Baxley, Tenen Holtz, John St. Polis, Lloyd Whitlock.

See: THE SHADOW STRIKES [essay].

IT'S A WONDERFUL WORLD (Metro-Goldwyn-Mayer, 1939) 86 minutes.

Producer, Frank Davis; director, W. S. Van Dyke, II; story, Ben Hecht, Herman J. Mankiewicz; screenplay, Hecht; art director, Cedric Gibbons; costumes, Adrian; camera, Oliver Marsh; editor, Harold F. Kress.

Claudette Colbert (Edwina Corday); James Stewart (Guy Johnson); Guy Kibbee (Captain Streeter); Nat Pendleton (Sergeant Koretz); Frances Drake (Vivian Tarbel); Edgar Kennedy (Lieutenant Meller); Ernest Truex (Willie Heyward); Richard Carle (Major Willoughby); Cecilia Callejo (Dolores Gonzales); Sidney Blackmer (Al Mallon); Andy Clyde (Gimpy); Cliff Clark (Captain Haggerty); Cecil Cunningham (Madame Chambers); Leonard Kibrick (Herman Plotka); Hans Conreid (Stage Manager); Grady Sutton (Bupton Peabody).

None-too-honest, and still wet behind the ears, young private eye Guy Johnson (James Stewart) gets a job guarding millionaire playboy Willie Heyward (Ernest Truex), who ends up drinking far too much and being accused of committing murder. Johnson finds himself named as an accessory to the crime and is convicted. He is on his way to the penitentiary when he escapes from the prison train. He aims to clear himself and Heyward by finding the real murderer. En route to freedom he abducts starchy poetess Edwina Corday (Claudette Colbert) and steals her car for a getaway. The intellectual

James Stewart and Claudette Colbert in IT'S A WONDERFUL WORLD (1939).

and beautiful woman does not appreciate being kidnapped, but she finds herself attracted to Johnson and quickly believes in his innocence. She aids him in gaining the needed evidence as he parades as a chauffeur, actor, and Boy Scout pack leader. It is usually she who extricates him from various jams he gets into. Finally he uncovers the killer's identify, leaving him free to romance Edwina.

In this ingratiating mixture of slapstick and homicide, director W. S. Van Dyke, II returned to the detective film genre, having previously directed THE THIN MAN (1934) and AFTER THE THIN MAN (1936), *qq.v.*, the latter featuring James Stewart in a supporting role. Here Stewart assumes the lead as the befuddled detective who learns to follow the straight and narrow after falsely being accused of a double murder. The *New Republic* magazine called the film ". . . one of the few genuinely comic pieces in a dog's age." In addition to stars Claudette Colbert and James Stewart, the feature was enhanced by a fine supporting cast, especially Nat Pendleton, Guy Kibbee and Edgar Kennedy as the cops in the case and Ernest Truex as the pint-sized, tipsy millionaire. On the other side of the coin, Frank S. Nugent (*New York Times*) insisted, "The story's destination is obvious from the start" and "No one is permitted to take the picture's two murder victims seriously, or the playboy languishing in the death house. Just comic props." Nugent summarized the plot of this film (and too many like it) as ". . . a killing farce about a private detective, an unwanted feminine assistant (who finally, of course, effects the murderer's capture) and a couple of comedians from the Homicide Bureau."

In retrospect, a fitting analysis of this pleasing madcap murder mystery is provided by Don Miller in his article "Private Eyes" for *Focus on Film* magazine (August 1975), "It's a breathless affair, directed with Van Dyke's unerring sense of timing (and reportedly shot in eleven days), written by Hecht with his flair for farce well in evidence. Hecht also deftly fashioned a good murder sequence. . . . The picture is played for comedy, and succeeds."

THE JADE MASK (Monogram, 1945) 69 minutes.

Producer, James S. Burkett; director, Phil Rosen; based on the character created by Earl Derr Biggers; screenplay, George Callahan; art director, Dave Milton; assistant director, Eddie Davis; sound, Tom Lambert; camera, Harry Neumann; editor, Dick Currier.

Sidney Toler (Charlie Chan); Mantan Moreland (Birmingham Brown); Edwin Luke (Tommy Chan); Janet Warren (Jean); Edith Evanson (Louise); Alan Bridge (Sheriff Mack); Ralph Lewis (Kimball); Frank Reicher (Harper); Hardie Albright (Meeker); Cyril Delevanti (Roth); Dorothy Granger (Stella); Jack Ingram (Archer); Lester Dorr (Mitchell); Henry Hall (Godfrey); Joe Whitehead (Peabody).

"Chan Versus A Mad Genius! It's Charlie's Strangest And Most Dangerous Case. . . . He Matches Wits With a Diabolical Mastermind of Crime!" and "A Mystery Mansion . . . Where death lurks in every dark corner and a mad genius runs loose!" boasted the poster blurbs for THE JADE MASK, the first of a quartet of Charlie Chan features released by Monogram Pictures in 1945. Well directed by Phil Rosen, with a gripping script by George Callahan, this feature, the fourth since Monogram took over the series the prior year, proved to be a flavorful and engrossing mystery with good pacing and suspense.

Charlie Chan (Sidney Toler), now working undercover for the government in the war effort, is about to return to Washington, D.C. when the police ask him to investigate the murder of scientist Harper (Frank Reicher), who was involved in secret government work. Chan, along with chauffeur Birmingham Brown (Mantan Moreland) and number three son Tommy (Edwin Luke), arrives at the man's mansion to find a houseful of suspects who all hated the nasty, murdered man. Trying to assist Chan in the investigation (but mostly blundering the assignment) is local law enforcer Sheriff Mack (Alan Bridge). After two additional murders are committed, Chan realizes he is dealing with an evil genius who wants to keep for himself Harper's formula for making wood as strong as steel. Undaunted, Chan brings the killer to justice.

Like several other entries in the Monogram Chan series (BLACK MAGIC, DARK ALIBI, DOCKS OF NEW ORLEANS), THE JADE MASK contains a tinge of science fiction (in this case the formula for making treated wood hard as steel) along with such mystery film motifs as a dark mysterious house, hidden room, alleged walking dead people—all of which, of course, turn out to be red herrings.

One point to be noted in this film is the similarity between the sheriff (Alan Bridge) here and the Nevada lawman (Slim Summerville) in CHARLIE CHAN IN RENO (1939), *q.v.* Both law enforcers are depicted as hick sheriffs who are overly suspicious of Chan's capacity to deduce crimes. Chan's successful ratiocination is played against their bumbling attempts to outdo the Oriental sleuth. This type of conflict was a sub-genre convention, usually complemented by a mixture of racial intolerance, in the standard detective film stricture in which the bonafide lawman is impatient with the (amateur) sleuth, but eventually relies on the latter to solve the caper.

THE KENNEL MURDER CASE (Warner Bros., 1933) 73 minutes.

Director, Michael Curtiz; based on the novel by S. S. Van Dine [Willard Huntington Wright]; screenplay, Robert N. Lee, Peter Milner; art director, Jack Okey; costumes, Orry-Kelly; camera, William Reese; editor, Harold McLarnin.

William Powell (Philo Vance); Mary Astor (Hilda Lake); Eugene Pallette (Sergeant Ernest Heath); Ralph Morgan (Raymond Wrede); Helen Vinson (Doris Delafield); Jack LaRue (Eduardo Grassi); Paul Cavanagh (Sir Bruce MacDonald); Robert Barrat (Archer Coe); Arthur Hohl (Gamble); Henry O'Neill (Dubois); Robert McWade (District Attorney John F. X. Markham); Frank Conroy (Brisbane Coe); Etienne Girardot (Dr. Doremus); Spencer Charters (Snitkin); Charles Wilson (Hennessey); James Lee (Liang); Harry Allen (Sandy, the Dog Trainer); George Chandler (Reporter); Milton Kibbee (Charlie Adler the Reporter); Wade Boteler (Sergeant); Leo White (Desk Clerk); Don Brodie (Photographer); James Burke (Cop); Monte Vandergrift (Detective).

Produced as THE RETURN OF PHILO VANCE, THE KENNEL MURDER CASE, based on S. S. Van Dine's 1933 novel, brought William Powell back to the role of Philo Vance, a part he had played to perfection at Paramount in THE "CANARY" MUR-

DER CASE (1929), THE GREENE MURDER CASE (1929), THE
BENSON MURDER CASE (1930), *qq.v.*, and PARAMOUNT ON
PARADE (1930). Many viewers and critics consider this to be the
acme of the seventeen feature films based on the Philo Vance
character and today it is the most accessible of all the Vance screen
canon.

Hostile Archer Coe (Robert Barrat), who reneges on business
deals, refuses to allow his niece Hilda Lake (Mary Astor) to marry.
He insults his Chinese servant Liang (James Lee) and has a falling out
with his brother, Brisbane Coe (Frank Conroy). Following his
success at the dog track races, at which debonair sleuth Philo Vance
(William Powell) is in attendance, a dog is found murdered on Coe's
estate and the man himself is discovered killed behind the locked
doors of his study. Hilda, Liang and Brisbane are the prime suspects,
although the latter had left on a trip before his brother's demise.
Baffled and brusque Sergeant Ernest Heath (Eugene Pallette) and
punctilious District Attorney John F. X. Markham (Robert McWade)
ask Philo Vance's help and he promptly uncovers other suspects.
They include: Eduardo Grassi (Jack LaRue), a crooked agent, covet-
ous of Coe's Chinese porcelain collection; the victim's high class
prostitute girlfriend, Doris Delafield (Helen Vinson); family friend
Raymond Wrede (Ralph Morgan); the sinister butler Gamble (Arthur Hohl); and Sir Bruce MacDonald (Paul Cavanagh), Coe's rival
at the dog races and Hilda's lover. The case becomes even more
complicated when the body of Brisbane is found secreted in the
house; he too has been murdered. Finally, with the aid of a pedigreed
Doberman Pinscher and a Scotty, Vance solves the crimes by noting
that two individuals attempted to kill Archer Coe on the same night
and the two had a fatal meeting. He exposes the survivor.

At the time of its release Mordaunt Hall (*New York Times*)
championed that this film offers "an ingenious and always interesting
story" and lauded star William Powell, "whose experience as a
screen criminologist is second to none." Rotund, raspy-voiced
Eugene Pallette was on hand for his final go-round as Inspector
Heath while Robert McWade was the prim Markham for the first
time—he would return to the assignment in THE DRAGON
MURDER CASE (1934), *q.v.* Etienne Girardot was again on hand as
waspish Medical Examiner Doremus. Spencer Charters and Charles
Wilson made appearances as police detectives, with Wilson repeating his role in THE DRAGON MURDER CASE.

Ray Cabana, Jr., in "Murder Mythology and Mother Goose"
(*Kaleidoscope* magazine, Vol 2, No. 3, 1967), noted that Michael
Curtiz directed the film, " . . . employing all manner of artistic
photography (bits of action caught in angled mirrors; keyhole of a

locked room; shots taken from inside a closet, from outside a window, through parked cars, a staircase, and glass-enclosed antique cases). The final disclosures concerning the diabolic catenation of circumstances involve flashbacks (done in part with subjective technique) accompanied by narrative explanations by Vance, so that the viewer actually sees how two separate people planned the murder of Archer Coe for the same night . . . and how their paths crossed with startling results." William K. Everson reported in *The Detective in Film* (1972), "The beauty of the film is that it succeeds despite the limitations of its breed, and without really departing from a formula which was then very popular. Van Dine's novel is beautifully constructed and, unlike most movie adaptations, this one follows its parent novel to the letter."

In 1940 THE KENNEL MURDER CASE was remade as CALLING PHILO VANCE, this Warner Bros.-First National release starring James Stephenson as Philo Vance. The script updating has Vance as a government agent investigating the murder of Archer Coe (Richard Kipling), pictured here as an airplane manufacturer who has a decided lack of patriotism. Bosley Crowther (*New York Times*) rated this unflavorful rehash a " . . . tiresomely routine and unexciting whodunit." *Variety* added, "James Stephenson in the title role is all cerebral, mostly deadpanish and so cocksure at every step of the way that the spectator in quick time begins to feel that what he is witnessing is more of a guided tour through a murder than a dramatic enactment."

THE KEYHOLE (Warner Bros., 1933) 69 minutes.

Director, Michael Curtiz; based on the story "Adventuress" by Alice D. G. Miller; screenplay, Robert Presnell; dialogue director, Arthur Greville Collins; art director, Anton Grot; gowns, Orry-Kelly; music director, Leo F. Forbstein; camera, Barney McGill; editor, Ray Curtiss.

Kay Francis (Anne Brooks); George Brent (Neil Davis); Glenda Farrell (Dot); Allen Jenkins (Hank Wales); Monroe Owsley (Maurice Le Brun); Helen Ware (Portia Brooks); Henry Kolker (Schuyler Brooks); Ferdinand Gottschalk (Brooks' Lawyer); Irving Bacon (Grover the Chauffeur); Clarence Wilson (Weems, the Head of the Detective Agency); George Chandler (Joe, the Desk Clerk); Heinie Conklin (Departing Guest); Renee Whitney (Cheating Wife); John Sheehan (Bartender); William [Bill] Elliott (Dancing Extra); George Humbert, Gino Corrado (Waiters); Maurice Black (Salesman); Leo White (Porter).

Private detectives have usually been romanticized in fiction, films, radio and TV, but in reality most private investigators work unglamorously and ploddingly as skip tracers or in divorce cases. Rarely have they been shown as such on film but THE KEYHOLE, the first of two detective yarns directed by Michael Curtiz for Warner Bros. in 1933 (the other being PRIVATE DETECTIVE 62, *q.v.*), follows just this plotline. However, the sleuth ends romantically entwined with the enticing and chic young woman he is trailing.

Private eye Neil Davis (George Brent) is hired by wealthy Schuyler Brooks (Henry Kolker) to surveil his young, beautiful wife Anne (Kay Francis) while she is on holiday in Havana. The older husband fears that his wife may be involved with her ex-husband and former dancing partner, Maurice Le Brun (Monroe Owsley). Davis' pursuit uncovers that Le Brun is blackmailing Anne (their divorce was never official) and after he dies mysteriously, the engaging Anne is the prime suspect. Davis, however, has fallen in love with Anne and she reciprocates the feeling, leaving the dapper private eye to solve the case, live up to his commitment to his employer, and yet keep his new love.

THE KEYHOLE, taken from the Alice Duer Miller short story "Adventuress," was the first of six feature films to team handsome George Brent with luscious fashion plate Kay Francis. The film, however, was merely a showcase for its headliners. "It's a cinch from the start which way the wind will blow, and the details of the plot, as the story presses in its routine way, are never very interesting. Entertainment is confined to the personal performances of the lead pair and the generous wardrobe worn unaffectedly by Miss Francis," wrote *Variety*. Richard Watts, Jr. (*New York Herald-Tribune*) added, "Of all the unpleasant gentlemen who surround the unhappy heroine this lover [George Brent] is probably the least alluring. He is, you see, a private detective who has been hired to test her virtue—the idea being that, since he is portrayed by George Brent, if any woman can resist him she must be beyond suspicion. Miss Francis resists for quite a while." For comedy relief there are Hank Wales (Allen Jenkins) as Davis' Brooklynese assistant and roving golddigger Dot (Glenda Farrell); together they enjoy an assortment of smart-mouthed dialogue exchanges.

KISS ME DEADLY (United Artists, 1955) 105 minutes.

Executive producer, Victor Saville; producer/director, Robert Aldrich; based on the novel by Mickey Spillane; screenplay, A. I. Bezzerides; art director, William Glasgow; music/song/music conductor, Frank DeVol; assistant director, Robert Justman; camera, Ernest Laszlo; editor, Mike Luciani.

Ralph Meeker (Mike Hammer); Albert Dekker (Dr. Soberin); Paul Stewart (Carl Evello); Juano Hernandez (Eddie Yeager); Wesley

Addy (Pat); Marian Carr (Friday); Maxine Cooper (Velda); Cloris Leachman (Christina); Gaby Rodgers (Lily Carver); Nick Dennis (Nick); Jack Lambert (Sugar); Jack Elam (Charlie Max); Jerry Zinneman (Sammy); Leigh Snowden (Girl at Pool); Percy Helton (Morgue Doctor); Madi Comfort (Nightclub Singer); Fortunio Bonanova (Trivaco); James McCallian (Super); Silvio Minciotti (Old Man); Robert Cornthwaite, James Seay (FBI Men); Mara McAfee (Nurse); Jesslyn Fax (Mrs. Super); Mort Marshall (Ray Diker); Strother Martin (Harvey Wallace the Truck Driver); Marjorie Bennett (Manager); Art Loggins (Bartender); Bob Sherman (Gas Station Man); Keith McConnell (Athletic Club Clerk); Paul Richards (Attacker); Eddie Beal (Sideman).

Following the critical lambasting given to his initial Mike Hammer feature film, I, THE JURY (1953), *q.v.*, producer Victor Saville hired Robert Aldrich to helm his second Hammer offering, KISS ME DEADLY, based on Mickey Spillane's 1952 novel. Ralph Meeker was cast as the tough Hammer and he suited the role admirably. The film also allows for much more of a relationship between the detective and his secretary/companion Velda (Maxine Cooper), something only touched on in the initial venture.

While driving along a deserted stretch of road, Los Angeles private eye Mike Hammer (Ralph Meeker) picks up a distraught blonde woman, Christina (Cloris Leachman), who has escaped from a mental institution. A gang of thugs captures and tortures them and the woman dies. Surviving, Hammer sets out to find out why they were attacked and why the woman was killed. Because of something the deceased said to him, Hammer believes she was involved in something very important and was murdered to hush her up. Knowing he will get no help from the law, Hammer goes it alone and learns that a scientist (Albert Dekker) and a gangster (Paul Stewart) have secreted an atomic device for use by a foreign power. Hammer obtains the metal box containing the device and when the crooks, who want the box back, kidnap Hammer's secretary/lover Velda (Maxine Cooper), he rescues her from the beach house where she is held captive. He causes the box to be opened and the explosions kill the corruptors as he and Velda escape.

"Like GUN CRAZY, KISS ME DEADLY seems to be one of those films that get better as the years go by. The screenwriter, A. I. Bezzerides, transformed Spillane's book so that the film takes on a partial anti-Spillane quality," wrote Robert Ottoson in *A Reference Guide to the American Film Noir: 1940-1958* (1981). Don Miller reported in "Private Eyes" (*Focus on Film* magazine, Autumn 1975) that the picture ". . . was passed aside as confused by American critics, but Europeans quickly pounced upon it as political, and allegorical, with a Pandora's box sought after by various forces . . . standing in for the secret of atomic power. . . . Exported, the film became a favorite of near cult proportions, and remains so." For many, this is the best depiction of the egocentric Mike Hammer on screen, engulfed in a trap of crime and fighting viciously any way he knows to escape the brutality.

For the record, Nat "King" Cole sings "Rather Have the Blues" during the title credits and, in the course of the story, Madi Comfort sings what is known as "The Blues from Kiss Me Deadly."

LADY IN CEMENT (Twentieth Century-Fox, 1968) Color 93 minutes.

Producer, Aaron Rosenberg; director, Gordon Douglas; based on the novel by Anthony Rome [Marvin H. Albert]; screenplay, Albert, Jack Guss; art director, Leroy Deane; set decorators, Walter M. Scott, Jerry Wunderlich; costumes, Moss Mabry; makeup, Dan

Advertisement for LADY IN CEMENT (1968).

Striepeke; music/music conductor, Hugo Montenegro; orchestrator, Billy May; assistant director, Richard Lang; sound, Howard Warren, David Dockendorf; special camera effects, L. B. Abbott, Art Cruickshank; camera, Joseph Biroc; editor, Robert Simpson.

Frank Sinatra (Tony Rome); Raquel Welch (Kit Forrest); Richard Conte (Lieutenant Santini); Martin Gabel (Al Mungar); Lainie Kazan (Maria Baretto); Pat Henry (Rubin); Dan Blocker (Gronsky); Steve Peck (Paul Mungar); Virginia Wood (Audrey); Richard Deacon (Arnie Sherwin); Frank Raiter (Danny Yale); Peter Hock (Frenchy); Alex Stevens (Shev); Christina Todd (Sandra Lomax); Mac Robbins (Sidney, the Organizer); Tommy Uhlar (Tighe Santini); Ray Baumel (Paco); Pauly Dash (McComb); Andy Jarrell (Pool Boy); Joe E. Lewis (Himself).

During the late 1960s Frank Sinatra sought a new screen image for his mature screen years and emerged in a trio of tough private eye features, beginning with TONY ROME (1967). He followed it with the police caper, THE DETECTIVE (1968), and the same year peformed in a sequel to the first actioner, called LADY IN CEMENT. This latter feature was from the 1960 Anthony Rome [Marvin H. Albert] novel of the same title and, like TONY ROME, was set in and filmed on location at Miami Beach. Gordon Douglas directed all three of these entries. The *New York Times* did not find this hastily-constructed sequel appealing: "Continuing as a flinty private-eye, but not nearly so effectively as in THE DETECTIVE, Frank Sinatra has some fairly crude material, this time carelessly handled, with Miami as a background—or playground, for a familiar-type crime melodrama. . . . Sinatra himself is all right, no more."

Freewheeling Miami gumshoe Tony Rome (Frank Sinatra) is enjoying his hobby of diving for sunken treaure when he finds the nude body of a young woman with her feet in hardened cement off the city's coastline. An autopy reveals that the girl was knifed to death and hoodlum Gronsky (Dan Blocker) hires Rome to find out if the deceased was his missing go-go dancer-lover, Sandra. Tony visits Sandra's roommate, Maria (Lainie Kazan), who reveals that she last saw Sandra at a party given by socialite Kit Forrest (Raquel Welch) but the sleuth finds she is a lush who remembers nothing of the party. Meanwhile, Kit's neighbor, Al Mungar (Martin Gabel), a former Mafia leader, warns Tony to leave the beautiful Kit alone. Maria is murdered and two of Mungar's hired men attempt to kill Gronsky. Tony uses a sketch artist (Richard Deacon) to prove that the dead girl was Sandra. He also learns that both Kit and Sandra were in love with Mungar's son, Paul (Steve Peck), and had fought over him. As the situation snowballs, Rome is accused of murdering Maria's gay club owner boss Danny Yale (Frank Raiter), but he escapes from his friend, Lieutenant Santini (Richard Conte), to prove his innocence. Rome returns to Kit and and she tells him she was framed for Sandra's murder. He forces Gronsky to confess that he and the younger Mungar stole part of the money from a robbery committed by Al Mungar's gang. When Gronsky admits he had given Sandra part of the money, the detective realizes who the actual killer is and they save Kit from being eliminated by the murderer. With the guilty party now captured, Rome calls Santini and provides him with the details. At the end Rome and Kit go hunting for sunken treasure.

LADY IN THE LAKE (Metro-Goldwyn-Mayer, 1946) 105 minutes.
    Producer, George Haight; director, Robert Montgomery; based on the novel by Raymond Chandler; screenplay, Steve Fisher, (uncredited) Chandler; art directors, Cedric Gibbons, Preston Ames; set decorators, Edwin B. Willis, Thomas Theuerkauf; music, David Snell; assistant director, Dolph Zimmer; sound, Douglas Shearer; camera, Paul C. Vogel; editor, Gene Ruggiero.
    Robert Montgomery (Philip Marlowe); Lloyd Nolan (Lieutenant DeGarmot); Audrey Totter (Adrienne Fromsett); Tom Tully (Captain Kane); Leon Ames (Derace Kingsby); Jayne Meadows

Robert Montgomery and Audrey Totter in LADY IN THE LAKE (1946).

(Mildred Haveland); Morris Ankrum (Eugene Grayson); Lila Leeds (Receptionist); Richard Simmons (Chris Lavery); Ellen Ross (Elevator Girl); William Roberts (Artist); Kathleen Lockhart (Mrs. Grayson); Cy Kendall (Jaibi); Ralph Dunn (Sergeant); Wheaton Chambers (Property Clerk); Frank Orth (Greer); William McKeever Riley (Bunny); Robert Williams (Detective); Fred E. Sherman (Reporter); Jack Davis, John Gallaudet, Tom Murray, George Magrill, Budd Fine, John Webb Dillon (Policemen); Robert Spencer (Marlowe's Double); Billy Newell (Drunk); Eddie Acuff (Coroner); Nina Ross, Charles Bradstreet, George Travell, William O'Leary, Bert Moorhouse, Florence Stephens, Sandra Morgan, Fred Santley, Laura Treadwell, Kay Wiley, Frank Dae, David Cavendish, James Nolan, Sherry Hall, Ann Lawrence, Roger Cole (Christmas Party Guests).

In 1945 MGM purchased the screen rights to Raymond Chandler's fourth Philip Marlowe book, *Lady in the Lake* (1943), and hired the writer to develop a screenplay for the studio. Chandler's script, however, proved too lengthy and divergent and Steve Fisher was brought in to rewrite it. Robert Montgomery maneuvered the studio into assigning him the role of Marlowe. He also made his solo directorial debut* with this film, which was shot in fifty days of actual production. In addition, the creative Montgomery used the subjective camera technique of having the camera become Marlowe's eyes. Thus the audience sees what Marlowe sees through the camera and not Montgomery as Marlowe. He actually appears in only a few scenes when not shown in mirror reflections. *Newsweek* magazine noted that this motion picture is "a brilliant tour de force" and it ". . . indicates that Hollywood isn't beyond exploring the uncharted boundaries of its medium." Shot on a $1,000,000 budget, the film grossed more than four times that amount in its initial release.

Tired of his low-paying work as a private eye, Hollywood gumshoe Philip Marlowe (Robert Montgomery) writes a pulp magazine story and on the day before Christmas takes it to Kingsby Publications. There, story editor Adrienne Fromsett (Audrey Totter) hires him to find Chrystal, the missing wife of her boss, Derace Kingsby (Leon Ames), because the latter intends to divorce her. Marlowe learns that Chrystal had been seeing Chris Lavery (Richard Simmons) but the young man denies this. When Marlowe presses the issue, Lavery knocks him out. The detective wakes up in the Bay City Jail on a drunk charge, but Lieutenant DeGarmot (Lloyd Nolan) and Captain Kane (Tom Tully) release him. Adrienne tells Marlowe

---

*During the filming of MGM's THEY WERE EXPENDABLE (1945) director John Ford had been taken ill and co-star Robert Montgomery stepped in to help complete the helming chores.

that Chrystal was last seen at the Little Fawn Lake resort and he goes there, finds the owner's wife, Muriel Chess, has been drowned and her husband held for the crime. Since Adrienne thinks Chrystal may have killed Muriel because she hated the woman, Marlowe investigates further and discovers that Muriel was really Mildred Haveland (Audrey Meadows) and that she had gone to the lake to get away from the law. Returning to Hollywood the sleuth goes to see Lavery and finds his landlady instead. He also finds Lavery dead after the woman leaves.

Marlowe is convinced that Adrienne killed Lavery and Kingsby tries to buy him off, but the detective refuses. The publisher later hires him to locate Chrystal, as he too feels Adrienne may have murdered Lavery. Back at Lavery's apartment, Marlowe calls in DeGarmot and Kane and then accuses the former of having gone to Little Fawn Lake searching for Mildred, with whom he was involved. The cop beats up Marlowe and then arrests him, but lets him go when he tells them that DeGarmot knew both Mildred and Lavery. Adrienne confides to Marlowe that Mildred once worked for a doctor whose wife had died mysteriously and that DeGarmot had been the investigating officer who had ruled the death a suicide. Marlowe questions the dead woman's parents (Morris Ankrum and Kathleen Lockhart), but they refuse to talk. He is trailed by DeGarmot who knocks Marlowe's car off the road and then reports him as a drunk driver. Marlowe, however, substitutes a real drunk in his place and goes to Adrienne's apartment. She admits she loves him and wants him off the case. Kingsby arrives to say that Chrystal needs money and he wants Marlowe to take it to her. Marlowe agrees and when he meets Chrystal, the pieces fall into place. Before the wrap-up Marlowe and Adrienne pursue their romance.

The use of the subjective camera* and the convoluted plotline make LADY IN THE LAKE difficult to follow at times. Moreover, while this is a slick production, full of all the usual MGM gloss, it fails to capture the true flavor of Raymond Chandler's novel, one of his best Philip Marlowe yarns. A main reason for this inadequacy is the film's complete deletion—except in explanatory dialogue—of the Little Fawn Lake sequences, the most flavorful part of the original narrative.

---

*"YOU accept an invitation to a blonde's apartment. YOU get socked in the jaw by a murder suspect," insisted the film's advertising campaign. At the opening of LADY IN THE LAKE, Philip Marlowe (Robert Montgomery) informs the viewer, "You'll see it just as I saw it. You'll meet the people. You'll find the clues. And maybe you'll solve it quick and maybe you won't."

LADY IN THE MORGUE (Universal, 1938) 70 minutes.

Producer, Irving Starr; director, Otis Garrett; based on the novel by Jonathan Latimer; adaptors, Eric Taylor, Robertson White; camera, Stanley Cortez; editor, Ted Kent.

Preston Foster (Bill Crane); Patricia Ellis (Mrs. Sam Taylor); Frank Jenks (Doc Williams); Barbara Pepper (Kay Renshaw); Thomas Jackson (Inspector Storm); Rollo Lloyd (Coroner); Gordon [Bill] Elliott (Chauncey Courtland); Roland Drew (Sam Taylor); Joseph Downing (Steve Collins); James Robbins (Frankie French); Morgan Wallace (Leyman); Al Hill (Spitzy); Brian Burke (Johnson); Donald Kerr (Greening); Don Brodie (Taxi Driver); Gordon Hart (Colonel Black).

Jonathan Latimer wrote five novels about the exploits of cynical gumshoe Bill Crane and his free-wheeling associate, Doc Williams. Three of these literary exploits were filmed by producer Irving Starr for Universal as part of the studio's low-budget "Crime Club" series, all of the films being based on Crime Club novels published by Doubleday Doran. *Headed for a Hearse* (1935) was made as the initial Bill Crane feature, THE WESTLAND CASE (1937), while *The*

Frank Jenks and Preston Foster in LADY IN THE MORGUE (1938).

Dead Don't Care (1938) became THE LAST WARNING (1938), the last of the trio of Crane entries. *Lady in the Morgue* (1936) appeared under its own title as the second in the screen adventures. The first and last books in the series, *Murder in the Madhouse* (1935) and *Red Gardenias* (1939) remain unfilmed.

LADY IN THE MORGUE presents private eye Bill Crane (Preston Foster) and his cohort Doc Williams (Frank Jenks) researching a supposed suicide which Crane believes is a homicide. While on the trail he comes across three additional killings and finds that gangsters, including moll Kay Renshaw (Barbara Pepper), are involved. It seems that the body Crane was sent to investigate at the morgue, that of a young blonde woman, has disappeared and the gumshoe is promptly accused by police Inspector Storm (Thomas Jackson) of committing the murder and then filching the corpse. When he realizes that gangsters are also hunting the corpse, Crane unravels the case.

Variety judged the film "easily superior to the average run of film" and added "film makes up in merit for the overcomplication of plot." Don Miller discussed this breezy production in his essay, "The American B Film," in *Focus on Film* magazine (Winter 1970): "Given a bright script with which to work, [director Otis] Garrett's handling of the film is worth study, for it shows a cohesion seldom found even in the top-budgeted product of the period. Apparently, in the midst of an era when the dissolve and wipe were *de rigueur*, Garrett as an ex-film editor planned his transitions in advance, building them right into the camerawork. . . . Despite the morbid title, the film is free of blood or gruesome scenes. The plot is complicated but entertaining while the dialogue, cleansed of Latimer's more Rabelaisian humor, is tart and crackling. . . . Foster and Jenks suited their roles perfectly, and Barbara Pepper had a chance to shine in all her Mae Westian glory."

Preston Foster as Bill Crane and Frank Jenks as Doc Williams appeared in all three episodes in the series.

A.k.a.: CORPSE IN THE MORGUE. British release title: CASE OF THE MISSING BLONDE.

LADY OF BURLESQUE (United Artists, 1943) 91 minutes.

Producer, Hunt Stromberg; director, William A. Wellman; based on the novel *The G-String Murders* by Gypsy Rose Lee; screenplay, James Gunn; art director, Bernard Herzbrun; Miss Stanwyck's costumes, Edith Head; other costumes, Natalie Visart; music, Arthur Lange; songs, Sammy Cahn and Harry Akst; choreography, Danny Dare; assistant director, Sam Nelson; sound,

Charles Althouse; camera, Robert De Grasse; editor, James E. Newcomb.

Barbara Stanwyck (Dixie Daisy); Michael O'Shea (Biff Brannigan); J. Edward Bromberg (S. B. Foss); Iris Adrian (Gee Gee Graham); Gloria Dickson (Polly Baxter); Victoria Faust (Lolita La Verne); Stephanie Bachelor (Princess Nirvena); Charles Dingle (Inspector Harrigan); Marion Martin (Alice Angel); Eddie Gordon (Officer Pat Kelly); Frank Fenton (Russell Rogers); Pinky Lee (Mandy); Frank Fenton (Russell Rogers); Frank Conroy (Stacchi); Lew Kelly (The Hermit); Claire Carleton (Sandra); Janis Carter (Janine); Gerald Mohr (Louie Grindero); Bert Hanlon (Sammy); Sid Marion (Joey); Lou Lubin (Moey); Lee Trent (Lee); Don Lynn (Don); Beal Wong (Wong); Freddie Walburn (Messenger Boy); Isabel Withers (Teletype Operator); George Chandler (Jake the Stagehand); Kit Guard (Hank, the Stagehand); Eddie Borden (Man in Audience); David Kashner (Cossack); Florence Auer (Policewoman); and: Joe Devlin, Louise La Plance, Elinor Troy, Virginia Gardner, Carol Carrollton, Dallas Worth, Mary Gail, Barbara Slater, Noel Neill, Marjorie Raymond, Jean Longworth, Joan Dale, Gerry Coonan, Valmere Barman, Josette Robinson.

Following the success of his outstanding comedy, ROXIE HART (1942), starring Ginger Rogers, director William A. Wellman returned to the medium with a mystery-tinged whodunit, LADY OF BURLESQUE, based on Gypsy Rose Lee's flavorsome novel, *The G-String Murders* (1941). Budgeted at a then-expensive one million dollars, this feature was producer Hunt Stromberg's first independent production after being employed at Metro-Goldwyn-Mayer for nearly twenty years.

A burlesque stock company has its headquarters in an opera house, and the place is raided by the police. When the entertainers are out on bail the show continues with the various cast members engrossed in petty rivalries and jealousies. Stooge comedian Biff Brannigan (Michael O'Shea) tries to romance headline stripper Dixie Daisy (Barbara Stanwyck), who is getting heavy career promotion from gruff manager S. B. Foss (J. Edward Bromberg). One of the strippers is murdered and police Inspector Harrigan (Charles Dingle) investigates, as do Dixie and Brannigan. However, before that crime can be solved another of the girls is killed. Among the suspects are the other over-heated strippers: Gee Gee Graham (Iris Adrian), Polly Baxter (Gloria Dickson), Lolita La Verne (Victoria Faust), Princess Nirvena (Stephanie Bachelor), and Alice Angel (Marion Martin). Since the two murders utilized a G-string as a weapon, Dixie and Brannigan set a trap for the killer and capture the guilty party.

Much of the peppery entertainment value of this spirited feature comes in its depiction of the denizens of the burlesque field, as Frank T. Thompson notes in *William A. Wellman* (1983). "The characters in LADY OF BURLESQUE are professionals, as are most typical Wellman people, and even the tensest moment in the murder mystery does not keep them from going to work. From a commercial point of view, it's quite obvious why Wellman spends so much time showing the bad burlesque comedy skits, dance numbers, and pseudo-Ziegfeld productions: it gives the picture some songs, some laughs, and a lot of beautiful girls with not much to wear." Due to the Hays Office intervention, the bumps and grinds of real striptease acts could not be depicted in authentic detail. As an alternative, audience reaction shots are used to convey their appeal and effect.

Among the musical production numbers presented in this offbeat murder mystery is Barbara Stanwyck cavorting through "Take It Off the E-String, Play It On the G-String." For the record, a G-string has *nothing* whatever to do with a string on a violin.

British release title: STRIPTEASE LADY.

LADY OF DECEIT   *see*   BORN TO KILL.

LANIGAN'S RABBI (NBC-TV, 6/17/76) Color 100 minutes.

Executive producer, Leonard B. Stern; producers, Robert C. Thompson, Roderick Paul; director, Lou Antonio; based on the novel *Friday the Rabbi Slept Late* by Harry Kemelman; teleplay, Don M. Mankiewicz, Gordon Cotler; art director, Norman R. Newberry; costume designer, Nolan Miller; music, Leonard Rosenman; camera, Andrew Jackson; editor, Howard Volney III.

Art Carney (Police Chief Paul Lanigan); Stuart Margolin (Rabbi David Small); Janis Paige (Kate Lanigan); Janet Margolin (Miriam Small); Lorraine Gary (Myra Galen); Robert Reed (Morton Galen); Andrew Robinson (Willie Norman); Jim Antonio (Jim Blake); David Sheiner (Al Becker); Barbara Carney (Bobbi Whittaker); Robert Doyle (Osgood); William Wheatley (Stanley); Steffen Zacharias (Basserman); Barbara Flicker (Mrs. Blake); Don Keefer (Mr. Kogan); Ray Ballard (Store Detective); Rudy Ranton (Santos).

When a young woman is found dead inside his auto which is parked in front of a small town (Cameron, California) synagogue, Rabbi David Small (Stuart Margolin) is the chief suspect in the case. Irish police Chief Paul Lanigan (Art Carney), however, feels he is innocent and looks into other avenues while investigating the homicide. Now implicated, amateur criminologist Small also delves into

Bruce Solomon and Art Carney in LANIGAN'S RABBI (1976).

the matter and turns up pertinent information. He and Lanigan work as an unlikely team to solve the murder and in doing so uncover adultery and a clandestine love affair which have led to the untimely death.

This offbeat mystery-comedy telefeature did surprisingly well in the TV ratings and spawned a TV series, "Lanigan's Rabbi," which ran on NBC-TV from 1976 to 1977 as part of "The NBC Sunday Mystery Movie," with Art Carney continuing as Lanigan and Bruce Solomon taking over the role of Rabbi Small. (The telefilm's co-star, Stuart Margolin, was by then a regular on another ongoing TV detective series, "The Rockford Files," with James Garner). LANIGAN'S RABBI was based on Harry Kemelman's novel *Friday* *the Rabbi Slept Late* (1964), one in a series of Rabbi David Small detective novels.*

A.k.a.: FRIDAY THE RABBI SLEPT LATE.

LARCENY IN HER HEART (Producers Releasing Corp., 1946) 68 minutes.

Producer, Sigmund Neufeld; director, Sam Newfield; based on the character created by Brett Halliday [Davis Dresser]; screenplay, Raymond L. Schrock; art director, Edward C. Jewell; set decorator, Elias H. Rief; music director, Leo Erdody; camera, Jack Greenhalgh; editor, Holbrook N. Todd.

Hugh Beaumont (Michael Shayne); Cheryl Walker (Phyllis Hamilton); Ralph Dunn (Sergeant Rafferty); Paul Bryar (Tim Rorke); Charles Wilson (Chief Gentry); Douglas Fowley (Doc Patterson); Gordon Richards (Burton Stallings); Charles Quigley (Arch Dubler); Julia McMillan (Lucille); Marie Harmon (Helen Stallings); Lee Bennett (Whit Marlow); Henry Hall (Dr. Porter); Milton Kibbee (Joe Morell); Gene Roth (Orderly).

Wealthy Burton Stallings (Gordon Richards) hires detective Michael Shayne (Hugh Beaumont) to locate his missing stepdaughter, right on the eve of the shamus's planned trip to Niagara Falls with secretary/girlfriend Phyllis Hamilton (Cheryl Walker). The trip called off, Shayne accepts the case, but the missing girl shows up dead in his apartment and he has a tough time keeping the police, especially persistent Sergeant Rafferty (Ralph Dunn), from finding the corpse. With the aid of pal Tim Rorke (Paul Bryar), Shayne transports the body to the missing persons' bureau, where Stallings identifies her. Shayne learns Stallings' wife was once committed to Doc Patterson's (Douglas Fowley) sanitarium and the gumshoe has himself admitted there as a drunk. Once inside, he finds the stepdaughter a prisoner. He alerts Rorke, who brings in the police just as Stallings and Patterson start to carry out their plan to eliminate Shayne for knowing too much about Stallings' scheme. The culprits are arrested and the supposedly deceased girl is reunited with her spouse. As for Shayne, he has been knocked out in an altercation with a hospital orderly (Gene Roth). Phyllis intends driving her unconscious suitor to Niagara Falls.

The second (preceded by MURDER IS MY BUSINESS, 1946)

---

*Other novels in the Rabbi David Small detective series by Harry Kemelman are: *Saturday the Rabbi Went Hungry* (1966), *Sunday the Rabbi Stayed Home* (1969), *Monday the Rabbi Took Off* (1972), *Tuesday the Rabbi Saw Red* (1974), *Wednesday the Rabbi Got Wet* (1976), *Thursday the Rabbi Walked Out* (1978), *Conversations with Rabbi Small* (1982), *Someday the Rabbi Will Leave* (1985), *One Fine Day the Rabbi Bought a Cross* (1987).

in PRC's Michael Shayne series starring Hugh Beaumont in the title role, LARCENY IN HER HEART is a congenial, fast-paced actioner with lots of plot twists to keep the viewer guessing. Beaumont (who gained fame later as the extremely patient father on the "Leave It to Beaver" teleseries) is quite believable as the peanut-eating shamus and the programmer moves at a pleasing clip.

In the early 1950s this feature would be re-edited into a thirty-minute 16mm home version entitled STAND-IN FOR MURDER by Official Films.

THE LAST CROOKED MILE (Republic, 1946) 67 minutes.

Associate producer, Rudolph E. Aliel; director, Philip Ford; based on the radio play by Robert L. Richards; screenplay, Jerry Sackheim; additional dialogue, Jerry Guskin; art director, Frank Hotaling; set decorators, John McCarthy, Jr., George Milo; sound, Victor Appell; special effects, Howard and Theodore Lydecker; camera, Alfred Keller.

Donald Barry (Tom Dwyer); Ann Savage (Sheila Kennedy); Adele Mara (Bonnie); Tom Powers (Floyd Sorelson); Sheldon Leonard (Ed MacGuire); Nestor Paiva (Ferrara); Harry Shannon (Lieutenant Blake); Ben Welden (Haynes); John Miljan (Lieutenant Mayrin); Charles D. Brown (Detrich); John Dehner (Jarvis); Anthony Caruso (Charlie).

With the increasing interest in the *film noir*, or dark cinema, movement of the 1940s and early 1950s, it is surprising that THE LAST CROOKED MILE is not a better known feature film. Not only does it include the various plot motifs and settings of such genre pictures, but it is a very Raymond Chandler-like melodrama (adapted from Robert L. Richards' radio play), with a gumshoe involved in an intricate robbery and murder case. The film also features Ann Savage, a favorite actress of the *film noir* clique, best known for her screen work in the near-no-budget genre classic, DETOUR, issued the same year.

A $300,000 payroll robbery is carried out by hoodlum Jarvis (John Dehner) and his three associates. However, one of the men is killed at the scene of the heist and the rest are killed when their car is wrecked as they flee the police. The loot is not recovered, however, and Los Angeles private eye Tom Dwyer (Donald Barry) is hired by unscrupulous Floyd Sorelson (Tom Powers), representative of the insurance company for the bank, to find the stolen payroll. Dwyer's fee is to be ten percent of the amount recovered. Since the getaway auto is now part of a carnival exhibit owned by Ferrara (Nestor Paiva) in Ocean City, Dwyer goes there to examine the vehicle. There he encounters his former girlfriend, beautiful Bonnie (Adele

Mara), who insists on helping him solve the mystery. They interview a mechanic who worked on the car after Ferrara purchased it, and then the repairman turns up dead. Dwyer crosses paths with Jarvis' girlfriend, cabaret thrush Sheila Kennedy (Ann Savage), who also wants the loot, as does gangster Ed MacGuire (Sheldon Leonard). Sheila eventually turns on hard-pressed Dwyer and tries to do him in before he is saved by Bonnie and together they unravel the riddle.

Cowboy film star Donald Barry (also known as Don "Red" Barry) is especially effective as the flippant Philip Marlowe-type shamus and is nicely supported by Adele Mara as his scatterbrained girlfriend. For contrast Ann Savage is the slinky, murderous Sheila (who, in a club sequence, sings "The One I Love Belongs to Somebody Else"). Full of the gritty flavor of locales typical of Raymond Chandler novels and with similar type characters, THE LAST CROOKED MILE is a *film noir* worth definite reappraisal.*

LAST OF THE LONE WOLF (Columbia, 1930) 70 minutes.

Producer, Harry Cohn; director, Richard Boleslavsky; based on the story by Louis Joseph Vance; adaptor, John Thomas Neville; screenplay, Dorothy Howell; dialogue, James Whittaker; technical director, Edward Shulter; art director, Edward Jewell; assistant director, C. C. Coleman; sound, Russell Malmgren; camera, Ben Kline; editor, David Berg.

Bert Lytell (Michael Lanyard, the Lone Wolf); Patsy Ruth Miller (Stephanie); Lucien Prival (Varril); Otto Matieson (Prime Minister); Alfred Hickman (The King); Maryland Morne (Queen); Haley Sullivan (Camilla the Queen's Maid); Pietro Sosso (Master of Ceremonies); Henry Daniell (Count von Rimpau); James Liddy (Hoffman).

In the European monarchy of Saxonia, jewel thief Michael Lanyard, alias the Lone Wolf (Bert Lytell), is detained for nefarious activities. The Prime Minister (Otto Matieson) offers him his freedom if he recovers a valuable ring given by the Queen (Maryland Morne) to Count von Rimpau (Henry Daniell). The King (Alfred Hickman) wants the ring returned so that scandal will not result if the Queen's actions are ever known. The Queen, not knowing of the prime Minister's offer, sends her lady-in-waiting, Stephanie (Patsy Ruth Miller), to recover the gem. On the train to von Rimpau's

---

*At the time of its release Bosley Crowther (*New York Times*) reacted strongly to the feature, warning that this film is ". . . the end of the road for movie-goers." He labeled it a "heavy and hackneyed whodunnit." *Variety* was more charitable: "There are several implausible developments in view of the final denouement but these are largely covered up by the smart scripting . . . and expert direction. . . ."

embassy, Varril (Lucien Prival), the Count's henchman, attempts to molest the young woman, and Lanyard comes to her rescue. At the embassy Lanyard obtains the ring but returns it when he is suspected of the theft. Stephanie tells Lanyard the Queen must have the ring to wear at a royal ball, but he is captured by Varril and his men. Escaping with Stephanie, Lanyard returns the precious jewelry to Saxonia in time to avoid any royal scandal.

With a plot that owes (far too) much to Alexandre Dumas' *The Three Musketeers*, LAST OF THE LONE WOLF is Bert Lytell's fifth and final screen appearance as the smooth, slippery Michael Lanyard. He was the screen's first Lone Wolf in Selznick's 1917 release, THE LONE WOLF, *q.v.*, and he would return to the part for Columbia in THE LONE WOLF RETURNS (1926), *q.v.*, followed by ALIAS THE LONE WOLF (1927), and THE LONE WOLF'S DAUGHTER (1929), in which he became the screen's first talking Lanyard. This 1930 feature ended Lytell's association with the part. The movie itself is a creaky offering with its aged Graustarkian storyline. In addition, it wastes lovely Patsy Ruth Miller in a minor co-starring assignment. At least it provides flashy roles for Henry Daniell (as the villainous Count) and for Lucien Prival (as his corrupt associate).

Another silent screen idol, Thomas Meighan, next took over the Lone Wolf characterization in Fox's CHEATERS AT PLAY (1932), *q.v.*

THE LATE SHOW (Warner Bros., 1977) Color 94 minutes.

Producer, Robert Altman; associate producers, Scott Bushnell, Robert Eggenweiler; director/screenplay, Robert Benton; music, Ken Wannberg; lyrics, Stephen Lehner; set decorator, Bob Gould; assistant director, Tommy Thompson, Tony Bishop; sound, Sam Gemette; camera, Chuck Rosher; editors, Lou Lombardo, Peter Appleton.

Art Carney (Ira Wells); Lily Tomlin (Margo); Bill Macy (Charlie Hatter); Eugene Roche (Ron Birdwell); Joanna Cassidy (Laura Birdwell); John Considine (Lamar); Ruth Nelson (Mrs. Schmidt); John Davey (Sergeant Dayton); Howard Duff (Harry Regan).

One of the most surprisingly delightful detective feature films of the 1970s—or any other decade—is THE LATE SHOW, one of the few comprehensible motion pictures with which Robert Altman has yet been involved. Here, however, he is the producer and the driving force behind the production is writer/director Robert Benton, who fashioned an outstanding and satisfying film around the off-kilter casting of Art Carney as a retired private eye and Lily Tomlin as his strung-out *vis-à-vis*. Carney received the National Society of Film Critics Award for his acting in this feature.

Time has not been kind to retired Los Angeles private investigator Ira Wells (Art Carney). He is deaf in one ear, has bad feet, and is doing none too well financially. He finds his ex-partner Harry Regan (Howard Duff) dying on his doorstep and sets out to trap those responsible for his pal's demise. At the same time he meets semi-hippie Margo (Lily Tomlin), an oddly attractive youngish woman who peddles marijuana for a living while thinking she is an artist. She wants Wells to find her kidnapped cat. Margo latches onto the chagrined senior citizen and tries to aid him in the case. So, too, does her grubby little friend Charlie Hatter (Bill Macy), who makes a living doing anything which pays money or the promise of it. Through Hatter they become enmeshed with wealthy fence Ron Birdwell (Eugene Roche) and his forceful cohort Lamar (John Considine), while Birdwell's attractive wife Laura (Joanna Cassidy) attempts to persuade Wells to get rid of her husband. Eventually Wells realizes that Regan was murdered because he knew too much about a certain individual's crooked dealings. When the guilty party endeavors to silence Wells, there is a shootout. The detective and the bewildered Margo survive to start a new, if uneasy, life together.

F. Maurice Speed determined in *Film Review 1979-80* (1979), "The most successful attempt yet to recapture the style and, more especially, the spirit of those classic private-eye films of the forties and thereabouts; with a highly involved and complicated story of murder, solved with dogged persistence and brilliant calculation by 'retired private' detec Ira Wells. . . ." Marc Sigoloff concurred in *The Films of the Seventies* (1984), rating the film a "Superb detective thriller." He added, "THE LATE SHOW is far more than just a comedy as Robert Benton has created one of the screen's finest detective films with an exciting, but never overly confusing story, many wonderfully odd characters and a moody film noir atmosphere."

One of the big assets of the unpretentious THE LATE SHOW is its variety of well-played and diverse characters. Art Carney is superbly understated as Ira Wells in what is perhaps his finest screen role. For once, Lily Tomlin is totally believable in her quirky part and she and Carney complement each other in scenes of near perfection. The supporting cast is equally effective, especially Bill Macy as the seedy, sleazy Charlie Hatter, whose wretched pink Cadillac convertible has to be one of the most memorable autos in movie history. Eugene Roche is fine as the bloated crook and Howard Duff (once radio's famous "Sam Spade") makes the most of his brief role as the murdered private eye.

THE LEAGUE OF FRIGHTENED MEN (Columbia, 1937) 71 minutes.

Director, Alfred E. Green; based on the novel by Rex Stout; screenplay, Eugene Soplow, Guy Endore; camera, Henry Freulich; editor Gene Liford.

Walter Connolly (Nero Wolfe); Lionel Stander (Archie Goodwin); Eduardo Ciannelli (Paul Chapin); Irene Hervey (Evelyn Hibbard); Victor Kilian (Pitney Scott); Nana Bryant (Agnes Burton); Allen Brook (Mark Chapin); Walter Kingsford (Ferdinand Bowen); Leonard Mudie (Professor Hibbard); Kenneth Hunter (Dr. Burton); Charles Irwin (Augustus Farrell); Rafaela Ottiano (Dora Chapin); Edward McNamara (Inspector Cramer); Jameson Thomas (Michael Ayers); Ian Wolfe (Nicholas Cabot); Jonathan Hale (Alexander Drummond); Herbert Ashley (Fritz); James Flavin (Joe).

Following the success of MEET NERO WOLFE (1936), q.v., Columbia Pictures made its second Nero Wolfe entry, THE LEAGUE OF FRIGHTENED MEN, from Rex Stout's 1935 novel of the same title. By then Edward Arnold had left Columbia to work at other studios and he was replaced by Walter Connolly, who had previously had the title role in Paramount's FATHER BROWN, DETECTIVE (1935), q.v. Prior to that, in 1933, he had portrayed Charlie Chan in a series on the NBC Blue radio network. Connolly, however, was better noted for his comedy interpretations and did not easily fit the image of Nero Wolfe although the New York Times agreed that the film is "a well knit-mystery, and well played out." Lionel Stander, who had portrayed faithful Archie Goodwin in the initial production, repeated his role, but here the character is used for comedy relief, a type-casting which would have better fit the screen work of Nat Pendleton.

Three members of a Harvard University fraternity have been murdered and the seven survivors persuade Nero Wolfe (Walter Connolly) to look into the troublesome matter. Years before, the ten men had been involved in the hazing of another student and as a result of the trick they played on him, the man (Eduardo Ciannelli) was left a cripple for life. He is now a noted mystery writer and the survivors insist he is the cause of the killings, getting revenge on them for what they did in college. Wolfe, with the aid of assistant Archie Goodwin (Lionel Stander), unearths the killer's identity and the motive for the murders. "The film was in no way the equal to its predecessor," Jon Tuska determined in The Detective in Hollywood (1978).

Following this film Columbia made no further Nero Wolfe escapades due to Walter Connolly's fragile health (he would die in 1940), and after that Rex Stout refused to allow his characters to be filmed. In 1943 "The Adventures of Nero Wolfe" was heard on radio, with Santos Ortega as Wolfe and Louis Vittes as the irrepressible Archie Goodwin. Sydney Greenstreet, who became famous as The Fat Man in THE MALTESE FALCON (1941), *q.v.*, later played Nero Wolfe in the radio series. In 1979 Thayer David was Wolfe in the made-for-television feature film, NERO WOLFE, *q.v.*, and in 1980-81 William Conrad played the part in the NBC-TV series, "Nero Wolfe."

LEAVE IT TO THE IRISH (Monogram, 1944) 71 minutes.

Producer, Lindsley Parsons; director, William Beaudine; story/ screenplay, Tim Ryan, Eddie Davis; art director, David Milton; assistant directors, William Strohbach, Eddie Davis; camera, Ira Morgan; editor, Dick Currier.

James Dunn (Terry Moran); Wanda McKay (Nora O'Brien);

Barbara Woodell, James Dunn and Wanda McKay in LEAVE IT TO THE IRISH (1944).

Jack LaRue (Maletti); Arthur Loft (Timothy O'Brien); Vince Barnett (Harry); Barbara Woodell (Mrs. Hamilton); Joseph Devillard (Gus); Olaf Hytten (Butler); Ted Stanhope (Joe); Eddie Allen (Slim); Dick Scott (Biff).

Jovial James Dunn portrayed a private eye in the 1942 Monogram programmer, THE LIVING GHOST, *infra*, and two years later he and director William Beaudine, who had helmed the 1942 quickie, re-teamed for another Monogram detective cheapie, LEAVE IT TO THE IRISH. While the former film had been a straight melodrama with science fiction elements, LEAVE IT TO THE IRISH has as much comedy as drama and Dunn plays sleuth Terry Moran as a cheerful sort of guy full of blarney.

When a series of fur thefts occur and a furrier is murdered, private investigator Terry Moran (James Dunn) is hired to investigate and is aided by distaff sleuth Nora O'Brien (Wanda McKay). Several more murders occur and Moran learns that the police suspect him of being the perpetrator, so he and Nora intensify their efforts to solve the riddle.

It is too bad that the pleasing presence of James Dunn and Wanda McKay is undermined by such a hackneyed screenplay.

LEND ME YOUR EAR *see* THE LIVING GHOST.

THE LITTLE SISTER *see* MARLOWE.

THE LIVING GHOST (Monogram, 1942) 61 minutes.

Producer. A. W. Hackel; director, William Beaudine; based on the story by Howard Dimsdale; screenplay, Joseph Hoffman; music director, Frank Sanucci; camera, Mack Stengler; editor, Jack Ogilvie.

James Dunn (Nick Trayne); Joan Woodbury (Betty Hilton); Jan Wiley (Tina Craig); George Eldredge (Tony Weldon); Gus Glassmire (Walter Craig); Edna Johnson (Helen Craig); J. Arthur Young (George Phillips); and: Howard Banks, Danny Beck, Harry Depp, Vera Gordon, Lawrence Grant, J. Farrell MacDonald, Paul McVey, Frances Richards, Minerva Urecal, Norman Willis.

When millionaire Walter Craig (Gus Glassmire) disappears, private eye Nick Trayne (James Dunn) is hired to find him. One night the sleuth and Craig's secretary, Betty Hilton (Joan Woodbury), find the millionaire in the library of his home, but his mental capabilities have been greatly diminished. An examination by physicians reveals that one-half of his brain has been destroyed and that he will require constant care forever. Family friend Tony Weldon

(George Eldredge) lives on the estate in a small cottage and assists in taking care of Craig. However, another family friend, George Phillips (J. Arthur Young), is found dead by Trayne, with Craig standing over the corpse. Trying to find out who caused the brain damage to Craig, Trayne and Betty learn that a mysterious man named Carson has purchased chemicals and rented the house in which Craig underwent his debilitation. Carson can only be identified by his voice so Trayne brings the entire Craig family together to make voice recordings. When one of the assembled is thwarted from killing Trayne it proves that this person is Carson. He admits that he and Craig's wife Helen (Edna Johnson) are in love but that because Craig's estate is left to daughter Tina (Jan Wiley), they have kept Craig alive in the hope that he will alter his will in favor of Helen.

"Is He Man or Zombie? Strange secrets of a scientific Killer!" emblazoned the ads for THE LIVING GHOST, which mixed the detective genre with a mild touch of science fiction. Don Miller in *B Movies* (1973) termed it ". . . a whodunit with James Dunn's clowning boosting it over the hurdles."

THE LIVING GHOST was directed by William Beaudine and two years later at Monogram, Beaudine and James Dunn were teamed again for another detective yarn, LEAVE IT TO THE IRISH, *supra*, with Dunn again portraying a gumshoe.

British release title: LEND ME YOUR EAR.

THE LODGER (Woolf & Freedman Film Service, 1926) 88 minutes.
Producer, Michael Balcon; director, Alfred Hitchcock; based on the novel by Mrs. Marie Belloc Lowndes; screenplay, Eliot Stannard, Hitchcock; art directors, C. Wilfred Arnold, Bertram Evans; assistant director, Alma Reville; camera, Baron Ventimiglia, Hal Young; editor/titles, Ivor Montagu.

Ivor Novello (Jonathan Drew the Lodger); June (Daisy Bunting); Malcolm Keen (Joe Chandler); Marie Ault (Mrs. Bunting); Arthur Chesney (Mr. Bunting).

U.S. release title: The CASE OF JONATHAN DREW.

THE LODGER (Woolf & Freedman Film Service, 1932) 85 minutes.
Producer, Julius Hagen; director, Maurice Elvey; based on the novel by Mrs. Marie Belloc Lowndes; screenplay, Ivor Novello, Miles Mander, Paul Rotha, H. Fowler Mear; art director, Jamers Carter; music director, W. L. Trytel; camera, Basil Emmot; editor, Jack Harris.

Ivor Novello (Angeloff); Elizabeth Allen (Daisy Bunting); A. W. Baskcomb (Mr. Bunting); Jack Hawkins (Joe Martin); Barbara Everest (Mrs. Bunting); Peter Gawthorne (Lord Southcliffe); P.

Kynaston Reeves (Bob Mitchell); Shayle Gardner (Snell); Drusilla Wills (Mrs. Coles); Antony Holles (Sylvano); George Merritt (Commissioner); and: Mollie Fisher, Andrea Malandrinos, Iris Ashley.

U.S. release title: THE PHANTOM FIEND.

THE LODGER (Twentieth Century-Fox, 1944) 84 minutes.

Producer, Robert Bassler; director, John Brahm; based on the novel by Marie Belloc Lowndes; screenplay, Barre Lyndon; art directors, James Basevi, John Ewing; set decorators, Thomas Little, Walter M. Scott; music, Hugo W. Friedhofer; music director, Emil Newman; choreography, Kenny Williams; assistant director, Sam Schneider; sound, E. Clayton Ward, Roger Heman; special camera effects, Fred Sersen; camera, Lucien Ballard; editor, J. Watson Webb.

Merle Oberon (Kitty); George Sanders (John Garrick); Laird Cregar (The Lodger); Sir Cedric Hardwicke (Robert Burton); Sara Allgood (Ellen); Aubrey Mather (Superintendent Sutherland); Queenie Leonard (Daisy); David Clyde (Sergeant Bates); Helena Pickard (Anne Rowley); Lumsden Hare (Dr. Sheridan); Frederick Worlock (Sir Gerald); Olaf Hytten (Harris); Colin Campbell (Harold); Anita Bolster (Wiggy); Billy Bevan (Publican); Forrester Harvey (Cobbler); Skelton Knaggs (Costermonger); Charles Hall (Comedian); Edmund Breon (Manager); Harry Allen (Conductor); Raymond Severn (Boy); Heather Wilde (Girl); Colin Kenny, Bob Stephenson, Les Sketchley, Clive Morgan (Plainclothesmen); Crauford Kent, Frank Elliott (Aides); Stuart Holmes (King Edward); Walter Tetley (Call Boy); Boyd Irwin (Policeman); Herbert Clifton (Conductor); Jimmy Aubrey (Cab Driver); Will Stanton (Newsboy); Gerald Hamer (Milkman); Montague Shaw (Stage Manager); Cyril Delevanti (Stage Hand); Connie Leon (Woman); Kenneth Hunter (Mounted Inspector); Donald Stuart (Concertina Player); John Rogers (Down and Outer); Wilson Benge (Vigilante); Alec Harford (Conductor); Yorke Sherwood, Colin Hunter (Policemen); Dave Thursby (Sergeant); John Rice (Mounted Police); Herbert Evans (Constable); Charles Knight (Vigilante); Douglas Gerrard (Porter); Ruth Clifford (Hairdresser); Harold De Becker (Charlie); Doris Lloyd (Jennie).

Although Alfred Hitchcock had directed four feature films (two of which were unfinished) prior to THE LODGER in 1926, it is this feature which began his screen reputation as a master of the thriller movie. Based on Mrs. Marie Belloc Lowndes' 1914 novel, a fictionalized account of the Jack the Ripper murders, the project was adapted to the screen by Eliot Stannard and Hitchcock. Here the Ripper is dubbed "The Avenger" and the story takes place in

London, where a number of young women (all blondes) have been murdered violently. The film opens with the now famous sequence of a woman screaming. The plot then switches to focus on mysterious Jonathan Drew (Ivor Novello), who rents a room from the Buntings (Marie Ault, Arthur Chesney). He is attracted to their pretty daughter Daisy (June) who, however, is romanced by young police detective Joe Chandler (Malcolm Keen), the policeman on the trail of The Avenger. As the romance between Drew and Daisy intensifies, jealous Chandler begins to suspect the lodger is the killer, especially since the newcomer carries a black medical bag and the murders have been committed with surgical instruments. Due to circumstantial evidence, Drew is arrested and almost killed by a mob, but the real Avenger strikes again and Drew's innocence is established. Ironically, it is Chandler who saves Drew from the crowd, only to lose Daisy to the wealthy man. The latter reveals that his obsession with the killer is due to the fact that his sister was one of The Avenger's victims.

Ivan Butler wrote in *Cinema in Britain* (1973), "The first 'real' Hitchcock, and a landmark in the British silent period. . . . It is, in fact, the treatment rather than the story which is memorable. The atmosphere is heavily Germanic, full of heavily symbolic shadows and chiaroscuro lighting effects. . . . The film encountered some resistance from renters on its first appearance, and now seems tame, but there is no denying its historical importance." John Belton commented in *Cinema Stylists* (1983), "Strangely enough, Hitchcock blends expressionism (low-key lighting, distorted mirror reflections) with realism, documenting the gathering, reporting, and dissemination to the hysterical populace of news of the Avenger's latest murder. Here, as later with his incorporation of montage and mise-en-scène into a single visual aesthetic, Hitchcock reveals an interest in synthesizing disparate styles."

THE LODGER was issued in the U.S. in 1928 by Artlee Pictures as THE CASE OF JONATHAN DREW. *Variety* was not impressed by the production. "The best thing about the picture is that despite its outrageous crudities, it somehow does manage to suggest that in its script form it probably had literary and dramatic excellence. And the worst thing about it is that the studio was not equal to developing its artistic merit on the screen."

In 1932 Ivor Novello teamed with Miles Mander (an actor who was quite impressive as the villainous Giles Conover in THE PEARL OF DEATH [1944], *q.v.*), Paul Rotha (the author of *The Film Till Now*, 1930), and H. Fowler Mear, for a modernized remake of THE LODGER. Novello again appeared in the title role. The plot was changed somewhat to adapt the story to the sound medium. The revamped narrative involves attractive telephone operator Daisy Bunting (Elizabeth Allen), who dates Scotland Yard detective Joe Martin (Jack Hawkins). However, she falls for musician Michel Angeloff (Ivor Novello), who has rented a room from her parents, George and Helen Bunting (A. W. Baskcomb, Barbara Everest). Meanwhile, a number of young women have been murdered brutally by a man known as The Avenger and foreign psychologist Sylvano (Antony Holles) believes the killer to be a madman who escaped from an asylum in his country after committing a series of similar crimes due to his hatred of women. Jealous of Daisy's infatuation with Angeloff, Martin begins to focus on the possibility that the lodger may be the killer, as he matches the description provided by Sylvano. On a tip, the police trace the latest killing to Angeloff but he escapes, although handcuffed. Later a strange man attacks Daisy in the park at night and Angeloff saves her, strangling the man with his cuffed hands. He tells her the attacker was The Avenger, his deranged brother whom he has traced to London. With The Avenger's death, Angeloff and Daisy are free to marry.

An almost forgotten thriller, especially in light of the highly regarded Hitchcock rendition, the remake of THE LODGER is an entertaining melodrama highlighted by Ivor Novello's suave performance as the mysterious Angeloff and by Elizabeth Allen as the appealing heroine. The film is filled with scenes of foggy, dark streets, screams in the night, Angeloff's seemingly threatening behavior, and the moody interiors of the Bunting house itself, where the Lodger appears to take refuge from his crimes. Only the static of the soundtrack detracts from the mystery flavor of the remake. It was released in the U.S. in 1935 by Olympic Pictures as THE PHANTOM FIEND.* That title comes from words used by the Scotland Yard police commissioner (George Merritt) to describe The Avenger in the feature.

Mrs. Lowndes' enduring thriller came to the screen for yet a third time in 1944, with direction by John Brahm for Twentieth Century-Fox. Here Jack the Ripper is named as the arch murderer although the story remains fairly close to the two earlier screen adaptations. The Burtons (Cedric Hardwicke, Sara Allgood) rent a vacant room to a young man (Laird Cregar) who becomes very attentive to their beautiful niece, Kitty (Merle Oberon), a music hall performer. Several actresses have been murdered recently and it

---

*When THE LODGER (1932) was released, *Variety* reviewed the film in London and reported of the offering, "Despite its subject of 'Jack the Ripper,' this is an eerie, absorbing story without being morbid—at least it has been so prepared and produced as to eliminate the suggestion of ghoulishness."

turns out that the lodger, a sexual psychopath, is the madman—an actress had led his young brother astray and to his demise. The lodger plans to murder Kitty but the young woman is also romanced by John Garrick (George Sanders), a Scotland Yard detective investigating the Jack the Ripper murders. Before the lodger can dispatch Kitty, Garrick and his men corner him and kill him. The *New York Times* commented, ". . . If it was intended as a sly travesty on the melodramatic technique of ponderously piling suspicion upon suspicion (and wrapping the whole in a cloak of brooding photographic effects), then THE LODGER is eminently successful." On the other hand, *PM* found the elaborately mounted feature quite atmospheric: "It's Whitechapel setting is story-book London to the Queen's taste—bowlered bobbies materializing in fog-shrouded byways, glistening cobblestones and clopping cabs, toffs and slatterns slinking in and out of pubs, and finally an Old Vic interior of backdrops, high-spiraling airways and lofty catwalks for the final closing in."

Laird Cregar is especially impressive in the title role and, despite his large frame, he developed quite a coterie of feminine followers as a result of his portrayal of the mesmerizing lodger. This led to his re-teaming with director John Brahm and co-star George Sanders for a very similar follow-up, HANGOVER SQUARE (1945), for Twentieth Century-Fox. In this gaslight-era thriller Cregar is cast as a psychopathic killer/composer who is attracted to a conductor's daughter (Faye Marlowe) and a music hall chirp (Linda Darnell) while carrying out a series of killings, which are investigated by a Scotland Yard detective/psychiatrist (George Sanders). The film is highlighted by Cregar's array of talents but by the time of release he had died from excessive dieting.

THE LONE WOLF (Selznick, 1917) eight reels.
   Producer, Lewis Selznick; director, Herbert Brenon; based on the novel by Louis Joseph Vance; screenplay, Brenon; camera, George Edwardes Hall.
   Hazel Dawn (Lucy Shannon); Bert Lytell (Michael Lanyard, the Lone Wolf); Cornish Beck (Marcel, the Waif); Stephen Grattan (Burke); Alfred Hickman (Eckstrom); Ben Graham (Thibaut, the Inventor); Robert Fisher (Bannon); William Riley Hatch (De Moriban); Joseph Challies (Popinot); William E. Shay (Wertheimer); Edward Abeles (Ducroy, the Minister of War); Florence Ashbrooke (Mme. Troyon); Juliet Brenon (Tribault's Maid).

THE LONE WOLF (Associated Exhibitors, 1924) 5,640'
   Producer, John McKeown; director, S. E. V. Taylor; based on

the novel by Louis Joseph Vance; screenplay, Taylor; camera, Jack Brown, Albert Wilson, Dal Clawson.

Dorothy Dalton (Lucy Shannon); Jack Holt (Michael Lanyard, the Lone Wolf); Wilton Lackaye (William Burroughs); [Frederick] Tyrone Power (Bannon); Charlotte Walker (Clare Henshaw); Lucy Fox (Annette Dupre); Edouard Durand (Popinot); Robert T. Haines (Solon); Gustav von Seyffertitz (Wertheimer); Alphonse Ethier (Eckstrom); William Tooker (Ambassador); Paul McAllister (Count de Morbihan).

Louis Joseph Vance introduced the character of Michael Lanyard, alias The Lone Wolf, a reformed jewel thief, in his 1914 novel, *The Lone Wolf*. In the next two decades he was to write seven additional books about the character.* The initial novel was first brought to the screen in 1917 and was remade in 1924. Here Lanyard is *not* a detective; instead, the sleuth is the leading lady, who in reality is a secret operative. Although the Lone Wolf's various screen adventures do sometimes have him solving crimes, Lanyard did not evolve into an out-and-out detective until the Columbia Pictures series with Warren William (and later Gerald Mohr) in the late 1930s and 1940s.

Trained as a thief by his mentor, the latter having been killed in a row with a female member of his gang, Michael Lanyard (Bert Lytell) continues his life of crime but as The Lone Wolf, always working alone. He carries out a large jewel heist under the nose of his old gang, The Pack, and the crooks vow revenge. Lanyard steals the plans to a weapon which will stop German submarine warfare, and an Axis spy, Eckstrom (Alfred Hickman), tries to regain them. Also after the plans is pretty Lucy Shannon (Hazel Dawn), who is in reality a Scotland Yard detective. Lanyard and Lucy fall in love and when The Lone Wolf realizes the enormity of the plans he has stolen, he fights to turn them over to the Allied powers while simultaneously holding off members of The Pack. Lanyard and Lucy secure the plans and The Lone Wolf defeats the crooks singlehandedly. With the case closed, he vows to go straight and wins Lucy as his bride.

"A rattling good melodrama is something to be thankful for. The eight-reel screen version of THE LONE WOLF . . . is such a picture," applauded *The Moving Picture World*. The same reviewer added, "There are two murders, slides for life down ropes and across

---

*In *Detectionary* (1977), edited by Otto Penzler, Chris Steinbrunner and Marvin Lachman, Michael Lanyard is described as ". . . an expert mathematician, a connoisseur of armour-plate and an adept with explosives. He could grade precious stones at a glance, developed a passion for good paintings and learned to be at ease in every grade of society." As The Lone Wolf he is ". . . a sophisticated, debonair gentleman by day and a daring, debonair burglar by night."

the roofs of houses, and a sensational auto chase that ends with one machine taking a drawbridge at dare-devil risk, and the other machine plunging from the end of the bridge into the water. There are also a realistic fire scene that burns a trifle too long, and a race and battle in the air that is the best thing of its kind to be shown on the screen. . . . THE LONE WOLF is full of excellent acting."

In 1919 Michael Lanyard (Henry B. Walthall) returned in THE FALSE FACES, again at odds with German spy Karl Eckstrom (Lon Chaney), and the same year screen vamp Louise Glaum had the title role in THE LONE WOLF'S DAUGHTER, with Bertram Grassby as Lanyard. Neither was a detective yarn.

Louis Joseph Vance's initial Lone Wolf novel was remade in 1924 by Associated Exhibitors, with Dorothy Dalton as Lucy Shannon and Jack Holt as Michael Lanyard; Alphonse Ethier appears as Eckstrom. The plot is fairly faithful to the 1917 version except that Lucy, still a Scotland Yard detective, infiltrates The Pack and she and Lanyard join forces to bring in his old gang as well as to save stolen defense plans from the clutches of spy Eckstrom. Here, however, Lanyard has taken the plans from Eckstrom originally to use them in exchange for asylum in America. *Photoplay* magazine noted, "A revival of an old favorite with plenty of intrigue and adventure and love interest. Worth seeing."

Bert Lytell would return as Michael Lanyard in a quartet of hastily-assembled Columbia releases: THE LONE WOLF RETURNS (1926), *infra*; ALIAS THE LONE WOLF (1927), *q.v.*; THE LONE WOLF'S DAUGHTER (1929), a remake of the 1919 film; and THE LAST OF THE LONE WOLF (1930), *q.v.*, thus making him the screen's first and last silent Lone Wolf and its first talking Michael Lanyard.

THE LONE WOLF RETURNS (Columbia, 1926) 61 minutes.

Supervisor, Harry Cohn; director, Ralph Ince; based on the novel by Louis Joseph Vance; screenplay, J. Grubb Alexander; camera, J. O. Taylor.

Bert Lytell (Michael Lanyard, alias The Lone Wolf); Billie Dove (Marcia Mayfair); Freeman Wood (Mallison); Gustav von Seyffertitz (Morphew); Gwen Lee (Liane De Lorme); Alphonse Ethier (Inspector Crane).

THE LONE WOLF RETURNS (Columbia, 1936) 68 minutes.

Director, Roy William Neill; based on the novel by Louis Joseph Vance; screenplay, Joseph Krumgold, Bruce Manning, Lionel Houser; music director, Howard Jackson; camera, Henry Freulichy; editor, Viola Lawrence.

Melvyn Douglas (Michael Lanyard, alias The Lone Wolf); Gail Patrick (Marcia Stewart); Tala Birell (Liane De Lorme); Henry Mollison (Mallison); Thurston Hall (Inspector Crane); Raymond Walburn (Jenkins); Douglass Dumbrille (Morphew); Nana Bryant (Aunt Julie); Robert Middlemass (McGowan); Robert Emmet O'Connor (Benson); Wyrley Birch (Mr. Cole); Eddy Chandler, John Thomas, William Howard Gould (Detectives); Arthur Rankin, Harry Depp (Men); George McKay (Maestro) Frank Reicher (Coleman); Harry Holman (Friar); Archie Robbins (Terry); Lois Lindsey (Baby); Fred Malatesta (French Official); Olaf Hytten (The Bancrofts' Butler); Monte Vandergrift, Lew Kelly (Customs Officials); Maude Truax (Fat Woman); Thomas Pogue (Old Man); Pat West (Mugg); Jack Clifford, Roger Gray, Hal Price, Jack Gray, Kernan Cripps, Lee Shumway (Cops); Gennaro Curci (Flute Player); John Piccori (Assistant to Official); Henry Roquemore, Ned Norton (Suburbanites); Arthur Loft (Oscar); Lloyd Whitlock (Drunk); Mort Greene (Crooner); Eddie Fetherston (Reporter); Harry Harvey (Photographer); Vesey O'Davoren (The Stewarts' Butler); Dorothy Bay (Marjorie); Pat Somerset (Gladiator); Arthur Stuart Hull (Jackson); George Webb (Tarzan); David Horsley (Robin Hood); Ivan Christy, Tony Merlo, Arthur Raymond Hill (Waiters), Harry Hollingsworth (Doorman); Helen Leyser (Young Girl); Earl Pingree (New York Traffic Cop).

Bert Lytell first portrayed Michael Lanyard, the Lone Wolf, in the 1917 Selznick release THE LONE WOLF, *supra*, and in 1926 returned to the part in THE LONE WOLF RETURNS (reviewed as RETURN OF THE LONE WOLF), based on Louis Joseph Vance's 1924 novel of the same title. The film proved successful for the fledgling Columbia Pictures and Lytell would portray Lanyard in three more features for the studio: ALIAS THE LONE WOLF (1927), THE LONE WOLF'S DAUGHTER (1929), and LAST OF THE LONE WOLF (1930), *q.v.*, making him the screen's first talking Michael Lanyard.

THE LONE WOLF RETURNS has Michael Lanyard (Bert Lytell) being stalked by detectives as he robs a safe and hides the necklace he finds there in a cigarette case before leaving. He crashes a masquerade ball at a nearby house, conceals himself in the bedroom of Marcia Mayfair (Billie Dove), and then joins the festivities and dances with the pretty young socialite. When the police arrive they force everyone to unmask. However, Marcia does not reveal that Lanyard is a stranger and he replaces the jewels he had pilfered from her boudoir. The two begin a romance and go to Morphew's (Gustav von Seyffertitz) resort where Lanyard deduces that the man is the head of a gang of crooks. The police raid the place, with the

Lone Wolf and Marcia barely escaping. After Marcia's jewels are again stolen, Inspector Crane (Alphonse Ethier), who had suspected Lanyard of the initial theft, feels that he has committed the new robbery. But Lanyard captures Morphew and his confederates and proves they were responsible for the filching. "Well-managed polite crook story, done in the polite and casual style and with the high-toned society background of the 'Raffles' series. . . . From the box-office angle the story has value from the large following built up by Vance for his romantic hero through enormous magazine circulation" (*Variety*).

A decade later, in the wake of the success of The Thin Man series at MGM, Columbia Pictures dusted off the Vance property and refilmed it with direction by Roy William Neill, who would later produce and direct the popular Universal Sherlock Holmes features with Basil Rathbone and Nigel Bruce in the 1940s. Here Michael Lanyard (Melvyn Douglas) arrives in the U.S. and promptly plans to steal society girl Marcia Stewart's (Gail Patrick) emerald necklace. However, seeing her picture, he takes it instead. He tells Inspector Crane (Thurston Hall) he has abandoned crime because he has found the woman of his dreams. Crooks Morphew (Douglass Dumbrille) and Mallison (Henry Mollison), frame Lanyard so that he will help them execute a robbery. But he outsmarts them and brings them to justice, allowing him to pursue Marcia.

Variety endorsed this picture as a "deft society crook comedy" and added of its debonair leading man, "Melvyn Douglas in the title role contributes one of his happiest performances. . . . Raymond Walburn in the droll character of the Lone Wolf's butler and partner in crime is a standout. Grabs nearly half of laughs. . . ." Frank S. Nugent (*New York Times*) chided Columbia Pictures for having resurrected "The international jewel thief, one of Hollywood's most overworked brain children. . . ." As to the hero/crook, he noted that urbane Melvyn Douglas ". . . strolls through the new photoplay with the self-assurance of a man whose position in the cinematic scheme of things is unquestioned and whose course—from A to Z—has been defined so carefully by tradition that deviation is not merely impossible, but unthinkable." Thurston Hall would resume the adversarial role of Inspector Crane in Columbia's Lone Wolf series with Warren William in the 1940s.

THE LONE WOLF SPY HUNT (Columbia, 1939) 71 minutes.

Associate producer, Joseph Sistrom; director, Peter Godfrey; based on the novel *Red Masquerade* by Louis Joseph Vance; screenplay, Jonathan Latimer; music director, Morris Stoloff; art director,

Lionel Banks; gowns, Kalloch; camera, Allen G. Siegler; editor, Otto Meyer.

Warren William (Michael Lanyard, alias The Lone Wolf); Ida Lupino (Val Carson); Rita Hayworth (Karen); Virginia Weidler (Patricia Lanyard); Ralph Morgan (Gregory); Tom Dugan (Sergeant Devan); Don Beddoe (Inspector Thomas); Leonard Carey (Jamison); Ben Welden (Jenks); Brandon Tynan (Senator Carson); Helen Lynd (Marie Templeton); Irving Bacon (Sergeant); Mark Windheim (Waiter); Jack Norton (Charlie Fenton, the Drunk); Dick Elliott (Little Cop); Marc Lawrence (Heavy Leader); James Craig (Guest); Adrian Booth (Girl Whom Lanyard Meets in Club); I. Stanford Jolley (Doorman); Edmund Cobb (Police Clerk); Eddie Hearn (Police Sergeant).

Angular and glib Warren William, who had previously portrayed Perry Mason and Philo Vance on the screen, took over the role of Michael Lanyard, The Lone Wolf, in THE LONE WOLF SPY HUNT in 1939, and proved perfectly cast in the role of the fast-talking debonair, ex-jewel thief, now on the side of the law. He was so popular in the part that he portrayed the glib Lanyard in another eight economy features before leaving the series in 1943. This film is loosely based on Louis Joseph Vance's 1914 novel, *Red Masquerade,* which had been produced in 1919 and 1929 as THE LONE WOLF'S DAUGHTER. The script is by Jonathan Latimer, who had written five books centered around private eye Bill Crane, three of which (THE WESTLAND CASE, WOMAN IN THE MORGUE [*q.v.*], and THE LAST WARNING) were filmed by Universal as part of its ongoing "Crime Club" series.

Foreign spies working in Washington, D.C. kidnap one-time jewel thief Michael Lanyard (Warren William), known as The Lone Wolf, and force him to steal the plans for an anti-aircraft weapon from the vaults of the War Department. Lanyard succeeds in obtaining the plans but they turn out to be only a part of what the spies require and exotic agent Karen (Rita Hayworth) tries to romance The Lone Wolf into acquiring the rest of the plans. He thwarts her scheme with the aid of girlfriend Val Carson (Ida Lupino) and her wisecracking daughter Patricia (Virginia Weidler). The Lone Wolf then sets out to gain the remaining plans on his own and at the same time round up the spy ring.

The Motion Picture Herald noted, "Picture hits the level of fundamental slapstick in many spots, but has a moderate amount of laugh content. . . . [Director Peter] Godfrey is handicapped by the script provided him." *Variety* pointed out, ". . . [The] picture leans too heavily toward the Thin Man formula, and combo of screwball comedy with dramatic episodes is intermixed too haphazardly to provide more than mild entertainment." In retrospect, this Lone Wolf entry has special merit for the intriguing appearances of two vital 1940s screen leading ladies, Ida Lupino and Rita Hayworth.

British release title: THE LONE WOLF'S DAUGHTER.

THE LONE WOLF STRIKES (Columbia, 1940) 66 minutes.

Producer, Fred Kohlmar; director, Sidney Salkow; based on the character created by Louis Joseph Vance; story, Dalton Trumbo; screenplay, Harry Segall, Albert Duffy; camera, Henry Freulich; editor, Al Clark.

Warren William (Michael Lanyard, alias The Lone Wolf); Joan Perry (Delia Jordan); Eric Blore (Jamison, the Butler); Alan Baxter (Jim Ryder); Astrid Allwyn (Binnie Weldon); Montagu Love (Emil Gorlick); Robert W. Wilcox (Ralph Bolton); Don Beddoe (Conroy); Fred A. Kelsey (Dickens); Addison Richards (Stanley Young); Roy Gordon (Phillip Jordan); Harland Tucker (Alberts); Peter Lynn (Dorgan); Murray Alper (Peter the Bartender); Edmund Cobb (Cop).

THE LONE WOLF STRIKES is the second of nine feature films made between 1939 and 1943 at Columbia in which Warren William essays The Lone Wolf, better known as Michael Lanyard. It also set a pattern for the assembly-line budget series with the welcome additions of Eric Blore as Lanyard's faithful and acid-tongued valet, Jamison, and Fred Kelsey as the perennially bumbling police officer, Dickens. "Latest entry in the Lone Wolf series being turned out by Columbia is one of the best of the group. Its content of suspense and suave detecting will provide adequate program entertainment for the secondary audiences. . . . Warren William grooves neatly as the suave and personable reformed crook" (*Variety*).

When her wealthy father (Roy Gordon) is killed following the theft of a valuable pearl necklace, heiress Delia Jordan (Joan Perry) enlists the aid of one-time crook Michael Lanyard (Warren William), The Lone Wolf, in retrieving the jewelry and capturing her father's murderer. Delia attempts to assist Lanyard in the case, as does his valet, Jamison (Eric Blore). The Lone Wolf locates a fence, Emil Gorlick (Montagu Love), who had purchased the stolen necklace from the thieves, Jim Ryder (Alan Baxter) and Binnie Weldon (Astrid Allwyn). With little help from thick-headed policemen Conroy (Don Beddoe) and Dickens (Fred Kelsey), The Lone Wolf seeks to solve the mystery, but is blamed when another murder occurs involving the coveted necklace. Finally Lanyard recoups the necklace and brings in the thieves and the killer.

B. R. Crisler (*New York Times*) acknowledged that the " . . . super-intellectual of reformed cracksmen, who wears a Homburg hat on the back of his head with all the superb, devil-may-care grace of a veritable Warren William, is rapidly becoming the cinema's most delightful detective. . . . He's pretty coy about taking a case . . . but when he takes one you may settle back in your chair in the cozy certainty that it will be solved with maximum urbanity and a charm on his part and with a minimum of brain fatigue on yours."

THE LONE WOLF TAKES A CHANCE (Columbia, 1941) 72 minutes.

Director, Sidney Salkow; based on the character created by Louis Joseph Vance; story/screenplay, Earl Felton, Salkow; camera, John Stumar; editor, Viola Lawrence.

Warren William (Michael Lanyard, alias The Lone Wolf); June Storey (Gloria Foster); Henry Wilcoxon (Frank Jordan); Eric Blore (Jamison, the Butler); Thurston Hall (Inspector Crane); Don Beddoe (Sheriff Haggerty); Evalyn Knapp (Evelyn Jordan); Fred Kelsey (Dickens); William Forrest (Vic Hilton); Walter Kingsford (Dr. Hooper Tupman); Lloyd Bridges (Johnny Baker); Ben Taggart

Lloyd Bridges, June Storey and Warren William in THE LONE WOLF TAKES A CHANCE (1941).

(Conductor); Richard Fiske (Brakeman); Regis Toomey (Wallace); Irving Bacon (Projectionist); Tom London (Cop).

This is the fourth of nine programmers in which Warren William effortlessly plays the ex-jewel thief turned detective. It is the second of a trio of the series episodes to be released in 1941: sandwiched between THE LONE WOLF KEEPS A DATE and SECRETS OF THE LONE WOLF. "The Lone Wolf Can't Leave Crime Alone! . . . It may be a cops' conspiracy, but once more he's knee-deep in homicide, robbery and exciting villainy!" insisted the poster advertising for this feature.

Michael Lanyard (Warren William), better known as The Lone Wolf, and his valet Jamison (Eric Blore) find a corpse on their apartment fire escape and the victim proves to be a private detective. Blustering police Inspector Crane (Thurston Hall) charges the duo with the crime but lacks sufficient evident to arrest them. With a telegram as a clue, Lanyard and Jamison seek the reason why this man was killed. They discover a shipment of American currency plates is about to be transported in a train's burglar-proof baggage car, and that the car's inventor, Johnny Baker (Lloyd Bridges), has been kidnapped. Lanyard locates Baker in the hands of a gang which includes Evelyn Jordan (Evalyn Knapp) among its members. The lawbreakers are after the currency plates and they place Baker on a poison-filled car on the train, but Lanyard rescues him and brings in the gang.

In order to save on this film's budget, a scene in which Michael Lanyard overtakes the special train with the burglar-proof baggage car attached to it was borrowed from the 1934 Columbia feature, SPEED WINGS, which starred Tim McCoy and Evalyn Knapp, the latter conveniently being one of the gang members in this film.

THE LONE WOLF'S DAUGHTER *see* THE LONE WOLF SPY HUNT.

THE LONG GOODBYE (United Artists, 1973) Color 112 minutes.

Executive producer, Elliott Kastner; producer, Jerry Bick; associate producer, Robert Eggenweiler; director, Robert Altman; based on the novel by Raymond Chandler; screenplay, Leigh Brackett; music, John Williams; song, Johnny Mercer and Williams; assistant director, Tommy Thompson; sound, John V. Speak; camera, Vilmos Zsigmond; editor, Lou Lombardo.

Elliott Gould (Philip Marlowe); Nina Van Pallandt (Eileen Wade); Sterling Hayden (Roger Wade); Mark Rydell (Marty Augustine); Henry Gibson (Dr. Verringer); David Arkin (Harry); Jim

Bouton (Terry Lennox); Warren Berlinger (Morgan); Jo Ann Brody (Jo Ann Eggenweiler); Jack Knight, Vince Palmieri, Arnold Strong (Hoods); Pepe Callahan (Pepe); Rutanya Alda, Tammy Shaw (Marlowe's Neighbors); Jack Riley (Piano Player); Ken Sansom (Colony Guard); Danny Goldman (Bartender) Sybil Scotford (Real Estate Lady); Steve Coit (Detective Farmer); Jerry Jones (Detective Green); Tracy Harry (Detective); Rodney Moss (Supermarket Clerk); Pancho Cordoba (Doctor); Enrique Lucero (Jefe); John Davies (Detective Davies); Herb Kerns (Herbie).

The Long Goodbye (1953) is Raymond Chandler's sixth Philip Marlowe novel and in 1955 it won the Mystery Writers of America Award for the Best Mystery Novel of 1954. That year the project was dramatized for the first time on television as the opening episode of the CBS-TV program, "Climax!" (October 7, 1954). Dick Powell, who first portrayed Philip Marlowe to perfection in MURDER, MY SWEET (1944), *q.v.*, reprised the gumshoe role and Teresa Wright co-starred. The hour telecast, done live, is best remembered for the scene when an actor playing a murdered man thought the segment was over and walked off camera in full view of millions of TV watchers!

In the early 1970s the Chandler novel was brought to the screen by director Robert Altman. It was badly hampered by the disastrous casting* of sad-faced comedian Elliott Gould as Philip Marlowe, along with the modernization of the story and the general irreverence to Chandler and his subject matter. The film cost $1,700,000 to produce, but failed to generate even $1,000,000 in domestic film rentals. Critical reception, at best, was very mixed. *Time* magazine commented, "Altman's lazy, haphazard putdown is without affection or understanding, a nose-thumb not only at the idea of Philip Marlowe but at the genre that his tough-guy-soft-heart character epitomized." On the other hand, Pauline Kael in *The New Yorker* magazine called it "a knockout of a movie." She added, "Altman tells a detective story all right, but he does it through a spree—a high-flying rap on Chandler and the movies and L.A. The film drives you a little crazy, turns you on the way some musicals . . . and some comedies . . . do."

Private eye Philip Marlowe (Elliott Gould) is asked by long-time friend Terry Lennox (Jim Bouton) to drive him to Tijuana because he has had an argument with his wife Sylvia. When Marlowe returns to L.A. alone, the police question him because Sylvia has been murdered. When he refuses to talk, he is arrested. Marlowe is released, however, because Lennox has written a confession before committing suicide in Mexico. The detective receives his own letter from Lennox along with $5,000. Eileen Wade (Nina Van Pallandt) then hires Marlowe to find her writer husband Roger (Sterling Hayden), and he locates the author at Dr. Verringer's (Henry Gibson) clinic and returns him to his wife. Gangster Marty Augustine (Mark Rydell) tells Marlowe that Lennox had money belonging to him when he went to Mexico and orders the sleuth to find this loot. Trailing Augustine, Marlowe discovers that the man knows Eileen. Roger Wade informs Marlowe that the gangster owes him $50,000. The gumshoe heads to Mexico to learn more details of Lennox's suicide and later, back in Los Angeles, he attends a party hosted by the Wades. There Dr. Verringer demands the money due him by Roger. (Marlowe learns from Eileen that her husband actually owes Augustine $10,000.) Meanwhile, Wade walks into the sea and drowns. The detective pieces together that Wade was having an affair with Sylvia, but the police already know that, and also that Wade had an alibi for the homicide. The money Lennox took with him suddenly turns up while Marlowe is being questioned by Augustine. The sleuth observes Eileen leaving the scene but while pursuing her, he is hit by an auto. Once again back in Mexico, Marlowe discovers that Lennox is still alive and that he killed Sylvia because Wade had informed her that it was her husband who was carrying on with Eileen. Sylvia planned to go to the law about the loot Lennox was carrying for Augustine and he silenced her for that reason. Lennox and Eileen intend to run away together but Marlowe shoots his former friend who has used him unmercifully as a patsy.

With its combination of a hopelessly convoluted script (by comparison that of THE BIG SLEEP, *q.v.* seems simplicity personified), Robert Altman's self-indulgent direction and the damaging casting of Elliott Gould as Philip Marlowe, THE LONG GOODBYE is certainly the nadir among the films based on the works of Raymond Chandler.*

---

*A semi-champion of THE LONG GOODBYE is film critic Roger Ebert. In his *Movie Home Companion 1989* (1988) he details, "It tries to be all genre and no story, and it almost works. . . . It just takes all the characters out of that novel and lets them stew together in something that feels like a private-eye movie." It is Ebert's contention that "The private eye is, I suppose, a fairly obsolete institution in our society. . . . The private eye as a fiction device was essentially a way to open doors; the best novels of Chandler and the others are simply hooks for a cynical morality." And as to this film's star, "Gould has enough of the paranoid in his acting style to really put over Altman's revised view of the private eye."

LORD EDGWARE DIES (Radio, 1934) 82 minutes.

Producer, Julius Hagen; director, Henry Edwards; based on the novel by Agatha Christie; screenplay, H. Fowler Mear; camera, Sydney Blythe.

Austin Trevor (Hercule Poirot); Jane Carr (Lady Edgware); Richard Cooper (Captain Hastings); John Turnbull (Inspector Japp); Michael Shepley (Captain Ronald Marsh); Leslie Perrins (Bryan Martin); C. V. France (Lord Edgware); Esme Percy (Duke of Merton).

Austin Trevor had portrayed Agatha Christie's Belgian sleuth, Hercule Poirot in two 1931 Twickenham British productions, ALIBI and BLACK COFFEE, *qq.v.*, and in the latter film Richard Cooper played Poirot's friend, Captain Hastings. Trevor and Cooper repeated these parts for the final time in 1934's LORD EDGWARE DIES, based on Ms. Christie's 1933 novel, which is also known as *13 At Dinner*. It was the last Poirot film for three decades and when the character returned in 1966's THE ALPHABET MURDER, *q.v.*, with Tony Randall as Poirot, Austin Trevor had a supporting part in that lackluster production.

Actress Lady Edgware (Jane Carr) consults detective Hercule Poirot (Austin Trevor) about obtaining a divorce from her rich but elderly husband, Lord Edgware (C. V. France), because she wants to marry the Duke of Merton (Esme Percy). Poirot and friend Captain Hastings (Richard Cooper) consult the Lord on the matter but he is soon found stabbed to death. His wife, who was overheard to say she wanted her husband dead, has an alibi, since she was a guest at a formal dinner party at the time of the murder. Police Inspector Japp (John Turnbull) is brought into the case and the other suspects include: the dead man's nephew, Captain Ronald Marsh (Michael Shepley), with whom he had argued over money, and Lady Edgware's intended next spouse, plus a mysterious woman who looked and sounded like the new widow. Poirot, using his deductive reasoning, brings forth the murderer.

David Quinlan in *British Sound Films: The Studio Years: 1928-1959* (1984), rated this film "a workmanlike if wordy whodunnit." It was not a popular entry and received only limited U.S. release by RKO in 1935. It was remade in 1985 as the TV movie, THIRTEEN AT DINNER, *q.v.*, with Peter Ustinov as the indomitable, eccentric Hercule Poirot.

LYING LIPS (Sack Attractions, 1939) 55 minutes.

Producer/director/screenplay, Oscar Micheaux; music, Jack Skilkrit; camera, Lester Lang; editor, Leonard Weiss.

Edna Mae Harris (Elsie Bellwood); Carmen Newsome (Benjamin Hadnott); Earl Jones (Detective Wanzer); Frances Williams

(Elizabeth Green); Cherokee Thornton (John); Slim Thompson (Clyde); Gladys Williams (Aunt Josephine); Juano Hernandez (Reverend Bryson); Henry "Gang" Gines (Ned Green); Don Delese (Farina); Charles LaTorre (Garotti); Robert Paquin (District Attorney); George Reynolds (Police Lieutenant); Amanda Randolph (Matron); Teddy Hall (Boy).

Singer Elsie Bellwood (Edna Mae Harris) will not participate in racially mixed parties for her boss, gangster Farina (Don Delese) and his cousin Garotti (Charles LaTorre). Musician Benjamin "Benny" Hadnott (Carmen Newsome) sides with her and quits his job at the club to join the District Attorney's office in breaking up the notorious "Cabaret Racket." When Elsie's aunt is murdered Elsie is arrested for the crime. Hadnott and Detective Wanzer (Earl Jones) try to help her but she is convicted and sentenced to life in prison based on the testimony of John (Cherokee Thornton) and Clyde (Slim Thompson), two brothers of Elizabeth Green (Frances Williams). They insist they saw Elsie leaving the club at the time the deceased was killed. The two detectives discover that Elizabeth was jealous of Elsie's aunt because her late husband had loved the woman for many years and because Mrs. Green had forced her husband to marry her, insisting she was pregnant. After the trial Elizabeth makes a claim on the murdered woman's insurance money from a policy Elsie had purchased for her. Enterprising Hadnott and Wanzer take John to a supposedly haunted house and scare a confession out of him. He relates how Mr. Green had killed the woman and then committed suicide, and that Elizabeth had then forced him and his brother to frame Elsie for the insurance proceeds. Elsie is set free and she and Hadnott marry.

This all-black cast (except for a few white players in minor roles, including the gangsters and a police lieutenant) was made by pioneer black filmmaker Oscar Micheaux, on a shoestring budget, and it shows. The acting is raw at best and the film is cluttered with lots of diverting music and dance numbers utilizing popular standards of the day. The mystery angle, however, is engaging on its own, out of the ordinary, and difficult to solve. Considering its production background, the film contains surprisingly stereotypical situations, such as the suspect being taken to a haunted house to force his confession. There is also the dialogue passage where the hero explains to the heroine, "Some Negro in this will talk. They always talk. They can't keep a secret." *No* 1930s Hollywood production, even with full-fledged cliched characters, would have dared to use such dialogue.

THE MALTESE FALCON (Warner Bros., 1931) 75 minutes.

Director, Roy Del Ruth; based on the novel by Dashiell

Hammett; screenplay, Maude Fulton, Lucien Hubbard, Brown Holmes; camera, William Rees; editor, George Marks.

Bebe Daniels (Ruth Wonderly); Ricardo Cortez (Sam Spade); Dudley Digges (Casper Gutman); Una Merkel (Effie Perine); Robert Elliott (Dundy); Thelma Todd (Iva Archer); Otto Matieson (Joe Cairo); Oscar Apfel (District Attorney); Walter Long (Miles Archer); Dwight Frye (Wilmer Cook); J. Farrell McDonald (Detective Polhaus); Augustino Borgato (Captain Jacobi).

U.S. TV title: DANGEROUS FEMALE.

THE MALTESE FALCON (Warner Bros., 1941) 100 minutes.*

Executive producer, Hal B. Wallis; associate producer, Henry Blanke; director, John Huston; based on the novel by Dashiell Hammett; screenplay, Huston; art director, Robert Haas; music, Adolph Deutsch; orchestrator, Arthur Lange; music director, Leo F. Forbstein; assistant director, Claude Archer; dialogue director, Robert Foulk; makeup, Perc Westmore; gowns, Orry-Kelly; sound, Oliver S. Garretson; camera; Arthur Edeson; editor, Thomas Richards.

Humphrey Bogart (Sam Spade); Mary Astor (Brigid O'Shaughnessy); Gladys George (Iva Archer); Peter Lorre (Joel Cairo); Barton MacLane (Detective Lieutenant Dundy); Lee Patrick (Effie Perine); Sydney Greenstreet (Casper Gutman); Ward Bond (Detective Tom Polhaus); Jerome Cowan (Miles Archer); Elisha Cook, Jr. (Wilmer Cook); James Burke (Luke); Murray Alper (Frank Richman); John Hamilton (District Attorney Bryan); Emory Parnell (Mate of the La Paloma); Robert E. Homans (Policeman); Creighton Hale (Stenographer); Charles Drake, William Hopper, Hank Mann (Reporters); Jack Mower (Announcer); Walter Huston (Captain Jacobi).

No film is more associated with the detective genre than John Huston's 1941 production of THE MALTESE FALCON, actually the third filming of Dashiell Hammett's 1930 novel. Warners initially made it in 1931 (that version now is shown as DANGEROUS FEMALE) and in 1936 the disastrous SATAN MET A LADY, q.v., was issued by the same studio—in it the character names were changed, the falcon became a ram's horn and the fat man became a hefty woman! It is the first and third productions of the novel, however, which remain true to the original work. While the Huston work far outweighs the first film in critical acclaim and audience acceptance, both are well worth seeing. Had not the 1941 film been produced, the 1931 edition would have remained the definitive screen rendering of Hammett's classic novel.

Both the 1931 and 1941 motion pictures are fairly true to the

---

*Computer colorized version now available.

novel in plot, although both deviate in various ways, mostly through omission of certain elements. Roy Del Ruth directed the initial screen version and the *New York Times* felt he ". . . has done splendidly by an excellent mystery story." Pictorially the feature nicely captures the feel of the book original—almost as well as the Huston film. In casting it is somewhat weaker than the remake although part of this may be due, in retrospect, to audience acceptance of the 1941 cast as "the players" of the parts.

Silent film idol Ricardo Cortez makes a most interesting Sam Spade in the 1931 version. His Spade is handsome, slick, perhaps a bit oily, and is able to imbue the character with the underlying cruelty Hammett suggested of Spade, something Humphrey Bogart failed to achieve in the remake. Walter Long is especially good as the womanizing partner, Miles Archer, whom Spade detests, and Long's interpretation of the role is superior to the later performance by Jerome Cowan, which verges on the effete. Just as good in the 1931 rendering is Dwight Frye as Wilmer Cook. Frye specialized on camera in degenerate types, mainly in horror films like DRACULA (1931), FRANKENSTEIN (1931) and THE BRIDE OF FRANK-ENSTEIN (1935) where he etched out solid performances as hapless and mentally twisted characters. His Wilmer in THE MALTESE FALCON is no exception, reeking of underlying and unstated perversity. Elisha Cook, Jr. would be equally memorable in the 1941 remake. Otto Matieson's Joel Cairo in the 1931 rendering lacks the effeminate twist given to the role by Peter Lorre in the remake. J. Farrell MacDonald and Robert Elliott, of the earlier version, are the equal of their successors—Barton MacLane and Ward Bond—as the cops on the case. However, it is the rest of the casting of the first movie which pales considerably in comparison to the 1941 offering. While Bebe Daniels is an adequate (if too genteel) Brigid O'Shaughnessy she does not invest the part with the sexy, breathless, edgy feeling that Mary Astor gives to the role; nor is the lighthearted characterization of Iva Archer by Thelma Todd a match for the hard-as-nails work done by Gladys Cooper in the remake, although Ms. Todd certainly, at least in pulchritude, provides a more lustful allure to the part. Another weakness of the first THE MALTESE FAL-CON is the casting of Una Merkel as Spade's secretary, Effie Perrine, a part played to perfection by Lee Patrick in the remake. Of course, the biggest casting discrepancy is Dudley Digges as the villainous Casper Gutman, The Fat Man, in the first film, in comparison to Sydney Greenstreet's interpretation (in his screen debut!) in the remake. Digges, while handling the assignment in fine fashion, simply does not get across the innate evil of character—also he is *not* fat! Greenstreet, who was nominated as Best Supporting Actor in

Above: Ricardo Cortez, J. Farrell MacDonald, Bebe Daniels and Robert Elliott in THE MALTESE FALCON (1931).

Below: Humphrey Bogart, Peter Lorre, Mary Astor and Sydney Greenstreet in THE MALTESE FALCON (1941).

the Academy Award sweepstakes for his performance, *is* the Fat
Man. He was born to play the part and his performance as Casper
Gutman is one of the finest characterizations ever put on film.
William K. Everson notes in *The Detective in Film* (1972), "Greenstreet's
rich delivery of his classic dialogue, the punctuation provided by his
distinctive and hearty laugh, and the subtle use of expression and
that enormous body itself—the traditional jolly fat man turning
suddenly into a monster, Santa Claus becoming Satan via fleeting
change of expression or stance—all these things make his Gutman
one of the most enjoyable and also one of the most memorable of all
movie villains."

As noted, both the 1931 and 1941 versions provide fairly
accurate screen translations of the Hammett work. After attractive
Brigid O'Shaughnessy comes to San Francisco to hire private eyes
Sam Spade and Miles Archer for a rather foggy assignment, Archer is
murdered and Spade, although hating the man and having an affair
with his wife Iva, vows to bring in the killer; after all, his professional
code of ethics is at stake. Although not trusting Brigid, Spade is
physically attracted to the woman and eventually falls in love with
her. He finds she is involved with several shady characters: effeminate Joel Cairo, grotesquely overweight Casper Gutman, and his
gunsel/gunman Wilmer Cook. They all are in search of an elusive art
object, which turns out to be a jewel-encrusted Falcon. The police
suspect Spade in Archer's killing and he must clear himself of that
charge as well as settle the case with Brigid. Throughout he is
supported by his faithful secretary Effie. Treachery, double-crosses
and more murders take place before Spade finally latches onto the
Falcon and makes a deal with Gutman and Cairo to frame Wilmer for
the murders. The Falcon turns out to be a fake, however, and Spade
has to turn in Brigid, who actually killed Archer.

It is claimed that when John Huston was planning his remake of
the Hammett work, he had his secretary paste up pages from the
novel from which the script for the new film was developed. In the
process, some portions of the novel were deleted and others changed.
The 1931 film also deviates from the book, especially in its finale
when Spade reveals he has a Chinese witness to Archer's murder and
there are hints that Brigid may not be behind bars for long, as Sam
takes a job in the District Attorney's office, a plot ploy which causes
Effie's alienation from Sam in the novel. One character from the
book is completely overlooked by both films and her part in the
literary proceedings is quite intriguing: she is the Fat Man's teenage
daughter, Rhea Gutman, who appears briefly toward the finale of
the book as Spade finds her while trailing her father and Cairo.
Hammett leaves her presence in the story ambiguous. Much has

been made by critics of the allegedly physical relationship between Gutman and Wilmer, but Rhea's inclusion in the plot adds a whole new dimension to their "family." Hammett indicates that the nubile girl was used by Wilmer as a punching bag at times, but also hints that both Wilmer and Gutman used the girl sexually. Certainly they used her sadistically. In the scene where Spade finds the girl in Gutman's otherwise vacant hotel rooms, she is heavily drugged. In that state she innocently reveals her body to the detective and she has literally been carved from her breasts to her pelvis. In the final confrontation in Spade's apartment, the detective caustically tells Gutman his daughter's belly is far too pretty to be so cut up. Gutman agrees but says the action was regrettably necessary, while Wilmer, who hates Spade anyway, seems angry and very jealous.

It was the 1941 version of THE MALTESE FALCON which made Humphrey Bogart a film star, although the part had first been offered to George Raft. John Huston always maintained that Raft would have been a superb Spade; he was probably correct. Interestingly, Bogart looked no more like the Spade of the novel than did Ricardo Cortez. Jon Tuska wrote in *The Detective in Hollywood* (1978), "If THE MALTESE FALCON isn't Bogart's best picture, it is certainly one of his most endurable. It can be viewed repeatedly. The outcome isn't important. Huston managed to achieve in film what Hammett had achieved in fiction: he made us more interested in the character than in the plot."

Like most detective works, THE MALTESE FALCON (in both versions) is a fairy tale look at a profession which is basically mundane. If novels were written about the true activities of detecting (divorce case clues, skip tracing, hunting runaways) few would be published or read. The same is true for films and TV episodes or series and, in days gone by, even radio. Like the Western and the gangster genres, detective fiction must embellish to enthrall and entertain. THE MALTESE FALCON does this to perfection, making it perhaps the most enduring detective film ever produced.

Dashiell Hammett also wrote a trio of short stories involving Sam Spade, published in *The Adventures of Sam Spade and Other Stories* in 1944, and on June 3, 1946, Humphrey Bogart, Mary Astor and Sydney Greenstreet repeated their roles in a 30-minute radio adaptation of "The Maltese Falcon" on CBS' "Academy Award Theatre." The same year CBS presented Howard Duff as Sam Spade and Lurene Tuttle as Effie in "The Adventures of Sam Spade," a highly popular weekly radio program. In 1951 the show was broadcast on NBC with Steve Dunne as Spade. Plans to reunite director John Huston with the stars of his 1941 film for a feature to be called THE FURTHER ADVENTURES OF THE MALTESE FALCON never materialized. However, in 1975 a quasi-sequel to the 1941 film, THE BLACK BIRD, *q.v.*, was issued, with poor results.

MAN KILLER   *see*   PRIVATE DETECTIVE 62.

THE MAN WHO WOULDN'T DIE (Twentieth Century-Fox, 1942) 73 minutes.

Producer, Sol Wurtzel; director, Herbert I. Leeds; based on the character created by Brett Halliday [Davis Dresser] and the novel *No Coffin for the Corpse* by Clayton Rawson; screenplay, Arnaud d'Usseau; music director, Emil Newman; art directors, Richard Day, Lewis Creber; camera, Joseph P. McDonald; editor, Fred Allen.

Lloyd Nolan (Michael Shayne); Marjorie Weaver (Catherine Wolff); Helene Reynolds (Anne Wolff); Richard Derr (Roger Blake); Paul Harvey (Dudley Wolff); Billy Bevan (Phillips); Olin Howland (Chief Meek); Robert Emmett Keane (Alfred Dunning); LeRoy Mason (Zorah Bey); Jeff Corey (Coroner Larsen); Francis Ford (Caretaker).

The fifth entry in producer Sol M. Wurtzel's Michael Shayne detective series for Twentieth Century-Fox, the man who wouldn't die was based on the book *No Coffin for the Corpse* (1942) by Clayton Rawson, which had featured the sleuth-magician, The Great Merlini. Here Michael Shayne takes over as the lead character and Merlini is reduced to little more than a walk-on. To provide a horror film flavor to this mystery, the events occur in a spooky old house on a stormy night. The set had been used previously by the studio for its classic detective thriller, THE HOUND OF THE BASKERVILLES (1939), *q.v.*, with Basil Rathbone as Sherlock Holmes and Nigel Bruce as Dr. Watson. *Variety* termed this newest Michael Shayne film ". . . a standard whodunit mystery programmer. . . . [It] carries the usual quota of weird and mysterious happenings always associated with this type of picture."

A prowler is seen at the remote Wolff mansion and Catherine Wolff (Marjorie Weaver), at the behest of her father Dudley Wolff (Paul Harvey), calls in private eye Michael Shayne (Lloyd Nolan) to investigate. A murder takes place and local lawman Sheriff Meek (Olin Howland) investigates, but his inept efforts do little to resolve the case. Shayne continues to look into the matter and finds himself at odds with a mystic who can simulate death. In addition, the fakir is blackmailing Mr. Wolff. Shayne reveals the killer's identity to the sheriff.

Don Miller in "Private Eyes" (*Focus on Film* magazine, Autumn 1975) complained that the film ". . . wasn't much good; no suspense, no thrills, nothing. Adding insult to injury, Merlini was retained, but in an insignificant scene with no bearing on the plot." In the only other screen adaptation of a Clayton Rawson novel about The Great Merlini, MIRACLES FOR SALE (1939), *q.v.*, the magician/detective was deleted entirely from the scenario.

THE MANDARIN MYSTERY (Republic, 1937) 65 minutes.

Producer, Nat Levine; director, Ralph Staub; based on characters created by Ellery Queen [Frederic Dannay, Manfred B. Lee]; story, Gertrude Orr, Cortland Fitzsimmons; screenplay, John Francis Larkin, Rex Taylor; music supervisor, Harry Grey; camera, Jack Marta; editor, Grace Goddard.

Eddie Quillan (Ellery Queen); Charlotte Henry (Josephine Temple); Rita La Roy (Martha Kirke); Wade Boteler (Inspector); Franklin Pangborn (Mellish); George Irving (Dr. Alexander Kirk); Kay Hughes (Irene Kirk); William Newell (Guffy); George Walcott (Donald Trent); Edwin Stanley (Bronson); Edgar Allen, Richard Beach (Reporter); Anthony Merrill (Craig); Monte Vandergrift (Detective).

One of the all time worst detective feature films is THE MANDARIN MYSTERY, based on the 1934 Ellery Queen mys-

Advertisement for THE MANDARIN MYSTERY (1937).

tery, *The Chinese Orange Mystery*. The reason for the feature's failure was noted by Don Miller in *B Movies* (1973), "Whoever suggested Eddie Quillan to portray the sleuth knew not his casting directory. Quillan, a popeyed little comedian, was fine for character roles or breezy leads, but as a brain-user he was far out of place. Not that it mattered—four scripters had mangled the story beyond repair and the film would have been a turkey no matter who was doing the deducing." Jon Tuska agreed in *The Detective in Hollywood* (1978): "You cannot really film an Ellery Queen plot, and the characters as yet were so undeveloped that a producing company ended up simply buying the title of a book. So it was felt the screenplay should be a comedy of the absurd. . . . The picture was so terrible I really would prefer to say no more about it."

Beautiful Josephine Temple (Charlotte Henry) arrives in Gotham as the custodian of the Chinese Mandarin postage stamp, worth $50,000, and it is promptly stolen. Detective Ellery Queen (Eddie Quillan) is hired to retrieve it, but two murders result and he ends up falling in love with Josephine. One of the victims (Rita La Roy) is the supposed daughter of a "collector" (George Irving) who covets the stamp. Queen brings in the killer, recovers the stamp, and wins the affection of winsome Josephine.

Although THE MANDARIN MYSTERY is a mess plotwise, its production values were more than adequate. As *Variety* reported, "Producer Nat Levine has given the film superb backgrounding. Musical direction of Harry Grey is a highlight. Flawless photography is furnished by Jack Marta." Regarding Quillan as Queen, the same trade paper noted, "Eddie Quillan partially overcomes the handicap of being made a smart-alecky detective. Only his clever handling of the role makes it believable."

THE MANDARIN SECRET *see* SHADOWS OVER CHINATOWN [essay].

MANHUNTER (DeLaurentiis Entertainment Group, 1986) Color 119 minutes.

Producer, Richard Roth; director, Michael Mann; based on the novel *Red Dragon* by Thomas Harris; screenplay, Mann; production designer, Mel Bourne; art director, Jack Blackman; costumes, Colleen Atwood; makeup, Stefano Fava; music, The Reds, Michel Rubini; songs, Rubini, Kitaro, Klaus Schulze, David Allen, Barry Andrews, Carl Marsh, Martyn Baker, Severs Ramsay, Gary Putnam, Curt Lichter, Gregory Markel, Doug Ingle, Gene Stashuk; stunt coordinator, Bud Davis; special effects, Joseph DiGaetano, II; camera, Dante Spinotti; editor, Dov Heonig.

William Petersen (Will Graham); Kim Greist (Molly Graham); Joan Allen (Reba); Brian Cox (Dr. Lektor); Dennis Farina (Jack Crawford); Stephen Lang (Freddie Lounds); Tom Noonan (Francis Dollarhyde); David Seaman (Kevin Graham); Benjamin Hendrickson (Dr. Chilton); Michael Talbott (Geeham); Dan E. Butler (Jimmy Price); Michele Shay (Beverly Katz); Robin Moseley (Sarah); Paul Perri (Dr. Sidney Bloom); Patricia Charbonneau (Mrs. Sherman); Bill Cwikowski (Ralph Dandridge); Alex Neil (Eileen); Norman Snow (Springfield); Jim Zubiena (Spurgen); Frankie Faison (Lieutenant Fisk); Garcelle Beavais (Young Woman House Buyer); Joanne Camp (Mother on Plane); David A. Brooks (Mr. Leeds); Lisa Ryall (Mrs. Leeds); Chris Elliot (Zeller); Gary Chavaras (Guard); Chris Cianciolo (Attendant); Ken Colquitt (Husband House Buyer); Ron Fitzgerald, Dennis Quick (Storage Guards); David Meeks (Dr. Warfield); Sherman Michaels (Technician); Robin Trapp, Lisa Winters (Secretaries); Daniel T. Snow (State Trooper); Cynthia Chvatal (Airport Waitress); King White (SWAT Man); Mickey Lloyd (Atlanta Detective); Dawn Carmen (Child on Plane); David Fitzsimmons (Bill); Robert A. Burton (Doctor); Steve Hogan (Helicopter Pilot); Mickey Pugh (Lear Jet Technician); Kin Shriner (Mr. Sherman); John Posey (Mr. Jacobi); Kristin Holby (Mrs. Jacobi); Greg Kelly, Brian Kelly, Ryan Langhorne (Jacobi Boys); Hannah Cacciano, Lindsey Fonora (Sherman Children); Jason Frair, Bryant Arrants, Christopher Arrants (Leeds Children); Captain Melvin Clark, Officer Renee Ayala, Officer Dana Dewey, Officer Stephen Hawkins, Officer Leonard Johnson, Officer Keith Pyles, Officer Michael Russell, Officer Michale Vitug , Officer Pat Williams, Officer Charles Yarbaugh (SWAT Team Members); Bill Smigrovich (Lloyd Bowman); Peter Maloney (Dr. Dominick Princi); Michael D. Roberts (The Runner).

"Somewhere between dream and reality lies the key to a killer's identity and hunting in that dangerous place is F.B.I. agent Will Graham," announced the advertisement for MANHUNTER, taken from Thomas Harris' novel, *Red Dragon* (1981). Despite its brutal plotline, the film is surprisingly lacking in overt and grossly exploited violence and gore, but it does appear to derive much of its pacing, communication, and music from small screen cops-and-robbers stories. The plotline moves very quickly, apparently to mask the many obvious plot holes and contrivances.

Southern detective Will Graham (William L. Petersen), a former F.B.I. agent, has recently captured a psychotic murderer. Former friend and cohort, Jack Crawford (Dennis Farina), also with the Bureau, asks Graham to resume his old job and bring in a maniac who has brutally slaughtered two families. Graham agrees and, while investigating the perplexing cases, realizes that the killer acts only during the cycle of the full moon. The detective then uses his special method of putting himself so deeply into the killer's shoes that he thinks like the madman. He comes to realize that the next victim will be a blind woman and tries to prevent her killing and bring in the murderer.

Walter Goodwin (*New York Times*) judged, ". . . Attention keeps being diverted away from the story to odd camera angles, the fancy lighting, the crashing music, and you realize you're being had. It's like catching a glimpse of the gimmicks in a magician's bag." Goodwin, however, did agree that scripter/director Michael Mann ". . . builds to his climax with considerable force." In *Playboy* magazine, Bruce Williamson judged the film, "Eerie, unnerving. . . ." *Variety* was more basic, ". . . [It] is an unpleasantly gripping thriller that rubs one's nose in a sick criminal mentality for two hours . . . builds up an unhealthy head of dread, result of which is that the viewer is kept constantly on edge."

MARLOWE (Metro-Goldwyn-Mayer, 1969) Color 100 minutes.

Producers, Gabriel Katzka, Sidney Beckerman; director, Paul Bogart; based on the novel *The Little Sister* by Raymond Chandler; screenplay, Stirling Silliphant; art directors, George W. Davis, Addison Hehr; set decorators, Henry Grace, Hugh Hunt; music director, Peter Matz; song, Matz and Norman Gimbel; assistant directors, Bud Grace, Richard Oxford, Michael Daves; makeup, William Tuttle, Phil Rhodes; stunt coordinator, Bruce Lee; recording supervisor, Franklin Milton; sound, Bruce Wright; camera William Johnson; editor, Gene Riggiero.

James Garner (Philip Marlowe); Gayle Hunnicutt (Mavis Wald); Carroll O'Connor (Lieutenant Christy French); Rita Moreno (Dolores Gonzales); Sharon Farrell (Orfamay Quest); William Daniels (Mr. Crowell); H. M. Wynant (Sonny Steelgrave); Jackie Coogan (Grant W. Hicks); Kenneth Tobey (Sergeant Fred Beifus); Bruce Lee (Winslow Wong); Christopher Cary (Chuck); George Tyne (Oliver Hady); Corinne Camacho (Julie); Paul Stevens (Dr. Vincent Lagardie); Roger Newman (Orrin Quest); Read Morgan (Gumpshaw); Warren Finnerty (Haven Clausen); Nate Esformes (Pale Face); and: Pauline Gest, Tracy Bogart.

Raymond Chandler's character Philip Marlowe was beginning to show signs of age by the time the sixth Marlowe adventure, *The Little Sister,* was published in 1949, although it is perhaps the last really interesting book about the famous sleuthing character. Two decades after publication it was brought to the screen as MAR-LOWE and updated, omitting some of the more memorable characters as well as Chandler's caustic view of the movie industry, replaced by big-time television. Two of the novel's most intriguing people, fat man Joseph P. Toad and his drug-addicted nephew Alfred, were entirely eliminated from the film's script and in their place was Chinese martial arts expert, Winslow Wong, portrayed by Bruce Lee in a part which predates his screen success in this type of role. *Variety* pegged MARLOWE (later retitled THE LITTLE SIS-TER), "Plodding . . . for less discriminating situations."

Hollywood private investigator Philip Marlowe (James Garner) is hired by beautiful Orfamay Quest (Sharon Farrell) to locate her brother Orrin (Roger Newman). At the Bay City Hotel he finds its manager, Haven Clausen (Warren Finnerty), has been murdered with an ice pick, and one of the people who might know of Orrin's whereabouts, Dr. Lagardie (Paul Stevens), denies knowing Orrin or Clausen. Marlowe receives a call from Grant Hicks (Jackie Coogan) and goes to the Alvarado Hotel, where a woman in Hicks' room knocks out the detective. When he awakens Hicks is dead and Marlowe locates a photo claim check. He calls in policemen Christy French (Carroll O'Connor) and Sergeant Beifus (Kenneth Tobey) and they investigate Hicks' killing. The claim check leads Marlowe to photos of TV star Mavis Wald (Gayle Hunnicutt) with gangster Sonny Steelgrave (H. M. Wynant). Marlowe realizes it was Mavis who was in Hicks' room, and also that Sonny's gang had used ice picks to carry out their hit jobs. Marlowe goes to question Mavis and there meets Dolores Gonzales (Rita Moreno), the actress' friend. Later, Sonny's thugs beat him senseless. Returning to his office, Marlowe is called on by Winslow Wong (Bruce Lee), who offers him $500 to forget the cases. When he refuses, the martial arts expert makes a shamble of his office. After Marlowe takes his girlfriend Julie (Corinne Camacho) to Steelgrave's nightclub, Marlowe dodges the death-dealing Wong and the latter lunges out through a high window to his death. Orfamay tells Marlowe she has learned that Orrin is with Dr. Lagardie and she fears for his life. Marlowe interrogates Crowell (William Daniels), Mavis's agent, and is soon hired to protect the TV star's interests. Marlowe informs Dr. Lagardie that he knows the physician once worked for Steelgrave. This leads to the detective being doped and later awakening to find Orrin dying. The law questions the gumshoe about Orrin's death but releases him because they feel that Orrin committed the two murders. At Steelgrave's house Marlowe finds the hoodlum murdered, and back at his apartment he interrupts Orfamay ransacking the place. Mavis arrives and it is revealed that she is really Orfamay's sister. At the strip club where Dolores performs, she admits to Marlowe that she killed Steelgrave so that Mavis could not marry him, and that she was once married to Dr. Lagardie. The medical man arrives, shoots his ex-wife and then turns the gun on himself. Marlowe decides *not* to reveal the full story in order to protect Mavis' career.

The best ingredient of MARLOWE is James Garner's breezy interpretation of the title role. Later he would have great popularity on the small screen in a similar part in "The Rockford Files" (1974-80).

A.k.a.: THE LITTLE SISTER.

THE MASKS OF DEATH (Tyburn Entertainment, 1985) Color 82 minutes.

Executive producer, Kevin Francis; producer, Norman Priggen; director, Roy Ward Baker; story, John Elder [Anthony Hinds]; screenplay, N. J. Crisp; art director, Geoffrey Tozer; music, Malcolm Williamsom; music supervisor, Philip Martell; story/research editor, Gillian Garrow; camera, Brendan J. Stafford; editor, Christopher Barnes.

Peter Cushing (Sherlock Holmes); John Mills (Dr. John H. Watson); Ray Milland (British Home Secretary); Anne Baxter (Irene Adler); Anton Diffring (Graf Udo Von Felseck); Gordon Jackson (Alec MacDonald); Susan Penhaligon (Miss Derwent); Marcus Gilbert (Anton Von Felseck); Jenny Laird (Mrs. Hudson); Russell Hunter (Alfred Toombs); James Cossins (Frederick Barnes); Eric Dodson (Lord Claremont); Georgia Coombs (Lady Claremont); James Head (Chauffeur); Dominic Murphy (Boot Boy).

Sherlock Holmes (Peter Cushing) comes out of retirement at the behest of Scotland Yard's Alex MacDonald (Gordon Jackson). Three victims have been found in the East End of London, all of whom appear to have been frightened to death. With the aid of Dr. Watson (John Mills), Holmes begins investigating the murders and is visited by the British Home Secretary (Ray Milland) and German diplomat Graf Udo Von Felseck (Anton Diffring). They ask Holmes to find a German envoy who has disappeared from Von Felseck's Buckinghamshire home. Unless this man, on a secret mission, is found, war is bound to break out between the two nations. Holmes drops the first case and goes to Von Felseck's home and establishes that the envoy was abducted before his arrival there. To his surprise Holmes also finds his lover and one-time adversary, Irene Adler (Anne Baxter), there, and he suspects she is implicated in the disappearance. That night Holmes and Watson narrowly escape being killed and this convinces the detective that he was lured to Buckinghamshire to keep him from investigating more important affairs. Holmes comes to realize that the supposed envoy was really

Von Felseck's son Anton (Marcus Gilbert) and he leaves a false trail for the German diplomat. He is nearly done in by the man's chauffeur (James Head) but is saved by the intervention of Irene Adler. Now feeling that the East End deaths and the German case are very much intertwined, Holmes returns to his earlier investigation, and beneath a low-class public house he and Watson locate an underground laboratory. There Holmes deduces that the Germans are manufacturing deadly gas to kill Londoners when war breaks out between England and Germany. The Germans resist but Holmes has called MacDonald and his men, and the spies are corralled and their plot foiled. Holmes realizes the original three victims were killed by the poison gas and their frightened looks came from seeing the Germans in gas masks just before they died. For saving his nation, Holmes is called to Windsor Castle by the King.

This British film is an engrossing Sherlock Holmes feature in several ways. Peter Cushing is considered by many purists to be the best screen Holmes, having played the part in THE HOUND OF THE BASKERVILLES (1959), *q.v.*, and in fifteen BBC-TV programs in 1968. His return to the part was a welcome one and his deft work as Holmes did not disappoint his fans or those of the immortal sleuth. John Mills, too, was quite effective as Dr. Watson and the film presented Anne Baxter and Ray Milland in two of the final roles of their distinguished careers. The plot has Cushing as an older Holmes and also delved somewhat into his shadowy relationship with Irene Adler. In plot and performances, the offering is one of the more ingratiating Sherlock Holmes films in recent years.

A MASTERPIECE OF MURDER (NBC-TV, 1/27/86) Color 100 minutes.

Executive producer, Andrew J. Fenady; producer, Terry Morse; associate producer, Duke Fenady; director, Charles S. Dubin; story, Fenady; teleplay, Fenady, Terry Nation; art director, Steven Geaghan; music, Richard Markowitz; camera, Laszlo George; editor, Art Seid.

Bob Hope (Dan Dolan); Don Ameche (Frank Aherne); Jayne Meadows (Matilda Hussey); Claudia Christian (Julia Forsythe); Yvonne De Carlo (Mrs. Murphy); Anne Francis (Ruth Beekman); Frank Gorshin (Pierre Rudin); Steven Keats (Lieutenant Simon Wax); Kevin McCarthy (Jonathan Hire); Anita Morris (Lola Crane); Clive Revill (Vincent Faunce); Stella Stevens (Della Vance/Deb Potts); Jamie Farr (Himself); Penny Baker (Christine Manning); Peter Palmer (Bronson); Eddie Ryder (Jerry Page); Louise Sorel (Louise); Joseph Della-Sorte (Ugarti Van Meer); Jason Wingreen (Williams); Richard Sargent (Maurice Beekman).

One of the alleged great "events" of network TV early in 1986 was the TV movie debut of Bob Hope and his teaming with Oscar winner Don Ameche for a masterpiece of murder. "Hope and Ameche together in their first TV movie! Who'll find the missing masterpiece? Who'll catch the killer? Who'll get the girl? May the best man win . . . by a nose!" read the advertising for this highly touted telefilm which backed the two show business greats with a relatively strong supporting cast. The results, however, were sadly tepid, as noted by *TV Movies and Video Guide* (1988): "A tired walk-through by Hope who used to toss off this kind of vehicle with relish in years gone by. Below average."

Veteran private eye Don Dolan (Bob Hope) is at the end of his financial trail (he has a penchant for making bad bets at the race track), and he cannot even pay the rent owed to his lustful landlady, Mrs. Murphy (Yvonne De Carlo). On the other hand, his one-time nemesis, former cat burglar Frank Aherne (Don Ameche), is now a highly successful business tycoon. When a murder occurs, these two former foes unite to track down the culprit and expose an underground art-collection scam in the midst of car chases and blackmail.

Daily Variety opined that the film is a ". . . rather listless venture, a whodunit lacking any real excitement or suspense. . . . One has the feeling all this has been seen before, and it has, many times, but with more polish and vigor. The dialog is old-hat, like the vehicle. Hope and Ameche go through their paces, but are let down by the confusing, uninspired script."

Originally written to be shot in Palm Springs, the misfire was lensed on location in Vancouver, British Columbia.

MEET MISS MARPLE *see* MURDER SHE SAID [essay].

MEET NERO WOLFE (Columbia, 1936) 70 minutes.

Producer, B. P. Schulberg; director, Herbert Biberman; based on the novel *Fer de Lance* by Rex Stout; adaptor, Howard J. Green, Bruce Manning, Joseph Anthony; camera, Henry Freulich; editor, Otto Meyer.

Edward Arnold (Nero Wolfe); Lionel Stander (Archie Goodwin); Joan Perry (Ellen Barstow); Victor Jory (Claude Roberts); Nana Bryant (Sarah Barstow); Dennie Moore (Mazie Gray); Russell Hardie (Manuel Kimball); Walter Kingsford (E. J. Kimball); Boyd Irwin, Sr. (Professor Barstow); John Qualen (Olaf); Gene Morgan (O'Grady); Rita Cansino [Hayworth] (Maria); Frank Conroy (Dr. Bradford); Juan Toreno (Carlo Maringola); Martha Tibbetts (Anna); Eddy Waller (Golf Starter); George Offerman, Jr. (Mike); William Benedict (Johnny); Raymond Borzage (Tommy); William Anderson (Bill); Al Matthews (Attendant); David Worth (Kimball's Chauffeur); Roy

Bloss (Messenger Boy); and: Arthur Stewart Hull, Jay Owen, Henry Roquemore, Arthur Rankin.

Columbia Pictures obtained the screen rights to three of Rex Stout's Nero Wolfe novels and one story in the mid-1930s in the hopes of building a series around the character to rival Fox's popular Charlie Chan features. Stout's initial novel, *Fer de Lance* (1934), was made as MEET NERO WOLFE and the studio cast Edward Arnold as the reclusive, orchid-growing, gourmet food fancier detective, and Lionel Stander as his right hand man, Archie Goodwin. The production met with a good reception but rotund Arnold bowed out of the series and was replaced by Walter Connolly in the second and final outing, THE LEAGUE OF FRIGHTENED MEN (1937), *q.v.*

Professor Barstow (Boyd Irwin, Sr.) is murdered while playing on a golf course and a gunsmith wanted by the law is also killed. The professor's wife, Sarah Barstow (Nana Bryant), and daughter Ellen (Joan Perry) offer $50,000 to find the murderer. Detective Nero Wolfe (Edward Arnold) takes up the case with the aid of his associate, Archie Goodwin (Lionel Stander), who is about to wed Mazie Gray (Dennie Moore). Wolfe uncovers the fact that the professor was silenced by the means of a pin shot from the handle of a golf club, and associates the two killings with similar ones in Argentina. He then has Goodwin round up all the suspects and bring them to his New York City penthouse home. The killer, meanwhile, sends Wolfe a bomb, but he uses it to his own advantage and points out the murderer.

The *Motion Picture Herald* reported, "Melodrama and comedy are adroitly balanced . . . production is wholly adequate to story requirements as to settings, cast and technical aspects." *Variety* printed, "The comedy and the guessing elements have been deftly mixed, the well-knit narrative precludes any dropping interest and the cast disports itself in crack whodunit fashion." Jon Tuska wrote in *The Detective in Hollywood* (1978), "The film was one of the finest detective films produced in the Thirties. Unfortunately, it has not been seen since its original theatrical release. Arnold's characterization is superb; he may not keep Wolfe's hours in the plant rooms, but he's there much of the time and, atypically, that's where he solves the case with all the suspects gathered together."

MEETING AT MIDNIGHT *see* BLACK MAGIC.

MICHAEL SHAYNE, PRIVATE DETECTIVE (Twentieth Century-Fox, 1940) 77 minutes.

Producer, Sol M. Wurtzel; director, Eugene Forde; based on the novel *Dividend of Death* by Brett Halliday [Davis Dresser];

screenplay, Stanley Rauh, Manning O'Connor; music director, Emil Newman; camera, George Schneiderman; editor, Al De Gaetano.

Lloyd Nolan (Michael Shayne); Marjorie Weaver (Phyllis Brighton); Joan Valerie (Marsha Gordon); Walter Abel (Elliott Thomas); Elizabeth Patterson (Aunt Olivia); Donald MacBride (Chief Painter); Douglass Dumbrille (Gordon); Clarence Kolb (Brighton); George Meeker (Harry Grange); Charles Coleman (Ponsby); [Adrian] Michael Morris (Al); Robert Emmett Keane (Larry Kincaid); Frank Orth (Steve); Irving Bacon (Fisherman).

One of the most prolific writers of detective fiction was Brett Halliday [Davis Dresser] (1904-1977), who turned out more than six dozen novels centered around the character of tough private eye Michael Shayne.* The first Shayne novel, *Dividend of Death* (1938), was adapted to the screen in 1940 as MICHAEL SHAYNE, PRIVATE DETECTIVE and although a series followed with flippant Lloyd Nolan as Shayne, none of Halliday's works were ever again adapted to the screen. In the Nolan series the works of other detective writers (Raymond Chandler, Clayton Rawson, Frederick Nebel) were used as the basis of the programmers. Other Shayne screen adventures were built upon original stories. Shayne had better success on radio with the CBS series, "Michael Shayne, Private Detective," with Jeff Chandler in the title role; it debuted in 1949. In 1960 Richard Denning played Shayne for the one-season run of "Michael Shayne, Private Detective," on NBC-TV. Next to the many books, Shayne's most enduring popularity has come from the monthly *Mike Shayne Mystery Magazine,* which Davis Dresser began editing in 1956 and which is still being published.

Rich businessman Brighton (Clarence Kolb) hires private detective Michael Shayne (Lloyd Nolan) to keep his spoiled daughter, Phyllis (Marjorie Weaver), out of trouble. Shayne is aided by detective story fancier Aunt Olivia (Elizabeth Patterson). The case, however, soon brings Shayne and Phyllis into proximity with race-track corruption, gambling, and two murders, leaving them at odds with none too bright policemen Chief Painter (Donald MacBride) and Al ([Adrian] Michael Morris) before the sleuth solves the case and romances his client's daughter.

Variety noted that the film "looks good enough to be the start of a new series," and added, "Lloyd Nolan is ideally suited to play the tough-skinned Irish detective." Don Miller in *B Movies* (1973)

---

*In *Detectionary* (1977), edited by Otto Penzler, Chris Steinbrunner, and Marvin Lachman, Mike Shayne is detailed as "... tough, two-fisted, cognac-swigging redhead from Miami. He is tall, handsome, and almost as fond of beautiful girls as they are of him."

Marjorie Weaver, Clarence Kolb, Charles Coleman and Lloyd Nolan in MICHAEL SHAYNE, PRIVATE DETECTIVE (1940).

assessed, "Equipped with a more elaborate looking production than many 'B' films, with a fine cast . . . and a script with superior dialogue, the opener was well received by the trade press and local film critics, seemingly overpraised in retrospect."

In the next two years, Lloyd Nolan would play Shayne in six more economy installments for producer Sol M. Wurtzel: SLEEPERS WEST (1941), DRESSED TO KILL (1941), *q.v.*, BLUE, WHITE AND PERFECT (1941), *q.v.*, THE MAN WHO WOULDN'T DIE (1942), *q.v.*, JUST OFF BROADWAY (1942) and TIME TO KILL (1942), *q.v.*

MICKEY SPILLANE'S MARGIN FOR MURDER (CBS-TV, 10/15/81) Color 100 minutes.

Executive producers, Robert Hamner, Jay Bernstein, Larry Thompson; producer, Alex Lucas; supervising producer, Biff Johnson; director, Daniel Haller; based on characters created by Mickey Spillane; story, Lucas; teleplay, Calvin Clements, Jr.; art director, Kenneth S. Davis; music, Nelson Riddle; camera, Michael Margulies; editor, John M. Woodcock.

Kevin Dobson (Mike Hammer); Charles Hallahan (Pat Chambers); Cindy Pickett (Velda); Donna Dixon (Daisy); Asher Brauner (Jerry Adams); Floyd Levine (Geraldo Machetti); Aarika Wells (Lindsey Brooks); John Considine (Lou Krone); Renata Vanni (Mama DeFellita); Charles Picerni (Glover); Nicholas Hormann (John O'Hare); and: John Alderman, Tybee Brascia, Katia Christine, Christina Cummings, David Downing, Dock P. Ellis, Jr., Carol Hamner, Marilyn Faith Hickey, Zacky Murphy, Mary Reynolds, Elizabeth Robinson, Ivan Saric, A. Gerald Singer, Ralph Strait, Chuck Tamburro, Christine Wagner, Elizabeth Wickenshaw, Glenn Wilder.

MICKEY SPILLANE'S MIKE HAMMER: MORE THAN MURDER (CBS-TV, 1/26/84) Color 100 minutes.

Supervising producers, Daniel H. Blatt, Robert Singer; producer, Lew Gallo; associate producer, Jon C. Andersen; director, Gary Nelson; based on characters created by Mickey Spillane; story, William Stratton; teleplay, Stratton, Stephen Downing; art directors, Ross Bellah, William L. Campbell; music, Earle Hagen; camera, James Crabe; editor, Michael F. Anderson.

Stacy Keach (Mike Hammer); Lindsay Bloom (Velda); Don Stroud (Captain Pat Chambers); Kent Williams (Assistant District Attorney Lawrence Barrington); Tim McIntire (Malcolm Dobbs); Lynn-Holly Johnson (Sandy); Sam Groom (Phillips); Richard Romanus (Bordante); Denny Miller (Tallahassee); Robyn Douglass (Eve Warwick); Danny Goldman (Ozzie); Gail Rae Carlson (Linda); Kevin King (Davey); Ingrid Anderson (Angela); John Hancock (Judge); Stephanie Blackmore (Roz); David Haskell (Titus); Martin West (Ellison); Lee Meredith (Marty); Nora Gaye (Nicky); Jineane Ford (Honey); Mindi Iden (Bonnie); Darcy Lee (Jolene); Michelle Michaels (Maisy); Jinaki (Millie); Carol Pritikin (Bidder); Leroy Applebaum III (Norman Matlock); Jay Bernstein (Sprague).

MICKEY SPILLANE'S MIKE HAMMER: MURDER ME, MURDER YOU (CBS-TV, 4/9/83) Color 100 minutes.

Executive producers, Jay Bernstein, Larry Thompson; producer, Lew Gallo; associate producer, Lana Wood; director, Gary Nelson; based on characters created by Mickey Spillane; teleplay, William Stratton; art directors, Fredric P. Hope, Ross Bellah; music, Earle Hagen; camera, Gayne Rescher; editor, Donald R. Rode.

Stacy Keach (Mike Hammer); Tanya Roberts (Velda); Don Stroud (Captain Pat Chambers); Delta Burke (Paula Corey); Tom Atkins (Jack Vance); Jonathan Banks (Janos Saracen); Kent Williams (Lawrence Barrington); Lisa Blount (Michelle Jameson); Michelle

Phillips (Chris Jameson); Bert Rosario (Durardo); Randi Brooks (Arla); Lee Meredith (Marty); Ric Mancini (Cal Pope); Eddie Egan (Hennessey); Madison Arnold (Conlin); Ava Lazar (Janice Wells); James Arone (Bumpo); Michelle Avonne (Betty Beraldo); Julid Hayek (French Courier); Quinn Kessler (Karen Marshall); William Vincent Kulak (Paramedic); Carol Pritiken (Receptionist); Timothy Stack (Natty); Michael A. Andrews (Sadora Shepperton).

In 1981 Mickey Spillane's I, THE JURY, *q.v.*, was remade with Armand Assante as Mike Hammer; the same year, the character came to television* with Kevin Dobson as Hammer in CBS-TV's MICKEY SPILLANE'S MARGIN FOR MURDER. This telefeature, which served as a pilot for a series which did not sell, was the first Hammer production not to be based on a Spillane novel. Instead, it was taken from a story by Alex Lucas which used Spillane's cast of characters. When his best friend is killed while driving his car, private eye Mickey Spillane (Kevin Dobson) sets out to bring in the murderer with the aid of his secretary/lover Velda (Cindy Pickett) and police pal Pat Chambers (Charles Hallahan). "He's every crook's nightmare—every woman's fantasy. He's Mike Hammer—and they don't make private detectives like him anymore!" bragged the advertising for this adult telefeature. In *TV Guide* magazine, Judith Crist endorsed that Kevin Dobson ". . . emerges as a jim-dandy, toughest-of-'em-all private eye . . . with the Calvin Clements Jr. teleplay and Daniel Haller's direction doing full justice to the genre and Cindy Pickett as charming Velda to Dobson's Mike Hammer."

A second Mike Hammer pilot was telecast in the spring of 1983 by CBS-TV, with Stacy Keach in the title role. MICKEY SPILLANE'S MIKE HAMMER; MURDER ME, MURDER YOU was so good that it was awarded the Mystery Writers of America's Edgar Award and Gayne Rescher's cinematography was given an Emmy Award nomination. In *TV Guide* magazine, Judith Crist reported that Keach ". . . is probably the classiest incarnation to date of Mike Hammer, that toughest of tough private eyes. . . . The character's also older and softer in this teleplay. . . ." *TV Movies and Video Guide* (1988) opined, "Keach is aces as private eye Mike Hammer. . . . Above Average." The promotional copy for this production insisted, "Mike Hammer is Back! Stalked by Danger, Deadly Killers, and Gorgeous Women. Stacy Keach is Mike Hammer." Mike Hammer is hired by former lover Chris James (Michelle Phillips), who needs protection since she is to testify before a grand jury about a $2,000,000 payoff and an all-girl courier service in which she is a

---

*Darren McGavin had the title role in the 1958-59 NBC-TV series, "Mike Hammer, Detective."

partner. Through Chris, Hammer learns that they have a nineteen-year-old daughter. Chris, however, dies while testifying and Hammer is determined to solve her death and find his daughter (Lisa Blount). This leads him into the world of pornography, business corruption and murder. He is aided by ever loyal and loving secretary Velda (Tanya Roberts) and always helpful police captain Pat Chambers (Don Stroud).

"Mickey Spillane's Mike Hammer" became a TV series early in 1984 on CBS-TV, with Stacy Keach continuing as Hammer, Lindsay Bloom as Velda, and Don Stroud as Captain Pat Chambers. Before the one-hour series got underway, however, it was introduced by a two-hour TV movie, MICKEY SPILLANE'S MIKE HAMMER: MORE THAN MURDER, telecast on January 26, 1984. "Don't Mess With Hammer! He can't be bought. He won't be pushed. He always gets his way!" the ads informed. The plotline has Hammer's (Stacy Keach) friend Captain Chambers, (Don Stroud), being shot during a big poker game and then framed as a drug trafficker. Hammer comes to his defense as well as romancing undercover agent Eve Warwick (Robyn Douglass), who is killed before Hammer rounds up the real crooks and clears his buddy. *Daily Variety* decided this third Hammer telefilm was "considerably below" the first Keach-Hammer feature, ". . . primarily because the scripting kept pretty close to standard private eye plot devices of the past. This gave it an old-hat quality, despite production efforts to outfit the film with a contemporary look. Keach, however, continued to give a strong performance as Hammer, despite the more leisurely pace of MORE THAN MURDER."

The TV series proved quite popular but production was halted in 1985 after star Stacy Keach was arrested in England for drug possession and was sentenced to a short prison stay. Amidst much publicity, in 1986 Keach returned to the role in the CBS-TV series, "The New Mike Hammer," but it only had a brief run.

The second Mike Hammer television series with Stacy Keach was ushered in by still another telefeature, THE RETURN OF MICKEY SPILLANE'S MIKE HAMMER, for which the ads exclaimed, "The plot to kidnap a movie star's daughter holds a deeper and more terrifying secret!" Telecast April 18, 1986 on CBS-TV, the telefilm has Mike Hammer (Stacy Keach) involved in a Central Park kidnapping and the attempted grabbing of movie star Joanna Lake's (Lauren Hutton) small daughter while on a film location not far from the detective's Gotham office. After thwarting the second kidnapping, Hammer accepts the job of being the little girl's bodyguard and he goes with her to Hollywood. There the child is abducted and Hammer must find her. The suspects include Nick

(Stephen Macht), the little girl's father. Hammer is aided by an "expert" (John Karlin) on missing children and soon finds that the case also involves hit men, gangsters, and a half-million-dollar ransom. In *TV Guide* magazine, Judith Crist allowed that the telefeature is a "complex adventure," and added, "It's stylish, sharp-tongued and sophisticated, with a sensational helicopter sequence." As in the TV show, program regulars Lindsay Bloom (Velda, the secretary), Don Stroud (Hammer's police pal, Captain Pat Chambers) and Kent Williams (nemesis Assistant District Attorney Barrington) repeated their assignments.

MIDNIGHT LIMITED (Monogram, 1940) 61 minutes.

Producer, T. R. Williams; director, Howard Bretherton; screenplay, Harrison Carter, C. B. Williams; lyrics, Carter; camera, Harry Neumann; editor, Karl Zint.

John King (Val Lennon); Marjorie Reynolds (Joan Marshall); George Cleveland (Professor [Ben Miller]); Edward Keane (Harrigan); Pat Flaherty (Conductor); Monte Collins (Abel Kranz); Herb Ashley (Trainman); I. Stanford Jolley (Frenchie); Buck Woods (Willy).

On a train from New York City to Toronto a courier is robbed of $75,000 in diamonds and the young woman, Joan Marshall (Marjorie Reynolds), in the next compartment sees the thief and is also robbed of valuable papers regarding an inheritance her family is to receive. Later, railroad detective Val Lennon (John King) tells Joan that secrecy is necessary in the case. She asks to help in the investigation since she saw the robber, and Lennon's superior, Harrigan (Edward Keane), agrees. The next day a gambler is robbed on the same train and an old man, Ben Miller, known as the Professor (George Cleveland), is aboard as he had been during the first heist. A railroad detective is killed during the theft and Lennon and Harrigan vow revenge. They find that the Professor had been hired to escort coffins to Toronto and he now agrees to be used as a decoy on his next assignment. For the next trip Lennon masquerades as a Frenchman with $10,000 and he makes train reservations at the same place as did the other two men who were robbed, at the New York Ritz Hotel. That evening Lennon is robbed during the train ride, and Harrigan and Joan are in the next compartment. After the robbery Lennon leads them to the train's baggage compartment where he confronts baggage car attendant Abel Kranz (Monte Collins); a shootout ensues in which Krantz is killed. An inspection of the coffin aboard finds the robber (I. Stanford Jolley) inside; he has been killed by a stray bullet. The case now solved, Lennon and Joan marry and honeymoon on the same train.

MIDNIGHT LIMITED is a compact minor actioner with the

crooks and their mode of robbery hard to spot. *Variety* labeled the film "the usual bit of romantic taffy" and noted a couple of production and plot errors: "Probably few spectators even in New York will notice the incongruity of a steam locomotive pulling the train out of Grand Central (when actually only electric engines are used in the station), but a more obvious mistake is the pointless song number which John King, as the moony detective, warbles at the heroine."

THE MIDNIGHT PHANTOM (Reliable, 1935) 63 minutes.

Associate producer, Harry S. Webb; director, Bernard B. Ray; screenplay, Jack Neville; art director, Ira Webb; assistant director, S. Gordon; sound, J. S. Westmoreland; camera, Pliny Goodfriend; editor, Arthur Hilton.

Reginald Denny (Professor David Graham); Claudia Dell (Diane Sullivan); Lloyd Hughes (Lieutenant Dan Burke); James Farley (Chief James A. Sullivan); Barbara Bedford (Kathleen Ryan); Mary Foy (Mary Ryan); John Elliott (Captain Bill Withers); Francis Sayles (Lieutenant Kelly); Al St. John (Radio Officer Jones); Henry Roquemore (Dr. McNeil); Lee Prather (Captain Perkins); Robert Walker (Captain Phillips); Jack Kenny (Lieutenant Silverstein).

In trying to keep politics and corruption out of his police department, Chief James A. Sullivan (James Farley) has acquired many enemies both on and off the force. In addition, his romance with his secretary, Kathleen Ryan (Barbara Bedford), has raised the ire of her policewoman mother (Mary Foy), who demands that they marry. Sullivan has given consent for his own daughter Diane (Claudia Dell) to marry Lieutenant Dan Burke (Lloyd Hughes), although he prefers her other suitor, criminologist/detective Professor David Graham (Reginald Denny). After Burke tries to hide the fact that his younger brother was killed following participation in a bank robbery, Sullivan demands that he break off his engagement to Diane and the two quarrel. Diane consults Graham on the matter and he tells her to follow her heart; she and Burke decide to remain engaged. At midnight that night Graham gives a lecture to the police department on various criminal types and at the end of the talk Sullivan is found in his chair, dead. Graham says he was murdered and that the killer had been in the room. Graham deduces that the chief was murdered by the use of an Amazon jungle poison and he questions the various suspects. After Lieutenant Kelly (Francis Sayles) is killed in the same manner, Graham accuses Burke of the crime because he had possession of a cigar which was used as a blow gun to carry the poisoned needles. Burke fakes his own death to prove the real killer's identity. Diane and Burke can now wed.

This obscure poverty row dual biller is a slow-moving, talk-filled affair which takes too much of its running time in building up suspects and motives for the killing of Chief Sullivan. It concludes with a too talky epilogue in which the hero and heroine discuss the murderer's psychological motivations and his execution. The prime interest engendered by this feature is that it is one of the few detective movies in which a sleuth is also the culprit, putting it in a league with MURDER AT MIDNIGHT (1931) and SO DARK THE NIGHT (1946), *qq.v.*

MIDNIGHT SHADOW (Sack Amusement Enterprises, 1939) 50 minutes.

Producer/director, George Randol; screenplay, no credit given; music, Johnny Lange and Lew Porter; camera, Arthur Reed; editor, Robert Johns.

Frances Redd (Margaret Wilson); Buck Woods (Lightfoot); Richard Bates (Junior Lingley); Ollie Ann Robinson (Emma Wilson); Clinton Redmont (Dan Wilson); Jesse Lee Brooks (Detective Sergeant Ramsey); Edward Brandon (Buster); John Criner (Prince Alihabad); Pete Webster (Mr. Mason); Ruby Dandridge (Mrs. Lingley); Napoleon Simpson (Ernest Lingley).

This all-black-cast feature was made specifically for the segregated black theaters which prospered in urban areas in the 1930s and 1940s. Production-wise, the film is acceptable, but except for a few instances (i.e., Ruby Dandridge), the action is subpar, the comedy forced, and the true criminal's identity too hazy. The film, however, abounds with detectives: Jesse Lee Brooks plays the forceful police detective investigating the case, while Richard Bates and Buck Woods are "amateur" private eyes, out to settle the matter. Bates, in particular, wears a deerstalker cap and smokes a curved pipe while always hunting for fingerprints.

In the South a fake swami, Prince Alihabad (John Criner), is courting oil heiress Margaret Wilson (Frances Redd), who is also loved by Buster (Edward Brandon). That night Margaret refuses to run away with the swami, her father (Clinton Redmont) is murdered and the deed to his oil lands is stolen. The swami is immediately the chief suspect. Amateur crime solvers Junior Lingley (Richard Bates) and Lightfoot (Buck Woods) are called into the caper by the family, over the objections of the investigating police officer, Detective Sergeant Ramsey (Jesse Lee Brooks). Junior and Lightfoot theorize the swami will try to sell the oil deed and they head to Oklahoma to the headquarters of the La-Tex-Okla Oil Company, operated by Mr. Mason (Pete Webster), who agrees to help trap the killer. When a culprit (unbilled) tries to rob Mason, the police intervene and Junior and Lightfoot return him home for trial, the man having been an intruder in the Wilson home and not the swami. Margaret, in the end, rejects the swami for the love of Buster.

THE MIDNIGHT WARNING (Mayfair, 1933) 63 minutes.

Supervisor, Ciff Broughton, director, Spencer Gordon Bennet; story, Norman Battle; adaptor, J. T. Neville; assistant director, Ralph Black; music director, Lee Zahler; sound, Homer Ackerman; camera, Jules Cronjager; editor, Byron Robinson.

William "Stage" Boyd (William Cornish); Claudia Dell (Enid Van Buren); Huntley Gordon (Mr. Gordon); Hooper Atchley (Dr. Stephen Walcott); John Harmon (Erich); Lloyd Whitlock (Rankin); Phillips Smalley (Dr. Brown); Lloyd Ingraham (Adolph Klein); Henry Hall (Dr. Barris); and: Art Winkler, Lon Poff.

Noted detective William Cornish (William "Stage" Boyd) visits his old friend, neurologist Dr. Stephen Walcott (Hooper Atchley), at a stylish Gotham hotel and during their reunion Walcott suddenly faints. Cornish summons the house doctor, Brown (Phillips Smalley), who arrives with manager Gordon (Huntley Gordon) and clerk Rankin (Lloyd Whitlock). Brown says Walcott fainted from the heat and cut his forehead in the fall, but Cornish deduces that he was shot through the room's open window. He later learns the shot was fired from across the street by Erich (John Harmon), the boyfriend of Enid Van Buren (Claudia Dell). Enid's brother had disappeared in the hotel when the two had stopped there after returning from Southeast Asia, where they had lived since childhood. To add to the mystery, Walcott had found a human ear bone among the ashes in his hotel room fireplace. Cornish agrees to aid Enid and Erich in locating the missing sibling. Later Gordon, Brown and Rankin kidnap Enid and take her to Adolph Klein's (Lloyd Ingraham) mortuary, where they try to drive her insane. Cornish, Walcott and Erich, however, arrive with the law to save the girl. The kidnappers admit that the brother died in their hotel of bubonic plague. They burned his body and covered up his demise to prevent a public panic and to save the hotel's reputation. Cornish advises Enid and Erich to drop the matter and to go to his country place for a rest.

THE MIDNIGHT WARNING belies its poverty row origins in several respects, especially in William "Stage" Boyd's strong performance as the detective and Spencer Gordon Bennet's solid direction of John Thomas Neville's script, which was based on an actual incident. Although stage-bound, with just a few indoor locations, the movie moves well and the denouement is surprising: the villains are *not* punished, despite covering up a death and trying to drive the heroine crazy. Especially eerie are the scenes in which the leading lady is locked in a mortuary embalming room lined with corpses on each side of her as Rankin intones sounds through a loudspeaker, all to make the girl believe that her brother is beckoning her. The girl slowly unravels as she bumps into dangling white arms and feet from sheet-covered corpses in the dark room.

MIRACLES FOR SALE (Metro-Goldwyn-Mayer, 1939) 70 minutes.

Director, Tod Browning; based on the novel *Death from a Top Hat* by Clayton Rawson; adaptors, Harry Ruskin, Marion Parsonnet, James Edward Grant; art directors, Cedric Gibbons, Gabriel Scognamillo; set decorator, Edwin B. Willis; wardrobe, Dolly Tree; makeup, Jack Dawn; sound, Douglas Shearer; camera, Charles Lawton; editor, Frederick Y. Smith.

Robert Young (Michael Morgan); Florence Rice (Judy Barclay); Frank Craven (Dad Morgan); Henry Hull (Dave Duvallo); Lee Bowman (La Claire); Cliff Clark (Inspector Gavigan); Astrid Allwyn (Mrs. Zelma La Claire); Walter Kingsford (Colonel Watrous); Frederick Worlock (Dr. Sabbatt); Gloria Holden (Madame Rapport); William Demarest (Quinn); Harold Minjir (Tauro); Charles Lane (Hotel Clerk); Richard Loo (Chinese Soldier); Suzanne Kaaren (Girl); Edward Earle (Man); Chester Clute (Waiter); Truman Bradley (Master of Ceremonies); Cyril Ring (Numbers Man); William Norton Bailey (Man in Box); Manuel Paris (Sinister Man); Paul Sutton (Captain R. Z. Storm); Armand Kaliz (Francois); Fred Warren (Police Surgeon); John Davidson (Strange Voice); Claire McDowall (Woman); Alphonse Martell (Headwaiter); Monte Vandergrift (Bergin); Edward Kilroy (Attendant); Harry Vejar (Citizen); Margaret Bert (Mary); Frances McInemey (Magician's Assistant); and: Amelia Stone.

MIRACLES FOR SALE is remembered today chiefly as being the final film of masterly director Tod Browning, who helmed many of Lon Chaney's silent classic melodramas and such talkie chillers as: THE THIRTEENTH CHAIR (1929), DRACULA (1931), FREAKS (1932), MARK OF THE VAMPIRE (1935), and THE DEVIL DOLL (1936). This motion picture is based on Clayton Rawson's 1938 novel, *Death from a Top Hat,* but the name of the magician/detective in the book, The Great Merlini, is altered for the film.

Rich society folk are being amused by those involved in the black arts (magic, telepathy, demonology) when two of the presenters are murdered. Magician Michael Morgan (Robert Young) fears for the life of pretty maid Judy Barclay (Florence Rice) and tries to prevent her from being killed. Meanwhile, police Inspector Gavigan (Cliff Clark) must ferret out the killer from an array of likely suspects, including magician Dave Duvallo (Henry Hull), spiritualist Madame Rapport (Gloria Holden), telepathy expert La Claire (Lee

Bowman), his wife Zelma (Astrid Allwyn), and Dr. Sabbatt (Frederick Worlock), a demonologist. Also involved is Morgan's dad (Frank Craven), who is visiting the big city for the first time. He gets embroiled in the murder case, but Michael succeeds in unmasking the killer.

Frank S. Nugent (*New York Times*) granted, "While it has enough loose ends to fringe a Spanish shawl, the tale has been rather ingeniously contrived and jogs along briskly. . . ." But, added the reviewer, "The identity of the murderer is fairly obvious from the start, but the motive and the methods are not. . . ." *Variety* explained, "Most of the diverting moments derive from the business tipoff stuff. [Robert] Young not only reveals the gimmicks of the illusions that clutter up his shop, but discloses the mechanical devices that some mental telepathy performers use. There is also a gesture toward exposing the spiritualism thing, with one scene showing how ectoplasm can be produced during a seance."

One other Clayton Rawson book about magician/detective The Great Merlini was brought to the screen, but when *No Coffin for the Corpse* (1942) was filmed it became a Michael Shayne mystery, THE MAN WHO WOULDN'T DIE (1942), *q.v.*, and the character of Merlini was greatly abbreviated in the plotline.

THE MIRROR CRACK'D (Associated Film Distribution, 1980) Color 105 minutes.

Producers, John Brabourne, Richard Goodwin; director, Guy Hamilton; based on the novel by Agatha Christie; screenplay, Jonathan Hales, Barry Sandler; music, John Cameron; production designer, Michael Stringer; costumes, Phyllis Dalton; art director. John Roberts; assistant director, Derek Cracknell; camera, Christopher Challis; editor, Richard Marden.

Angela Lansbury (Miss Jane Marple); Wendy Morgan (Cherry); Margaret Courtenay (Mrs. Bantry); Charles Gray (Bates the Butler); Maureen Bennett (Heather Babcock); Carolyn Pickles (Miss Giles); Eric Dodson (The Major); Charles Lloyd-Pack (Vicar); Richard Pearson (Dr. Haydock); Thick Wilson (Mayor); Pat Nye (Mayoress); Peter Woodthorpe (Scoutmaster); Geraldine Chaplin (Ella Zielinsky); Tony Curtis (Marty N. Fenn); Edward Fox (Inspector Craddock); Rock Hudson (Jason Rudd); Kim Novak (Lola Brewster); Elizabeth Taylor (Marina Rudd); Marella Oppenheim (Margot Bence); Anthony Steel (Sir Derek Ridgeley); Dinah Sheridan (Lady Amanda Ridgeley); Oriana Grieve (Kate Ridgeley); Kenneth Fortescue (Charles Foxwell); Hildegard Neil (Lady Foxcroft); Allan Cuthbertson (Peter Montrose); George Silver (DaSilva); John Bennett (Barnsby); Nigel Stock (Inspector Gates).

A film called MURDER AT MIDNIGHT, about Sir Derek Ridgeley (Anthony Steel) and Lady Amanda (Dinah Sheridan) being involved in a murder, is being shown, and when the film breaks, Miss Jane Marple (Angela Lansbury) leaves, since she has deduced who committed the crime. A short time later an American movie company arrives near Miss Marple's home in Kent, England to produce a remake of MARY, QUEEN OF SCOTS and, after drinking a poisoned daiquiri, a local busybody dies. Miss Marple is asked to investigate, since the drink was really meant for one of the film's players. Although Miss Marple is actively engaged in the case, it is her nephew, Scotland Yard Inspector Craddock (Edward Fox), who does most of the leg work, elderly Miss Marple having sprained her ankle. Among the suspects are anxious screenwriter/director Jason Rudd (Rock Hudson) and his self-absorbed wife Marina (Elizabeth Taylor), who is making a screen comeback in the project as Mary of Scots, and her long-time rival, actress Lois Brewster (Kim Novak), who will play Queen Elizabeth. Catty Lois is married to the film's slimy producer, Marty N. Fenn (Tony Curtis). Also bound into the production is the prim unit secretary, Ella Zielinsky (Geraldine Chaplin). Sedentary Miss Marple puzzles out the motive and the killer.

Vincent Canby (*New York Times*) explained, "That THE MIRROR CRACK'D never builds up much momentum has less to do with Guy Hamilton's direction and the performers than with the screenplay . . . which promises more sophistication than it delivers." Regarding Angela Lansbury's star turn as Miss Marple, Canby wrote, "Her's is a sweet-natured, quick witted but not especially eccentric Miss Marple, a character who comes close to self-effacing. It's an intelligent, legitimate performance but nowhere as entertaining as Miss Lansbury can be when she's playing to the top balcony."

The film was based on Agatha Christie's 1962 novel, *The Mirror Crack'd from Side to Side,* and in *The New Bedside, Bathtub and Armchair Companion to Agatha Christie* (1986), Michael Tennenbaum comments, ". . . Jane and the entire plot take a back seat to the real point of the film—the back-biting bitchiness of Taylor and Novak as the fading, feuding movie queens in town to outdo each other in an unlikely remake of MARY, QUEEN OF SCOTS. In an interesting attempt to establish a sense of time and style (1950s British drawing-room mystery) the movie opens with a scene from MURDER AT MIDNIGHT, a supposed film from that period. Unfortunately, some reviewers found the clever pastiche more interesting than the actual film that followed. Never mind. Angela Lansbury's clever and charming portrayal of Miss Marple no doubt led indirect-

Angela Lansbury in THE MIRROR CRACK'D (1980).

ly to the notion that she would be wonderful in a Christie-style television series, which became the highly successful 'Murder, She Wrote'."

It should be noted that THE MIRROR CRACK'D is a leisurely, absorbing, and cinematically stunning murder mystery in which a white-haired Angela Lansbury is as close to Agatha Christie's version of Miss Marple as the movies have yet come. The film also provides a stunning (if overweight) Elizabeth Taylor with one of her better screen assignments in some time.

MISS PINKERTON (First National, 1932) 66 minutes.

Producer, Hal B. Wallis; director, Lloyd Bacon; based on the novel by Mary Roberts Rinehart; screenplay, Lillian Hayward, Niven Busch; camera, Barney McGill; editor, Ray Curtiss.

Joan Blondell (Miss Adams [Miss Pinkerton]); George Brent (Inspector Patten); Mae Madison (Nurse); John Wray (Hugo); Ruth Hall (Paula Brent); Allan Lane (Herbert Wynne); C. Henry Gordon (Dr. Stewart); Donald Dillaway (Charles Elliott); Blanche Frederici (Mary); Mary Doran (Florence Lenz); Holmes Herbert (Arthur Glenn); Eulalie Jensen (Miss Gibbons); Treva Laler, Luana Walter (Nurses); Lucien Littlefield (Henderson); Nigel de Brulier (Coroner); Walter Brennan (Police Broadcaster); Lyle Talbot (Editor).

Mary Roberts Rinehart, author of THE BAT, *q.v.*, was a former nurse and she fashioned a quartet of works around a sleuthing nurse named Miss Adams, whom she dubbed "Miss Pinkerton." The First National release, MISS PINKERTON, was based on the 1932 novel by Ms. Rinehart and was released in the summer of that year. Although very much a detective story, the movie was made in the popular mode of the time: it is set in a mysterious old house where a murder is committed by a stalking, hooded figure and most of the plot elements of these creakers are present, such as a spiritualistic housekeeper, a nervous maid, a house full of suspects and a menacing thunderstorm.

When a suicide occurs at a remote estate, Detective Inspector Patten (George Brent) is brought into the case and receives much unwanted help from Miss Adams (Joan Blondell), a nurse on duty there, who insists the death is actually a murder, with the $100,000 insurance policy on the deceased a very good motive. The detective comes to realize that the the young woman has a penchant for unearthing vital clues and before long he accepts her leads. It is Miss Adams who winds up solving the tangled case and assisting in the killer's capture.

At the time of release, Andre Sennwald (*New York Times*) complained, ". . . The aging handmaidens of the murder melodrama perform their grisly dance in the gloomy mansion of old Juliet Mitchell, but the sound and the fury have gone out of them . . . there isn't a good, wholesome shudder in the whole of MISS PINKERTON." On the other hand, William K. Everson in *The Detective in Film* (1972) decided, in retrospect, "Although no world beater at the box-office, MISS PINKERTON had the stuff for a sustaining series, and presumably only the monetary obstacles of paying for the story and character rights prevented this."

THE MISSING GUEST (Universal, 1938) 68 minutes,.
    Producer, Barney A. Sarecky; director, John Rawlins; based on the screenplay to SECRET OF THE BLUE ROOM by Erich Philippi; camera, Milton Krasner; editor, Fran Gross.
    Paul Kelly (Scoop Hanlon); Constance Moore (Stephanie Kirkland); William Lundigan (Larry Dearden); Edwin Stanley (Dr. Carroll); Selmer Jackson (Frank Baldrich); Billy Wayne (Vic); George Cooper (Jake); Patrick J. Kelly (Edwards, the Butler); Florence Wix (Linda Baldrich); Harlan Briggs (Frank Kendall, the Editor); Pat C. Flick (Inventor); John Harmon (Baldrich's Guard).
    See: SECRET OF THE BLUE ROOM [essay].

THE MISSING PEOPLE (Monogram, 1940) 71 minutes.
    Producer, Charles Q. Steele; director, Jack Raymond; based on the novel *The Mind of Mr. Reeder* by Edgar Wallace; screenplay, Ludia Hayward; camera, George Stretton.
    Will Fyffe (J. G. Reeder); Kay Walsh (Peggy Gillette); Lyn Harding (Joseph Branstone); Ronald Shiner (Sam Hackett); Ronald Adam (Surtees); Patricia Roc (Doris Bevan); Anthony Holles (Ernest Branstone); Reginald Purdell (Harry Morgan); Marie O'Neill (Housekeeper); and: O. B. Clarence, Lawrence Hanray.
    Although Edgar Wallace (1875-1932) penned over 170 novels, he had few continuing characters in his works. One of these few was Mr. J. G. Reeder, an inspector for the Public Prosecutor's Office in London, and the subject of several Wallace novels and short stories. Wallace himself first brought the character to the screen in 1928 in England when he directed his novel RED ACES for Beaconsfield, with Geoffrey Swyther as Reeder. In 1936 Gibb McLaughlin played the part in MR. REEDER IN ROOM 13, and in 1939 the British Grand National studio headlined Will Fyffe in two Reeder adventures, THE MIND OF MR. REEDER (issued in the United States in 1940 by Monogram as THE MYSTERIOUS MR. REEDER) and

Will Fyffe and Lyn Harding in THE MISSING PEOPLE (1940).

THE MISSING PEOPLE, both based on the Wallace novel *The Mind of Mr. Reeder* (1925).

Retired Mr. Reeder (Will Fyffe) is looking into the disappearance of more than two dozen women who were all receiving a monthly income by registered post. Reeder feels that Doris Bevan (Patricia Roc) will be the next victim and he enlists her aid in solving the case. It turns out that the disappearances are due to a solicitor's brother (Lyn Harding) and his murderous ring of cohorts.

Variety judged THE MISSING PEOPLE ". . . a delightfully naive and amiable, though implausible, melodrama, all on one key, with macabre musical accompaniment." *Film Daily* weighed it as ". . . moderately entertaining screenfare. Story is well concocted and maintains a certain amount of suspense right to the climax; the cast is agreeable and the production value is okay for the budget limitations."

Unfortunately this was to be Mr. Reeder's last theatrical film appearance to date, although Hugh Burden played the part in the 1972 Thames Television series, "The Mind of Mr. Reeder." *Room 13*

(1924) was remade in West Germany in 1963 as ZIMMER 13, but the Reeder character was eliminated.

THE MISSING REMBRANDT (First Division, 1932) 72 minutes.
  Producer, Julius Hagen; director, Leslie Hiscott; based on the story "The Adventure of Charles Augustus Milverton" by Sir Arthur Conan Doyle; adaptors, Cyril Twyford, H. Fowler Mear; camera, Sydney Blythe, Basil Emmott; editor, Jack Harris.
  Arthur Wontner (Sherlock Holmes); Ian Fleming (Dr. Watson); Minnie Raynor (Mrs. Hudson); Francis L. Sullivan (Baron von Guntermann); Dino Galvani (Carlo Ravelli); Miles Mander (Claud Holford); Jane Welsh (Lady Violet Lumsden); Philip Howland (Inspector Lestrade); Anthony Hollis (Marquis de Chaminade); Herbert Lomas (Manning); Ben Welden (Pinkerton Man); Kenji Takase (Chang Wu).
  The second of five British films in which Arthur Wontner played Sherlock Holmes, THE MISSING REMBRANDT is based on Sir Arthur Conan Doyle's story, "The Adventure of Charles Augustus Milverton." The original story was greatly expanded for the big screen, with several additional characters being incorporated, including a Pinkerton agent and a swarthy Italian co-villain. In *Holmes of the Movies* (1976), David Stuart Davies wrote, ". . . Although the early part of the film is very slow in tempo, the atmosphere of Limehouse and Baker Street is realistic and all through there is an air of respect for the Holmes tradition. . . . Holmes' deductions tend to be a little far fetched . . . and Wontner in this feature began to deviate slightly from his original conception of the character, portraying the detective with a marked air of facetiousness. Nevertheless, he was the best Holmes around at the time. . . ."
  Art treasures have been disappearing and French authorities summon Sherlock Holmes (Arthur Wontner). At the same time he and Dr. Watson (Ian Fleming) take the case of Lady Violet Lumsden (Jane Welsh) who is being blackmailed by an American, Baron von Guntermann (Francis L. Sullivan). He has letters belonging to her which, if offered to the public, would cause a scandal. Inspector Lestrade (Philip Howland) has been given a tip that one of the stolen French paintings, a Rembrandt, has been smuggled into England in a chest of tea. The police raid a Chinese opium den in Limehouse but fail to find the work. Lestrade asks Holmes to check the rumor about the painting and Holmes ties both cases to art dealer von Guntermann, who is aided in his nefarious activities by his secretary, Carlo Ravelli (Dino Galvani), and an artist, Claude Holford (Miles Mander), whom he has been using to steal the priceless paintings. A Pinkerton agent (Ben Welden) from the United States is also on the case, but

von Guntermann murders him. Holmes manages to steal the incriminating letters from the villain's safe and later finds Holford dead from an overdose of poison. Holmes proves von Guntermann's criminal activities and reveals the whereabouts of the missing Rembrandt treasure.

THE MISSING REMBRANDT, made by Twickenham Films, was originally released in England with an 84-minute running time by Producers Distributing Corporation.

MR. AND MRS. NORTH (Metro-Goldwyn-Mayer, 1941) 68 minutes.

Producer, Irving Asher; director, Robert B. Sinclair; based on

William Post, Jr. and Gracie Allen in MR. AND MRS. NORTH (1941).

stories by Richard and Frances Lockridge and the play by Owen Davis; screenplay, S. K. Lauren; camera, Harry Stradling; editor, Ralph Winters.

Gracie Allen (Pamela North); William Post, Jr. (Gerald P. North); Paul Kelly (Lieutenant Weigand); Rose Hobart (Carol Brent); Virginia Grey (Jane Wilson); Tom Conway (Louis Berex); Felix Bressart (Arthur Talbot); Porter Hall (George Reyler); Millard Mitchell (Mullins); Lucien Littlefield (Barnes); Inez Cooper (Mabel Harris); Keye Luke (Kumi); Jerome Cowan (Ben Wilson); Stuart Crawford (Stuart Blanton); Fortunio Bonanova (Buano); Harry Strang (Cop); and: James Flavin, Lee Phelps, Tim Ryan.

Richard and Frances Lockridge created the ingratiating husband-and-wife amateur sleuths, Pamela and Jerry North, in a series of *New Yorker* magazine stories, and in 1939 "Mr. and Mrs. North" came to radio on CBS with Peggy Conklin and Carl Eastman in the leads. In 1941, a play about the duo by Owen Davis, also called *Mr. and Mrs. North,* was on Broadway. Later in the year, Metro-Goldwyn-Mayer, which had bankrolled the stage production, filmed it with Gracie Allen and William Post, Jr. in the top roles. Previously Gracie Allen (also without her partner/spouse George Burns) had headlined another comedy murder mystery, THE GRACIE ALLEN MURDER CASE, *q.v.,* which had her in tandem with ace sleuth Philo Vance (Warren William).

After being separated for the weekend, Pamela (Gracie Allen) and Jerry North (William Post, Jr.) return to their Greenwich Village apartment to discover a dead body in the closet. Police detective Lieutenant Weigand (Paul Kelly) is called in to investigate the homicide and the Norths propose bringing together all their friends, since one of them must have done the killing. The suspects arrive and scatterbrained Pamela relates prior events which involved them. With the aid of brush salesman Arthur Talbot (Felix Bressart) the Norths pinpoint the murderer.

"Too much Gracie for so little meat" was Bosley Crowther's (*New York Times*) verdict. *Variety* judged of this very talky whodunit, "It gets off to a slow start, picks up momentum in several episodes along the way, but is handicapped by bumpy tempo. . . . Miss Allen carries the major portion of attention as the pivotal factor in the proceedings."

In 1942 the "Mr. and Mrs. North" radio series transferred to NBC with Alice Frost and Joseph Curtin playing the leads, and in 1952 returned to CBS with Richard Denning and Barbara Britton as the detective couple. This later revival was in tandem with the popular video series of the same title which the two stars performed on CBS from 1952 to 1953 and on NBC in the first half of 1954.

MR. DYNAMITE (Universal, 1935) 75 minutes.

Producer, E. M. Asher; director, Alan Crosland; based on the story "On the Take" by Dashiel Hammett; adaptor, Doris Maloy, Harry Clark; camera, George Robinson.

Edmund Lowe (T. N. Thompson [Mr. Dynamite]); Jean Dixon (Lynn); Esther Ralston (Charmion); Victor Varconi (Dvorjak); Verna Hillie (Mona); Minor Watson (Lewis); Robert Gleckler (King); Jameson Thomas (Williams); Matt McHugh (Sunshine); G. Pat Collins (Rod); Greta Meyer (Jane); Bradley Page (Felix); James Burtis (Joe).

San Francisco gambler Dvorjak (Victor Varconi) hires none-too-honest private eye T. N. Thompson—better known as Mr. Dynamite (Edmund Lowe)—to probe a murder which took place in his casino. Dynamite, who has been in and out of trouble with the law, is at odds with police Chief King (Robert Gleckler) about the case, but he continues his search with the aid of his trustworthy secretary Lynn (Jean Dixon). Along the way the detective romances pretty Mona (Verna Hillie) but after he solves the caper and brings in the killer, the police provide Mr. Dynamite with a one-way ticket out of town and Lynn follows her boss.

Dashiell Hammett wrote the original story for MR. DYNA-MITE and the detective, as enacted by Edmund Lowe, is a close relative of Nick Charles, especially in the fast and witty dialogue. *Variety* pegged it as a ". . . breezy whodunit told in the modern sophisticated manner now popular in Hollywood. . . . It's an okay run-of-the-mill release that keeps close enough to plausibility, or is smart enough when crossing the line to cover the liberties with wit." Frank S. Nugent (*New York Times*) reminded, "Mr. Hammett's distinction among mystery tale spinners is that he never takes his corpse as seriously as his detective; and he never lets his detective take himself seriously at all." The reviewer rated the picture "an amiable excursion into homicide."

MR. MOTO IN DANGER ISLAND (Twentieth Century-Fox, 1939) 70 minutes.

Producer, Sol M. Wutzel; associate producer, John Stone; director, Herbert I. Leeds; based on the character created by John P. Marquand and the novel *Murder in Trinidad: A Case in the Career of Bertram Lynch* by John W. Vandercook; story, John Reinhardt, George Bricker; screenplay, Peter Milne; art directors, Richard Day, Chester Gore; costumes, Herschel; music director, Samuel Kaylin; camera, Lucien Andriot; editor, Harry Reynolds.

Peter Lorre (Mr. Moto); Jean Hersholt (Sutter); Amanda Duff (Joan Castle); Warren Hymer (Twister McGurk); Richard Lane

(Commissioner Gordon); Leon Ames (Commissioner Madero); Douglass Dumbrille (Commander La Costa); Charles D. Brown (Colonel Thomas Castle); Paul Harvey (Governor John Bentley); Robert Lowery (Lieutenant George Bentley); Eddie Marr (Captain Dahlen); Harry Woods (Grant); Don Douglas (Petty Officer); Ward Bond (Sailor Sam the Wrestler); Eddie Marr (Captain Dahlen); Harry Woods (Grant); Paul Harvey (Governor John Bentley); Harry Strang (Smuggler).

This penultimate entry in the Mr. Moto series is not based on the works of John P. Marquand, other than the use of the title character, but is taken from the 1933 murder mystery, *Murder in Trinidad: A Case in the Career of Bertram Lynch* by John W. Vandercook; a property which Fox first filmed in 1934, *q.v.*, and remade for the third time in 1945 as CARIBBEAN MYSTERY, *q.v.*

For this Moto excursion, the setting has been altered from Trinidad to Puerto Rico, where Japanese Mr. Moto (Peter Lorre) is on the trail of diamond smugglers. They kidnap the inscrutable Oriental almost as soon as his ship docks on the island. He escapes and is aided by dimwitted wrestler Twister McGurk (Warren Hymer)—a man full of malapropisms—in tracking the crooks and suspects including two commissioners (Richard Lane, Leon Ames), a local called La Costa (Douglass Dumbrille), and a mysterious ship owner named Sutter (Jean Hersholt). Also involved in the case is pretty Joan Castle (Amanda Duff), who romances Navy Lieutenant George Bentley (Robert Lowery). Moto and McGurk corner the crooks and capture them after a speedboat chase in and out of the Great Selinas Swamp, once reputed to be a pirates' hideout and now the headquarters for smugglers.

As in the other budget entries in the eight-feature series, which ran from 1937 to 1939 for producer Sol M. Wurtzel, the main attracton of this film is Peter Lorre's fine interpretation of the wily Japanese sleuth. Bosley Crowther (*New York Times*) reported, "This corner has long since allowed that Peter Lorre is super-human in every conceivable respect when he slicks down his hair, stains his face, puts on those steel-rimmed 'specks' and goes around playing Mr. Moto, the yellow peril among sleuths. . . . This corner has seldom quibbled about little things like logic." *Variety* agreed, "Lorre is again the suave, calmly calculating Sherlock Holmes, whose size belies his ability to overcome aggressors having twice his apparent stamina."

A.k.a.: DANGER ISLAND. British release title: MR. MOTO ON DANGER ISLAND.

MR. MOTO ON DANGER ISLAND *see* MR. MOTO IN DANGER ISLAND.

MR. MOTO'S GAMBLE *see* CHARLIE CHAN AT MONTE CARLO [essay].

MR. MOTO'S LAST WARNING (Twentieth Century-Fox, 1939) 71 minutes.

Producer, Sol M. Wurtzel; director, Norman Foster; based on the character created by John P. Marquand; screenplay, Philip MacDonald; art directors, Bernard Herzbrun, Lewis Creber; set decorator, Thomas Little; costumes, Helen A. Myron; music/music director, Samuel Kaylen; sound, E. Clayton Ward, William H. Anderson; camera, Virgil Miller; editor, Norman Colbert.

Peter Lorre (Mr. Moto); Ricardo Cortez (Fabian, the Ventriloquist); Virginia Field (Connie Porter); John Carradine (Danforth [Richard Burke]); George Sanders (Eric Novel); Joan Carol (Mary Delacour); Robert Coote (Rollo Venables); Margaret Irving (Mme. Delacour); Leyland Hodgson (Captain Hawkins); John Davidson (Hakim); Teru Shimada (Fake Mr. Moto); Georges Renavent (Admiral Delacour); E. E. Clive (Commandant); Holmes Herbert (Bentham); C. Montague Shaw (First Lord of Admiralty).

Filmed under the working title of MR. MOTO IN EGYPT, this sixth entry (of eight) in the Mr. Moto series has the wily Japanese detective in Port Said, Egypt, posing as an Oriental curio dealer. In reality the sleuth is in the employee of the International Police (Agent #673) and is on the trail of a gang of Axis spies who are plotting to catapult the world into a new war. The scheme is being hatched by Fabian (Ricardo Cortez), who covers his covert activities by being employed as a ventriloquist at the Sultana Theatre. He is in league with turncoat Britisher Eric Morvel (George Sanders). The duo plan to blow up the French fleet as it travels through the Suez Canal and then blame the British for the disaster, thus breaking a vital allied bond. With the aid of secret service agent Danforth (John Carradine), who sacrifices his life, Moto thwarts the scheme and brings in the spies from the unnamed country.

Thomas M. Pryor (*New York Times*) observed, "A Philo Vance probably would have solved it [the mystery] in two reels, but Mr. Moto apparently does not believe in direct action. Perhaps that is because he belongs to the leisurely school of Oriental screen sleuths whose motto seems to be 'give the culprit enough rope and he'll hang himself.'" A top-notch cast is the chief asset of this Mr. Moto installment, with star Peter Lorre delivering a sleek performance as he continues to use assorted disguises and jiu-jitsu along with his innate sleuthing abilities to capture the villains. But by this time the series was beginning to pale, despite solid production values. Without its splendid cast, the movie would have been mundane indeed.

Historically this film has interest in that it is a Japanese hero who saves the day for the Allies, something which could hardly have sat well with some segments of the movie's audience. (By 1939 it was evident that the Japanese had world conquest plans of their own and that they were more at home with the Axis than the Allies.) The political undertones of the Moto series have often been suggested as the prime reason why the property faded after two additional entries, leaving Charlie Chan and Mr. Wong—*both Chinese*—to handle the Oriental detection work on screen.

MR. WONG, DETECTIVE (Monogram, 1938) 70 minutes.

Producer, Scott R. Dunlap; director, William Nigh; based on the stories by Hugh Wiley; screenplay, Houston Branch; music director, Art Meyer; makeup, Gordon Bau; camera, Harry Neuman; editor, Russell Schoengarth.

Boris Karloff (Mr. James Lee Wong); Grant Withers (Captain Street); Maxine Jennings (Myra); Evelyn Brent (Olga); Lucien Prival (Mohl); William Gould (Meisel); John Hamilton (Dayton); Tchin (Lea Tong Foo); John St. Polis (Karl Roemer); Hooper Atchley (Wilk); Frank Bruno (Lascarl); George Lloyd (Devlin); and: Wilbur Mack, Grace Wood, Lynton Brent.

Boris Karloff had performed the role of a Chinese warlord in Warner Bros.' WEST OF SHANGHAI (1937) and the next year he was hired by Monogram Pictures to portray Chinese detective James Lee Wong in a series of low-costing features based on the character created by Hugh Wiley in *Collier's* magazine; the series being designed to take advantage of the box-office popularity of Twentieth Century-Fox's Charlie Chan and Mr. Moto properties. MR. WONG, DETECTIVE would be followed by THE MYSTERY OF MR. WONG (1939), MR. WONG IN CHINATOWN (1939), THE FATAL HOUR (1940), *q.v.*, and DOOMED TO DIE (1940), *q.v.* Keye Luke, who was seen as Charlie Chan's Number One son in the Fox offerings, played Wong himself in one further installment, PHANTOM OF CHINATOWN (1940).

MR. WONG, DETECTIVE has the San Francisco-based Chinese sleuth (Boris Karloff) hired by Dayton (John Hamilton) when his life is threatened by Karl Roemer (John St. Polis), who claims the chemical manufacturer stole his formula for an invisible, odorless gas. When he goes to meet Dayton, Wong finds the man murdered by gas poisoning. Roemer is arrested but Dayton's partners, Meisel (William Gould) and Wilk (Hooper Atchley), are killed by the same means. Police Captain Street (Grant Withers) and Wong look into the murders and find that foreign spies are involved in the shenanigans. This group committed the murders by the use of a glass bulb which contained the poison and which was broken by vibrations caused by the sound of police sirens. The inventor of the gas then tries to murder both Wong and Street, but fails and is apprehended.

Variety complained that the ". . . picture suffers from directorial and writing troubles, plus a combination of careless acting and haphazard casting. Despite these handicaps, Karloff shows he is suited for this new type role and doesn't need a grotesque makeup to register." The British publication, *The Cinema,* prophesied, "Noteworthy for introducing Boris Karloff as a Chinese detective in what may well prove a popular series."

Monogram would remake the film in 1948 as DOCKS OF NEW ORLEANS, *q.v.,* a segment in its Charlie Chan series with Roland Winters as Chan.

MRS. O'MALLEY AND MR. MALONE (Metro-Goldwyn-Mayer, 1950) 69 minutes.

Producer, William H. Wright; director, Norman Taurog; based on the story "Once Upon a Train" by Craig Rice, Stuart Palmer; screenplay, William Bowers; art directors, Cedric Gibbons, Daniel B. Cathcart; set decorator, Edwin B. Willis, Richard A. Pefferle; assistant director, Jack Greenwood; music/music director, Adolph Deutsch; sound, Douglas Shearer, J. Edmondson; camera, Ray June; editor, Gene Ruggiero.

Marjorie Main (Hattie O'Malley); James Whitmore (John J. Malone); Ann Dvorak (Connie Kepplar); Phyllis Kirk (Kay); Fred Clark (Tim Marino); Dorothy Malone (Lola Gillway); Clinton Sundberg (Donald); Douglas Fowley (Steve Kepplar); Willard Waterman (Mr. Ogle); Don Porter (Myron Brynk); Jack Bailey (Announcer); Nancy Saunders (Joanie); Basil Tellou (The Greek); James Burke (Conductor); Eddie Walter (Rigger); Regis Toomey, Herbert Vigran (Reporters); Fred Brady (Orchestra Leader); Henry Corden (Sascha); Edward Earle (Mr. Fillion); Elizabeth Flournoy (Mrs. Fillion); Noreen Mortensen (Margie); Mae Clarke, Thelma Rigdon, Stanley Blystone, Bette Arlen, Lisa Lowry, Philo McCullough, Jerry Lacoe, Jr. (Passengers); Pat Williams (Pirate Girl); Jeffrey Sayre, J. Lewis Smith (Photographers); Diana Norris (Jessie); Donna Norris (Bessie).

Mystery writers Stuart Palmer and Craig Rice teamed to combine their fictional sleuths, Hildegarde Withers and John J. Malone, in several short stories, one of which, "Once Upon a Train" (1950), was the basis for this film. By the time the property was transferred to the screen, however, school teacher Miss Withers had been replaced by Hattie O'Malley, enacted by boisterous Marjorie Main, while Mr. Malone was portrayed by James Whitmore. MGM was hopeful of creating a series built around these two diverse characters, and the advertising announced, "They'll tickle the nation's funny bone. . . . MGM's new screen team." The picture even provides Miss Main with a musical interlude in which she sings "Possum Up a Gum Stump."

Mrs. Hattie O'Malley (Marjorie Main), housewife of Proudfoot, Montana, has won the Treasure Ship radio contest by naming the final mystery tune and is en route by train to Gotham to collect her prize. At the Chicago stopover, lawyer John J. Malone (James Whitmore) boards the luxury train on the trail of crook Steve Kepplar (Douglas Fowley), who has run out on Malone owing him $10,000 in bail money. Also on the train are Kepplar's ex-wife Connie (Ann Dvorak); a private eye, Tim Marino (Fred Clark), who is on his trail; Myron Brynk (Don Porter), Kepplar's crooked ex-employer, and his girlfriend Lola Gillway (Dorothy Malone); bookie Donald (Clinton Sundberg); and Malone's loyal secretary, Kay (Phyllis Kirk). It develops that Kepplar is on the lam with $100,000 and he is bumped off and his body put in Malone's compartment. By this time Malone and the mystery-loving Mrs. O'Malley have become pals. The two, determined to unmask the killer, keep the police from finding Kepplar's body. When Lola is also murdered, Mrs. O'Malley and Mr. Malone are arrested and handcuffed together, but the two solve the crime and place the onus on the real culprit.

Played for laughs—and very broadly at that—MRS. O'MALLEY AND MR. MALONE failed to engender filmgoer enthusiasm, chiefly because there is little chemistry between the two stars. A second O'Malley-Malone pairing, CHERCHEZ LA FRAME, again based on a Palmer-Rice collaboration, was shelved.

MURDER (British International, 1930) 90 minutes.

Producer, John Maxwell; director, Alfred Hitchcock; based on the play *Enter Sir John* by Clemence Dane, Helen Simpson; screenplay, Hitchcock, Alma Reville, Walter C. Mycroft; art director, J. F. Mead; music, John Reynders; camera, Jack J. Cox; editor, Emile DeRuelle.

Herbert Marshall (Sir John Menier); Norah Baring (Diana Baring); Phyllis Konstam (Dulcie Markham); Edward Chapman (Ted Markham); Miles Mander (Gordon Druce); Esme Percy (Handel Fane); Donald Calthrop (Ion Stewart); Amy Brandon Toimas (Defense); Marie Wright (Miss Mitcham); Hannah Jones (Mrs. Didsonme); Una O'Connor (Mrs. Grogram); R. E. Jeffrey (Foreman); Violet Farebrother (Mrs. Ward); Kenneth Kove (Matthews); Gus McNaughton (Tom Trewitt); and: William Fazan, Clare Greet, Joynson Powell, S. J. Warmington.

Some critics consider MURDER to be director Alfred Hitchcock's only true whodunit movie, as opposed to thrillers like THE LODGER (1926) and BLACKMAIL (1929), *qq.v.*, which use the detective motif but whose plots rely more on action and characterization than true mystery. John Belton writes in *Cinema Stylists* (1983), "Hitchcock is generally less interested in mystery—a high-mimetic mode in which the audience is slightly inferior to the plot and character—than in suspense—an ironic mode in which the audience knows more than, and is thus superior to, the plot and characters. The unsuitability of the genre for Hitchcock is reflected in the way his direction struggles against its restrictions, employing a logic that is more ironic than deductive."

Pretty Diana Baring (Norah Baring) is entertaining a friend at her flat for tea when Diana suddenly passes out. When she awakens she is surrounded by neighbors and police, and learns that her friend has been murdered. She is charged with the crime and placed on trial. One of the jurors is a famous actor, Sir John Menier (Herbert Marshall). Since the evidence against her is so great, he goes along with the rest of the jurors in voting for her conviction, but Sir John is convinced of her innocence. Diana is sentenced to be executed and Sir John sets out to break the case and trap the real killer. To do so, he writes a play in which the actual murder is recreated, and knowing the identity of the murderer, he invites him to do a reading of the work. As a result the killer reveals his guilt and Sir John follows him to his job at the circus, where the man falls to his death while performing a high wire act.

MURDER was Alfred Hitchcock's third sound feature film and the killer's identity is hard to fathom because the culprit is a transvestite.

When originally released by Wardour in England in 1930 the film had a 108-minute running time. SIR JOHN GREIFT IN!, a German-language version of MURDER, was shot simultaneously with Alfred Abel in the key role of the actor-juror.

MURDER AHOY! (Metro-Goldwyn-Mayer, 1964) 93 minutes.

Producer, Lawrence P. Bachmann; associate producer, Ben Arbeid; director, George Pollock; based on the character created by Agatha Christie; screenplay, David Pursall, Jack Seddon; art director, Bill Andrews; assistant director, David Tomblin; music/music conductor, Ron Goodwin; recording supervisor, A. W. Watkins; sound, Fred Turtle; sound editor, Allan Stones; camera, Desmond Dickinson; editor, Ernest Walter.

Margaret Rutherford (Miss Jane Marple); Lionel Jeffries (Captain de Courcy Rhumstone); Charles Tingwell (Detective Inspector

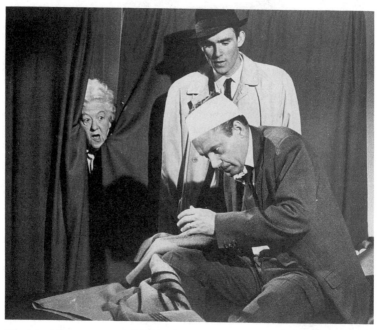

Margaret Rutherford, Terence Edmund and Charles Tingwell in MURDER AHOY!
(1964).

Craddock); William Mervyn (Commander Breeze-Connington);
Joan Benham (Matron Alice Fanbraid); Stringer Davis (Mr. Stringer);
Nicholas Parsons (Dr. Crump); Miles Malleson (Bishop Faulkner);
Henry Oscar (Lord Rudkin); Derek Nimmo (Sub-Lieutenant
Humbert); Gerald Cross (L. W. Brewer Dimchurch); Norma Foster
(Assistant Matron Shirley Boston); Terence Edmond (Sergeant
Bacon); Francis Matthews (Lieutenant Compton); Lucy Griffiths
(Millie); Bernard Adams (Dusty Miller); Tony Quinn (Kelly a
Tramp); Edna Petrie (Miss Pringle); Roy Holder (Petty Officer
Lamb); Henry Longhurst (Cecil Ffolly-Hardwicke).
See: MURDER SHE SAID [essay].

MURDER AT MALIBU BEACH *see* THE TRAP.

MURDER AT MIDNIGHT (Tiffany, 1931) 69 minutes.
Producer, Phil Goldstone; director, Frank R. Strayer; story/
screenplay, Strayer, W. Scott Darling; art director, Ralph M. DeLacy;
costumes, Elizabeth Coleman; music director, Val Burton; camera,
William Rees; editor, John Rawlins.

Aileen Pringle (Mrs. Kennedy); Alice White (Millie Scripps); Hale Hamilton (Montrose the Criminologist); Robert Elliott (Inspector Taylor); Clara Blandick (Aunt Mildred); Brandon Hurst (Lawrence the Butler); Leslie Fenton (Grayson); William Humphrey (Colton); Tyrell Davis (Englishman); Aileen Carlisle (Maid); Kenneth Thomson (Mr. Kennedy); Robert Ellis (Channing).

A charade game involving a murder takes place at a society party and one of the players is actually murdered, with suspicion falling on his employer, Kennedy (Kenneth Thomson). One of the party guests, private investigator/criminologist Montrose (Hale Hamilton), takes over the investigation while awaiting the arrival of police Inspector Taylor (Robert Elliott). Kennedy is shot to death in his study but before he dies he tells the murderer he has written a letter which will implicate the killer. The brother (Leslie Fenton) of the dead man's wife (Aileen Pringle) is found in another room near the murder scene, and the butler, Lawrence (Brandon Hurst), tells the police he heard both murdered men arguing that morning. The police also learn that housemaid Millie (Alice White) loves the brother and that Kennedy's new will, which would disinherit his spouse, has disappeared . Both Millie and Lawrence are murdered after locating the missing letter, which falls into the hands of Aunt Mildred (Clara Blandick), another party guest. She is nearly killed by the villain because the letter implicates him in an affair with Kennedy's wife. The lawbreaker is thwarted, however, by the arrival of Taylor, and the killer dies by his own lethal device, a deadly needle fitted into a telephone receiver.

MURDER AT MIDNIGHT is a well done murder mystery which has an entertaining plot twist, providing unexpected turns pertaining to the killer's identity. The atmospheric sets and the fine cast keep the mystery element moving along and the opening, with a staged murder which turns out to be real, is very realistic. George E. Turner and Michael H. Price assessed in *Forgotten Horrors* (1979), "Tiffany provided its usual solid production values, particularly in obtaining William Rees from Warner Brothers to handle the photography. [Frank R.] Strayer's direction is noteworthy for its avoidance of heavy-handedness that could easily have turned a pleasing mystery into a morbid affair."

MURDER AT THE BASKERVILLES (Astor Films, 1941) 70 minutes.

Producer, Julius Hagen; director, Thomas Bentley; based on the story "Silver Blaze" by Sir Arthur Conan Doyle; screenplay, Arthur Macrae, H. Fowler Mear; camera, Sydney Blythe, William Luff; editor, Alan Smith.

Arthur Wontner (Sherlock Holmes); Lyn Harding (Professor Moriarty); Judy Gunn (Diana Baskerville); Ian Fleming (Dr. Watson); Lawrence Grossmith (Sir Henry Baskerville); Arthur Macrae (Jack Trevor); Eve Gray (Mrs. Straker); Martin Walker (John Straker); John Turnbull (Inspector Lestrade); Robert Horton (Colonel Ross); Arthur Goullet (Colonel Sebastian Moran); Minnie Rayner (Mrs. Hudson); D. J. William (Silas Brown); Ralph Truman (Bert Prince).

Arthur Wontner portrayed Sherlock Holmes in five well-executed British features in the 1930s and the series finished out with SILVER BLAZE,* in which Ian Fleming again is Dr. Watson and Lyn Harding reprises the Professor Moriarty role. "SILVER BLAZE was, despite the consummate playing by the trio of leading actors, the weakest and dreariest of the series and on its release in Britain in 1937 it received such a cool reception that it was thought not worth releasing in the States," according to David Stuart Davies in *Holmes of the Movies* (1976). Actually the film is rather diverting, although not as good as the other films in the Wontner series. When it was issued in the U.S. in 1941 by Astor Pictures the title was altered to MURDER AT THE BASKERVILLES, no doubt to cash in on the popularity of Twentieth Century-Fox's THE HOUND OF THE BASKERVILLES (1939), *q.v.*, but this new title was legitimate since the bulk of the action occurs at Baskerville Hall.

Evil mastermind Professor Moriarty (Lyn Harding) and cohort Colonel Sebastian Moran (Arthur Goullet) plot another wicked scheme. Sherlock Holmes (Arthur Wontner) tells Scotland Yard Inspector Lestrade (John Turnbull) that Moriarty is up to no good, but the policeman refuses to believe him. Holmes and Watson (Ian Fleming) are invited by Sir Henry Baskerville (Lawrence Grossmith) to journey to Baskerville Hall to celebrate the tenth anniversary of the famous case of the Hound and to enjoy the running of the Barchester Cup. Upon arrival, Holmes learns that neighbor Colonel Ross' (Robert Horton) horse, Silver Blaze, a favorite in the race, has disappeared and its groom has been murdered. The chief suspect is Jack Trevor (Arthur Macrae), who is in love with Diana Baskerville (Judy Gunn), Sir Henry's daughter. Investigating, Holmes finds the horse on a nearby farm; it has been disguised by paint. That night Moran attempts to kill Holmes and Watson with an air rifle but fails, and when the race is run the next day, Silver Blaze appears, but his jockey is shot. Back in London, Moriarty kidnaps Watson but Holmes and Lestrade save the doctor and once again arrest the master criminal.

---

*Conan Doyle's original story, "Silver Blaze," is far simpler in plot than the movie; Moriarty, Moran, and Lestrade do not appear in the tale, and there are *no* Baskervilles.

MURDER AT THE GALLOP (Metro-Goldwyn-Mayer, 1963) 81 minutes.

Executive producer, Lawrence P. Bachmann; producer, George H. Brown; director, George Pollock; based on the novel *After the Funeral* by Agatha Christie; screenplay, James P. Cavanagh, David Pursall, Jack Seddon; art director, Frank White; music/music conductor, Ron Goodwin; assistant directors, Basil Rayburn, Edward Dorian; makeup, Eddie Knight; recording supervisor, A. W. Watkins; sound, David Bowen; sound editor, Ed Dennis Rogers; special effects, Tom Howard; camera, Arthur Ibbetson; editor, Bert Rule.

Margaret Rutherford (Miss Jane Marple); Robert Morley (Hector Enderby); Flora Robson (Miss Gilchrist); Charles Tingwell (Detective Inspector Craddock); Stringer Davis (Mr. Stringer); Duncan Lamont (Hillman); James Villiers (Michael Shane); Robert Urquhart (George Crossfield); Katya Douglas (Rosamund Shane); Gordon Harris (Sergeant Bacon); Noel Howlett (Mr. Trundell); Finlay Currie (Old Enderby); Kevin Stoney (Dr. Markwell).

See: MURDER SHE SAID [essay].

MURDER BY AN ARISTOCRAT (Warner Bros., 1936) 60 minutes.

Producer, Bryan Foy; director, Frank McDonald; based on the novel by Mignon G. Eberhart; screenplay, Luci Ward, Roy Chanslor; costumes, Orry-Kelly; camera, Arthur Todd; editor, Louis Hasse.

Lyle Talbot (Dr. Allen Carick); Marguerite Churchill (Sally Keating); Claire Dodd (Janice Thatcher); Virginia Brissac (Adela Thatcher); William B. Davidson (Bayard Thatcher); John Eldredge (John Tweed); Gordon [Bill] Elliott (Dave Thatcher); Joseph Crehan (Hilary Thatcher); Florence Fair (Evelyn Thatcher); Stuart Holmes (Higby); Lottie Williams (Emeline); Mary Treen (Florrie); Milton Kibbee (Cab Driver); Henry Otho (Sheriff).

See: WHILE THE PATIENT SLEPT [essay].

MURDER BY DEATH (Columbia, 1976) Color 94 minutes.

Producer, Ray Stark; associate producer, Roger M. Rothstein; director, Robert Moore; screenplay, Neil Simon; production designer, Stephen Grimes; art director, Harry Kemm; set decorator, Marvin March; costumes, Ann Roth; makeup, Joseph De Bella; music, Dave Grusin; assistant director, Fred T. Gallo; sound, Tex Rudloff, Jerry Jost; special effects, Augie Lohman; camera, David M. Walsh; editors, Margaret Booth, John F. Burnett.

Eileen Brennan (Tess Skeffington); Truman Capote (Lionel Twain); James Coco (Milo Perrier); Peter Falk (Sam Diamond); Alec Guinness (Bensonumum, the Butler); Elsa Lanchester (Jessica Marbles); David Niven (Dick Charleston); Peter Sellers (Sidney Wang);

Peter Sellers, Maggie Smith and David Niven in MURDER BY DEATH (1976).

Maggie Smith (Dora Charleston); Nancy Walker (Yetta, the Maid); Estelle Winwood (Nurse Withers); James Cromwell (Marcel, the Chauffeur); Richard Narita (Willie Wang); Myron (The Dog).

Neil Simon penned this none-too-amusing and very blatant spoof of detective movies in which numerous fictional sleuths are satirized, using phony names: Milo Perrier (Hercule Poirot), Miss Jessica Marbles (Miss Jane Marple), Sidney Wang (Charlie Chan), Dick and Dora Charleston (Nick and Nora Charles), and Sam Diamond (Sam Spade). The result was ". . . a popular film, though not a terribly intelligent one, and [it] seemed to indicate that audiences really were hungry to see mystery movie comedies. Of course the Neil Simon name helped at the box-office" (Ron Haydock, *Deerstalker! Holmes and Watson on Screen,* 1978).

Mystery author Lionel Twain (Truman Capote) invites the world's greatest detectives to his remote mansion for "dinner and murder." Arriving are Belgian sleuth Miles Perrier (James Coco), eccentric British detective Miss Jessica Marbles (Elsa Lanchester) and her elderly nurse (Estelle Winwood), Chinese detective Sidney

Wang (Peter Sellers) and his adopted number two son Willie (Richard Narita), socialites Dick and Dora Charleston (David Niven, Maggie Smith) and their pet dog Myron, and tough investigator Sam Diamond (Peter Falk) and his equally tough girlfriend, Tess Skeffington (Eileen Brennan). Twain informs them someone will be murdered at midnight by being stabbed twelve times and says that whoever solves the crime before it happens will get one million tax-free dollars and the accolade of the world's greatest crime solvers. The five sleuths agree to the challenge and embark on solving the crime and claiming the prizes.

William Avery wrote in *Films in Review* magazine (August-September 1976), "Though the one-liners have the Simon seal, the script occasionally falters to the vulgarly witty, giving both director Robert Moore and the cast's professionalism a few uneasy moments. . . . Truman Capote . . . gives a revolting caricature of himself. . . . The movie contains too many plot twists. It's really a movie *à clef,* very 'in' in its demands that you recognize all the cross references."

Actually two versions of the absurd MURDER BY DEATH were issued. The one which received only minor issuance included a scene where Sherlock Holmes (Keith McConnell) and Dr. Watson (Richard Peel) arrive at the mansion late in the proceedings, solve the caper, refuse to divulge the identity of the murderer and then leave. Apparently some of the film's stars objected to having their characters so upstaged. Thus an alternate ending was written which played down Holmes' deductive powers. But this was not enough and Holmes and Watson were then excised from most release prints.

MURDER BY DECREE (Avco Embassy, 1979) Color 121 minutes.

Executive producer, Len Herberman; producers, Rene Dupont, Bob Clark; director/story, Clark; screenplay, John Hopkins; production designer, Harry Pottle; costumes, Judy Moorcroft; assistant director, Ariel Levy; sound, John Mitchell; camera, Reg Morris; editor, Stan Cole.

Christopher Plummer (Sherlock Holmes); James Mason (Dr. Watson); Donald Sutherland (Robert Lees); Genevieve Bujold (Annie Crook); David Hemmings (Inspector Foxborough); Susan Clark (Mary Kelly); Anthony Quayle (Sir Charles Warren); John Gielgud (Lord Salisbury); Frank Finlay (Inspector Lestrade); Teddi Moore (Mrs. Lees); Peter Jonfield (William Slade); Roy Lansford (Sir Thomas Smiley); Catherine Kessler (Carrie); Ron Pember (Makins); Ken Jones (Dock Guard); and: June Brown, Hilary Sesta, Chris Wiggins.

Sherlock Holmes and Jack the Ripper had been foes in the quality production, A STUDY IN TERROR (1965), *q.v.*, and the two remarkable fictional characters were reunited in this Canadian-produced feature which is highlighted by a stylish recreation of the gaslight era. Otherwise, the confused and overlong script seems to be taking the Watergate Conspiracy and tossing it back to Victorian times, using the infamous Ripper murders as a plot focus. "Handsome-bland production is short on substance—the revelations of conspiracy and cover-up seem anti-climactic," wrote Donald C. Willis in *Horror and Science Fiction Films II* (1982). The film was shot under the working title, SHERLOCK HOLMES AND SAUCY JACK.

Three women are found brutally murdered in London's Whitechapel area and a citizens' committee asks Sherlock Holmes (Christopher Plummer) to look into the matter. When another murder takes place that night, Holmes and Dr. Watson (James Mason) go to the scene where Inspector Lestrade (Frank Finlay) and Inspector Foxborough (David Hemmings) are in charge. Sir Charles Warren (Anthony Quayle), the head of Scotland Yard, arrives and orders Holmes away from the scene. The resolute detective consults Robert Lees (Donald Sutherland), who has had visions of the murders. When one of the men who hired Holmes is murdered, it turns out that he was a radical and Sir Charles threatens to charge Holmes with the killings if he does not stay out of the Jack the Ripper case. Holmes, however, confronts Sir Charles as a Freemason and notes that a cipher left by the Ripper makes reference to that order. Consulting Lees again, Holmes discerns that the man has led the police to the killer but has been told to remain silent. Watson goes to Whitechapel and the prostitutes there tell him that one of the murdered street walkers knew a Mary Kelly (Susan Clark). When Holmes meets the woman they are attacked and she escapes after being abducted. Recovering, Holmes goes to a mental institution to visit Annie Crook (Genevieve Bujold), whom Mary had mentioned. Holmes uncovers that Annie had a baby which was entrusted to Mary and that its father was the Duke of Clarence, the heir to the British throne. Later Holmes finds Mary being brutally murdered by two men (Peter Jonfield, Roy Lansford) and in a lengthy battle along the waterfront he kills one of them. Holmes takes his case to the Prime Minister (John Gielgud) with evidence of the clandestine royal marriage, and accuses the government of conspiracy in killing the prostitutes who knew of it and the child. He exposes Jack the Ripper as a myth created by the government as a smokescreen to cover up its own crimes. The charges are not denied and Holmes agrees to remain silent as long as the child is safe, the mother having committed suicide.

In analyzing this presentation, Pauline Kael in *500 Nights at the*

Movies (1984) noted, "The mellifluous-voiced Christopher Plummer makes a good-looking Holmes, but, as usual, Plummer, though accomplished, is totally unconvincing. . . . Holmes seems less a master of deduction than a wet-eyed saintly firebrand trying (ineffectively) to save mankind from the corruption of those in power. This Holmes also patronizes the common man, in the form of Dr. Watson, with whom he lives in an 'odd couple' relationship that is the film's best comic resource."

MURDER BY THE BOOK (CBS-TV, 3/17/87) Color 100 minutes.

Producer, Peter Nelson; director, Mel Damski; based on the novel *Alter Ego* by Mel Arrighi; teleplay, Michael Norell; production designer, Gavin Mitchell; makeup, Patricia Green; music, Mark Snow; stunt coordinator, Ernie Orsatti; sound, Rod Haykin; camera, Don H. Birnkrant; editor, Joanna D'Antonio.

Robert Hays (D. H. "Hank" Mercer/Biff Deegan); Catherine Mary Stewart (Merissa Winfield); Christopher Murney (Lieutenant Stanley Greenberg); Fred Gwynne (Victor Greville); Celeste Holm (Mrs. Claire Mercer); Lewis J. Stadlen (Norman Wagstaff); Gavin Reed (Roger); Jacques Sandulescu (Timothy); Jonathan Moore (Nicholas Rubenstein); Martin Neufeld (Peter Winfield); Bunty Webb (Stout Woman); Eric Keenleyside (Sergeant); Robin Ward (Harold Bordagaray); Eric Fink (Martinez, the Doorman); Thick Wilson (Dream Sequence Victim); Al Bernardo (Taxi Driver); Louis DiBianco (Limousine Driver); Marc Gomes (Captain); Robbie Baker (Half-Dressed Blonde).

Filmed in New York City and Toronto, Canada in late 1985 and based on the novel *Alter Ego* (1983) by Mel Arrighi, this light-hearted telefeature has the catchy premise of a mystery writer being aided by his invented character, in this case a hard-boiled detective of the Sam Spade-Philip Marlowe school. The result is a pleasing murder mystery which pokes fun at the genre while at the same time being laced with all the ingredients which make detective movies fun to watch.

Wimpy mystery writer D. H. "Hank" Mercer (Robert Hays) has just completed another book about his successful literary creation, rugged gumshoe Biff Deegan (Robert Hays), called *The Dead Bimbo's Return,* and his mother (Celeste Holm) convinces him to set his literary sights higher by creating a more refined sleuth. Agreeing, Mercer meets with his publisher to discuss the matter and during the dinner session the writer witnesses what appears to be the abduction of vulnerable Merissa Winfield (Catherine May Stewart) by the overly refined Victor Greville (Fred Gwynne). The publisher informs Mercer that if he can solve this baffling case himself, he will be allowed to redo his fictional creation. Mercer now must find out if what he witnessed was truly a kidnapping. He is aided by the unseen Deegan, who has become a reality (i.e., an alter ego) to his author and can only be seen by him. Mercer (and Deegan) uncover the fact that the suspect is rich, rapacious art dealer Victor Greville and that he is holding an ancient statue which belonged to Merissa's brother. When several murders occur, police Lieutenant Stanley Greenberg (Christopher Murney) jumps into the case.

Miles Beller (*The Hollywood Reporter*) decided, "There's a casual likability Hays brings to the roles played in BOOK, an understated affability, a quality Jimmy Stewart made so much a part of his screen persona." *Daily Variety* judged the TV film ". . . a merry romp about murders and murder mystery styles. It's a pleasure."

MURDER IN THE BLUE ROOM (Universal, 1944) 61 minutes.

Associate producer, Frank Gross; director, Leslie Goodwins; based on the screenplay to SECRET OF THE BLUE ROOM by Erich Philippi; new screenplay, I. A. L. Diamond, Stanley Davis; art directors, John B. Goodman, Harold H. MacArthur; costumes, Vera West; music director, Sam Freed, Jr.; choreography, Carlos Romero; special effects, John P. Fulton; camera, George Robinson; editor, Charles Maynard.

Anne Gwynne (Nan Kirkland); Donald Cook (Steve Randall); John Litel (Frank Baldrich); Grace McDonald (Peggy); Betty Kean (Betty); June Preisser (Jerry); Regis Toomey (Inspector McDonald); Nella Walker (Linda Baldrich); Andrew Toombes (Dr. Carroll); Ian Wolfe (Edwards the Butler); Emmett Vogan (Hannagan); Bill MacWilliams [Williams] (Larry Dearden); Frankie Marlowe (Curtin); Victoria Horne (Maid).

See: SECRET OF THE BLUE ROOM [essay].

MURDER IN THE MUSEUM (Progressive, 1934) 60 minutes.

Producer, Willis Kent; director, Melville Shyer; screenplay, E. B. Grosswhite; assistant director, George Curtner; camera, James Diamond, editor, Roy Luby.

Henry B. Walthall (Professor Mysto the Magician); Phyllis Barrington (Lois Brandon); John Harron (Jerry Rose); Joseph Girard (Police Commissioner Brandon); Donald Kerr (Barker); John Elliott (Snell); Symonia Boniface (Fortune Teller); Sam Flint (Newgate); Clinton Lyle (Judson); Steve Clemente (Knife Thrower); Albert Knight (King Kiku); Lynton Brent (Carr); Si Jenks (Rube); Al Hill (Detective).

Poverty row producer Willis Kent made his films as economically as possible, having a penchant for "B" Westerns and exploitation items (e.g., THE COCAINE FIENDS, 1935). Occasionally, however, he turned to the detective motif, as with SINISTER HANDS (1932), *q.v.*, and MURDER IN THE MUSEUM. Unfortunately, his meagre production funds led to rather stage-bound efforts which rely on their casts to carry out a talky, and not always literate, plotline. Such is the case with MURDER IN THE MUSEUM, which is blessed with Henry B. Walthall's fine work in a leading assignment, although the detective, here played as a newshound, is weak and appears to stumble onto the solution to the crime rather than puzzle it out on his own.

The police, led by Inspector Brandon (Joseph Girard) and morals-minded Councilman Newgate (Sam Flint), plan to raid and close down Carr's (Lynton Brent) carnival freak show. Brandon's niece, Lois (Phyllis Barrington), comes to the show to see magician professor Mysto (Henry B. Walthall), so Brandon intends to delay the raid. However, he is urged on by Newgate when newsman Jerry Rose (John Harron) appears. Soon thereafter, Newgate is shot and killed, and when liquor is found on the premises, Carr escapes. Jerry files his story and decides to investigate the mystery. By now he and Lois are falling in love. The next day Jerry and Lois hide themselves in an attic room overlooking the museum. They are attacked by a hooded figure but the police arrive to save them. Jerry agrees to meet Mysto at a remote house and when he keeps the appointment, he is captured, as is Lois, who has followed him. The place turns out to be Carr's headquarters. When rivals attack Carr he is able to kill them. He next plans to abduct Lois but is himself killed. Jerry escapes and confronts the killer, who admits he has developed a weapon which can change bullet calibers and thus was able to disguise his crime while thrusting suspicion on Carr. The killer commits suicide, leaving Jerry and Lois free to wed.

MURDER IN TRINIDAD (Fox, 1934) 74 minutes.

Director, Louis King; based on the novel *Murder in Trinidad: A Case in the Career of Bertram Lynch* by John W. Vandercook; adaptor, Seton I. Miller; music director, Samuel Kaylin; camera, Barney McGill; editor, Al De Gaetano.

Nigel Bruce (Bertram Lynch); Heather Angel (Joan Cassell); Victor Jory (Howard Sutter); Murray Kinnell (Major Bruce Cassell); Douglas Walton (Gregory Bronson); J. Carrol Naish (Duval); Claude King (Sir Ellery Bronson); Pat Somerset (Inspector Henley); Francis Ford (Davenant).

John W. Vandercook's 1933 novel, *Murder in Trinidad: A Case in the Career of Bertram Lynch,* was used as the basis for three Fox theatrical features, although the Lynch character appears only in the initial filming, with the character undergoing name and character changes in the two remakes.

MURDER IN TRINIDAD was issued in 1934 and it tells of London detective Bertram Lynch (Nigel Bruce) being sent to Trinidad to study the activities of a diamond smuggling operation. Once there he uncovers three murders and a host of suspects and eventually ferrets out the killer while trying to avoid the island's natural danger—a huge swamp filled with crocodiles.

Nigel Bruce, the screen's best known Dr. Watson, here plays the sleuth and does so in fine fettle, as noted by *Variety*: "Nigel Bruce's performance . . . is not only refreshing but also played as to overshadow everyone else. . . . Bruce, who has a soft English accent, moves slowly through the picture in keeping with the character he plays, never getting excited, never voicing the many opinions average detective roles are cluttered up with. That helps." Naturally the film has a romantic angle and here it is supplied by Victor Jory (who later had the title role in the 1940 serial, THE SHADOW, *q.v.*) and Heather Angel (later the leading lady of several of Paramount's Bulldog Drummond programmers). Jory's character, who aids Lynch in investigating the case, is bent on saving his lady love from the villains.

In 1939 the Vandercook novel was remade as MR. MOTO IN DANGER ISLAND, *q.v.*, and Lynch became Mr. Moto (Peter Lorre) and the locale was changed to Puerto Rico. The third rendition occurred in 1945 as CARIBBEAN MYSTERY, headlining James Dunn, who had just won a Best Supporting Actor Oscar for his work in A TREE GROWS IN BROOKLYN (1945). Here he was not Bertram Lynch either, but a Mr. Smith, an ex-Brooklyn policeman who is assigned the role as special investigator for a large oil company. He is to look into the disappearance of several geologists the company had dispatched to a Caribbean island jungle in search of oil deposits. On the island Smith receives scant cooperation from local officials and when the hotel hostess (Sheila Ryan) tries to provide him with important information she is killed. Prior to the poorly-executed CARIBBEAN MYSTERY James Dunn had played a private eye in two William Beaudine-directed Monogram features, THE LIVING GHOST (1942) and LEAVE IT TO THE IRISH (1944), *qq.v.*

MURDER MOST FOUL (Metro-Goldwyn-Mayer, 1964) 90 minutes.

Executive producer, Lawrence P. Bachmann; producer, Ben

Arbeid; director, George Pollock; based on the novel *Mrs. McGinty's Dead* by Agatha Christie; screenplay, David Pursall, Jack Seddon; art director, Frank White; music/music conductor, Ron Goodwin; assistant director, David Tomblin; recording supervisor, A. W. Watkins; sound, Cyril Swern; sound editor, Allan Sones; camera, Desmond Dickinson; editor, Ernest Walter.

Margaret Rutherford (Miss Jane Marple); Ron Moody (Driffold Cosgood); Charles Tingwell (Inspector Craddock); Andrew Cruickshank (Justice Crosby); Megs Jenkins (Mrs. Thomas); Dennis Price (Theatrical Agent); Ralph Michael (Ralph Summers); James Bolam (Bill Hanson); Stringer Davis (Mr. Stringer); Francesca Annis (Sheila Upward); Allison Seebohm (Eva McGonigall); Terry Scott (Police Constable Wells); Pauline Jameson (Maureen Summers); Maurice Good (George Rowton); and: Annette Kerr, Windsor Davies, Neil Stacey, Stella Tanner.

See: MURDER SHE SAID [essay].

MURDER, MY SWEET (RKO, 1944) 95 minutes.

Executive producer, Sid Rogell; producer, Adrian Scott; direc-

Margaret Rutherford and Stringer Davis in MURDER MOST FOUL (1964).

tor, Edward Dmytryk; based on the novel *Farewell My Lovely* by Raymond Chandler; screenplay, John Paxton; art directors, Albert S. D'Agostino, Carroll Clark; set decorators, Darrell Silvera, Michael Ohrenbach; music, Roy Webb; music director, C. Bakaleinikoff; assistant director, William Dorfman; dialogue director, Leslie Urbach; sound, Bailey Fester; montages, Douglas Travers; special effects, Vernon L. Walker; camera, Harry J. Wild; editor, Joseph Noriega.

Dick Powell (Philip Marlowe); Claire Trevor (Mrs. Grayle); Anne Shirley (Ann Grayle); Otto Kruger (Jules Amthor); Mike Mazurki (Moose Malloy); Miles Mander (Mr. Grayle); Douglas Walton (Marriott); Don Douglas (Lieutenant Randall); Ralf Harolde (Dr. Sonderborg); Esther Howard (Mrs. Jesse Florian); John Indrisano (Chauffeur); Jack Carr (Short Guy); Shimen Ruskin (Elevator Operator); Ernie Adams (Bartender); Dewey Robinson (The Boss); Larry Wheat (Butler); Sammy Finn (Headwaiter); Bernice Ahi (Dancer); Don Kerr (Cab Driver); Paul Phillips (Detective Nulty); Ralph Dunn, George Anderson (Detectives); Paul Hilton (Boy).

In 1941 RKO Radio paid $2,000 for the screen rights to Raymond Chandler's second Philip Marlowe novel, *Farewell, My Lovely* (1940) and filmed it as THE FALCON TAKES OVER in 1943 with George Sanders' Gay Falcon substituting for the Marlowe role. Otherwise, the film was a fairly literate retelling of the Chandler story. In 1945 director Edward Dmytryk remade the vehicle as MURDER, MY SWEET, with crooner Dick Powell drastically changing his screen image in the role of hard-nosed gumshoe Philip Marlowe. The result ". . . is unquestionably one of the best private eye films ever made" (Stephen Pendo, *Raymond Chandler on Screen*, 1976).

Hollywood detective Philip Marlowe (Dick Powell) is being questioned by policemen Randall (Don Douglas) and Nulty (Paul Phillips) about several unsolved murders and relates how he became involved in the cases. While on assignment in one of the seedier sections of Los Angeles, Marlowe encounters giant Moose Malloy (Mike Mazurki) who strongarms him into locating his girlfriend Velma. They head to a bar called Florian's where the girl used to work, but the place is now a black joint, and Moose ends up thrashing the new owner. Moose has not seen Velma for eight years, since he has been in prison, and he orders Marlowe to locate her. The detective talks with Jesse Florian (Esther Howard), the widow of the bar owner, but she is a drunk who insists that Velma is deceased. Back at his office Marlowe is hired by Lindsay Marriott (Douglas Walton) to act as a bodyguard when he buys back stolen jade. At the transaction site, Marlowe is knocked out and Marriott is murdered. Marlowe informs the police and although they suspect him of the killing, they let him go, warning him to stay away from Marriott's friend, psychic Jules Amthor (Otto Kruger). Ann Grayle (Anne Shirley) comes to Marlowe's office claiming to be a journalist needing information about the Marriott killing and the missing jade necklace. The sleuth discovers that she is really the daughter of jade collector Grayle (Miles Mander) and that the necklace had been stolen from her stepmother, Mrs. Grayle (Claire Trevor). Ann takes Marlowe to meet her father and stepmother but he learns little from them other than that Mrs. Grayle knows Amthor. Both Mrs. Grayle and Ann want Marlowe off the case and Malloy appears to take the detective to see Amthor, who wants the necklace. When Marlowe says he does not have it, he is beaten up by Malloy and the psychic. Drugged, Marlowe spends three days incarcerated at Amthor's sanitarium, but manages to escape. He encounters Malloy again and is told to continue the search for Velma. Finally, meeting again with Mrs. Grayle, Marlowe is informed that Amthor has been blackmailing her because he knew of her extramarital affairs and that he had supposedly killed Marriott for the jewelry. Marlowe agrees to aid the woman in getting rid of Amthor, but the latter is already dead—killed by Malloy. The next night Marlowe takes Malloy to the beach house where he is to meet Mrs. Grayle and she gives him the necklace, which had never been stolen. Marlowe accuses her of killing Marriott and the woman draws a gun on him as her husband and stepdaughter arrive. In the mayhem that follows Mrs. Grayle, who was actually Velma, is shot by her husband, as is Moose. Grayle himself dies in the scuffle. After the police interrogation, Marlowe is freed because Ann confirms his story. Marlow and Anne leave together.

In adapting Chandler's novel to the screen for its second filming, John Paxton made several plot alterations: a major character from the novel, gangster Laird Burnette, was eliminated; aged Judge Grayle becomes a somewhat younger jade collector; and newspaperwoman Anne Riordan becomes Ann Grayle, the collector's daughter. Otherwise the film remains close to the novel's origins except for the ending, which is even more convoluted than the book, where Velma kills Malloy and then escapes, only to later kill herself in Baltimore. Richard B. Jewell and Vernon Harbin wrote in *The RKO Story* (1982), "Director Edward Dmytryk explored the full vocabulary of film to convey the descent of private eye Marlowe into the nether world of homicide, blackmail, charlatanism, thievery, sadistic violence, sexual enslavement, and, above all else, Mystery. The film's dream and drug sequences . . . were especially effective in the visualization of Marlowe's confused and paranoic state of mind. One of the refreshing aspects of MUR-

DER, MY SWEET was its notable lack of clean-living, soft-spoken heroes and heroines."

MURDER, MY SWEET greatly benefits from being filmed in Raymond Chandler's contemporary Los Angeles and it beautifully captures the flavor of the landscape, always an important ingredient of the author's work. In addition, Dick Powell was especially fine as the semi-seedy private investigator and his performance was matched by Claire Trevor as the bitch heroine, Anne Shirley in the good girl assignment, Esther Howard as the booze hound, and, especially, wrestler Mike Mazurki in his expert handling of the Moose Malloy character. The film ended forever Dick Powell's typecasting as a movie crooner, although ironically, when the picture was released in Manhattan, Powell appeared on stage with the production and sang a few songs! He reprised the Marlowe role in two radio adaptations of "Murder, My Sweet": on "Lux Radio Theatre" on CBS on June 11, 1945 with Claire Trevor; and on June 8, 1946 on CBS' "Hollywood Star Time" with Mary Astor. He played Marlowe for the last time in 1954 on "The Long Goodbye" segment of CBS-TV's "Climax!" series in its premiere episode.

MURDER, MY SWEET was issued in England under the novel's title, FAREWELL, MY LOVELY, and it was under that title that the property was filmed yet a third time, *q.v.*, in 1975 with Robert Mitchum as Marlowe.

THE MURDER OF DR. HARRIGAN (Warner Bros., 1936) 66 minutes.

Producer, Bryan Foy; director, Frank McDonald; based on the novel *From This Dark Stairway* by Mignon G. Eberhart; screenplay, Peter Milne, Sy Bartlett, Charles Belden; art director, Robert M. Haas; music director, Leo F. Forbstein; camera, Arthur Todd; editor, William Clemens.

Kay Linaker (Sally Keating); Ricardo Cortez (Dr. George Lambert); Mary Astor (Lillian Ash); John Eldredge (Dr. Harrigan); Joseph Crehan (Lieutenant Lamb); Frank Reicher (Dr. Coate); Anita Kerry (Agnes); Phillip Reed (Simon); Robert Strange (Peter Melady); Mary Treen (Margaret Brody); Gordon Elliott (Ladd); Don Barclay (Jackson); Johnny Arthur (Wentworth); Joan Blair (Ina).

See: WHILE THE PATIENT SLEPT [essay].

MURDER OF THE THIRTEENTH GUEST (Monogram, 1943) 61 minutes.

Producer, Lindsley Parsons; director, William Beaudine; based on the novel *The Thirteenth Guest* by Armitage Trail; screenplay,

Charles Marion, Arthur Hoerl, Tim Ryan; art director, Dave Milton; music, Edward Kay; camera, Mack Stengler; editor, Dick Currier.

Dick Purcell (Johnny); Helen Parrish (Marie); Tim Ryan (Burke); Frank Faylen (Speed); John Duncan (Harold); John Dawson (Jackson); Paul McVey (Morgan); Jacqueline Dalya (Marjory); Cyril Ring (Barksdale); Addison Richards (District Attorney); and Lloyd Ingraham.

See: THE THIRTEENTH GUEST [essay].

MURDER ON A BRIDLE PATH (RKO, 1936) 63 minutes.

Producer, William Sistrom; directors, Edward Killy, William Hamilton; based on the novel *The Puzzle of the Red Stallion* by Stuart Palmer; adaptor, Dorothy Yost, Thomas Lennon, Edmund North, James Gow; music director, Roy Webb; camera, Nick Musuraca; editor, Jack Hively.

James Gleason (Inspector Oscar Piper); Helen Broderick (Hildegarde Martha Withers); Louise Latimer (Barbara Foley); Owen Davis, Jr. (Eddie Fry); John Arledge (Joey); John Carroll (Latigo Wells); Leslie Fenton (Don Gregg); Christian Rub (Thomas); Sheila Terry (Violet); Willie Best (High Pockets); John Miltern (Pat Gregg); Harry Jane (Addle); James Donlan (Kane); Gustav Von Seyffertitz (Dr. Bloom); Frank Reicher (Dr. Peters); Spencer Charters (Mahoney).

Angular Edna May Oliver proved to be the epitome of Stuart Palmer's fictional old maid school teacher sleuth, Miss Hildegarde Withers, in a trio of films—THE PENGUIN POOL MURDER, 1932, MURDER ON THE BLACKBOARD, 1934, and MURDER ON A HONEYMOON, 1935, *qq.v.*—before withdrawing from the part due to recurring ill health. She was replaced by acerbic Helen Broderick and the result was a near disaster. Not even the continuation of frazzled James Gleason in the role of Inspector Oscar Piper, which fitted him as well as the Withers role did Miss Oliver, could help matters. MURDER ON A BRIDLE PATH proved to be Miss Broderick's sole appearance in the series before she was replaced by fluttery ZaSu Pitts for two more, but not much better, entries, THE PLOT THICKENS (1936) and FORTY NAUGHTY GIRLS (1937), *qq.v.*

A nasty young woman is murdered while horseback riding in Central Park and Gotham homicide Inspector Oscar Piper (James Gleason) is assigned to the case. He soon finds himself burdened with the unwanted help of his sometime ally, maiden school teacher Hildegarde Withers (Helen Broderick). Both find a myriad of suspects, including the murdered woman's ex-husband (Leslie Fenton), his father (John Miltern), her sister (Louise Latimer), the latter's fiancée (Owen Davis, Jr.) and the dead woman's lover (John

Carroll). The plot thickens when the father-in-law is found dead and the killer nearly does in the nosy Miss Withers before she assembles sufficient evidence to name the villain.

Variety explained, "On the surface it looks like too many cooks spoiled the picture. Four writers were concerned with the screenplay, and two directors with the actual staging, with the final result a strickly-for-the-dualers film that will do moderately at best. It's a murder mystery which pulls its punches, showing how the fine comedy abilities of Helen Broderick and James Gleason can be thoroughly submerged by a poor script."

The film, at best, is a mediocre adaptation of Stuart Palmer's 1935 novel, *The Puzzle of the Red Stallion,* which was issued in Britain as *The Puzzle of the Briar Pipe.* The novel was reprinted by Bantam Books in the U.S. in 1987.

MURDER ON A HONEYMOON (RKO, 1935) 73 minutes.

Producer, Kenneth MacGowan; based on the novel *Puzzle of the Pepper Tree* by Stuart Palmer; screenplay, Seton I. Miller, Robert Benchley; special camera effects, Vernon L. Walker, camera, Nick Musuraca; editor, William Morgan.

Edna May Oliver (Hildegarde Martha Withers); James Gleason (Inspector Oscar Piper); Lola Lane (Phyllis La Font); Chick Chandler (Pilot French); George Meeker (Kelsey); Dorothy Libaire (Kay Deving); Harry Ellerbee (Marvin Deving); Spencer Charters (Chief Britt); DeWitt Jennings (Captain Beegle); Leo G. Carroll (Joseph B. Tate); Arthur Hoyt (Dr. O'Rourke); Matt McHugh (Pilot Madden); Sleep 'n' Eat [Willie Best] (Porter); Morgan Wallace (Arthur J. Jack); Brooks Benedict (Forrest); Rollo Lloyd (Hotel Clerk); and: Robert E. Homans, Irving Bacon.

Stuart Palmer's *Puzzle of the Pepper Tree* (1933) was the basis for this feature, the third screen teaming of Edna May Oliver as Hildegarde Withers and James Gleason as Inspector Oscar Piper, following THE PENGUIN POOL MURDER (1932) and MURDER ON THE BLACKBOARD (1934), *qq.v. Variety* called the feature, ". . . better than average. . . . Edna May Oliver and James Gleason team . . . equally effectively. Plot is just a once over lightly proposition, but jammed with laughs and with the one important element— a surprise finish."

At the start of the story Miss Hildegarde Withers (Edna May Oliver) is found flying to Catalina Island for a vacation. When the plane lands, one of the passengers, Forrest (Brooks Benedict), is found dead. Mrs. Withers goes to the local police, believing that foul play has taken place, but gets little help from Chief Britt (Spencer Charters) or the coroner, Dr. O'Rourke (Arthur Hoyt). She telegraphs New York city police Inspector Oscar Piper (James Gleason) about the case and he realizes that the murdered man has been sought by the city's district attorney to testify against racketeers, who have vowed to kill him. Piper arrives on Catalina to claim the body but it is stolen and a mysterious figure named Mack (Morgan Wallace) appears, with Miss Withers insisting that he is the hired killer the mob has sent to murder Forrest. Miss Withers and Piper search the local casino and find two other passengers, honeymooners Kay (Dorothy Libaire) and Marvin Deving (Harry Ellerbee), and as the latter is about to tell Piper something he is shot and killed. The next day Forrest's body is found buried beneath a tree and Tommy Kelsey (George Meeker), who has been romancing another passenger, actress Phyllis La Font (Lola Lane), is arrested for Forrest's murder. He advises Piper that he is really Forrest and that the murdered man was his bodyguard, Kelsey. Miss Withers searches Mack's room and when he finds her there, he ties her up and leaves her in the closet. Several hours later Piper and Britt rescue the school teacher and find Mack murdered in another room. Miss Withers figures out that the killers had murdered the bodyguard by mistake and that when Mack had killed one of them to keep him quiet, the other had killed Mack in revenge. They then capture the killer. The real Forrest, after leaving a complete report for Piper on the racketeers, departs with Phyllis for Mexico where they plan to wed.

MURDER ON A HONEYMOON is the least satisfying of the first three Hildegarde Withers features but it is still entertaining, and is highlighted by many red herrings. The movie takes some rather acid pokes at the film industry, with one of the suspects being film director Joseph B. Tate (Leo G. Carroll) who has come to Catalina Island to film his latest epic, a jungle picture.

When ill health forced Edna May Oliver out of this series, she was replaced first by Helen Broderick (MURDER ON THE BRIDLE PATH, 1935) and then by ZaSu Pitts (THE PLOT THICKENS, 1936 and FORTY NAUGHTY GIRLS, 1937) before the faltering property was brought to a halt.

MURDER ON DIAMOND ROW (United Artists, 1937) 75 minutes.

Producer, Alexander Korda; director, William K. Howard; based on the novel *The Squeaker* by Edgar Wallace; adaptors, Bryan Edgar Wallace, Edward O. Berkman; songs, William Kernell and Berkman; camera, Georges Perinal; editor, Russell Lloyd.

Edmund Lowe (Barrabal); Sebastian Shaw (Frank Sutton); Ann Todd (Carol Stedman); Tamara Desni (Tamara); Robert Newton (Larry Graeme); Allan Jeayes (Inspector Elford); Alastair Sim (Joshua

Collie); Stewart Rome (Superintendent Marshall); Mabel Terry-Lewis (Mrs. Stedman); Gordon McLeod (Mr. Field).

One-time police Inspector Barrabal (Edmund Lowe) has become a drunk and is on the skids when shipper Frank Sutton (Sebastian Shaw) tries to rehabilitate him with a job. Meanwhile, gambler Larry Graeme (Robert Newton) is murdered for double-crossing a notorious underworld figure known only as "The Squeaker" and Scotland Yard Inspector Elford (Allen Jeayes) is not able to bring in the criminal. He wants Barrabal to do the dirty job. Also investigating the case is newspaperman Joshua Collie (Alastair Sim). At a society party Barrabal meets Carol Stedman (Ann Todd) and they are attracted to each other although she is Sutton's fiancée. In reality, Barrabal is working undercover to catch The Squeaker and he seeks out Graeme's girlfriend, nightclub entertainer Tamara (Tamara Desni), for information, but she too is murdered. Winning Carol's confidence and eventual love, Barrabal unmasks The Squeaker and traps him in the confines of Scotland Yard.

American star Edmund Lowe came to England to star in this well-paced and "Slick thriller" (David Quinlan, *British Sound Films,* 1984) which Bryan Edgar Wallace co-adapted to the screen from the popular 1927 novel by his father, Edgar Wallace. When United Artists debuted the film in England in August 1937, as THE SQUEAKER, *Variety* reported, "Barest framework of Wallace, Sr., remains, but it has been changed from a whodunit to a newer formula, that of revealing early in the unreeling the identity of the arch criminal . . . interest in the film is wholly dependent on how the Yard unravels the crime." When United Artists released the film in the United States in November of 1937 it changed the title to MURDER ON DIAMOND ROW, since neither American exhibitors nor filmgoers were familiar with the derivation of the film's title (i.e., squeaker, which is underworld parlance for a police informer). Four minutes had been shorn from the running time, but, said *Variety,* "Even more could have been trimmed, including the two mediocre songs ["He's Gone" and "I Can't Get Along Without You"] in night club scenes." The trade paper forecast, ". . . may get by in America, though distinctly for the dualers."

Edgar Wallace's THE SQUEAKER was first filmed in England in 1930 with Wallace himself adapting the film to the screen and directing. Percy Marmont was the detective on the trail of the master supercriminal. The next year Fritz Rasp starred in a German version of the novel, DER ZINKER [The Squeaker], and in the supporting cast was S. Z. "Cuddles" Sakall, long before his successful Hollywood career. In 1963 the property was remade in West Germany by director Alfred Vohrer as DER ZINKER [The Squeaker] but it was issued directly to the U.S. in a dubbed version called THE SQUEAKER. The revamped and contemporized plot has a writer, the head of a newspaper syndicate, and a reporter marked for death after having seen the mysterious master criminal, The Squeaker.

MURDER ON THE BLACKBOARD (RKO, 1934) 72 minutes.

Associate producer, Kenneth MacGowan; director, George Archainbaud; based on the novel by Stuart Palmer; adaptor, Willis Goldbeck; music director, Max Steiner; camera, Nick Musuraca; editor, Archie Marshek.

Edna May Oliver (Hildegarde Martha Withers); James Gleason (Inspector Oscar Piper); Bruce Cabot (Addison Stevens); Gertrude Michael (Janey Davis); Regis Toomey (Smiley North); Edgar Kennedy (Sergeant Donahue); Tully Marshall (MacFarland); Jackie Searle (Leland); Fredrik Vogeding (Olaf Sweitzer); Barbara Fritchie (Louise Halloran); Gustav von Seyffertitz (Dr. Max Bloom); Tom Herbert (McTeague); Jed Prouty (Dr. Lewis).

At a Gotham grammar school principal, MacFarland (Tully

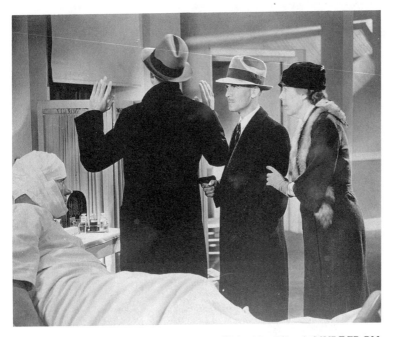

Edgar Kennedy, Bruce Cabot, James Gleason and Edna May Oliver in MURDER ON THE BLACKBOARD (1934).

Marshall) is attracted to his pretty secretary, Janey Davis (Gertrude Michael), who has taken a gun from the desk of one of the teachers, Louise Halloran (Barbara Fritchie), because she fears for Louise, who is ill and depressed. Janey loves science teacher Addison Stevens (Bruce Cabot) who admits to her that he once had a romance with Louise. While staying after school with a disobedient pupil (Jackie Searle), Miss Hildegarde Withers (Edna May Oliver) discovers Louise's dead body in the school cloak room. She sends for police Inspector Oscar Piper (James Gleason), who arrives with Sergeant Donahue (Edgar Kennedy) and Officer Smiley North (Regis Toomey). The corpse has disappeared but later reappears in the furnace, leading Piper to arrest school janitor Olaf Sweitzer (Fredrik Vogeding). Miss Withers learns that Louise's roommate, Janey, had staked the dead girl to a winning lottery ticket worth $300,000 and it was Sweitzer who had sold her the ticket. When principal MacFarland asks Miss Withers to investigate the murder, she finds a fragment of a love letter the man had written to the dead girl. However, he claims he broke off his relationship with her when she began dating Stevens. During the subsequent investigation, an attempt is made on Miss Wither's life, and, later, Withers, Piper and North find a tunnel leading from the school into a liquor warehouse where Sweitzer stole the liquor he sold to Louise. Miss Withers determines who murdered Louise by consulting Dr. Max Bloom (Gustav von Seyffertitz). She and Piper set a trap for the killer by having the hospitalized Sergeant Donahue announce that he knows who injured him. It develops that the killer had been poisoning Louise with an oil derivative in her liquor. When she had not died quickly enough for him, the murderer killed her outright.

Based on Stuart Palmer's 1932 novel of the same title, MURDER ON THE BLACKBOARD is the second of three movies in which Edna May Oliver enacts the role of snoopy school teacher sleuth Miss Hildegarde Withers—the first being THE PENGUIN POOL MURDER (1932) and the third, MURDER ON A HONEYMOON (1935), *qq.v.* These three are among the best detective films produced by Hollywood in the 1930s, mainly because of their strong plots, polished production values and the chemistry of Edna May Oliver as Miss Withers and James Gleason as her slow-witted nemesis, Oscar Piper. Of the trio, MURDER ON THE BLACKBOARD is the best, as it presents Miss Withers* solving a murder

---

*Mordaunt Hall (*New York Times*) enthused, "Having established herself as a criminologist with amazing powers of observation and deduction . . . the willowy Edna May Oliver continues her rivalry of Sherlock Holmes, Father Brown, Philo Vance and Charlie Chan. . . . What might mean nothing to any one with an average mentality is a link in the chain of evidence to Miss Withers. She goes so far as to map

occurring in the (home) environment of her school. The supporting cast is also superior, especially Gertrude Michael as the lovely Janey, Regis Toomey as the policeman subordinate, and Tully Marshall as the lecherous principal.

MURDER ON THE CAMPUS (Chesterfield, 1934) 73 minutes.

Producer, George R. Batcheller; director, Richard Thorpe; based on the novel *The Campanile Murders* by Whitman Chambers; adaptor; Andrew Moses; art director, Edward Jewell; music director, Abe Meyer; assistant director, Melville Shyer; sound, L. E. Clark; camera, M. A. Anderson.

Shirley Grey (Lillian Voyne); Charles Starrett (Bill Bartlett); J. Farrell MacDonald (Captain Ed Kyne); Ruth Hall (Ann Michaels); Edward Van Sloan (Professor Hawley); Maurice Black (Blackie Atwater); Harry Bowen (Reporter); Dewey Robinson (Charlie Lorrimer); Jane Keckley (Hilda Lund); Harrison Greene (Brock).

Screen sleuths have come in many guises other than professional gumshoes and one of the most common types is the newspaper reporter snooping out a story and solving the case. This occurs in MURDER ON THE CAMPUS, in which future cowboy star Charles Starrett is cast as a newshound who clears up several homicides. "Presenting in stirring drama a ridiculously simple solution of the mystery of three seemingly impossible murders," read the poster advertisement for this flavorful and fast-moving poverty row effort.

Young newspaperman Bill Bartlett (Charles Starrett) is researching a series of articles on co-eds working their way through college. One of them is nightclub thrush Lillian Voyne (Shirley Grey), who refuses to be interviewed in depth by Bartlett because of her gangster boss Blackie Atwater (Maurice Black). Bartlett tells Lillian he thinks she loves a goldbricking school athlete who has a campus job ringing the college's belltower chimes nightly. That evening the chimes ring and, when a shot is heard, Bartlett rushes to the tower, finds the athlete murdered and awaits the arrival of police Captain Ed Kyne (J. Farrell MacDonald). When a gun, with the same calibre bullet which killed the student, is found in Lillian's off-campus apartment, she is implicated in the crime, as is another co-ed, Ann Michaels (Ruth Hall), who turns out to be the murdered

---

out various phases of the killing. . . . This bright woman can make almost any one change his mind by a word or two." As for the movie itself, the reviewer added, ". . . When most such yarns depend largely on spine-chilling effects and screams this MURDER ON THE BLACKBOARD has the saving grace of a sense of humor. Miss Withers affords plenty of laughter, both by the gravity with which she approaches her task and the manner in which she is enabled to chuckle over the bolstered-up evidence of Piper and his underlings."

man's secret wife. Later, a crooked lawyer involved in the case is found dead and Bartlett asks chemistry professor and amateur detective Professor Hawley (Edward Van Sloan) for assistance. When Lillian is arrested for the crime, Bartlett, with or without Hawley's help, must solve the case.

Based on Whitman Chambers' 1933 novel, *The Campanile Murders,* the film's weakness is that it does not live up pictorially to its title. Outside of a brief studio-bound campus scene at the time of the initial murder, there is little of the ambiance of a college. Director Richard Thorpe would have been wise to have sent a second unit to a nearby campus for insert shots to better depict a college setting.

MURDER ON THE ORIENT EXPRESS (Paramount, 1974) C 128 minutes.

Producers, John Brabourne, Richard Goodwin; director, Sidney Lumet; based on the novel by Agatha Christie; screenplay, Paul Dehn; production designer/costumes, Tony Walton; art director, Jack Stephens; music, Richard Rodney Bennett; assistant director,

Martin Balsam, Lauren Bacall, George Coulouris and Albert Finney in MURDER ON THE ORIENT EXPRESS (1974).

Ted Sturgis; sound, Peter Handford, Bill Rowe; camera, Geoffrey Unsworth; editor, Anne V. Coates.

Albert Finney (Hercule Poirot); Lauren Bacall (Mrs. Hubbard); Martin Balsam (Bianchi); Ingrid Bergman (Greta Ohlsson); Jacqueline Bisset (Countess Andrenyi); Jean-Pierre Cassel (Pierre Paul Michel); Sean Connery (Colonel Arbuthnot); John Gielgud (Beddoes); Wendy Hiller (Princess Dragomiroff); Rachel Roberts (Hildegarde Schmidt); Anthony Perkins (Hector McQueen); Vanessa Redgrave (Mary Debenham); Richard Widmark (Ratchett); Michael York (Count Andrenyi); Colin Blakely (Hardman); George Coulouris (Dr. Constantine); Denis Quilley (Foscarelli); Vernon Dobtcheff (Concierge); Jeremy Lloyd (A.D.C.); John Moffatt (Chief Attendant).

Fearing what filmmakers might do to her 1934 novel (called *Murder on the Calais Coach* in the U.S.), Agatha Christie would not permit filming of *Murder on the Orient Express* for three decades. However, in the early 1970s she gave producers John Brabourne and Richard Goodwin her approval. Under Sidney Lumet's direction they assembled a huge cast of stars and provided a sumptuous production for the author's red-herring-laden story of murder on a train. The feature grossed over $19,000,000 at the box-office and became "the most successful British film ever made" (Michael Tennenbaum, *The New Bedside, Bathtub & Armchair Companion to Agatha Christie,* 1986).

In the 1930s, meticulous Belgian detective Hercule Poirot (Albert Finney), with the aid of his friend Bianchi (Martin Balsam), an Italian train company director, is able, at the last minute, to get a berth on the Orient Express, in the Calais Coach, on its way to Constantinople. A number of rather wealthy people, from various backgrounds, are also aboard, but the coterie is dominated by crooked and nasty Ratchett (Richard Widmark), an American millionaire, traveling with his secretary, Hector McQueen (Anthony Perkins) and butler Beddoes (John Gielgud). When Ratchett is found murdered, repeatedly stabbed, in his berth, Poirot is given the go-ahead to investigate. The suspects include both the murdered man's employees plus obnoxious Mrs. Hubbard (Lauren Bacall), a rich American; Greta Ohlsson (Ingrid Bergman), a missionary from Sweden; Hungarian Count (Michael York) and Countess Andrenyi (Jacqueline Bisset); British Colonel Arbuthnot (Sean Connery); and Russian Princess Dragomiroff (Wendy Hiller) and her servant Hildegarde Schmidt (Rachel Roberts). Poirot finds the situation filled with clues and in the desolate and snow-covered expanse of Yugoslavia he has the coach detached from the rest of the train and sets about solving the murder, realizing that all the suspects have solid motives for the killing. A chance clue leads to information about the dead man's nefarious past and to Poirot's final solving of the complicated web of murder, deceit and revenge.

Albert Finney was nominated for an Academy Award for his work as Hercule Poirot, he of the slicked down hair and the curled moustache. Certainly he has been the screen's most substantial Poirot to date, bringing alive Ms. Christie's eccentric little Belgian detective to perfection, both in looks and action. Ingrid Bergman won a Best Supporting Actress Award. Oscar nominations went to John Gielgud for Best Supporting Actor, to Paul Dehn for his script, to Geoffrey Unsworth for cinematography, to Tony Walton for costumes, and to Richard Rodney Bennett for the music. (Bergman, Gielgud and Bennett won British Academy Awards for their contributions to this production.)

"This isn't a 'thriller,' because we're not thrilled, or scared— only amused. The murder itself has a certain antiseptic, ritualistic quality. . . . The movie provides a good time, high style, a loving salute to an earlier period of filmmaking. . . . It ends with a very long scene in which Poirot asks everyone to be silent, please, while he explains his various theories of the case. He does in great detail, and it's fun of a rather malicious sort watching a dozen high-priced stars keep their mouths shut and just listen while Finney masterfully dominates the scene" (Roger Ebert's *Movie Home Companion-1988,* 1987).

MURDER OVER NEW YORK (Twentieth Century-Fox, 1940) 65 minutes.

Producer, Sol M. Wurtzel; director, Harry Lachman; based on the character created by Earl Derr Biggers; screenplay, Lester Ziffren; art directors, Richard Day, Lewis Creber; music director, Emil Newman; camera, Virgil Miller; editor, Louis Loeffler.

Sidney Toler (Charlie Chan); Marjorie Weaver (Patricia West); Robert Lowery (David Elliott); Ricardo Cortez (George Kirby); Donald MacBride (Inspector Vance); Melville Cooper (Herbert Fenton); Joan Valerie (June Preston); Kane Richmond (Ralph Percy); Victor Sen Yung (Jimmy Chan); John Sutton (Richard Jeffrey); Leyland Hodgson (Boggs); Clarence Muse (Butler); Frederick Worlock (Hugh Drake); Lal Chand Mehra (Ramullah); Frank Coghlan, Jr. (Gilroy); Shemp Howard (Shorty McCoy); Trevor Bardette (Suspect).

Charlie Chan (Sidney Toler) is about to fly to New York City for a police convention. On his flight he encounters an old friend, former Scotland Yard Inspector Hugh Drake (Frederick Worlock), who is working for British military intelligence in trying to find Paul

Harvo, the head of a spy ring which has been sabotaging bombers. Drake is on the flight to New York City as he hopes to locate Narvo's wife, who has left him. In Manhattan Chan is greeted by number two son Jimmy (Victor Sen Yung), who has arrived to see the World's Fair. Drake is staying with airplane manufacturing company president George Kirby (Ricardo Cortez) and when Chan goes to see him, he and Kirby find Drake dead, the victim of poison gas. Chan calls in police Inspector Vance (Donald MacBride) and the suspects include many of the guests who attended a party Kirby hosted for Drake. They are: actress June Preston (Joan Valerie); Herbert Fenton (Melville Cooper), Drake's school chum; airplane designer Ralph Percy (Kane Richmond); stockbroker Richard Jeffrey (John Sutton); and Kirby's valet, Boggs (Leyland Hodgson). The butler (Clarence Muse) informs Chan and Vance that chemist David Elliott (Robert Lowery) had visited Drake before he died. From Miss Preston, Chan learns that Drake was searching for her friend, Patricia West (Marjorie Weaver), who is in love with Elliott. Visiting Miss West, Chan discovers that she is Narvo's ex-wife, and while he is there an attempt is made on their lives. The assailant turns out to be Ramullah (Lal Chand Mehra), Narvo's Hindu servant, but he is killed at the police station by a bullet fired from a nearby building. Later Kirby is found dead in his apartment and the following day Charlie invites all the suspects to the metropolitan airport to watch a test of a new bomber designed by Percy for Kirby's company. Chan, Jimmy and the suspects go up in the plane along with Fenton, who stops a gas bomb, which spies had planted aboard, from exploding. When the plane lands he is arrested. He confesses to being part of the operation but when he is about to name Narvo, who has undergone plastic surgery, an attempt is made on his life. At this juncture Chan singles out Narvo from among the remaining suspects.

"Story is regulation formula for the Chan series, and will satisfy the followers of the series as whodunit entertainment," declared *Variety*. Overall this feature presents a fair mystery with a goodly collection of red herring suspects, and the killer is particularly hard to identify. One amusing scene details a police lineup as the cops look for the Hindu servant. Among the suspects on the lineup is one of The Three Stooges, Shemp Howard, here cast as Shorty McCoy, a crook masquerading as a fakir.

MURDER OVER NEW YORK has its full complement of Chan wise sayings: "Same leopard can hide beneath different spots," "Faces may alter but fingerprints never lie," "Needle can be found when correct thread located," "Coincidence like ancient egg—leave unpleasant odor," "Nut easy to crack often empty," "Aid from number two son like interest on mortgage—unable to escape,"

"Person who asks riddle should know answer," and "Wishful thinking sometimes lead to blind alley."

MURDER SHE SAID (Metro-Goldwyn-Mayer, 1961) 87 minutes.
Producer, George H. Brown; director, George Pollock; based
on the novel *4:50 From Paddington* by Agatha Christie; adaptor,
screenplay, David Pursall, Jack Seddon; art director, Harry White;
wardrobe, Felix Evans; makeup, Eddie Knight; assistant director,
Douglas Hickox; music/music conductor, Ron Goodwin; recording
supervisor, A. W. Watkins; sound, Cyril Swern, J. B. Smith; dubbing
editor, Robert Carick; camera, Geoffrey Faithfull; editor, Ernest
Walter.

Margaret Rutherford (Miss Jane Marple); Arthur Kennedy (Dr.
Quimper); Muriel Pavlow (Emma Ackenthorpe); James Robertson-
Justice (Ackenthorpe); Thorley Walters (Cedric Ackenthorpe);
Charles Tingwell (Inspector Craddock); Conrad Phillips (Harold);
Ronald Howard (Brian Eastley); Joan Hickson (Mrs. Kidder); Stringer
Davis (Mr. Stringer); Ronnie Raymond (Alexander Eastley); Gerald
Cross (Albert); Michael Golden (Hillman); Barbara Leake (Mrs.
Stainton); Gordon Harris (Bacon); Peter Butterworth (Ticket Col-
lector); Richard Briers ("Mrs. Binster"); Lucy Griffiths (Lucy).

In 1960 Metro-Goldwyn-Mayer purchased the screen rights to
most of Agatha Christie's published novels and short stories for
$3,000,000, planning to develop a television series around them.
However, the studio decided to make a film called MEET MISS
MARPLE, taken from the 1957 novel *4:50 From Paddington*,* and
cast Margaret Rutherford (who initially declined the part) as the
spinster detective Miss Jane Marple, who lives in St. Mary's Mead. In
the cast was Miss Rutherford's husband, Stringer Davis, as the local
librarian, Mr. Stringer, who aids Miss Marple in the case. Margaret
Rutherford would do three more entries in the series and her
husband would continue to play Mr. Stringer. Ironically, the physically large Miss Rutherford (with the pop-owl eyes and multi-chins)
did not resemble the Christie character; Miss Marple was a tall, thin
woman with blue eyes and a wrinkled countenance.

MURDER SHE SAID (the film's release title) has Miss Jane
Marple (Margaret Rutherford) riding a train from London and
reading a mystery novel when she happens to see a man strangling a
lady on a passing train. She reports the bizarre incident to the police
but Inspector Craddock (Charles Tingwell) does not believe her.

---

*Agatha Christie's novel *4:50 From Paddington*, the basis for MURDER SHE SAID,
was re-titled *What Mrs. McGillicuddy Saw!* for its American publication and in 1961
was reprinted as *Murder She Said.*

Insulted by his abrupt dismissal of her wild story, Miss Marple determines to investigate the matter. She takes a job at the estate of the elderly Ackenthorpe (James Robertson-Justice), working as a maid. Miss Marple believes the dead woman's body was thrown off the train near the estate and she is proved correct when she locates the corpse hidden in an outbuilding on the estate. At first it is suspected that the victim was from France and during the last war had been wed to Ackenthorpe. The deceased makes suspects of Ackenthorpe's relatives, but two of his sons are also killed. Setting a trap, Miss Marple outmaneuvers the killer, who had murdered his own wife on the train and then planned to kill off all the other Ackenthorpe relatives except daughter Emma (Muriel Pavlow), whom he planned to wed to gain the estate.

The *New York Times* endorsed, "Yes, it is an Agatha Christie special, sprinkled with the whodunit queen's matchless red herrings and dominated, start to finish, by the grand comic sweep and rubber-faced sparkle of Margaret Rutherford, whose blustery presence underscores both the humor and suspense. The general treatment is pleasantly, wryly wise, British style, under George Pollock's direction of a frightfully apt cast."

The black-and-white lensed MURDER SHE SAID proved to be a box-office success, though more so in Britain, where it was issued in the fall of 1961, than in its 1962 general U.S. playdates. Next came MURDER AT THE GALLOP, which was based on a Hercule Poirot novel, *After the Funeral* (1953), with Miss Marple replacing the Belgian sleuth. The narrative has Jane Marple (Margaret Rutherford) and Mr. Stringer (Stringer Davis) collecting charity money (for The Reformed Criminals Assistance League) when they see the elderly Mr. Enderby (Finlay Currie) fall to his death, allegedly being frightened by a cat (he feared felines). Miss Marple attends the reading of the will at his estate and finds that his wealth will be divided among four relatives. She also notices a cat on the premises. The dead man's sister (Katya Douglas) believes her brother was murdered and she too is killed. Her companion (Flora Robson) blames the crime on Miss Marple, who is absolved by Inspector Craddock (Charles Tingwell). To be closer to the case Miss Marple moves to The Gallop, a riding academy operated by the murdered man's nephew, Hector Enderby (Robert Morley). She finds out that the three surviving relatives seek a painting belonging to the murdered sister; while it is presumed worthless, the picture is actually a priceless French masterpiece. Another relative, George Crossfield (Robert Urquhart), is killed and Miss Marple pinpoints the killer but lacks the necessary evidence for an arrest. She establishes a plan in which she will be the next victim. When the murderer strikes, the police arrest the culprit. As she leaves The Gallop, Enderby asks Miss Marple to marry him, but she declines.

MURDER AT THE GALLOP is a sparkling mystery highlighted by Margaret Rutheford's ingratiating (if broad) work as snoopy Miss Marple; her riding sequence is particularly amusing. Also lighthearted is the sequence in which she dances the Twist and then feigns a heart attack to obtain the necessary evidence to convict the murderer.

Next came 1964's MURDER AHOY, which was not issued in Great Britain until 1965, and then minus almost twenty minutes of running time. It is also the only feature of the quartet of Miss Marple entries starring Margaret Rutherford to be based on an original screenplay and not a Christie work. Miss Christie would say of the film, it is ". . . one of the silliest things you ever saw! It got very bad reviews, I'm delighted to say."

The plot has Miss Marple (Margaret Rutherford) as a trustee of an organization (Cape of Good Hope Reclamation Trust) devoted to the rehabilitation of juvenile delinquents. At a board meeting one of the other trustees (Henry Longhurst) dies and Miss Marple finds out there had been poison in his snuff. Since the information the dead man was to present concerned the *H.M.S. Battledore,* a ship used by the group to house the juveniles, Miss Marple goes aboard, leaving her friend Mr. Stringer (Stringer Davis) ashore. Miss Marple finds out that the young men are not being reformed on the ship but are being taught larcenous activities. Compton (Francis Matthews), who has been instructing the boys in house robbing, and matron Shirley Boston (Norma Foster) are murdered. The amateur sleuth deduces that the commander (William Mervyn) has been embezzling money from the charity for years and has committed the crimes to hide his thefts. When Miss Marple confronts him, the commander engages her in a fencing match, but she holds him at bay until Police Inspector Craddock (Charles Tingwell) rescues her.

Regarding MURDER AHOY, *Variety* reported, "In spite of . . . clichés, including people creeping along dark corridors, sudden screams, and quick searches of empty rooms, the story sparkles. . . ."

The last of the four Miss Marple/Margaret Rutherford features is MURDER MOST FOUL, issued in 1965. It had been made prior to MURDER AHOY but was released after it. Like MURDER AT THE GALLOP it was taken from a Hercule Poirot mystery, *Mrs. McGinty's Dead* (1952), not a Miss Marple work. This adventure has bull-headed Miss Marple (Margaret Rutherford) as the member of a jury trying the case of a man accused of murdering his landlady. When Miss Marple is the sole juror to vote for acquittal a mistrial is declared and she embarks on tracking the real murderer. With ever-willing Mr. Stringer (Stringer Davis) offering his bumbling help, she searches the victim's home and finds she was once an actress who worked with a touring company owned by Driffold Cosgood (Ron Moody). Miss Marple pretends to be an actress and applies for a job with the repertory group. Cosgood accepts her, thinking he might be able to bilk money out of her to save the financially ailing outfit. Miss Marple relays her suspicions about the murder to Inspector Craddock (Charles Tingwell) who, of course, believes the original accused man is guilty and refuses to help her. When two members of the repertory troupe are then murdered Miss Marple suspects another in the group as the culprit, as well as being the killer of the landlady. With more investigation she is able to place the criminal responsibility on one of the performers whose mother had been hanged for murder. The landlady had been blackmailing him to keep this information secret.

Variety acknowledged, "Miss Marple is beginning to wear a little thin as she retraces many of the same comedy situation and even some similar dialog. Audiences who have seen the other pix can pretty well guess the tale. . . ."

In retrospect, the quartet of films in which Margaret Rutherford (who won a Best Supporting Actress Academy Award for THE V.I.P.s, 1963) enacted Miss Jane Marple are delicious comedy mysteries held together by the engaging, if eccentric, acting style of the imposing star. Following these features she returned to the role yet one more time when she and Stringer Davis made cameo appearances as Miss Marple and Mr. Stringer in another Agatha Christie comedy-mystery, THE ALPHABET MURDERS (1966), *q.v.*

Angela Lansbury, who has had great success in the 1980s as a contemporary Miss Marple-like detective on CBS-TV's "Murder, She Wrote," played Miss Marple in THE MIRROR CRACK'D (1980), *q.v.* Helen Hayes would play the intrepid crime solver in two TV movies, A CARIBBEAN MYSTERY (1983), and MURDER WITH MIRRORS (1985), *qq.v.* In 1987 Joan Hickson, who had played a subordinate role in MURDER SHE SAID, was a solid Miss Marple in the British teleseries, "Agatha Christie's Miss Marple," which was serialized in the U.S. on PBS-TV's "Mystery!" series.

MY FAVORITE BRUNETTE (Paramount, 1947) 88 minutes.

Producer, Daniel Dare; director, Elliott Nugent; screenplay, Edmund Beloin, Jack Rose; art directors, Hans Dreier, Earl Hedrick; set decorators, Sam Comer, John MacNeil; music/music director, Robert Emmett Dolan; song, Jay Livingston and Ray Evans; assistant director, Mel Epstein; sound, Harold Lewis, Gene Garvin; special effects, Gordon Jennings; camera, Lionel Lindon; editor, Ellsworth Hoagland.

Bob Hope (Ronnie Jackson); Dorothy Lamour (Carlotta Montay); Peter Lorre (Kismet); Lon Chaney (Willie); John Hoyt (Dr. Lundau); Charles Dingle (Major Simon Montague); Reginald Denny (James Colling); Frank Puglia (Baron Montay); Ann Doran (Miss Rogers); Willard Robertson (Prison Warden); Jack LaRue (Tony); Charles Arnt (Crawford); Garry Owen, Richard Keane (Reporters); Tony Caruso ("Raft" Character); Matt McHugh ("Cagney" Character); George Lloyd (Prison Guard—Sergeant); Jack Clifford (Prison Guard—Captain); Ray Teal, Al Hill (State Troopers); Boyd Davis (Mr. Dawsen); Clarence Muse (Man in Condemned Row); Helena Evans (Mabel); Roland Soo Hoo (Baby Fong); Jean Wong (Mrs. Fong); Charley Cooley (Waiter); John Westley (Doctor); Ted Rand (Waiter Captain); Tom Dillon (Policeman); Harland Tucker (Room Clerk); Reginald Simpson (Assistant Manager); James Flavin (Mac, the Detective); Jim Pierce, Budd Fine (Detectives); John Tyrrell

Lon Chaney, Jr. and Peter Lorre in MY FAVORITE BRUNETTE (1947).

(Bell Captain); Joe Recht (Newsboy); Bing Crosby (Executioner); Alan Ladd (Sam McCloud); Eddie Johnson (Caddy); Betty Farrington (Matron); Brandon Hurst (Butler); Jack Chefe (Henri, the Waiter).

Exotic Carlotta Montay (Dorothy Lamour) appears at the office of San Francisco baby photographer Ronnie Jackson (Bob Hope), thinking he is private eye Sam McCloud (Alan Ladd), who is away on a case. Carlotta wants Jackson to find her missing uncle, Baron Montay (Frank Puglia), who has come to the U.S. on a secret mission and has been kidnapped. Attracted to Carlotta and always wanting to be a detective, rambunctious Jackson takes the dangerous case. Before long he has possession of the secret plan for a uranium mine, which is sought by a gang of international uranium smugglers led by Kismet (Peter Lorre) and his dim-witted, but hulking associate, Willie (Lon Chaney). The gang frames bumbling, wise-cracking Jackson for the Baron's murder and he is tried and convicted, but ends up saving himself (much to the chagrin of San Quentin prison executioner Bing Crosby!), by bringing in the spy gang and winning Carlotta's affections.

This spunky burlesque (in production for 54 days) of private eye films received critical endorsements. *Time* magazine acknowledged that the film ". . . is a well-roasted rib of the fancy talk and fancy incident served up by Raymond Chandler and other whodunit authors of the rough & tough school. . . ." *Newsweek* magazine decided Bob Hope's detective character was "a Raymond Chandler's Philip Marlowe who has been raised on Winnie-the-Pooh."

MY GUN IS QUICK (United Artists, 1957) 91 minutes.

Executive producer, Victor Saville; producers/directors, George A. White, Phil Victor; based on the novel by Mickey Spillane; screenplay, Richard Powell, Richard Collins; art director, Boris Leven; music, Marlin Skiles; camera, Harry Neuman; editor, Frank Sullivan.

Robert Bray (Mike Hammer); Whitney Blake (Nancy); Pat Donahue (Dione); Donald Randolph (Holloway); Pamela Duncan (Velda); Booth Colman (Captain Pat); Jan Chaney (Red); Gina Core (Maria); Richard Garland (Lou); Charles Boaz (Gangster); Peter Mamakos (La Roche); Claire Carleton (Proprietress); Phil Arnold (Shorty); John Dennis (Al); Terrence De Marney (Jean); Jackie Paul (Stripper); Leon Askin (Teller); Jack Holland (Hotel Clerk).

Producer Victor Saville had brought Mickey Spillane's private eye Mike Hammer to the screen in I, THE JURY (1953) and KISS ME DEADLY (1955), *qq.v.*, plus a non-Hammer Spillane opus called THE LONG WAIT (1954). In 1957 he produced his final Mike Hammer adventure, MY GUN IS QUICK, based on Spillane's

Whitney Blake, Donald Randolph, Patricia Donahue and Robert Bray in MY GUN IS QUICK (1957).

1950 novel, the second of the Mike Hammer books. This film, however, does not boast the solid production values of the previous Hammer exercises and despite its popular hero and the then-in-vogue brutality, the feature was unsuccessful. Mike Hammer would not reappear on film until 1963, when Mickey Spillane himself played his detective hero in THE GIRL HUNTERS, *q.v.*

Private eye Mike Hammer (Robert Bray) becomes entangled in a case concerning the recovery of a fortune in gems which were taken from the enemy during World War II by Holloway (Donald Randolph). Aided by secretary Velda (Pamela Duncan), Hammer gets onto his trail but realizes that two gangs are also after the jewels. Several murders take place, including those of several beautiful women. Eventually Hammer meets Nancy (Whitney Blake) and she attempts to aid him and his policeman pal, Captain Pat (Booth Colman), locate the treasure. Finally Hammer corners both sets of hoodlum on a fishing boat and in a fight one gang is done in by the detective. At that point he discovers Nancy is behind the other operations and he turns her over to the law.

MY GUN IS QUICK maintained the Mike Hammer quota for violence, with the plot boasting seven murders and two fights, plus the detective's involvement with a quintet of attractive females. As a result, *Variety* opined, ". . . senseless brutality, murky plotting and unsubtle sex seems to have diminishing appeal and prospects for this outing seem milder." Don Miller commented in "Private Eyes" (*Focus on Film* magazine, Autumn 1975), "The film story was a routine one, as was Robert Bray's performance as the third Mike Hammer. Saville's production wasn't as tidy as his previous efforts, with a lot of tedious car pursuits taking up too much time, and a tatty physical look."

MYSTERIOUS INTRUDER (Columbia, 1946) 62 minutes.

Producer, Rudolph C. Fothow; director, William Castle; based on the radio series "The Whistler"; story/screenplay, Eric Taylor; assistant director, Carl Hiecke; art director, Hans Radon; set decorator, Robert Priestley; music director, Mischa Bakaleinikoff; camera, Philip Tannura; editor, Dwight Caldwell.

Richard Dix (Don Gale); Barton MacLane (Detective Taggart); Nina Vale (Joan Hill); Regis Toomey (James Summers); Helen Mowery (Freda Hanson); Mike Mazurki (Harry Pontos); Pamela Blake (Elora Lund); Charles Lane (Detective Burns); Paul Burns (Edward Stillwell); Kathleen Howard (Rose Denning); Harlan Briggs (Brown).

MYSTERIOUS INTRUDER is the fifth entry in the diverse but entertaining The Whistler series, based on the popular radio program. It is a highly satisfying "B" detective thriller and *Variety* reported, ". . . This film paces itself with a nicety that should prove attractive to meller fans. With its surprise ending, frequent plot twists and generally excellent casting, MYSTERIOUS INTRUDER proves a consistently entertaining hour's performance. . . . Direction of William Castle is nicely done. He keeps the action moving at a lively pace. . . ."

Private detective Don Gale (Richard Dix) is hired to locate a missing girl who purportedly has possession of a valuable treasure. Several murders have occurred regarding the treasure and police Detective Taggart (Barton MacLane) is pursuing the killer. Gale learns that a Swedish millionaire has offered a hefty reward for the treasure, which turns out to be original Jenny Lind recordings. The investigation brings Gale into contact with a thug killer, Harry Pontos (Mike Mazurki), who works for the person responsible for the murders. Gale confronts the culprit behind all the trouble.

Don Miller observed in "Private Eyes" (*Focus on Film* magazine,

Autumn 1975), "Perhaps the best of the non-[Raymond] Chandler private eyes of the period came in a Columbia Grade-B. . . . [It] possessed a haunting atmosphere all of its own . . . and some unforgettable characters, such as Mike Mazurki's brutish killer, without a word of dialogue. Most haunting of all was the sleuth, Don Gale, as played by Richard Dix. 'I'm an unusual kind of detective,' says Dix early in the film, which is pure understatement. . . . Since the film was structured for supporting slots, the 62-minute running time didn't allow for any subtle or detailed character development . . . so there are certain aspects of Gale's psyche only hinted at, or at best sketched in . . . the effect is unsettling yet fascinating."

MYSTERY BROADCAST (Republic, 1943) 63 minutes.

Associate producer/director, George Sherman; screenplay, Dane Lussier, Gertrude Walker; art director, Russell Kimball; set decorator, Otto Siegel; costumes, Adele; music director, Morton Scott; assistant director, Kenneth Holmes; camera, William Bradford; editor, Arthur Roberts.

Frank Albertson (Michael Jerome); Ruth Terry (Jan Cornell); Nils Asther (Ricky Moreno); Wynne Gibson (Eve Stanley); Paul Harvey (A. J. Stanley); Mary Treen (Smitty); Addison Richards (Bill Burton); Joseph Crehan (Chief Daniels); Alice Fleming (Mida Kent); Francis Pierlot (Crunch); Ken Carpenter (Announcer); Emmett Vogan (Don Fletcher).

Jan Cornell (Ruth Terry) writes a weekly radio program in which bogus mysteries are solved for the listening audience. When the ratings for the show tumble, she decides to air the solutions to actual cases to bring back the listeners. She becomes intrigued with a long unsolved murder case and after she airs it, several murders occur which are tied to the original case. With the aid of her boyfriend, Michael Jerome (Frank Albertson), a rival mystery show writer, Jan embarks on solving the mystery herself, much to the chagrin of the local police chief (Joseph Crehan). Also enmeshed in the situation is bandleader Ricky Moreno (Nils Asther), who has been romancing Eve Stanley (Wynne Gibson), the wife of the show's sponsor (Paul Harvey). The crime solving writers get to the bottom of the case and bring in the guilty party.

MYSTERY BROADCAST was one of eight programmers producer/director George Sherman turned out for Republic in the 1941-43 period. Another was also a private eye mystery, X MARKS THE SPOT, *q.v. Variety* judged of MYSTERY BROADCAST, "George Sherman has taken a mystery script loaded with the usual mechanics and tailored an acceptable short-end dualer. . . . Film moves with good pace in spite of hackneyed story."

It should be noted that the film's premise may have been affected by the success of Red Skelton's trio of films: WHISTLING IN THE DARK (1941), *q.v.*, WHISTLING IN DIXIE (1942), and WHISTLING IN BROOKLYN (1943), in which he portrayed a radio sleuth called The Fox, who got embroiled in murder cases. Those MGM films, however, were comedies, while MYSTERY BROADCAST supplied equal doses of mystery and comedy. And for a change, it offered the obvious suspect as the actual killer.

MYSTERY HOUSE (Warner Bros., 1938) 56 minutes.

Associate producer, Byran Foy; director, Noel Smith; based on the novel *The Mystery of Hunting's End* by Mignon C. Eberhart; screenplay, Sherman L. Lowe, Robertson White; camera, L. William O'Connell; editor, Frank Magee.

Dick Purcell (Lance O'Leary); Ann Sheridan (Sarah Keate); Anne Nagel (Gwen Kingery); William Hopper (Lal Killian); Anthony Averill (Julian Barre); Dennie Moore (Annette); Hugh O'Connell (Newell Morse); Ben Welden (Gerald Frawley); Sheila Bromley (Terice Von Elm); Elspeth Dudgeon (Aunt Lucy Kingery); Anderson Lawlor (Joe Paggi); Trevor Bardette (Bruker); Eric Stanley (Huber Kingery); Jean Benedict (Helen Page); Jack Mower (Coroner); Stuart Holmes (Jury Foreman); Loia Cheaney (Secretary); John Harron (Director).

See: WHILE THE PATIENT SLEPT [essay].

THE MYSTERY OF EDWIN DROOD (Universal, 1935) 85 minutes.

Producer, Edmund Grainger; director, Stuart Walker; based on the novel by Charles Dickens; adaptors, Leopold Atlas, Bradley King; screenplay, John L. Balderston, Gladys Unger; camera, George Robinson.

Claude Rains (John Jasper); Douglass Montgomery (Neville Landless/Datchery); Heather Angel (Rosa Bud); David Manners (Edwin Drood); Valerie Hobson (Helena Landless); Francis L. Sullivan (Mr. Crisparkle); Walter Kingford (Hiram Grewglous); E. E. Clive (Thomas Sapsea); Vera Buckland (Tope); Forrester Harvey (Durdles); Louise Carter (Mrs. Crisparkle); Ethel Griffies (Miss Twinkleton); George Ernest (Deputy); Zeffie Tilbury (Opium Den Hag); George Breakston (Boy); and: J. M. Kerrigan.

Charles Dickens wrote *The Mystery of Edwin Drood* in 1870. It was intended to be printed in twelve monthly installments but only half of them were finished when the author died, leaving no notes as to the conclusion of the mystery which friend and fellow writer Wilkie Collins had urged him to write. The solution to the story has always enticed mystery fans and in 1935 Universal filmed the novel, with scripters John L. Balderson and Gladys Unger supplying their own finish to the literary work. The results are fairly engaging and are highlighted by an extremely good cast, with an outstanding performance by Forrester Harvey as the comical Durdles, the drunken cemetery caretaker. The feature, however, lacks the Dickensian flavor of Universal's previous effort, GREAT EXPEC-TATIONS (1934). For the screen adaptation of THE MYSTERY OF EDWIN DROOD the script writers made the mysterious character of Datchery into a detective who tracks down the mystery of the disappearance of Drood. Datchery, in reality, is the prime suspect, Neville Landless, disguised as an old man. The results led Andre Sennwald (*New York Times*) to decide, "Since the scenarists have elected to be orthodox in their solution, the photoplay wisely presents itself as a tale of horror rather than a hide-and-seek mystery."

Two young people, Edwin Drood (David Manners) and Rosa Bud (Heather Angel), are engaged because their parents had be-trothed them as children, although the two are not in love. Drood's uncle and guardian, John Jasper (Claude Rains), a cantor in the church, is a secret opium addict. Jasper also is Rosa's music teacher and lusts after his pupil. Half-caste Neville Landless (Douglass Montgomery) and his beautiful sister Helena (Valerie Hobson) come to live in the village and Landless is attracted to Rosa, which causes him and Drood to become sworn enemies. Thinking that Drood and Rosa will really wed, Jasper gives a dinner for Landless and Drood so that they will become friends. That night, Christmas Eve, is a terrible one, with a violent ice storm, and the next day Jasper reports Drood missing. A search is made but the young man is not found. Since Landless is the last person to have been seen with Drood he is accused of killing him. Landless runs away and soon an elderly man, Datchery, comes to the village and begins making inquiries into the case. He watches Jasper's house closely, and when an old woman (Zeffie Tilbury), who runs an opium den frequented by Jasper, arrives and tries to blackmail him, Jasper kills her and the old man is aware of the crime. The trail leads Datchery to Durdles (Forrester Harvey), the alcoholic caretaker of the local cemetery and crypts. Durdles takes the old man into the crypts, saying he had done the same earlier for Jasper. When it is discovered that one of the graves thought empty actually contains a body, the old man tries to open the grave as Durdles rushes for the law. Jasper has followed the two and tries to kill the old man, but in the scuffle Datchery's wig and beard are torn off, revealing Landless. The officials open the grave, find a body, and on it is a ring belonging to Drood. Now completely insane, Jasper confesses to the crime and, trying to escape, falls to his death from a high tower.

It is important to note that at least one person did try to complete the Dickens work. A printer, Thomas P. James, published his "finished" version of the novel in 1873, claiming that Dickens had revealed the remainder of the tale to him while he was in trances. Critics scoffed at the reconstructed narrative, but as late as 1927 Sir Arthur Conan Doyle (the author of Sherlock Holmes) investigated the case and reported James' work closely matched the feel of that of Dickens, although the finished manuscript was the young man's only literary work and was not in keeping with his limited education.

THE MYSTERY OF THE GOLDEN EYE   *see*   THE GOLDEN EYE.

NANCY DREW—DETECTIVE (Warner Bros., 1938) 67 minutes.

Associate producer, Bryan Foy; director, William Clemens; based on the novel *The Password to Larkspur Lane* by Carolyn Keene [Harriet Stratemeyer Adams]; screenplay, Kenneth Gamet; dialogue director, John Langan; costumes, Milo Anderson; camera, L. William O'Connell; editor, Frank Magee.

Bonita Granville (Nancy Drew); John Litel (Carson Drew); James Stephenson (Challon); Frankie Thomas (Ted Nickerson); Frank Orth (Inspector Milligan); Renie Riano (Effie Schneider); Helena Phillips Evans (Mary Eldridge); Charles Trowbridge (Hollister); Dick Purcell (Keifer); Ed Keane (Adam Thorne); Brandon Tynan (Dr. Spires); Vera Lewis (Miss Van Deering); Mae Busch (Miss Tyson); Tommy Bupp (Spud Murphy); Lottie Williams (Mrs. Spires).

Edmund Stratemeyer wrote the first trio of Nancy Drew books in 1930 before his death that year and his daughter, Harriet S. Adams, writing as Carolyn Keene, took over the series and turned out scores of popular books about the teenage detective before her death in 1983. As popular as ever, with copies sold around fifty million, the Nancy Drew books continue to be produced by anonymous writers using the Carolyn Keene moniker. Nancy Drew's screen career, however, was as brief as her literary career has been lengthy.

Warner Bros. purchased the screen rights to the Nancy Drew character and, in 1938, commenced a brief series about the teenager with NANCY DREW, DETECTIVE issued late that year. The plot has a wealthy woman giving $250,000 to a girl's school and then disappearing. People believe she has reneged on the gift but teenager Nancy Drew (Bonita Granville) thinks the woman has been abducted. She and her next door neighbor/boyfriend Ted Nickerson

(Frankie Thomas) intend to locate her. They find out that she has been kidnapped by a gang that is after the money and that she is being held prisoner in a remote country home. The lawbreakers learn Nancy is on their trail and they threaten her lawyer father, Carson Drew (John Litel). Nevertheless, he aids his daughter and Nickerson in finding the woman. With the assistance of police Inspector Milligan (Frank Orth) and his men, they arrest the gang leader, Keifer (Dick Purcell). *Variety* termed the effort, "Fairly worthwhile kid stuff. . . . Too light for adult fare. . . . Direction is acceptable, since it keeps the action spinning and doesn't let subtleties impede the story. Miss Granville is forthright and refreshing as the bright-eyed heroine. . . ."

In March, 1939 NANCY DREW, REPORTER was released, Bonita Granville, John Litel, and Frankie Thomas were back in their roles and director William Clemens and scripter Kenneth Gamut repeated their chores from the initial feature. In fact, all five would remain with the series throughout its four-picture run. Here Nancy (Bonita Granville) wins a newspaper writing contest and becomes a fledgling reporter. She is soon engulfed in a murder case which she solves eventually. In the fall of 1939 came NANCY DREW AND THE HIDDEN STAIRCASE, with Nancy (Bonita Granville) and Ted Nickerson (Frankie Thomas) looking into the murder of two old ladies who had willed their remote home to a children's hospital. Eventually, the two teenagers find that hoodlums want the land for a new racetrack. The *New York Journal-American* thought the entry a "diverting piece" but *Variety* countered that the plot was "shaky." The final Nancy Drew screen adventure was released at the end of 1939 and NANCY DREW—TROUBLE SHOOTER found the enterprising young lady trying to help one of her father's clients falsely accused of a killing he did not commit.

In 1977 the earnest juvenile crime solver returned for the ABC-TV series, "The Hardy Boys-Nancy Drew Show," with Pamela Sue Martin as Nancy and William Schallert as Carson Drew. In 1978 Janet Louise Johnson took over the Nancy Drew part but her stint was short-lived as Nancy's adventures were dropped from the series that year.

NANCY DREW AND THE HIDDEN STAIRCASE   *see*   NANCY DREW—DETECTIVE [essay].

NANCY DREW, REPORTER   *see*   NANCY DREW—DETECTIVE [essay].

NANCY DREW—TROUBLE SHOOTER *see* NANCY DREW—
DETECTIVE [essay].

NERO WOLFE (ABC-TV, 12/19/79) Color 100 minutes.
  Executive producer, Emmett G. Lavery, Jr.; producer, Everett
Chambers; director, Frank D. Gilroy; based on the novel *The
Doorbell Rang* by Rex Stout; teleplay, Gilroy; art director, John
Beckman; music, Leonard Rosenman; camera, Ric Waite; editor,
Harry Keller.
  Thayer David (Nero Wolfe); Tom Mason (Archie Goodwin);
Anne Baxter (Rachel Bruner); Brooke Adams (Sarah Dacos); Biff
McGuire (Inspector Cramer); Sarah Cunningham (Mrs. Athaus);
John Randolph (Lou Cohen); David Hurst (Fritz); Allen Case (Agent
Fredericks); and: Frank Campanella, Katherine Charles, Jim Gerstead,
John Hoyt, David Lewis, John O'Leary, Robert Phalen, Sam Weisman.
  Rex Stout (1886-1975) wrote* nearly fifty books on the
exploits of home-bound detective Nero Wolfe, a corpulent, self-
indulgent man who raised orchids and fancied fine foods and good
beer. He was aided in his exploits by right-hand man Archie
Goodwin and operatives like Saul Panzer and Orrie Cather. In the
mid-1930s two attempts were made to bring Nero Wolfe to the big
screen: Edward Arnold in MEET NERO WOLFE (1936), *q.v.*, and
Walter Connolly in THE LEAGUE OF FRIGHTENED MEN
(1937), *q.v.*; but Stout was unhappy with the results and no further
screen exploits of Wolfe ensued. In 1977, two years after Stout's
death, ABC-TV/Paramount Television produced a pilot movie
called NERO WOLFE, based on Stout's 1965 novel, *The Doorbell
Rang*, with Thayer David as the oversized sleuth. Unfortunately
Thayer David died soon after the film was made and the project lay
dormant for two years until the property was aired on December 19,
1979 on ABC.
  Nero Wolfe (Thayer David) lives in a brownstone on New
York City's West 35th Street and raises orchids (he has 10,000
plants!) on his brownstone roof while enjoying gourmet cooking by
private chef Fritz Brenner (David Hurst) and enjoying flavorful
beer. To maintain his costly life style, Wolfe works as a private
detective, with all his outside legwork done by assistant Archie
Goodwin (Tom Mason). Wealthy Mrs. Rachel Bruner (Anne Baxter)

*Rex Stout's *Death Times Three* (containing three Nero Wolfe adventures) was
published posthumously in 1985. Stout's widow and estate (as well as his official
biographer) have condoned and agreed to a continuation of the Nero Wolfe mysteries
as written by Robert Goldsborough. The following new adventures have appeared to
date: *Murder in E Minor* (1986), *Death on Deadline* (1987), and *The Bloodied Ivy*
(1988).

offers Wolfe the highest retainer of his career to find out why she and members of her family are being followed by FBI agents, Wolfe learns that the Bureau is investigating a murder case which it does not want publicized. His knowledge of this not only puts him at loggerheads with the G-men but also with local Inspector Cramer (Biff McGuire) and his department. Wolfe gathers all the suspects in the case at his home and reveals the murderer.

Stephen Scheuer's *Movies on TV* (1987) acknowledged, "[Thayer] David is perfectly cast as Rex Stout's stout sophisticated sleuth. . . . [Tom] Mason makes a favorable impression as Wolfe's sidekick, Archie Goodwin."

NEW FACE IN HELL   *see*   P.J.

NICK CARTER—MASTER DETECTIVE (Metro-Goldwyn-Mayer, 1939) 60 minutes.

Producer, Lucien Hubbard; director, Jacques Tourneur; story, Bertram Millhauser, Harold Buckley; screenplay, Millhauser; camera, Charles Lawton; editor, Elmo Vernon.

Walter Pidgeon (Nick Carter/Robert Chalmers); Rita Johnson (Lou Farnsby); Henry Hull (John Keller); Donald Meek (Bartholomew); Stanley Ridges (Dr. Frankton); Addison Richards (Hiram Streeter); Henry Victor (J. Lester Hammil); Milburn Stone (Dave Krebs); Martin Kosleck (Otto King); Wally Maher (Cliff Parson); Frank Faylen (Pete Foley); Frank Ball (Peake); George Meeker (Hartley); Richard Terry (Cain); Paul Ellis (Faber); Don Castle (Ed); Sterling Holloway (Youth); Louis V. Arco (Captain of Cruiser).

Detective Nick Carter (Walter Pidgeon) is on the trail of a gang stealing blueprints from a West Coast airplane factory and is aided by friend Bartholomew (Donald Meek). Along the way he meets Lou Farnsby (Rita Johnson), a stewardess-nurse, whom he romances. Using the alias of Robert Chalmers, Carter infiltrates the organization and finds out that the gang are actually foreign spies who intend to steal military secrets. Following a waterfront plane chase, Carter rounds up the gang.

NICK CARTER, MASTER DETECTIVE was the first of an intended series of economy features based on the popular turn-of-the-century pulp-fiction hero. *Variety* commented, "Subsequent releases of the series will have to have strong and more thrilling content, if Carter's screen life is to carry along for any length of time." On the other hand, William K. Everson noted in *The Detective in Film* (1972), "The role, as rewritten, was perfectly suited to the cool nonchalance of Walter Pidgeon. In the first film . . . Pidgeon goes to great pains to debunk his own reputation, and in a lengthy speech to Addison Richards enumerates all of the meticulous deductions from small clues that he is *not* capable of. It was a sober, not too exciting, but solidly satisfying little mystery."

MGM issued two further Nick Carter features with Walter Pidgeon before he graduated to class "A" pictures. Jonathan Latimer, the author of the Bill Crane detective character, wrote PHANTOM RAIDERS (originally called NICK CARTER IN PANAMA), issued in the summer of 1940. Like the first film it deals with foreign spies and has Carter investigating Panama Canal ship sinkings for a marine insurance firm. Late in 1940 came SKY MURDER, which finds Nick Carter investigating a murder aboard a flight from Washington, D.C. to Manhattan.

Nick Carter had a successful radio run in the 1940s on the Mutual network series, "Nick Carter, Master Detective," with Lon Clark in the title assignment. It debuted in 1943 and, three years later, Nick's adopted son, Chick Carter, was featured in Mutual's "Chick Carter, Boy Detective," with Billy Lipton (later Leon Janney) as Chick. In 1972 Robert Conrad would portray the title role in the ABC-TV film, THE ADVENTURES OF NICK CARTER, *q.v.*

NIGHT CLUB LADY (Columbia, 1932) 70 minutes.

Director, Irving Cummings; based on the novel *About the Murder of the Night Club Lady* by Anthony Abbot [Fulton Oursler]; screenplay, Robert Riskin; sound, George Cooper; camera, Teddy Tetzlaff.

Adolphe Menjou (Thatcher Colt); Mayo Methot (Lola Carewe); Skeets Gallagher (Tony); Ruthelma Stevens (Kelly); Blanche Frederici (Mrs. Carewe); Gerald Fielding (Everett); Nat Pendleton (Mike); Albert Conti (Vincent Rowland); Greta Granstedt (Eunice); Ed Brady (Bill); Lee Phelps (Joe); George Humbert (Andre); Niles Welch (Dr. Baldwin); William Von Brincken (Dr. Lengle); Teru Shimada (Mura).

Anthony Abbot [Fulton Oursler] wrote a series of detective novels centered around the character of Thatcher Colt, the chief inspector of the New York Police Department. With a penchant for trying out wrestling holds, Colt sets about unraveling a variety of homicides. The character proved to be a deft detective in the Sherlock Holmes mold. Three films were made revolving around Colt, the first two starring suave Adolphe Menjou in what appeared to be a promising, but sadly short-lived, series.

NIGHT CLUB LADY, released in the late summer of 1932, is based on Anthony Abbot's 1931 novel, *About the Murder of the Night Club Lady*. The plot has nasty club entertainer Lola Carewe (Mayo Methot) receive a warning that she will die shortly after midnight.

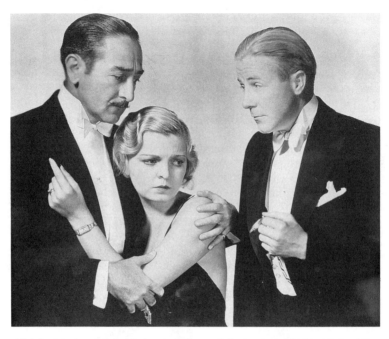

Adolphe Menjou, Mayo Methot and Skeets Gallagher in NIGHT CLUB LADY (1932).

She immediately asks the aid of the police and is protected by police commissioner Thatcher Colt (Adolphe Menjou), his assistant Tony (Skeets Gallagher), and several policemen. Despite their presence, the woman drops dead at the appointed time. Colt traces all her close relationships and finds them to be of the international sort. It also seems that all the men she knew had prison records and she had been blackmailing them; thus each had a motive for removing her. A friend of Lola's is also murdered, as is the doctor who examined her shortly after she was killed. Colt pieces the puzzle together and deduces the ingenious way Lola was dispatched and by whom. Writing in the *New York Times*, Mordaunt Hall stated, "It is a better mystery tale than most and one that keeps one guessing until the end . . . the picture moves rapidly and interestingly, with effective backgrounds."

THE CIRCUS QUEEN MURDER, *q.v.*, based on Abbot's *About the Murder of the Circus Queen* (1932), followed in the spring of 1933. The film deviates from the novel in that it is set around a small traveling circus in a hinterland town instead of a large unit working at

Madison Square Garden. Here Gotham police commissioner Thatcher Colt (Adolph Menjou) is on vacation and comes to see a circus. During the high wire act, the chief attraction, Josie La Tour (Greta Nissen), falls to her death and it is discovered she has a poison arrow in her back. Colt takes over the investigation and learns, among other things, that the woman's late husband, Flandrin (Dwight Frye), did not commit suicide as she believed. It may be he who also threatened the life of her lover, high wire performer Sebastian (Donald Cook). Colt catches the killer with dispatch. *Variety* noted, "Faster moving than the average picture based on a circusing story. . . . Picture obviously did not cost much, but it is well cast and directed. Editing is exceptionally good." The reviewer, like others, also praised debonair Adolphe Menjou's smooth work as Thatcher Colt: "Adolphe Menjou, as the police commissioner on vacation, proves one of the screen's best bets for detective roles. He does the job so realistically that the audience mind is distracted from the usual bromidic strains." Unfortunately Columbia made no further Thatcher Colt pictures following this outing.

Thatcher Colt, however, did return to the screen in the summer of 1942 in Producers Releasing Corporation's THE PANTHER'S CLAW, *q.v.*, based on an Anthony Abbot short story. Here Colt (Sidney Blackmer) is called in to investigate the murder of opera diva Nina Politza (Gerta Rozan), with Everett Digberry (Byron Foulger) being the prime suspect. Digberry wanted to loan $1,000 to Nina but could not explain the matter to his wife, so he wrote extortion notes to all the members of the opera troupe, including himself. When the diva is murdered he is blamed for the crime, but Colt proves him innocent and unmasks the real killer. "This is a tight, fast-moving murder mystery without marquee names. . . . With an operatic background, film is exceedingly well acted and carries a punch in dialog and situations" (*Variety*). Don Miller decided in *B Movies* (1973), "Byron Foulger walked away with the acting honors as a milquetoast murder suspect, while Blackmer invested Colt with his usual authority. The mystery wasn't very mysterious, but the film was good enough to have merited a sequel and even a series, but no further ones were made."

NIGHT MOVES (Warner Bros., 1975) Color 99 minutes.

Producer, Robert M. Sherman; associate producer, Gene Lasko; director, Arthur Penn; screenplay, Alan Sharp; production designer, George Jenkins; set decorator, Ned Parsons; costume supervisor, Rita Riggs; makeup, Bob Stein; music, Michael Small; assistant director, Jack Roe; sound, Richard Vorisek; camera, Bruce Surtees;

underwater camera, Jordan Klein; editors, Dede Allen, Stephen A. Rotter.

Gene Hackman (Harry Moseby); Jennifer Warren (Paula); Edward Binns (Ziegler); Harris Yulin (Marty Heller); Susan Clark (Ellen Moseby); Kenneth Mars (Nick); Janet Ward (Arlene Iverson); James Woods (Quentin); Anthony Costello (Marv Ellman); John Crawford (Tom Iverson); Melanie Griffith (Delly Grastner); Ben Archibek (Charles); Maxwell Gail, Jr. (Tony); Victor Paul, Louis Elias, Carey Loftin, John Moio (Policemen); Susan Barrister, Larry Mitchell (Airline Ticket Clerks); Tim Haldeman (Delivery Boy); Jacque Wallace (Man); Dennis Dugan (Young Man); C. J. Hincks (Girl); Phil Altman, Bob Templeton (Crewmen); Avril Gentles, Sandra Diane Seacat, Rene Enriquez, Simon Deckard, Michael Ebert (Voices).

Director Arthur Penn and scripter Alan Sharp struck out badly in their effort to make a 1970s *film noir* detective film, harking back to the movie genre so popular in the post-World War II era. NIGHT MOVES (filmed under the working title of THE DARK TOWER and which sat on the shelf many months before release)

Gene Hackman in NIGHT MOVES (1975).

suffers from a meandering plot, basically murky performances, and a too mundane premise. Further Gene Hackman is miscast as the Sam Spade-Philip Marlowe type gumshoe and, outside of John Crawford as the lecherous stepfather,* the movie lacks sufficient emoting to carry its convoluted, rickety storyline. Not even added violence and R-rated sex could save the financial day for NIGHT MOVES, nor could the partial on-location shooting off the coast of Florida.

When he discovers that his lonely wife Ellen (Susan Clark) is having an affair with Marty Heller (Harris Yulin), former football hero turned small time private eye Harry Moseby (Gene Hackman) is distraught. As with his earlier search to track his long lost father (after discovering him, he would not speak to the man) and now with Ellen, he is a man obsessed with a desire for knowledge, but suffers from an emotional inability to act upon such knowledge. Moseby accepts a case from fading movie star Arlene Iverson (Janet Ward) to locate her promiscuous runaway teenage daughter Delly (Melanie Griffith), who also has a drug problem. (The unstated prime reason Arlene wants her back is to maintain control of her trust fund.) From the girl's boyfriend, Quentin (James Woods), a stuntman, Moseby learns that she has run off with one of his cohorts, Marv Ellman (Anthony Costello), after the two men had fought over her for her sexual favors. Since Quentin thinks the girl may now be in Florida with Tom Iverson (John Crawford), her stepfather, Harry flies there and meets film producer Ziegler (Edward Binns), who informs him that Iverson resides on a small island. Iverson lives with a young woman named Paula (Jennifer Warren). In the process, Moseby also finds Delly, who is hysterical after finding a body in the water near the isle. Moseby and Paula go to the spot and locate a crashed plane with its dead pilot. Back in California, Harry receives a call from Paula telling him that Delly is dead after being involved in a movie stunt, and that Ziegler has been injured. Determined to put the pieces together, Moseby returns to Florida where he discovers that Quentin is dead and that he and Iverson were in a scheme with Ziegler to obtain a $500,000 statue through their smuggling operation. Iverson is killed in a fight with Moseby. The detective and Paula agree to recover the sunken statue but the rest of Iverson's men arrive and in a shootout Moseby is the sole survivor, left helpless in a motorboat making widening arcs in the water.

Variety assessed one of this production's major problems. "It is said that the final scenes were not revealed even to the cast in order

---

*In one of the few intriguing scenes in this downbeat and meandering melodrama, Tom Iverson laments to Moseby about being seduced by his nubile stepdaughter. "There ought to be a law," he sighs. "There is," Moseby retorts.

to keep the [plot] secret. Well, the curtain disclosure isn't that hard to figure out, since by the end of 99 minutes, nearly everyone but Mister Big is either dead . . . injured . . . or else dismissed from the plot. . . ."

While NIGHT MOVES is a very flawed film indeed, it does highlight the transition that has occurred in the arena of private investigation. "The traditional detective derived his power not just from the ability to track one clue to the next but from the insight that enabled him to see the larger picture, to justify the sordidness of his search by creating meaning out of mystery. . . . Harry [Moseby] stands under the light of modern psychologizing; and what was once investigation is now recognized as cheap spying and a vicarious emotional life" (Eileen McGarry, *Film Noir: An Encyclopedic Reference to the American Style*, 1979).

A NIGHT OF MYSTERY (Paramount, 1937) 66 minutes.

Director, E. A. DuPont; based on the novel *The Greene Murder Case* by S. S. Van Dine; screenplay, Frank Partos, Gladys Unger; sound, Walter Oberst; music director, Boris Morros; camera, Harry Fischbeck; editor, James Smith.

Grant Richards (Philo Vance); Roscoe Karns (Sergeant Ernest Heath); Helen Burgess (Ada Greene); Ruth Coleman (Sibella) Elizabeth Patterson (Mrs. Greene); Harvey Stephens (Dr. Von Blon); June Martel (Barton); Purnell B. Pratt (Inspector John F. X. Markham); Colin Tapley (Chester); James Bush (Rex); Ivan Simpson (Sproot); Greta Meyer (Mrs. Manheim); Leonard Corey (Lister); Nora Cecil (Hemming); George Anderson (Snitkin); Barlowe Borland (Medical Examiner); Myra Marsh (Police Nurse).

A remake of the third S. S. Van Dine Philo Vance novel, *The Greene Murder Case* (1927), which Paramount had filmed originally under that title as the second Vance movie in 1929, *q.v.*, A NIGHT OF MYSTERY rather closely follows the book. However, it was made on a small budget by director E. A. Dupont, whose Hollywood work failed to revive the critical acclaim or popularity he had known in Europe during the previous decade.

Philo Vance (Grant Richards) aids Inspector Ernest Heath (Roscoe Karns) and District Attorney F. X. Markham (Purnell B. Pratt) in solving the murder of rich Chester Greene (Colin Tapley). The deceased's mansion is filled with suspects and is now run by wicked Mrs. Tobias Greene (Elizabeth Patterson) along with the other heirs, including Ada (Helen Burgess) and Sibella (Ruth Coleman). The guilty party, Vance determines, is a crazed family member.

Don Miller in *B Movies* (1973) weighed this remake as a "weak reworking" of the novel and added, "Grant Richards, a new recruit, did nothing to make audiences forget William Powell in the Vance role, and the proceedings were reeled off in a soggy manner. Not helping production troubles was the unfortunate demise of Helen Burgess, who succumbed to pneumonia midway through shooting and whose role was pivotal to the film. . . . Her part in MYSTERY was completed by use of a double and some desperate editorial juggling of scenes. It didn't help." Ray Cabana, Jr. in "Murder, Mythology and Mother Goose" (*Kaleidoscope* magazine, Vol 2, No. 3, 1967) noted that the production " . . . tried to incorporate too much of the original novel, and was spoiled by an all-too-weak and abrupt ending in which hasty and unsatisfactory answers are given as explanations with many aspects of the case being completely ignored."

It should be noted that the film cast Purnell B. Pratt as District Attorney Markham. It was the second time he enacted the role, having done it previously in THE CASINO MURDER CASE (1935), *q.v.*, for MGM.

A NIGHT TO REMEMBER (Columbia, 1943) 92 minutes.

Producer, Samuel Bischoff; director, Richard Wallace; story, Kelley Roos; screenplay, Richard Flournoy, Jack Henley; art director, Lionel Banks; music, Werner R. Heymann; music director, Morris Stoloff; camera, Joseph Walker; editor, Charles Nelson.

Loretta Young (Nancy Troy); Brian Aherne (Jeff Troy); Jeff Donnell (Anne Carstairs); William Wright (Scott Carstairs); Sidney Toler (Inspector Hankins); Gale Sondergaard (Mrs. DeVoe); Donald MacBride (Bolling); Lee Patrick (Polly Franklin); Don Costello (Eddie Turner); Blanche Yurka (Mrs. Walter); Richard Gaines (Lingle); James Burke (Pat Murphy); Billy Benedict (Messenger Boy); Cyril Ring (Man); Eddie Dunn (Mathews); George Chandler (Taxi Driver); John H. Dilson (Coroner); Cy Kendall (Louis Kaufman); Ralph Curly (Detective); Ralph Peters (Taxi Driver); Gary Owen (Mailman); and: William "Billy" Newill.

Nancy (Loretta Young) is married to mystery writer Jeff Troy (Brian Aherne) but she wants him to quit writing thrillers and compose a love story. For atmosphere they take a basement apartment in Greenwich Village and all goes well until a dead man is found in their back yard. Police Inspector Hankins (Sidney Toler) investigates the killing and the suspects include a young couple (Jeff Donnell, William Wright) in the apartment above the Troys' as well as several other suspicious occupants (Lee Patrick, Blanche Yurka, Gale Sondergaard) of the building. With little information to go on, Nancy and Jeff set out to solve the caper and discover that the killing involved a blackmail scheme.

By this juncture every studio had worn out the imitative Thin

Man premise of a husband-and-wife team as amateur sleuths, and A NIGHT TO REMEMBER was at the near end of the lengthy cycle. In addition, it was hampered by a haphazard script. "The company is thoroughly adequate," stated Bosley Crowther (*New York Times*), "but the plot is tedious and involved. So the film is largely a succession of looming shadows, conversations and mediocre gags and people creeping out of the darkness and saying 'Boo!' (or something similar) right under your nose."

Brian Aherne was debonair and Loretta Young too shrill, and it remained for Sidney Toler (more famous as Charlie Chan) and Donald MacBride (he of the exasperated fast-burn expression) as the law enforcers to provide the film with its energy.

NO HANDS ON THE CLOCK (Paramount, 1941) 76 minutes.

Producers, William H. Pine, William C. Thomas; director, Frank McDonald; based on the novel by Geoffrey Homes [Daniel Mainwaring]; screenplay, Maxwell Shane; camera, Fred Jackman, Jr.; editor, William Ziegler.

Chester Morris (Humphrey Campbell); Jean Parker (Louise); Rose Hobart (Mrs. West); Dick Purcell (Red Harris); Astrid Allwyn (Gypsy Toland); Rod Cameron (Tom Reed); George Watts (Oscar Flack); James Kirkwood (Warren Benedict); Billie Seward (Rose Madden); Robert Middlemass (Chief Bates); Grant Withers (Harry Belding); Loren Raker (Copley); George Lewis (Paulson); Ralph Sanford (Officer Gimble); and Frank Faylen, Keye Luke.

Producers William H. Pine and William C. Thomas headed a "B" unit at Paramount in the 1940s and churned out a series of satisfying programmers with such stars as Chester Morris, Richard Arlen and Robert Lowery. One of the best of their outings was NO HANDS ON THE CLOCK, based on the 1939 novel of the same title by Geoffrey Homes [Daniel Mainwaring]. The plot centered around the character of detective Humphrey Campbell, enacted by Chester Morris, who was also starring at Columbia Pictures as Boston Blackie.

In Reno pretty Louise (Jean Parker) becomes the wife of gumshoe Humphrey Campbell (Chester Morris). Before they can enjoy their conjugal bliss the duo are knee deep in kidnapping and murder. The local police ask Campbell to get on the trail of a rich rancher's abducted son and, with the deft aid of Louise, he finds that the culprits are gangsters from the Midwest who have committed several murders. The detective rounds up several suspects as he puzzles out the mystery and spotlights the guilty party.

Variety judged, "Picture, scaled on moderate budget proportions, is a well-sustained whodunit. . . . Story is geared for speedy

action, getting life from good direction by Frank McDonald." Don
Miller noted in *B Movies* (1973), "[Chester] Morris lent himself well
to the role, and [Maxwell] Shane's screenplay stuck closely to the
novel. The plotting was intricate but rich in characterization and
[Frank] McDonald directed it stylishly." Miller further discussed the
feature in "Private Eyes" (*Focus on Film* magazine, Autumn 1975):
"By the time the explanations and unmasking of the killer rolled
around, the film had built up a laudable amount of interest, and the
end results were pleasant indeed. . . . The title, incidentally, was
explained in a pre-credit scene, unusual in itself in 1941: a passer-by
on the local boulevard stops to admire the ultra-modern new clock
erected over the entrance of an undertaking emporium. 'But where
are the hands?' asks the passer-by of the head of the establishment,
who answers with a smile, 'Death is timeless.'"

NO PLACE FOR A LADY (Columbia, 1943) 66 ins.
  Producer, Ralph Cohn; director, James Hogan; story/adaptor,
Eric Taylor; art director, Richard Irvine; music, Lee Zahler; assistant
director, Carl Hieckle; camera, James S. Brown; editor, Dwight
Caldwell.
  William Gargan (Jess Arno); Margaret Lindsay (June Terry);
Phyllis Brooks (Dolly Adair); Dick Purcell (Rand Brooke); Jerome
Cowan (Eddie Moore); Edward Norris (Mario); Frank Thomas
(Webley); Thomas Jackson (Captain Baker); Tom Dugan (Rawlins);
Doris Lloyd (Mrs. Harris); Ralph Sanford (Hal); William Hunter
(Thomas); Chester Clute (Yvonne).
  The team consisting of director James Hogan, scripter Eric
Taylor, stars William Gargan and Margaret Lindsay—all of whom
had been involved previously in Columbia Pictures' Ellery Queen
detective series—joined together in still another sleuthing pro-
grammer. Unfortunately NO PLACE FOR A LADY was a ". . . murder mystery of mediocre quality. . . . Picture is tinged with romance
and some comedy but these factors fail to lift it out of the ordinary
class. The story is hackneyed and the dialog lacks force or color. . ."
(*Variety*).
  A wealthy woman is murdered and detective Jess Arno (William Gargan) investigates, with the aid of his fiancée June Terry
(Margaret Lindsay). Pretty Dolly Adair (Phyllis Brooks) is accused
of the killing and Arno, believing her innocent, hides her out in a
beach house. He has a solid hunch that the homicide involves a
stolen tire ring using the lucrative black market in rubber. The
suspects include newspaperman Rand Brooke (Dick Purcell), night
club gangster Mario (Edward Norris), and night club crooner Eddie

Moore (Jerome Cowan). While at odds with police detective Captain Baker (Thomas Jackson), Arno solves the murder case.

William Gargan went on to play another private eye in the Columbia programmer, FOLLOW THAT WOMAN, *q.v.*, the next year.

NOCTURNE (RKO, 1946) 88 minutes.

Executive producer, Jack Gross; producer, Joan Harrison; director Edwin L. Marin; story, Frank Fenton, Rowland Brown; screenplay, Jonathan Latimer; art directors, Albert D'Agostino, Robert Boyle; set decorators, Darrell Silvera, James Altwies; music, Leigh Harline; songs: Harline and Mort Greene, Eleanor Rudolph; music director, Constantin Bakaleinikoff; technical adviser, Lieutenant Barney Ruditsky; sound, Jean Speak, Terry Kellum; special effects, Russell A. Cully; montage, Harold Palmer; camera, Harry J. Wild; editor, Elmo Williams.

George Raft (Lieutenant Joe Warne); Lynn Bari (Frances Ransom); Virginia Huston (Carol Page); Joseph Pevney (Fingers); Myrna Dell (Susan); Edward Ashley (Paul Vincent); Walter Sande (Halberson); Mabel Paige (Mrs. Warne); Bernard Hoffman (Torp); Queenie Smith (Queenie); Mack Gray (Gratz); Pat Flaherty (Cop with Susan); Lorin Raker (Police Chemist); William Challee (Police Photographer); Greta Grandstedt (Clara); Lilian Bond (Mrs. Billings); Carol Forman (Receptionist); Robert Malcolm (Earl); Jim Pierce, William Bloom, Ed Dearing, Roger Creed (Cops); Phil Baribault (Darkroom Assistant); John Banner (Shawn); Rudy Robles (Eujemio); Janet Shaw (Grace); Ted O'Shea (Dancer); Tex Swan, Mel Wixon, Bob Terry (Men); Harry Harvey (Police Doctor); Lee Frederick (Attendant); Robert Anderson (Pat); Will Wright (Mr. Billings); Broderick O'Farrell (Billings' Butler); Virginia Edwards (Mrs. O'Rourke); Virginia Keiley (Lotus Evans); James Carlisle (Elderly Man); Paul Stader (Practical Life Guard); Antonio Filauri (Nick Pappas); Jack Norton (Drunk); Betty Farrington, Connie Evans, Doris Stone, Monya Andre, Eleanor Counts, Norma Brown (Women); John Rice (Doorman); Al Hill (Cop at the Brown Derby Restaurant); Edward Clark (Apartment House Clerk); Dorothy Adams (Woman Tenant); Lillian Bronson (Cashier at the Gotham); Gladys Blake (Ticket Seller); Betty Hill, Carol Donell (Girls); Al Rhein (Keyboard Club Waiter); Benny Burt (Keyboard Club Bartender); Matt McHugh (Coffee Attendant); Lucille Casey (Bessie); Donald Kerr (Gaffer); Dick Rush (Studio Cop); Bert Moorehouse (Director); George Goodman (Keyboard Club Manager).

Sometimes the instinctual urge to solve a mystery can lead a person into deep trouble, as proved to be the case in the very atmospheric NOCTURNE, one of George Raft's finest 1940s films.

Playboy/composer Paul Vincent (Edward Ashley) is found dead in his plush Hollywood Hills home and all evidence points to suicide. Police detective Lieutenant Joe Warne (George Raft), however, has a hunch the man was murdered, since he was composing a new song at the time of death. His superiors insist that Warne lay off the case but he is urged on by his mother (Mabel Paige) to do the right thing. His persistent investigation leads him to one of Vincent's many girlfriends, movie bit player Frances Ransom (Lynn Bari), for whom he develops a compulsive attraction. Frances' pretty sister, Carol Page (Virginia Huston), is a night club thrush. Warne feels he is on to something when Carol's boyfriend, Torp (Bernard Hoffman), tails him. However, after an altercation with the huge thug, plus other problems with his inflexible superiors, Warne is suspended from the force. Undaunted, he dogs after clues which lead him to portrait photographer Shawn (John Banner). Shawn promises to provide Warne with information but at the man's studio Warne finds him hanged. At Frances' apartment the ex-cop finds the fireplace gas jet turned full on, and the girl unconscious. He saves her and after locating a photo of Carol before she changed her hair color, he drives to the club where she entertains. There he singles out the killer, who had also murdered Shawn and tried to eliminate Frances. After turning the guilty party over to the law, Warner can look forward to reinstatement on the force and to a relationship with Frances.

NOCTURNE is a moody, *film noir* feature with a solid murder mystery plot and a cast brimming with interesting characterizations, especially the detective's mother and her good friend Mrs. O'Rourke (Virginia Edwards) who speculate on the progress of the murder case using all kinds of police and gangster jargon. Filling out the engaging scenario are the thug Torp and his bulldog faithfulness to a woman who only uses him (very similar in concept to Moose Malloy of MURDER, MY SWEET, *q.v.*), and Fingers (Joseph Pevney) the distraught pianist. Also adding to the overall success is the haunting title theme composed by Leigh Harline. The Hollywood settings add zest to the proceedings, as do the shadowy cinematography and windy environs of the film capital. George Raft is effective as the methodical detective who has only a hunch that a murder was committed (although film viewers have witnessed the killing) and persistently follows through to prove his point, despite losing his job and receiving two terrible beatings from Torp, whom he dispatches finally by splashing him in the face with scalding coffee.

NUMBER SEVENTEEN (Woolf and Freedman, 1928) 72 minutes.
Producer, Josef Somlo; Director, Geza M. Bolvary; based on the play by J. Jefferson Farjeon; screenplay, Bolvary.

Guy Newall (Ben); Lien Dyers (Elsie Ackroyd); Carl de Vogt (Gilbert Fordyce); Fritz Greiner (Shelldrake); Ernst Neicher (Harold Brant); Hertha von Walter (Nora Brant); Craighall Sherry (Sam Ackroyd); Frederick Solm (Henry Jobber).

NUMBER SEVENTEEN (Wardour, 1932) 65 minutes.
Producer, John Maxwell; director, Alfred Hitchcock; based on the play by J. Jefferson Farjeon; screenplay, Hitchcock, Alma Reville, Rodney Ackland; art director, C. W. Arnold; camera, Jack Cox, Bryan Langley; editor, A. C. Hammond;

Leon M. Lion (Ben Tramp); Anne Grey (Nora Brant); John Stuart (Gilbert Fordyce); Donald Calthrop (Brant); Barry Jones (Henry Doyle); Ann Casson (Rose Ackroyd); Henry Caine (Ackroyd); Garry Marsh (Sheldrake); Herbert Langley (Guard).

J. Jefferson Farjeon's stage play provided the basis for two detective films, both of British origin. The first version was done in 1928 and was made in Germany by a British company. Initially filmed as a silent, it had sound added to it to make it a part-talkie for re-release in the summer of 1929. The plot has detective Gilbert Fordyce (Carl de Vogt) on the trail of jewel thieves and being helped by a sailor (Guy Newall).

In 1932, director Alfred Hitchcock, with scripters Alma Reville and Rodney Ackland, remade NUMBER SEVENTEEN, turning it into an engrossing, if slow moving, thriller. Detective Gilbert Fordyce (John Stuart) is pursuing a jewel theft gang and believes their hideout is an abandoned house near a railroad depot. He investigates and finds tramp Ben (Leo M. Lion) and the gang, which includes Nora Brant (Anne Grey). The crooks escape by boarding a freight train on its way to the Continent and Fordyce follows. During his quest he and Nora fall in love and it is the girl who aids him in rounding up the gang, although not until the train has crashed into a ferry boat and sunk.

At the time of its issuance *Variety* complained, ". . . the story is vague and, despite its intended eeriness, unconvincing. It is asking a lot of an audience—even a picture one—to make them believe a woman accomplice of a band of thieves will fall in love at first sight with a detective and prevent his being done in by her associates."

In *The Detective in Film* (1972), William K. Everson called NUMBER SEVENTEEN "cheap but marvelously stylish" and added that it was ". . . already a deliberate spoof of the thriller genre that was to become Hitchcock's permanent stamping ground. He gives us a 'detective' who turns out to be the villain—and an innocent bystander who turns out to be the detective. . . . It can be considered one of Hitchcock's most enjoyable thrillers; the first half all expressionistic shadow and lighting camerawork in the old house, a heritage of Hitchcock's German period, the second half all thrills and chase."

ONE FRIGHTENED NIGHT (Mascot, 1935) 67 minutes.

Producer, Nat Levine; director, Christy Cabanne; story, Stuart Palmer; screenplay, Wellyn Totman; music director, Arthur Kay; special effects, Jack Coyle, Howard Lydecker; camera, Ernie Miller, William Nobles; editor, Joseph Lewis.

Charley Grapewin (Jasper Whyte); Mary Carlisle (Doris Waverly); Arthur Hohl (Arthur Proctor); Evalyn Knapp (First Doris); Wallace Ford (Joe Luvalle); Hedda Hopper (Laura Proctor); Lucien Littlefield (Dr. Denham); Regis Toomey (Tom Dean); Rafaela Ottiano (Elvira); Clarence H. Wilson (Felix, the Lawyer); Adrian Morris (Deputy Sheriff); Fred Kelsey (Jenks).

Convinced that his time has come, aged Jasper Whyte (Charley Grapewin) brings all of his grasping relatives together for the reading of his will. They will divide the inheritance unless his granddaughter, Doris Waverly, whom he has never seen, should be found. If that happens, the proceeds would go to her. The various relatives arrive at the Whyte mansion on a stormy night, as does a vaudeville magician, Joe Luvalle (Wallace Ford), who brings a girl (Evelyn Knapp) he claims is Doris; attorney Felix (Clarence H. Wilson) also brings a girl and claims *she* is Doris. One of the relatives, great nephew Tom Dean (Regis Toomey), is attracted to the Doris (Mary Carlisle) brought by the lawyer. The first Doris, however, is soon found murdered and detective Jenks (Fred Kelsey) arrives with a deputy (Adrian Morris) to investigate the killing. The relatives blame one another for the crime and a mysterious, cloaked figure attempts to kill the "other" Doris with a blowgun; he is unsuccessful although he does eliminate Luvalle. Later, the phantom attempts to knife Doris but again fails and, when his mask is found, Dean is thought to be the murderer. When relative Arthur Proctor (Arthur Hohl) is found to have embezzled bank funds, the suspicion shifts to him, but then the mysterious phantom abducts Doris. Dean and Whyte join forces to save her and eventually unmask one of the surviving guests as the killer.

"Mascot's Mirthful Mystery" read the poster blurb for this old-house murder mystery tinged with comedy, the studio's only outing in this area before becoming part of the newly formed Republic Pictures the same year. Bolstered by a top-notch cast, the feature

presents two detectives: the dim-witted type as exemplified by
Jenks, and a character (Tom Dean) suddenly thrust into the role of
sleuth to save his lady love. The film story is by Stuart Palmer, the
creator of the fictional sleuth, Hildegarde Withers. Jon Tuska
commented in *The Vanishing Legion: A History of Mascot Pictures:
1927-1935* (1982), "But even with Palmer to recommend it, the
plot was strictly derivative." Tuska complained that a room in the
house which was supposed to be locked for two decades had modern
light fixtures and added, "Another production ineptitude was the
capricious rain. One minute it would be raining a torrent, the next
the suspects would be wandering through garden shrubbery, both
the shrubbery and the suspects as dry as if they were in the midst of a
drought." On the other hand, George E. Turner and Michael H.
Price noted in *Forgotten Horrors* (1979), "The picture opens impres-
sively with an excellent miniature of a storm-battered old house.
Credit titles—including photographs of the principal actors—appear behind flapping shutters; the Dunworth-de la Roche misterioso
theme that also opened THE VAMPIRE BAT [1933] is heard
between peals of thunder. Photography maintains this forbidding
atmosphere throughout, and the effect is heightened by startling
bursts of venerable music. . . . As always in any Mascot mystery, the
identity of the villain is a secret well kept until the last moments."

P.I. PRIVATE INVESTIGATIONS (Polygram, 1987) Color 90
minutes.

Executive producers, Michael Kuhn, David Hockman, (with)
Art Dalhuisen; producers, Steven Golin, Sigurjon Sighvatsson;
associate producer, David Warfield; director/story, Nigel Dick;
screenplay, John Dahl, Warfield; production designer, Piers Plowden;
art director, Nick Rafter; set decorator, Deborah Evans; wardrobe,
Charmin Espinoza; makeup, Vilborg Aradottir; music, Murray Munro;
music consultant, Andy Murray; music coordinators, Peter Olliff,
Tony Powell; assistant director, Warfield, Bruce Carter; stunt coordinator, Alan Oliney; sound, Bob Dreebin; supervising sound editors, Barry Rubinow, Peter Austin; sound effects editors, E. J.
Lachmann, Daniel P. Tripoli; digital sound effects, Dane Davis;
camera, David Bridges; additional camera, Bryan Duggan; second
unit camera, Beth-Jana Friedberg; editor, Scott Chestnut.

Clayton Rohner (Joey Bradley); Ray Sharkey (Ryan); Paul
LeMat (Detective Wexler); Talia Balsam (Jenny Fox); Phil Morris
(Eddie Gordon); Martin Balsam (Cliff Dowling); Anthony Zerbe
(Charles Bradley); Robert Ito (Kim); Vernon Wells (Detective
North); Anthony Geary (Larry) Justin Lord (Howard White); Rich-
ard Cummings, Jr. (Hollister); Desiree Boschetti (Denise); Andy

Romano (Mr. Watson); Sydney Walsh (Janet); Jon St. Elwood (Gil); Rex Ryon (Lou); Richard Herkert (Kim's Driver); Frank Gargani (Wire Tapper); Big Yank (Clay); Nigel Dick (Photographer); Robert Torti, Jean Glaude (Burglars); Dennis Phung (Cafe Owner); Sharonlee McLean (Cafe Waitress); Michelle Seipp (Woman in Restaurant); Stan Yale (Bum); Hugh Slate (Himself); Del Zamora, Luis Manuel ("Car Thieves").

Los Angeles architect Joey Bradley (Clayton Rohner) complains to his friend Eddie Gordon (Phil Morris) about his failure to get a promotion. When he returns to his apartment he finds a corpse in the bathroom and a strange message on his telephone answering machine. It develops that the dead man is a private detective who has been hired by Joey's father, Charles Bradley (Anthony Zerbe), the editor of a large San Francisco newspaper, who is investigating alleged police involvement in drug trafficking. The telephone message is to tell the senior Bradley that the police are wise to his investigations, and Ryan (Ray Sharkey), a police assassin, is assigned to kill Joey before he reveals what he knows. Realizing he is in deep trouble, Joey goes to detective Wexler (Paul LeMat), who has him stay with his sister, even though Joey does not know for sure whether Wexler is in cahoots with Ryan. Trying to elude Ryan, Joey is hit by kookie driver Jenny Fox (Talia Balsam), who takes him to her apartment. Joey then steals Gordon's car and goes to an oil field where another detective (Vernon Wells) advises him that his dad is about to meet with a police informant. However, the man is shot and Joey escapes. He is later arrested for possession of a stolen car. Gordon bails him out but Ryan and Wexler spot him and he takes refuge in Jenny's apartment. Finally realizing the full meaning of the mysterious phone message, Joey and Jenny attempt to warn his father that the crooked cops are on to his activities and plan to kill him. However, in a shootout it is Ryan and Wexler who are killed, with the newspaper editor getting the story. Joey, however, is now alienated from his father and departs with his new love, Jenny.

The initial theatrical feature of director, Nigel Dick, who also plays a photographer in the film, P.I. PRIVATE INVESTIGATIONS is a typically fluffy melodrama with the typical dense hero, his light-headed girlfriend, a thug cop assassin (well played by Ray Sharkey) and a stalwart journalist trying to expose police corruption. *Variety* explained, "Its furious intensity cannot overcome the mostly sterile and empty characters." More enthusiastic was Mark Finch (British *Monthly Film Bulletin*): "A cheerfully telegrammatic, love-and-bullets stand-them-up and knock-'em-down, PRIVATE INVESTIGATIONS is the sort of film whose energies are solely and rewardingly devoted to pushing its unlikely narrative forward."

P.J. (Universal, 1968) Color 109 minutes.

Producer, Edward J. Montague; director, John Guillermin; story, Philip Reisman, Jr., Montagne; screenplay, Reisman; art directors, Alexander Golitzen, Walter M. Simonds; set decorators, John McCarthy, Robert Priestley; gowns, Jean Louis; makeup, Bud Westmore; music, Neal Hefti; music supervisor, Joseph Gershenson; song, Percy Faith and Reisman; assistant directors, Phil Bowles, Skip Cosper; sound, Waldon O. Watson, Lyle Cain; matte supervisor, Albert Whitlock; camera, Loyal Griggs; editor, Sam E. Waxman.

George Peppard (P. J. Detweiler); Raymond Burr (William Orbison); Gayle Hunnicutt (Maureen Preble); Brock Peters (Police Chief Waterpark); Wilfrid Hyde-White (Billings-Browne); Jason Evers (Jason Grenoble); Coleen Gray (Betty Orbison); Susan Saint James (Linette Orbison); Severn Darden (Shelton Quell); H. Jane Van Duser (Elinor Silene); George Furth (Sonny Silene); Barbara Dana (Lita); Herbert Edelman (Charlie); John Qualen (Poppa); Bert Freed (Police Lieutenant); Ken Lynch (Thorson); Jim Boles (Landlord's Agent); Arte Johnson (Jackie); King Charles MacNiles (Calypso Singer); Don Haggerty (Ape); Kay Farrington (Mrs. Thorson); Lennie Bremen (Greavy).

Needing work, Gotham private eye P. J. Detweiler (George Peppard) accepts a job as the bodyguard of beautiful Maureen Preble (Gayle Hunnicutt), the mistress of business magnate William Orbison (Raymond Burr). When several attempts are made on the young woman's life, Orbison moves her to a Bahamas island along with his wife Betty (Coleen Gray), business associates and other relatives. P.J. fears another attempt will be made to silence Maureen and when it appears that such is about to happen, he kills the assailant, who turns out to be Orbison's business associate, Jason Grenoble (Jason Evers). P. J. is arrested for homicide but apparently Orbison uses his political power to get him freed. However, upon release the detective finds the isle deserted by Orbison and his clan. Realizing that he has been double-crossed and tricked into murdering Jason, P. J. returns to Manhattan and confronts both Orbison and Maureen with proof of their complicity in Grenoble's demise. The two acknowledge the fact and now they want the detective out of the way. In the melee, the man and his mistress kill each other and P. J. emerges unharmed.

Made as CRISS CROSS (with location filming at Catalina Island) and given the pre-release title NEW FACE IN HELL, this film is sometimes called P.J.: A NEW FACE IN HELL. At the time of its mild release, *Variety* termed it an "Action-packed but confusing meller. . . ." When shown on TV the feature is cut by nine minutes, deleting several violent sequences.

Don Miller noted in "Private Eyes" (*Focus on Film* magazine, Autumn 1975), ". . . Phil Reisman, a writer of ability, polished the familiarities to a sheen that made them seem fresh, and Peppard had the right blend of boyishness in looks and cynicism in demeanor. Some minor characters were also sharply etched. It was a Universal assembly-line product, but head and shoulders above the rest of the private eyes of the period."

P.J.: A NEW FACE IN HELL   *see*   P.J.

THE PANTHER'S CLAW (Producers Releasing Corp., 1942) 72 minutes.

Producer, Lester Cutler; associate producer, T. R. Williams; director, William Beaudine; based on the story by Anthony Abbot [Fulton Oursler]; screenplay, Martin Mooney; dialogue director, Edward Kaye; camera, Marcel Le Picard; editor, Fred Bain.

Sidney Blackmer (Thatcher Colt); Byron Foulger (Everett Digberry); Rick Vallin (Anthony Abbot); Herbert Rawlinson (District Attorney); Gerta Rozan (Nina Politza); Lynn Starr (Miss Spencer); Barry Bernard (Edgar Walters); John Ince (Captain Flynn); Martin Ashe (Officer Murphy); Joaquin Edwards (Endico Lombardi); Walter James (Captain Henry).

See: NIGHT CLUB LADY [essay].

THE PATIENT IN ROOM 18 (Warner Bros., 1938) 58 minutes.

Associate producer, Byran Foy; directors, Bobby Connolly, Crane Wilbur; based on the novel by Mignon G. Eberhart; screenplay, Eugene Solow, Robertson White; camera, James Van Trees; editor, Lou Hesse.

Patric Knowles (Lance O'Leary); Eric Stanley (Hentley); Ann Sheridan (Nurse Sarah Keate); Rosella Towne (Maida Day); Jean Benedict (Carol Lethany); Charles Trowbridge (Dr. Balman); Cliff Clark (Inspector Foley); John Ridgely (Jim Warren); Harland Tucker (Dr. Arthur Lethany); Edward Raquelo (Dr. Fred Hajek); Vicki Lester (Nurse); Ralph Sanford (Donahue); Frank Orth (John Higgins); Greta Meyer (Hilda); Walter Young (Coroner); Ralph Dunn (Hotel Clerk); George Offerman, Jr. (Newsboy); Glen Cavender (Doorman); Jack Richardson (Cabby); Cliff Saum, Jack Mower (Policemen); Spec O'Donnell (Elevator Operator); William Hopper (Grabshot); Owen King (Day Clerk).

See: WHILE THE PATIENT SLEPT [essay].

THE PEARL OF DEATH (Universal, 1944) 67 minutes.

Producer/director, Roy William Neill; based on the story "The Six Napoleons" by Sir Arthur Conan Doyle; screenplay, Bertram Millhauser; art directors, John B. Goodman, Martin Obzine; set decorator, Russell A. Gausman; music director, Paul Sawtell; assistant director, Melville Shyer; sound, Joe Lapis; camera, Virgil Miller; editor, Ray Snyder.

Basil Rathbone (Sherlock Holmes); Nigel Bruce (Dr. John H. Watson); Dennis Hoey (Inspector Lestrade); Evelyn Ankers (Naomi Drake); Miles Mander (Giles Conover); Ian Wolfe (Amos Hodder); Charles Francis (Digby); Holmes Herbert (James Goodram); Richard Nugent (Bates); Mary Gordon (Mrs. Hudson); Rondo Hatton (The Creeper); Audrey Manners (Teacher); Harold de Becker (Boss); Leland Hodgson (Customs Officer); Charles Knight (Bearded Man); Connie Leon (Ellen Carey); Al Ferguson, Colin Kenny (Guards); Billy Bevan (Constable); Lillian Bronson (Major Harker's Housekeeper); Leslie Denison (Constable Murdock); John Merkyl (Dr. Boncourt); Harry Cording (George Gelder); Eric Wilton (Chauffeur); Harold de Becker (Boss); Arthur Mulliner (Sandeford); Wilson Benge, Arthur Stenning (Stewards); Leyland Hodgson (Customs Officer).

"The Creeper Stalks to Kill!" exclaimed the advertising for this

Nigel Bruce, Ian Wolfe, Evelyn Ankers and Basil Rathbone in THE PEARL OF DEATH (1944).

Sherlock Holmes series outing, the seventh Universal film with Basil Rathbone and Nigel Bruce as Holmes and Watson. Screenwriter Bertram Millhauser based the film on Sir Arthur Conan Doyle's story, "The Six Napoleons," and then deftly weaved in a series of interesting villains, most notably the Oxton Creeper, to provide the film with real flavor and thrills.

Scotland Yard is baffled by a series of brutal murders in which the victim's spine is broken and around the corpse are strewn bits of pottery. Sherlock Holmes (Basil Rathbone) and Dr. Watson (Nigel Bruce) come into the case to aid Inspector Lestrade (Dennis Hoey). Holmes learns that each victim had purchased a statue of Napoleon and that one of them contained the infamous Borgia pearl, secreted in it years before by Giles Conover (Miles Mander), who had stolen it from the London Museum. Now Conover, in league with beautiful Naomi Drake (Evelyn Ankers), is determined to locate the bust with the pearl and dispatches his hired killer, the monstrous Oxton Creeper (Rondo Hatton), to find the pearl. Unable to prevent five killings, Holmes traces the last statue to the home of an elderly doctor and poses as the physician when the Creeper arrives with Conover. When Conover threatens to give Naomi, whom the Creeper loves, to the law, the Creeper turns on him and kills him. Holmes is forced then to shoot the maniac.

Wanda Hale (*New York Daily News*) wrote that THE PEARL OF DEATH "is one of the best" of the Universal series, and added, "The appeal of these Sherlock Holmes who-done-its is that they never insult your intelligence. Without cheap trickery, you are allowed to follow the mastermind at work, tracking down clues and piecing together bits that relate to the crime until the answer is within sight. In the end, you're never shocked or disappointed by the detective pointing the finger of guilt at the last person you suspect of the crime. THE PEARL OF DEATH is a workmanlike baffler and therefore intriguing!"

The most engaging aspect of this production is the use of Rondo Hatton as the Creeper. A small man who was deformed by the glandular disease acromegaly, he is revealed mostly in shadows and his evil deeds (he likes to crack spines!) amplify the horror of his appearance. Hatton caused a sensation in the role and Universal quickly put him to work in THE SPIDER WOMAN STRIKES BACK in 1946 (a follow-up to the earlier Holmes entry, THE SPIDER WOMAN, *q.v.*) and then returned him to the Creeper role in THE HOUSE OF HORRORS (1946). He performed the assignment a third time in THE BRUTE MAN (1946), but he died shortly after it was completed and Universal sold the feature to Producers Releasing Corp.

THE PENGUIN POOL MURDER (RKO, 1932) 70 minutes.

Associate producer, Kenneth MacGowan; director, George Archainbaud; based on the novel by Stuart Palmer and the story by Lowell Brentano; adaptor, Willis Goldbeck; music, Max Steiner; sound, Hugh McDowell, Jr.; camera, Henry Gerrard; editor, Jack Kitchin.

Edna May Oliver (Hildegarde Martha Withers); James Gleason (Inspector Oscar Piper); Mae Clarke (Gwen Parker); Robert Armstrong (Barry Costello); Donald Cook (Philip Seymour); Clarence H. Wilson (Bertrand B. Hemingway); Edgar Kennedy (Donovan); Mary Mason (Secretary); Rochelle Hudson (Telephone Operator); Guy Usher (Gerald Parker); James Donlan (Fink); Joe Hermano (Chicago Lew); William Le Maire (MacDonald); Gustav von Seyffertitz (Dr. Max Bloom).

When schoolteacher Hidegarde Martha Withers takes her grade school class to the New York City aquarium she finds the body of a stock broker, Gerald Parker (Guy Usher), floating in the penguins' tank. Several suspects are also present, including the dead man's estranged wife, Gwen (Mae Clarke), and her ex-lover, Philip

Donald Cook, Mae Clarke and Clarence Wilson in THE PENGUIN POOL MURDER (1932).

Seymour (Donald Cook), as well as the aquarium director, Bertrand B. Hemingway (Clarence H. Wilson), who vowed revenge on Parker because the Wall Street man had lost Hemingway's money in the market. Miss Withers calls the police and Inspector Oscar Piper (James Gleason) arrives to investigate, while another patron, lawyer Barry Costello (Robert Armstrong), offers to represent Gwen. When questioned, Seymour confesses to the crime in order to protect Gwen and is arrested. However the medical examiner (Gustav von Seyffertitz) reports that Parker did not drown but was murdered by a thin instrument through the brain before being dumped into the tank. The murder weapon turns out to have belonged to Miss Withers who lost the hat pin when she tripped escaping pickpocket Chicago Lou (Joe Hermano). He escaped when guard Fink (James Donlan) and policeman Donovan (Edgar Kennedy) were arguing over who gets the reward for his apprehension. Donovan finds Chicago Lou, a deaf mute, in the rafters of the aquarium and he is taken to jail with Seymour.

The next day Costello informs Piper that Gwen will turn state's evidence against Seymour, and when Miss Withers and Piper visit him in jail, Seymour admits that he thinks it was Gwen who killed her husband. Both are indicted by the grand jury. Miss Withers next tells Piper to give the newspapers an incorrect account of how Parker was killed, so that the killer might make a telling error. That night Miss Withers and Costello return to the aquarium and she finds a clue but it is stolen just as Piper and his men arrive on the scene. Costello announces that Chicago Lou can identify the killer, but when they return to the jail Lou is found hanging in his cell and Seymour is blamed for the new murder. At the trial of Gwen and Seymour, Costello questions Miss Withers and accuses her of being the dead man's jilted lover who won her revenge by sticking her hat pin through his right ear. By this point, Miss Withers knows who the real killer is and the person is apprehended. With everything settled, Miss Withers and Piper depart for the marriage license bureau.

THE PENGUIN POOL MURDER is based on Stuart Palmer's initial Miss Withers novel, published in 1931.* The casting of Edna

---

*The Hildegarde Withers mystery novels are: *The Penguin Pool Murders* (1931), *Murder on Wheels* (1932), *Murder on the Blackboard* (1932), *The Puzzle of the Pepper Tree* (1933), *The Puzzle of the Silver Persian* (1934), *The Puzzle of the Red Stalion* (1936), *The Puzzle of the Blue Banderilla* (1937), *The Puzzle of the Happy Hooligan* (1954), *Miss Withers Regrets* (1947), *Four Lost Ladies* (1949), *The Green Ace* (1950), *Nipped in the Bud* (1951), *Cold Poison* (1954), and *Hildegarde Withers Makes the Scene* (1969) [written with Fletcher Flora]. The Hildegarde Withers short stories published in book form are: *The Riddles of Hildegarde Withers* (1947) (edited by Ellery Queen), *The Monkey Murder and Other Hildegarde Withers Stories* (1950) [edited by Ellery Queen), and *People vs. Withers and Malone* (1963) [written with Craig Rice].

May Oliver as Miss Withers was an ideal one as she captures beautifully the eccentric, but very likable, spirit of the sleuthing old-maid schoolmarm.* In every way the stately, angular woman looked the part. James Gleason, too, was admirably cast as Oscar Piper, the cigar chewing police inspector who is always one step behind the brainy Miss Withers in solving the caper. Public reaction to the film was so enthusiastic that two follow-ups were made, MURDER ON THE BLACKBOARD (1934) and MURDER ON A HONEY-MOON (1935), *qq.v.*, and others were planned but Miss Oliver's illness forced them to be curtailed. When her health returned, Miss Oliver signed with MGM and Helen Broderick took over for the poorly done MURDER ON A BRIDLE PATH (1936), q.v, while ZaSu Pitts did the equally mediocre THE PLOT THICKENS (1936) and FORTY NAUGHTY GIRLS (1937), *qq.v.* In all these entries James Gleason continued as the harassed police inspector.

It should be noted that Hildegarde Withers and Oscar Piper never marry, despite the ending of THE PENGUIN POOL MUR-DER. The nuptials were called off in the second Miss Withers book, *Murder on Wheels* (1932), but it was never filmed.

British release title: THE PENGUIN POOL MYSTERY.

THE PENGUIN POOL MYSTERY   *see*   THE PENGUIN POOL MURDER.

PERRY MASON RETURNS (NBC-TV, 12/1/85) Color 100 minutes.

Executive producers, Fred Silverman, Dean Hargrove; producer, Barry Steinberg; associate producer, Jeff Peters; director, Ron Satlof; based on characters created by Erle Stanley Gardner; teleplay, Hargrove; art director, David Jaquest; set decorator, Jardo Dick; costume designer, Ronn Rynhart; makeup, Irene Kent; music, Dick De Benedictis; "Perry Mason" theme by Fred Steiner; music editor, Ted Roberts; assistant directors, Richard Flower, Ross Clyde; camera, Albert J. Dunk; editors, Robert L. Kimble, Edwin F. England.

Raymond Burr (Perry Mason); Barbara Hale (Della Street); William Katt (Paul Drake, Jr.); Patrick O'Neal (Arthur Gordon);

---

*In *Twentieth-Century Crime and Mystery Writers* (1985), Hildegarde Withers is described as "... a snoopy old mail sleuth extraordinaire ... a schoolteacher, of the sharp-tongued, knuckle-wrapping variety, with a take-charge attitude and a tendency to treat suspects and police alike as if they were little boys caught cheating in class. She is lean and horsefaced, and given to wearing ghastly hats ... beneath the formidable exterior there is a great deal of kindness and sentimentality."

Richard Anderson (Ken Braddock); Cassie Yates (Barbara Scott); James Kidnie (Bobby Lynch); Holland Taylor (Paula Gordon); David McIlwraith (David Gordon); Roberta Weiss (Laura Gordon); Kerrie Keane (Kathryn Gordon); Al Freeman, Jr. (Lieutenant Cooper); Paul Hubbard (Sergeant Stratton); Lindsay Merrithew (Chris); Kathy Lasky (Lianne); Charles Macaulay (Judge Norman Whitewood); Mag Huffman (Salesgirl); Carolyn Hetherinton (Mrs. Jeffries); Cec Linder (District Attorney Jack Welles); John MacKenzie (Gas Station Attendant); David Bolt (Dr. Henderson); Doug Lennox (Vinnie); Frank Adamson (Mr. Williams); Lee Miller (Security Guard); Nerene Virgin (Minicam Reporter); Ken Pogue (Frank Lynch); Doris Petrie (Mrs. Lynch); Lillian Lewis (Customer); Perek Keurworst (Court Clerk).

PERRY MASON: THE CASE OF THE AVENGING ACE (NBC-TV, 2/28/88) Color 100 minutes.

Executive producers, Fred Silverman, Dean Hargrove; executive supervising producer, Philip Saltzman; supervising producer, Joel Steiger; producer, Peter Katz; associate producer, David Solomon; executive in charge of production, Mike Moder; director, Christina I. Nyby, II; based on characters created by Earl Stanley Gardner; teleplay, Lee David Zlotoff; art director, Paul Staheli; music, Dick De Benedictis; "Perry Mason" theme by Fred Steiner; sound, James Emerson; camera, Arch Bryant; editor, David Solomon.

Raymond Burr (Perry Mason); Barbara Hale (Della Street); William Katt (Paul Drake, Jr.); David Ogden Stiers (District Attorney Michael Reston); Gary Hershberger (Lieutenant Wilkins); Don Galloway (General Hobart); Larry Wilcox (Lieutenant Colonel Kevin Parks); and: Patty Duke, Gary Hershberger, James McEachin, Richard Sanders, Charles Siebert, James Sutorius, Arthur Taxier.

PERRY MASON: THE CASE OF THE LADY IN THE LAKE (NBC-TV, 5/15/88) Color 100 minutes.

Executive producers, Fred Silverman, Dean Hargrove; executive supervising producer, Philip Saltzman; supervising producer, Joel Steiger; producer, Peter Katz; director, Ron Satlof; based on characters created by Erle Stanley Gardner; teleplay, Shel Willens; art director, Paul Staheli; music, Dick De Benedictis; "Perry Mason" theme by Fred Steiner; sound, James Emerson; camera, Arch Bryant; editor, David Solomon.

Raymond Burr (Perry Mason); Barbara Hale (Della Street); William Katt (Paul Drake, Jr.); David Hasselhoff (Billy Travis); Doran Clark (Sara Wingate Travis); John Beck (Doug Vickers); David Ogden Stiers (District Attorney Michael Reston); Liane

Advertisement for PERRY MASON: THE CASE OF THE LADY IN THE LAKE (1988).

Langland (Lisa Blake); Audra Lindley (Mrs. Chaney); Darrell Larson (Skip Wingate); George Deloy (Frank Travis); and: Jim Beaver, Terrance Evans, Michael Flynn, John Ireland, Ric Jury, Wendy MacDonald, Carl Morrow, Michael Preston, Nadya Starr, David Watson.

PERRY MASON: THE CASE OF THE LOST LOVE (NBC-TV, 2/23/87) Color 100 minutes.

Executive producers, Fred Silverman, Dean Hargrove; producer, Barry Steinberg; supervising producer, Joel Steiger; associate producer, Jeff Peters; executive in charge of production, Mike Moder; director, Ron Satlof; based on characters created by Erle Stanley Gardner; story, Hargrove, Steiger; teleplay, Anne Collins; art director, Paul Staheli; costumes, Ronn Rynhart; makeup, Dee Sandela, Patti Dallas; music, Dick De Benedictis; "Perry Mason" theme by Fred Steiner; assistant director, Jim Masella; sound, Paul Clay; camera, Arch Bryant; editor, David Solomon.

Raymond Burr (Perry Mason); Barbara Hale (Della Street); William Katt (Paul Drake, Jr.); Jean Simmons (Laura Robertson); Gene Barry (Glen Robertson); Robert Mandan (Dr. Emmett Michaels); David Ogden Stiers (District Attorney Michael Reston); Robert Walden (Robert Lane); Stephen Elliott (Elliott Moore); Robert F. Lyons (Peter Dickson); Gordon Jump (Arthur Wellman); Jonathan Banks (Luke Dickson); Leslie Wing (Sergeant Linda Austin); Stephanie Dunnam (Jennifer Parker); and: Lucien Berrier, Julian Gamble, Virginia Gregory, Dee Dee Olinsky, Norvell Rose, Pam Ward.

PERRY MASON: THE CASE OF THE MURDERED MADAM (NBC-TV, 10/4/87) Color 100 minutes.

Executive producers, Fred Silverman, Dean Hargrove; executive supervising producer, Philip Saltzman; supervising producer, Joel Steiger; producer, Peter Katz; director, Ron Stalof; based on characters created by Earl Stanley Gardner; teleplay, Patricia Green; art director, Paul Staheli; music, Dick De Benedictis; "Perry Mason" theme by Fred Steiner; camera, Arch Bryant; editor, David Solomon.

Raymond Burr (Perry Mason); Barbara Hale (Della Street); William Katt (Paul Drake, Jr.); Ann Jillian (Suzanne Dominico); Vincent Baggetta (Tony Dominico); Daphne Ashbrook (Miranda Bonner); Bill Macy (Richard Wilson); John Rhys-Davies (Edward Tremayne); Anthony Geary (Steve Reynolds); David Ogden Stiers (District Attorney Michael Reston); and: Wendeline Harstone, Jamie Horton, Mike Moroff, John Nance, Michael Osborn, Richard Portnow, Kim Ulrich.

PERRY MASON: THE CASE OF THE NOTORIOUS NUN (NBC-TV, 5/25/86) Color 100 minutes.

Executive producers, Fred Silverman, Dean Hargrove; supervising producer, Joel Steiger; producer, Barry Steinberg; associate producer, Jeff Peters; director, Ron Satlof; based on characters created by Erle Stanley Gardner; teleplay, Steiger; production designer, Richard Wilcox; set decorator, Jim Erickson; costume designer, Ronn Rynhart; makeup, Jamie Brown; music, Dick De Bendictis; "Perry Mason" theme by Fred Steiner; music editor, Ted Roberts; assistant director, Jacques Methe; sound editor, William Westrom; camera, Hector Figueroa; editors, Robert Kimble, George Chanian.

Raymond Burr (Perry Mason); Barbara Hale (Della Street); William Katt (Paul Drake, Jr.); Timothy Bottoms (Father Thomas O'Neill); Jon Cypher (Dr. Peter Lattimore); Michele Greene (Sister Margaret); James McEachin (Detective Brock); Gerald S. O'Loughlin (Monsignor Kyser); William Prince (Archbishop Stefan Corro); Edward Winter (Jonathan Eastman); Barbara Parkins (Ellen Cartwright); David Ogden Stiers (District Attorney Michael Reston); Tom Bosley (Father DeLeon); Arthur Hill (Thomas Shea); Hagan Beggs (Richard Logan); and: Donna Cox, Alex Diakun, Dennis Kelli, Jane Mortifee, David Petersen, Marie Stillin.

PERRY MASON: THE CASE OF THE SCANDALOUS SCOUNDREL (NBC-TV, 11/15/87) Color 100 minutes.

Executive producers, Fred Silverman, Dean Hargrove; executive supervising producer, Philip Saltzman; supervising producer, Joel Steiger; producer, Peter Katz; based on characters created by Erle Stanley Gardner; teleplay, Anthony Spinner; art director; music, Dick De Benedictis; "Perry Mason" theme by Fred Steiner; camera, Arch Bryant; editor, David Solomon.

Raymond Burr (Perry Mason); Barbara Hale (Della Street); William Katt (Paul Drake, Jr.); Morgan Brittany (Marianne Clayman); Yaphet Kotto (General Sorensen); Robert Guillaume (Harlan Wade); Rene Enriquez (Oscar Ortega); George Grizzard (Dr. Clayman); Wings Hauser (James Rivers); Susan Wilder (Michele).

PERRY MASON: THE CASE OF THE SHOOTING STAR (NBC-TV, 11/9/86) Color 100 minutes.

Executive producers, Fred Silverman, Dean Hargrove; supervising producer, Joel Steiger; producer, Barry Steinberg; associate producer, Jeff Peters; based on characters created by Erle Stanley Gardner; story, Hargrove, Steiger; teleplay, Anne C. Collins; art director, Charles Dunlop; makeup, Irene Kent; music, Dick De

Benedictis; "Perry Mason" theme by Fred Steiner; camera, Hector Figueroa; editor, David Solomon.

Raymond Burr (Perry Mason); Barbara Hale (Della Street); William Katt (Paul Drake, Jr.); Joe Penny (Robert McCay); Ron Glass (Eric Brenner); Alan Thicke (Steve Carr); Ivan Dixon (Judge); Wendy Crewson (Michelle Benti); David Ogden Stiers (District Attorney Michael Reston); Jennifer O'Neill (Alison Carr); Ross Petty (Peter Towne); Mary Kane (Kate Huntley); Lisa Howard (Sharon Loring): and: J. Kenneth Campbell, Michael Donaghue, Jon Evans, Bryan Genesse, Ken James, Cec Linder, Mag Ruffman, Lee Wilkof.

PERRY MASON: THE CASE OF THE SINISTER SPIRIT (NBC-TV, 5/24/87) Color 100 minutes.

Executive producers, Fred Silverman, Dean Hargrove, producer, Barry Steinberg; supervising producer, Joel Steiger; associate producer, Jeff Peters; executive in charge of production, Mike Moder; director, Richard Lang; based on characters created by Erle Stanley Gardner; story, Hargrove, Steiger, Glenn Benest, Timothy Wurtz; teleplay, Anne Collins; art director, Paul Staheli; costume designer, Ron Rynhart; music, Dick De Benedictis; "Perry Mason" theme by Fred Steiner; stunt coordinator, Roy Harrison; sound, James Emerson; sound editor, Michael Graham; camera, Arch Bryant; editor, David Solomon.

Raymond Burr (Perry Mason); Barbara Hale (Della Street); William Katt (Paul Drake, Jr.); Robert Stack (Jordan White); Dwight Schultz (Andrew Lloyd); Kim Delaney (Susan Warrenfield); Dennis Lipscomb (Michael Light); Leigh Taylor-Young (Maura McGuire); Jack Bannon (Donald Sayer); David Ogden Stiers (District Attorney Michael Reston); Matthew Faison (David Hall); Percy Rodriquez (Dr. Froman).

From 1957 to 1966 Raymond Burr portrayed Erle Stanley Gardner's lawyer detective on CBS-TV's highly successful series, "Perry Mason." Barbara Hale co-starred as loyal, efficient secretary Della Street while William Hopper was Mason's private investigator, Paul Drake. Ray Collins was Lieutenant Tragg and William Talman was prosecutor Hamilton Burger, his nemesis on the side of the law. The series had a brief, unsuccessful revival on CBS-TV in 1973-74, with Monte Markham as Mason. With the late 1970s and 1980s success of telefilms based on once-popular TV shows, it was only reasonable to bring Perry Mason back to TV. This was done in 1985 with PERRY MASON RETURNS, with Raymond Burr now a heavier and (grey) bearded Mason. Barbara Hale returned also as Della Street, and her son, William Katt, played detective Paul

Drake, Jr., William Hopper having died since the earlier series. The production was shot on location in Toronto, Canada.

"The Accused: Della Street. The Solution: Perry Mason. Only One Thing could bring him back: his lifelong friend's framed for murder! PERRY MASON RETURNS is his toughest case!" read the advertising for this telefilm in which Perry Mason (Raymond Burr) resigns his judgeship to defend former secretary Della Street (Barbara Hale), who is charged with killing her new boss for his money. Mason enlists the aid of Paul Drake, Jr. (William Katt), the son of his former private investigator, to ferret out why Della has been set up in this case. He soon finds himself pitted against an aggressive female district attorney (Cassie Yates). In *TV Guide* magazine, Judith Crist reported that the production " . . . sets the old nostalgia afire. . . . It's all pleasantly old hat. . . ." *TV Movies and Video Guide* (1988) noted, "Writer Dean Hargrove's script is given the time and space to evoke the real Erle Stanley Gardner. Above average. . . ."

PERRY MASON RETURNS proved to be an enormous success in the TV ratings and as a result eight more Mason telefeatures have followed to date, beginning with PERRY MASON: THE CASE OF THE NOTORIOUS NUN. Here Perry Mason (Raymond Burr) takes the case of Sister Margaret (Michele Greene), a nun accused of killing Father O'Neill (Timothy Bottoms), a priest with whom she may have been linked romantically. Snide District Attorney Michael Reston (David Ogden Stiers) believes the nun is guilty and accuses her of killing the priest because he rejected her advances. Judith Crist, in *TV Guide* magazine, called the film " . . . very good and the whodunit engrossing." At the time the film was in production, NBC-TV announced that another half-dozen movies with Raymond Burr would be produced. As with the first two Mason TV movies, Barbara Hale was cast as Della Street and William Katt played Paul Drake, Jr. The teleplays were all original stories, as would be the case with each of the new installments.

The second Mason TV movie was shown in the spring of 1986 and late that fall came PERRY MASON: THE CASE OF THE SHOOTING STAR. The story has self-centered actor Robert McCay (Joe Penny) killing smart-mouthed TV talk show host Steve Carr (Alan Thicke) before an audience of forty million people. Mason (Raymond Burr) is called in to defend the accused and is opposed again by District Attorney Michael Reston (David Ogden Stiers). "What adds zest to the comfortably familiar red-herringed plot is the New York City seething with 'inside' views of moviemaking and telecasting," wrote Judith Crist in *TV Guide* magazine. The casting of TV host-turned-actor Alan Thicke as the victim provided additional interest.

Early in 1987 NBC-TV telecast PERRY MASON: THE CASE OF THE LOST LOVE in which Perry Mason's (Raymond Burr) former lover, Laura Robertson (Jean Simmons), is being black-mailed by a man (Jonathan Banks) who has information that she once had a nervous breakdown and underwent shock treatments in a mental institution. The information would obviously jeopardize her upcoming senatorial campaign. When the blackmailer is murdered, Laura's husband (Gene Barry) is charged with the killing and Laura asks Mason to defend him. "Will a passion from 30 years ago finally get the better of him? It's a murder that's left even him without a clue!" read the advertising for the TV film. Miles Beller (*The Hollywood Reporter*) decided, "Admittedly, this Masonry doesn't stack up quite as high as the previous three TV projects. However, it is imminently [*sic*] watchable, despite its rather implausible claims. . . . [It] is a solid chunk of entertainment, as durable and dependable as the TV attorney, a TV courtroom figure who continues to cast a long shadow."

In the spring of 1987 NBC-TV presented PERRY MASON: THE CASE OF THE SINISTER SPIRIT, which seemed to borrow its premise from Agatha Christie's TEN LITTLE INDIANS, *q.v.* Mystery novelist David Hall (Matthew Faison) invites diverse guests for a holiday at the remote Briarcliff Hotel to celebrate the publica-tion of his latest book. The invitees include Hall's secretary, Andrew Lloyd (Dwight Schultz); his publisher, Jordan White (Robert Stack); psychic Donald Sayer (Jack Bannon); movie star Maura McGuire (Leigh Taylor-Young) and astrologer Michael Light (Dennis Lipscomb). Once there the guests are tormented by Hall for past incidents in their lives, but the writer ends up falling to his death from a bell tower. Susan Warrenfield (Kim Delaney), the hotel's assistant manager, points the finger of guilt at White, who then asks Perry Mason to defend him against a murder case. "These Mason movies have got so ubiquitous they're starting to blend into the TV landscape. Yet expertly and stolidly fashioned (script-writer Anne Collins has masterfully handled this mystery), they are like Volkswagens of the airwaves, good, sturdy entertainment vehicles that are trustwor-thy and dependable" (Miles Beller, *The Hollywood Reporter*). More blunt in its assessment was *Daily Variety,* which pinpointed, "Diffi-culty here is attempting to tell a one-hour tale in twice that time. Events move at an excruciatingly slow pace, with dialog almost comically deliberate—as though main concern was to fill the minutes."

The next Mason TV production, shown in the fall of 1987 was

PERRY MASON: THE CASE OF THE MURDERED MADAM: "When the wife of a friend turns out to be a call girl, it's more than scandalous. . . . It's murder," exclaimed the advertising for this telefeature. An ex-madam (Ann Jillian) who became a public relations executive is found murdered and her jealous husband (Vincent Baggetta) is accused of the crime. Perry Mason (Raymond Burr) comes to his defense. He unravels the case with the aid of a former prostitute (Daphne Ashbrook) and finds out that the murdered woman was done in because she electronically bugged a luncheon meeting in which four businessmen discussed a planned bank-fraud operation. "It's pleasant enough and just a bit mechanical," admitted Judith Crist in *TV Guide* magazine, while *Daily Variety* opined, "Pic is not up to norm for the Mason mysteries, long on talk, short on action."

PERRY MASON: THE CASE OF THE SCANDALOUS SCOUNDREL was telecast November 15, 1987. Here Mason (Raymond Burr) is the defense attorney for a newswoman (Susan Wilder) who is accused of killing the publisher (Robert Guillaume) of a tacky tabloid newspaper. Mason realizes the case includes a number of other suspects, including a banker smeared by the murdered man and the woman he rejects. He sets out to win acquittal for his client by disclosing the real killer. "This one doesn't play quite fair with mystery-lovers, but in this series it's the old familiars who count," said *TV Guide* magazine's Judith Crist.

"The beautiful victim always got what she wanted . . . except one," announced the promotional for the eighth Perry Mason TV movie, PERRY MASON: THE CASE OF THE AVENGING ACE, telecast by NBC-TV on February 28, 1988. Perry Mason (Raymond Burr) is called upon to defend a famous Air Force officer (Larry Wilcox) who is accused of murdering a young woman. Mason knows he has been framed and sets out to prove his innocence. As in the preceding six Mason telefeatures, David Ogden Stiers is the near-obnoxious chief opponent, District Attorney Michael Reston. *TV Guide* magazine complained, "Each time out, it seems these efforts get more predictable and (no offense to Raymond Burr intended) more flabby. This one is just a run-of-the-mill PERRY MASON episode rattling around in a two-hour time slot."

The ninth Perry Mason TV movie, and the third one for the 1987-88 season, was telecast May 15, 1988 by NBC-TV. PERRY MASON: THE CASE OF THE LADY IN THE LAKE has *nothing* to do with Raymond Chandler's novel, *q.v.* Instead it has Perry Mason (Raymond Burr), with the aid of Della Street (Barbara Hale) and private investigator Paul Drake, Jr. (William Katt), defending former tennis star Billy Travis (David Hasselhoff) who is accused of murdering his rich wife Sara (Doran Clark) by drowning her at the lake near her remote lodge estate—the same lake where her sister disappeared fifteen years before. Mason, however, uncovers a number of other suspects including Travis' embittered ex-girlfriend, waitress Lisa Blake (Liane Langland); Sara's uncle/guardian (John Ireland); her no-good cousin Skip Wingate (Darrell Larson); Doug Vickers (John Beck), Sara's former boyfriend and president of her mining company; estate manager Mrs. Chaney (Audra Lindley); and Billy's gambler brother, Frank Travis (George Deloy). Opposing Mason on the case is belligerent District Attorney Michael Reston (David Ogden Stiers). *The Hollywood Reporter* felt the film was "as ponderous as Raymond Burr's physique," while *Daily Variety* opined, "Barnaby Jones solved cases tougher than this many times—and in one hour. . . . Telefilm has deteriorated into a routine two-hour telefilm with the case sorted out in about the same fashion as the last one and the one before." On the other hand, *TV Guide* magazine decided, "This one is less predictable than any of the others."

And there are definite promises of several more telefeature installments of PERRY MASON to come.

THE PHANTOM FIEND *see* THE LODGER (1932).

PHILO VANCE RETURNS (Producers Releasing Corp., 1947) 64 minutes.

Producer, Howard Welsch; director, William Beaudine; based on the character created by S. S. Van Dine [Willard Huntington Wright]; screenplay, Robert E. Kent; art director, Perry Smith; set decorator, Armor Marlow; music, Albert Glasser; music director, Irving Friedman; assistant director, Emmett Emerson; dialogue director, William Kunell; sound, J. N. A. Hawkins, Percy Townsend; camera effects, George Teague; camera, Jackson Rose; editor, Gene Fowler.

William Wright (Philo Vance); Terry Austin (Lorena Simms); Leon Belasco (Alexis); Clara Blandick (Stella Blendon); Ramsey Ames (Virginia); Damian O'Flynn (Larry Blendon); Frank Wilcox (George Hullman); Iris Adrian (Choo-Choo Divine); Ann Staunton (Helen Sandman); Tim Murdock (Policeman); Mary Scott (Maid).

The character of detective Philo Vance was portrayed by S. S. Van Dine [Willard Huntington Wright] as a debonair, sophisticated sleuth with an upper-crust background. For most of his screen career a succession of actors (William Powell, Basil Rathbone, Warren William, Paul Lukas, Grant Richards) portrayed him in this stylized manner. In 1940 James Stephenson played Vance as a tough guy in CALLING PHILO VANCE for Warner Bros., and in 1947

William Wright (keeping in tune with the post-World War II aim of more pragmatic realism in films) made him an even more hard-boiled detective in PHILO VANCE RETURNS. Regarding this 1947 production *Film Daily* noted, "For the film mystery-murder fan PHILO VANCE RETURNS has what it takes to provide an hour's diversion. . . . William Beaudine's direction supplies required whodunit elements in proper, effective style."

When wealthy playboy Larry Blendon (Damian O'Flynn) plans to marry for the fifth time, his fiancée and an ex-wife are murdered. The man's aunt, Stella Blendon (Clara Blandick), calls Philo Vance (William Wright) into the case and the detective learns that the man's three surviving ex-wives all had strong motives for the killings. With the aid of art dealer Alexis (Leon Belasco) Vance tries to get to the bottom of the homicides, but the affair becomes even more muddled when Blendon himself is murdered. Besides the ex-wives, fan dancer Choo-Choo Divine (Iris Adrian) becomes a prime suspect because she is named in Blendon's will. As the killer closes in on another female victim (Terry Austin), Vance apprehends the murderer, a close relative of Blendon's.

PHILO VANCE RETURNS, which was ten days in production, was successful enough at the box-office to warrant PRC producing two follow-ups: PHILO VANCE'S GAMBLE and PHILO VANCE'S SECRET MISSION (both 1947). However, William Wright was replaced by Alan Curtis as Vance, with Frank Jenks playing his cohort, Ernie Clark. Again Vance was played in the rough guy image and not as the urban sophisticate of the polished Van Dine novels.

PITFALL (United Artists, 1948) 85 minutes.

Producer, Samuel Bischoff; director, Andre De Toth; based on the novel *The Pitfall* by Jay Dratler; screenplay, Karl Lamb; music director, Louis Forbes; assistant director, Joseph Depew; art director, Arthur Lonergan; set decorator, Robert Priestley; makeup, Robert Cowan; assistant director, Joe Depew; sound, Frank Webster; camera, Harry Wild; editor, Walter Thompson.

Dick Powell (John Forbes); Lizabeth Scott (Mona Stevens); Jane Wyatt (Sue Forbes); Raymond Burr (MacDonald); John Litel (District Attorney); Byron Barr (Bill Smiley); Jimmy Hunt (Tommy Forbes); Ann Doran (Maggie); Selmer Jackson (Ed Brawley); Margaret Wells (Terry); Dick Wessel (Desk Sergeant).

Los Angeles insurance man John Forbes (Dick Powell) is after stolen property. He finds it with beautiful Mona Stevens (Lizabeth Scott); she got it from her boyfriend (Byron Barr) who is now in prison. Forbes and Mona begin an affair but he keeps it secret from his wife (Jane Wyatt) and their young son Tommy (Jimmy Hunt). Private detective MacDonald (Raymond Burr), an obese man, lusts for Mona and wants Forbes out of the way. He visits the woman's former boyfriend in prison and informs him about her link with Forbes. After Barr is released from prison MacDonald gets him drunk and takes him to Forbes' home, where the insurance man shoots him, allegedly in self-defense. Forbes' wife agrees to protect him and they tell the police that the man was a burglar. Forbes also wants to break up with Mona, who kills MacDonald when he tries to force his attentions on her. Forbes confesses to the prosecutor (John Litel) about killing the man but he is not held. Mona is arrested and charged with murdering MacDonald.

A *film noir* melodrama, PITFALL (36 days in production) reflects the disillusionment of the post-World War II period. Insurance man Forbes is unhappy with his job and his suburban life until he meets siren-like Mona, whom he never tells he is married. Like most *film noir* characters, Forbes has little if any control over the world around him and his life seems run by others: his wife, his girlfriend, and the grasping detective MacDonald who wants him out of the way so he can have Mona for himself. Here the detective is definitely a villainous character and, as per the Hays Office standards, he is killed before the film's finale.

"A double standard is at work in PITFALL. Scott is prosecuted for the killing of Burr, while Powell, who is morally responsible and confesses everything to the District Attorney, is not tried for the killing of Barr. But then, going back to his former lifestyle is perhaps enough punishment for him. PITFALL is a moralistic film which ultimately reaffirms middle-class life," decided Robert Ottoson in *A Reference Guide to the American Film Noir: 1940-1958* (1981).

Dick Powell, Lizabeth Scott, Jane Wyatt, and Raymond Burr would repeat their screen roles in the "Lux Radio Theatre" adaptation of PITFALL, broadcast on November 8, 1948.

THE PLOT THICKENS (RKO, 1936) 67 minutes.

Producer, William Sistrom; director, Ben Holmes; based on the story "The Riddle of The Dangling Pearl" by Stuart Palmer; screenplay, Clarence Upson Young, Jack Townley; camera, Nick Musuraca; editor, John Leckert.

James Gleason (Inspector Oscar Piper); ZaSu Pitts (Hildegarde Martha Withers); Owen Davis, Jr. (Robert Wilkins); Louise Latimer (Alice Stevens); Arthur Aylesworth (Kendall); Richard Tucker (John Carter); Paul Fix (Joe); Barbara Barondess (Marie); James Dolan (Jim); Agnes Anderson (Dagmar); Oscar Apfel (Robbins).

Wealthy John Carter (Richard Tucker) is killed in his car by one person and then taken to his garage and from there transported to his library, the last two times by a different individual. Gotham police Inspector Oscar Piper (James Gleason) investigates with the unsolicited aid of snoopy school teacher Hildegarde Martha Withers (ZaSu Pitts). Piper believes the murder was the result of a love triangle, but Miss Withers finds a clue which puts them on the trail of an international jewel theft operation. After another murder occurs it becomes apparent that the thieves are after the Cosmopolitan Museum's priceless Cellini Cup, and when the killer attempts to plant a bogus one in place of the real object, he is captured, thanks to a ruse planned and executed by Miss Withers.

Based on Stuart Palmer's short story "The Riddle of the Dangling Pearl," THE PLOT THICKENS is the first of two RKO entries with ZaSu Pitts as Hildegarde Withers (James Gleason continues in his role of police investigator Oscar Piper). Usually known for her roles as a flighty comedienne, ZaSu Pitts was badly miscast as Hildegarde Withers, a part played to perfection by Edna May Oliver in THE PENGUIN POOL MURDER (1932), murder on the blackboard (1934) and MURDER ON A HONEYMOON (1935), *qq.v.*, and by Helen Broderick in the letdown MURDER ON A BRIDLE PATH (1936), *q.v.* "Thanks to the miscasting of Pitts, and Ben Holmes' sub-standard direction, this was the most anaemic chapter in an otherwise felicitous RKO series," determined Richard B. Jewell and Vernon Harbin in *The RKO Story* (1982).

Frank S. Nugent commented in the *New York Times,* "It is a reasonably entertaining baffler, barring our faint wince at the sight of ZaSu Pitts trying to fill the saturnine shoes of Edna May Oliver and Helen Broderick. Miss Pitts is better as a midnight screamer during the unreeling of these detective epics than she is as an inquisitive and reliable amateur Philo [Vance]."

ZaSu Pitts and James Gleason continued the Hildegarde Withers series for one more tepid entry, FORTY NAUGHTY GIRLS (1937), *q.v.*

British release title: THE SWINGING PEARL MYSTERY.

PRIVATE DETECTIVE (Warner Bros., 1939) 57 minutes.

Producer, Bryan Foy; director Noel Smith; based on the story "Invitation to Murder" by Kay Krause; screenplay, Earle Snell, Raymond Schrock; assistant director, William Kissell; camera, Ted McCord; editor, Harold McLernon.

Jane Wyman (Myrna Winslow); Dick Foran (Jim Rickey); Gloria Dickson (Mona Lannon); Maxie Rosenbloom (Brody); John Ridgely (Donald Norton); Morgan Conway (Nat Flavin); John Eldredge (Millard Lannon); Joseph Crehan (Murphy); William Davidson (Evans); Selmar Jackson (Sanger); Vera Lewis (Mrs. Widner); Julie Stevens (Mona's Maid); Jack Mower (Officer Dolan); Henry Blair (Bobby Lannon); Earl Dwire (Justice of the Peace); Willie Best (Valet); Creighton Hale (Coroner); Leo Gorcey (Newsboy); Maris Wrixon (Telephone Operator); Sol Gorss (Taxi Driver); Lottie Williams (Mrs. Smith); Frank Dae (Judge).

Saucy Jane Wyman had played female sleuth/newspaper reporter Torchy Blane in the last entry of that series, TORCHY PLAYS WITH DYNAMITE (1939), and the formula for that series was continued in PRIVATE DETECTIVE, based on an original story by Kay Krause. Apparently the mixture of having private eye Wyman outwit her policeman boyfriend, also the premise of the Torchy Blane films, was to be continued into a new series, but only PRIVATE DETECTIVE materialized.

Myrna Winslow (Jane Wyman) is the owner of a private detective agency is the lady love of policeman Jim Rickey (Dick Foran), who is fed up with her meddling in his cases. Myrna takes the case of

Jane Wyman and Dick Foran in PRIVATE DETECTIVE (1939).

a pretty young widow Mona Lannon (Gloria Dickson) who, along with boyfriend Donald Norton (John Ridgely), is accused of murdering her late millionaire husband for his money. Also involved is a large trust fund intended for the millionaire's young son (Henry Blair). The police are convinced that Mona and Norton are the culprits but Myrna investigates and finds crooked legal machinations have occurred. She pinpoints the killer, thus exonerating her client.

Variety reported, "Plot unwinds according to formula, but provides some actionful and suspenseful moments, although the situations are obviously elemental and far-fetched. . . . Picture is up to par for nominal budgeter." Added relief to the proceedings is provided by boxing champ Maxie Rosenbloom in another of his comical dumb-guy roles.

PRIVATE DETECTIVE 62 (Warner Bros., 1933) 67 minutes.

Director, Michael Curtiz; story, Raoul Whitfield; screenplay, Rian James; dialogue director, Arthur Greville Collins; art director, Jack Okey; camera, Tony Gaudio; editor, Harold McLernon.

William Powell (Donald Free); Margaret Lindsay (Janet Reynolds); Ruth Donnelly (Amy Moran); Gordon Westcott (Tony Bandor); James Bell (Whitey); Arthur Hohl (Dan Hogan); Arthur Byron (Tracey); Natalie Moorhead (Helen Burns); Sheila Terry (Mrs. Wright); Hobart Cavanaugh (Harcourt S. Burns); Theresa Harris (Maid); Renee Whitney (Alice); Ann Hovey (Rose); Irving Bacon (Cab Driver); Georges Renavent (Captain La Farge); Eddie Phillips (Lover); Toby Wing (Girl Friend); Pat Wing (Secretary); Eddie Dunn (Doorman); George Brent (Club Extra); [William] Bill Elliott (Gambling Kibitzer); Rolfe Sedan (Casino Man); Harry Seymour (Gambler); Charles Wilson, Heinie Conklin (Bartenders); Charles Lane (Process Server).

Between playing Philo Vance and Nick Charles (in the Thin Man series), William Powell sandwiched in the role of a private eye in this limp detective feature which director Michael Curtiz churned out for Warner Bros., following another sleuthing assignment (also with Powell), THE KEYHOLE (1933), *q.v.* Not only is PRIVATE DETECTIVE 62 a weak film but at no time is it explained why the number 62 appears in the title. It should be noted, though, that the production is based on a story by Raoul Whitfield, himself a one-time regular writer for *Black Mask* magazine.

Former Paris-based government operative and spy Donald Free (William Powell), who has been discredited for shady dealings, takes up the profession of private detective in New York City. He joins a disreputable firm that specializes in divorce matters. Free's unethical agency is hired by a gambling club to prevent a lucky winner, Janet Reynolds (Margaret Lindsay), from collecting her $50,000 winnings. Thanks to a frame-up, she becomes the chief suspect in a murder case. Free becomes involved innocently in the proceedings and soon realizes that she has been framed and the job was done by someone with whom he is closely associated. The detective solves the case, wins Janet's affection, and regains his government post.

Variety noted, "As it unfolds on the screen it's episodic and disconnected. Powell does some admirable work, both in the comedy moments and elsewhere, but so much of the action is implausible that it curtails real customer satisfaction which could have reacted to Powell under better story conditions."

TV title: MAN KILLER.

PRIVATE EYE (NBC-TV, 9/13/87) Color 100 minutes.

Executive producer, Anthony Yerkovich; co-producer, Frederick Lyle; supervising producer, Scott Brazil; director, Mark Tinker; teleplay, Yerkovich; production designer, John Vallone; art director, Michael Corenblith; set decorator, Robert Gould; makeup, Cheri Minns; costume supervisors, Karen Bellamy, Michael Voight; music, Joe Jackson; stunt coordinator, Ernie Orsatti; sound, Bill Marky; camera, Bradford May; editor, David Rosenbloom.

Michael Woods (Jack Cleary); Josh Brolin (Johnny Betts); Faye Grant (Lana); Jay O. Sanders (Nick Cleary); Bill Sadler (Detective Charlie Fontana); Lisa Jane Persky (Dottie); Frederick Coffin (Dan Dibble); Stanley Kamel (Bobby Bator); Anthony Carnota (Battista); Robert Picardo, (Eddie Rosen); and: Jeannine Bisignano, Andrew Block, Simmy Bow, Don Calfa, Gary Lee Davis, Keith Joe Dick, Lisa Dunsheath, Hogan H. Evans, Tom Finnegan, Maria Frumkin, Roy Galloway, Michael Gerard, Hugh Gillin, Joe Horvath, Ron Karabetsos, James Intveld, Bruno Marcotulli, William Moore, Lee Shaef, Peter A. Stelzer, Tom Mustin, Josef Powell, Luther Waters, Oren Waters.

The telefeature pilot for the NBC-TV series, "Private Eye," this outing, set in 1956 Los Angeles, proved to be an actionful, if rather mundane, film. In fact, the production at times is so tiresome that one wonders how it was to spawn a credible series. The script is by Anthony Yerkovich, who created the popular small-screen action program, "Miami Vice."

When his gumshoe brother Nick (Jay O. Sanders) is murdered while working on a case, former policeman Jack Cleary (Michael Woods) investigates and enlists the aid of his late sibling's partner, Betts (Josh Brolin). The puzzle-solving becomes more complex when Lana (Faye Grant) shows up drunk at Cleary's door begging for help. It seems her record promoter husband has been murdered and this was the case on which Cleary's brother was working when he too was killed. Despite trouble with dishonest former cohorts on the police force, Cleary uncovers that the killings were centered around surveillance tapes and he and Betts bring in the criminals.

Daily Variety complained, "Telefilm . . . for some reason, employs gangsters, whiskey and cigarettes, head bashing and a good-pal secretary, wealth spread over rottenness, a crooked cop or two, and a good-looking femme client who needs some investigating. To make up for the tiresome plotting, the vidpic uses dialog so contrived or artificial it matches the action."

On the other hand, Miles Beller (*The Hollywood Reporter*) was more positive in his reaction. "The preview of PRIVATE EYE makes for stylish television (distinguished by a great look and superb music that frequently is more '40s than '50s) but is a bit bloated in this 120-minute intro. However, Woods and Brolin get the chemistry going, and one expects that in its shorter, regular hour timeslot PRIVATE EYES will perform more sharply."

The NBC network teleseries debuted on September 13, 1987 and was off the air by January 8, 1988.

PRIVATE EYES (Allied Artists, 1953) 64 minutes.

Producer, Ben Schwalb; director, Edward Bernds; screenplay, Elwood Ullman, Bernds; art director, David Milton; set decorator, Charles Steenson; wardrobe, Smoke Kring; makeup, Norman Pringle; music director, Marlin Skiles; assistant director, Austin Jewell; sound, Charles Cooper; camera, Carl Gutherie; editor, Lester A. Sansom.

Leo Gorcey (Terrence Aloysius "Slip" Mahoney); Huntz Hall (Horace Debussy "Sach" Jones); David Condon (Chuck); Bennie Bartlett (Butch); Bernard Gorcey (Louie Dumbrowski); Rudy Lee (Herbie); Joyce Holden (Myra Hagen); Robert Osterloh (Professor Damon); William Forrest (John Graham); Peter Marnakos (Chico); Myron Healey (Karl); Tim Ryan (Andy the Cop); Lou Lubin (Oskar); Emil Sirka (Wheelchair Patient); William Phillips (Soapy); Gil Perkins (Al); Edith Leslie (Aggie the Nurse); Chick Chandler (Eddie the Detective); Lee Van Cleef (Man).

The budget features of the Bowery Boys (who evolved from The Dead End Kids, The Little Tough Guys and The East Side Kids) were exceedingly popular programmer fodder in the 1940s and 1950s, and their shenanigans touched almost every film genre. PRIVATE EYES proved to be the Bowery Boys excursion into the realm of detection and the results are surprisingly good. The film's speedy plot gives stars Leo Gorcey and Huntz Hall plenty of opportunity to indulge in their unique brand of burlesque-type antics and slapstick.

When his pal Herbie (Rudy Lee) punches him in the nose, Sach Jones (Huntz Hall) finds out he can read minds, and he and his buddy Slip Mahoney (Leo Gorcey) open the Eagle Eye Detective Agency. They take the case of Myra Hagen (Joyce Holden) who leaves evidence with the two sufficient enough to jail members of a mink-coat theft racket which once employed the young woman. When the gangsters attempt to gain possession of the envelope with the information they are unsuccessful, since Sach has locked it in a safe and forgotten the combination. The hoodlums then kidnap Herbie and Myra and use them as hostages to retrieve the envelope. But Slip and Sach find out that the two are being held at a sanitarium. Slip pretends to be Dr. Hockenlopper from Vienna, Sach becomes wealthy Mrs. Abernathy, and the two march into the sanitarium. Their true identities are soon discovered and after a fracas in which the hoodlums are trapped in a mineral bath, the crooks are turned over to the police and the victims released.

"PRIVATE EYES is the fastest-paced entry in the Bowery Boys series and one of the funniest. Transcending its meager budget, the film is consistently brisk and does not let up for a moment, allowing Gorcey and Hall to romp freely. Much of the credit must be given to director Edward Bernds, who let the boys perform without too much plot interference," judged David Hayes and Brent Walker in *The Films of The Bowery Boys* (1984).

THE PRIVATE LIFE OF SHERLOCK HOLMES (United Artists, 1970) Color 125 minutes.

Producer, Billy Wilder; associate producer, I. A. L. Diamond; director, Wilder; based on the characters created by Sir Arthur Conan Doyle; screenplay, Wilder, Diamond; production designer, Alexander Trauner; art director, Tony Inglis; set decorator, Harry Cordwell; costumes, Julie Harris; makeup, Ernest Gasser; music, Miklos Rozsa; dances arranger/ballet adviser, David Blair; assistant director, Tom Pevsner; sound, J. W. N. Daniel, Dudley Messenger, Gordon MacCallum; special effects, Wally Veevers, Cliff Richardson; camera, Christopher Challis; editor, Ernest Walter.

Robert Stephens (Sherlock Holmes); Colin Blakely (Dr. John H. Watson); Irene Handl (Mrs. Hudson); Stanley Holloway, Eric Francis (Gravediggers); Christopher Lee (Mycroft Holmes); Genevieve Page (Gabrielle Valladon); Clive Revill (Rogozhin); Tamara Toumanova (Petrova); George Benson (Inspector Lestrade); Catherine Lacey (Old Lady); Mollie Maureen (Queen Victoria); Peter Madden (Von Tirpitz); Robert Cawdron (Hotel Manager); Michael

Elwyn (Cassidy); Michael Balfour (Cabby); Frank Thornton (Porter); James Copeland (Guide); Alex McCrindle (Baggage Man); Kenneth Benda (Minister); Graham Armitage (Wiggins); John Garrie, Godfrey James (Carters); Ina De La Haye (Petrova's Maid); Ismet Hassan, Charlie Young Atom, Teddy Kiss Atom, Willie Shearer (Submarine Crew); Daphne Riggs (Lady-in-Waiting); John Gatrell (Equerry); Martin Carroll, John Scott (Scientists); Philip Anthony (Lieutenant Commander); Phillipi Ross (McKellar); Annette Kerr (Secretary); Kynaston Reeves (Old Man); Anne Blake (Madame); Marilyn Head, Anna Matisse, Wendy Lingham, Penny Brahms, Sheena Hunter (Girls); Tina Spooner, Judy Spooner (Twins); and: Paul Hansard, David Kossoff, Paul Stassino.

Billy Wilder's production of THE PRIVATE LIFE OF SHERLOCK HOLMES, which Wilder co-wrote with his long-time associate I. A. L. Diamond, is probably the most unpopular Sherlock Holmes motion picture ever made. The public stayed away in droves, making it a box-office dud. Almost everything about the film, except the recreation of the gaslight era, was made contrary to the well-known literary origins of Holmes. Here Robert Stephens portrays the sleuth as near-effeminate, Dr. Watson is rather scatterbrained, and brother Mycroft (played by gaunt Christopher Lee in contrast to the corpulent Mycroft of literature) was shown as the real brains of the picture. To cement the fiasco, Sherlock Holmes is depicted as being completely deceived by a German spy and drowning his idle hours and failures in drugs.

Lacking in substantial cases, Sherlock Holmes (Robert Stephens) returns to his cocaine habit, much to the chagrin of his friend Dr. John H. Watson (Colin Blakely). The two receive tickets to the Russian ballet and after the performance the famous ballerina Petrova (Tamara Toumanova) sexually propositions Holmes, hoping to conceive a child of great beauty and intelligence. The detective declines and hints that he is familiar with Watson, much to the latter's distaste. A new case arises involving some disappearing midgets and a nearly drowned woman who appears at 221B Baker Street. The latter is Belgian Gabrielle Valladon (Genevieve Page), who is seeking her missing husband. Holmes and Watson travel to Scotland to consult Holmes' older brother, Mycroft (Christopher Lee), who tells him to steer clear of the case. While crossing Loch Ness in a small boat, Holmes and Watson are attacked by what appears to be the legendary Loch Ness monster, but the two manage to get ashore. Mycroft shows Holmes plans for a submarine headquartered in the Loch which will be run by the midgets but says that Queen Victoria (Mollie Maureen) has ordered the project halted. Mycroft informs him that Gabrielle is in reality a German spy who has used him to find the whereabouts of the submarine, although the Japanese have killed her because of her spy work. Dejected because of his failure, Holmes returns to his Baker Street flat and his drugs.

Arlene Kramborg reported in *Films in Review* magazine (November 1970), "The bulk of the action is unbelievable. . . . It's so flat-footed, crudely put together, and unfunny, one is amazed that Wilder and his collaborator were its authors. Ditto for the dialogue, once a Wilder-Diamond forte."

On Wilder's behalf, it should be noted that a major sequence was deleted from the film's final release prints. It had Holmes confiding to Watson that years before he had been jilted by a young woman, hence his current mistrust of women. The scene sheds new light on his rejection of Petrova and makes it even more ironic that he should be tantalized and duped by the beautiful spy.

PURSUIT TO ALGIERS (Universal, 1945) 65 minutes.

Executive producer, Howard Benedict; producer/director, Roy William Neill; based on the story "The Return of Sherlock Holmes" by Sir Arthur Conan Doyle; screenplay, Leonard Lee; art directors, John B. Goodman, Martin Obzina; set decorators, Russell A. Gausman, Ralph Sylos; music, Edgar Fairchild; songs, Jack Brooks and Milton Rosen; Everett Cutler and Rosen; dialogue director, Raymond Kessler; assistant director, Seward Webb; sound, Bernard Brown, Robert Pritchard; camera, Paul Ivano; editor, Saul A. Goodkind.

Basil Rathbone (Sherlock Holmes); Nigel Bruce (Dr. John H. Watson); Marjorie Riordan (Sheila Woodbury); Rosalind Ivan (Agatha Dunham); Martin Koslek (Mirko); John Abbott (Jodri); Frederick Worlock (Prime Minister); Morton Lowry (Sanford, the Ship's Steward); Leslie Vincent (Prince Nikolas); Gerald Hamer (Kingston); Rex Evans (Gregor); Tom Dillon (Restaurant Proprietor); Sven Hugo Borg (Johanssen); Wee Willie Davis (Gubec); Wilson Benge (Mr. Arnold, the Clergyman); Gregory Gay (Ravez); Dorothy Kellogg (Fuzzy Looking Woman); Olaf Hytten (Simpson, the Gunsmith).

Sherlock Holmes (Basil Rathbone) and Dr. Watson (Nigel Bruce) are hired to protect the young Prince of Rovenia, whose father has just been murdered. Holmes and the Prince are to fly to the Mediterranean where they are to meet Watson, who will be aboard a ship. On board, Watson meets several people, including singer Sheila Woodbury (Marjorie Riordan) and gun-carrying British spinster Agatha Dunham (Rosalind Ivan). When Watson calls on a sick passenger he finds out that Holmes is on board with Prince Nikolas (Leslie Vincent), the plane trip having been a ruse. Watson becomes uneasy about the actions of a young steward, Sanford (Morton Lowry), and in Lisbon three men board the vessel: Gregor (Rex Evans), Mirko (Martin Kosleck), and the giant Gubec (Wee Willie Davis). Holmes, whose presence is now known to the passengers, stops Mirko from hurling a knife at Nikolas, and when they reach Algiers Holmes learns from Sheila that she is an unwilling messenger for an international crook. At a party hosted by Agatha, Holmes finds a concealed bomb and throws it overboard. Later he is waylaid and Nikolas is kidnapped. The victim, however, is the wrong person; the steward is really the young prince, Holmes leads in rounding up the gang that is out to kill him.

PURSUIT TO ALGIERS, the tenth film in Universal's Sherlock Holmes adventures with Basil Rathbone and Nigel Bruce, is one of the weaker installments. While not uninteresting in plot or execution, the movie provides few thrills and only the switching of the Prince for a steward has any final impact. It should be noted, though, that wrestler Wee Willie Davis imparts a quiet menace as the hulking villain, Gubec.

David Stuart Davies observes in *Holmes of the Movies* (1976), "PURSUIT TO ALGIERS showed a decided decline in inventiveness and proved to be the weakest of the series. . . . The plot which gives Holmes little opportunity for making many deductions is heavily padded with the inclusion of two musical numbers and some amusing but unnecessary comedy scenes with Watson." Michael B. Druxman wrote in *Basil Rathbone: His Life and His Films* (1975), "The fact that the villains are captured off-screen is typical of the second-rate treatment this project received. The audience is only told of this event, presumably because the producers did not wish to spend the time and money required to film it."

QUIET PLEASE, MURDER (Twentieth Century-Fox, 1942) 70 minutes.

Producer, Ralph Dietrich; director, John Larkin; story, Lawrence G. Blochman; screenplay, Larkin; art directors, Richard Day, Joseph C. Wright; music director, Emil Newman; camera, Joseph MacDonald; editor, Louis Loeffler.

George Sanders (Fleg); Gail Patrick (Myra Blanding); Richard Denning (Hal McByrne); Lynne Roberts (Kay Ryan); Sidney Blackmer (Martin Cleaver); Kurt Katch (Eric Pahsen); Margaret Brayton (Miss Oval); Charles Tannen (Hollis); Byron Foulger (Mr. Walpole); Arthur Space (Vance); George Wolcott (Benson); Chick Collins (Webley); Bud McCallister (Stock Boy); Bud Geary (Gannett); Harold R. Goodwin (Stover); James Farley (Detective); Jack Cheatham (Policeman); Minerva Urecal (Housewife); Bert Roach (Husband);

Paul Porcasi (Rebescu); Theodore von Eltz (Lucas); Frank O'Connor (Library Guard); W. R. Deming (Mr. Daly); Hooper Atchley, Arthur Tahlasso (Air Raid Wardens); Mae Marsh (Miss Hartwig); Monica Bannister (Bit); Fern Emmett (Miss Philbert); Bobby Larsen (Boy); Pat O'Malley (Guard); Jill Warren (Girl); Charles Cane (Inspector Henderson); Matt McHugh (Taxi Driver).

Script writer John Larkin made his feature film directorial debut and star George Sanders closed out his Twentieth Century-Fox contract with this efficient programmer, about which the *New York Sun* opined, "The title is better than the story, which strays from probability too often." On the other hand, Don Miller in *B Movies* (1973) felt, "To Larkin's credit, he got more excitement from a library setting than other directors with a whole war to work with." Miller labeled the film "a suspenseful crime yarn."

Rare book dealer and Freudian fancier Fleg (George Sanders) has come up with an artful scheme to make money: he steals rare books, carefully duplicates them and then sells the bogus books in America to gain money to buy the art treasure he covets. He is in league with Myra Blanding (Gail Patrick) in the successful ruse. Fleg has made a contract with a Washington, D.C. library to deliver a copy of the Richard Burbage edition of *Hamlet* but he finds himself at odds with Nazi agents Martin Cleaver (Sidney Blackmer) and Eric Pahsen (Kurt Katch) who are in America to steal art treasures for the Third Reich. As the Nazis begin leaving victims in their wake, private eye Hal McByrne (Richard Denning) gets on the case and enlists the aid of pretty assistant librarian Kay Ryan (Lynne Roberts) in cracking the murderous affair. When the Germans attempt to murder Fleg, Myra allies herself with them but eventually pays with her life for her duplicity. Finally Fleg and the Nazis have a showdown and both sides are eliminated, leaving McByrne to romance Kay.

The ever-observant Bosley Crowther (*New York Times*) pointed out, "One of the many things about this picture which is very hard to understand is how a model of the village in HOW GREEN WAS MY VALLEY happens to be in the art room of a public library in Washington, D.C. Maybe it is because Twentieth Century-Fox made that picture, too."

RAFFLES (United Artists, 1930) 71-1/2 minutes.

Producer, Sam Goldwyn; directors, Harry D'Abbadie D'Arrast, George Fitzmaurice; based on the novel *Raffles: The Further Adventures of The Amateur Cracksman* by Ernest William Hornung and the play *Raffles, the Amateur Cracksman* by Eugene Wiley Presbrey; screenplay, Sidney Howard; assistant director, H. Bruce Humberstone; technical directors, Gerald Grove, John Howell; art director, William Cameron Menzies; sound, Oscar Lagerstrom; camera, George Barnes, Gregg Toland; editor, Stuart Heisler.

Ronald Colman (Raffles); Kay Francis (Lady Gwendolyn Amersteth); Bramwell Fletcher (Bunny Manners); Frances Dade (Ethel); David Torrence (Inspector McKenzie); Alison Skipworth (Lady Melrose); Frederick Kerr (Lord Melrose); John Rogers (Crawshaw); Wilson Benge (Barraclough); Virginia Bruce (Blonde).

RAFFLES (United Artists, 1939) 71 minutes.

Producer, Samuel Goldwyn; directors, Sam Wood, William Wyler; based on the novel *Raffles, The Further Adventures of The Amateur Cracksman* by Ernest William Hornung; screenplay, John Van Druten, Sidney Howard; set decorator, Julie Heron; costumes, Travis Banton; music, Victor Young; camera, Greg Toland; editor, Sherman Todd.

David Niven (Raffles); Olivia de Havilland (Lady Gwendolyn Amersteth); Dame May Whitty (Lady Melrose); Dudley Digges (Bunny MacKenzie); Douglas Walton (Bunny Manners); Lionel Pape (Lord Melrose); E. E. Clive (Barraclough); Peter Godfrey

Dame May Whitty, Olivia de Havilland, David Niven and Lionel Pape in RAFFLES (1939).

(Crawshay); Margaret Seddon (Maud Holden); Gilbert Emery (Bingham); Hilda Plowright (Wilson); Vesey O'Davoren (The Butler); Keith Hitchcock (Morton); Forrester Harvey (Umpire); James Finlayson (Cabby); George Atkinson, Eric Wilton, Frank Baker (Attendants); Gibson Gowland, George Kirby, Herbert Clifton (Villagers); Wilfred Lucas, Larry Dodds, John Power, Colin Kenny, Charles Coleman (Bobbies); David Thursby (Passenger); Elspeth Dudgeon (School Mistress); and: Harry Allen, Douglas Gordon, Olaf Hytten, John Graham Spacey.

RAFFLES, THE AMATEUR CRACKSMAN (Hiller & Wilk, 1917) seven reels.

Director, George Irving; based on the play by Eugene Wiley Presbrey; screenplay, Anthony Kelly.

John Barrymore (Raffles); Evelyn Brent (Lady Gwendolyn Amersteth); Frank Morgan (Bunny Manners); Christine Mayo (Mrs. Clarice Vidal), and: H. Cooper Cliffe, Mike Donlin.

RAFFLES, THE AMATEUR CRACKSMAN (Universal, 1925) 65 minutes.

Director, King Baggot; based on the novel *Raffles: Further Adventures of the Amateur Cracksman* by Ernest William Hornung and the play *Raffles, the Amateur Cracksman* by Eugene Wiley Presbrey; screenplay, Harvey Thew; camera, Charles Stumar.

House Peters (A. J. Raffles); Miss Du Pont (Gwendolyn Amersteth); Hedda Hopper (Mrs. Clarice Vidal); Frederick Esmelton (Captain Belford); Walter Long (Crawshay); Winter Hall (Lord Amersteth); Kate Lester (Lady Amersteth); Freeman Wood (Bunny Manners); Roland Bottomley (Lord Crowley); Lillian Langdon (Mrs. Tilliston); Robert Bolder (Mr. Tilliston).

Ernest William Hornung wrote *The Amateur Cracksman* in 1899 and followed it with *Raffles; Further Adventures of the Amateur Cracksman* in 1901. In 1903 Eugene Wiley Presbrey's play *Raffles, the Amateur Cracksman* debuted on Broadway. Raffles was a character to baffle the law with his slick robberies and the detectives involved in the storylines were usually unsuccessful in stopping him, although they were always on his trail with dogged determination. Thus in the Raffles story it is not the sleuth who is the hero but the devil-may-care robber who most often outwits him.

The character was first brought to the screen in September 1905 by Vitagraph in the New York City-filmed THE ADVENTURES OF RAFFLES, THE AMATEUR CRACKSMAN, a one-reeler starring J. Barney Sherry in the title role. Raffles next showed up in three entries in Nordisk Film Company's Sherlock Holmes series from Denmark. They starred Viggo Larsen, who also wrote and directed a baker's dozen one- and two-reelers about the Conan Doyle character. Forrest Holger-Madsen played Raffles in SHER-LOCK HOLMES IN DEADLY DANGER, RAFFLES ESCAPES FROM PRISON and THE SECRET DOCUMENT, all 1909 releases. Each film had Holmes on the trail of the renowned Raffles and putting him in jail, only to have him out and up to his old tricks again in the ensuing onscreen adventures.

In 1917 Hiller & Wilk issued RAFFLES, THE AMATEUR CRACKSMAN, which reveals Raffles (John Barrymore) on a weekend holiday at a country estate. He is lifting jewels in order to rescue a friend (Frank Morgan) who is contemplating suicide over a financial misadventure. Also at the party is a detective who has been on Raffles' trail for years, but he is thwarted in capturing the elusive master thief. In *The Detective in Film* (1972), William K. Everson called it "delightful and spritely" and noted, "By far the most prolific group of silent detective films were those in which the detective was the secondary character, did little real sleuthing, but was an ever present potential nemesis to the hero. . . ." Such was the case with RAFFLES, THE AMATEUR CRACKSMAN.

King Baggot directed RAFFLES, THE AMATEUR CRACKSMAN (1925), a six-reeler issued by Universal and based on both the 1901 novel and the 1903 play. The plot has Raffles (House Peters), once the talk of England for his daring jewel robberies, on a ship from India. He tells beautiful Gwendolyn Amersteth (Miss Du Pont) to be on guard so that her valuable necklace will not be stolen. It disappears but is later returned to her when the boat docks in England. Gwendolyn invites Raffles to a house party at which noted detective/criminologist Captain Belford (Frederick Esmelton) is present and the detective makes a bet that a string of pearls cannot be stolen. When Raffles steals them Belford uses a paroled crook to aid him in setting a trap, but Gwendolyn finds out and warns Raffles. The two elope, Raffles sends back the pearls and promises his new bride he will reform. *Photoplay* magazine called the film, "A good crook story marred by some slow direction."

The best known version of the E. W. Hornung character is RAFFLES, which Samuel Goldwyn produced for United Artists release in 1930. Ronald Colman, who had just scored a success for Goldwyn as BULLDOG DRUMMOND, *q.v.*, the year before, played the title character. Here Raffles (Ronald Colman) is a safecracker whom Scotland Yard cannot seem to capture. He falls in love with beautiful Gwen (Kay Francis), an heiress, and plans to abandon his dishonest trade. However, when his close pal Bunny Manners (Bramwell Fletcher) contemplates suicide due to a financial loss, Raffles plots one final big robbery to get the money his friend desperately needs. He plans to steal a valuable diamond necklace from Lady Melrose (Alison Skipworth) but Scotland Yard detective Inspector MacKenzie (David Torrence) learns of the scheme. Knowing the Yard is fast on his trail, Raffles acquires the necklace and returns to London where he convinces Gwen of his good intentions. Mac-Kenzie corners Raffles and he admits to the theft but makes a getaway through a hidden opening in a floor clock. He plans to meet Gwen in Paris.

Harry D'Arrast began the direction of RAFFLES but due to a falling out with Goldwyn was replaced by George Fitzmaurice, who finished the production. *Cinema* magazine commented, "Those who look for the white-haired Raffles of the Hornung stories, cool and serenely unscrupulous, will be disappointed. . . . But, if not the original package, we have Ronald Colman, who can suggest that all sorts of things can happen, though in the end it has turned out to be nothing more thrilling than outwitting an unusually stupid gentleman from Scotland Yard. Colman keeps the interest up more than would seem possible, and Kay Francis manages to give the impression the most entertaining part of the story will come after she and Raffles are safely on the Continent." *Photoplay* magazine dubbed RAFFLES "A talkie that moves, and entertainingly!"

In 1932 George Barraud played the title role in THE RETURN OF RAFFLES, a British film, which had the reformed crook framed for a jewel theft at a country party. Silent film star Camilia Horn was his German lady love, while Claude Allister played Bunny.

Samuel Goldwyn produced a remake of his 1930 production with RAFFLES (1939), nearly a decade later, with Sam Wood directing David Niven in the title role. The plot is much the same: to save pal Bunny Manners (Douglas Walton) from being booted out of the army, Raffles (David Niven) plans to obtain funds for him by stealing a priceless necklace from his hosts (Dame May Whitty, Lionel Pape) while a guest at their weekend party. Here Bunny is the brother of Raffles' lady love, Gwen (Olivia de Havilland). On Raffles' trail is Scotland Yard sleuth MacKenzie (Dudley Digges). Raffles is thwarted in his attempt to steal the necklace by another thief, but he then lifts the jewels from that man (Peter Godfrey) and hides them in his apartment, making it impossible for the law to find the necklace. *Variety* remarked, "The Hornung tale has moments of interest and suspense in its present telling, but overall is able to generate only slight reaction for a familiar yarn. Too many copies have been struck off the original in the past decade to provide spontaneity and sustain interest. . . . RAFFLES has been given Class

A production values throughout, with photography and sound recording excellent. But on the entertainment side, it's a lower A."

Although the outdated Raffles has had no more screen adventures to date, Horace Braham did play the part in the 1940 radio series, "Raffles."

THE RARE BOOK MURDERS   *see*   FAST COMPANY.

THE RED DRAGON (Monogram, 1946) 64 minutes.

Producer, James B. Burkett; director, Phil Rosen; based on the character created by Earl Derr Biggers; screenplay, George Callahan; art director, David Milton; camera, Vincent Farrar; editor, Ace Herman.

Sidney Toler (Charlie Chan); Fortunio Bonanova (Inspector Luis Carvero); Benson Fong (Tommy Chan); Robert E. Keane (Alfred Wyans); Willie Best (Chattanooga Brown); Carol Hughes (Marguerite Fontan); Marjorie Hoshelle (Countess Irena); Barton Yarborough (Joseph Bradish); George Meeker (Edmond Slade); Don Costello (Charles Masack); Charles Trowbridge (Prentiss); Mildred Boyd (Josephine); Jean Wang (Iris); Donald Dexter Taylor (Walter Dorn).

The last of four Charlie Chan films James S. Burkett produced for Monogram Pictures in 1945, THE RED DRAGON (made as CHARLIE CHAN IN MEXICO) interpolated the current headline theme of atomic energy in its plot. "The Case of The Atomic Murders! Chan tracks down a gang seeking to steal the secrets of the atom bomb!" announced the film's poster blurbs.

A detective who has obtained important atomic secrets is murdered in Mexico City but before he dies the man writes a clue in a rare Chinese ink called Red Dragon. Police Inspector Luis Carvero (Fortunio Bonanova) asks his old friend, Chinese detective Charlie Chan (Sidney Toler), to help him in the investigation. Chan arrives in Mexico City with his Number Three son, Tommy, and a new chauffeur, Chattanooga Brown (Willie Best). When several guests staying at the same hotel as the detective die in the same mysterious manner as the murdered man, Chan deduces that they were all involved in the case. He finds out that the killings were accomplished by a device placed on the victim's person and set off by electric impulses. As a result, Chan captures the killer.

THE RED DRAGON is one of the better entries in Monogram's Charlie Chan series with Sidney Toler. Despite its downbeat theme the film includes quite a bit of comedy, much of it supplied by Willie Best, here replacing Mantan Moreland in the recurring chauffeur role. Willie Best is particularly amusing in the scenes where he courts the maid (Mildred Boyd) of a murdered actress. Tommy Chan also has a romantic interlude with hotel worker Jean (Iris Wang), a comely young lady who engages the elder Chan in a rumba dance as he tries to extricate information from her. At the finale both father and son agree not to tell Mrs. Chan of their indiscretions.

Poster art for this feature quotes Charlie Chan as calling THE RED DRAGON "My Weirdest Case!"

REMEMBER LAST NIGHT? (Universal, 1935) 85 minutes.

Producer, Carl Laemmle, Jr.; director, James Whale; based on the novel *The Hangover Murders* by Adam Hobhouse; screenplay, Doris Malloy, Harry Clark, Dan Totheroh; camera, James Valentine; editor, Ted J. Kent.

Edward Arnold (Inspector Danny Harrison); Constance Cummings (Carlotta Milburn); Sally Eilers (Bette Huling); Robert Young (Tony Milburn); Robert Armstrong (Fred Flannagan); Reginald Denny (Jack Whitridge); Monroe Owsley (Billy Arnold); George Meeker (Vic Huling); Ed Brophy (Maxie); Jack LaRue (Baptiste Bouclier); Louise Henry (Penny Whitridge); Gustav von Seyffertitz (Professor Carl Herman Eckhart Jones); Gregory Ratoff (Faronea); Arthur Treacher (Clarence Phelps); Rafaela Ottiano (Mme. Bouclier); Louise Henry (Penny Whitridge); Monte Montague (Mechanic); Ted Billings (Sailor); Tiny Sandford (Truck Driver); E. E. Clive (Photographer); Kate Price (Cook); Wade Boteler, James Flavin (Cops); and: Alice Ardell, Frank Reicher.

Adam Hobhouse's 1935 novel, *The Hangover Murders* appears to be greatly influenced by Dashiell Hammett's *The Thin Man,* published the previous year, in that it dealt with a husband and wife team of amateur sleuths who solve a murder following a drunken high society party. Alcohol and a devil-may-care attitude pervade both works. In fact, thanks to Hammett, it seemed that most 1930s debonair detectives—always garbed in impeccable haberdashery— did as much drinking and cigarette smoking as they did sleuthing.

Young socialites Tony (Robert Young) and Carlotta Milburn (Constance Cummings) wake up from a drunken all-night binge and discover that their host has been murdered. They had been guests at a Long Island house party and none of the other people present can recall anything—all of them were drunk. The other guests include Bette (Sally Eilers) and Vic Huling (George Meeker), Fred Flannagan (Robert Armstrong), Jack (Reginald Denny) and Penny Whitridge (Louise Henry), and Faronea (Gregory Ratoff). Police Inspector Danny Harrison (Edward Arnold), who knows all the participants, is called in to investigate, assisted by detective Maxie (Edward Brophy).

None of the guests, nor butler Clarence Phelps (Arthur Treacher), can remember any helpful details. Harrison calls in hypnotist Professor Carl Jones (Gustav von Seyffertitz) to help refresh their memories but the professor is murdered, as are several more guests. By a process of elimination, the killer is revealed.

Andre Sennwald (*New York Times*) quipped, "The film is good minor fun, even though you come away from it with the feeling that one or two additional murders among the madcap principals would have made Long Island a still better place to live in." In *The Detective in Film* (1972), William K. Everson noted that director James Whale ". . . brought to it many additional ingredients, including his own macabre sense of humor, a photographic and lighting style reminiscent of his great horror films for Universal, and a zany, almost surrealist sense of speed and comedy. REMEMBER LAST NIGHT?, virtually forgotten today, was one of the most enjoyable mysteries of the thirties."

THE RETURN OF FRANK CANNON (CBS-TV 11/1/80) Color 100 minutes.

Producer, Michael Rhodes; director, Corey Allen; teleplay, James D. Buchanan, Ronald L. Austin; art director, George B. Chan; music, Bruce Broughton; music supervisor, John Elizalde; "Cannon" theme, John Parker; camera, William Cronjager; editor, Donald Hoskinson.

William Conrad (Frank Cannon); Allison Argo (Jessica Bingham); Burr DeBenning (Charles Kirkland); Taylor Lacher (Sheriff Lew Garland); Diana Muldaur (Sally Bingham); Ed Nelson (Mike Danvers); Joanna Pettet (Alana Richardson); William Smithers (Wilson Barrett); Arthur Hill (Dr. Curtis McDonald); Hank Brandt (Pearson); Rafael Campos (Luis Barrientos); Hector Elias (Paparazzo); Rene Enriquez (Salvador Cruz); Gary Grubbs (Mechanic); Evelyn Guerrero (Inez); James Hong (Yutong); John Steadman (Zoo Guard); James Gavin (Helicopter Pilot); Luca Bercovici (Club Employee); Tom Morga (Marine); Ross Rhodes (Waiter); Paul Sorensen (Spook); Diane Takai (Waitress).

After years as a character actor in films, radio and TV, William Conrad became a star with the television series "Cannon" (CBS-TV, 1971-77), in which he portrayed portly Los Angeles detective Frank Cannon, a high-priced sleuth who values fine cars and good food and whose detection is more cerebral than physical. Following the practice of reviving once-popular TV shows as television movies, Cannon returned in the telefeature, THE RETURN OF FRANK CANNON (1980), which *TV Movies and Video Guide* (1988) dubbed "Average."

Blubbery private investigator Frank Cannon (William Conrad) has retired and runs a restaurant for which he spends most of his time catching his own fish. Jessica Bingham (Allison Argo) asks Cannon to investigate the death of his old Army buddy, her father. The man supposedly committed suicide but Jessica believes he was murdered. Complicating the case is the fact that Cannon once loved Jessica's mother, Sally Bingham (Diana Muldaur). Cannon agrees to study the facts as a favor to Jessica and finds that the C.I.A. is involved in the affair, as is a mysterious doctor (Arthur Hill). Finally Cannon cracks the case, proving Jessica's theory.

Regarding Cannon's investigation, John J. O'Connor (*New York Times*) commented, "But off he goes, pipe clenched between teeth and stomach thrust about two feet forward. . . . [The plot is] fairly well contrived, spliced with bits of hard-boiled dialogue. . . . Mr. Conrad can play the part with his eye shut, and he almost does. . . . [The film] is a pleasant and undemanding way to pass a couple of hours."

THE RETURN OF MICKEY SPILLANE'S MIKE HAMMER (CBS-TV, 4/18/86) Color 100 minutes.

Executive producer, Jay Bernstein; producer, Gray Frederickson; associate producer, Jeff Morton; director, Ray Danton; based on characters created by Mickey Spillane; teleplay, James M. Miller, Larry Brody, Janis B. Hendler; art directors, Ross Bellah, Bill Campbell; music/song, Earle Hagen; camera, Hector Figueroa (New York), Warren Rothenberg (Hollywood); editor, Richard E. Rabjohn.

Stacy Keach (Mike Hammer); Lindsay Bloom (Velda); Don Stroud (Captain Pat Chambers); Kent Williams (Lawrence D. Barrington); Vince Edwards (Inspector Frank Walker); Lauren Hutton (Joanna Lake); John Karlen (Simon Chapel); Frank McRae (Herschel Dean); Leo Penn (Leo Hawkins); Mike Preston (DAK [David Anson Kohler]); Stephen Macht (Nick Anton); Mickey Rooney (Jack Bergen); Bruce Boxleitner (Himself); Dabney Coleman (Himself); Dionne Warwick (Herself); Tom Everett (Orville Tate); Emily Chance (Megan Lake); Lee Benton (Jenny); David Chow (Professor Lai); Peter Iacangelo (Norwood Ritz); Kieu Chinh (Sai Luhn); Hunter Von Leer (Sneakers Man); Dawn Mangrum (Dancer); Don Lewis (Mime); Andre "Rosey" Brown (Big Man); Andre Feijoo (Bus Driver); Jeannie Marie Austin (PA); Danny Goldman (Ozzie the Answer); John Karlen (Simon Chapel); Jo Ann Pflug (TV Reporter); Julie Hayek (Ticket Chaser); Joseph DiSante (Lieutenant); Frank Romano (Postman); Malgosia Tomassi (Nun); Corinne Wahl (Sandra); Otto Felix (Agent Adler); Christina Jenson (Carla Arnell);

Kathy Chaffin (Wanda); Tony Mann (Second Bus Driver); Laurie Cantwell (Sergeant Hooper); Laura Dankel (Sasha Davison); Gregory Chase (George); Donna Snow (Paula); Ron Foster (Forensic Man); Bobby Bass (Bruiser); Fianni Russo (Card Player); Larry Grant (Camera Assistant).

See: MICKEY SPILLANE'S MIKE HAMMER: MARGIN FOR MURDER [essay].

THE RETURN OF MR. MOTO (Twentieth Century-Fox, 1965) 71 minutes.

Producers, Robert L. Lippert, Jack Parsons; director, Ernest Morris; based on the character created by John P. Marquand; story/continuity, Randall Hood; screenplay, Fred Eggers; music, Douglas Gamley; assistant director, Gordon Gilbert; art director, Harry White; wardrobe supervisor, Jean Fairlie; makeup, Harold Fletcher; sound, Jock May; sound editor, Clive Smith; camera, Basil Emmott; editors, Robert Winter, Dave Bennett.

Henry Silva (Mr. Moto); Terence Longdon (Jonathan Westering); Suzanne Lloyd (Maxine Powell); Marne Maitland (Wasir Hussein); Martin Wyldeck (Dargo); Brian Coburn (Magda); Stanley Morgan (Inspector Halliday); Peter Zander (Ginelli); Harold Kasket (Shahrdar); Anthony Booth (Hovath); Gordon Tanner (McAllister); Henry Gilbert (David Lennox); Richard Evans (Chief Inspector Marlow); Dennis Holmes (Chapel); Ian Fleming (Rogers); Tracy Connell (Arab); Alister Williamson (Maitre d'Hotel); Sonya Benjamin (Belly Dancer).

John P. Marquand's famous Japanese sleuth, Mr. Moto, returned to the screen in this mid-1960s Robert L. Lippert production among the spurt of spy/espionage films engendered by the success of the James Bond movie series. The results are tepid at best. Moto had been immortalized on film in the late 1930s by Peter Lorre and this rehash outing is just a tired cloak and dagger dual-biller which received scant notice. Veteran director Ernest Morris turned the film out in quick fashion and its prime highlight is veteran cinematographer Basil Emmott's sharp black and white photography. Henry Silva, a near cult star for his many villainous roles, is only passable in the title part.

Interpol agent Mr. Moto (Henry Silva) investigates sabotage at the Beta Oil Company in London after former Nazi Dargo (Martin Wyldeck) and his henchman Hovath (Anthony Booth) murder oil executive McAllister (Gordon Tanner) during an oil conference at the home of British Intelligence agent Jonathan Westering (Terence

Henry Silva in THE RETURN OF MR. MOTO (1965).

Longdon). Dargo has Moto abducted and placed in a sack and thrown into the Thames River. The wily sleuth escapes, although the ex-Nazi believes his adversary drowned. Beta oil chief Lennox (Henry Gilbert) is successful in persuading the Shahrdar (Harold Kasket) of a Middle East oil country to renew with his firm, and Moto arrives, disguised as a Japanese oil man. He learns that the murdered McAllister may have tried to involve Beta with an oil trust scheme along the Persian Gulf. To gain Beta's secrets, Dargo and Horvath abduct Lennox's secretary, Maxine Powell (Suzanne Lloyd), and hold her hostage. Moto traces them to the night club hideout and Dargo is killed in a shootout. Westering and the Shahrdar's advisor, Wasir Hussein (Marne Maitland), are arrested for their part of the plot. Moto rescues Maxine and closes the case.

The film was made as MR. MOTO AND THE PERSIAN OIL

CASE, a title more relevant in the 1980s than in the time it was discarded.

THE RETURN OF RAFFLES (Williams and Pritchard, 1932) 72 minutes.

Producer/director, Nasfield Markham; based on the character created by Ernest William Hornung; screenplay, W. J. Balef; camera, Emil Schunemann, Geoffrey Faithful.

George Baraud (A. J. Raffles); Camilia Horn (Elga); Claud Allister (Bunny Manner); A. Bromley Davenport (Sir John Truwode); Sydney Fairbrother (Lady Truwode); H. Saxon-Snell (Von Spechen); and: Philip Strange.

See: RAFFLES [essay].

THE RETURN OF SHERLOCK HOLMES (Paramount, 1929) 71 minutes.

Director, Basil Deane; based on the stories "The Dying Detective" and "His Final Bow" by Sir Arthur Conan Doyle; screenplay, Deane, Garrett Ford; camera, William Steiner; editor, Helene Turner.

Clive Brook (Sherlock Holmes); H. Reeves-Smith (Dr. John H. Watson); Donald Crisp (Colonel Sebastian Moran); Harry T. Morey (Professor Moriarty); Phillips Holmes (Roger Longmore); Betty Lawford (Mary Watson); Hubert Druce (Sergeant Gripper); Charles Hay (Captain Longmore); and: Arthur Mack.

Staid Britisher Clive Brook was the sound era's first Sherlock Holmes in the surprisingly ultra-modern THE RETURN OF SHERLOCK HOLMES, which Paramount shot at its Long Island Astoria Studios. Brook's Holmes is pictured as an older man, as the film depicts him coming out of retirement to aid Dr. Watson's grown daughter, a part originally assigned to sultry Evelyn Brent. A "Big All-Talking Mystery Thriller" is how the studio promoted this feature, but in reality it is a mundane affair. It did establish Brook in the Sherlock Holmes characterization and he would repeat it in a comedy turn in PARAMOUNT ON PARADE in 1930 (the segment also had William Powell as Philo Vance) and in SHERLOCK HOLMES (1932), *q.v.*, for Fox. THE RETURN OF SHERLOCK HOLMES is loosely adapted from two Conan Doyle stories, "The Dying Detective" and "His Last Bow."

Captain Longmore (Charles Hay) writes a confession in which he admits that he worked for the notorious criminal mastermind, Professor Moriarty (Harry T. Morey), and his equally nefarious henchman, Colonel Sebastian Moran (Donald Crisp). Moriarty poisons the man but before Longmore dies he tells his son, Roger (Phillips Holmes), the truth and urges him to get both his killers and the confession they have stolen. Roger trails Moran to an ocean liner sailing between the U.S. and Europe. On it Moran is the ship's doctor and Moriarty is incognito as one of the passengers. Meanwhile, one of Moriarty's minions uses the ship's wireless to get information his boss needs for his various international crimes. Roger is kidnapped by Moriarty's men and the police suspect that he killed his father. Roger's fiancée, Mary Watson (Betty Lawford), appeals to Sherlock Holmes (Clive Brook) to investigate and he and her father, Dr. Watson (H. Reeves-Smith), board the vessel in France. Holmes masquerades as a member of the ship's orchestra and, later, doing a sleight of hand trick, gets the late captain's confession from Moriarty and replaces it with blank paper. Disguising himself as a steward, Holmes traces Moriarty to Roger's whereabouts and rescues the young man. Later Moriarty tries to kill Holmes with a poisoned cigarette case and Holmes fakes his own death, only to be at the dock in New York City when Moriarty is arrested for his crimes.

While the public—still entranced with talkie films—took rather well to THE RETURN OF SHERLOCK HOLMES, the critics lambasted it. *Motion Picture News* rated it "a slow draggy affair" and *Photoplay* magazine complained, "The greatest sleuth of them all wouldn't recognize himself in this faint reincarnation." For the record, Holmes does intone, "Elementary, my dear Watson, elementary." And Watson does respond, "Amazing, Holmes."

THE RETURN OF SHERLOCK HOLMES (CBS-TV, 1/10/87) Color 100 minutes.

Producer, Nick Gillot; supervising producer, Bob Shayne; director, Kevin Connor; teleplay, Shayne; production designer, Keith Wilson; art director, Simon Wakefield; costume designer, Graham Williams; music, Ken Thorne; technical consultant, Sean Wright; assistant director, Bill Westley; sound, Tony Dawe; camera, Tony Imi; editor, Bernard Gribble.

Michael Pennington (Sherlock Holmes); Margaret Colin (Jane Watson); Lila Kaye (Mrs. Houston); Connie Booth (Violet Morstan); Nicholas Guest (Tobias Gregory); Barry Morse (Carter Morstan); Shane Rimmer (Lysander Stark); Paul Maxwell (Hopkins); Olivier Pierre (Hampton); Ray Jewers (Singer); Daniel Benzali (Michael Ross); Sheila Brand (Kitty Horowitz); Tony Steedman (Doctor); William Hootkins (Spelman).

Marking the one-hundredth anniversary of the literary birth of Sherlock Holmes with *A Study in Scarlet* (1887), this telefeature inaugurated the celebration with the literal revival of the character, placing him in modern times to solve a murder. *TV Movies and Video*

Advertisement for THE RETURN OF SHERLOCK HOLMES (1987).

Guide (1988) judged it an "original bit of Holmesiana," and Judith Crist (*TV Guide* magazine) described it as "a delightfully lighthearted and literate mystery."

Jane Watson (Margaret Colin), the great-granddaughter of Dr. John Watson, is going over an old piece of real estate owned by the family and there, in a state of suspended animation, she finds Sherlock Holmes (Michael Pennington). She learns that in 1901 Holmes became a victim of the bubonic plague and that her grandfather placed the sleuth in a frozen state, planning to revive him when a cure was found. However, Watson died before this occurred. Jane herself revives Holmes and with modern medicine cures him. The great detective is enlisted by the U.S. government to solve a murder which turns out to involve corrupt FBI agents, counterfeit currency, a hijacker, and a beautiful client (Connie Booth). Adopting various disguises, Holmes is forced to trek across the Arizona desert before bringing the case to a satisfactory conclusion.

Daily Variety commented, "Silly, farcical and affectionate, the study of Holmes in contemporary America owes as much to the Basil Rathbone films as it does to Doyle; no apologies necessary. . . . The vidpic looks and sounds good, and the sheer daring of the work lifts it out of the ordinary." Miles Beller (*The Hollywood Reporter*) enthused, "Never mind that Sherlock's return doesn't fully jibe with Holmesian history, for Shayne's literary liberties go a long way to making this two-hour movie one of the more enjoyable TV films seen in a long time. RETURN takes some devilishly good twists, playing with the Holmes legend and infusing it with a fresh viewpoint. Moreover, Michael Pennington as the level-headed Holmes makes a smashing sleuth. Urbane and thorough, he is Holmes, possessing an incisive mind that would be as sharp in any age as it was decades ago."

THE RETURN OF SHERLOCK HOLMES was filmed on location in London and Arizona.

THE RETURN OF THE TERROR (Warner Bros., 1934) 65 minutes.

Director, Howard Bretherton; based on the play *The Terror* by Edgar Wallace; adaptors, Eugene Solow, Peter Milne; art director, John Hughes; costumes, Orry-Kelly; dialogue director, Arthur Collins; camera, Arthur Todd; editor, Owen Marks.

Mary Astor (Olga Morgan); Lyle Talbot (Dr. Goodman); John Halliday (Dr. Redmayne); Frank McHugh (Joe, the Reporter); Irving Pichel (Burke); Frank Reicher (Reinhardt); J. Carroll Naish (Steve Scola); Renee Whitney (Virginia Mayo); Robert Barrat (Pudge); George E. Stone (Soapy); Robert Emmett O'Connor (Bradley, the

Detective); Etienne Girardot (Mr. Tuttle); and: Frank Conroy, George Cooper, Cecil Cunningham, Maude Eburne, Charles Grapewin, George Humbert.

See: THE TERROR [essay].

THE RETURN OF THE WORLD'S GREATEST DETECTIVE (NBC-TV, 6/16/76) Color 78 minutes.

Producers, Roland Kibbee, Dean Hargrove; director, Hargrove; teleplay, Kibbee, Hargrove; art director, William L. Campbell; music, Dick De Benedictis; camera, William Nendenhall; editor, John Kaufman, Jr.

Larry Hagman (Sherman Holmes); Jenny O'Hara (Dr. Joan Watson); Nicholas Colasanto (Lieutenant Nick Tinker); Woodrow Parfrey (Himmel); Helen Verbit (Landlady); Ivor Francis (Spiner); Charles Macaulay (Judge Clement Harley); Ron Silver (Dr. Collins); Sid Haig (Vince Cooley); Boothe Colman (Psychiatrist); Lieux Dressler (Mrs. Slater); Fuddle Bagley (Detective); Benny Rubin (Klinger); Robert Snively (Manager); Jude Farese (Caretaker); George Brenlin (Sergeant); Al Dunlap (Bailiff); Jefferson Kibbee (Delivery Man).

Prior to his becoming an international favorite via TV's suds melodrama, "Dallas," Larry Hagman portrayed a Sherlock Holmes-type in THE RETURN OF THE WORLD'S GREATEST DETECTIVE, a TV movie pilot for an unsold series which was quite similar to the earlier theatrical feature, THEY MIGHT BE GIANTS (1971), *q.v.* "Hagman romped through the show in fine Holmesian tradition, and he even sounded like Holmes—that is, he sounded like Basil Rathbone. It was all good fun, and the reaction from both viewers and critics was very favorable," Ron Haydock wrote in *Deerstalker! Holmes and Watson on Screen* (1978).

Los Angeles policeman Sherman Holmes (Larry Hagman) is a fancier of the Sherlock Holmes stories and while reading them one day he is hit by a motorcycle, which causes him to wake up believing he is really Sherlock Holmes. Dressing like the great detective, he takes up rooms at 221B Baker Street in an abode run by Mrs. Hudson (Helen Verbit) and sets out to solve serious cases. His own case comes to the attention of Dr. Joan Watson (Jenny O'Hara), a psychiatric social worker, and the two find themselves falling in love. Meanwhile, Holmes tries to aid Lieutenant Nick Tinker (Nicholas Colasanto) with a case which appears to be a simple auto accident, but which Sherman believes to be a homicide. In court he proves the entire case is centered around a huge embezzlement scheme.

Chris Steinbrunner and Norman Michaels in *The Films of Sherlock Holmes* (1978) rated this telefeature "an affectionate parody."

THE ROGUES' TAVERN (Puritan, 1936) 65 minutes.

Producer, Edward W. Rote; director, Bob Hill; screenplay, Al Martin; music director, Abe Meyer; set decorator, Fred Preble; camera, Bill Hyer; editor, Dan Milner.

Wallace Ford (Jimmy Flavin); Barbara Pepper (Marjorie Burns); Joan Woodbury (Gloria Rohloff); Clara Kimball Young (Mrs. Jamison); Jack Mulhall (Bill); John Elliott (Mr. Jamison); Vincent Dennis (Bert Hughes); Arthur Loft (Wentworth); Ivo Henderson (Harrison); Edward Cassidy (Mason); Earl Dwire (Morgan); Silver Wolf (The Dog).

One of the most enjoyable of the poverty row 1930s murder mysteries is THE ROGUES' TAVERN, which is set at a remote inn where a series of baffling murders occur. The affair is solved eventually by a detective and his fiancée who are about to be married. With a top-notch cast, fine direction and script and eerie atmosphere, the movie holds attention from start to finish and is one of the better productions to be issued by the short-lived Puritan Pictures Corporation.

Traveling incognito, detective Jimmy Flavin (Wallace Ford) and his fiancée, Marjorie Burns (Barbara Pepper), a department store detective herself, end up at the remote Red Rock Tavern, expecting to find a justice of the peace to marry them. Instead they encounter a storm which cuts off all communications. As a result they are stranded at the inn with the managers—the wheelchair-ridden Jamison (John Elliott) and his wife (Clara Kimball Young)—and assorted guests, including exotic card reader Gloria Rohloff (Joan Woodbury), Bill (Jack Mulhall), Bert Hughes (Vincent Dennis) and Harrison (Ivo Henderson). When Harrison is murdered and canine teeth marks are found on his throat, a local dog (Silver Wolf) is blamed, but Flavin is sure the animal is innocent. Arriving at the inn is Mason (Edward Cassidy), and Fowler and Marjorie find out that the other guests are members of a smuggling racket who have been lured to the inn, one by one. It appears that the owner of the hostel, scientist Morgan (Earl Dwire), is responsible, since the gang cheated him out of a valuable formula and he plans revenge. Flavin, however, finds a fake wolf's claw in one resident's dresser drawer and that person confesses to the crime. Morgan arrives and hides in the basement, and when the rest of the guests find him, they realize that they are trapped there. The killer and the confederate are found out and all the gang members go to jail. The justice of the peace arrives to marry Flavin and Marjorie.

George E. Turner and Michael H. Price commented in *Forgotten Horrors* (1979), "The script contains a number of surprises, not the least being the denouement. . . . The method used in the killing is unusual, perhaps unique, in films. While Wallace Ford and Barbara Pepper aren't exactly William Powell and Myrna Loy, they give lively performances patterned after those of the protagonists in M-G-M's highly successful THE THIN MAN (1934). . . . Unusual in low-budget production is the mobility of the camera work, in which fluid dolly and lateral tracking shots enhance many scenes. The dialogue has treats galore for lovers of wisecracking arrogance and lowbrow comedy."

THE ROSARY MURDERS (New Line, 1987) Color 105 minutes.

Producer, Robert G. Laurel; director, Fred Walton; based on the novel by William X. Kienzle; screenplay, Elmore Leonard, Fred Walton; music, Bobby Laurel, Don Sebersky; camera, David Golia; editor, Sam Vitale.

Donald Sutherland (Father Bob Koesler); Charles Durning (Father Ted Nabors); Josef Sommer (Lieutenant Walt Koznicki); Belinda Bauer (Pat Lennon, the Reporter); James Murtaugh (Javison); John Danelle (Detective Harris); Addison Powell (Father Killeen); Kathleen Tolan (Sister Ann Vania); Tom Mardirosian (Detective Fallon); Anita Barone (Irene Jiminez).

As Easter Week begins in cold metropolitan Detroit a series of bizarre murders occurs in which all the victims are priests and nuns whose corpses are left clutching rosaries. Police Lieutenant Walt Koznicki (Josef Sommer) is baffled by the serial killings. Meanwhile, Father Bob Koesler (Donald Sutherland), a progressive clergyman, is at odds with his superior, Father Ted Nabors (Charles Durning), over the baptizing of an illegitimate baby. During confession, Koesler listens to the recanting of a young individual who confesses to the killings and promises there will be more. Koesler, not always loyal to church doctrine in every matter, is at odds with himself over whether or not to reveal the man's horrific confession to the police. In the meantime, a young reporter (Belinda Bauer) from the *Detroit Free Press* comes to Koesler (himself the editor of the local Catholic paper) for help in finding the killer. The police also enlist his aid and Koznicki feels that the priest knows more than he is willing to admit. Koesler then decides the only way out of dilemma is to become a detective and track down the killer himself, thus avoiding the betrayal of the sanctity of the confessional.

Released about the time of the Papal visit of Pope John Paul II to the United States, THE ROSARY MURDERS has some contemporary interest and as a murder mystery it has flavor, although it is a far cry from G. K. Chesterton's Father Brown. The film is based on former priest William X. Kienzle's 1979 novel, which mystery novelist Elmore Leonard and director Fred Walton adapted to the

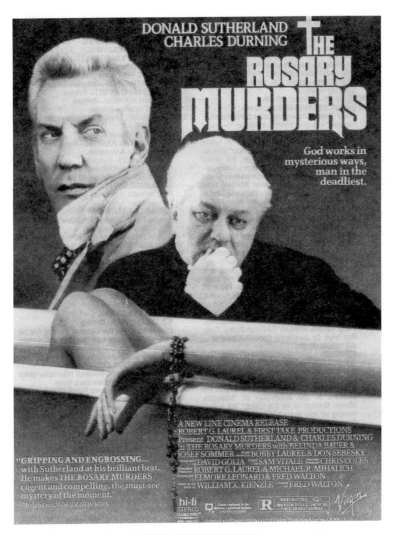

Advertisement for THE ROSARY MURDERS (1987).

screen. "Their earnest attempt to breathe cinematic life into this unexceptional serial murder mystery meets with mediocre success. In their hands, the homicides don't just fall into place, they stampede," wrote Dwight Brown in *The Hollywood Reporter*. On the other hand, Kevin Thomas (*Los Angeles Times*) opined, "It is most persuasive in its depiction of the everyday working of the American Roman

Catholic Church. . . . For once we're spared long-winded ecclesias-
tic debates and endless wranglings over the conflict between the
spirit and the flesh. The Catholic Church of this film emerges as a
very human institution and therefore, is involving rather than repel-
ling for non-Catholics. Indeed, there's a certain irony in the
realization that one of the most convincing and detailed portraits of
modern-day Catholicism merges in a murder mystery."

THE SAINT IN LONDON (RKO, 1939) 77 minutes.
    Producer, William Sistrom; director, John Paddy Carstairs;
based on the novel *The Million Pound Day* by Leslie Charteris;
screenplay, Lynn Root, Frank Fenton; camera, Claude Friese-Greene.
    George Sanders (Simon Templar, The Saint); Sally Gray
(Penelope Parker); David Burns (Dugan); Gordon McLeod (Inspec-
tor Teal); Henry Oscar (Bruno Lang); Ralph Truman (Kusetla); Carl
Jaffe (Stengler); Ben Williams (Wilkins); Nora Howard (Mrs. Mor-
gan); Ballard Berkeley (Richard Blake); Hugh McDermott (Tim);
John Abbott (Count Duni); Athene Seyler (Mrs. Buckley); and:
Charles Paton.
    Louis Hayward first played Leslie Charteris' character Simon
Templar, The Saint, in THE SAINT IN NEW YORK (1938), *infra*,
and George Sanders took over the role for THE SAINT STRIKES
BACK the following year. Closing out 1939 came THE SAINT IN
LONDON, the first Saint movie to be filmed in the environs of the
Charteris novels. George Sanders continued in the lead role and the
project was based on the Saint novelette, *The Million Pound Day*,
which had been published in Britain in 1932 in *The Holy Terror* and
then issued in the U.S. as *The Saint vs. Scotland Yard*.
    Simon Templar, The Saint (George Sanders) returns to his
homeland after cleaning up crime in America and British Intelligence requests him to look into the matter of a supposed nobleman,
Bruno Lang (Henry Oscar), who is suspected of stealing money
borrowed by a foreign dignitary. Scotland Yard Inspector Teal
(Gordon McLeod) believes Lang is behind a gang which is planning
to place five million pounds of bogus currency on the open market,
thus destroying the British monetary system. The Saint finds himself
aided in the case by lovely Penelope Parker (Sally Gray) and
reformed American gunman Dugan (David Burns). Despite their
"help," Templar accomplishes his mission.
    Variety commented, ". . . generally, it's a workmanlike job. . . .
Sanders is excellent as usual." The *New York Daily News* opined,
". . . this series is the best of the Grade B detective films."
    After three more Saint entries, THE SAINT'S DOUBLE
TROUBLE (1940), THE SAINT TAKES OVER (1940), and THE

SAINT IN PALM SPRINGS (1941), George Sanders abandoned
the part for The Falcon series, but RKO made two more Saint films
in England with Hugh Sinclair now as Templar. RKO issued THE
SAINT'S VACATION in 1941 but sold THE SAINT MEETS THE
TIGER to Republic Pictures and that studio issued it in 1943.

THE SAINT IN NEW YORK (RKO, 1938) 72 minutes.
    Producer, William Sistrom; director, Ben Holmes; based on the
novel by Leslie Charteris; adaptors Charles Kaufman, Mortimer
Offner; art director, Van Nest Polglase; costumes, Edward Steven-
son; camera, Joseph August, Frank Rediman; editor, Harry Marker.
    Louis Hayward (Simon Templar, The Saint); Kay Sutton (Fay
Edwards); Sig Rumann (Hutch Rellin); Jonathan Hale (Inspector
Henry Fernack); Jack Carson (Red Jenks); Paul Guilfoyle (Hymie
Fanro); Frederick Burton (William Valcross); Ben Welden (Papinoff);
Charles Halton (Vincent Nather); Cliff Bragdon (Sebastian Lipke);
Frank M. Thomas (Prosecutor); George Irving (Judge); Paul Fix
(Hoodlum); Lew Phelps (Cassidy the Detective).
    Leslie Charteris first introduced his debonair, crime-fighting
detective Simon Templar, The Saint,* in *Meet the Tiger* in 1928, and
followed it with a string of successful books over the next twenty
years or so, including the 1935 novel, *The Saint in New York,* on
which this film, the first in the RKO series about the charming
sleuth, is based. Louis Hayward was cast initially as Templar and did
quite well in the part, but in ensuing features at RKO, contractee
George Sanders handled the role, followed by Hugh Sinclair in two
British productions. Hayward, however, returned to the characterization in 1954 with THE SAINT'S GIRL FRIDAY. However,
Roger Moore is probably the best known The Saint, having starred
in the British television program of the same title in the 1960s prior
to his screen association with James Bond. In late 1978 there
appeared a teleseries, "The Return of the Saint," starring Ian Ogilvy
as the intrepid gentleman sleuth.
    When New York City is overrun with racketeers and the law
proves ineffective, a citizen's committee led by Red Jenks (Jack
Carson) hires Simon Templar (Louis Hayward) to either bring six
gangsters to justice or get them out of the way . . . *permanently.* The
Saint sets out to do his job, with quasi-aid from police Inspector

---

*In *Detectionary* (1977), editors Otto Penzler, Chris Steinbrunner, and Marvin
Lachman describe Simon Templar as ". . . tall, lean, broad-shouldered, his face is
clean-cut with deep-set blue eyes. His dark hair is patent-leather smooth and his
bronzed skin gives him a healthy, ruddy look. His voice—a low, gentle drawl—
conveys cavalier insolence. He is, indisputably, the most immaculate and elegant
adventurer in London."

Henry Fernack (Jonathan Hale). During the course of his mission he meets and falls for gangster's moll Fay Edwards (Kay Sutton), but she is killed when she tries to aid Templar. Finally The Saint eliminates all the gangsters except for the "big fellow," whom he eventually tracks down. He discovers he is one of the men who hired him initially for the case.

Variety ranked the film, "A rugged gangster melodrama, highly fantastic in plot but intriguing. . . . Makes no pretensions in being more than a B picture, this happens to be one of the top B's of the current crop of film fare."

SATAN MET A LADY (Warner Bros., 1936) 75 minutes.

Producer, Henry Blanke; director, William Dieterle; based on the novel *The Maltese Falcon* by Dashiell Hammett; screenplay, Brown Holmes; music director, Leo F. Forbstein; gowns, Orry-Kelly; camera, Arthur Edeson; editors, Max Parker, Warren Low.

Bette Davis (Valerie Purvis); Warren William (Ted Shayne); Alison Skipworth (Madame Barabbas); Arthur Treacher (Anthony Travers); Winifred Shaw (Astrid Ames); Marie Wilson (Murgatroyd); Porter Hall (Mr. Ames); Maynard Holmes (Kenneth); Charles Wilson (Pollock); Olin Howland (Dunhill); Joseph King (McElroy); Barbara Blane (Babs); Eddie Shubert, Stuart Holmes, Francis Sayles, James Burtis (Detectives); Billy Bletcher, Alice La Mont (Parents of Sextuplets); Alphonse Martell (Headwaiter); John Elliott (City Father); Edward McWade (Richards).

Between the fine 1931 version and the classic detective melodrama a decade later, Warner Bros. churned out still another remake of Dashiell Hammett's *The Maltese Falcon.* It was called SATAN MET A LADY (working titles: THE MAN IN THE BLACK HAT and MEN ON HER MIND). Not only does the plot differ from the novel, but names are altered and even a sex change takes place, as the Fat Man becomes Madame Barabbas (or The Fat Woman!). "So disconnected and lunatic are the picture's ingredients, so irrelevant and monstrous its people, that one lives through it in a constant expectation of seeing a group of uniformed individuals appear suddenly from behind the furniture and take the entire cast into protective custody. There is no story, merely a farrago of nonsense representing a series of practical studio compromises with an unworkable script," opined Bosley Crowther (*New York Times*).

Private investigator Ted Shayne (Warren William) is en route to San Francisco on a train when he meets Valerie Purvis (Bette Davis), who quickly hires him to locate a woman named Madame Barabbas (Alison Skipworth), although her reasons for wanting to meet the mystery person are vague. Finding out that Shayne is looking for her,

Madame Barabbas sends her underling (Maynard Holmes) to his office but Shayne's zany secretary, Miss Murgatroyd (Marie Wilson), divulges no information. Upon meeting Shayne, Madame Barabbas offers to employ him at a higher price; she wants to find Valerie, who knows when an art treasure, the ram's horn, is due to arrive in the bay city. She insists that Valerie stole it from her in the Orient. Shayne has his partner, Ames (Porter Hall), track Valerie but she kills him, assuming that he works for Madame Barabbas. Valerie then has Shayne obtain the ram's horn, but when he does so, Madame Barabbas and her minions steal it back. At the city pier, Valerie arrives and uses a gun to regain the treasure, but Miss Murgatroyd shows up with the police. Shayne is saved and the crooks are arrested.

SATAN MET A LADY was quite a comedown for its co-stars. Bette Davis was an Oscar winner for DANGEROUS (1935) and critically acclaimed for OF HUMAN BONDAGE (1934) and THE PETRIFIED FOREST (1936). Warren William, whom Warners had cast previously as Perry Mason, played Philo Vance at MGM (and would later be Vance at Paramount and then win lasting fame as The Lone Wolf at Columbia in the early 1940s). At least in SATAN MET A LADY Alison Skipworth is delightfully venal as the female counterpart of Casper Gutman.

THE SCARAB MURDER CASE (British and Dominions/Paramount British, 1936) 68 minutes.

Producer, Anthony Havelock-Allan; director, Michael Hankinson; based on the novel by S. S. Van Dine [Willard Huntington Wright]; screenplay, Selwyn Jepson; camera, Claude Friese-Greene.

Kathleen Kelly (Angela Hargreaves); Wilfrid Hyde-White (Philo Vance); Wally Patch (Inspector Moor); Henri de Vries (Dr. Bliss); John Robinson (Donald Scarlett); Wallace Geoffrey (Salveter); Stella Moya (Meryt Amen); Grahame Chesewright (Makeham); Rustum Medora (Hani); Shaun Desmond (Detective).

In 1930 Paramount Pictures purchased the film rights to S. S. Van Dine's [Willard Huntington Wright] fifth Philo Vance novel, *The Scarab Murder Case* intending to star William Powell in a continuation of the studio's popular Philo Vance series of detective films which had already included THE "CANARY" MURDER CASE (192), THE GREENE MURDER CASE (1929) and THE BENSON MURDER CASE (1930). However, Powell went on to other studio properties and then in 1932 moved over to Warner Bros. and the project was shelved. In the mid-1930s, as a part of the studio's quota plan for producing a few feature films annually in Britain, the concept was revived and Wilfred Hyde-White, making his film debut, was cast as Vance. He proved to be not very convincing either as an American or as a detective.

American Philo Vance (Wilfred Hyde-White) and his secretary Angela Hargreaves (Kathleen Kelly), are taking a London vacation and Vance visits Scotland Yard to examine their latest crime detection methods. He soon become enmeshed in solving the murder of a wealthy man who was the backer of archaeologist Dr. Bliss (Henri de Vries). The archaeologist is an obvious suspect, along with young Donald Scarlett (John Robinson). Vance uncovers the killer but in the process loses a secretary as Angela has fallen in love with Scarlett.

THE SCARAB MURDER CASE was a quickly done affair, made by British Paramount at its Pinewood Studios, and the youthful Wilfred Hyde-White hardly fit the bill as Vance. The film itself, which was shown only in the British Empire and received no U.S. bookings, was a slow, ponderous entry.

THE SCARLET CLAW (Universal, 1944) 74 minutes.

Producer/director, Roy William Neill; based on the characters created by Sir Arthur Conan Doyle; story, Paul Gangelin, Brenda Weisberg; screenplay, Edmund L. Hartmann, Neill; art directors, John B. Goodman, Ralph M. DeLacy; set decorators, Russell A. Gausman, Ira S. Webb; music director, Paul Sawtell; assistant director, Melville Shyer; sound, Robert Pritchard; special effects, John P. Fulton; camera, George Robinson; editor, Paul Landres.

Basil Rathbone (Sherlock Holmes); Nigel Bruce (Dr. John H. Watson); Gerald Hamer (Potts/Tanner/Alastair Ransom); Paul Cavanagh (Lord Penrose); Arthur Hohl (Emile Journet); Miles Mander (Judge Brisson); Kay Harding (Marie Journet); David Clyde (Sergeant Thompson); Ian Wolfe (Drake, Lord Penrose's Butler); Victoria Horne (Nora); George Kirby (Father Pierre); Frank O'Connor (Cab Driver); Harry Allen (Taylor, the Storekeeper); Olaf Hytten (Hotel Desk Clerk); Gertrude Astor (Lady Penrose); William Desmond (Spectator).

Universal's group of a dozen Sherlock Holmes feature films in the 1940s is considered to be one of the best overall detective series ever made. Like any collection of films, the entries had their ups and downs, but overall they were classy offerings. Even though these pictures were produced on modest budgets (in black and white) and often played as dual-bill items, the Sherlock Holmes motion pictures with Basil Rathbone and Nigel Bruce were nevertheless highly regarded by contemporary audiences. Their popularity increased in the 1950s when they were issued to television, and since that time they have continued to be telecast repeatedly, winning new and faithful audiences with each generation viewing them. Today they are all available in videocassette versions. Many consider the best of the Universal dozen to be THE SCARLET CLAW, the sixth entry in the series.

Sherlock Holmes (Basil Rathbone) and Dr. Watson (Nigel Bruce) are in Quebec to attend an Occult Society meeting addressed by Lord Penrose (Paul Cavanagh), who is at odds with Holmes over the existence of the supernatural. During the seminar, Penrose receives word from his home, the small village of La Morte Rouge, that his wife (Gertrude Astor) has been found murdered in the village church with her throat ripped open. The local citizens think a ghostly apparition seen on the nearby marshes is responsible for the crime but Holmes believes there must be a logical explanation for the grizzly matter. After the meeting Holmes receives a missive that Lady Penrose had written to him earlier that day requesting help, for she feared for her safety. Holmes and Watson go to La Morte Rouge and take up residence at the inn. Holmes finds out that the murdered woman was once known as actress Lillian Gentry, who had disappeared years before. Holmes examines Lady Penrose's body and is convinced she was killed by some kind of tearing instrument, such as a garden weeder. Meanwhile, Penrose orders him off the estate. In the village, postman Potts (Gerald Hamer) informs Holmes and Watson about the legend of the marsh ghosts, and that night Holmes spots a ghostly apparition and fires at it. Later, he finds a bit of cloth covered by phosphoresence. The clue leads them to the home of retired Judge Brisson (Miles Mander), who fears for his life behind the walls of his barricaded estate. Brisson explains to Holmes that the cloth came from a shirt he had given to a worker who lives in an abandoned boathouse. Holmes and Watson visit the boathouse and find a man named Tanner there, but he flees, leaving behind phosphorescent clothing, proof he is the alleged ghost. Holmes also locates a photograph inscribed to one Alastair, an actor. Researching the case, Holmes uncovers that Alastair Ransom had been a performer in Lillian Gentry's company and had killed a man over her. He had gone to jail and had supposedly been killed attempting to escape. Holmes realizes that Ransom is the killer and that he is masquerading as one of the villagers. However, Holmes is too late to save Judge Brisson, who presided over Ransom's trial, and he then learns that innkeeper Emile Journet (Arthur Hohl) was a guard at the prison where Ransom was incarcerated. Journet goes into hiding and Holmes and Watson discover the body of the man's young daughter,

Marie (Kay Harding), another victim of the madman. Journet agrees to help Holmes set a trap for the killer and, using the innkeeper as bait, Holmes captures the madman in the marshes. In trying to escape the criminal runs into the quicksand and is sucked under.

With its horror film trappings, THE SCARLET CLAW is an atmospheric and eerie movie which moves at a fine clip and never loses audience interest. Especially effective is actor Gerald Hamer, who enacts four different roles in the films: Potts the postman, the bearded Tanner, actor Ransom, and in one scene he masquerades as the judge's housekeeper as he murders the man. The movie also nicely handles the pathos in the murder of the young girl and it is balanced with amusing comedy byplay between Holmes and Watson over the good doctor's remembrances of his father.

THE SCARLET CLUE (Monogram, 1945) 65 minutes.

Producer, James S. Burkett; director, Phil Rosen; based on the character created by Earl Derr Biggers; screenplay, George Callahan; art director, David Milton; music director, Edward J. Kay; assistant director, Eddie Davis; camera, William A. Sickner; editor, Richard Currier.

Sidney Toler (Charlie Chan); Benson Fong (Tommy Chan); Mantan Moreland (Birmingham Brown); Helen Devereaux (Diane Hall); Robert Homans (Captain Flynn); Virginia Brissac (Mrs. Marsh); I. Stanford Jolley (Ralph Brett); Reid Kilpatrick (Wilbur Chester); Jack Norton (Willie Rand); Charles Sherlock (Sergeant McGraw); Janet Shaw (Gloria Bayne); Milton Kibbee (Herbert Sinclair); Ben Carter (Ben); Victoria Faust (Hulda Swenson); Charles Jordan (Nelson); Leonard Mudie (Horace Carlos); Kernan Cripps (Detective).

THE SCARLET CLUE is the second of a quartet of Charlie Chan featured produced by Monogram Pictures in 1945 and the fifth film in the series since the Earl Derr Biggers character was revived by the studio the previous year. It is worth noting that of the first five Monogram Chans, three had the Chinese sleuth investigating the murder of a scientist doing war work. This topical plot ploy was used for the initial revival feature, CHARLIE CHAN IN THE SECRET SERVICE and in the film issued prior to this one, THE JADE MASK (qq.v.). Setting the tone for some of the entries to follow, THE SCARLET CLUE also stopped the action frequently to permit series co-star Mantan Moreland to revive on camera some of his vaudeville routines with sometimes stage partner Ben Carter. The light moments aided the programmer, which is nicely paced with a fairly good mystery plot and competent direction by Phil Rosen, who had helmed the previous four series outings.

A scientist involved in secret government radar experiments is murdered and federal agent Charlie Chan (Sidney Toler) investigates. The only clue is a footprint in blood at the scene of the homicide. Since the scientist's laboratory was in the basement of an office building which houses both a radio and an experimental television station, Chan suspects there may be a connection. He questions the people employed there, with the unwanted aid of number three son Tommy Chan (Benson Fong) and chauffeur Birmingham Brown (Mantan Moreland). After Willie Rand (Jack Norton) and Gloria Bayne (Janet Shaw), radio station actors, are murdered, Chan discovers that the manager of the station, Ralph Brett (I. Stanford Jolley) is an employee of a mysterious leader of a gang that is after secret radar plans. After Brett is also eliminated, Chan realizes the culprit is using a gas secreted in a microphone to do the killings. Thereafter, the gang leader traps Chan in a falling elevator. However, the crime solver uses a remote control device to turn the tables on the killer and bring about the villain's demise.

SCOTLAND YARD (Fox, 1930) 65 minutes.

Presenter, William Fox; producer, Ralph Block; director, William K. Howard; based on the play by Denison Clift; screenplay/dialogue, Garrett Fort; art director, Duncan Cramer; costumes, Sophie Wachner; assistant directors, R. L. Hough, Ray Flynn; technical director, Gerald L. G. Samson; sound, Al Protzman; camera, George Schneiderman; editor, Jack Murray.

Edmund Lowe (Sir John Lasher/Dakin Barrolles); Joan Bennett (Xandra, Lady Lasher); Donald Crisp (Charles Fox); Georges Renevant (Dr. Dean); Lumsden Hare (Sir Clive Heathcote); David Torrence (Captain Graves); Barbara Leonard (Nurse Cecilia); Halliwell Hobbes (Lord St. Arran); J. Carrol Naish (Dr. Remur); Arnold Lucy (McKillop).

SCOTLAND YARD (Twentieth Century-Fox, 1941) 68 minutes.

Producer, Sol M. Wurtzel; director, Norman Foster; based on the play by Denison Clift; screenplay, Samuel G. Engel, John Balderston; camera, Virgil Miller; editor, Al De Gaetano.

Nancy Kelly (Lady Sandra Lasher); Edmund Gwenn (Inspector Cork); John Loder (Sir John Lasher); Henry Wilcoxon (Dakin Barrolles); Melville Cooper (Dr. Crownfield); Gilbert Emery (Sir Clive Heathcote); Norma Varden (Lady Heathcote); Leyland Hodgson (Henderson); Lionel Pape (Hugh Burnalde); Lillian Bond (Lady Constance); Leo G. Carroll (Craven); Frank Dawson (Kinch); Eugene Borden (Tony); Edward Fielding (Pickering); Robert de Bruce (Jeffries); Denis Green (Scott-Bishop); Jimmy Aubrey (Cockney); Yorke Sherwood (Lorry Driver); Lester Matthews (Dr. Gilbert); Doris Lloyd (Miss Harcourt).

Denison Clift's 1929 London stage success, *Scotland Yard,* was the basis for three films: the 1930 Fox production of the same title and its Spanish-language counterpart, and the 1941 remake by Twentieth Century-Fox as a programmer.

Crook Dakin Barrolles (Edmund Lowe) is on the run from Scotland Yard detectives and takes refuge in the houseboat of weak-willed Sir John Lasher (Edmund Lowe), whom he somewhat resembles. The crook is attracted to the portrait of Sir John's bride, Xandra (Joan Bennett), and he steals a locket containing her picture. The police trace Dakin to his hideout and the only way he can escape is to join the army. During a battle in France he is badly injured and it takes plastic surgery to restore his face, the doctor using Lasher's picture in the locket as a guide. Now looking totally like Lasher, Dakin returns to the man's home, intent on robbing him. He finds that Sir John has been missing in action and that Xandra thinks the crook is really her lost spouse. Staying with Xandra, Dakin pretends to be Lasher and plans to fleece the man's ex-partner, Charles Fox (Donald Crisp). However, the latter learns the truth and blackmails Dakin, who has now fallen in love with Xandra. When Scotland Yard detective Captain Graves (David Torrence) finds out the truth about Dakin, the latter helps him capture Fox. As a reward he is placed in Xandra's custody, since she too now knows his real identity.

Mordaunt Hall (*New York Times*) assessed, "There are a number of surprises in this film, and while it is hardly ever convincing, it at least possesses the spice of originality. . . . Lumsden Hare's interpretation of the knowledgeable Scotland Yard commissioner is intelligent and well-spoken."

Fox also filmed a Spanish-language version of SCOTLAND YARD as EL IMPOSTER [The Imposter], which was issued south of the border in 1931. Lewis Seiler directed and Juan Torena, Blanca de Castejon and Carlos Villarias (who portrayed the title role in the Spanish version of DRACULA the same year) co-starred.

The 1941 low-budget remake was produced by Sol M. Wurtzel, who handled the Charlie Chan, Mr. Moto and other quickie detective films at Twentieth Century-Fox, with direction by Norman Foster. Here the plot remains close to the 1930 version except that the villains are changed to a German spy ring out to steal the gold in Lasher's London bank, with reformed Dakin Barrolles thwarting them. While Edmund Lowe handled the dual role in the 1930 feature, Henry Wilcoxon essays the part of crook Dakin and, after the plastic surgery, John Loder portrays him as Lasher. Nancy Kelly is the object of his affection, and Edmund Gwenn is the persistent Scotland Yard detective, with Gilbert Emery as his boss. *Variety* reported, "Script, with its up-to-the-minute revisions to take advantage of present war events, is an exceptionally fine job, compactly handling the dramatic situations and highlighting the mystery element."

SCOTLAND YARD INVESTIGATOR (Republic, 1945) 66 minutes.

Associate producer/director, George Blair; screenplay, Randall Faye; art director, Frank Hotaling; set decorator, Charles Thompson; music, Charles Maxwell; music director, Richard Cherwin; assistant director, Joe Dill; sound, Ed Borschell; special effects, Howard Lydecker, Theodore Lydecker; camera, Ernest Miller, William Bradford; editor, Fred Allen.

Sir C. Aubrey Smith (Sir James Collison); Erich Von Stroheim (Carl Hoffmeyer); Stephanie Bachelor (Tony Collison); Forrester Harvey (Sam Todworthy); Doris Lloyd (Ma Todworthy); Eva Moore (Mary Collison); Richard Fraser (Inspector Cartwright); Victor Varconi (Jules); Frederic Worlock (Colonel Brent); George Metaza (Henri); Emil Rameau (Professor Renault); Colin Campbell (Waters).

Stephanie Bachelor and Sir C. Aubrey Smith in SCOTLAND YARD INVESTIGATOR (1945).

George Blair, who directed the detective programmer EX-POSED (1947), *q.v.*, for Republic, produced and directed this Republic release which employed C. Aubrey Smith as a museum curator who becomes a detective trying to track down a stolen masterpiece. Meanwhile, an actual sleuth, Scotland Yard's Inspector Cartwright (Richard Fraser), also works on the case. In addition to having two detectives, the film also boasts two villains: Erich Von Stroheim as a crazed art collector and Forrester Harvey as a corrupt antique dealer. "Here's a case where a mediocre, yet successful script, is made to appear like a well-polished project, simply because it was excellently cast, shrewdly produced," said *Variety*, adding, "Charles Thompson's set decorations really contribute an air of authenticity to the production."

The Mona Lisa has been hidden for safekeeping during World War II in London's National Art Gallery and now that the hostilities have ended, the French request its return. Sir James Collison (C. Aubrey Smith), the gallery's curator, receives two Louvre repre-sentatives who have come for the painting and since their credentials are in order he hands it over to them. The two men, however, are in the employ of Carl Hoffmeyer (Erich Von Stroheim), a madman art collector who covets the Mona Lisa, and other prize works, for his own private collection. Hoffmeyer examines the painting and finds he has obtained a very good forgery. Collison then is visited by antique dealer Sam Todworthy (Forrester Harvey), who insists he has the real Mona Lisa. He asks a huge amount of money for its return so that he and his wife (Doris Lloyd) can retire in luxury. Realizing he has been duped and not wanting to tarnish the gallery's reputation if news of the loss of the Mona Lisa is made known, Collison calls in Scotland Yard detective Inspector Cartwright (Richard Fraser) and together they search for the painting. Meanwhile, Hoffmeyer sends his goons to obtain the real picture and two murders ensue before he is finally stopped and the priceless Mona Lisa is retrieved.

SECRET OF THE BLUE ROOM (Universal, 1933) 61 minutes.

Director, Kurt Neumann; story, Erich Phillipi; screenplay/dialogue, William Hurlbut; camera, Charles Stumar; editor, Philip Cohn.

Lionel Atwill (Robert von Hellsdorf); Gloria Stuart (Irene von Hellsdorf); Paul Lukas (Captain Walter Brink); Edward Arnold (Commissioner Foster); Onslow Stevens (Frank Faber); William Janney (Thomas Brandt); Robert Barrat (Paul, the Butler); Muriel Kirkland (Betty); Russell Hopton (Max); Elizabeth Patterson (Mary); Anders van Haden (Stranger); James Durkin (Foster's Assistant).

At a chateau in a Middle European country, Irene von Hellsdorf (Gloria Stuart) is celebrating her twenty-first birthday and her boyfriend Thomas Brandt (William Janney) asks her to marry him. In the chateau is the "blue room," which has been locked for two decades, ever since three people died there mysteriously: the best friend of Irene's father, Robert (Lionel Atwill), her aunt and a detective, the latter from fright. To prove he has come of age, Brandt decides he will sleep in the blue room and challenges fellow suitors Captain Walter Brink (Paul Lukas) and Max (Russell Hopton) to do the same. The next morning the room is found locked and Brandt has disappeared. A mysterious stranger later frightens Irene in the blue room and reporter Frank Faber (Onslow Stevens) decides to spend the night there and capture the assailant. However, Faber is shot and killed during the vigil. The next day Commissioner Foster (Edward Arnold) arrives to cross-examine everyone in the chateau. An enigmatic stranger (Anders von Haden) is captured by Foster's men and Robert confesses that the stranger is really his brother and Irene's real father. Irene had grown up believing Robert was her parent, only the butler (Robert Barrat) having been aware of the secret. Brink tells Foster he will sleep in the blue room and he and the police detective make plans to capture the killer. A dummy is set up and when the killer shoots at it from a hidden panel in the wall, Brink and Foster follow through a tunnel. After a struggle the murderer is corralled.

A well-executed murder mystery, THE SECRET OF THE BLUE ROOM is a handsomely mounted production with horror trappings. "Swan Lake" is used as the film's opening and closing music theme and the film's eerie old castle, with a storm setting, adds much to the film's flavor. Lionel Atwill is effective as the mysterious-acting Robert von Heldorf, and Edward Arnold is fine as the homicide squad detective looking in on the case—although he arrives on the scene after one murder has already been committed. It should be noted that the revelation of the killer's identity predates AFTER THE THIN MAN (1936), *q.v.*, by three years.

Never a studio to let a good property (in this case a story by Erich Phillipi) alone, Universal did two remakes of THE SECRET OF THE BLUE ROOM. The first came in 1938 as THE MISSING GUEST. Here the locale was in an American mansion where a killing had taken place two decades before. Newspaperman Scott Hanlon (Paul Kelly) takes on the guise of a psychic when Stephanie Kirkland (Constance Moore) and her family reopen the house, and sets out to find the killer. Lacking the spookiness of the Hollywood original, the film was pale indeed compared to the 1933 version. However, worse was to follow in 1944 with MURDER IN THE

BLUE ROOM. Now running barely one hour, the film has detective Steve Randall (Donald Cook) out to solve the murder of his fiancée's (Anne Gwynne) first husband in a mansion's blue room. A number of suspects arrive, including a female singing trio (Grace McDonald, Betty Kean, June Preisser) called "The Three Jazzybelles" who perform "The Boogie Woogie Boogie Man." Anne Gwynne also sings "One Starry Night." (In all fairness it should be noted that Gloria Stuart [dubbed] sang "I Can't Help Dream of You" at the beginning of SECRET OF THE BLUE ROOM.) The 1944 film was even worse than it sounds, with hokey sound effects and a ghost running amok.*

SECRETS OF CHINATOWN (Syndicate Films, 1935) 63 minutes.

Producer, Kenneth J. Bishop; director, Fred Newmeyer; based on the novel by Guy Morton; screenplay, Morton; camera, William Beckway; editor, William Austin.

Nick Stuart (Robert Rand); Lucille Browne (Zenobia); Raymond Lawrence (Donegal Dawn); James Flavin (Brandhma); Harry Hewitson (Chan Tow Ling); James McGrath (Commissioner); Reginald Hincks (Dr. Franklin); John Barnard (Doverscourt); Arthur Legge-Willis (Yogi of Madrada).

Noted detective Donegal Dawn (Raymond Lawrence) is consulted by the police commissioner (James McGrath) concerning a series of baffling tong murders disrupting Chinatown. Dawn feels the tong is not responsible for the murders, meanwhile his pal Robert Rand (Nick Stuart) ventures into the Oriental area because he is attracted to Zenobia (Lucille Browne), a white girl who works at a Chinese curio shop. An attempt is made on Rand's life after he romances the young woman, and she then disappears. Returning to the curio shop, Rand finds the girl, apparently in a trance, presiding over an elaborate, exotic ceremony with masked and robed worshippers who capture him. When he realizes that Rand has disappeared, the detective gets on his trail, which leads him to the area of the cult's temple. Getting the aid of the police, Dawn rescues Rand and Zenobia while the police capture the worshippers after a gun battle.

The most appealing aspect of this Chinatown detective yarn is that it was produced in Canada, specifically by Kenneth J. Bishop's Northern Films in Victoria, British Columbia. Issued in the United States by Syndicate Pictures, the film is a belabored one, helped only

---

*Some years ago, one of this book's authors (Michael R. Pitts) told actress Betty Kean he had once seen her in MURDER IN THE BLUE ROOM and she replied, "And you're still speaking to me?"

by some scenic locales and the emoting of its Hollywood stars, Nick Stuart, Lucille Browne, and her husband, James Flavin. The detective character of Donegal Dawn is a Sherlock Holmes-type without the innate interest engendered by that granddaddy of sleuths. Unfortunately, Dawn is basically snobbish and boring as a detective and lead character.

Producer Kenneth J. Bishop also starred Nick Stuart and Lucille Browne in THE FIGHTING PLAYBOY (1935), and later made an engaging Canadian Mountie programmer, DEATH GOES NORTH (1938), with Rin Tin Tin, Jr., Edgar Edwards, Sheila Bromley, Jameson Thomas and Walter Byron.

THE SEVEN PER-CENT-SOLUTION (Universal, 1976) Color 113 minutes.

Executive producers, Alex Winitsky, Arlene Sellers; producer, Herbert Ross; associate producer, Stanley O'Toole; director, Ross; based on the novel by Nicholas Meyer; screenplay, Meyer; music, John Addison; song, Stephen Sondheim; assistant director, Scott Wodehouse; production designer, Ken Adam; costumes, Alan Barrett; camera, Oswald Morris; editor, Chris Barnes.

Alan Arkin (Sigmund Freud); Vanessa Redgrave (Lola Devereaux); Robert Duvall (Dr. John H. Watson); Nicol Williamson (Sherlock Holmes); Laurence Olivier (Professor Moriarty); Joel Grey (Lowenstein); Samantha Eggar (Mary Watson); Jeremy Kemp (Baron von Leinsdorf); Charles Gray (Mycroft Holmes); Georgia Brown (Mrs. Freud); Regine (Madame); Anna Quayle (Freda); Jill Townsend (Mrs. Holmes); John Bird (Berger); Alison Leggatt (Mrs. Hudson); Erik Chitty (Butler); Jack May (Dr. Schultz); Gertan Klauber (The Pasha); Leon Greene (Squire Holmes); Ashley House (Young Freud); Sheila Shand Gibbs (Nun); Erich Padalewsky (Station Master); John Hill (Train Engineer).

"The film is somewhere between the genial 'little' English comedies of the 50s, with their nifty plots and overqualified performers, and the splashy, stylized James Bond pictures" (Pauline Kael, 5001 Nights at the Movies, 1982).

Nicholas Meyer's 1974 novel, The Seven-Per-cent-Solution (referring to the amount of Sherlock Holmes' cocaine addiction), brought forth a literal flood of updatings of the Holmes character, most of which drew only passing interest from Baker Street enthusiasts while being denounced by purists. Many consider Meyer's initial work to be one of the best of these pastiche works and it resulted in a 1976 feature film for which the author developed the script. In Deerstalker! Holmes and Watson on Screen (1978), Ron Haydock judged the picture, ". . . a grand, first-class adventure that easily

Robert Duvall and Samantha Eggar in THE SEVEN-PER-CENT-SOLUTION (1976).

ranks as one of the best Sherlock Holmes films ever made; in its own way, perhaps the best one of all."

In 1894, three years after his supposed fatal encounter with Professor Moriarty at Reichenbach Falls, Sherlock Holmes (Nicol Williamson) is found by his friend Dr. Watson (Robert Duvall) in a cheap hotel room, addicted to cocaine and suffering from severe hallucinations. He persuades Holmes, with the help of Sherlock's brother Mycroft (Charles Gray), to go to Vienna to see analyst Dr. Sigmund Freud (Alan Arkin), and there Holmes is cured of his drug addiction. A former patient of Freud's, noted actress Lola Devereaux (Vanessa Redgrave), is kidnapped by evil Baron von Leinsdorf (Jeremy Kemp) and his henchman Lowenstein (Joel Grey), and Holmes and Watson go to her rescue. Holmes becomes embroiled in a frantic train chase along the Austrian border before completing his mission. Finally, through psychoanalysis, he understands the reasons for his fear and hatred of the dastardly but hardly criminal Moriarty.

"If style were the sole criterion for the excellence of a picture, this one would be tops," wrote *Films in Review* magazine. "Herbert Ross has given it loving care . . . but he is stuck with Nicholas Meyer's script . . . and his own direction."

THE SEVEN-PER-CENT-SOLUTION grossed almost $6,000,000 at the box-office but it did not draw sufficient audience interest to warrant an intended follow-up, a filming of Meyer's even better *The West End Horror* (1976).

THE SHADOW (Columbia, 1940) fifteen chapters.

Producer, Larry Darmour; director, James W. Horne; based on the radio program and Maxwell Grant [Walter B. Gibson] stories published in *Shadow* magazine; screenplay, Joseph Poland, Ned Dandy, Joseph O'Donnell; music, Lee Zahler; camera, James S. Brown, Jr.; editor, Dwight Caldwell.

Victor Jory (Lamont Cranston [The Shadow/Lin Chang]); Veda Ann Borg (Margot Lane); Robert Moore (Vincent); J. Paul Jones (Turner); Jack Ingram (Marshall); Charles Hamilton (Roberts); Edward Peil, Sr. (Inspector Cardona); Frank La Rue (Commissioner Weston); ???? (The Black Tiger).

Chapters: 1) The Doomed City; 2) The Shadow Attacks; 3) The Shadow's Peril; 4) In the Tiger's Lair; 5) Danger Above; 6) The Shadow's Trap; 7) Where Horror Waits; 8) The Shadow Rides the Rails; 9) The Devil in White; 10) The Underground Trap; 11) Chinatown at Dark; 12) Murder by Remote Control; 13) Wheels of Death; 14) The Sealed Room; 15) The Shadow's Net Closes.

Criminologist/scientist Lamont Cranston (Victor Jory) is enlisted by several civic and government leaders to combat the evil machinations of a mysterious hoodlum, known as The Black Tiger, and his gang. The Black Tiger's identity is unknown as he sabotages railroads, airplanes and industrial plants to gain electrical equipment and chemicals for his weaponry, which includes a death ray. Even the Black Tiger's gang does not know his identity or whereabouts, as he speaks to them only through the head of a cat statuette. With the aid of girlfriend Margot Lane (Veda Ann Borg) Cranston takes on the guise of The Shadow in combatting the villain. Disguising himself as Chinese merchant Lin Chang, The Shadow infiltrates The Black Tiger's gang and locates his headquarters. In a showdown, The Black Tiger is electrocuted accidentally and his identity revealed. He proves to be one of the civic leaders who had hired Cranston.

"The 1940 Columbia serial, THE SHADOW, followed the line of the pulp character fairly faithfully, even though the invisible man of radio was familiar to *millions* of fans, while the magazine version was shown only to a few hundred thousand readers," noted Jim Harmon and Donald F. Glut in *The Great Movie Serials* (1972), regarding the Shadow's lack of invisibility in the cliffhanger. Nonetheless, the chapterplay has some excitement: among its plot twists are The Shadow as Lin Chang framing Lamont Cranston on a murder charge; the Shadow's escape from boiling steam, ammonia, X-rays and an exploding radio; and his saving lady love Margot from being killed by a falling elevator. Still, the cliffhanger could have been staged better and with more genre atmosphere, as Harmon and Glut further note in their reference book: "The film serial proceeded in a singularly unimaginative fashion. All the mystery and menace of The Shadow was lost by having him often appear in broad daylight and brightly lit rooms. The weapons and schemes of the Black Tiger were far from fantastic. All in all, the serial was simply a detective story in which the hero chose to wear a black cloak and slouch hat for no justifiable motive." One can imagine how much superior the production would have been had it been conceived at Republic Pictures.

SHADOW OF THE THIN MAN (Metro-Goldwyn-Mayer, 1941) 97 minutes.

Producer, Hunt Stromberg; director, W. S. Van Dyke, II; based on the characters created by Dashiell Hammett; story, Harry Kurnitz; screenplay, Irving Brecher, Kurnitz; music, David Snell; art director Cedric Gibbons; sound, Douglas Shearer; camera, William Daniels; editor, Robert J. Kern.

William Powell (Nick Charles); Myrna Loy (Nora Charles);

Barry Nelson (Paul Clarke); Donna Reed (Molly Ford); Sam Levene (Lieutenant Abrams); Alan Baxter (Whitey Barrow); Dickie Hall (Nick Charles, Jr.); Loring Smith (Link Stephens); Joseph Anthony (Fred Macy); Henry O'Neill (Major Jason I. Sculley); Stella Adler (Claire Porter); Lou Lubin ("Rainbow" Ben Loomis); Louise Beavers (Stella); Will Wright (Maguire); Edgar Dearing (Motor Cop); Noel Cravat (Baku); Tito Vuolo (Luis); Oliver Blake (Fenster); John Dilson, Arthur Aylsworth (Coroners); James Flavin, Edward Hearn, Art Belasco, Bob Ireland, Robert Kellard (Cops); Cliff Danielson, J. Louis Smith, Jerry Jerome, Roger Moore, Buddy Roosevelt, Hal Le Sueur (Reporters); Cardiff Giant (Bouncing Tschekov); Richard Frankie Burke (Buddy Burns); Tor Johnson (Jack the Ripper); Johnnie Berkes (Paleface); John Kelly (Meatballs Murphy); Joe Oakie (Spider Webb); Jody Gilbert (Lana); Dan Tobey (Announcer); Tommy Mack (Soft Drink Vendor); Joe Devlin (Mugg); Bill Fisher, Aldrich Bowker (Watchmen); Charles Calvert (Referee); Joey Ray (Stephen's Clerk); Inez Cooper (Girl in Cab); Adeline deWalt Reynolds (Landlady); Duke York (Valentino); Seldon Bennett (Mario); Sidney Melton (Fingers); George Lloyd (Pipey); Patti Moore (Lefty's Wife); Jerry Mandy (Waiter); Hardboiled Haggerty, Eddie Simms, Abe Dinovitch, Wee Willie Davis, Sailor Vincent, Jack Roper, Harry Wilson (Mugs); Ray Teal (Cab Driver); Sam Bernard (Counterman); Ken Christy (Detective); David Dornack (Lefty's Kid); Lyle Latell, Matt Gilman, Fred Graham (Waiters with Steaks); Harry Burns (Greek Janitor); Fred Walburn (Kid on Merry-Go-Round); Arch Hendricks (Photographer); Pat McGee (Handler).

Nick (William Powell) and Nora Charles (Myrna Loy) go to the racetrack for a day's pleasure. After a jockey is thrown from his horse, it is realized he has been shot in the neck. Nick wants nothing to do with investigating the homicide but police Inspector Abrams (Sam Levene) talks him into helping with the baffling case. Nick's pal, reporter Paul Clarke (Barry Nelson), believes that gangster Link Stephens (Loring Smith), whose moll, Claire Porter (Stella Adler), claims to be high society, is implicated in the killing. Clarke has his girlfriend, Molly Ford (Donna Reed), become Link's private secretary to gain information about his activities. Clarke goes to Link's office and finds fellow newshawk Whitey Barrow (Alan Baxter), who had worked as a stooge for the gangster, murdered, and the police blame Clarke for the homicide. Nick must clear his pal, as well as unravel the mystery behind the jockey's killing. After a racketeer is silenced, Nick traces the murders to syndicate bosses who are killing those who might uncover their protection benefactor, a high-ranking government official.

This fourth film in MGM's aristocratic Thin Man series, SHAD-

OW OF THE THIN MAN, is as light, sophisticated and amusing as its well-regarded predecessors and it has an unusually good mystery plotline. Among the more amusing scenes are suave Nick Charles supposedly reading the funny papers to his six-year-old son, Nick, Jr. (Dickie Hall), while the youngster knows full well he is looking at the racing form. Also chic Nora attends a wrestling match where patrons mock her new hat while Nick gossips with the combatants, Jack the Ripper (Tor Johnson) and Spider Webb (Joe Oakie). *Variety* printed, "Harry Kurnitz has fashioned the story with a good deal of ingenuity, using the characters of the private detective and his wife. . . . Irving Brecher collaborated on the screenplay with Kurnitz. Between them they have turned out a lively script, with spirited dialog and some amusing situations." Don Miller wrote in "Private Eyes" (*Focus on Film* magazine, Autumn 1975), ". . . By now, the husband-and-wife-cum-sleuths had borne the brunt of many imitators, and what was once genuine sophisticated comedy was now largely veneer, with the sweat of mechanics visible underneath."

THE SHADOW STRIKES (Grand National, 1937) 61 minutes.
  Producers, Max Alexander, Arthur Alexander; director, Lynn Shores; based on the radio series created by Maxwell Grant; screenplay, Al Martin; camera, Marcel Picard; editor, Charles Henkel.
  Rod La Rocque (Lamont Cranston, the Shadow); Lynn Anders (Marcia Delthern); Walter McGrail (Winstead Comstock); James Blakely (Jasper Delthern); Kenneth Harlan (Captain Breen); Norman Ainsley (Kendricks); John Carnavale (Warren Berrenger).
  Maxwell Grant's [Walter B. Gibson] The Shadow was first popular in pulp fiction before coming to radio in the early 1930s. It became an airwaves fixture in 1936 with Orson Welles as the elusive Lamont Cranston, and remained on the air for two more decades, with Bret Morrison probably being the most remembered actor to handle the role. Due to the radio show's enduring popularity, The Shadow came to the screen in 1937 with former silent film idol Rod La Rocque cast in two Grand National releases—THE SHADOW STRIKES and INTERNATIONAL CRIME. While The Shadow took the guise of invisibility to fight his foes on radio, in print and in these early films he is *not* invisible, but wears a dark cloak and hat and remains in the shadows.
  THE SHADOW STRIKES is an original screen story in which Lamont Cranston (Rod La Rocque) as The Shadow thwarts a bank robbery but police Captain Breen (Kenneth Harlan) thinks he is behind the attempted heist. Pretending to be a lawyer tied into the case, Cranston becomes embroiled in two murders. He believes a

gangland kingpin (Walter McGrail) is the culprit and traces the hoodlum's activities with a concealed wireless. The actual killer is also after Cranston but that individual and the gangster lord end up killing one another as The Shadow wraps up the puzzle and is cleared by the law. Along the way he romances pretty Marcia Delthern (Lynn Anders).

This initial The Shadow film is weak, as noted by *Variety*, which commented, ". . . what might have been an entertaining sleuth yarn is marred by stupid dialog, feeble acting, misdirection and dangling continuity. When the film goes mysterious, the point is smothered beyond recognition, and when it is not following the detective slant, the yarn becomes extremely boring."

INTERNATIONAL CRIME, *q.v.*, the second of The Shadow features, is based on Maxwell Grant's short story, "The Fox Hound," and in it Lamont Cranston (Rod La Rocque), alias The Shadow, is both a newspaper crime columnist and a radio commentator. He is at odds with the inept local police led by Commissioner Weston (Thomas Jackson). When a wealthy businessman is murdered, Cranston delves into the crime with the dubious aid of his girlfriend, Phoebe Lane (Astrid Allwyn), a reporter on the newspaper for which Cranston does his column. Eventually Cranston, as The Shadow, determines that a foreign agent and his cohorts are in cahoots with the gangsters in thwarting the passage of a huge bond issue. They eliminated the wealthy businessman to stop his efforts on behalf of the bond issue. Cranston obtains the needed proof to bring in the villains.

INTERNATIONAL CRIME, by comparison, is quite a bit better than THE SHADOW STRIKES, as noted by *Variety*: "The Alexander Brothers [Max and Arthur] have given their meller good backgrounds, considerable movement of action, suspense and some romantic flavor, plus a few splotches of comedy. While occasionally too much is given over to detail and occasionally some liberties are taken, on the whole the interest is well held. The dialog fails to rise above the ordinary for this type of production but otherwise the adaptation is capable." Despite the improvement, INTERNATIONAL CRIME was Grand National's final entry in its brief The Shadow series.

The Shadow, however, continued to appear on film. Victor Jory had the title part in the 1940 Columbia serial, THE SHADOW, *q.v.*, and in 1946 Kane Richmond played the part in a trio of second-string features for Monogram Pictures* in the late 1950s. Richard

---

*The three Monogram Pictures featuring The Shadow are: THE SHADOW RETURNS (1946), BEHIND THE MASK (1946), THE MISSING LADY (1946).

Derr was Cranston in two theatrical features* from Republic Pictures which were culled from episodes of an unsold TV series.

Finally, it should be noted that the 1937 Columbia programmer, THE SHADOW, with Charles Quigley and Rita Hayworth, is a crime drama and has nothing to do with the Maxwell Grant character.

SHADOWS OVER CHINATOWN (Monogram, 1946) 64 minutes.

Producer, James S. Burkett; director, Terry Morse; based on the character created by Earl Derr Biggers; screenplay, Raymond Schrock; art director, David Milton; camera, William Sickner; editor, Ralph Dixon.

Sidney Toler (Charlie Chan); Mantan Moreland (Birmingham Brown); Victor Sen Yung (Tommy Chan); Tanis Chandler (Mary Conover); John Gallaudet (Jeff Hay); Paul Bryar (Mike Rogan); Bruce Kellogg (Jack Tilford); Alan Bridge (Captain Allen); Mary Gordon (Mrs. Conover); Dorothy Granger (Joan Mercer); Jack Norton (Cosgrove); Charlie Jordan (Jenkins); John Hamilton (Bus Passenger); and: Mira McKinney, George Eldredge, Harry Depp, Gladys Blake, Jack Mower, Tyra Vaughn, Lyle Latell.

Charlie Chan (Sidney Toler), number three son Tommy (Victor Sen Yung) and chauffeur Birmingham Brown (Mantan Moreland) are on a bus trip during a terrible storm. On board they meet several people including a businessman (John Hamilton) and a pickpocket called Cosgrove (Jack Norton). Also on board is Mrs. Conover (Mary Gordon), who is heading to San Francisco in search of her missing daughter Mary (Tanis Chandler), who may be the victim of a torso murder. The bus develops engine problems and pulls into a terminal where an attempt is made on Chan's life. Mysterious Jack Tilford (Bruce Kellogg) appears at the terminal and is blamed for the attempted murder, but is soon cleared. When they reach San Francisco, Chan agrees to aid Mrs. Conover in locating her daughter and soon finds out that Tilford is Mary's fiancé, although she has left him. Chan discovers Mary working in a restaurant and learns she was employed by an escort service which involved her in an insurance-for-murder scheme in which she was to entice and marry Tilford. He was then to be killed for his insurance policy. Mary refused to carry out orders and fled. She tells Chan the gang is now hunting her. With the assistance of the police, Chan uncovers the identity of the corrupt operations chief and brings the killer to justice.

SHADOWS OVER CHINATOWN, produced as THE MANDARIN SECRET, the second of a trio of Charlie Chan-Monogram

---

*The two Republic Pictures featuring The Shadow are: INVISIBLE AVENGER (1958) and BOURBON STREET SHADOWS (1962).

features in 1946, is an atmospheric entry, especially in its early storm sequence and later as Chan ferrets out the murderer in the heart of exotic Chinatown. Victor Sen Yung, who had played number two son Jimmy Chan in the Twentieth Century-Fox Charlie Chan films with Sidney Toler from 1938 to 1942, returned to the series, but now assumed the name of Tommy Chan, which had been performed in earlier installments by Benson Fong. "There's Terror in Every Clue!" read the ads for this budget feature which has a well-staged comedy sequence with Tommy and Birmingham as (literally) bulls in a china shop as they wreak havoc in a curio establishment while the elder Chan searches for clues.

SHAFT (Metro-Goldwyn-Mayer, 1971) Color 100 minutes.

Producer Joel Freedman; associate producer, David Golden; director, Gordon Parks; based on the novel by Ernest Tidyman; screenplay, Tidyman, John D. F. Black; music, Isaac Hayes; assistant director, Ted Zachary; costumes, Joe Aulisi; sound, Lee Bost, Bob Rogow; camera, Urs Furrer; editor, Hugh A. Robertson.

Richard Roundtree (John Shaft); Moses Gunn (Bumpy Jonas); Charles Cioffi (Lieutenant Vic Androzzi); Christopher St. John (Ben Buford); Gwenn Mitchell (Ellie Moore); Lawrence Pressman (Sergeant Tom Hannon); Sherri Brewer (Marcy); Rex Robbins (Rollie); Camille Yarbrough (Dina Greene); Margaret Warnecke (Linda); Joseph Leon (Byron Leibowitz); Arnold Johnson (Cul); Dominic Barto (Patsy); George Strus (Carmen); Edmund Hashim (Lee); Drew Bundi Brown (Willy); Tommy Lane (Leroy); Al Kirk (Sims); Shimen Ruskin (Dr. Sam); Antonio Fargas (Bunky); Gertrude Jeannette (Old Lady); Lee Steele (Blind Vendor); Damu King (Mal); Donny Burks (Remmy); Tony King (Davies); Benjamin R. Rixson (Newfield); Ricardo Brown (Tully); Alan Weeks (Gus); Glenn Johnson (Char); Dennis Tate (Dotts); James Hainesworth, Adam Wade (Brothers); Clee Burtonya (Sonny); Ed Bernard (Peerce); Ed Barth (Tony); Joe Pronto (Dom); Robin Nolan (Waitress); Ron Tannas (Billy); Betty Bresler (Mrs. Androzzi); Gonzalo Madurga (Counterman); Paul Nevens (Elevator Man); Jon Richards (Starter).

SHAFT IN AFRICA (Metro-Goldwyn-Mayer, 1973) Color 112 minutes.

Producer, Roger Lewis; associate producer, Rene Dupont; director, John Guillermin; based on characters created by Ernest Tidyman; screenplay, Stirling Silliphant; production designer, John Stoll; art director, Jose Maria Tapiador; music/music director, Johnny Pate; song, Dennis Lambert and Brian Potter; second unit director, David Tomblin; assistant director, Miguel Angel Gil, Jr.;

Edmund Hashim and Richard Roundtree in SHAFT (1971).

stick fight arranger, Takahuki Kubota; action coordinator, Miguel Pedregosa; special effects, Antonio Molena; sound, Peter Sutton, Hal Walker; camera, Marcel Grignon; editor, Max Benedict.

Richard Roundtree (John Shaft); Frank Finlay (Amafi, the Slave Dealer); Vonetta McGee (Aleme); Neda Arneric (Jazar); Debebe Eshetu (Wassa); Spiros Focas (Sassari); Jacques Herlin (Perreau); Jho Jhenkins (Ziba); Willie Jonah (Oyo); Adolfo Lastretti (Piro); Marne Maitland (Colonel Gondar); Frank McRae (Osiat); Zenebech Tadesse (Prostitute); A. V. Falana (Ramila's Son); James E. Myers (Detective Williams); Nadim Sawalha (Zubair); Thomas Baptiste (Kopo); Jon Chevron (Shimba); Glynn Edwards (Vanden); Cy Grant (Emir Ramila); Jacques Marin (Inspector Cusset); Nick Zaran (Sadi); Aldo Sambreill (Angelo).

SHAFT'S BIG SCORE (Metro-Goldwyn-Mayer, 1972) Color 105 minutes.

Producers, Roger Lewis, Ernest Tidyman; associate producer, David Golden; director, Gordon Parks, Sr.; based on characters created by Tidyman; screenplay, Tidyman; art director, Emanuel Gerard; set decorator, Robert Drumheller; costumes, Joe Aulisi; makeup, Martin Bell; music/songs, Parks; orchestrators, Dick Hazard, Tom McIntosh, Jimmy Jones, Dale Oehler; assistant director, William C. Gerrity; stunts, Alex Stevens, Marvin Walters; special effects, Tony Parmalee; sound, Lee Bost, Hal Watkins; camera, Urs Furrer; editor, Harry Howard.

Richard Roundtree (John Shaft); Moses Gunn (Bumpy Jonas); Drew Bundini Brown (Willy); Joseph Mascola (Gus Mascola); Kathy Imrie (Rita); Wally Taylor (Kelly); Julius W. Harris (Captain Bollin); Rosalind Miles (Arna Ashby); Joe Santos (Pascal); Angelo Nazzo (Al); Don Blakely (Johnson); Melvin Green, Jr. (Junior Gillis); Thomas Anderson (Preacher); Evelyn Davis (Old Lady); Richard Pittmann (Kelly's Hood); Robert Kya-Hill (Cal Ashby); Thomas Brann (Mascola's Hood); Bob Jefferson (Harrison); Dan P. Hannafin (Cooper); Jimmy Hayeson (Caretaker); Henry Ferrentino (Detective Salmi); Frank Scioscia (Rip); Kitty Jones (Cabaret Dancer); Gregory Reese (Foglio); Marilyn Hamlin (Mascola's Girl); John Foster (Jerry); Joyce Walker (Cigarette Girl); Gordon Parks, Sr. (Croupier).

In the early 1970s Ernest Tidyman penned a half dozen novels about the exploits of tough black private detective John Shaft, and three theatrical films were produced by MGM about the character as well as a short-lived network TV series. The first of the theatrical series, SHAFT, proved so explosively popular that it is credited with defining and extending the blaxploitation motion picture craze that engulfed Hollywood until the mid-1970s. So closely identified did Richard Roundtree become with his casting as the emancipated, gritty black detective (who is equally adept in street warfare or in bed with a curvacious playmate), that to this date—two decades later—it remains the fine actor's most noteworthy screen part.

SHAFT, issued in 1971, was directed by Gordon Parks on a $1,500,000 budget with Harlem location lensing. The rough and dirty narrative finds Gotham private eye John Shaft (Richard Roundtree), who is a devil with women, hired by uptown gangster Bumpy Jonas (Moses Gunn) to retrieve his kidnapped daughter, who has been taken hostage by the downtown Mafioso. Handsome Shaft is given occasional help in the caper by his acquaintance, white police Lieutenant Vic Androzzi (Charles Cioffi) and direct assistance by his childhood friend, Ben Buford (Christopher St. John), who now leads a black revolutionary movement in Harlem. Before the case is concluded, Shaft and Buford have locked horns with the mobster organization in bloody shootouts. With matters resolved, Shaft (in an amusing turnabout on standard procedures), calls Androzzi to advise him that *he* can now clean up the dirty end pieces of the case.

SHAFT, thanks in part to Isaac Hayes' exciting musical score (which won an Academy Award), proved tremendously popular with its liberated approach to a black screen hero. This salty detective action film grossed nearly $8,000,000 and led to SHAFT'S BIG SCORE (1972). Here Shaft is at odds with a crook and a Mafia group in Queens; both are after a quarter of a million dollars. The cache was secreted by the criminal's associate, the latter intending it to be used for a Harlem child welfare group. Hubbell Robinson wrote in *Films in Review* magazine (October 1972), "For ninety-six minutes the contending factions beat and murder each other and climb in and out of bed, briefly and dangerously, with a succession of lovely, larcenous and lascivious dames, black and white. Shaft emerges in this version as a highly lethal and effective weapon of destruction and not much else." Costing $2,000,000, this derivative film—despite the lack of Isaac Hayes as music composer and minus the breathtaking innovations of the series' opener—grossed twice its expenses upon release, leading to yet a third outing, SHAFT IN AFRICA (1973). By this juncture, Gordon Parks, Sr. dropped out of the project and the studio, anxious to find new avenues to explore by removing the storyline from the now overexposed Harlem turf, has Shaft return to his roots, traveling to the dark continent to track a slave labor consortium which is shipping black natives to France to be exploited as cheap manual labor. As directed by John Guillermin, Shaft (Richard Roundtree) opposes slave trafficker Amafi (Frank Finlay) and along the way seduces Aleme (Vonetta McGee), his employer's daughter, and Amafi's randy girlfriend, Wassa (Debebe Eshetu). Costing over $2,000,000. the well-mounted feature grossed less than $1,500,000 at the box-office, a victim of the oversaturation of black action features sweeping the country. It was the end of the theatrical series.

During the 1973-74 television season Richard Roundtree portrayed black gumshoe John Shaft in the ABC-TV series "Shaft," thus becoming the small screen's first full-time black detective. However, the small-screen version sanitized Shaft's character and the storyline removed all the ethnic grit that had made the theatrical versions so popular. It faded quickly from the network lineup.

SHAMUS (Columbia, 1973) Color 93 minutes.

Producer, Robert M. Weitman; director, Guzz Kulik; screenplay, Barry Beckerman; art director, Philip Rosenberg; music, Jerry Goldsmith; assistant director, Ted Zachary; sound, Christopher Newman; camera, Victor J. Kemper; editor, Walter Thompson.

Burt Reynolds (McCoy); Dyan Cannon (Alexis); John Ryan (Colonel C. C. Hardcore); Joe Santos (Lieutenant Promuto); Georgio Tozzi (Dottore); Ron Weyand (Hume); Larry Block (Springly); Beeson Carroll (Bolton); Kevin Conway (The Kid); Kay Frye (Bookstore Girl); John Glover (Johnnie); Marwin Goldsmith (Schook); Melody Santangelo (Woman); Irving Seibert (Heavy); Alex Wilson (Felix); Tony Amato, Jr. (Willie); Lou Martell (Rock); Marshall Anker (Dealer); Bert Bertram (Doorman); Jimmy Kelly (Gifter).

Tough Brooklyn private investigator McCoy (Burt Reynolds) is hired by wealthy Hume (Ron Weyand) to locate a man allegedly involved in a diamond heist. Finding himself at odds with the law as well as the underworld, McCoy discovers he is actually caught up in an illegal game of exporting government arms. Also involved is Colonel C. C. Hardcore (John Ryan), who is profiteering in tank sales. Along the way McCoy meets and beds beautiful Alexis (Dyan Cannon), the sister of a cohort of the millionaire. In addition, he also takes several beatings and avoids being murdered before resolving the complicated situation.

"BURT REYNOLDS is the SHAMUS!" announced the poster blurb for this feature which aided in cementing Reynolds' place as one of the box-office champions of the 1970s. In the *New York Times*, Roger Greenspun called SHAMUS ". . . a game but not especially good movie that means to put the private eye back into some kind of current relevance. . . . Just possibly, the private eye, that last refuge of unfettered consciousness, is a less immortal pop-culture hero than some would like to imagine. . . ." Still, Greenspun added that the film is "... workmanlike, well-paced, modest, sometimes scary and sometimes genuinely funny." In *The Films of the Seventies* (1984), Marc Sigoloff calls SHAMUS a "Fine detective thriller. ... The plot is extremely convoluted and confusing, and there are many extraneous characters and plot developments. SHAMUS, however, remains interesting because of its brisk pace and its exciting action focusing on numerous attempts on Reynolds' life."

The film's main interest lies in the title character as enacted by Burt Reynolds. Hugh James notes in *Films in Review* magazine (April 1973), "Sleeping on a pool table in his one-room walkup apartment where he suggests to his lady friends that they stretch their legs with the help of the sidepockets, Burt Reynolds as Shamus has finally reaped the rewards of his 'Cosmopolitan' picture. Rather like an American James Bond, Reynolds is equal to every situation, whether it's a penthouse on Sutton Place or a barroom. He can beat up a man with a chain as well as the best of them. Lest we think he's perfect, however, he's afraid of dogs."

THE SHANGHAI CHEST (Monogram, 1948) 65 minutes.

Producer, James S. Burkett; director, William Beaudine; based on the character created by Earl Derr Biggers; story, Sam Newman; screenplay, W. Scott Darling, Newman; art director, David Milton; set decorator, Raymond Boltz, Jr.; music, Edward Kay; camera, William Sickner; editors, Otto Lovering, Ace Herman.

Roland Winters (Charlie Chan); Mantan Moreland (Birmingham Brown); Deannie Best (Phyllis Powers); John Alvin (Vic Armstrong); Victor Sen Yung (Tommy Chan); Tim Ryan (Lieutenant Ruark); Pierre Watkin (Judge Armstrong); Russell Hicks (District Attorney Bronson); Philip Van Zandt (Pindello); George Eldredge (Finley); Willie Best (Willie); Tristram Coffin (Ed Seward); Milton Parsons (Mr. Grail); Edward I. Coke (Cartwright); Olaf Hytten (Bates); Erville Alderson (Walter Somervale); Charlie Sullivan (Officer Murphy); Paul Scardon, Louis Mason (Custodians); William Ruhl (Jailer); Lola Austin (Landlady); Chabing (Miss Lee); John Shay (Stacey).

Roland Winters' third Charlie Chan feature, and the first *not* to be a remake of a Mr. Wong film, THE SHANGHAI CHEST is the first of a trio of Chan features to be directed by William Beaudine. It would be followed by THE GOLDEN EYE (*q.v.*) and THE FEATHERED SERPENT (*q.v.*), both in 1948. The film also introduced Tim Ryan, who provided the screenplay's additional dialogue, in the role of police Lieutenant Ruark, a role he would repeat in THE GOLDEN EYE and the final series entry, SKY DRAGON (1949), *q.v.*

District Attorney Bronson (Russell Hicks) is found brutally murdered and at the scene is a young man, Vic Armstrong (John Alvin), who had earlier argued with Bronson over marrying his niece, Phyllis Powers (Deannie Best). Charlie Chan (Roland Winters) takes the case as the evidence mounts against Armstrong and, as usual, he receives unneeded help from number three son Tommy Chan (Victor Sen Yung) and chauffeur Birmingham Brown (Mantan Moreland), the latter meeting old friend Willie (Willie Best) when the trio go behind bars to interview the accused. Eventually Chan fathoms the depths of the case and pinpoints the killer.

An appealing plot ploy in THE SHANGHAI CHEST is that the killer's fingerprints are in plain sight after the homicide but go overlooked. The interlude between Mantan Moreland and Willie Best adds comedy zest to the proceedings.

THE SHANGHAI COBRA (Monogram, 1945) 64 minutes.

Producer James B. Burkett; director, Phil Karlson; based on the character created by Earl Derr Biggers; screenplay, George Callahan, George Wallace Sayre; art director, Vin Taylor; sound, Tom Lambert; camera, Vince Farrar; editor, Ace Herman.

Sidney Toler (Charlie Chan); Benson Fong (Tommy Chan); Mantan Moreland (Birmingham Brown); Walter Fenner (Inspector Harry Davis); James Cardwell (Ned Stewart); Joan Barclay (Pauline Webster [Paula Webb]); James Flavin (Jarvis); Addison Richards (John Adams [Jan Van Horn]); Arthur Loft (Bradford Harris [Hume]); Gene Stutenroth [Roth] (Morgan); Joe Devlin (Taylor); Roy Gordon (Walter Fletcher); Janet Warren (Lorraine); George Chandler (Short Order Cook); Paul Newlan (Bank Guard); Cyril Delevanti (Larkin, the Undercover Agent).

During a storm, a man dies mysteriously after meeting with a young woman named Pauline Webster who is being trailed by private eye Ned Stewart (James Cardwell). The deceased was an employee of a bank and two others who worked there have also died, all by the same means—the venom of a cobra. Police Inspector Harry Davis (Walter Fenner) calls in government agent Charlie Chan (Sidney Toler), who can identify Jan Van Horn, a man he arrested in Shanghai eight years before when a special agent named Howe had charged him with robbery and the use of cobra venom to commit murder. Chan explains to Davis that Van Horn had escaped and had changed his looks by plastic surgery. In addition, the government has also assigned him, Chan, to check on the radium stored in the bank. Chan meets with bank president Walter Fletcher (Roy Gordon) and vice president Bradford Harris (Arthur Loft) and then he and number three son Tommy (Benson Fong) and chauffeur

Birmingham Brown (Mantan Moreland) visit Stewart. With the aid of Davis they plant a story that Stewart has been charged with the murders and Paula Webb (Joan Barclay) meets with Chan to clear the detective, since she was the woman who called herself Pauline Webster. Later, a police undercover agent (Cyril Delevanti) placed in the bank is found murdered and Chan deduces that all of the prior homicide victims had died after leaving a soda shop operated by a young woman (Janet Warren). The shop's juke box, Chan finds, contains a needle which injects the victims with cobra venom, and the young lady claims Jan Van Horn is the murderer. Chan also finds out that engineer Jarvis (James Flavin) and henchmen Morgan (Gene Roth) and Taylor (Joe Devlin) are planning to steal the radium from the bank vault. That night Chan, Tommy and Birmingham Brown are trapped in a sewer tunnel explosion beneath the bank, but Chan uses Morse code over a telephone cable to send a message to the police. The law captures the gang and rescues the trio. Chan points out the man who is really Van Horn and the woman who is his daughter. The Chinese sleuth next reveals the murderous brains behind the theft.

The sixth Monogram Charlie Chan feature, THE SHANGHAI COBRA is a complicated, slowly paced mystery in which director Phil Karlson employs the *film noir* motif to decent effect, especially in the opening storm scenes during which the first murders occurs. The actual killer in this narrative is also difficult to spot.

SHED NO TEARS (Eagle Lion, 1948) 70 minutes.

Producer, Robert Frost; director, Jean Yarbrough; based on the novel by Don Martin; screenplay, Brown Holmes, Virginia Cook; art director, Walter Koessler; set decorator, Fay Babcock; costumes, Lon Anthony; makeup, Don Donaldson, Lon Anthony; music/music director, Ralph Stanley; assistant director, Eddie Stein; sound, Ben Winkler; camera, Frank Redman; editor, Norman R. Cerf.

Wallace Ford (Sam Grover); June Vincent (Edna Grover); Robert Scott (Ray Belden); Jonathan White (Huntington Stewart); Dick Hogan (Tom Grover); Frank Albertson (Hutton).

Based on Don Martin's 1948 novel, the low-budget SHED NO TEARS (in production for only ten days) tells of a scheme cooked up by Sam Grover (Wallace Ford) and his wife Edna (June Vincent) to fake the former's death in order to collect on his $50,000 life insurance policy. After the scheme is carried out, Sam's son by a former marriage, Tom Grover (Dick Hogan), suspects something phony is taking place. He hires private eye Huntington Stewart (Jonathan White) to investigate and Edna bribes him to stay out of the case. Stewart shows that Edna and her new lover, Ray Belden

(Robert Scott), are out to pull further double-crosses, all leading to additional murders before the case is concluded.

In "Private Eyes" (*Focus on Film* magazine, Autumn 1975), Don Miller labels SHED NO TEARS a " . . . practically unknown crime yarn. . . . The downbeat drama saved the ironic best for last. . . ."

It is well to note that the private eye within SHED NO TEARS is not a typical screen crime solver. Here Huntington Stewart is hardly more honest than the crooks he is supposed to be trailing, even to the taking of a bribe to supplement his income.

SHERLOCK AND ME *see* WITHOUT A CLUE [essay].

SHERLOCK HOLMES (Goldwyn, 1922) 8,200'

Producer, F. J. Godsol; director, Albert Parker; based on the play by William Gillette and the stories by Sir Arthur Conan Doyle; screenplay, Marian Fairfax, Earl Browne; camera, J. Roy Hunt.

John Barrymore (Sherlock Holmes); Roland Young (Dr. John H. Watson); Carol Dempster (Alice Faulkner); Gustav von Seyffertitz (Professor Moriarty); Louis Wolheim (Craigin); Percy Knight (Sid Jones); William Powell (Forman Wells); Hedda Hopper (Madge Larrabee); Peggy Bayfield (Rose Faulkner); Margaret Kemp (Therese); Anders Randolf (James Larrabee); Robert Schable (Alf Bassick); Reginald Denny (Prince Alexis); David Torrence (Count Von Stalburg); Robert Fischer (Otto); Lumsden Hare (Dr. Leighton); Jerry Devine (Billy); John Willard (Inspector Gregson).

SHERLOCK HOLMES (Fox, 1932) 68 minutes.

Director, William K. Howard; based on the play by William Gillette and the stories by Arthur Conan Doyle; screenplay, Bertram Millhauser; art director, John Hughes; costumes, Rita Kaufman; assistant director, Philip Ford; sound, Albert Protzman; camera, George Barnes.

Clive Brook (Sherlock Holmes); Miriam Jordan (Alice Faulkner); Ernest Torrence (Professor Moriarty); Reginald Owen (Dr. John H. Watson); Howard Leeds (Little Billy); Alan Mowbray (Inspector Gore-King); Herbert Mundin (Pub Keeper); Montague Shaw (Judge); Arnold Lucy (Chaplain); Lucien Prival (Hans, the Hun); Roy D'Arcy (Manuel Lopez); Stanley Fields (Tony Ardetti); Eddie Dillon (Ardetti's Henchman); Robert Graves, Jr. (Gaston Roux); Brandon Hurst (Secretary to Erskine); Claude King (Sir Albert Hastings).

William Gillette's stage play *Sherlock Holmes* was produced initially in 1899* and for nearly three decades Gillette toured the boards as the Baker Street sleuth, even filming the property for Essanay in 1916, although that feature is lost to the ages. In 1922 Samuel Goldwyn produced another screen version of the Gillette play, casting John Barrymore as the intrepid Holmes. It was shot on location in London and Switzerland and was released in Great Britain as MORIARTY. *Photoplay* magazine enthused, "It is one of the most artistic and unusual films ever made. Its settings and photography are amazingly fine. Its cast is one of the few real all-star affairs."

In London Sherlock Holmes (John Barrymore), a student, is recommended by classmate John H. Watson (Roland Young) to Prince Alexis (Reginald Denny), who has been falsely accused of pilfering athletic funds. The actual criminal is Professor Moriarty (Gustav von Seyffertitz), who works out of his Limehouse den. Holmes also meets pretty Alice Faulkner (Carole Dempster) and falls in love with her. He locates Moriarty in Limehouse and vows to bring in the master criminal. A few years later Holmes and Dr. Watson now share quarters at Baker Street and Alice asks Holmes to aid her family; her sister Rose has committed suicide in Switzerland because Moriarty was blackmailing her over letters she had written to Alexis. The letters are in the hands of Moriarty's ally, James Larrabee (Anders Randolf), and Holmes journeys to Switzerland where he employs several disguises before apprehending the devious Moriarty. Holmes plans to wed Alice.

Although star John Barrymore was drinking heavily during much of the film's production, he gives a superb performance as Holmes and seems especially to enjoy the opportunity the role allows him to don various disguises. With a fine cast and handsome production values, the movie proved to be highly commercial and it still exists today, although it is currently not available for exhibition. Gustav von Seyffertitz was acknowledged to be especially effective as Moriarty, playing the character as a human monster both in looks and action.

A decade after the Samuel Goldwyn film, the William Gillette play was again used as the basis for a film entitled SHERLOCK HOLMES, but most of the plot was conceived by scripter Bertram Millhauser who would later write a number of the 1940s Universal Holmes films with Basil Rathbone and Nigel Bruce. Here Professor

---

*When actor and playwright William Gillette was preparing Sherlock Holmes for the Broadway stage, he asked Sir Arthur Conan Doyle what "liberties" he could take in his theater version. Doyle is said to have responded, "Marry him, murder him, do anything you please with him."

Moriarty (Ernest Torrence) is sentenced to die for his crimes and vows revenge on Holmes (Clive Brook) and Scotland Yard Inspector Gore-King (Alan Mowbray). Holmes receives this news from Dr. Watson (Reginald Owen) but is mainly involved in his work, teaching his apprentice, Little Billy (Howard Leeds), and romancing his fiancée, Alice Faulkner (Miriam Jordan). Moriarty escapes from prison and Holmes' friend Erskine, who prosecuted the madman, disappears. The great detective sets out to find him, although he is at odds with Gore-King over his scientific methods. Erskine is found murdered at the same time that Moriarty begins importing international gangsters to terrorize London as a cover for his real goal, the robbery of the London bank operated by Alice's father. To complicate matters, Moriarty kidnaps both Alice and Little Billy. Disguising himself as one of the workers Moriarty uses to tunnel into the bank, Holmes infiltrates the gang and with the aid of the police— Holmes had earlier used the ruse of killing Gore-King to get himself publicly embarrassed and to offset Moriarty's plans—the gang is captured and Moriarty is shot and killed. Holmes and Alice plan to wed and to move to the country to run a chicken farm.

SHERLOCK HOLMES cast Clive Brook in the title role for the third time. (He had played the part originally in Paramount's THE RETURN OF SHERLOCK HOLMES [1929], *q.v.*, and had made a guest appearance as the sleuth in PARAMOUNT ON PARADE [1930].) The Fox film, like the 1929 feature, is set in modern times and it should be noted that while Reginald Owen has little to do here as Watson, he would play Holmes himself in the next year's A STUDY IN SCARLET, *q.v.* While Clive Brook makes an engaging Holmes (including his moments in disguise as an elderly matron), the film itself is a disappointment and did not fare well with the critics. ". . . . It is doubtful whether the Sherlock Holmes stories can stand the test of being modernized," insisted Mordaunt Hall (*New York Times*). Ron Haydock, in *Deerstalker! Holmes and Watson on Screen* (1978), refers to the 1932 film as "an embarrassing exploit."

SHERLOCK HOLMES   *see*   THE ADVENTURES OF SHER-LOCK HOLMES (1939).

SHERLOCK HOLMES AND A STUDY IN SCARLET   *see*   A STUDY IN SCARLET [essay].

SHERLOCK HOLMES AND THE SECRET WEAPON (Universal, 1942) 68 minutes.

Associate producer, Howard Benedict; director, Roy William Neill; based on the story "The Dancing Men" by Sir Arthur Conan

Doyle; adaptor/screenplay, Edward T. Lowe, W. Scott Darling, Edmund L. Hartmann; art director, Jack Otterson; music, Frank Skinner; music director, Charles Previn; camera, Lester White; editor, Otto Ludwig.

Basil Rathbone (Sherlock Holmes); Nigel Bruce (Dr. John H. Watson); Kaaren Verne (Charlotte Eberli); Lionel Atwill (Professor Moriarty); William Post, Jr. (Dr. Franz Tobel); Dennis Hoey (Inspector Lestrade); Harry Woods (Kurt); George Burr MacAnnan (Gottfried); Paul Fix (Mueller); Holmes Herbert (Sir Reginald); Mary Gordon (Mrs. Hudson); Henry Victor (Hoffner); Harold de Becker (Peg Leg); Harry Cording (Jack Brady/Carpenter); Leyland Hodgson (Royal Air Force Officer); Robert O. Davis (Braun); Phillip Van Zandt (Kurt); Paul Bryar (Waiter); Vicki Campbell (Aviatrix); Gerard Cavin (Scotland Yard Man); Guy Kingsford (London Bobby); George Eldredge (Policeman); John Burton, Leslie Denison, James Craven (Bits).

The second of a dozen entries in Universal's successful Sherlock Holmes series, this outing is the first of eleven to be helmed by director Roy William Neill. It also introduces series regular Dennis Hoey as the bungling, thick-skulled Scotland Yard Inspector Lestrade. Like its predecessor, SHERLOCK HOLMES AND THE VOICE OF TERROR (1942), *q.v.*, and its successor, SHERLOCK HOLMES IN WASHINGTON (1943), *q.v.*, it deals with war-time espionage. The film also brings back Holmes' old nemesis, Professor Moriarty, here played to near perfection by Lionel Atwill. The film was very loosely based on the Arthur Conan Doyle story, "The Adventure of the Dancing Men."

Masquerading as a Swiss book dealer working for the Nazis, Sherlock Holmes (Basil Rathbone) smuggles Swiss scientist Dr. Franz Tobel (William Post, Jr.) out of that country and into England with the plans for his bomb site invention. In London, Tobel visits his lady love, Charlotte Eberli (Kaaren Verne), and leaves a cipher with her. Thereafter, an attempt is made on his life but it fails. The next day Holmes and Tobel go to the Office of the Minister of War, Sir Reginald (Holmes Herbert), where Tobel announces his plan to give four parts of the bomb site plans to Swiss workers in London, much to the chagrin of the British government. Tobel disappears and Holmes questions Charlotte and finds that the message the scientist gave her has been replaced. Holmes realizes that Professor Moriarty (Lionel Atwill) is behind all the trouble. Dressed as an Oriental, Holmes locates Moriarty in Soho and asks him for the sake of patriotism to give up his scheme to sell the bomb site plans to the Germans. The master criminal refuses and tries to murder Holmes. However, Dr. Watson (Nigel Bruce) thwarts his plan. From Charlotte, Holmes obtains the note pad on which Tobel made the cipher. He traces the impressions made on the next sheet of paper and reads the names of three men who have the crucial bomb site plan parts. Moriarty abducts the fourth man and takes him to his waterfront headquarters, but the man turns out to be Holmes, who has left an obvious trail for Scotland Yard Inspector Lestrade (Dennis Hoey) to follow. Moriarty decides to eliminate Holmes by slowly draining off his blood but it takes so much time that the police arrive. While escaping, Moriarty falls through a trap door and into the Thames River.

Bosley Crowther (*New York Times*) enthused, " . . . Universal Pictures, disregarding the literary traditions and time, has given those two beloved gentlemen the blessing of eternal youth and has set them to chasing Nazi villains in the war-consumed London of today with the same hale and vigorous tenacity as they showed toward opium smugglers years ago."

SHERLOCK HOLMES AND THE SPIDER WOMAN (Universal, 1944) 62 minutes.

Producer/director, Roy William Neill; based on the novel *The Sign of Four* by Sir Arthur Conan Doyle; screenplay, Bertram Millhauser; art director, John B. Goodman; camera, Charles Van Enger; editor, James Gibbon.

Basil Rathbone (Sherlock Holmes); Nigel Bruce (Dr. John H. Watson); Gale Sondergaard (Adrea Spedding); Dennis Hoey (Inspector Lestrade); Vernon Downing (Norman Locke); Alec Craig (Radlik); Mary Gordon (Mrs. Hudson); Arthur Hohl (Gilflower); Teddy Infuhr (Larry); Stanley Logan (Colonel); Donald Stuart (Artie); John Roche (Croupier); John Burton (Announcer); Lydia Bilbrook (Colonel's Wife); Belle Mitchell (Fortune Teller); Harry Cording (Fred Garvin); John Rogers (Clerk); Teddy Infuhr (Boy); Marie de Becker (Charwoman); Angelo Rossitto (Pygmy); Gene Stuttenroth [Roth] (Taylor).

While Sherlock Holmes (Basil Rathbone) and Dr. Watson (Nigel Bruce) are on a fishing excursion in Scotland, London is plagued with a number of deaths in which people suddenly expire during the night. On reading the newspaper accounts, Holmes believes it is murder, but he suffers a dizzy spell and supposedly drowns. Back in London, Dr. Watson (Nigel Bruce) is about to donate Holmes' belongings to the British Museum when the detective appears, masquerading as a bad-tempered postman. He informs Watson and Scotland Yard Inspector Lestrade (Dennis Hoey) that his "death" was merely a ruse to convince the killer that he was out of the way permanently. Next the crime solver disguises himself as an

Oriental and heads to a gambling casino where he suffers heavy losses and pretends he is about to kill himself. However, he is saved by exotic Adrea Spedding (Gale Sondergaard), who informs him that he can acquire easy money by taking out an insurance policy and borrowing on it, but making a new beneficiary. Soon the crafty woman realizes the man is Holmes and the detective understands that she and her half-brother (Vernon Downing) are behind the murders-for-insurance money scheme. Holmes fathoms that they use poisonous spiders to carry out their murders. Later Adrea and a young boy (Teddy Infuhr) visit Holmes at Baker Street, the woman allegedly looking for the Oriental gambler. As they leave, the boy tosses candy wrappers into the lit fireplace and the resulting fumes are so poisonous that they nearly kill Holmes and Watson. After finding out that an elderly spider breeder has been murdered by Adrea's minions, the trail leads to a carnival, where Holmes is captured by the woman and her evil pygmy henchman (Angelo Rossitto). Holmes is placed behind a cutout of Hitler at the arcade shooting gallery. Dr. Watson and Lestrade arrive and Watson ends up by shooting at the cutout. However, Holmes works himself free and the trio arrest Miss Spedding and her henchmen.

"Trapped in the Deadly Web of a Silken Killer!" boasted the advertising for this feature which is composed of bits and pieces of various Arthur Conan Doyle works such as the stories, "The Adventure of the Speckled Band" and "The Adventure of the Dying Detective," as well as the novel, *The Sign of Four* (1890). Engrossing in parts, overall this film, the fifth of twelve installments, is one of the weakest in the series. Academy Award winner Gale Sondergaard proved to be a most striking and formidable foe for Holmes and she would repeat the same type of character in a non-Holmes feature, Universal's THE SPIDER WOMAN STRIKES BACK (1946).

A.k.a.: THE SPIDER WOMAN.

SHERLOCK HOLMES AND THE VOICE OF TERROR (Universal, 1942) 65 minutes.

Associate producer, Howard Benedict; director, Jack Rawlins; based on the story "His Last Bow" by Sir Arthur Conan Doyle; screenplay, Lynn Riggs, Robert D. Andrews; art director, Jack Otterson; music, Frank Skinner; music director, Charles Previn; camera, Woody Bredell; editor, Russell Schoengarth.

Basil Rathbone (Sherlock Holmes); Nigel Bruce (Dr. John H. Watson); Evelyn Ankers (Kitty); Reginald Denny (Sir Evan Barham); Montagu Love (General Jerome Lawford); Henry Daniell (Sir Anthony Lloyd); Thomas Gomez (Meade); Olaf Hytten (Fabian Prentiss)

Basil Rathbone and Evelyn Ankers in SHERLOCK HOLMES AND THE VOICE OF TERROR (1942).

Leyland Hodgson (Captain Ronald Shore); Arthur Blake (Crosbie); Harry Stubbs (Taxi Driver); Mary Gordon (Mrs. Hudson); Hillary Brooke (Jill Grandis); Edgar Barrier (Voice of Terror); Robert O. Davis (Nazi); Harry Cording (Ex-Convict); Leslie Denison (Air Raid Warden).

Basil Rathbone and Nigel Bruce had portrayed Sherlock Holmes and Dr. Watson in the Twentieth Century-Fox features, THE HOUND OF THE BASKERVILLES (1938) and THE ADVENTURES OF SHERLOCK HOLMES (1939), qq.v., and since 1938 they had also starred on the "Sherlock Holmes" radio series. In 1942, enterprising Universal signed the duo to repeat their roles in a series of programmers which lasted for a dozen entries.* Overall,

---

*Basil Rathbone and Nigel Bruce also played Holmes and Watson respectively in a guest appearance in Universal's Olsen and Johnson comedy CRAZY HOUSE (1943).

this set is one of the most satisfying, and continually popular, film series ever produced in Hollywood.

Britain is being plagued by a radio voice of terror from Germany which predicts imminent destruction. At a loss as to what to do, Sir Evan Barham (Reginald Denny), a member of the country's Intelligence Inner Council, summons Sherlock Holmes (Basil Rathbone) and Dr. Watson (Nigel Bruce), an action opposed by fellow member Sir Anthony Lloyd (Henry Daniell). Holmes agrees to investigate and, after one of his agents is murdered, he and Watson go to Limehouse where he consults singer Kitty (Evelyn Ankers). With her aid Holmes appeals to the inhabitants of the area to aid in thwarting the menace of the voice of terror. The voice continues to make accurate predictions of destruction but Holmes deduces that the voice is a recording done in England, not Germany. Kitty leads Holmes to the Limehouse docks where he and Watson and Sir Anthony Lloyd, who has followed them, are captured by a gang led by Meade (Thomas Gomez), a German agent. However, the waterfront dwellers free them as Holmes allows Meade to escape. Kitty has now become Meade's lover at Holmes' direction and she learns about the Nazis' plan to carry out something at Barham's country estates. Holmes arrives there and soon an enemy plane flies overhead, but Barham fires at it, causing it to leave. The voice promises an invasion of England as Kitty leaves a message which leads Holmes, Watson and the police to a bombed church on the British coast where the Nazis are waiting for an invasion vanguard. Holmes surprises them and announces to the police and the council members—who are also present—that the voice's broadcast about the invasion was merely a trick to shift British defenses. Holmes names the actual voice of terror—a member of the council—who is a Nazi spy planted in England following Germany's defeat at the end of the First World War.

Michael B. Druxman wrote in *Basil Rathbone: His Life and His Films* (1975), "SHERLOCK HOLMES AND THE VOICE OF TERROR was the only episode of the Universal series that was *not* directed by Roy William Neill. John Rawlins handled these duties on this film and, although *his* work was adequate, the project suffered from a dull screenplay. It was one of the series' weakest segments. Rathbone, abandoning the deerstalker hat he had worn in the two entries at Fox, and Bruce were at their best in the roles, which they were, by now, quite familiar with. Mary Gordon, who had played Mrs. Hudson, the landlady of 221 Baker Street, in the earlier films, repeated the part in this picture." Mary Gordon, who also did Mrs. Hudson in the radio series, would remain in the part throughout the Universal series.

SHERLOCK HOLMES FACES DEATH (Universal, 1943) 68 minutes.

Associate producer/director, Roy William Neill; based on the story "The Musgrave Ritual" by Sir Arthur Conan Doyle; screenplay, Bertram Millhauser; art directors, John Goodman, Harold MacArthur; set decorators, Russell A. Gausman, E. R. Robinson; music director, H. J. Salter; assistant director, Melville Shyer; sound, B. Brown, Edwin Wetzel; camera, Charles Van Enger; editor, Fred Feitchans.

Basil Rathbone (Sherlock Holmes); Nigel Bruce (Dr. John H. Watson); Hillary Brooke (Sally Musgrave); Milburn Stone (Captain Vickery); Arthur Margetson (Dr. Sexton); Halliwell Hobbes (Brunton); Dennis Hoey (Inspector Lestrade); Gavin Muir (Philip Musgrave); Frederick Worlock (Geoffrey Musgrave); Olaf Hytten (Captain MacIntosh); Gerald Hamer (Major Langford); Vernon Downing (Lieutenant Clavering); Minna Phillips (Mrs. Howells); Mary Gordon (Mrs. Hudson); Peter Lawford (Sailor); Harold de Becker (Pub Proprietor); Holmes Herbert (Man); Norma Varden (Grace, the Pub Proprietress); Ian Wolfe (Antique Store Clerk).

The fourth film in Universal's dozen Sherlock Holmes episodes, this outing, based on Arthur Conan Doyle's short story, "The Musgrave Ritual," is one of the very best of the group. It is an eerie, spooky, atmospheric motion picture, as much of a horror tale as a detective story, and it captures beautifully the feel of the haunted house murder mysteries of the early 1930s. The film is laced with red herrings, along with its setting in the ancient Hulstone Towers in Northumberland and its use of the ancient puzzle, the Musgrave Ritual. Ray Cabana, Jr. wrote in "Always Holmes" (*Kaleidoscope* magazine, Vol 2, No.1, 1965), "[Bertram] Millhauser took Doyle's 'The Musgrave Ritual' and built a truly remarkable story around it, utilizing howling winds, a mansion of secret passages, a subterranean crypt first seen in Universal's DRACULA (1931), a huge tower clock that warns of approaching death by striking 13, and a giant chessboard using live humans as pieces. Peopled with the strangest of suspects—some of them mental cases from the War—the tale moves along briskly." In addition to the DRACULA crypt, the film also utilizes the village set Universal had constructed for its Frankenstein series. In the pub sequence newcomer Peter Lawford can be spotted in a quick bit as a sailor.

As part of the war effort, Dr. Watson (Nigel Bruce) is ministering to recovering soldiers with combat mental problems at the remote and ghostly Hulstone Towers in Northumberland, an ancient castle owned by the Musgrave family. Dr. Sexton (Arthur Margetson), Watson's assistant, is stabbed and Watson returns to London to enlist Sherlock Holmes' (Basil Rathbone) aid in the case. Upon their arrival at Hulstone Towers they find the body of Geoffrey Musgrave (Frederick Worlock), an ill-tempered man who had argued with his younger brother Philip (Gavin Muir) over their sister Sally's (Hillary Brooke) romance with visiting American soldier, Captain Vickery (Milburn Stone). Besides the various patients, other suspects include mysterious butler Alf Brunton (Halliwell Hobbes) and maid Mrs. Howells (Minna Phillips). Scotland Yard Inspector Lestrade (Dennis Hoey) arrives to investigate the murder and the next day Sally, by family tradition, is forced to recite an ancient ritual on the tiled floor of the castle's large hallway. A terrible storm, however, frightens the girl and she cannot continue. That night Brunton disappears and the next day Philip's corpse is found in the back of Sally's roadster. Holmes finds out that the butler and maid are really married and, despite the presence of several suspects, he believes that the answer to the riddle lies in the Musgrave Ritual. Realizing that the floor tile in the hall is actually a large chess board, he has the inhabitants of the house stand as chess pieces, and following the ritual he locates the tile over the entrance to an underground crypt. There he finds Brunton's body and an old parchment. Using himself as a decoy, Holmes captures the killer, who had planned to wed Sally and then use the parchment, an ancient land grant, to attain great wealth.

Chris Steinbrunner and Norman Michaels noted in *The Films of Sherlock Holmes* (1978), "What all the critics took pains to admire . . . and what *is* admirable about the film is the wonderful sense of atmosphere, of mystery, of sepulchral gloom that oozes like a fog throughout the melodrama. . . . Despite his [Holmes] being contemporized by the studio right up to the minute, this adventure was, paradoxically, a return to all of the shadowy Victorian trappings of a richly old-fashioned mystery. That the mood is so well sustained is due in no small measure to the talents of Roy [William] Neill, and we note this is the first film in the series he produces as well as directs."

SHERLOCK HOLMES' FATAL HOUR (First Division, 1931) 84 minutes.

Producer, Julius Hagen; director, Leslie Hiscott; based on the stories "The Empty House" and "The Final Problem" by Sir Arthur

Conan Doyle and (uncredited) the play by William Gillette; screenplay, Cyril Twyford, H. Fowler Mear; art director, James Carter; camera, Sidney Blythe; editor, Jack Harris.

Arthur Wontner (Sherlock Holmes); Norman McKinnell (Colonel Henslowe/Professor Moriarty); Jane Welsh (Kathleen Adair); Ian Fleming (Dr. John H. Watson); Louis Goodrich (Colonel Sebastian Moran); Philip Hewland (Inspector Lestrade); Charles Paton (J. J. Godfrey); Minnie Rayner (Mrs. Hudson); Leslie Perrins (Ronald Adair); William Frazer (Thomas Fisher); Gordon Begg (Marston); Norman McKinnell (Colonel Henslowe); Sidney King (Tony Rutherford); Harry Terry (#16).

During the 1930s Arthur Wontner portrayed Sherlock Holmes in five satisfying British feature films. The English series was inaugurated in 1931 by Twickenham Studios, which produced four of the five films, with THE SLEEPING CARDINAL (the title refers to a painting of sleeping Cardinal Richelieu, from behind which Professor Moriarty gives orders to his minions). When First Division distributed the film in the U.S. that same year, the title was altered to SHERLOCK HOLMES' FATAL HOUR. Upon its American release, *Variety* termed it " . . . one of the best programmers ever turned out in England. Maybe the best. . . . [The] film has a fine piece of acting by Arthur Wontner in the title part. He not only looks like a detective but handles the role beautifully throughout, and makes him more human than the stories did."

A London bank is robbed and a murder takes place while Foreign Office worker Ronald Adair (Leslie Perrins) is playing cards for high stakes and cheating to win. His sister, Kathleen (Jane Adair), worries about him and goes to her friend Dr. Watson (Ian Fleming) for assistance. Meanwhile, Sherlock Holmes (Arthur Wontner) tells Scotland Yard Inspector Lestrade (Philip Hewland) that Professor Moriarty (Norman McKinnell) is behind the recent outbreak of lawlessness. Adair has been captured by Moriarty's men and the master criminal, from behind a picture, orders him to smuggle a suitcase to Paris or his card cheating will be made known. In disguise, Moriarty confronts Holmes at Baker Street and Holmes makes special note of the man's boots and traces them to their maker. He finds one of Moriarty's hideouts, but the evil genius is not there. Adair commits suicide and Kathleen is charged with his murder. Holmes next interviews one of Adair's card playing chums, the one-armed Colonel Henslowe (Norman McKinnell). That night Moriarty tries to kill Holmes by shooting at him from a window in the empty house across the street from 221B Baker Street, but Holmes' landlady, Mrs. Hudson (Minnie Rayner), has been moving a decoy bust figure of Holmes which Moriarty fires at, breaking it to pieces. Holmes, Watson and Lestrade soon arrest Moriarty, who has been masquerading as Henslowe.

Arthur Wontner would again play Holmes in THE MISSING REMBRANDT (1932), THE SIGN OF FOUR (1932), THE TRIUMPH OF SHERLOCK HOLMES (1935), and SILVER BLAZE (MURDER AT THE BASKERVILLES) (1937), *qq.v.*

SHERLOCK HOLMES GROSSTER FALL   *see*   A STUDY IN TERROR.

SHERLOCK HOLMES IN NEW YORK (NBC-TV, 10/18/76) Color 100 minutes.

Executive producer, Nancy Malone; producer, John Cutts; director, Boris Sagal; based on characters created by Sir Arthur Conan Doyle; teleplay, Alvin Sapinsley; music, Richard Rodney Bennett; art director, Lawrence G. Paul; camera, Michael Margulies; editor, Samuel E. Beetley.

Roger Moore (Sherlock Holmes); John Huston (Professor James Moriarty); Patrick Macnee (Dr. John H. Watson); Gig Young (Mortimer McGraw); Charlotte Rampling (Irene Adler); David Huddleston (Inspector Lafferty); Signe Hasso (Frau Reichenbach); Leon Ames (Daniel Furman); John Abbott (Heller); Jackie Coogan (Hotel Haymarket Proprietor); Maria Grimm (Nicole Romaine); Marjorie Bennett (Mrs. Hudson); Geoffrey Moore (Scott Adler).

Roger Moore was internationally known for portraying Simon Templar, "The Saint," on television and James Bond on the big screen. In 1976 he undertook another famous hero role when he became Sherlock Holmes in the made-for-television movie (issued theatrically in Europe), SHERLOCK HOLMES IN NEW YORK. While hardly looking the part of the traditional Holmes, Moore acquitted himself well in the role and the TV movie, overall, was a good one. *TV Guide* magazine's Judith Crist called it "first-class entertainment" while Steven H. Scheuer's *Movies on TV and Videocassette* (1987) opined, "Cast, costumes, and production are conceived in the grand manner, and Boris Sagal's direction makes the film an entertaining diversion."

Sherlock Holmes' (Roger Moore) one-time lover, actress Irene Adler (Charlotte Rampling), reveals to him that they have a young son, Scott (Geoffrey Moore), and that the boy has been kidnapped by Professor Moriarty (John Huston) and taken to America. Holmes and Dr. Watson (Patrick Macnee) accompany Irene to New York City and learn that the evil mastermind has used the boy as a decoy for his master plan: the destruction of Holmes and the theft of the world's gold supply. Moriarty warns Holmes to stay away from the gold case or Scott will die, but the detective corners his quarry atop the madman's hideout. Moriarty falls to his death in the swirling water below.

Not everyone was pleased with the telefilm, however, as Ron Haydock indicates in *Deerstalker! Holmes and Watson on Screen* (1978): " . . . some critics wished that director Sagal would have let Moore and Patrick Macnee simply be themselves in the film, rather than come off as actors *trying* to play Holmes and Watson. . . ." Haydock also commented on the production's technical deficiencies, including the poor sound quality.

SHERLOCK HOLMES IN WASHINGTON (Universal, 1943) 71 minutes.

Associate producer, Howard Benedict; director, Roy William Neill; based on the characters created by Sir Arthur Conan Doyle; story, Bertram Millhauser; screenplay, Millhauser, Lynn Riggs; music, Frank Skinner; art directors, Jack Otterson, Martin Obzina; music director, Charles Previn; technical adviser, Tom McKnight; assistant director, William Tummel; camera, Lester White; editor, Otto Ludwig.

Basil Rathbone (Sherlock Holmes); Nigel Bruce (Dr. John H. Watson); Marjorie Lord (Nancy Partridge); Henry Daniell (William Raster); George Zucco (Stanley); John Archer (Lieutenant Peter Merriam); Gavin Muir (Bart Lang); Edmund Macdonald (Detective Lieutenant Grogan); Don Terry (Howe); Bradley Page (Cady); Holmes Herbert (Mr. Ahrens); Thurston Hall (Senator Henry Babcock); Gilbert Emery (Sir Henry Marchmont); Gerald Hamer (John Grayson/Alfred Pettibone); Clarence Muse (George, the Train Steward); Ian Wolfe (Antique Clerk); Margaret Seddon (Miss Pringle, the Lady with a Mouse); Mary Forbes (Alfred Pettibone's Mother).

Like the previous SHERLOCK HOLMES AND THE VOICE OF TERROR (1942) and SHERLOCK HOLMES AND THE SECRET WEAPON (1943), *qq.v.*, SHERLOCK HOLMES IN WASHINGTON, the third of twelve Universal Holmes programmers, also dealt with World War II espionage and German spies. While it may have been a bit stronger than the first two entries, the outing was still not up to some of the later features in the series. However, the two stars, Basil Rathbone and Nigel Bruce, carried off the weak script admirably, as noted by *The Hollywood Reporter*: "Basil Rathbone is just what he should be in the title role, and Nigel Bruce as Doctor Watson is supplied with much bright comedy of which he is quick to make the most."

The British Home Office informs Sherlock Holmes (Basil

Rathbone) that a courier (Gerald Hamer) carrying a vital document has been abducted in America. Holmes and Dr. Watson (Nigel Bruce) head to the U.S., but not before Holmes visits the man's home and determines that the document has been secreted as microfilm in a pack of paper matches. In Washington, D.C., the two find that the courier's body has been shipped to them in a crate and the train club car in which he had been riding has been searched. Holmes determines that among the passengers the courier talked with were attractive Nancy Partridge (Marjorie Lord) and long-winded Senator Henry Babcock (Thurston Hall). It turns out that the girl has been kidnapped. After examining the blanket used to wrap the courier's corpse, Holmes visits Richard Stanley's (George Zucco) antique shop and soon realizes that the man and his cohort, William Raster (Henry Daniell), are German spies. The detective allows himself to be captured by the Nazis, who also have the young woman. Watson and the police rescue the duo, but Stanley escapes. Realizing the latter will now search out the senator, Holmes reaches him first and the two work out a plan resulting in the man's capture.

George Zucco, who had made such a wonderful Moriarty in THE ADVENTURES OF SHERLOCK HOLMES (1939), *q.v.*, here does a marvelous turn as a Nazi spy villain and is assisted ably by lanky Henry Daniell, who would make a very solid Moriarty in the later series outing, WOMAN IN GREEN (1945), *q.v.* Also adding to the enjoyment is Thurston Hall's performance as the bombastic Senator Babcock. This film concludes Holmes' war-time counter-espionage activities, the following installments using a more ortho-dox mystery flavor.

SHERLOCK JR. (Metro, 1924) 4,065'
    Presenter, Joseph M. Schenck; directors, Buster Keaton, Clyde Bruckman; screenplay, Clyde Bruckman, Jean Havez, Joseph Mitchell; art director, Fred Gabourie; costumes, Clare West; camera, Byron Houck, Elgin Lessley.
    Buster Keaton (Sherlock, Jr.); Kathryn McGuire (The Girl); Ward Crane (The Rival); Joseph Keaton (The Father); and: Erwin Connelly, Jane Connelly, George Davis, Ruth Holly, Horace Morgan, John Patric, Ford West.
    A young man, dubbed Sherlock, Jr. (Buster Keaton) because of his fascination with the illustrious detective, works as a projectionist and janitor at a small town movie theater, and he becomes an amateur sleuth via a correspondence course. When his rival (Ward Crane) for the affection of the girl (Kathryn McGuire) he loves steals her father's watch, the young man hopes to retrieve it, although he is unaware of who took the jewelry. It is the girl who informs him who

Kathryn McGuire and Buster Keaton in SHERLOCK, JR. (1924).

stole the watch and he becomes depressed at his inadequacy. While projecting a film he dreams he is part of the on-screen action. When he awakens he realizes he is his own brand of hero and has won his young lady's heart.

At the time SHERLOCK JR. was issued, *Photoplay* magazine enthused of the short feature, "Buster Keaton, with a new bag of tricks. Don't miss it if you like Buster." In *Classics of the Silent Screen* (1959), Joe Franklin wrote, "If any one Buster Keaton feature comedy can really be said to be his best, then SHERLOCK JR. is that one. . . . The film zipped along at a merry pace, getting all of its characters and basic plots set up in the first reel, and leaving the last four reels for a non-stop parade of truly inventive gags, all worked out by Keaton himself (who also directed) and by his writer and co-director friend Clyde Bruckman." In *The Great Movie Comedians* (1978), Leonard Maltin observed, "This is the film in which Keaton plays a film projectionist who dreams himself into the action of the picture he's showing but first has trouble coordinating his 'real' existence with the happenings on-screen. Backgrounds suddenly change behind him, so that as he's walking along a street he suddenly discovers he's on the edge of a cliff, which then cuts to a jungle scene and so on and on. The trickery is impossible to detect."

In a film loaded with top-notch, and very funny, comedy moments, perhaps one of the best is the sequence in which Buster and Ward Crane shoot a game of pool, with Keaton unaware that one of the pool balls has a bomb in it! Just as good is the wild chase scene which concludes the feature. Then too, at the heart of SHERLOCK JR. is the premise that being a real detective is one of man's most recurring twentieth century fantasies.

THE SIGN OF FOUR (Stoll, 1923) 6,750'
    Director, Maurice Elvey; based on the novel by Sir Arthur Conan Doyle; screenplay, Elvey.
    Eille Norwood (Sherlock Holmes); Isobel Elsom (Mary Morstan); Fred Raynham (Prince Abdullah Khan); Arthur Cullin (Dr. John H. Watson); Norman Page (Jonathan Small); Humberston Wright (Dr. Sholto); Henry Wilson (Pygmy); Mme. D'Esterre (Mrs. Hudson); Arthur Bell (Inspector Athelney Jones).

THE SIGN OF FOUR (Associated Radio, 1932) 75 minutes.
    Producer, Basil Dean; directors, Rowland V. Lee, Graham Cutts; based on the novel by Sir Arthur Conan Doyle; screenplay, W. P. Lipscomb; camera, Robert G. Martin, Robert DeGrasse.
    Arthur Wontner (Sherlock Holmes); Isla Bevan (Mary Morstan); Ian Hunter (Dr. John H. Watson); Graham [Ben] Soutten (Jonathan

Small); Miles Malleson (Thaddeus Sholto); Herbert Lomas (Major Sholto); Gilbert Davis (Athelney Jones); Roy Emerton (Bailey); Kynaston Reeves (Bartholomew Sholto); Edgar Norfolk (Captain Marstan); Clare Greet (Mrs. Hudson); Moore Marriott (Mordecai Smith); Togo (Tonga); Mr. Burnhett (Tattoo Artist).

THE SIGN OF FOUR (Mapleton Films, 1983) Color 100 minutes.

Executive producer, Sy Weintraub; producer, Otto Plaschkes; director, Desmond Davis; based on the novel by Sir Arthur Conon Doyle; screenplay, Charles Pogue; art director, Eileen Diss, Fred Carter; costume designer, Julie Harris; makeup, Tom Smith, John Webber; music, Harry Rabinowitz; special effects, Alan Whibley; camera, Denis Lewiston; editor, Timothy Gee.

Ian Richardson (Sherlock Holmes); David Healy (Dr. John H. Watson); Thorley Walters (Major John Sholto); Terence Rigby (Inspector Layton); Joe Melta (Jonathan Small); Cherie Lunghi (Mary Morstan); Michael O'Hagan (Mordecai Smith); John Pedrick (Tonga) and: Clive Merrison.

Sir Arthur Conan Doyle's second Sherlock Holmes novel, *The Sign of Four* (also known as *The Sign of the Four*), was published in 1890 and has been brought to the screen five times, twice as a silent and three times as a talkie, as well as being televised as one of the British series on Sherlock Holmes televised in the U.S. in 1988 as part of the PBS-TV's "The Return of Sherlock Holmes" on the ongoing program, "Mystery!"

The initial screen version was produced by Thanhouser in 1913 as SHERLOCK HOLMES SOLVES "THE SIGN OF FOUR" and it featured Harry Benham as Holmes; it was a two-reeler. *The Moving Picture World* called it, "A strong production of a famous narrative. . . ." In 1921 the British company, Stoll Films, starred Eille Norwood in fifteen two-reelers called "The Adventures of Sherlock Holmes" and these were so popular that the next year Stoll and Norwood reunited for fifteen more two-reelers, "The Further Adventures of Sherlock Holmes," followed by fifteen additional ones entitled "The Last Adventures of Sherlock Holmes." Following this extended series, Stoll starred Eille Norwood in the feature film, THE SIGN OF FOUR, which was issued in 1923. In *Deerstalker! Holmes and Watson on Screen* (1978), Ron Haydock called it, "A faithful, entertaining version of the novel," while David Stuart Davies in Holmes of the Movies (1976) judged it "tame."

Arthur Wontner portrayed Sherlock Holmes in four films for the British Twickenham Studios in the 1930s: SHERLOCK HOLMES' FATAL HOUR (1931, THE MISSING REMBRANDT (1932),

THE TRIUMPH OF SHERLOCK HOLMES (1935), and SILVER
BLAZE (1937), *qq.v.*, and in addition he starred in the third screen
adaptation—and the first talking one—of THE SIGN OF FOUR
for Associated Radio Pictures in 1932. Like the silent edition, this
version of the Doyle work stayed quite close to the book's plotline.
Beautiful Mary Morstan (Isla Bevan) comes to Sherlock Holmes
(Arthur Wontner) with a most baffling account. Alone in London
after the disappearance of her father, she has received a huge pearl
from an unknown person. Holmes accepts her case and Dr. Watson
(Ian Hunter) is smitten with the young lady. The investigation leads
Holmes to Thaddeus Sholto (Miles Malleson) and information
about a hidden treasure to which Miss Morstan may have some
claim, although a series of murders have taken place because of it.
Holmes deduces that the killings were the act of another claimant of
the treasure, a one-legged criminal and his murderous pygmy
henchman. With the aid of the police, Holmes traps the culprit as he
attempts to leave London by boat. The wealth reverts to the Crown
and Miss Morstan and Dr. Watson plan to wed.

   In *Holmes of the Movies* (1976), David Stuart Davies said, "It
relies heavily on the Conan Doyle novel and tends to lose most of its
grip by presenting a prologue which gives the whole plot away,
leaving the matter of detection too obvious to be of any great
interest." While some contemporary critics were not overly impressed with THE SIGN OF FOUR, the British *Picturegoer* commented, "Arthur Wontner is as usual, a perfect Holmes."

   In 1968 England's BBC-TV network produced fifteen Sherlock Holmes adventures for the small screen, starring Peter Cushing
as Holmes and Nigel Stock as Dr. Watson. One of the episodes was
an adaptation of *The Sign of Four,* telecast December 16, 1968.

   The most recent British theatrical adaptation of the Doyle work
came in 1983 from Mapleton Films. It was the first of a planned
baker's dozen Holmes screen adventures, but only one other, THE
HOUND OF THE BASKERVILLES, *q.v.*, followed. This version
of THE SIGN OF FOUR is a stylish entry, with Ian Richardson
offering a fine interpretation of Holmes while David Healy is
resourceful as the love-smitten Dr. Watson and Cherie Lunghi is
quite lovely as Mary Morstan, the object of his affections. The
narrative opens with the murder of Major John Sholto (Thorley
Walters) over a stolen treasure and the eventual appearance of
Jonathan Small (Joe Melta) and the vicious savage, Tonga (John
Pedrick). *Variety* noted, " . . . period details are loving[ly] recreated
and settings such as fairground, riverside and chambers decorated in
Indian style provide plenty of scope for atmosphere." But the same
reviewer unjustly complained that the film "makes do as a tepid

adventure story," and added, "Some of the performances would embarrass even a college thespian."

In 1984, Peter O'Toole was the voice of Holmes in the animated featurette SHERLOCK HOLMES AND THE SIGN OF FOUR, a 48-minute rendering of the Doyle work. In the fall of 1988 the PBS-TV series, "Mystery!" presented a two-part Thames Television of London production of *The Sign of Four* with Jeremy Brett as Holmes and Edward Hardwicke as Watson.

SINISTER HANDS (Capitol, 1932) 66 minutes.

Producer, Willis Kent; director, Armand Schaeffer; based on the novel *The Seance Mystery* by Norton Parker; screenplay, Parker, Oliver Drake; camera, William Nobles.

Jack Mulhall (Detective Captain Devlin); Phyllis Barrington (Ruth Frazer); Crauford Kent (Judge McLeod); Mischa Auer (Swami Yomurda); Jimmy Burtis (Watkins); Phillips Smalley (Richard Lang); Louis Natheaux (Nick Genna); Gertrude Messenger (Betty Lang); Lloyd Ingraham (John Frazer); Helen Foster (Vivian Rogers); Lillian West (Mrs. Lang); Fletcher Norton (Lefty Lewis the Butler); Bess Flowers (Mary Browne); Russell Collar (Tommy Lang).

At a seance in his home, the much disliked Richard Lang (Phillips Smalley) is stabbed to death with an Oriental dagger. Detectives Devlin (Jack Mulhall) and his none-too-bright assistant, Watkins (Jimmy Burtis), are called in to investigate and they find the mansion full of likely suspects. These include the widow (Lillian West), who detested her husband and who has a lover, an un-named guest; daughter Betty Lang (Gertrude Messenger), who was estranged from her father because of her love affair with gangster Nick Genna (Louis Natheaux), also present; Judge McLeod (Crauford Kent) who was apparently blackmailed by Lang; a handicapped neighbor (Lloyd Ingraham) who resented Lang's lust for his young wife (Phyllis Barrington); the butler (Fletcher Norton), who is an ex-convict; Lang's secretary (Helen Foster), who has been stealing from him; and bogus Swami Yomurda (Mischa Auer), who had been blackmailing Lang's wife. During the investigation the dagger disappears and is used later to kill the butler, who knew the real culprit. Finally Devlin deduces who is the real killer, because he knew him previously and realizes he has the strongest motive for the murder.

"The 'B' detective film quickly became as standardized as the 'B' western. A typical product is SINISTER HANDS, an extremely economy-conscious Willis Kent production of 1932," wrote William K. Everson in *The Detective in Film* (1972). He added, "Dapper detective Jack Mulhall investigates the crime more by intuition than by sleuthing. . . . Indian swami Mischa Auer faces a particularly rampant case of minority persecution when Mulhall tells him, 'You're a Hindu, and have been trained to sneak stealthily through a darkened room.'" George E. Turner and Michael H. Price wrote in *Forgotten Horrors* (1979), "A typical mystery of the period, with the added weirdness of a seance killing. . . . Jack Mulhall's Irish pep and Mischa Auer's menace are well exploited. . . ." Interestingly, Mischa Auer again played the role of the fake swami Yomurda the next year in another Willis Kent production, SUCKER MONEY, an expose of the fake spiritualist racket.

THE SKY DRAGON (Monogram, 1949) 64 minutes.
    Producer, James S. Burkett; director, Lesley Selander; based on the character created by Earl Derr Biggers; story, Clint Johnston; screenplay, Oliver Drake, Johnston; art director, David Milton; set decorator, Ray Boltz; makeup, Webb Overlander; music director, Edward J. Kay; assistant directors, Wesley Barry, Ed Morey, Jr.; sound, Tom Lambert, John Kean; camera, William Sickner; editor, Roy Livingston.
    Roland Winters (Charlie Chan); Keye Luke (Lee Chan); Mantan Moreland (Birmingham Brown); Noel Neill (Jane Marshall); Tim Ryan (Lieutenant Ruark); Iris Adrian (Wanda LaFern); Elena Verdugo (Marie Burke); Milburn Stone (Tim Norton); Lyle Talbot (Andy Barrett); Paul Maxey (John Anderson); Joel Marston (Don Blake); John Eldredge (William French); Eddie Parks (Mr. Tibbets); Louise Franklin (Lena); Lyle Latell (Ed Davidson); George Eldredge (Stacey); Bob Curtis (Watkins); Steve [Gaylord] Pendleton (Ben Edwards); Emmett Vogan (Doctor); Edna Holland (Old Maid); Joe Whitehead (Doorman); Frank Cady (Clerk); Lee Phelps (Plainclothesman); Charlie Jordan (Assistant Stage Manager); Louise Franklin (Lena); Suzette Harbin (Strange Dark Girl).
    THE SKY DRAGON is the forty-seventh and final Charlie Chan series film, and the sixth in the series to star Roland Winters as Chan. Many writers claim that this low-budget offering (shot in seven days) is a terrible film, but in reality it is a more than passable entry in the series. It has an exciting climax and it proved to be a fitting finale to the long-running property.
    Lee Chan (Keye Luke) awakens while on board a plane in flight and finds that all the passengers, including his sleuth father, Charlie Chan (Roland Winters), are in a drug-induced sleep. He manages to awaken his dad and they find the plane is on automatic pilot, a bank guard on board has been murdered, and the money he was carrying is missing. The plane lands in San Francisco and police Lieutenant Ruark (Tim Ryan) takes over the case, with all the plane passengers except the Chans considered as suspects. The policeman also sus-

Advertisement for THE SKY DRAGON (1949).

pects William French (John Eldredge), employed by the company whose money was stolen. Chan conducts his own investigation and, with Ruark's aid, gathers all the suspects together and reveals the culprits.

"It's Cargo Is Murder! Its Destination . . . Doom! Death strikes at 300 miles per hour . . . as Chan stalks a killer in the clouds!" read the poster blurbs promoting this film, which was lensed as MURDER IN THE AIR.

Actually THE SKY DRAGON was *not* planned to be the final Monogram Chan entry. In order to add fresh flavor to the Chan capers, Monogram intended to shoot several series segments in England; new locales could be had there and production costs would be cheaper. On the eve of commencing these new installments, Britain devalued the pound and this hurt Monogram's financial resources in that country's banks. The series was cancelled as being cost prohibitive.

THE SLEEPING CARDINAL   *see*   SHERLOCK HOLMES' FATAL HOUR.

SMART BLONDE (Warner Bros., 1937) 57 minutes.
Associate producer, Bryan Foy; director, Frank McDonald; based on the story "No Hard Feelings" by Frederick Nebel; screenplay, Don Ryan, Kenneth Gamet; songs, M. K. Jerome and Jack Scholl; camera, Warren Lynch; editor, Frank Magee.
Glenda Farrell (Torchy Blane); Barton MacLane (Inspector Steve McBride); Winifred Shaw (Dolly Ireland); Craig Reynolds (Tom Carney); Addison Richards (Fritz Mularkey); Charlotte Wynters (Marcia Friel); Jane Wyman (Dixie); David Carlyle (Lewis Friel); Joseph Crehan (Tiny Torgensen); Tom Kennedy (Sergeant Gahagan); John Sheehan (Blyfuss); Max Wagner (Chuck Cannon); George Lloyd (Pickney Sex); Cliff Saum (Conductor); Allen Pomeroy, Al Hill (Taxi Drivers); Joseph Cunningham (City Editor); Jack H. Richardson (Murphy); Chic Bruno (Bozo); Frank Faylen (Ambulance Driver); Wayne Morris (Information Clerk); Dennis Moore (Interne); Milton Kibbee (Harms, the Ballistics Expert); Fred "Snowflake" Toones, Martin Turner (Red Caps).
Frederick Nebel wrote for *Black Mask* magazine from the late 1920s through the mid-1930s and did a number of stories centering around a newshound named Kennedy and his cohort, the rather dull-witted policeman Steve McBride. When the stories were purchased for the screen by Warner Bros. in the mid-1930s, Kennedy became female reporter Torchy Blane and Glenda Farrell played the sharp-tongued sleuth in seven budget features between

1937 and 1939. Barton MacLane co-starred as Steve McBride and Tom Kennedy appeared as the addled Sergeant Gahagan for comedy relief.

SMART BLONDE, issued in January 1937, the initial feature in the series, was based on Nebel's story, "No Hard Feelings." Sticking very closely to its source, the film tells of reporter Torchy Blane (Glenda Farrell) getting aboard a train to interview Tiny Torgensen (Joseph Crehan), who is planning to purchase the Million Club from gangster Fritz Mularkey (Addison Richards). As Torchy and Torgensen leave the train and enter a cab, he is murdered and Torchy, who has scooped the other papers with the big story, gets on the trail of the killer. However, the main suspect (Max Wagner) is poisoned. Torchy's boyfriend, police Inspector Steve McBride (Barton MacLane), brings in all the gangsters in town for questioning but Torchy takes her own course and ends up solving the case, pinning the crimes on members of a confidence ring.

Although the *New York Times* branded it "a static and listless little piece," the premise struck the public's fancy, due mainly to Glenda Farrell's pleasing work as the acerbic Torchy and her inter-

Jane Wyman, Barton MacLane, Glenda Farrell and Addison Richards in SMART BLONDE (1937).

play with Barton MacLane and Tom Kennedy. She was back in a series of "predictable little programmers" (Ted Sennett, *Warner Brothers Presents,* 1972): FLY-AWAY BABY (1937), THE ADVENTUROUS BLONDE (1937), BLONDES AT WORK (1938), TORCHY GETS HER MAN (1938), TORCHY BLANE IN CHINATOWN (1939) and TORCHY RUNS FOR MAYOR (1939). In 1938 Lola Lane took over briefly for Farrell in TORCHY BLANE IN PANAMA, and in 1939 Jane Wyman (who had a small role in SMART BLONDE) was Torchy in the series finale, TORCHY PLAYS WITH DYNAMITE, with Allen Jenkins cast as McBride.

SO DARK THE NIGHT (Columbia, 1946) 71 minutes.

Producer, Ted Richmond; director, Joseph H. Lewis; story, Aubrey Wisberg; screenplay, Martin Berkeley, Dwight Babcock; music, Morris W. Stoloff; art director, Carl Anderson; set decorator, William Kiernan; camera, Burnett Guffey; editor, Jerome Thoms.

Steven Geray (Henri Cassin); Micheline Cheirel (Nanette Michaud); Eugene Borden (Pierre Michaud); Ann Codee (Mama Michaud); Egon Brecher (Dr. Boncourt); Helen Freeman (Widow Bridelle); Theodore Gottlieb (Georges); Gregory Gay (Commissaire Grande); Jean Del Val (Dr. Maset): Paul Marlon (Leon Achard); Emil Ramu (Pere Cortot); Louis Mercier (Jean Duval); Billy Snyder (Chauffeur); Frank Arnold (Antoine); Adrienne d'Ambricourt (Newspaper Woman); Marcelle Corday (Proprietress); Alphonse Martel (Bank President); Andre Marsaudon (Postmaster); Francine Bordeaux (Flower Girl); Esther Zeitlin (Peasant Woman); Cynthia Gaylor (Bootblack).

Over the decades director Joseph H. Lewis has developed a cult following for his imaginative handling of such features as MY NAME IS JULIA ROSS (1945), DEADLY IS THE FEMALE [GUN CRAZY] (1949) and THE HALLIDAY BRAND (1957). However, it must be remembered that he was very much a hit-and-miss helmsman, also responsible for such unmemorable cinema items as THE INVISIBLE GHOST (1941) and THE MAD DOCTOR OF MARKET STREET (1941). SO DARK THE NIGHT is one of the features for which he is praised for having created a top notch subject on a typical Columbia Pictures' minimal budget.

In France just after World War II, Henri Cassin (Steven Geray), a police detective from Paris, desperately needs a vacation and takes time off in a small, remote community. There he meets a pretty young woman (Micheline Cheirel). He quickly falls in love with her, only to learn that she is attached to a local young man (Eugene Borden). When the two young people are found murdered, Cassin

Paul Marion, Steven Geray and Micheline Cheirel in SO DARK THE NIGHT (1946).

takes it upon himself to investigate and his methodical work uncovers the killer, providing the film with its twist ending.

Based on an actual nineteenth-century murder case, SO DARK THE NIGHT " . . . is one of the prime examples of how a film destined to play the lower rungs of twin bills, can transcend itself through formal devices to create a work of complexity and originality," wrote Robert Ottoson in *A Reference Guide to the American Film Noir: 1940-1958* (1981). He adds, "Lewis took what is essentially shoddy material and through the use of camera movement and angles, deep focus, lighting, mirror images, sound, close-ups, and point-of-view shots constructed a film that presents a psychiatric case study." Don Miller opined in "The American B Film" (*Focus on Film* magazine, Winter 1970), "The script spins the tale methodically, garnished by Geray's meticulous portrayal of the detective and the tense direction of Lewis . . . [whose] penchant for shots above and below eye-level add greatly to the atmospheric, while the prevailing aura, as in all his most successful melodramas, is one of melancholia."

SONG OF THE THIN MAN (Metro-Goldwyn-Mayer, 1947) 86 minutes.

Producer, Nat Perrin; director, Edward Buzzell; based on the characters created by Dashiell Hammett; story, Stanley Roberts; screenplay, Steve Fisher, Perrin; additional dialogue, James O'Hanlon, Harry Crane; art directors, Cedric Gibbons, Randall Duell; set decorators, Edwin B. Willis, Alfred E. Spencer; music, David Snell; song, Herb Magidson and Ben Oakland; assistant director, Jerry Bergman; sound, Douglas Shearer; camera, Charles Rosher; editor, Gene Ruggiero.

William Powell (Nick Charles); Myrna Loy (Nora Charles); Keenan Wynn (Clarence "Clinker" Krause); Dean Stockwell (Nick Charles, Jr.); Phillip Reed (Tommy Drake); Patricia Morison (Phyllis Talbin); Gloria Grahame (Fran Page); Jayne Meadows (Janet Thayer); Don Taylor (Buddy Hollis); Leon Ames (Mitchell Talbin); Ralph Morgan (David L. Thayar); Warner Anderson (Dr. Monolaw); William Bishop (Al Amboy); Bruce Cowling (Phil Brant); Bess Flowers (Jessica Thayar); Connie Gilchrist (Bertha); James Burke (Callahan); Tom Trout (Lewie, the Shiv); Henry Nemo (The Neem); Marie Windsor (Helen Amboy); Asta, Jr. (Asta); Tom Dugan (Davis, the Cop); John Sheehan (Manager); Lennie Bremen, Lyle Latell (Mugs); Eddie Simms, Jimmy O'Gatty (Hoods); James Flavin (Reardon, the Cop); Bill Harbach (Whitley); George Anderson (Dunne); Donald Kerr (News Photographer); Alan Bridge (Nagle, the Policeman); Esther Howard (Counterwoman); Harry Burns (Italian); William Roberts (Pete); Clarke Hardwicke (Bert); Henry Sylvester (Butler); Matt McHugh (Taxi Driver); Clinton Sundberg (Desk Clerk); Gregg Barton (Nurse); Earle Hodgins (Baggage Man); Howard Negley (Kramer); George Sorel (Headwaiter); Charles Sullivan (Sergeant); Robert Strickland (Musician); Jeffrey Sayre (Croupier); Morris Ankrum (Inspector); Maria San Marco (Oriental Girl); George Chan (Chinese); Jerry Fragnol (Young Nick at Age Five).

After thirteen years and five previous features, MGM's uppercase Thin Man series came to a halt with SONG OF THE THIN MAN. It should have been entitled SWAN SONG OF THE THIN MAN because it not only was the final entry in the group but it also has a plot centered around music. The series had shown strains of wear with the two previous entries, SHADOW OF THE THIN MAN (1941) and THE THIN MAN GOES HOME (1944), *qq.v.*, and this final outing (shot over 52 days of production) was the most

Myrna Loy, Asta and William Powell in SONG OF THE THIN MAN (1947).

anemic of the trio. Also William Powell and Myrna Loy were tired of their roles—and apparently each other—and both were becoming too old for the parts, especially Ms. Loy, although Powell is still dapper as he sports a vast array of flashy clothes in the proceedings.

Nick Charles (William Powell) and his chic wife Nora (Myrna Loy) are aboard a gambling ship when the band leader is murdered and a bottle is shot out of Nick's hand. Nick investigates and learns that wealthy Mitchell Talbin's (Leon Ames) wife Phyllis (Patricia Morison) is being blackmailed by gangster Al Amboy (William Bishop). A bombastic member of the band, clarinet player Clarence "Clinker" Krause (Keenan Wynn), tries to help Nick resolve the case but mobsters threaten to harm the Charles' son Nick, Jr. (Dean Stockwell), unless Charles drops the matter. Nick, nevertheless, persists and solves the case, but not before Phyllis murders her husband.

More for nostalgic reasons than artistic merit, Thomas M. Pryor (*New York Times*) cheered, "The blind alleys that Nick and Nora run into in their quest of the slayer are all used to good advantage, and whatever the script lacks in the way of logic is more than compensated for by the lighthearted manner in which the incidental scenes are worked out."

It should be noted that the original Asta the dog had died in 1946 and was replaced by Asta Jr., but the publicity surrounding this event did little to help the film. By now (in the more somber post-World War II atmosphere) the plot has Nora Charles avoiding hard liquor in order to be a good mother to her eight-year-old son, played nicely by Dean Stockwell.

THE SPANISH CAPE MYSTERY (Republic, 1935) 72 mins

Producer, M. H. Hoffman; director, Lewis D. Collins; based on the novel by Ellery Queen [Frederic Dannay, Manfred B. Lee]; adaptor/screenplay, Albert DeMond; camera, Gilbert Warrenton; editor, Jack Ogilvie.

Helen Twelvetrees (Stella Godfrey); Donald Cook (Ellery Queen); Berton Churchill (Judge Macklin); Frank Sheridan (Godfrey); Harry Stubbs (Sheriff Moley); Guy Usher (Inspector Queen); Huntley Gordon (Kummer); Betty Blythe (Mrs. Godfrey); Olaf Hytten (Dupre); Ruth Gillette (Mrs. Constable); Jack LaRue (Gardner); Frank Leigh (Tiller); Barbara Bedford (Mrs. Munn); Donald Kerr (Hendricks); George Cleveland (Jorum); and: George Baxter, Arnold Gray, Katherine Morrow, Lee Prather.

New York City-based cousins Frederic Dannay and Manfred B. Lee introduced their fictional detective, Ellery Queen, in 1928 and the character became so popular that it took on an enduring identity of its own. In fact, many readers thought Ellery Queen was an actual person. Adding to this charade was the fact that Dannay and Lee wrote under the name Ellery Queen, even for literary exploits not involving the famous detective. The character of Ellery Queen first came to the screen in 1935 when M. H. Hoffman produced THE SPANISH CAPE MYSTERY, based on the 1935 novel of the same title, for his Liberty Pictures. It was issued by Republic after Liberty became part of that studio.

Tired from his strenuous detection work, Ellery Queen (Donald Cook) agrees to accompany friend Judge Macklin (Berton Churchill) on a vacation near Spanish Cape, on the coast, and comes across a murder in which the victim is covered by a Spanish cape. Queen begins investigating, as does local loud-mouthed Sheriff Moley (Harry Stubbs). Ellery's father, Inspector Queen (Guy Usher), also arrives on the scene. During the course of the investigation, Ellery meets another vacationer, lovely Stella Godfrey (Helen Twelvetrees), and the two fall in love. Three more murders ensue before Ellery solves the mystery. At the last minute he steps aside and allows Moley to take the credit for the solution Queen and Stella look forward to their future.

Variety called the film a "Fairly intriguing detective mystery," but added that it fails "to cash in on inherent possibilities, both through weak adaptation and wobbly direction. . . ." The reviewer further explained, "Detective Queen, however, fails to measure up to expectations of the character. Director and author have seen fit to play up bombastic sheriff intent on solving the murders. Loud expounding of this local gendarme's theories not only slow up the action, but are so absurd as to become irritating. Towards close the director builds suspense that clicks. . . . Rich settings as well as some excellent scenic stuff help."

Republic followed this feature with another Ellery Queen adventure, THE MANDARIN MYSTERY (1936), *q.v.*, with Eddie Quillan cast as Queen.

THE SPECKLED BAND (First Division-AmerAnglo, 1931) 66 minutes.

Producer, Herbert Wilcox; director, Jack Raymond; based on the story "The Adventure of the Speckled Band" by Sir Arthur Conan Doyle; screenplay, W. P. Lipscomb; sound, L. F. Odell; camera, Freddie A. Young; editor, P. M. Rogers.

Lyn Harding (Dr. Grimesby Rylott); Raymond Massey (Sherlock Holmes); Athole Stewart (Dr. John H. Watson); Angela Baddeley (Helen Stoner); Nancy Price (Mrs. Staunton); Marie Ault (Mrs.

Hudson); Stanley Lathbury (Rodgers); Charles Paton (Builder); Joyce Moore (Violet).

One of Sir Arthur Conan Doyle's finest Sherlock Holmes stories, "The Adventure of the Speckled Band," was successfully adapted for the London stage in 1910. Two years later it was filmed by the Franco-British Film Company as part of that organization's Sherlock Holmes series. M. George Treville played Holmes in the two-reeler. In 1923 the story was filmed again as part of the British Stoll Films' "The Last Adventures of Sherlock Holmes" series, with Eille Norwood as Holmes. The 1931 British and Dominion production of THE SPECKLED BAND was the first sound version of the story and the only feature-length film made from it to date. In it Raymond Massey makes his film debut as Holmes, but he takes second billing to Lyn Harding as the villain, Dr. Grimesby Rylott, a part Harding originated in the 1910 stage production. (Harding also played Moriarty in the 1930s British features about Holmes in which Arthur Wontner starred.)

At the remote manor house of Grimesby Rylott (Lyn Harding), his stepdaughter Violet (Joyce Moore) screams and dies in the arms of her sister, Helen Stoner (Angela Baddeley), saying only the words, "The speckled band." Dr. Watson (Athole Stewart) had known Rylott's late wife in India and Helen comes to him for help. He, in turn, takes the case to Sherlock Holmes (Raymond Massey). Helen has decided to marry but Holmes urges expediency in the matter and, after a confrontation with Rylott at Baker Street, Holmes and Watson go to his manor to survey the house and its environs. The survey includes visiting gypsies, a simian creature Rylott lets roam the estate and a flute-playing Indian servant. That night Holmes and Watson send Helen to another part of the house while they remain awake in her sleeping quarters (her room is being repaired, so she has to sleep in her late sister's room), and a huge snake comes slithering through a ventilator shaft. Holmes forces it back into its master's room where it turns on Rylott and kills him. Holmes had discerned that Rylott was killing off his stepdaughters to obtain their inheritance and was using the deadly snake he had imported from India for that purpose.

By today's standards, THE SPECKLED BAND is an exceedingly slow production, but it is not without interest. Holmes' Baker Street residence is shown to be a modernized affair (the film takes place in contemporary times) with a busy office full of secretaries and modern equipment, and even a recording device to preserve conversations. Lyn Harding's larger-than-life portrayal of the terrible Rylott adds much to the proceedings, as does the sinister atmosphere of the manor house. The latter was the work of director

Jack Raymond, and Chris Steinbrunner and Norman Michaels noted in *The Films of Sherlock Holmes* (1978), " . . . In THE SPECKLED BAND he [Raymond] is helped considerably in the establishing of a heavily Gothic, Germanic mood by the shadowy camerawork of Freddie Young, which is both brooding and superb."

Due to its short story length, "The Adventure of the Speckled Band" is best suited for radio and TV adaptations, and it has appeared in both mediums on several occasions. Perhaps the best of these is the 1986 Thames Television production, part of "The New Adventure of Sherlock Holmes" series starring Jeremy Brett as Holmes. It was telecast in the U.S. as part of the PBS-TV series "Mystery!"

When originally released in England in 1931 by Woolf and Freedman, THE SPECKLED BAND had a running time of 90 minutes.

LE SPECTRE VERT   *see*   THE UNHOLY NIGHT [essay].

THE SPIDER (Twentieth Century-Fox, 1945) 61 minutes.

Producer, Ben Silvey; director, Robert Webb; based on the play by Fulton Oursler, Lowell Brentano; screenplay, Jo Eisinger, W. Scott Darling; music, David Buttolph; camera, Glen MacWilliams; editor, Norman Colbert.

Richard Conte (Chris Conlon); Faye Marlowe (Lila Neilson); Kurt Kreuger (Garonne); John Harvey (Burns); Martin Kosleck (Barak); Mantan Moreland (Henry); Walter Sande (Lieutenant Castle); Cara Williams (Wanda); Charles Tannen (Lieutenant Tonti); Margaret Brayton (Jean); Harry Seymour (Bartender); Ann Savage (Florence Cain); Jean Del Val (Dutrelle); Odette Vigne (Mrs. Dutrelle); James Flavin (Johnny); Roy Gordon (Picket); William Halligan (Police Inspector); Lane Chandler, Eddie Hart (Radio Cops); Margo Woode (Pretty Girl).

Lovely Lila Neilson (Faye Marlowe) comes to private detective Chris Conlon (Richard Conte) and asks him to help locate her sister, who has been missing for a long time; she fears the girl has been murdered. Conlon's partner in the detective agency is a woman (Ann Savage) who gets the needed information in the case but ends up murdered. Police detective Lieutenant Castle (Walter Sande) feels that Conlon killed her, but lacks sufficient evidence for an arrest. Not long after the detective talks to another suspect, that person is also killed and the dragnet goes out for Conlon, who is aided reluctantly by his assistant, Henry (Mantan Moreland). Conlon believes the killer is Barak (Martin Kosleck), who, like Lila, works for magician Garonne (Kurt Kreuger). Events take a turn to prove that the culprit is not Barak.

THE SPIDER is an enjoyable "B" *film noir* melodrama which highlights a fine cast caught in the web of a complicated and at times hard-to-follow narrative. "Script fails suitably to explain why the villain started his series of murders but otherwise maintains casual interest in the melodramatic developments" (*Variety*). Less kind was Thomas M. Pryor (*New York Times*), who called the film a "ponderous and silly melodrama," and added, " . . . the authors forgot to provide the murderer with any discernible motive for his actions."

Richard Conte is particularly good as the determined detective who almost winds up as one of the case's victims. Also, this feature provides Ann Savage with a small but memorable assignment as the detective's crooked partner, Florence Cain, who is killed for failing to divulge what she knows before it is too late. Ann Savage majored in attractive, but hard and often corrupt roles, as exemplified in DETOUR (1944) and THE LAST CROOKED MILE (1946), *q.v.*

THE SPIDER WOMAN *see* SHERLOCK HOLMES AND THE SPIDER WOMAN.

THE SQUEAKER *see* MURDER ON DIAMOND ROW.

STAND-IN FOR MURDER *see* LARCENY IN HER HEART.

STAR OF MIDNIGHT (RKO, 1935) 90 minutes.

Producer, Pandro S. Berman; director, Stephen Roberts; based on the novel by Arthur Somers Roche; screenplay, Howard J. Green, Anthony Veiller, Edward Kaufman; art directors, Van Nest Polglase, Charles Kirk; costumes, Bernard Newman; makeup, Mel Burns; music director, Max Steiner; camera, J. Roy Hunt; editor, Arthur Roberts.

William Powell (Clay Dalzell); Ginger Rogers (Donna Martin); Paul Kelly (Jim Kinland); Gene Lockhart (Horatio Swayne); Ralph Morgan (Roger Classen); Leslie Fenton (Tim Winthrop); J. Farrell MacDonald (Inspector Doremus); Russell Hopton (Tommy Tennant); Vivien Oakland (Gerry Classon); Frank Reicher (Abe Ohlman); Robert Emmett O'Connor (Sergeant Cleary); Francis MacDonald (Kinland Gangster); Paul Hurst (Corbett); Spencer Charters (Doorman); George Chandler (Witness); Sid Saylor (Deliveryman); Charles McMurphy (Officer Lewis); John Ince (Doctor); Hooper Atchley (Hotel Manager).

Following the success of THE THIN MAN (1934), *q.v.*, RKO borrowed that film's star, William Powell, and teamed him with director Stephen Roberts for a fun-filled carbon copy of the Dashiell Hammett work. Here Powell is hard-drinking lawyer Clay Dalzell, who becomes mixed up in murder and with the affections of a spritely young woman (Ginger Rogers) who is trying to get him to the altar. The duo of William Powell and Ginger Rogers retained much of the on-screen chemistry that Powell and Myrna Loy had created in THE THIN MAN, and Andre Sennwald (*New York Times*) commented, "A sleek, witty and engaging entertainment, it contemplates its corpses with the charming air of just passing the time pleasantly until the bar opens . . . good, lovely fun, and it can be recommended both as humor and as melodrama."

Gossip columnist Tommy Tennant (Russell Hopton) has print-ed unflattering information about high-class lawyer Clay Dalzell (William Powell), and the attorney asks him to his apartment, intending to request a retraction. While there the writer is shot in the back; the police suspect Dalzell of the killing but lack evidence for an immediate arrest. Dalzell, with the aid of his lady love, Donna Martin (Ginger Rogers), learns that Tennant had information on a mysterious masked female entertainer who disappears when pur-sued. Police Inspector Doremus (J. Farrell MacDonald) keeps on Dalzell's trail and hinders his investigation of the murder, as does gangster Jim Kinland (Paul Kelly). The latter wants Dalzell kept safe because the lawyer has proof in his safety deposit box of the hoodlum's tax falsifying. Other suspects in the murder include Roger Classen (Ralph Morgan) and Tim Winthrop (Leslie Fenton), while Dalzell's butler/valet, Horatio Swayne (Gene Lockhart), tries to keep his daring and dashing employer from getting himself killed. Dalzell finally does pinpoint the killer and then he and Donna marry.

The effervescent STAR OF MIDNIGHT proved so successful that RKO reteamed William Powell and director Stephen Roberts for a follow-up, THE EX-MRS. BRADFORD (1936), *q.v.*; it was scripted by Anthony Veiller, who had co-written STAR OF MIDNIGHT.

STRANGE ADVENTURE (Monogram, 1932) 62 minutes.

Producer, I. E. Chadwick; supervisor, Trem Carr; directors, Phil Whitman, Hampton Del Ruth; story, Arthur Hoerl; screenplay, Lee Chadwick; camera, Leon Shamroy.

Regis Toomey (Lieutenant Mitchell); June Clyde (Toodles the Reporter); Lucille LaVerne (Mrs. Sheen); William V. Mong (Silas Wayne); Jason Robards [Sr.] (Dr. Bailey); Eddie Phillips (Claude Wayne); Dwight Frye (Robert Wayne); Isabelle Vecki (Sarah Boulter); Alan Roscoe (Stephen Boulter); Nadine Dore (Gloria); Fred "Snowflake" Toomes (Jeff); William J. Humphrey (Coroner); Harry Myers (Officer Kelly); Eddy Candler (Policeman).

The police are called out to the gloomy Wayne mansion by elderly Silas Wayne (William V. Mong), who plans to read his will to his relatives, informing them how they will share his estate once he is gone. Present are his nephews Claude Wayne (Eddie Phillips) and Robert Wayne (Dwight Frye) and niece Sarah Boulter (Isabelle Vecki), her husband Stephen (Alan Roscoe), housekeeper Mrs. Sheen (Lucille LaVerne), Wayne's doctor, Bailey (Jason Robards [Sr.]), and the old man's woman, Gloria (Nadine Dore). Just as he begins reading the will, Silas falls over and, upon examination, Dr. Bailey finds he has been stabbed to death. The police officers then call their superior, Lieutenant Mitchell (Regis Toomey), who arrives at the same time as newshound Toodles (June Clyde). Mitchell questions the suspects and Stephen Boulter tells him he heard Claude and Robert quarrel over Gloria. Claude cannot be found and Robert is locked up as Mitchell returns to headquarters and Toodles leaves to file her story. The reporter, however, sneaks back into the house and is stalked by a hooded, cloak-wearing menace. She hides in a closet where she finds Claude's corpse. Mitchell returns and believes that either the housekeeper or Robert is guilty, but when the hooded figure abducts Gloria and tries to murder her, Mitchell stops him and unmasks the fiend.

Although turned out on a limited budget, this old house murder mystery is quite flavorful and chilling and the hooded killer's identity is hard to spot. Regis Toomey is especially good as the police detective and the film's raft of suspects make an engaging set of red herrings. "There are some effective scares, comedy by a couple of inept policemen and a frightened servant played by the expressive, Fred ["Snowflake"] Toomes, romance, and a hooded killer" wrote George E. Turner and Michael H. Price in *Forgotten Horrors* (1979). They added, "The killer's costume, incidentally, did double duty in THE THIRTEENTH GUEST [*q.v.*] a few months earlier. . . . Leon Shamroy's photography sees the menacing tone very well."

This film was issued to television as THE WAYNE MURDER CASE.

STRANGE BARGAIN (RKO, 1949) 68 minutes.

Producer, Sid Rogell; director, Will Price; screenplay, Lillie Hayward; art directors, Albert S. D'Agostino, Carroll Clark; set decorators, Darrell Silvera, James Altweis; music, Frederick Hollander; music director, Constantin Bakaleinikoff; assistant director, Sam Ruman; sound, Frank Sarver, Terry Kellum; camera, Harry J. Wild; editor, Frederic Knudtson.

Martha Scott (Georgia Wilson); Jeffrey Lynn (Sam Wilson); Henry Morgan (Lieutenant Richard Webb); Katherine Emery (Edna Jarvis); Richard Gaines (Malcolm Jarvis); Henry O'Neill (Timothy Herne); Walter Sande (Sergeant Cord); Michael Chapin (Roddy Wilson); Arlene Gray (Hilda Wilson); Raymond Roe (Sydney Jarvis); Robert Bray (McTay).

Bankrupt businessman Malcolm Jarvis (Richard Gaines) plans to commit suicide. If he does, however, his wife (Katherine Emery) will not get the proceeds from his insurance policy. He devises a plan in which he asks his accountant, Sam Wilson (Jeffrey Lynn), who sorely needs money, to fire shots into Jarvis' library and make it look like he was murdered. Then, Mrs. Jarvis could collect on the policy. At first Wilson refuses to do as Jarvis asks, but feeling loyalty to the man and needing the $10,000 he is to be paid for carrying out the job, he goes through with the strange assignment. When another man is charged and convicted of the murder, Wilson feels remorse and tells his wife Georgia (Martha Scott) the truth. With the help of police Lieutenant Richard Webb (Henry "Harry" Morgan) they track down Jarvis' actual murderer, since it develops the man did not die at his own hands.

"Real detective buffs should have no trouble spotting the identity of the real murderer from the usual least likely corner, but in this instance the solution is of less importance that the gradual and logical building of a case for murder and interesting character study," William K. Everson wrote in *The Detective in Film* (1972).

An interesting footnote to STRANGE BARGAIN took place 38 years later when the solution of the film's finale was made as an episode of the ABC network television series, "Murder, She Wrote," starring Angela Lansbury as mystery novelist and amateur sleuth, Jessica Fletcher. The plot, which used flashbacks from the black-and-white-film, had waitress Georgia Wilson (Martha Scott) recognizing Mrs. Fletcher (Angela Lansbury) and asking her to clear her husband Sam's (Jeffrey Lynn) name in the killing of his boss—a crime for which he has just been released from prison after thirty years. Jessica agrees and with the help of Richard Webb (Harry Morgan), the original investigating police office, she puzzles out the real culprit and clears Wilson.

This TV series episode has a different solution to the crime from that of the original film, but the picture's three stars (Martha Scott, Jeffrey Lynn, Harry Morgan) were reunited to redo their roles in the small-screen follow-up.

STRANGERS OF THE EVENING (Tiffany, 1932) 70 minutes.

Producer, Sam Bischoff; director, H. Bruce Humberstone;

based on the novel *The Illustrious Corpse* by Tiffany Thayer; adaptor/ dialogue, Stuart Anthony, Warren B. Duff; settings, Ralph De Lacy; costumes, Elizabeth Coleman; music director, Val Burton; sound, Corson Jowett; camera, Arthur Edeson; supervising editor, Martin G. Cohn; editor, Dave Berg.

ZaSu Pitts (Sybil); Eugene Pallette (Detective Brubacher); Lucien Littlefield (Frank); Tully Marshall (Robert Daniels); Miriam Seegar (Ruth Daniels); Theodore von Eltz (Dr. Everette); Warner Richmond (Chandler); Harold Waldridge (Tommy); Mahlon Hamilton (Nathan Frisbee); Alan Roscoe (Sutherland); Charles Williams, William Scott (Men); James Burtis (Nolan); Francis Sayles (Roberts); Hal Price (Policeman).

When he is told that his daughter Ruth (Miriam Seegar) is to marry Dr. Raymond Everette (Theodore von Eltz), who works in an undertaker's laboratory, Frank Daniels (Lucien Littlefield) becomes upset and goes to see Everette. Later, his corpse is brought to the funeral parlor and an assistant, Tommy (Harold Waldridge), soon runs away. Brubacher (Eugene Pallette), a detective, is assigned to investigate Daniels' death, while Everette tries to get information from housekeeper Sybil (ZaSu Pitts). When Daniels is reported as being alive, his casket is exhumed and is found to contain the body of a politician who had been seen arguing with the undertaker, Chandler (Warner Richmond), over a double-cross with a henchman. Everette and Tommy follow a truck which is carrying the unearthed casket and apprehend Chandler and his men. Chandler admits that the corpses were switched and that the dead man is really the henchman, who was killed in a car crash. Ruth later recognizes an amnesiac, who had originally told Brubacher of the politician's murder, as her father. It seems thugs had ambushed him while en route to see Dr. Everette and he had lost his memory. With his past restored, Daniels agrees to his daughter's marriage and, at the same time, romances Sybil himself.

Taken from Tiffany Thayer's novel, *The Illustrious Corpse* (1930), this film, shot in nine days, marks the directorial debut of H. Bruce Humberstone, who followed it with The Crooked Circle, *q.v.*, also with ZaSu Pitts. In *Close Up: The Contract Director* (1976), Jon Tuska commented, "It was an offbeat picture. Some of the humor is obviously intentional, but some of it not . . . most scenes consisted of only master shots with no intercuts, making it seem longish today, however consistent this may have been with the prevailing techniques of the time." George E. Turner and Michael H. Price commented in *Forgotten Horrors* (1979), "The blackly funny STRANGERS OF THE EVENING anticipated a trend which persists today. Its depiction of comic occurrences in an undertaking establishment was attacked as tasteless in 1932; today the film seems, in light of macabre comedies more recently in vogue, a product of impeccable taste."

The film was later reissued as THE HIDDEN CORPSE.

STRIPTEASE LADY *see* LADY OF BURLESQUE.

A STUDY IN SCARLET (Fox, 1933) 71 minutes.

Producers, Burt Kelly, Samuel Bischoff, William Saul; director, Edwin L. Marin; based on the novel *Study in Scarlet* by Sir Arthur Conan Doyle; adaptor, Robert Florey; continuity/dialogue, Reginald Owen; art director, Ralph M. De Lacy; music director, Val Burton; sound, Hans Weeren; camera, Arthur Edeson; editor, Rose Loewinger.

Reginald Owen (Sherlock Holmes); Anna May Wong (Mrs. Pyke); June Clyde (Eileen Forrester); Alan Dinehart (Merrydew); John Warburton (John Stanford); Warburton Gamble (Dr. John H. Watson); J. M. Kerrigan (Jabez Wilson); Alan Mowbray (Inspector Lestrade); Doris Lloyd (Mrs. Murphy); Billy Bevan (Will Swallow); Cecil Reynolds (Baker); Wyndham Standing (Captain Pyke); Halliwell Hobbs (Malcolm Dearing); Tetsu Komai (Ah Yet); Tempe Pigott (Mrs. Hudson); Hobart Cavanaugh (Publican); Olaf Hytten (Butler); Lelia Bennett (Dolly).

Sir Arthur Conan Doyle's first Sherlock Holmes novel, *Study in Scarlet* (1887), came to the screen in two 1914 silent features, the British A STUDY IN SCARLET with James Braginton as Holmes, and its Hollywood counterpart, made by Universal and starring Francis Ford, who also directed, as Holmes. Interestingly, in the latter film, Dr. Watson was portrayed by Jack Francis, really Francis Ford's brother Jack, who later became famous as director John Ford. The only sound-era version of the novel came in 1933, in World Wide's A STUDY IN SCARLET, but only the title was used; the script (by Robert Florey, who was to direct it originally) was more akin to Edgar Wallace than to Conan Doyle. Reginald Owen, who had portrayed Watson the year before in Fox's SHERLOCK HOLMES, *q.v.*, here was cast as the intrepid sleuth and also provided the film's continuity and dialogue. World Wide folded not long after this film was made and it was distributed by Fox.

A baffling murder takes place in London's Victoria Station as Eileen Forrester (June Clyde) attends a meeting of a sinister group called "The Scarlet Ring," whose members share in a business the profits of which are divided among the surviving associates. Eileen's late father had been a member of the organization, which is presided over by corrupt lawyer Thaddeus Merrydew (Alan Dinehart). The widow (Doris Lloyd) of the man done in at the train station consults

Sherlock Holmes (Reginald Owen) because her husband was a member of the Ring and she was left without an inheritance. When another member, Captain Pyke (Wyndham Standing), is murdered, Eileen is a witness, but the police are baffled and Inspector Lestrade (Alan Mowbray) asks Holmes' help. The man's widow, Mrs. Pyke (Anna May Wong), identifies his body by a ring he had given her when they were married. In the disguise of an old man, Holmes visits the Grange, the Pykes' home, and finds Mrs. Pyke there with Eileen and another Ring member, Jabez Wilson (J. M. Kerrigan). Merrydew is also present and Holmes has Dr. Watson (Warburton Gamble) and Lestrade staked outside the country home. During the night an attempt is made to kill Eileen and Wilson. When a mysterious figure in black kidnaps Eileen, and Mrs. Pyke's servant, Ah Yet (Tetsu Komai), tries to kill Wilson, Holmes comes to the rescue and solves the case.

With its plot about a secret society, cryptic murder messages, a remote country house and a figure in black, A STUDY IN SCARLET is an eerie thriller with solid entertainment value. It is also well produced for a low-budget programmer, as George E. Turner and Michael H. Price note in *Forgotten Horrors* (1979): "In photographic terms, A STUDY IN SCARLET ranks among the best of its time— which is understandable in that the great Arthur Edeson was in charge of the cameras. Edeson's exquisite studies of foggy Limehouse, eerie hidden rooms, and a menacing country mansion are wonderfully atmospheric. Ralph De Lacy's settings likewise are of major-studio calibre. One interesting sequence puts the camera in the role of the mysterious killer when he pays a visit to his accomplice."

While the World Wide feature was the only film to use the Doyle novel title (if *not* the plot), there is a 1984 featurette cartoon called SHERLOCK HOLMES AND A STUDY IN SCARLET, with Peter O'Toole supplying the voice of Holmes as he and Watson look into the mysterious death of an American tourist on holiday in London.

A STUDY IN TERROR (Columbia, 1965) Color 94 minutes.

Presenter/executive producer, Herman Cohen; producer, Henry E. Lester; director, James Hill; based on characters created by Sir Arthur Conan Doyle; screenplay, Donald Ford, Derek Ford; production designer, Alex Vetchinsky; costumes, Motley; makeup, Tom Smith; music/music conductor, Johnny Scott; sound supervisor, John Cox; sound editor, Jim Roddan; special effects, Wally Veevers; camera, Desmond Dickinson; editor, Henry Richardson.

John Neville (Sherlock Holmes); Donald Houston (Dr. John H. Watson); John Fraser (Lord Edward Carfax); Anthony Quayle

(Dr. Murray); Robert Morley (Mycroft Holmes); Barbara Windsor (Annie Chapman); Adrienne Corri (Angela); Frank Finlay (Inspector Lestrade); Judi Dench (Sally); Cecil Parker (Prime Minister); Georgia Brown (Singer); Barry Jones (Duke of Shires); Kay Walsh (Cathy Eddowes); Edwina Ronay (Mary Kelly); Terry Downes (Chunky); Peter Carsten (Max Steiner); Charles Regnier (Joseph Beck); Dudley Foster (Home Secretary); John Cairney (Michael Osborne); Christiane Maybach (Polly Nichols); Avis Bunnage (Landlady); Barbara Leake (Mrs. Hudson); Patrick Newell (P. C. Bens); Norma Foster (Liz Stride); Donna White (Streetwalker).

When the corpses of three disemboweled prostitutes are found in the Whitechapel area of London, Sherlock Holmes (John Neville) and Dr. Watson (Donald Houston) become involved after Holmes receives a parcel containing surgical instruments with a scalpel missing. Watson helps Holmes trace the instruments to the Duke of Shires (Barry Jones). They find out that the instruments belong to a son (John Cairney) who was disinherited for marrying a prostitute

John Neville in A STUDY IN TERROR (1965).

named Angela (Adrienne Corri). Holmes discovers that the Duke's other son, Lord Edward Carfax (John Fraser), is paying blackmail to Angela's lover, bar owner Max Steiner (Peter Carsten). The detective then unravels a complicated plot which shows that Angela is the real blackmailer. He rescues the disinherited son, who has been working as an assistant to Dr. Murray (Anthony Quayle) at a Whitechapel clinic, and takes him home to the Duke. Using Angela as a decoy, Holmes sets a trap for the killer, whom the press has dubbed Jack the Ripper.

This British-lensed Sherlock Holmes adventure is one of the best Holmes films ever released. Also called FOG, it was issued in West Germany as SHERLOCK HOLMES GROSSTER FALL. John Neville is particularly effective as Holmes, as is Donald Houston as Watson, with Robert Morley beautifully cast as Holmes' corpulent brother Mycroft. *Films in Review* magazine (August-September 1966) wrote, "John Neville is a credible Holmes, and the direction of James Hill, the production design of Vetchninsky, and the costumes of Motley lift this inexpensive black-&-whiter above the level of routine entertainment." *Time* magazine endorsed the production as "sly and stylish."

As a tie-in for the feature Ellery Queen [Manfred B. Lee, Fredric Dannay] wrote the Lancer paperback book, *A Study in Terror,* but it did not rewrite the script. Instead it has contemporary detective Ellery Queen finding Dr. Watson's manuscript of the Holmes encounter with Jack the Ripper, with both detectives, in separate eras, trying to solve the case. In England the book was called *Sherlock Holmes vs. Jack the Ripper.*

SUPER SLEUTH (RKO, 1937) 75 minutes.

Producer, Edward Small; director, Ben Stoloff; based on the play by Harry Segall; screenplay, Gertrude Purcell, Ernest Pagano; art director, Van Nest Polglase; special effects, Vernon L. Walker; camera, Joseph H. August; editor, William Hamilton.

Jack Oakie (William "Bill" Martin); Ann Sothern (Mary Strand); Eduardo Ciannelli (Professor Horman); Alan Bruce (Larry Frank); Edgar Kennedy (Lieutenant Garrison); Joan Woodbury (Doris Dunne); Bradley Page (Ralph Waring); Paul Guilfoyle (Gibbons, the Film Director); Willie Best (Warts); William Corson (Beckett); Alec Craig (Eddie, the Doorman); Richard Lane (Barker); Paul Hurst (Motorcycle Cop); Philip Morris (Sullivan); Dick Rush (Grimes); Dewey Robinson (Film Gangster).

Movie star Bill Martin (Jack Oakie) specializes in starring in detective thrillers and considers himself a qualified detective. Suddenly Hollywood is plagued by a number of homicides committed by a mysterious figure called The Poison Pen. The local police, led by Lieutenant Garrison (Edgar Kennedy), are at a loss, so Martin decides to solve the caper himself, much to the chagrin of his studio and his lady love, publicist Mary Strand (Ann Sothern). Working with criminologist Professor Horman (Eduardo Ciannelli), Martin becomes enmeshed in the case, only to get a Poison Pen letter himself. It orders him to desist immediately from his sleuthing activities. The Poison Pen then attempts to shoot Martin, but misses, and the studio orders Mary to get her boyfriend back before the cameras. Finally Martin traces The Poison Pen to his lair, a mansion, and is nearly done in before unmasking the killer.

Based on a play by Harry Segall, SUPER SLEUTH provides fast-talking comic Jack Oakie with a good springboard for his patter and slapstick comedy antics, and he receives fine support from Ann Sothern as his girlfriend, Edgar Kennedy as a typically bumbling cop, and Eduardo Ciannelli's straight playing of the villain. The *New York Times* thought the feature "an amusing bit of nonsense" and it proved popular fluff at the box-office. In *Movies on Movies* (1978) Richard Meyers judged it "an enjoyable quickie," and Rudy Behlmer and Tony Thomas remarked in *Hollywood's Hollywood* (1975), "Most of the scenes in this better-than-average programmer take place inside the [RKO] studio, with a location unit of camera cars and sound trucks also prominent in the action."

In 1946 RKO remade SUPER SLEUTH as GENIUS AT WORK, a vehicle for the comedy team of Alan Carney and Wally Brown, who play radio show detectives on the trail of a mad killer called The Cobra. Lionel Atwill is the villain and Bela Lugosi his henchman, Stone. *Variety* termed it "Lightweight slapstick comedy. . . ."

THE SUSPECT (Universal, 1944) 85 minutes.

Producer, Islin Auster; director, Robert Siodmark; based on the novel *This Way Out* by James Ronald; adaptor, Arthur T. Horman; screenplay, Bertram Millhauser; music, Frank Skinner; music director, Martin Obzina; costumes, Vera West; camera, Paul Ivano; editor, Arthur Hilton.

Charles Laughton (Philip Marshall); Ella Raines (Mary); Dean Harcus (John); Stanley C. Ridges (Huxley); Henry Daniell (Mr. Simmons); Rosalind Ivan (Cora Marshall); Molly Lamont (Mrs. Simmons); Raymond Severn (Merridew); Eve Amber (Sybil); Maude Eburne (Mrs. Packer); Clifford Brooke (Mr. Packer).

"HIS Was a Strange Secret! HERS Was a Strange LOVE!" announced the poster-advertising for this mystery melodrama about a middle-aged man's love affair with a young woman leading to blackmail and murder. Based on James Ronald's 1939 novel, *This*

Way Out, it was directed by Robert Siodmark, who considered it one of his finest feature films. The movie also provides Charles Laughton with one of his best 1940s screen roles. He gives an admirably restrained performance as the man caught in the middle between love and murder. He is equalled by Ella Raines as the girl who loves him and by Henry Daniell as the devious blackmailer. Not to be overlooked is Rosalind Ivan, who steals the film as Laughton's shrewish spouse.

In 1902 London tobacco shop proprietor Philip Marshall (Charles Laughton) is unhappy in his middle-age with a sharp-tongued wife, Cora (Rosalind Ivan), and a humdrum existence. He meets young and attractive Mary (Ella Raines) and the two fall in love. Marshall tries to persuade his grasping wife to give him a divorce and, when she refuses, beats her to death with a cane, making the crime appear to be an an accident. His alcoholic neighbor, Simmons (Henry Daniell), however, suspects foul play and blackmails Marshall, who is then forced also to murder Simmons. Scotland Yard detective

Rosalind Ivan and Charles Laughton in THE SUSPECT (1944).

Huxley (Stanley Ridges) suspects Marshall of the crime but cannot collect the needed evidence. Marshall and Mary wed and plan to relocate to Canada, but when he finds out that Mrs. Simmons (Molly Lamont) has been arrested for her husband's murder, Marshall gives up his new-found happiness and turns himself over to Huxley.

Thomas M. Pryor (*New York Times*) noted, "This is a very leisurely excursion into crime, somewhat overburdened with politeness. . . . THE SUSPECT is by no means a dull picture, but it seems to lack that quality of excitement which in good melodrama keeps one on edge." Regarding Rosalind Ivan's memorable performance, G. B. Shallin wrote in *Movieland* magazine, " . . . she jolted the customers into such an enthusiastic hatred that during her screen tantrums, many audiences gave out with hisses and boos. So terrific was the impact of her characterization that nobody blamed Laughton at all when, finally driven beyond the limits of human control, he finished her off. Yet even after we had watched Cora's funeral services (with a guilty feeling of relief), her personality continued to dominate the story clear to the end."

THE SWINGING PEARL MYSTERY *see* THE PLOT THICKENS.

TELL NO TALES (Metro-Goldwyn-Mayer, 1939) 68 minutes.

Producer, Edward Chodorov; director, Leslie Fenton; story, Pauline London, Alfred Taylor; screenplay, Lionel Houser; music, Dr. William Axt; art director, Cedric Gibbons; montage, Peter Ballbusch; camera, Joseph Ruttenberg; editor, W. Donn Hayes.

Melvyn Douglas (Michael Cassidy); Louise Platt (Ellen Frazier); Gene Lockhart (Arno); Douglass Dumbrille (Matt Cooper); Florence George (Lorna Travers); Halliwell Hobbes (Dr. Lovelake); Zeffie Tilbury (Miss Mary); Harlan Briggs (Dave Bryant); Sara Haden (Miss Brendan); Hobart Cavanaugh (Charlie Daggett); Oscar O'Shea (Sam O'Neil); Theresa Harris (Ruby); Jean Fenwick (Mrs. Lovelake); Esther Dale (Mrs. Haskins); Joseph Crehan (Chalmers); Tom Collins (Phil Arno); Gladys Blake (Myra Haskins); Ernest Whitman (Elab Giffin); Mary Gordon (Mrs. Bryant); Ray Walker (Dell); Ernie Alexander (Johnson); Jack Carlton (Wilson); Thomas Jackson (Eddie); Frank Orth (Vic, the Bartender); Roger Imhof (Taxi Driver); Claire DuBrey (Miss Arnold); Chester Clute (Manders); Renie Riano (Swedish Maid); Charles D. Brown (Lieutenant Brandon); Norman Willis (Meves); Anthony Warde (Lewis); Ian Wolfe (Fritz); George Noisom (Office Boy); E. Alyn Warren (Janitor); Pat Flaherty (Printer); Fred Kelsey, James C. Morton, Jack Daley, Lee Phelps, Monte Vandergrift (Cops); Hilda Haywood, Bess Flowers (Teachers); Harry Depp (Robert E. More); James Flavin (Simmons); Gertrude Sutton (Gertrude); Harry Tyler (Man on Bus); Brandon Hurst (Butler); Everett Brown (Black Doorman); Mantan Moreland (Sporty Black); Mme. Sul-Te-Wan (Alley Cat's Mother); Florence O'Brien (Belle); Rosalie Lincoln (Girl); Ruby Elsy (Woman in Chair); Thad Jones (Preacher); Ben Carter (Politician); Phil Tead (Marty); James G. Blaine (Captain Hendry); Gladden James (Male Secretary); Nick Copeland (Attendant); Claire Rochelle (Girl at Phone); Ward Wing (Kammy); George Magrill (Alex); Ben Taggart (Lieutenant); John Marlowe (Pianist); Heinie Conklin, Billy Engle (Tramp Comics); Joseph E. Bernard (Man)

TELL NO TALES, the first feature directorial effort of ex-actor Leslie Fenton, is a diverting detective film in which the hero is not a gumshoe, but a newspaperman. William K. Everson notes in *The Detective in Film* (1972), "Perhaps it isn't technically a detective movie, since [Melvyn] Douglas plays a newspaper editor who follows up and solves a kidnapping case, but the plotting and construction is pure Philip Marlowe."

With his newspaper struggling to survive, managing editor Michael Cassidy (Melvyn Douglas), searching for a cause, hops on the trail of a well-publicized kidnapping case in which a hefty ransom is being paid. The investigation leads him along several lines and when he gets too close to the truth the gang kidnaps him and plans to murder him. However, Cassidy escapes and brings about the gang's capture. He writes the big story which saves his newspaper from extinction.

At the time of its release, *Variety* labeled this MGM film "a fast-paced melodrama, produced on a moderate budget. . . . Despite its melodramatic setup, picture carries credulity in its exciting passages and yarn has been developed with logical situations on the whole." In retrospect, Don Miller discussed the picture in his *Focus on Film* magazine (Winter 1970) article, "The American B Film": "Episodic in structure, TELL NO TALES contains some striking dramatic vignettes, especially a sequence wherein Theresa Harris plays the young widow of a slain prizefighter, mourning the loss of her man. Still powerful today, the scene was all the more remarkable in 1939, since it treated the Negro with decency, respect and understanding, a far cry from the shuffling comedy image prevalent on the screen. . . . The newspaper sequences are handled with more than the usual amount of authenticity. [Melvyn] Douglas lends his customary flair to the leading role. . . ."

TEMPLE TOWER (Fox, 1930) 58 minutes.

Presenter, William Fox; director, Donald Gallaher; based on the novel by Sapper [Herman Cyril McNeile]; screenplay, dialogue,

Llewellyn Hughes; assistant director, Horace Hough; sound, Frank MacKenzie; camera, Charles G. Clarke; editor, Clyde Carruth.

Kenneth MacKenna (Captain Hugh "Bulldog" Drummond); Marceline Day (Patricia Verney); Henry B. Walthall (Blackton); Cyril Chadwick (Peter Darrell); Peter Gawthorne (Matthews); Ivan Linow (Gaspard); Frank Lanning (The Nightingale); Yorke Sherwood (Constable Muggins).

Ronald Colman had been superb in the very successful BULLDOG DRUMMOND (1929), *q.v.*, so Fox Pictures made a followup, TEMPLE TOWER, based on Herman Cyril McNeile's [Sapper] 1929 novel of the same title. Because Colman was under contract to Samuel Goldwyn, Fox had to find a new leading man. They chose Kenneth MacKenna but he did not register well in the part. While *Photoplay* magazine called the film, "Burlesque and good, whether intentional or not," the feature was a disappointment, and when Drummond returned to the screen for Fox in 1934 with BULLDOG DRUMMOND STRIKES BACK, Ronald Colman was thankfully back in the title assignment.

After a gang of crooks move into a house in his neighborhood, Scotland Yard Captain Hugh "Bulldog" Drummond (Kenneth MacKenna) vows to bring them to justice. Drummond's patrician girlfriend, Patricia Verney (Marceline Day), works undercover to aid Bulldog by taking a job as secretary to Blackton (Henry B. Walthall), the gang leader. Blackton, however, is being stalked by the mysterious Masked Strangler, who wants revenge because Blackton had double-crossed him. Patricia also wants revenge on Blackton since he murdered her uncle and stole her family's jewelry. Drummond, with aid from pal Peter Darrell (Cyril Chadwick) and his own men from Scotland Yard, puts a stop to Blackton and his gang and unmasks the Strangler.

William K. Everson in *The Detective in Film* (1972) ranked TEMPLE TOWER as "dull" and added, "Its creepy old house setting was ill used in a turgidly written and directed script and Kenneth MacKenna, projecting both a lack of self-confidence and an absence of virility (the very antithesis of Drummond), was probably the weakest player ever to tackle the role . . . only Henry B. Walthall's villain had any strength."

TEMPLE TOWER was remade by Paramount in 1939 as part of its Bulldog Drummond programmer series as BULLDOG DRUMMOND'S SECRET POLICE, *q.v.*, with John Howard as Drummond.

TEN LITTLE INDIANS (Seven Artists, 1966) 92 minutes.

Producer, Harry Alan Towers, Oliver A. Unger; in association

Hugh O'Brian and Shirley Eaton in TEN LITTLE INDIANS (1966).

with Harry M. Popkin; director George Pollock; based on the novel *Ten Little Niggers* by Agatha Christie; screenplay, Peter Yeldham, Peter Welbeck [Harry Alan Towers]; art director, Frank White; assistant director, Barrie Melrose; music/music conductor, Malcolm Lockyer; sound, Peter Keen; sound recording, John Bormage, Ken Cameron; camera, Ernest Steward; second unit camera, Robert Thomson; editor, Peter Boita.

Hugh O'Brian (Hugh Lombard); Shirley Eaton (Ann Clyde); Fabian (Mike Raven); Leo Genn (General Mandrake); Stanley Holloway (William Blore); Wilfrid Hyde-White (Judge Cannon); Daliah Lavi (Ilona Bergen); Dennis Price (Dr. Armstrong); Marianne Hoppe (Frau Grohmann); Mario Adorf (Herr Grohmann).

See: AND THEN THERE WERE NONE [essay].

TEN LITTLE INDIANS (Avco Embassy, 1975) Color 105 minutes.

Producer, Harry Alan Towers; associate producers, Harry Benn, Tibor Reeves, Juan Esterlich; director, Peter Collinson; based on the novel *Ten Little Niggers* by Agatha Christie; screenplay, Peter Welbeck; music/music director, Bruno Nicholai; sound, Ivan

Sharrock; sound editor, Mike Le Mare; camera, Fernando Arribas; editor, John Trumper.

Oliver Reed (Hugh Lombard); Elke Sommer (Vera Clyde); Stephane Audran (Ilona Bergen); Charles Aznavour (Michael Raven); Richard Attenborough (Judge Cannon); Gert Froebe (Wilhelm Blore); Herbert Lom (Dr. Armstrong); Maria Rohm (Elsa Martino); Adolfo Celi (General Soule); Alberto de Mendoza (Martino), Nasser Malak Motii (Inspector Nuri); Orson Welles (Mr. Owen, the Voice on the Tape Recorder).

See: AND THEN THERE WERE NONE [essay].

THE TERROR (Warner Bros., 1928) 80 minutes.

Director, Roy Del Ruth; based on the play by Edgar Wallace; screenplay, Harvey Gates, Joseph Jackson; camera, Barney McGill; editors, Thomas Pratt, Jack Killier.

May McAvoy (Olga Redmayne); Louise Fazenda (Mrs. Elvery); Edward Everett Horton (Ferdinand Fane); Alec B. Francis (Dr. Redmayne); Matthew Betz (Joe Connors); Holmes Herbert (Goodman); John Miljan (Alfred Katman); Otto Hoffman (Soapy Marks); Joseph W. Girard (Superintendent Hallick); Frank Austin (Cotton); Conrad Nagel (Narrator); and: Carl Stockdale, Reed Howes, Lester Cuneo.

THE TERROR (Associated British, 1938) 73 minutes.

Producer, Walter C. Mycroft; director, Richard Bird; based on the play by Edgar Wallace; screenplay, William Freshman; camera, Walter Harvey; editor, Lionel Tomlinson.

Wilfred Lawson (Mr. Goodman); Bernard Lee (Ferdi Fane); Arthur Wontner (Colonel Redmayne); Linden Travers (Mary Redmayne); Henry Oscar (Connor); Alastair Sim (Soapy Marks); Iris Hoey (Mrs. Elvery); Lesley Wareing (Veronica Elvery); Stanley Lathbury (Hawkins); John Turnbull (Inspector Hallick); Richard Murdoch (P. C. Lewis); Edward Lexy (Inspector Dobie).

Edgar Wallace's most popular play, *The Terror*, debuted on the London stage in 1927. The property was purchased by Warner Bros., which made it as its second all-talkie feature film (the first was the gangster picture, LIGHTS OF NEW YORK) in 1928. It had the novel idea of having actor Conrad Nagel read the credits and introduce the story. *Photoplay* magazine called it "Mystery stuff, well presented," but in retrospect, in *An Illustrated History of the Horror Film* (1967), Carlos Clarens declared, "The picture may have been full of sound but it signified absolutely nothing. . . . [It] was the first all-talkie to receive lukewarm reviews." Still, the new novelty of sound aided the picture greatly as the Vitaphone soundtrack presented howling winds, creaking doors, endless screams into the night and a heavy music score.

At a remote English inn, which was once a country house containing underground dungeons, there are presently a number of guests, including attractive Olga Redmayne (May McAvoy), drunken Scotland Yard detective Ferdinand Fane (Edward Everett Horton), spiritualist Mrs. Elvery (Louise Fazenda), crazed cleric Dr. Redmayne (Alec B. Francis), Olga's father, and con men Joe Connors (Matthew Betz) and Soapy Marks (Otto Hoffman). The inn is the headquarters of a mysterious, black-cloaked mass murderer called The Terror, and the house is filled with sudden rushes of organ music and spooky sounds. The Terror attempts to frighten the guests away but Connors and Marks, just out of jail, are determined to gain revenge on the hooded figure for double-crossing them. After a night of fear in which several murders occur, the seemingly incompetent Fane unmasks The Terror.

In 1932, the year of his death, Edgar Wallace novelized *The Terror* and two years later Warner Bros. remade the property as THE RETURN OF THE TERROR. The plot remains close to the 1928 version, although without the elaborate production trappings of the original. The locale, however, is changed to a remote sanitarium, with heroine Olga Morgan (Mary Astor) being tormented by The Terror, while Dr. Goodman (Lyle Talbot) is a physician hero and Dr. Redmayne is played by John Halliday. *Photoplay* magazine endorsed it as a "Chilling mystery" while *Variety* appraised it as a "lukewarm feature."

A third cinema version of THE TERROR was produced in Great Britain in 1938 by Associated British Films. Here the action takes place in the Monks Hall Priory, which is haunted by the elusive hooded figure, The Terror. Bullion from a gold robbery has been secreted in the guest house by the master criminal, who has double-crossed his underlings, Connor (Henry Oscar) and Soapy Marks (Alastair Sim), who plot revenge. Also at the inn are Mary Redmayne (Linden Travers) and her father, Colonel Redmayne (Arthur Wontner), drunken detective Ferdy Fane (Bernard Lee), and the respectable Mr. Goodman (Wilfred Lawson). After Connor is found murdered and the guests terrorized, Fane reveals the killer's identity. "Very little subtlety but plenty of suspense," is how David Quinlan characterized this version in *British Sound Films: The Studio Years 1928-1959* (1984). In his filmography of Edgar Wallace screen work in *Films in Review* magazine (February 1967), Jack Edmund Nolan said of THE TERROR, "Artistically, this re-make was probably the best of the pre-World War II British films that utilized W [Wallace] material." Associated British reissued the film in 1942 but it appears to have had no U.S. distribution. Extracts from it appeared in the 1974 feature, ALL CREATURES GREAT AND SMALL.

TERROR BY NIGHT (Universal, 1946) 60 minutes.

Executive producer, Howard Benedict; producer/director, Roy William Neill; based on the characters created by Sir Arthur Conan Doyle and the Doyle story, "The Adventure of the Empty House"; screenplay, Frank Gruber; art directors, John B. Goodman, Abraham Grossman; set decorators, Russell A. Gausman, Carl Lawrence; music director, Mark Levant; camera, Maury Gertsman; editor, Saul A. Goodkind.

Basil Rathbone (Sherlock Holmes); Nigel Bruce (Dr. John H. Watson); Alan Mowbray (Major Duncan-Bleek); Dennis Hoey (Inspector Lestrade); Renee Godfrey (Vivian Vedder); Mary Forbes (Lady Margaret); Billy Bevan (Train Attendant); Frederic Worlock (Professor Kilbane); Leyland Hodgson (Conductor); Geoffrey Steele (Ronald Carstairs); Boyd Davis (Inspector McDonald); Janet Murdoch (Mrs. Shallcross); Skelton Knaggs (Sands); Gerald Hamer (Mr. Shallcross); Harry Cording (Mock); Charles Knight (Guard); Bobby Wissler (Mock, Jr.).

As film series begin to wane in viewer popularity, the final entries tend to pale. In the case of Universal's Sherlock Holmes features this was not true and TERROR BY NIGHT, the eleventh and penultimate series entry, is one of the best in the group. Scripter Frank Gruber used the murder-on-a-train motif to good effect and the plot, very slightly based on Conan Doyle's "The Adventure of the Empty House," was an exciting and compact one, as the film ran only one hour, making it the briefest of the series. The *New York Times* approved that the film is " . . . told in a tight continuity and with flavorsome atmosphere."

Wealthy Lady Margaret Carstairs (Mary Forbes) and her son Ronald (Geoffrey Steele) engage Sherlock Holmes (Basil Rathbone) and Dr. Watson (Nigel Bruce) to accompany them on a train trip to Edinburgh to protect their diamond, "The Star of Rhodesia." Also aboard the train are Vivian Vedder (Renee Godfrey), who is accompanying the body of her mother to Scotland for burial; Major Duncan-Bleek (Alan Mowbray), an old friend of Watson's in the Twelfth Indian Lancers; the nasty Professor Kilbane (Frederic Worlock); and a meek little man (Gerald Hamer) who is remorseful over stealing a teapot from a London hotel. Soon after the train's departure, Ronald Carstairs is found murdered and the diamond missing. Inspector Lestrade (Dennis Hoey), who is allegedly on the train for a fishing trip to Scotland, begins an investigation with Holmes' aid. Holmes informs Watson that Colonel Sebastian Moran, a henchman of the late Professor Moriarty, is on the train and is responsible for the killing. He also finds that the coffin carrying Vivian's mother has a false bottom that hid the murderer. In addition, he tells Watson and Lestrade that he holds the real diamond and the one stolen was merely a fake. The killer later obtains the actual diamond but his employer turns on him and kills him with the same air gun used to commit the first homicide. At an unscheduled stop, Scotland Yard Inspector McDonald (Boyd Davis) boards the train and things take a swift turn as Holmes confounds the culprits and completes his mission of transporting the diamond safely to Scotland.

In his article, "Always Holmes" (*Kaleidoscope* magazine, Vol. 2, No. 1, 1965), Ray Cabana, Jr. terms the film " . . . a tight-plotted story . . . the treatment was quite original. Once the express gets rolling so does the plot." Ron Haydock commented in *Deerstalker! Holmes and Watson on Screen* (1978), "Although it was strictly confined to the train and its various compartments, TERROR BY NIGHT was still a better film than usually credited to be. Incidents and dialogue raced along well, and the effective use of many camera dissolves and shots of the train hurtling through the black of the night to Scotland helped greatly in keeping the pace humming." David Stuart-Davies enthused in *Holmes of the Movies* (1976), "Not only is TERROR BY NIGHT one of the most effective of the Holmes series, but it is one of the most original murder-on-the-train movies ever made."

THERE'S ALWAYS A WOMAN (Columbia, 1938) 82 minutes.
Producer, William Perlberg; director, Alexander Hall; story, Wilson Collison; (uncredited) screen treatment, Joel Sayre, Philip Rapp; screenplay, Glady Lehman, (uncredited) Morrie Ryskind; art directors, Stephen Goosson, Lionel Banks; music director, Morris Stoloff; gowns, Kalloch; camera, Henry Freulich; editor, Viola Lawrence.

Joan Blondell (Sally Reardon); Melvyn Douglas (William Reardon); Mary Astor (Lola Fraser); Frances Drake (Anne Calhoun); Jerome Cowan (Nick Shane); Robert Paige (Jerry Marlowe); Thurston Hall (District Attorney); Pierre Watkin (Mr. Ketterling); Walter Kingsford (Grigson); Lester Matthews (Walter Fraser); Rita Hayworth (Ketterling's Secretary); Wade Boteler (Sam, the Radio Car Driver); Arthur Loft (Radio Patrolman); William H. Strauss (Rent Collector); Marek Windheim (Headwaiter); Bud Jamison (Jim, the Bartender); George Davis (Waiter); Robert Emmett Keane (*Dispatch* City Editor); John Gallaudet (Reporter); Eddie Fetherston (Photographer); Josef De Stefani (Cigar Stand Clerk); Ted Oliver,

Eddie Dunn, George McKay (Cops); Gene Morgan (Officer Fogarty); Tom Dugan (Detective Flannigan); Bud Geary (District Attorney's Assistant); Billy Benedict (Bellhop); Lee Phelps (Police Broadcaster).

THERE'S THAT WOMAN AGAIN (Columbia, 1939) 70 minutes.

Associate producer, B. B. Kahane; director, Alexander Hall; based on the characters created by Gladys Lehman, Wilson Collison; screenplay, Philip G. Epstein, James Edward Grant, Ken Englund; art director, Lionel Banks; set decorator, Babs Johnstone; music director, Morris W. Stoloff; camera, Joseph Walker; editor, Viola Lawrence.

Melvyn Douglas (Bill Reardon); Virginia Bruce (Sally Reardon); Margaret Lindsay (Mrs. Nacelle); Stanley Ridges (Tony Croy); Gordon Oliver (Charles Crenshaw); Tom Dugan (Flannigan); Don Beddoe (Johnson); Jonathan Hale (Rolfe Davis); Pierre Watkin (Mr. Nacelle); Paul Harvey (Stone); Marc Lawrence (Stevens); Charles Wilson (Police Captain); Don Barry, Jack Hatfield (Bellboys); Georgette Rhodes, Lillian Yarbo (Attendants); Vivien Oakland (Large Woman); William Newell (Waiter); Gladys Blake (Fran); Pat Flaherty (Husky Gent); Dick Curtis (Subway Guard); June Gittelson (Fat Woman); Lucile Lund (Receptionist); John Dilson (Coroner's Deputy); Eric Mayne (Bearded Man); Maurice Costello, Russell Heustis (Headwaiters); Lola Jensen (Hat Check Girl); Frank Hall Crayne, Charles McMurphy (Detectives); Mantan Moreland (Porter); George Turner (Delivery Boy); Lee Shumway (Policeman); Nell Craig, Lillian West (Women); Allen Fox (Taxi Driver); Charles McMurphy (Detective); Larry Wheat (Clerk).

Hoping to cash in on the continuing popularity of husband-and-wife detective teams which MGM had originated in its The Thin Man series, Columbia offered up THERE'S ALWAYS A WOMAN, based on characters created in stories by Wilson Collison. Pert Joan Blondell and suave Melvyn Douglas were cast as the leads, Sally and Bill Reardon. The *Motion Picture Herald* decided that this screwball detective mystery was " . . . an amusing show in which tomfoolery, mystery melodrama, suspense and surprise have been welded in expert fashion."

Failing to make a living as a private detective, sophisticated Bill Reardon (Melvyn Douglas) returns to his old job in the District Attorney's (Thurston Hall) office. When society woman Lola Fraser's (Mary Astor) husband (Lester Matthews) is murdered, it is Reardon's rattle-brained wife, Sally (Joan Blondell), who attempts to solve the case. She soon drags Bill into the chaos and adds to the confusion in her vain efforts to help. Eventually the murderer is singled out by Bill. *Variety* judged, "It's a briskly-paced, battle-of-the-sexes comedy against a background of a murder mystery. Smart production, and notably, the direction of Alexander Hall have imbued a basically incredible plot with the tempo and animation necessary to make people either believe or forget to disbelieve." On the other hand, Ted Sennett in *Lunatics and Lovers* (1973) decided, "Much of the humor in fact, has the edge of harshness and nastiness prevalent in comedies of the period," and felt the scenario "contains none of the bright repartee between the principals required to keep the film from collapsing." Of note is the fact that Rita Hayworth was to costar in this film, but her role was snipped so badly that she ended up with just a bit assignment.

Director Alexander Hall and Melvyn Douglas reteamed for a sequel, THERE'S THAT WOMAN AGAIN, in which Virginia Bruce took over the role of whimsical, vivacious Sally Reardon. Here Bill Reardon (Melvyn Douglas) is again working for the District Attorney's office. He fastens on the trail of a jewel thief, only to find that his zany wife Sally is also investigating the matter, which includes two homicides. They are aided by none-too-bright police detective Flannigan (Tom Dugan) in their pursuit of the guilty parties. Frank S. Nugent (*New York Times*) wondered where the movie craze for derivative sequels would stop, and added, "The murderer changes character more often than the famous chameleon on the plaid tablecloth; Fifth Avenue jewelry stores apparently are easier to open than sardine tins; . . . the District Attorney's investigators delight in accepting crumbs of information from the private detective and his wife. It is a case, in brief, of flimsy whimsy. . . . "

THERE'S THAT WOMAN AGAIN was not as popular as the series opener and no further screen adventures with the Reardons followed.

THEY MIGHT BE GIANTS (Universal, 1971) Color 91 minutes.

Producers, John Foreman, Paul Newman; associate producer, Frank Caffey; director, Anthony Harvey; based on the play by James Goldman; screenplay, Goldman; production designer, John Robert Lloyd; set decorator, Herbert Mulligan; costumes, Ann Roth, Fern Buchner; makeup, Vince Callaghan; music, John Barry; assistant director, Louis A. Stroller; camera, Victor J. Kemper; editor, Gerald Greenberg.

Joanne Woodward (Dr. Mildred Watson); George C. Scott (Justin Playfair/Sherlock Holmes); Jack Gilford (Wilbur Peabody); Lester Rawlins (Blevins Playfair); Rue McClanahan (Daisy); Ron Weyland (Dr. Strauss); Kitty Winn (Grace); Peter Fredericks (Her Boy Friend); Sudie Bond (Maud); Jenny Egan (Miss Finch); Theresa Merritt (Peggy); Al Lewis (Messenger); Oliver Clark (Mr. Small);

Jane Hoffman, Dorothy Greener (Telephone Operators); M. Emmett Walsh, Louis Zorich (Sanitation Men); Michael McGuire (Telephone Guard); Eugene Roche (Policeman); James Tolkan (Mr. Brown); Jacques Sandulescu (His Driver); Worthington Miner (Mr. Bagg); Frances Fuller (Mrs. Bagg) Matthew Cowles (Teenage Boy); Candy Azzara (Teenage Girl); John McCurry (Police Lieutenant); Tony Capodilupo (Chief); F. Murray Abraham (Usher); Staats Cotsworth (Winthrop); Paul Benedict (Chestnut Vendor); Ralph Clanton (Store Manager); Ted Beniades (Cab Driver).

Retired Manhattan judge Justin Playfair (George C. Scott), who has just lost his wife, has come to believe in his initial delusion that he is the reincarnation of Sherlock Holmes. He ventures about town dressed like the gaslight-era detective, making deductions and trying to solve cases. Meanwhile, his corrupt brother, Blevins Playfair (Lester Rawlins), seeks to have Justin committed so he can control the family funds to pay off a blackmailing vice ring. To aid his cause, Blevins hires Dr. Mildred Watson (Joanne Woodward), who specializes in abnormal psychology, to observe his brother and to gain the needed medical evidence to have him placed in an asylum. Dr. Watson studies Justin and is amazed at his deductive reasoning regarding her patients. He leads her through the city, obtaining clues which turn out to be evidence against the blackmailers. They also encounter many of the judge's eccentric friends, including a librarian (Jack Gilford) who thinks he is the Scarlet Pimpernel and a policeman (Oliver Clark) who regards Justin as Basil Rathbone. After a time, Dr. Watson finds herself falling in love with Justin and begins believing in his activities. In Central Park the two await the arrival of Professor Moriarty and their final fight to the finish.

A whimsical farce, THEY MIGHT BE GIANTS met with sharp critical rejection. Gwenneth Britt wrote in *Films in Review* magazine (May 1971), "No film with the pretensions of this one has a right to be so stupid. . . . [George C.] Scott would have been better advised had he refused this part in THEY MIGHT BE GIANTS instead of the Oscar for his performance in PATTON." On the other hand, Ron Haydock opined in *Deerstalker! Holmes and Watson on Screen* (1978), "All in all, George C. Scott's portrayal of Holmes was one of the better characterizations ever given the sleuth and the film itself was entertaining, if wacky."

A wild chase sequence in a supermarket involving Justin's nutty friends and the police was cut from the initial release print but restored to expand the film's running time when it was issued to TV.

THE THIN MAN (Metro-Goldwyn-Mayer, 1934) 91 minutes.
Producer, Hunt Stromberg; director, W. S. Van Dyke II; based

on the novel by Dashiell Hammett; screenplay, Albert Hackett, Frances Goodrich; assistant director, Lesley Selander; art directors, Cedric Gibbons, David Townsend; set decorator, Edwin B. Willis; costumes, Dolly Tree; music director, Dr. William Axt; sound, Douglas Shearer; camera, James Wong Howe; editor, Robert J. Kern.

William Powell (Nick Charles); Myrna Loy (Nora Charles); Maureen O'Sullivan (Dorothy Wynant); Nat Pendleton (Lieutenant John Guild); Minna Gombell (Mimi Wynant); Porter Hall (MacCauley); Henry Wadsworth (Tommy); William Henry (Gilbert Wynant); Harold Huber (Nunheim); Cesar Romero (Chris Jorgenson); Natalie Moorhead (Julia Wolf); Edward Brophy (Joe Morelli); Thomas Jackson, Creighton Hale, Phil Tead, Nick Copeland, Dink Templeton (Reporters); Ruth Channing (Mrs. Jorgenson); Edward Ellis (Clyde Wynant); Gertrude Short (Marion); Clay Clement (Quinn); Cyril Thornton (Tanner); Robert E. Homans (Bill the Detective); Raymond Brown (Dr. Walton); Douglas Fowley, Sherry Hall (Taxi Drivers); Polly Bailey, Dixie Laughton (Janitresses); Arthur Belasco, Ed Hearn, Garry Owen (Detectives); Fred Malatesta (Headwaiter); Rolfe Sedan, Leo White (Waiters); Walter Long (Stutsy Burke); Kenneth Gibson (Apartment Clerk); Tui Lorraine (Stenographer); Bert Roach (Foster); Huey White (Tefler); Ben Taggart (Police Captain); Charles Williams (Fight Manager); John Larkin (Porter); Harry Tenbrook (Guest); Pat Flaherty (Cop/Fighter).

THE THIN MAN is one of those motion pictures which struck a chord with the American public at just the right time. Issued in 1934, this story of the free-wheeling adventures of easy-going and always-partying Nick and Nora Charles* seemed a relief to Depression-weary filmgoers. Their somewhat hedonistic actions and devil-may-care lifestyles, coupled with their fondness for undiluted and frequent alcohol, made the Charles clan favorites with audiences from the start. Furthermore, the "perfect" casting of suave William Powell and chic Myrna Loy in the parts, plus their lovable white terrier Asta, made the whole package delectable and complete. Based on Dashiell Hammett's 1934 novel, THE THIN MAN was one of the year's most successful ventures, artistically and commercially. Made on a budget of a little over $200,000 (and shot in an economical 16 days), it grossed more than three times that amount at the box-office and netted William Powell an Academy Award nomination; the picture itself was also nominated. It should be noted

---

*In the 1970s, author Lillian Hellman stated that her close friend Dashiell Hammett had based much of Nora Charles' characteristics on her, an opinion hard to document one way or the other.

that the title does *not* refer to Nick Charles, but to a gaunt stranger he is trying to locate.

Nick Charles (William Powell), an ex-detective, spends his time drinking and looking after his wife Nora's (Myrna Loy) financial holdings. They live in lavish apartment surroundings and fully enjoy the good life. When inventor Clyde Wynant (Edward Ellis) disappears, his daughter, Dorothy (Maureen O'Sullivan), asks Nick to help find him. Although he is no longer sleuthing, he agrees to aid the grieved young woman. It seems that Clyde had a young girlfriend, Mimi (Minna Gombell), which caused the breakup of his marriage. The young woman, who had a lover, stole $50,000 from Clyde before he disappeared. When the mistress is murdered, the police, led by thick-headed Lieutenant Guild (Nat Pendleton), investigate, but the woman's lover, too, is soon found dead. Surrounded by the trimmings of the Christmas season, Nick tries to fathom out the case and finally points out the murderer after bringing all the suspects together.

In retrospect, Pauline Kael explained in *5001 Nights at the Movies* (1984), "It started a new cycle in screen entertainment . . . by demonstrating that a murder mystery could also be a sophisticated screwball comedy. . . . Powell and Loy startled and delighted the country by their heavy drinking (without remorse) and unconventional diversions. In one scene Nick takes the air-gun his complaisant wife has just given him for Christmas and shoots the baubles off the Christmas tree. . . . There's a lot of plot exposition and by modern standards the storytelling is very leisurely." Ted Sennett further explained in *Lunatics and Lovers* (1973), "THE THIN MAN was not the first film to blend murder with mirth, but in this case a dollop of engagingly frank husband-and-wife banter was added to the mixture, and the result surprised and pleased filmgoers. . . . Nick and Nora were obviously delighted to be married to each other and not at all taken aback by having to cope with a little homicide in their merry-go-round existence. When the two are exchanging quips . . . the film sparkles brightly, and the ostensible plot—a tangle of murder and deception—fades into the background."

THE THIN MAN was so successful that MGM reteamed director W. S. Van Dyke with William Powell and Myrna Loy for another fun-and-detection adventure two years later in AFTER THE THIN MAN, *q.v*, which was just as good as the original. The high-budgeted series was to continue for a total of a half-dozen features in the next thirteen years, although they began to pale after the second outing (by which time MGM and other studios had saturated the marketplace with distillations of the successful formula). In 1941 "the Thin Man" came to radio on NBC, with Les

Tremayne as Nick and Claudia Morgan as Nora. On September 27, 1957 "The Thin Man" debuted on NBC-TV, with Peter Lawford and Phyllis Kirk as Nick and Nora Charles. Over the two-season program run Stafford Repp, Tol Avery and Jack Albertson played the law enforcers exasperated by and benefitting from the chic Charles clan's efforts as amateur private detectives.

THE THIN MAN GOES HOME (Metro-Goldwyn-Mayer, 1944) 100 minutes.

Producer, Everett Riskin; director, Richard Thorpe; based on characters created by Dashiell Hammett; screenplay, Robert Riskin, Dwight Taylor; art directors, Cedric Gibbons, Edward Carfagno; set decorator, Edward B. Willis; assistant director, Al Jennings; music, David Snell; sound, James K. Burbridge; editor, Ralph E. Winters.

William Powell (Nick Charles); Myrna Loy (Nora Charles); Lucile Watson (Mrs. Charles); Gloria DeHaven (Laura Ronson); Anne Revere (Crazy Mary); Harry Davenport (Dr. Charles); Helen Vinson (Helena Draque); Lloyd Corrigan (Bruce Clayworth); Donald Meek (Willie Crump); Edward Brophy (Brogan); Leon Ames (Edgar Draque); Paul Langton (Tom Clayworth); Donald MacBride (Chief MacGregory); Minor Watson (Sam Ronson); Anita Bolster (Hilda); Charles Halton (Tatum); Morris Ankrum (Willoughby); Nora Cecil (Miss Peavy); Wally Cassell (Bill Burns); Arthur Hohl (Charlie); Anthony Warde (Captain); Bill Smith, Lucile Brown (Skating Act); Mickey Harris (Contortionist); Rex Evans (Fat Man); Harry Hayden (Conductor); Connie Gilchrist (Woman with Baby); Robert Emmet O'Connor (Baggage Man); Dick Botiller (Big Man's Companion); John Wengraf (Big Man); Ralph Brooks (Tom Burton); Jane Green (Housekeeper); Irving Bacon (Tom, the Proprietor); Virginia Sale (Tom's Wife); Garry Owen (Pool Player); Saul Gorss (Bartender); Bert May (Sailor); Chester Clute (Drunk); Clarence Muse (Porter); Tom Fadden, Joseph Greene, Sarah Edwards, Frank Jaquet (Train Passengers); Oliver Blake (Reporter); Don Wilson (Masseur); Etta McDaniel (Ronson's Maid); Tom Dugan (Slugs); Ed Gargan (Mickey); Thomas Dillon, Bill Hunter (Officers); Marjorie Wood (Montage-Shot Mother); Catherine McLeod (Montage Shot Daughter); Clancy Cooper (Butcher); Joe Yule (Barber); Robert Homans (Railroad Clerk); Lee Phelps (Cop); Helyn Eby Rock, Jean Acker (Tarts); Mike Mazurki, Mitchell Lewis, Ray Teal (Men).

After a three-year hiatus following 1941's SHADOW OF THE THIN MAN, *q.v.*, Nick and Nora Charles returned to the screen for the fifth time in THE THIN MAN GOES HOME, an almost apple-pie-and-motherhood concoction which has Nick's bucolic parents even living in the Hardy family house on the MGM backlot. Also thrown into the mix are foreign spies and saboteurs, plus the usual murders, and for a change Nick is forced to remain sober during the proceedings. (Mom and pop allow nothing stronger than apple cider to be imbibed at home.) For comic effect, there is even one scene where Nick turns Nora over his knees and paddles her. Obviously the makers of this entry had lost the feel of the original Dashiell Hammett characters and, with the death of director W. S. Van Dyke, who had helmed the first four series features, The Thin Man seemed almost lost at sea. It no longer seemed the leading example of the sophisticated, amusing murder mystery that its original audiences had come to expect.

Nick Charles (William Powell), wife Nora (Myrna Loy) and small son Nick, Jr. (Dickie Hall) return to Nick's parents' Sycamore Springs home for a visit. Nick's father and mother, Dr. (Harry Davenport) and Mrs. Charles (Lucile Watson), are still somewhat unhappy that their "boy" did not follow his father's footsteps into the medical profession instead of becoming an amateur sleuth, a professional drinker, and the custodian of his wife's wealth. Nick's detective abilities take hold, however, when he is forced to take the case of an artist murdered at his parents' home. He receives little help from the exasperated local police chief (Donald MacBride). Nick uncovers the fact that spies are sequestered at the local weapons manufacturing plant and are using fifth-column methods to hurt production. Nick and Nora round up the espionage agents and the killer.

THE THIN MAN GOES HOME is not without interest, but generally it appears limp and the repartee between Nick and Nora is no longer zestful. The plot itself is housed in scores of other wartime detective films and, outside of the novelty of giving Nick a hometown to return to, the aura is like having the Charles clan slumming in Andy Hardy's Carvel, U.S.A. Worse followed, however, three years later, when the series ended with SONG OF THE THIN MAN, *q.v.*

THE THIRTEENTH GUEST (Monogram, 1932) 69 minutes.

Producer, M. H. Hoffman; director, Albert Ray; based on the novel by Armitage Trail; adaptors, Francis Hyland, Arthur Hoerl; dialogue, Trail; art director, Gene Hornbostel; assistant director, Gene Anderson; camera, Harry Neumann, Tom Galligan; editor, Lester Brown.

Ginger Rogers (Marie Morgan/Lela); Lyle Talbot (Phil Winston); J. Farrell MacDonald (Captain Ryan); James Eagles (Harold "Bud" Morgan); Eddie Phillips (Thor Jensen); Erville Alderson (John Adams); Robert Klein (John Barksdale); Crauford Kent (Dr. Sherwood); Frances Rich (Marjorie Thornton); Ethel Wales (Aunt Joan

Stanley "Tiny" Sandford, James Eagles and Eddie Phillips in THE THIRTEENTH
GUEST (1932).

Thornton); Paul Hurst (Detective Grump); William Davidson (Captain Brown); Phillips Smalley (Uncle Dick Thornton); Harry Tenbrook (Cabby); John Ince (John Morgan); Allan Cavan (Uncle Wayne Seymour); Alan Bridge (Policeman); Tom London (Detective Carter); Henry Hall (Sergeant—Jailer); Stanley "Tiny" Sandford (Mike, the Jailer); Kit Guard, Lynton Brent (Prisoners); Adrienne Dore (Winston's Date); Charles Meacham (Marie's Father); Isobel LeMall (Marie's Mother); Robert Klein (Attorney John Barksdale); Bobby Burns (Photographer).

Pretty Marie Morgan (Ginger Rogers) returns to her family home on her twenty-first birthday to learn the secret of her inheritance, her father having died there at a dinner party thirteen years earlier. She disappears and her cab driver calls in police Captain Ryan (J. Farrell MacDonald) and his inept associate, Detective Grump (Paul Hurst). Ryan sends for private detective Phil Winston (Lyle Talbot), who arrives at the house to find the girl dead, apparently by electrocution. The family lawyer, John Barksdale (Robert Klein), is suspected of the crime since he had the electricity turned back on in the vacant house. The lawyer, however, dies by the identical method the next night in the same house, and Marie reappears. It is obvious that an impersonator of the girl was killed in her stead, and Winston questions Marie and six surviving guests of the thirteen-year-old dinner party. All of the suspects are jailed, yet the one missing relative (Allan Cavan) is later found murdered in the house. The suspects are released and Marie receives a call which leads her back to the old house; there she is abducted by a mysterious, cloaked figure. In a cellar below the house the phantom forces Marie to provide him with the combination to a safe. Soon thereafter, Winston and Ryan capture the fiend. The safe discloses over $1,000,000, which goes to Marie, and she and Winston begin a romance.

Ginger Rogers earned her first starring role in THE THIRTEENTH GUEST, although she does not often appear in the middle portion of the film. (The bulk of the action is in the capable hands of Lyle Talbot as the detective and J. Farrell MacDonald as the crusty police chief.) Paul Hurst is especially effective as the befuddled and incompetent police detective. The film derived from a work by Armitage Trail, the author of *Scarface*. George E. Turner and Michael H. Price detailed in *Forgotten Horrors* (1979), "In the original screen interpretation, the exterior of the old house is real, and the Pathé interiors were properly weird. The hooded killer, who could have stepped from the cover of one of the era's pulp mystery magazines, seems part of the setting. The murderer's devilish methods are presented so graphically that the scenes of electrocution would not have passed the stronger censorship regulations instituted in 1934."

THE THIRTEENTH GUEST was so successful that producer M. H. Hoffman followed it up with A SHRIEK IN THE NIGHT (1933), which reteamed Ginger Rogers and Lyle Talbot as two reporters on the trail of a revenge killer. While Ginger is nearly electrocuted in the first film, in the second she is almost tossed into a fiery furnace.

In 1943 Monogram Pictures remade THE THIRTEENTH GUEST as MYSTERY OF THE THIRTEENTH GUEST, *q.v.*, with Helen Parrish and Dick Purcell taking over the lead roles. Don Miller opined in *B Movies* (1973), ". . . While considerably less adept in production dress, the shoddy sets bespeaking of wartime necessity, the remake was . . . in some ways an improvement. Tim Ryan and Charles Marion had updated the old script, with Ryan and Frank Faylen doing a comedy-cop act. William Beaudine's direction . . .

caught much of the eerie suspense of Albert Ray's original work. Even Edward Kay's background score was unusually effective, purloined as it was from Kay's music from a previous horror thriller, REVENGE OF THE ZOMBIES."

THE THIRTEENTH HOUR (Metro-Goldwyn-Mayer, 1927) 53 minutes.

Director, Chester M. Franklin; based on the play by Douglas Furber, Franklin; continuity, Edward T. Lowe, Jr.; titles, Wellyn Totman; sets, Eugene Hornbostel; camera, Maximilian Fabian; editor, Dan Sharits.

Lionel Barrymore (Professor Leroy); Jacquelin Gadsdon (Mary Lyle); Charles Delaney (Matt Gray); Fred Kelsey (Detective Shaw); Polly Moran (Polly); Napoleon (The Dog).

THE THIRTEENTH HOUR (Columbia, 1947) 65 minutes.

Producer, Rudolph Flothow; director, William Clemens; story, Leslie Edgley; screenplay, Edward Bock, Raymond L. Schrock; art director, Hans Radon; set decorator, Albert Richard; music, Wilbur Hatch; music director, Mischa Bakaleinikoff; assistant director, Carter DeHaven; sound, Howard Fogette; camera, Vincent Farrar; editor, Dwight Caldwell.

Richard Dix (Steve Reynolds); Karen Morley (Eileen Blair); John Kellogg (Charlie Cook); Jim Bannon (Jerry Mason); Regis Toomey (Don Parker); Bernadene Hayes (Mabel Sawyer); Mark Dennis (Tommy); Anthony Warde (Ransford); Ernie Adams (McCabe); Cliff Clark (Captain Linfield); Jack Carrington (Stack); Nancy Saunders (Donna); Lillian Wells (Secretary); Michael Towne (Driver); Pat O'Malley, Frank O'Connor, Ralph Linn, Stanley Blystone (Detectives); Robert B. Williams (Berger); Robert Stevens [Kellard] (Man); George Lloyd (Waiter); Paul Campbell (Jimmy); Selmer Jackson (Judge); Charles Jordan (Bernie); Kernan Cripps (Cop); Eddy Parker (Trucker).

A killer with two missing fingers is terrorizing a city and is sought by detective Matt Gray (Charles Delaney) and his thickheaded associate Shaw (Fred Kelsey). They are joined by Matt's wonder dog, Napoleon (himself). A young woman, Mary Lyle (Jacquelin Gadsdon), takes a job as secretary to famous criminologist Professor Leroy (Lionel Barrymore), and soon finds out that he is the mad killer. Leroy imprisons Mary but she gets a message to Matt and he, along with Shaw and Napoleon, come to her rescue. In a fight with the dog, the madman falls to his death from a roof top.

Chester Franklin directed this fast-paced silent thriller, based on his stage play, and it proved to be an entertaining, atmospheric barn burner, much in the tradition of the old Pearl White chapterplays. William K. Everson wrote in *The Detective in Film* (1972), "Right away, THE THIRTEENTH HOUR gives evidence of real style, with elaborate camera angles, the use of zoom and slow motion effects, and above all the promise of a complex and bizarre mystery—all within the first reel. The title derives from the killer's consistent habit of committing his crimes at one in the morning. . . . The film provides colorful action all the way, rather like a crossing of Buster Keaton's THE HAUNTED HOUSE with one of the best silent serials." At the time of its release, *Photoplay* magazine noted, "In spite of trap doors, secret panels, and underground passages, Napoleon, the crafty canine, outsmarts the villains."

Two decades after the MGM silent feature was issued, Columbia used the title THE THIRTEENTH HOUR for its seventh entry in the popular The Whistler series starring Richard Dix. It proved to be Dix's last film, as he died two years later at the age of fifty-five. In it Dix is Steve Reynolds, the head of a trucking company who, during a run, makes a stop to see his girlfriend, cafe owner Eileen Blair (Karen Morley), and they have a drink together. Continuing the trip he gets into a road accident which is not his fault, but because he has been drinking his license is suspended for six months. During that time he tries a clandestine run and when he is a attacked by a mysterious man, a policeman named Don Parker (Regis Toomey) is killed and Reynolds is blamed for the homicide, especially since the law enforcer was vying with Reynolds for Eileen's affections. Afraid of arrest, Reynolds hides out at the home of his mechanic friend Charlie Cook (John Kellogg). His friend is now a night watchman for competing trucker Jerry Mason (Jim Bannon), who had tried to buy out Reynolds. Cook tells Reynolds that the killer is hiding out at Mason's garage, but when Reynolds arrives, he finds Mason murdered and Cook knocked out. A cache of diamonds is found by Eileen in a glove Reynolds found at the site of the wreck in which the cop died. Reynolds suspects that Eileen's new waitress, Mabel Sawyer (Bernadene Hayes), is involved in the heist and he and Cook go to see her. Soon the amateur detective reaches the solution to the mystery.

Columbia's THE THIRTEENTH HOUR, only seventeen days in production, was tossed out into the overcrowded double-bill market so quickly that it received scant critical comment.

THREE ON A TICKET (Producers Releasing Corp., 1947) 62 minutes.

Producer, Sigmund Neufeld; director, Sam Newfield; based on the character created by Brett Halliday [Davis Dresser]; screenplay,

Hugh Beaumont and Cheryl Walker in THREE ON A TICKET (1947).

Fred Myton; set decorator, Elias H. Reif; music, Emil Cadkin; music director, Dick Carruth; assistant director, Stanley Neufeld; sound, John Carter; camera, Jack Greenhalgh; editor, Holbrook N. Todd.

Hugh Beaumont (Michael Shayne); Cheryl Walker (Phyllis Hamilton); Paul Bryar (Tim Rourke); Ralph Dunn (Pete Rafferty); Louise Currie (Helen Brinstead); Gavin Gordon (Pearson); Charles Quigley (Kurt Leroy); Douglas Fowley (Marc Morgan); Noel Cravat (Trigger); Charles King, Sr. (Drunk); Brooks Benedict (Jim Lacy).

During the 1946-47 movie season Producers Releasing Corporation (PRC) issued five programmers based on the adventures of fictional detective Michael Shayne, whom Lloyd Nolan had played so jauntily in seven quickie films for Twentieth Century-Fox from 1940 to 1942. Here Hugh Beaumont (who later gained fame as Ward Cleaver on TV's "Leave It to Beaver") essayed the role of the tough sleuth, although he tended to smooth off the gumshoe's rough edges and give him a little more stalwart charm than had author Brett

Halliday [Davis Dresser]. While no world beaters, the quintet of Shayne budget films was more than adequate in both the action and detection departments. All but the final film in the series were produced by Sigmund Neufeld and directed by his brother, Sam Newfield. Very attractive Cheryl Walker played the role of Shayne's secretary/girlfriend in three of the films.

A fellow gumshoe drops dead in Michael Shayne's (Hugh Beaumont) office and on the corpse Shayne finds a baggage check. A gang of crooks is after the ticket, as are the police, the FBI and a pretty young woman (Louise Currie), whose husband (Douglas Fowley) is an escaped convict and wants her to fraternize with a wealthy suitor. The crooks kidnap Shayne's secretary, Phyllis Hamilton (Cheryl Walker), and when he attempts to rescue her the detective is dry-gulched by the thugs. Finally Shayne learns from the unfriendly police that the suitcase to which the baggage ticket belongs contains secret documents sought after by spies. Shayne rescues Phyllis and unravels the mystery.

The Film Daily tradepaper opined of this entry, "Okay Michael Shayne number effectively played by [Hugh] Beaumont . . . it all adds up to make sense." Shot in twelve days, THREE ON A TICKET was preceded by MURDER IS MY BUSINESS (1946), LARCENY IN HER HEART (1946), *q.v.*, and BLONDE FOR A DAY (1946). It was followed by TOO MANY WINNERS (1947), which ended the brief but engaging series.

TIME OUT FOR MURDER (Twentieth Century-Fox, 1938) 60 minutes.

Producer, Sol M. Wurtzel; associate producer, Howard J. Green; director, H. Bruce Humberstone; based on the story "Meridian 7-1212" by Irving Reis; screenplay, Jerry Cady; music director, Samuel Kaylin; camera, Virgil Miller; editor, Jack Murray.

Gloria Stuart (Margie Ross); Michael Whalen (Barney Callahan); Chick Chandler (Snapper Doolan); Douglas Fowley (Dutch Moran); Robert Kellard (Johnny Martin); Jane Darwell (Polly); Jean Rogers (Helen Thomas); June Gale (Muriel); Ruth Hussey (Peggy Norton): Cliff Clark (Captain Collins); Peter Lynn (Blackie); Edward Marr (Eddie); Lester Matthews (Phillip Gregory).

In 1938 Twentieth Century-Fox executive producer Sol M. Wurtzel began the Roving Reporters series, in which Barney Callahan (Michael Whalen) is a newspaper snoop who ferrets out murder mysteries with the aid of his photographer pal, Snapper Doolan (Chick Chandler). The first two in the economy series were helmed by H. Bruce Humberstone, who did several of the studio's Charlie Chan group, and who continued his expert work with this series.

One-time matinee idol Ricardo Cortez directed the third and last of the group in fine form. However, for some reason, the studio dropped the series in favor of the globe-trotting Camera Daredevils offering, which lasted for only two episodes.

TIME OUT FOR MURDER opened the series in the early fall of 1938 and in it ace reporter Barney Callahan (Michael Whalen) and photographer Snapper Doolan (Chick Chandler) arrive at the scene of the murder of a wealthy woman (Ruth Hussey). Police Captain Collins (Cliff Clark) jails a bank messenger, Johnny Martin (Robert Kellard), for the crime. Callahan, however, is skeptical and investigates the murder himself, and the trail leads to his acquaintance, gangster Dutch Moran (Douglas Fowley). Meanwhile, Callahan tries to dodge beautiful bill collector Margie Ross (Gloria Stuart) despite the fact that he has a yen for her. Finally, Callahan realizes that a banker (Lester Matthews) is involved in the killing and this leads him to solution of the case. Having one-upped the police, Callahan is now free to pursue—and yet flee from—pretty Margie. *Variety* described the picture as "hokish, hilarious and highly melodramatic." The film was initially titled MERIDIAN 7-1212, then New York's telephone number for the correct time.

Late in 1938 the second series outing, WHILE NEW YORK SLEEPS, *q.v.*, was released. Here Barney Callahan (Michael Whalen) and Snapper Doolan (Chick Chandler) find themselves at the scene of an apparent suicide which the newshound quickly realizes is a murder. The trail takes them into a case which involves gangster Joe Marco (Harold Huber) and moll Nora Parker (Joan Woodbury) as Callahan carries on a romance with comely Judy King (Jean Rogers). While almost going to jail, Callahan solves the case by proving the murder is tied into a bond racket. *Variety* termed it ". . . a fast moving newspaper-murder mystery yarn."

INSIDE STORY, *q.v.*, issued in the spring of 1939, is the third and last entry in the series. Ricardo Cortez, making his directorial debut, took over the helming chores from H. Bruce Humberstone and continued the solid quality of the previous entries. This time out reporter Barney Callahan (Michael Whalen) and photographer Snapper Doolan (Chick Chandler) are involved in a gangland killing in a nightclub. They try to protect clip joint hostess June White (Jean Rogers), who has witnessed the rub-out and fears for her life. The chief suspect is gangster Gus Brawley (Douglas Fowley) but again it is the newshound who brings in the actual murderer and then looks forward to domestic bliss with attractive June. Regarding Cortez's direction, Don Miller wrote in *B Movies* (1973), "As a director, Cortez gave the same quality found in his screen performances—smooth, workmanlike, steady, eschewing flamboyance but making certain everything was in place, all details attended to in good order."

TIME TO KILL (Twentieth Century-Fox, 1942) 62 minutes. Producer, Sol M. Wurtzel; director, Herbert I. Leeds; based on the novel *The High Window* by Raymond Chandler and on a character created by Brett Halliday [Davis Dresser]; screenplay, Clarence Upson Young; art directors, Richard Day, Chester Gore; music, Emil Newman; camera, Charles Clarke; editor, Alfred Day.

Lloyd Nolan (Michael Shayne); Heather Angel (Merle); Doris Merrick (Linda Conquest); Ralph Byrd (Louis Venter); Richard Lane (Lieutenant Breeze); Morris Ankrum (Alex Morney); Sheila Bromley (Lois Morney); Ethel Griffies (Mrs. Murdock); James Seay (Leslie Murdock); Ted Hecht (Phillips); William Pawley (Hench); Syd Saylor (Postman); Lester Sharpe (Washburn); Charles Williams (Dental Assistant); LeRoy Mason (Headwaiter); Phyllis Kennedy (Edna); Paul Guilfoyle (Manager); Helen Flint (Marge); Bruce Wong (Houseboy).

In 1942 Twentieth Century-Fox purchased the screen rights to Raymond Chandler's recently published novel *The High Window*, a Philip Marlowe story, and promptly filmed it as the final entry in the studio's Michael Shayne series with Lloyd Nolan. Despite the change of names for the detective, the film remains fairly close to Chandler's work, although it is condensed somewhat to get it into a 62-minute time slot. Of the seven Shayne adventures Nolan performed in, TIME TO KILL is considered one of the best, if not the best, of the lot.

Tough private eye Michael Shayne (Lloyd Nolan) is hired by Mrs. Murdock (Ethel Griffies) to find a rare coin, the Brasher Doubloon, missing from her valuable coin collection. Shayne is attracted immediately to her secretary Merle (Heather Angel) and notices that the old woman's son, Leslie (James Seay), seems to have the same feelings. The trail leads Shayne to gangland kingpin Alex Morney (Morris Ankrum) and the police, led by Lieutenant Breeze (Richard Lane), become involved in the case when a murder occurs involving the coin. Finally Shayne learns that a photographer, Louis Venter (Ralph Byrd), has been blackmailing Mrs. Murdock and that the theft of the coin is really a dodge to lead him (Shayne) away from the blackmail angle. All this helps Shayne to solve the caper and to continue his pursuit of Merle's affections.

In *The Detective in Hollywood* (1978), Jon Tuska thought it Nolan's best Michael Shayne effort. "The film, directed by Herbert I. Leeds, is in every way superior to the later remake, THE BRASHER DOUBLOON [*q.v.*] wherein George Montgomery portrayed a colorless Philip Marlowe. The plot is better presented in TIME TO KILL. . . . The comedy is better than in any other Shayne entry, and the scenes, the characters, and the plot constitute the strongest in the series." Don Miller added in "Private Eyes" (*Focus on Film* magazine, Autumn 1975), ". . . Leeds again used little touches to add to the enjoyment. Example: as Shayne is about to take a case, a camera angle shows the soles of his shoes in dire need of repair as his feet are propped up on his desk while phoning. Later we see him in the same position, after being paid a retainer fee—with new shoes."

TONY ROME (Twentieth Century-Fox, 1967) Color 110 minutes.

Producer, Aaron Rosenberg; director, Gordon Douglas; based on the novel *Miami Mayhem* by Anthony Rome [Marvin H. Albert]; screenplay, Richard Breen; action sequence director, Buzz Henry; assistant director, Richard Lang; art directors, Jack Martin Smith, James Roth; set decorators, Water M. Scott, Warren Welch; music/music conductor, Billy May; songs: Lee Hazlewood, Randy Newman; costumes, Moss Mabry; makeup, Ben Nye; sound, Howard Warren, David Dockendorf; camera, Joseph Biroc; editor, Robert Simpson.

Frank Sinatra (Tony Rome); Jill St. John (Ann Archer); Richard Conte (Lieutenant Santini); Sue Lyon (Diana Pines); Gena Rowlands (Rita Kosterman); Simon Oakland (Rudolph Kosterman); Jeffrey Lynn (Adam Boyd); Lloyd Bochner (Rood); Robert J. Wilke (Ralph Turpin); Virginia Vincent (Sally); Joan Shawlee (Fat Candy); Richard Krisher (Donald Pines); Lloyd Gough (Langley); Babe Hart (Oscar); Templeton Fox (Mrs. Schuyler); Rocky Graziano (Packy); Elisabeth Fraser (Irma); Shecky Greene (Catleg); Jeanne Cooper (Lorna); Harry Davis (Ruyter); Stan Ross (Sam Boyd); Buzz Henry (Nimmo); Deanna Lund (Georgia McKay); Michael Romanoff (Maitre d'Hotel); Tiffany Bolling (Photo Girl).

In Miami, Florida, cynical private detective Tony Rome (Frank Sinatra) agrees, for a fee, to aid his ex-partner, Ralph Turpin (Robert J. Wilke), in removing drunk Diana Pines (Sue Lyon) from Turpin's motel. Rome takes the young girl to her father, wealthy construction businessman Rudolph Kosterman (Simon Oakland), who asks him to look into the girl's recent marriage to very middle-aged Adam Boyd (Jeffrey Lynn). At the same time Kosterman's wife Rita (Gene Rowlands), the girl's stepmother, offers Rome money to inform her first of his findings. Looking into the complex case Rome finds a jewelry theft from Diana's collection and is attacked and nearly killed. Later, he learns that Turpin has been murdered. Rome's lady friend, divorcee Anne Archer (Jill St. John), helps him find out that Diana has been paying money to her drunken mother Lorna, (Jeanne Cooper), and that the young woman's jewelry cache has been

Advertisement for TONY ROME (1967).

replaced by paste imitations. The case leads Rome into contact with several unsavory underworld types, and his pal, police Lieutenant Santini (Richard Conte), wants to know what Rome has discovered regarding the case. Kosterman is nearly killed and Rome discovers that Turpin was murdered by a man who had been blackmailing Rita because his divorce from her was never legal. The pieces all fit together and the case is concluded. By now, Anne decides to return to her ex-spouse.

Filmed on location in Miami, this fast-paced actioner gave Frank Sinatra one of his most popular 1960s film roles, that of tough detective Tony Rome. The film is based on Anthony Rome's [Marvin H . Albert] 1960 novel, *Miami Mayhem. The New York Times* reported, "Sinatra Bogart-style, in a hard-nosed mystery melodrama. . . . The backgrounds include various hotels, night clubs, hippie hangouts, and purlieus of crime. Our sleuth gets hit, kicked, cut up, shot at, betrayed and almost seduced. It's brassy, trashy, vulgar and Miami Beach colorful. And under the direction of Gordon Douglas, it also has speed, dexterity and a nice running patter of gags."

With the favorable box-office results from TONY ROME, Sinatra, director Gordon Douglas, and co-star Richard Conte reunited for a less felicitous follow-up, Twentieth Century-Fox's LADY IN CEMENT (1968), *q.v.*, which concluded this series.

THE TRAP (Monogram, 1947) 62 minutes.

Producer, James S. Burkett; director, Howard Bretherton; based on the character created by Earl Derr Biggers; screenplay, Miriam Kissinger; art director, David Milton; music director, Edward J. Kay; camera, James Brown; editor, Ace Herman.

Sidney Toler (Charlie Chan); Mantan Moreland (Birmingham Brown); Victor Sen Yung (Jimmy Chan); Tanis Chandler (Adelaide); Larry Blake (Rick Daniels); Kirk Alyn (Sergeant Reynolds); Rita Quigley (Clementine); Anne Nagel (Marcia); Helen Gerald (Ruby); Howard Negley (Cole King); Lois Austin (Mrs. Thorn); Barbara Jean Wong (San Toy); Minerva Urecal (Mrs. Weebles); Margaret Brayton (Madge Mudge); Bettie Best (Winifred); Jan Bryant (Lois); Walden Boyle (Doc Brandt).

"It's The Height of Fright! Gorgeous Showgirls doomed to death! Chan hunts the weirdest killer of his career!" extolled the advertising for THE TRAP, Sidney Toler's final Charlie Chan feature. Toler, who controlled the screen rights to the famous Earl Derr Biggers' character, had played the role since Monogram resurrected the series with CHARLIE CHAN IN THE SECRET SERVICE (1944), *q.v.*, and he had done nine more feature before making THE TRAP. This film was released early in 1947 and Toler died in February of that year. Monogram replaced him with Roland Winters for six more Chan features.

Jimmy Chan (Victor Sen Yung) is visiting his latest girlfriend, San Toy (Barbara Jean Wong), who is a member of a group of show girls staying at a Malibu beach resort run by Mrs. Thorn (Lois Austin). When one of the young women is found murdered on the beach, Jimmy masquerades as his father in an attempt to solve the case. However, Charlie Chan (Sidney Toler) arrives with chauffeur Birmingham Brown (Mantan Moreland) and takes over the investigation. He is aided by local policeman Sergeant Reynolds (Kirk Alyn). As Chan examines the situation another of the show girls is found murdered. In addition, another troupe member, who has a nasty disposition, disappears. Chan reveals the culprit, who dies in a car crash following a high-speed chase.

THE TRAP is a noteworthy film in several respects. From the point of view of its plot, it is somewhat similar to THE FALCON AND THE CO-EDS (1943), *q.v.*, and, like that picture, boasts a moody, *film noir*-type atmosphere about it. Some cinema writers have claimed that Sidney Toler was physically moribund in the feature but a viewing of the film shows that he was still agile in the role of Charlie Chan. As usual it is his performance which provides the abiding interest in the film, which itself is a flavorful mystery. British release title: MURDER AT MALIBU BEACH.

TRAVIS McGEE (ABC-TV, 5/18/83) Color 100 minutes.

Producer, George Eckstein; associate producer, Maria Padilla; director, Andrew V. McLaglen; based on the novel *The Empty Copper Sea* by John D. MacDonald; art director, Gary Lee; music, Jerrold Immel; camera, Jack Whitman; editor, Richard Bracken.

Sam Elliott (Travis McGee); Gene Evans (Meyer); Barry Corbin (Sheriff Hack Ames); Richard Farnsworth (Van Harder); Geoffrey Lewis (John Tuckerman); Amy Madigan (Billy Jean Bailey); Vera Miles (Julie Lawless); Katharine Ross (Gretel Howard); Marshall Teague (Nicky Noyes); Maggie Wellman (Mishy Burns); Walter Olkewicz (Bright Fletcher); and: Greta Blackburn, Pilar Del Rey, Mack Murdock, Owen Orr.

John MacDonald (1916-1986) wrote a score* of books on the adventures of unofficial private eye Travis McGee, and the world-weary character came to the big screen in 1970 in DARKER THAN AMBER, *q.v.*, with Rod Taylor as the detective. It was not a successful translation and it was not until 1983 that the well-regarded fictional character—a Florida-based boat-loving sleuth who specializes in recovering stolen property for half the proceeds—came to the small screen. This ABC-TV telefeature, TRAVIS McGEE, was a pilot for a projected series which did not sell in the demanding marketplace of the 1980s. The locale for this outing was altered to southern California.

Based on John MacDonald's *The Empty Copper Sea* (1978), the made-for-television film focuses on charter boat skipper Van Harder (Richard Farnsworth), who has been charged with wrecking his boat while drunk and causing the death of a wealthy real estate developer whose body has not been recovered. Van Harder's pal, private eye Travis McGee (Sam Elliott), comes to his aid. McGee

---

*John McDonald's Travis McGee novels are: *The Deep Blue Goodbye* (1964), *Nightmare in Pink* (1964), *A Purple Place for Dying* (1964), *The Quick Red Fox* (1964), *A Deadly Shade of Gold* (1965), *Bright Orange for the Shroud* (1965), *Darker Than Amber* (1966), *One Fearful Yellow Eye* (1966), *Pale Gray for Guilt* (1968), *The Girl in the Plain Brown Wrapper* (1968), *Dress Her in Indigo* (1969), *The Long Lavender Look* (1970), *A Tan and Sandy Silence* (1972), *The Scarlet Ruse* (1973), *The Turquoise Lament* (1973), *The Dreadful Lemon Sky* (1975), *The Empty Copper Sea* (1978), *The Green Ripper* (1979), *Free Fall in Crimson* (1981), *Cinnamon Skin* (1982), *The Lonely Silver Rain* (1985).

believes in the man's innocence and is assisted by his financial whiz friend Meyer (Gene Evans). Investigating the case, McGee comes to believe that Van Harder was not drunk but had been drugged, and that the so-called accident may have been staged and the victim's demise faked. The inquiry leads McGee successfully to the missing man's partner, John Tuckerman (Geoffrey Lewis), to a confrontation with the local sheriff, Hack Ames (Barry Corbin), and to a romantic interlude with Gretel Howard (Katharine Ross), before the successful wrap-up of the mystery.

Judith Crist (*TV Guide* magazine) was "delighted that this is a pilot" and further commented, ". . . Sam Elliott is just fine as the moody macho, introspective yachtsman-detective. . . . It's more California than McGee's Florida, but small matter. . . ."

TRENT'S LAST CASE (Walturdaw, 1920) 5,550'
Director, Richard Garrick; based on the novel by Edmund Clerihew Bentley; screenplay, P. L. Mannock.

Gregory Scott (Philip Trent); Pauline Peters (Mabel Manderson); Clive Brook (John Marlow); George Foley (Sigsbee Manderson); Cameron Carr (Inspector Murch); P. E. Hubbard (Nathaniel Cupples); Richard Norton (Martin).

TRENT'S LAST CASE (Fox, 1929) 6,834'
Presenter, William Fox; supervisor, Bertram Millhauser; director, Howard Hawks; based on the novel by Edmund Clerihew Bentley; adaptor, Beulah Marie Dix; screenplay, Scott Darling; titles, Malcolm S. Boylan; assistant director, E. D. Leshin; camera, Harold Rosson.

Donald Crisp (Sigsbee Manderson); Raymond Griffith (Philip Trent); Raymond Hatton (Joshua Cupples); Marceline Day (Evelyn Manderson); Lawrence Gray (Jack Marlowe); Nicholas Soussanin (Martin); Anita Garvin (Ottilie Dunois); Edgar Kennedy (Inspector Murch).

TRENT'S LAST CASE (Republic, 1952) 90 minutes.
Producer/director, Herbert Wilcox; based on the novel by Edmund Clerihew Bentley; screenplay, Pamela Bower; art director, William C. Andrews; music, Anthony Collins; camera, Max Greene; editor, Bill Lewthwaite.

Margaret Lockwood (Margaret Manderson); Michael Wilding (Philip Trent); Orson Welles (Sigsbee Manderson); John McCallum (John Marlowe); Miles Malleson (Burton Cupples); Hugh McDermott (Calvin C. Bunner); Sam Kydd (Inspector Murch); Jack McNaughton

(Martin); Henry Edwards (Coroner); Kenneth Williams (Horace Evans); Eileen Joyce (Pianist).

Edmund Clerihew Bentley's British detective, Philip Trent, was the subject of several novels, with *Trent's Last Case* (called *The Woman in Black* in the U.S.) being the initial novel in 1913. The book is dedicated to G. K. Chesterton, the author of the Father Brown books who in turn called Bentley's fiction, "The finest detective story of modern times." The Bentley work was filmed three times but none of the three features have captured successfully the flavor of the author's plot or title character.

TRENT'S LAST CASE first was filmed in Britain in 1920 by director Richard Garrick for Broadwest Films and it detailed how detective Philip Trent (Gregory Scott) puzzles out how a millionaire commits suicide and yet frames his secretary for the crime of murder. Howard Hawks directed the first sound-era version of the novel in 1929 for Fox, with Bertram Millhauser supervising the project which Scott Darling had adapted to the screen in both sound and silent versions. The plotline remained similar to the British effort, with a man (Donald Crisp) apparently murdered and a police inspector (Edgar Kennedy) questioning the suspects. They included the dead man's wife (Marceline Day) and his secretary (Lawrence Gray), who is in love with the widow. All the evidence points to the secretary having murdered his boss but detective Philip Trent (Raymond Griffith) proves otherwise. *Photoplay* magazine called it "A mystery story, treated like a farce. And very good, too." On the other hand, William K. Everson reported in *The Detective in Film* (1972), ". . . that tremendously subtle silent comedian Raymond Griffith literally had a voice defect and could speak only in quiet and hoarse tones; to have cast him as Detective Trent in TRENT'S LAST CASE seems the height of folly. . . ."

In 1952 Britisher Herbert Wilcox produced and directed still a third version of the novel, this time with Philip Trent (Michael Wilding) as a newspaper reporter who comes to believe that a financier's (Orson Welles) death was not suicide, as initially ruled by a jury, after he finds out that the man's wife (Margaret Lockwood) loves the deceased man's secretary (John McCallum). *Variety* said, "While the suspense is adroitly kept going and the climax has all the elements of surprise, the film suffers from an excess of wordage."

TRIAL WITHOUT JURY (Republic, 1950) 60 minutes.

Producer, Stephen Auer; director, Philip Ford; based on the story by Rose Simon Kohn; adaptor, Lawrence Goldman; screenplay, Albert De Mond; camera, John Macburnie; editor, Harold Minter.

Robert Rockwell (Lieutenant Bill Peters); Barbara Fuller (Corinne Hollister); Kent Taylor (Jed Kilgore); Audrey Long (Myra Peters); K. Elmo Lowe (John Webb); Stanley Waxman (Arthur Gentry); John Whitney (Riley Wentworth); Barbara Billingsley (Rheta Mulford); Ruthelma Stevens (Mrs. Mannings); William Grueneberg (Turner); Christine Larson (Bernice Andrews); James Craven (Producer); William Haade (Kennedy); Bill Baldwin (Ticket Seller); Theodore Von Eltz (Phillip Mannings); Sid Marion (Shuffalong); Dabbs Greer (Jack, the Police Radio Operator); Jack Larson (Tommy).

After playwright Jed Kilgore (Kent Taylor) argues with theatrical producer Phillip Mannings (Theodore Von Eltz) over turning down his new play, the producer is found murdered. Kilgore visits his girlfriend, publicist Myra Peters (Audrey Long), who suggests he rewrite the play to take advantage of the producer's demise. Myra's brother, police Lieutenant Bill Peters (Robert Rockwell), is handling the case and, knowing he will be a suspect, Kilgore goes along with Myra's suggestion. In the process he attempts to catch the killer and clear his own name. Mannings had many enemies, among whom were his wife (Ruthelma Stevens), his junior business partner, Rheta Mulford (Barbara Billingsley), a theatrical backer (James Craven) and actress Corinne Hollister (Barbara Fuller), whom Mannings was trying to romance. When the revised play debuts, it leads the guilty party into revealing his identity.

In THE CRIME THAT NOBODY SAW (1936), q.v., three playwrights use an actual murder as a basis for their own play and at the same time a device to catch the killer, TRIAL WITHOUT JURY uses the same premise. Produced by Republic, the film is a slick, fast-paced programmer, with Kent Taylor very professional as the sleuthing writer on the spot. Robert Rockwell is cast as the thick-headed police detective, while Dorothy Patrick is his sister and Taylor's girlfriend who becomes an accessory to protect him. The same year the acting trio headlined another Republic programmer, the gangster film, FEDERAL AGENT AT LARGE.

THE TRIUMPH OF SHERLOCK HOLMES (Olympic, 1935) 75 minutes.

Producer, Julius Hagen; director, Leslie S. Hiscott; based on the novel *The Valley of Fear* by Sir Arthur Conan Doyle; screenplay, H. Fowler Mear, Cyril Twyford; camera, William Luff.

Arthur Wontner (Sherlock Holmes); Ian Fleming (Dr. John H. Watson); Lyn Harding (Professor Moriarty); Leslie Perrins (John Douglas); Jane Carr (Ettie Douglas); Charles Mortimer (Inspector Lestrade); Roy Emerton (Boss McGinty); Wilfred Caithness (Colonel Sebastian Moran); Charles Mortimer (Inspector Lestrade); Minnie

Rayner (Mrs. Hudson); Conway Dixon (Ames); Edmund D'Alby (Captain Marvin); Ernest Lynds (Jacob Shafter); Ben Welden (Ted Balding).

"The unquestioned best of all the five Arthur Wontner films in the Sherlockian saga, TRIUMPH was a close and reverential adaptation of the Conan Doyle novel which that Grand master of the mystery, John Dickson Carr, considered among the five best detective novels of all time: *The Valley of Fear*. THE TRIUMPH OF SHERLOCK HOLMES reproduces all the major incidents of the book so lovingly and so closely, it rivals even the Basil Rathbone HOUND OF THE BASKERVILLES as the most faithful Holmesian derivation from the Conan Doyle source" (Chris Steinbrunner, Norman Michael, *The Films of Sherlock Holmes*, 1978).

Sherlock Holmes (Arthur Wontner) announces he has retired as a consulting detective and his arch enemy, Professor Moriarty (Lyn Harding), comes to 221B Baker Street to be sure that his nemesis is truly gone. American gangster Ted Balding (Ben Welden) hires Moriarty to get rid of another American who has arrived in England. Holmes, meanwhile, has moved to Sussex to raise bees. He is visited by Dr. Watson (Ian Fleming) and, at the same time, receives a missive telling hm that John Douglas (Leslie Perrins) of Birlstone Castle has been murdered and that Inspector Lestrade (Charles Mortimer) is baffled by the case. Holmes and Watson journey to the castle and Sherlock informs a scoffing Lestrade that Moriarty is behind the trouble. Holmes deduces that Douglas was a member of a secret organization and his widow (Jane Carr) recounts that, years before, in the coal fields of Pennsylvania, he had been a member of a gang called the Scowlers, although, in reality, he had been a strike-breaking Pinkerton agent who had infiltrated the gang. When his identity became known, he and his wife were forced to flee and change their names. Holmes realizes that Douglas is alive and in hiding and that the dead man—his face was blown away by a gun blast—was his intended assassin. Douglas is found hiding in a secret room in the castle and that night Holmes, Watson and Lestrade set a trap for Moriarty. As the latter tries to escape, he falls to his death from one of Birlstone's high towers.

THE TRIUMPH OF SHERLOCK HOLMES is a good retelling of *The Valley of Fear* (1915) and in its construction it is even more entertaining than the book original. Doyle wrote the novel in two parts: first Holmes solving the chase and then a retelling of the events leading up to the case. The title of the novel refers to the Pennsylvania coal mining area where the second part of the book is situated. In fact, the Scowlers was Doyle's thinly veiled reference to the Molly Maguires. In the Gaumont-British film, instead of telling the story in two parts, the film has the second part of the novel interpolated into the middle of the picture in a long flashback, making the movie more cohesive and easier to follow than the novel.

In terms of its production values, THE TRIUMPH OF SHERLOCK HOLMES is top-notch and Arthur Wontner, Ian Fleming and Lyn Harding are superb in their continuing roles as Holmes, Watson, and Moriarty. The 84-minute British release was cut by nine minutes when distributed in the U.S. and received rather lukewarm reviews stateside as in this example from *Variety*: "It is considerably too talky, yet, aside from a prolonged flash-back section of the story, it should please many fans who like baffling detective pix."

Like most Sherlock Holmes properties, *The Valley of Fear* had more than one filming, the initial effort coming in 1916 with the British production of THE VALLEY OF FEAR starring H. A. Saintsbury as Holmes. Like the 1935 remake, this first version of Doyle's final Sherlock Holmes story faithfully followed its literary source. Unfortunately, a third screen rendition of the book, the West German-French-Italian co-production, SHERLOCK HOLMES AND THE DEADLY NECKLACE, starring Christopher Lee (Holmes), Thorley Walters (Dr. Watson), and Hans Sohnker (Moriarty), although allegedly based on the novel, had nothing whatsoever to do with its plot. In 1968 Nando Gazzolo played Holmes in an Italian television version of THE VALLEY OF FEAR, and in 1984 Peter O'Toole was the voice of Holmes in the 49-minute animated featurette, SHERLOCK HOLMES AND THE VALLEY OF FEAR.

TOUGH GUYS DON'T DANCE (Cannon, 1987) Color 108 minutes.

Executive producers, Francis Coppola, Tom Luddy; producers Menahem Golan, Yoram Globus; director, Norman Mailer, based on the novel by Mailer; screenplay, Mailer; production designer, Armin Ganz; set decorator, Gretchen Rau; costumes, Michael Kaplan; music, Angelo Badalamenti; camera, John Bailey; editor, Debra McDermott.

Ryan O'Neal (Tim Madden); Isabella Rossellini (Madeline); Debra Sandlund (Patty Lareine); Wings Hauser (Regency); John Bedford Lloyd (Wardley Meeks III); Clarence Williams III (Bolo); Lawrence Tierney (Doug Madden); Penn Jillette (Big Stoop); Frances Fisher (Jessica Pond); R. Patrick Sullivan (Lonny Pangborn); Stephen Morrow (Stoodie); John Snyder (Spider).

Brilliant but extremely iconoclastic Norman Mailer wrote the novel from which this offbeat feature was made; he also adapted it to the screen and made his directorial debut with the picture. The venture was lensed in Provincetown, Massachusetts, and is high-lighted by John Bailey's superior cinematography.

Ex-convict and former bartender, and now a fledgling writer, Tim Madden (Ryan O'Neal) awakens with a violent hangover and a new tattoo. He is at home in the house he once shared with his estranged wife, Patty Lareine (Debra Sandlund). Madden soon realizes that there was a murder near his auto the night before and, searching through his drug stash in the woods, he finds a severed head, which may belong to his ex-wife *or* to the woman he had picked up the night before. Madden finds himself involved in five murders and two suicides. The victims include southerner Patty Lareine, who had wanted him to murder her first husband, Wardley Meeks III (John Bedford Lloyd), Madden's one-time Exeter class-mate for whose family Madden had once worked as a chauffeur. Meeks is found murdered too, and also killed is the town's drunken assistant police chief Regency, (Wings Hauser). The only people Madden can turn to are his tough, cancer-dying father Doug (Lawrence Tierney), and his girlfriend Madeline (Isabella Rossellini), unhappily married to Regency.

Vincent Canby (*New York Times*) wrote that the film was ". . . Norman Mailer's Cape Cod film noir . . . no matter how hard Mr. Mailer tries, [the film] never seems more dangerous than a picturesque seafood restaurant that sells day-old lobsters." *Daily Variety* opined, "Norman Mailer's TOUGH GUYS DON'T DANCE is like a *film noir* thriller turned in as a film-school assignment by a very gifted student. He knows all the moves but it just doesn't have any heart. TOUGH GUYS is part parody and part serious with a nasty streak running right down the middle . . . it's certain to leave audiences cold." It did, and died a quick box-office death.

THE UNDERCOVER WOMAN (Republic, 1946) 56 minutes.

Producer, Herbert J. Yates; associate producer, Rudolph E. Abel; director, Thomas Carr; based on the story by Sylvia G. L. Dannett; adaptor, Robert Metzler; screenplay, Jerry Sackhelm, Sherman I. Lowe; art director, Hilyard Brown; set decorators, John McCarthy, Jr., Charles Thompson; costumes, Adele Palmer; music director, Richard Cherwin; sound, Bill Clark; special effects, How-ard Lydecker, Theodore Lydecker; camera, Bud Thackery; editor, Fred Allen.

Stephanie Bachelor (Marcia Conroy); Robert Livingston (Sher-iff Don Long); Richard Fraser (Gregory Vixon); Isabel Withers (Penny Davis); Helene Heigh (Laura Vixon); Edythe Elliott (Mrs. Grey); John Dehner (Walter Hughes); Elaine Lange (Juanita Gillette);

Betty Blythe (Cissy Van Horn); Tom London (Lem Stone); Larry Blake (Simon Gillette).

During the 1940s Republic Pictures produced several supporting features in the detective genre, and two of these featured female sleuths. THE UNDERCOVER WOMAN in 1946, the best of the two, was followed the next year by EXPOSED, *q.v.*

Beautiful private eye Marcia Conroy (Stephanie Bachelor) is hired by a woman (Elaine Lange) to get evidence on her two-timing husband (Larry Blake) for a pending divorce. The trail leads Marcia to a dude ranch where she becomes entangled romantically with the local sheriff, Don Long (Robert Livingston). During the investigation, the husband is killed and Marcia and Sheriff Long try to find the killer. Several of the guests have prime motives. Marcia and the sheriff receive minor aid from Marcia's assistant, Cissy Van Horn (Betty Blythe), and local newspaperman Walter Hughes (John Dehner). After the guilty party is apprehended, Marcia and Long are free to carry on their romance.

Variety commented, "Snappy dialog helps this mystery dualer to please. A modestly budgeted whodunit, UNDERCOVER WOMAN subordinates plot aspects to bright gags and laughable situations. Mystery elements, however, provide a neat framework for the production, heightening the chuckles with well-sustained suspense." Stephanie Bachelor is engaging as the comely detective and cowboy star Robert Livingston is an old hand at such "western" settings. Silent film star Betty Blythe offers good support as the detective's none-too-brave helper.

THE UNHOLY NIGHT (Metro-Goldwyn, Mayer, 1929) 92 minutes.

Director, Lionel Barrymore; based on the story "The Green Ghost" by Ben Hecht; adaptor, Dorothy Farnum; screenplay, Edwin Justus Mayer; titles, Joe Farnham; art director, Cedric Gibbons; gowns, Adrian; sound, Paul Neal, Douglas Shearer; camera, Ira Morgan; editor, Grant Whytock.

At Lord Montague's Home: Ernest Torrence (Dr. Ballou); Roland Young (Lord Montague); Dorothy Sebastian (Lady Efra); Natalie Moorhead (Lady Vi); Sidney Jarvis (Butler); Polly Moran (Maid); George Cooper (Orderly); Sojin (Mystic); Boris Karloff (Abdoul); *At Scotland Yard:* Claude Fleming (Sir James Ramsey); Clarence Geldert (Inspector Lewis); *At The Regiment:* John Miljan (Major Mallory); Richard Tucker (Colonel Davidson); John Loder (Captain Dorchester); Philip Strange (Lieutenant Williams); John Roche (Lieutenant Savor); Lionel Belmore (Major Endicott); Gerald Barry (Captain Bradley); Richard Travers (Major McDougal).

When four members of an English regiment die in similar ways, detective Sir James Ramsey (Claude Fleming) investigates and asks all the regiment survivors to meet with him at the home of Lord Montague (Roland Young). Among those arriving are Lady Efra (Dorothy Sebastian), whose late father, the Marquis of Cavendar, was dismissed from the regiment for misconduct. Lady Efra brings her father's will, which gives her and the survivors his fortune, with the men designated as her guardians, thus making the men he hated fight over the money and the young woman. All of the regiment members are suspected of the murders but Ramsey has a mystic (Sojin) perform a seance, during which, he uncovers the culprits.

Lionel Barrymore directed this early talkie from a story, "The Green Ghost," by Ben Hecht. *Photoplay* magazine opined, "Swell mystery story, artistically directed by Lionel Barrymore. Roland Young and Dorothy Sebastian are great." The film is well executed, with an eerie ambiance and an impeccable cast, even to the smallest roles, such as Boris Karloff as the mysterious Montague family servant, Abdoul, and Polly Moran as their skittish maid. When the film was issued in England in late 1929, *Bioscope* wrote, "The power and fascination of this picture is undeniable. The weirdly beautiful pictures of fogbound London, official announcements of tragedies, warnings to the populace, glimpses of assaults, screams, groans and pursuits, must make the hearts of many spectators knock at their ribs. The cast is a strong one. . . . Every performer speaks with remarkable distinctness."

The film was shot under the working title, THE GREEN GHOST, and a French-language version was issued in 1930 under that title in that country; in that version silent film star Jetta Goudal played Lady Efra. The French film, titled LE SPECTRE VERT, was directed by Jacques Feyder; Georges Renavent and Andre Luguet co-starred. The title refers to a legend about men dying of a disease—which allegedly plagues the regiment members—and turning green.

UNMASKED (Weiss Bros./Artclass, 1929) 5,559'

Producer, Louis Weiss; director, Edgar Lewis; story, Arthur B. Reeve; screenplay, Albert Cowles; dialogue, Bert Ennis, Edward Clark; camera, Thomas Malloy, Buddy Harris, Irving Browning; editor, Martin G. Cohn.

Robert Warwick (Craig Kennedy); Milton Krims (Prince Hamid); Sam Ash (Billy Mathews); Charles Slattery (Inspector Collins); Susan Conroy (Mary Wayne); Lyons Wickland (Larry Jamieson); William Corbett (Franklin Ward); Roy Byron (Cafferty); Marie Burke (Mrs. Brookfield); Kate Roemer (Madam Ramon); Helen

Mitchell (Mrs. Ward); Waldo Edwards (Gordon Hayes); Clyde Dillison (Imposter).

Arthur B. Reeve's scientific detective, Craig Kennedy, America's answer to Sherlock Holmes, was popular in literature from 1915 to the early thirties. Like Holmes, Kennedy had his "Watson" in the person of Walter Jameson (here called Larry Jamieson), a newspaper reporter. Kennedy was the hero of such silent cliffhangers as THE EXPLOITS OF ELAINE (1914), THE NEW EXPLOITS OF ELAINE (1915), THE ROMANCE OF ELAINE (1915), THE CARTER CASE (1919), and THE RADIO DETECTIVE (1926), before making his sound debut in this New York City-lensed feature, written by the author and based on one of his short stories.

At a fashionable party hosted by Mrs. Brookfield (Marie Burke), detective Craig Kennedy (Robert Warwick) and his associate, Jamieson (Lyons Wickland), are guests and Kennedy intends to spring a trap on East Indian mystic Prince Hamid (Milton Krims), who is present incognito. To entertain the guests, Kennedy explains how he foiled Hamid's fake seance in which the mystic tried to call Franklin Ward's (William Corbett) wife from the dead and how he also exposed the murderer of Ward's wife (Helen Mitchell). He relates how he proved that Mary Wayne (Susan Conroy) administered poison to the woman while under the hypnotic spell of Hamid. The young woman is now Kennedy's fiancée. Following his accounts, Kennedy unmasks Hamid as one of the party guests.

George E. Turner and Michael H. Price in *Forgotten Horrors* (1979) wrote, "The first feature to deal with Kennedy toned down the action and concentrated on mystery, romance, and an abundance of dialogue. UNMASKED, as such, moves slowly in comparison with the frantic pacing of the serials, although it is not so unimaginative as some other early talkies. The deadening effect of long takes and much dialogue is lessened by the film's construction, unusual for the time, which embraces a long flashback resolved only after a return to the framing story."

Craig Kennedy resumed his screen career in 1936 in the serial, THE CLUTCHING HAND, with Jack Mulhall as Kennedy. In 1954 Donald Woods essayed the part in the syndicated TV series, "Craig Kennedy, Criminologist."

A VERY MISSING PERSON (ABC-TV, 3/4/72) Color 78 minutes.

Executive producer, Richard Irving; producer, Edward J. Montagne; director, Russ Mayberry; based on the novel *Hildegarde Withers Makes the Scene* by Stuart Palmer, Fletcher Flora; teleplay,

Philip Reisman, Jr.; music, Vic Mizzy; art director, William H. Tuntke; costumes, Grady Hunt; camera, William Margulies; editor Richard M. Sprague.

Eve Arden (Hildegarde Martha Withers); James Gregory (Inspector Oscar Piper); Julie Newmar (Aletha Westering); Ray Danton (Captain Westering); Skye Aubrey (Sister Isobel/Leonore Gregory); Dennis Rucker (Al Fister); Robert Easton (Onofre); Woodrow Parfrey (Eberhardt); Bob Hastings (James Malloy); Pat Morita (Delmar Faulkenstein); Ezra Stone (Judge); Linda Gillin (Bernadine Toller); Dwan Smith (Ora); Peter Morrison Jacobs (Dr. Singer); Savannah Bentley (Mrs. Singer); Udana Power (Mariette).

Hildegarde Withers, the old maid school teacher/detective was the creation of Stuart Palmer (1905-1968) who wrote a dozen novels about her exploits between 1931 and 1954, plus many short stories, and also involved her with Craig Rice's John J. Malone in several short stories. Before his death in 1968 Palmer commenced another Miss Withers' book but died before it was completed; Fletcher Flora finished it and the result was the 1969 novel, *Hildegarde Withers Makes the Scene.* That book served as the basis for the 1972 TV movie, A VERY MISSING PERSON (filmed as HILDEGARDE WITHERS), starring Eve Arden in the title role in a pilot for an unsold series. James Gregory co-starred as Miss Withers' Gotham police rival and former boyfriend, Inspector Oscar Piper.

Filmed on location in New York City, the telefeature has Miss Hildegarde Withers (Eve Arden), who has a penchant for outlandish hats, retiring from her profession as a grammar school teacher. She becomes involved in the case of a missing heiress (Skye Aubrey) and attempts to find the young woman, much to the chagrin of police Inspector Oscar Piper (James Gregory), whom the schoolmarm has assisted on other cases. Finding little help from the police, Miss Withers enlists the aid of motorcyclist Al Fister (Dennis Rucker) and the two set out to find the young woman. They soon become embroiled in a murder. Eventually Miss Withers solves the complicated case.

Eve Arden is quite good as the spinster Miss Withers, although far too attractive for the part. (Edna May Oliver, who played the role in a trio of RKO films in the 1930s, was far closer to Palmer's description of the sleuth.) James Gregory is equally fine as Oscar Piper. However, they are let down by a dull and meandering script that is flavorless. "The story and the supporting cast aren't up to the star's level," reported *Movies on TV* (1981). *TV Movies and Video Guide* (1988) called it a ". . . standard detective thriller. . . . Another busted pilot. Average." Judith Crist, in *TV Guide to the Movies* (1976), complained that Miss Withers' fans ". . . will shudder at this inept updating thereof. . . . The plot . . . will barely satisfy even the least demanding mystery buff."

THE WAKEFIELD CASE (World Film, 1921) 6 reels.
Director, George Irving; story, Mrs. L. Case Russell; screenplay, Shannon Fife; camera, William S. Adams and/or Walter Young.
Herbert Rawlinson (Wakefield, Jr.); John P. Wade (Wakefield, Sr.); J. H. Gilmore (Gregg); Charles Dalton (Richard Krogan); Joseph Burke (James Krogan); Jerry Austin (Bryson); W. W. Black (Blaine); H. L. Dewey (Briggs); Florence Billings (Ruth Gregg [the Breen Girl]).

After his father (John P. Wade) is murdered mysteriously, playwright Wakefield, Jr. (Herbert Rawlinson) turns detective to bring in the culprits. He believes that they are two brothers (Charles Dalton, Joseph Burke) who have stolen four rubies from the British museum. The senior Wakefield nearly captured the two thieves before they murdered him and his son's only clue is a young woman known as the Breen Girl (Florence Billings) who is thought to be in cahoots with the men. Wakefield follows her from England to the U.S. and there he rounds up the crooks and finds out that the girl, with whom he has fallen in love, is really Ruth Gregg, a Secret Service agent working undercover to infiltrate the hoodlum gang.

William K. Everson in *The Detective in Film* (1971) notes that this silent feature shifted its ". . . emphasis from bona fide detecting to fast melodrama. It was well served, however, by the presence of Herbert Rawlinson as the detective hero . . . he looked good in a dressing gown, puffing at a pipe—obviously fulfilling all of the limited requirements for a silent era detective." Rawlinson, an early cinema matinee idol, later had the title role as the detective in the serial, BLAKE OF SCOTLAND YARD (1937), *q.v.*

THE WALLS CAME TUMBLING DOWN (Columbia, 1946) 82 minutes.
Producer, Albert J. Cohen; director, Lothar Mendes; based on the novel by Jo Eisinger; screenplay, Wilfrid H. Pettitt; art director, Stephen Goosson, A. Leslie Thomas; set decorator, Robert Priestley; music, Marlin Skiles; music director, Morris W. Stoloff; assistant director, Sam Nelson; sound, Jack Goodrich; camera, Charles Lawton, Jr.; editor, Gene Havlick.

Lee Bowman (Gilbert Archer); Marguerite Chapman (Patricia Foster); Edgar Buchanan (George Bradford); George Macready (Matthew Stoker); Lee Patrick (Susan); Jonathan Hale (Captain Griffin); J. Edward Bromberg (Ernest Heims); Elisabeth Risdon

(Catherine Walsh); Miles Mander (Dr. Marka); Moroni Olsen (Bishop Martin); Katherine Emery (Mrs. Stoker); Noel Cravat (Rausch); Bob Ryan (Detective Regan); Charles LaTorre (Bianca).

When a priest is found murdered, newspaper columnist Gilbert Archer (Lee Bowman) is drawn into the case by his association with pretty Patricia Foster (Marguerite Chapman). It appears the killing occurred during the disappearance of two collectible Bibles and may be connected with that disappearance. Archer finds out that crooks Matthew Stoker (George Macready) and Ernest Heims (J. Edward Bromberg) are also seeking the books because they contain a needed clue to the whereabouts of a valuable stolen painting. The newspaperman survives the caper's many twists and turns, finds the valuable objects and brings in the killer.

Although based on scripter Joe Eisinger's only novel (1943), THE WALLS CAME TUMBLING DOWN bears a heavy resemblance to THE MALTESE FALCON, *q.v.*, in both plot and charac-

Lee Bowman and Marguerite Chapman in THE WALLS CAME TUMBLING DOWN (1946).

terization. Here the elusive Black Bird becomes the two Bibles. The stories have several parallels: the newspaperman-turned-sleuth is named Gilbert Archer; in THE MALTESE FALCON Sam Spade's detective partner is Miles Archer. The villains Stoker and Heims are very similar in presentation to Joel Cairo and Caspar Gutman in THE MALTESE FALCON. And in a derivative casting ploy by Columbia Pictures, Lee Patrick here plays Archer's secretary, Susan (in the FALCON, of course, she was Effie Perrine, Spade's loyal office helper). Even the leading lady (Marguerite Chapman) of THE WALLS CAME TUMBLING DOWN is highly mysterious and her motives are not known until the film's end, à la Bridgett O'Shaugnessey in the Hammett work.

Despite its "relationship" to THE MALTESE FALCON, THE WALLS CAME TUMBLING DOWN is a solid low-budget detective yarn, steady of pace, nicely directed (it is Lothar Mendes' last directorial effort), and pleasantly entertaining. It is a detective movie that is unjustly forgotten.

THE WAYNE MURDER CASE   see   STRANGE ADVENTURE.

WHILE NEW YORK SLEEPS (Twentieth Century-Fox, 1938) 61 minutes.

Producer, Sol M. Wurtzel; director, H. Bruce Humberstone; story, Frank Fenton, Lynn Root; adaptors, Frances Hyland, Albert Ray; songs, Sidney Clare and Arthur Johnston; music director, Samuel Kaylin; choreography, Nicholas Castle, Geneva Sawyer; camera, Lucien Andriot; editor, Norman Colbert.

Michael Whalen (Barney Callahan); Jean Rogers (Judy King); Chick Chandler (Snapper Doolan); Robert Kellard (Malcolm Hunt); Joan Woodbury (Nora Parker); Harold Huber (Joe Marco); Marc Lawrence (Happy Nelson); Sidney Blackmer (Ralph Simmons); William Demarest (Red Miller); June Gale (Kitty); Cliff Clark (Inspector Cliff Collins); Edward Gargan (Sergeant White); Minor Watson (Charles MacFarland); Robert Middlemass (Sawyer).

See: TIME OUT FOR MURDER [essay].

WHILE THE PATIENT SLEPT (First National, 1935) 65 minutes.

Producer, Harry Joe Brown; director, Ray Enright; based on the novel by Mignon G. Eberhart; adaptors, Robert N. Lee, Eugene Solow, Brown Holmes; art director, Esdras Hartley; camera, Arthur Edeson; editor, Owen Marks.

Aline MacMahon (Sarah Keate); Guy Kibbee (Lance O'Leary); Lyle Talbot (Deke Lonergan); Patricia Ellis (March Federie); Allen Jenkins (Jackson); Robert Barrat (Adolphe Federie); Hobart

Aline MacMahon, Patricia Ellis and Brandon Hurst in WHILE THE PATIENT SLEPT (1935).

Cavanaugh (Eustace Federie); Dorothy Tree (Mittee Brown); Henry O'Neill (Elihu Dimuck); Russell Hicks (Dr. Jay); Helen Flint (Isobel Federie); Brandon Hurst (Grondal); Eddie Shubert (Muldoon); Walter Walker (Richard Federie).

Mignon Eberhart wrote a series of novels and stories centered around sleuthing nurse Sarah Keate and her compatriot Lance O'Leary. Miss Keate was a middle-aged woman, detective O'Leary was youngish, and Ms. Eberhart wrote about them between 1929 and 1954. In the mid-1930s Warner Bros. latched onto the literary property, probably in an attempt to rival RKO's popular Hildegarde Withers series. The result was five features—another was done by Twentieth Century-Fox—which were so convoluted that the nurse rarely had the same name in more than two features; also she was rarely portrayed as middle-aged and O'Leary was in only half the entries.

The initial Warners outing is WHILE THE PATIENT SLEPT,

from the 1930 novel of the same title. Aline MacMahon is nicely cast as Nurse Sarah Keate, while very middle-aged, and balding Guy Kibbee is seen as Lancy O'Leary. The film is one of five (BABBITT, 1934, being the most noted) in which the popular team of Aline MacMahon and Guy Kibbee starred for Warners at the time. WHILE THE PATIENT SLEPT finds a rich man in a coma with Nurse Keate (Aline MacMahon) in attendance as his wisecracking nurse and his greedy relatives flocking to his mansion. Eventually a murder takes place. Detective O'Leary (Guy Kibbee) and Miss Keate join forces to pin down the murderer and solve the case. Allen Jenkins is on hand as his usual dumb cop and Patricia Ellis and Lyle Talbot are cast as the romantic interest. The *New York Times* called this March 1935 release "Quite unsatisfactory." It is interesting to note it was issued at the same time as Edna May Oliver's final Hildegarde Withers starrer, MURDER ON A HONEYMOON, *q.v.*, a far superior mystery movie.

Next came THE MURDER OF DR. HARRIGAN, *q.v.*, taken from the 1931 novel, *From This Dark Stairway,* issued early in 1936. For this outing top-billed Kay Linaker is seen as young nurse Sally Keating. She is in love with Dr. George Lambert (Ricardo Cortez). At the hospital where they work, its founder (Frank Reicher) is about to undergo surgery when Dr. Harrigan (John Eldredge), the doctor who is scheduled to perform the operation, dies suddenly. The head man disappears and it is proved Harrigan has been murdered. Police Lieutenant Lamb (Joseph Crehan) investigates the case but, after an attempt is made on Sally's life, it is Dr. Lambert who ferrets out the killer. He finds out that the hospital's founder is alive. He had escaped being murdered by going to the morgue as a presumed corpse while Harrigan was murdered by a rival who thought he had stolen the formula for a new anesthetic from him. Another nurse (Mary Astor) had helped to conceal his identity. *Variety* dubbed the film, "A murder mystery that's too routine to inspire more than casual audience interest. . . . Most of the action, as usual, surrounds efforts of police to pin guilt upon a flock of persons after a lot of humdrum questioning. As usual, also, everyone looks suspicious except the cops."

Early in the summer of 1936, the third film in the series, MURDER BY AN ARISTOCRAT, *q.v.*, based on the 1932 novel of the same title, was issued. Again the nurse heroine is dubbed Sally Keating. As with the previous installment, Lance O'Leary is deleted from the scenario. The case involves a person who blackmails five members of the same family and ends up murdered. Nurse Sally Keating (Marguerite Churchill) and her boyfriend Dr. Allen Carick

(Lyle Talbot) become entangled in the case and it is Nurse Keating who unearths the various clues and reveals the killer. *Variety* judged it "A routine mediocrity. . . . It's flimsy entertainment. It belongs to and will discredit First National's so-called 'Crime Club' series."

Warner Bros.-First National made no entries in the Nurse Keate series in 1937, but Mignon Eberhart's story "Dead Yesterday" was employed as the basis for Twentieth Century-Fox's THE GREAT HOSPITAL MYSTERY, *q.v.*, in which Jane Darwell played hospital head nurse Miss Keats. The plot revolves around a young man who witnesses a gangland execution and is then shot himself. He is taken to a hospital and placed under police protection. The hoodlums still plan to kill him since he can identify the killers. Unknown to them, however, the witness has died and a policeman has taken his place; the law hopes to capture the hit man when he arrives to carry out his assignment. Romance between a doctor (Thomas Beck) and a young nurse (Sally Blane) is a sub-theme, but the tedium is best aborted by the ongoing antics of angular Joan Davis as a bumbling novice nurse.

Warners returned to the Miss Keate property in 1938 with two final entries, both starring Ann Sheridan as Nurse Sara Keate and both resurrecting the character of Lance O'Leary. The first is THE PATIENT IN ROOM 18, *q.v.*, issued in April and taken from the 1929 novel of the same title—the first Miss Keate book. A man is murdered in a hospital by radium, with the valuable mineral also being stolen. A police inspector (Cliff Clark) investigates. Also in the hospital as a patient is detective Lance O'Leary (Patric Knowles), who has suffered a nervous breakdown after failing to solve a recent case. The murder gives him a second chance and, together with his nurse, Miss Keate (Ann Sheridan), he reveals the killer. The *New York Times* dubbed it, "A modest little mystery-comedy."

In June 1938 the final series entry, MYSTERY HOUSE, *q.v.*, was released. This dual-biller is based on Eberhart's 1930 novel, *The Mystery of Hunting's End,* the second Miss Keate book, and it finds Nurse Sara Keate (Ann Sheridan) and detective Lance O'Leary (Dick Purcell) investigating a killing in which more murders result from the investigation. MYSTERY HOUSE proved to be an inconspicuous end to a tame whodunit series.

THE WHISTLER (Columbia, 1944) 59 minutes.

Producer, Rudolph Flothow; director, William Castle; based on the radio series; story, J. Donald Wilson; screenplay, Eric Taylor; art director, George Van Marter; set decorator, Sidney Clifford; music, Wilbur Hatch; assistant director, Richard Monroe; sound, Hugh McDowell; camera, James S. Brown; editor, Jerome Thoms.

Richard Dix (Earl Conrad); J. Carrol Naish (The Killer); Gloria Stuart (Alice Walker); Alan Dinehart (Gorman); Don Costello (Lefty Vigran); Joan Woodbury (Toni Vigran); Cy Kendall (Bartender); Trevor Bardette (The Thief); Robert E. Keane (Charles McNear); Clancy Cooper (Briggs); George Lloyd (Bill Tomley); Byron Foulger (Flophouse Clerk); Charles Coleman (Jennings); Robert E. Homans (Dock Watchman); Otto Forrest (The Whistler).

"The Whistler" was a popular radio mystery series which debuted on CBS in 1942 with Bill Forman (later Marvin Miller and then Everett Clarke) in the title role of the voice of fate involved in the lives of unsuspecting people. In 1944 Columbia Pictures acquired the screen rights to the character and initiated a programmer series with THE WHISTLER, which was expertly directed by William Castle. Veteran screen leading man Richard Dix was signed to star in the property and was to portray different characters in each installment. Between 1944 and 1947 Dix starred in seven features in the series. Besides the initial outing, two others—THE MYSTERIOUS INTRUDER (1946) and THE THIRTEENTH HOUR (1947), qq.v.—use the detective motif.

Businessman Earl Conrad (Richard Dix) is distraught over the death of his wife and pays an assassin $5,000 to end his misery. The go-between, Lefty Vigran (Don Costello), finalizes the contract but is gunned down by the police soon thereafter, although the killer (J. Carrol Naish) is aware of his latest victim-to-be. Conrad, then discovers that his wife is not dead but a prisoner in a Japanese internment camp. With the new reason to live, he tries to stop his own execution. Not knowing who is assigned to murder him, Conrad becomes a detective to find the man, while the killer—always devising new methods to get rid of his victims—plans to scare his high-strung victim to death. Thanks to Conrad's loyal secretary, Alice Walker (Gloria Stuart), the killer's plan is foiled and her boss is saved. Otto Forrest is The Whistler, the narrator/background voice whose whistle diverts the hero from impending peril on several occasions.

Don Miller in *B Movies* (1973) noted that the plot " . . . was not novel then and has been further shopworn by frequent repetition through the years. . . ." He added, " . . . [Eric] Taylor's script was suspenseful and without wasted motion, and Castle heightened the tenseness with excellent economy of means while eliciting exemplary performances from Dix and J. Carrol Naish as his killer. . . . THE WHISTLER attracted more than the normal amount of attention from the trade-press reviewers and commanded several glowing critiques from various newspaper critics."

WHISTLING IN THE DARK (Metro-Goldwyn-Mayer, 1941) 76 minutes.

Producer, George Haight; director, S. Sylvan Simon; based on the play by Laurence Gross, Edward Childs Carpenter; screenplay, Robert MacGunigle, Harry Clark, Albert Mannheimer; art director, Cedric Gibbons; camera, Sidney Wagner; editor, Frank E. Hull.

Red Skelton (Wally Benton); Conrad Veidt (Joseph Jones); Ann Rutherford (Carol Lambert); Virginia Grey (Fran Post); Rags Ragland (Sylvester); Henry O'Neill (Philip Post); Eve Arden (Buzz Baker); Paul Stanton (Jennings); Don Douglas (Gordon Thomas); Don Costello (Noose Green); William Tannen (Robert Graves);

Virginia Grey and Red Skelton in WHISTLING IN THE DARK (1941).

Reed Hadley (Beau Smith); Mariska Aldrich (Hilda); Lloyd Corrigan (Upshaw); George Carleton (Commissioner O'Neill); Will Lee (Herman); Ruth Robinson (Mrs. Robinson); John Wald (Announcer's Voice); Ken Christy (Inspector); Betty Farrington (Mrs. Moriarity); Paul Ellis (Captain); Dora Clement (Mrs. Upshaw); James Adamson (Attendant); Inez Cooper (Stewardess); Emmett Vogan (Producer); Barbara Bedford (Local Operator); Lester Dorr (Dispatcher); Mark Daniels (Co-Pilot); Leon Tyler (Gerry); Mel Ruick (Engineer); Dorothy Adams (Mrs. Farrell); Jenny Mac (Mrs. Kendall); John Dilson (Vanderhoff); Billy Bletcher (Effects Man); Larry Steers (Studio Manager); Ronnie Rondell (Waiter); Brick Sullivan, Al Hill, Robert E. Homans (Policemen).

In 1933 MGM starred Ernest Truex as a radio announcer who wants to become a mystery writer and who ends up involved with gangsters in WHISTLING IN THE DARK (called SCARED on TV). Eight years later the project was revamped for Red Skelton's first starring film role and was again titled WHISTLING IN THE DARK. It has Skelton playing Wally Benton, alias The Fox, a radio sleuth who solves complicated crimes for his adoring listening audience. Gangster Joseph Jones (Conrad Veidt) kidnaps Benton, along with girlfriend Carol Lambert (Ann Rutherford) and Fran Post (Virginia Grey), the sponsor's daughter. The trio are taken to a remote locale where Benton is ordered to write the perfect murder of a man who stands in Jones' way of collecting one million dollars. Benton devises a plan, along with a poison to carry it out, and then he and the two women escape, trying to thwart Jones and his henchmen from carrying out the plan. Along the way they are aided by Benton's pal, Sylvester (Rags Ragland). Thanks to a radio receiving set attached to a telephone which is hooked up to Wally's broadcast, the radio detective brings about the downfall of the gangsters and stops the crime.

The whole show is Red Skelton, as noted by *Variety*: "His timing and delivery of laugh lines and situations—despite the familiar hoke injected—catches maximum audience reaction. The liberal doses of broad comedy concocted by the scripting trio [Robert MacGunigle, Harry Clark, Albert Mannheimer], and paced in lively fashion by direction of Sylvan Simon, are delivered in expert fashion by Skelton." As Doug McClelland analyzed in *The Golden Age of "B" Movies* (1978), "Among the principals, Skelton was funny and likable, vulnerable but not moronic (something that could not be said of many later roles), Rutherford was cute and spirited, Grey a delicate-looking, pretty girl who packed a long-shoreman's wallop with a quip, Arden a joy, and Veidt a perfect villain who did not take himself too seriously—led away by the authorities at the end, he uttered the cult's standard farewell, 'We part in radiant contentment.'"

WHISTLING IN THE DARK proved so successful that two unpretentious sequels followed, both also directed by S. Sylvan Simon. In WHISTLING IN DIXIE (1942), Wally Benton (Red Skelton) and his new bride Carol (Ann Rutherford) become entangled in a murder case while on their honeymoon in the deep South. WHISTLING IN BROOKLYN (1943) has Benton (Red Skelton) tied into a murder and trying to elude the law by pretending to be a member of the Brooklyn Dodgers baseball team.

Regarding the trio of films, Leonard Maltin wrote in *The Great Movie Comedians* (1978), "In retrospect, the WHISTLING films are among Skelton's best screen endeavors, not only because they showcase him so well, but because they are such unpretentious and spirited outings. They benefit from M-G-M gloss but they are not drowned in M-G-M over-production, and Skelton is not obliged to share his screen time with musical stars or production numbers."

WHO FRAMED ROGER RABBIT (Buena Vista, 1988) Color 103 minutes.

Executive producers, Steven Spielberg, Kathleen Kennedy; producers, Robert Watts, Frank Marshall; associate producers, Don Hahn, Steve Starkey; director, Robert Zemeckis; based on the novel *Who Censored Roger Rabbit?* (1982) by Gary K. Wolf; screenplay, Jeffrey Price, Peter S. Seaman; production designers, Elliott Scott, Roger Cain; costume designer, Joanna Johnston; music, Alan Silvestri; animation director, Richard Williams; animation supervisor, Wes Takahashi; chief visual effects editor, Bill Kimberlin; optical camera supervisor, Edward Jones; visual effects supervisor, Ken Ralston; visual effects coordinator, Suella Kennedy; mechanical effects supervisor, George Gibbs; camera, Dean Cundey; editor, Arthur Schmidt. *U. K production:* art director, Stephen Scott; set decorator, Peter Howitt; second unit directors, Ian Sharp, Frank Marshall; assistant director, Michael Murray; sound, Tony Dawe; *U.S. production:* art director, William McAllister; set decorator, Robert R. Benton; set designers, Roy Barnes, LynnAnn Christopher; second unit director, Max Kleven; assistant directors, Marty Ewing, David McGiffert; sound, Michael Evje; re-recording mixers, Robert Knudson, John Boyd, Don Digirolamo;

Bob Hoskins (Eddie Valiant); Christopher Lloyd (Judge Doom); Joanna Cassidy (Dolores); Stubby Kaye (Marvin Acme); Alan Tilvern (R. K. Maroon); Joel Silver (Raoul, the Producer); *voices of:* Charles Fleischer (Roger Rabbit, Benny the Cab, Others); Kathleen Turner (Jessica—Speaking); Amy Irving (Jessica—Singing); Lou Hirsch

Roger Rabbit and Bob Hoskins in WHO FRAMED ROGER RABBIT (1988).

(Baby Herman); Mel Blanc (Daffy Duck, Tweety Bird, Others); Mae Questel (Betty Boop).

One of the mega-box-office successes of the summer of 1988, WHO FRAMED ROGER RABBIT successfully sewed live action and animation into an entertaining unit which appealed to both children and adults. While it was hardly the first feature film to mesh the animation and live action genres (e.g., The Muppet movies), it was the first attempt to graft the two areas within the stylistic framework of the *film noir*. Based on Gary Wolf's novel *Who Censored Roger Rabbit?* (1982), the project had first seen the light of day in the early 1980s but it was not until Steven Spielberg's Amblin Productions joined with the Disney organization—the owner of the screen rights—on this film that it began to show promise of realization. Following the success of BACK TO THE FUTURE (1985), director Robert Zemeckis began work on the feature with animation accomplished by Richard Williams, who used a crew of 320 animators to complete the complex movie. In *Movieline* magazine, Richard Natale noted the result: "Robert Zemeckis has made it tough on anyone who tries to mix animation and live-action in the future. WHO FRAMED ROGER RABBIT will be the film they're all compared to. It's a breakthrough technical achievement that borrows liberally from our collective cinematic past and fuses it all into an accomplished original work—part zany cartoon, part serious detective story. The one quibble about the film is that it's a sensory overload experience. So much happens so quickly and with such ease that it's impossible to sit back and totally enjoy the film in just one sitting."

In 1947, some years after the killing of his brother, who was also his partner, Hollywood private eye Eddie Valiant (Bob Hoskins) hits the bottle and loses all his clients. Down and out, Valiant gets an offer from Maroon Studios' chief (Alan Tilvern) to handle a case involving one of the company's most famous Toons stars, Roger Rabbit (voice of Charles Fleischer). Most sleuths avoid the Toons because the cartoon characters are extremely temperamental (in fact, one murdered Valiant's brother), but Valiant has no choice and accepts the case. It has him attempt to get blackmail data on Roger's sexy singer wife Jessica (speaking voice of Kathleen Turner; singing voice of Amy Irving) who, Roger is convinced, is playing around. The studio fears Roger's behavior will hurt him at the box-office and that incriminating evidence will keep Jessica in line and Roger happy. When rival movie studio owner (Stubby Kaye) of Acme Studios ("If it's an Acme, it's a gasser") is murdered, Roger is blamed. Delving into the case, Valiant finds it involves more than just hanky-panky. He uncovers graft and corruption involving Los

Angeles' dismantling of its Red Car (public trolley car transportation) System in order to construct freeways. Along the way Valiant becomes enmeshed with corrupt and dastardly Judge Doom (Christopher Lloyd)—who murders cartoon figures by dropping them in an acid solution he calls the "Dip"—as well as with such legendary cartoon characters as Betty Boop (voice of Mae Questel), Daffy Duck, Donald Duck, Bugs Bunny, Tweety Bird (voice of Mel Blanc) and many others.

Daily Variety opined, "The real stars are the animators, who have pulled off the technically amazing feat of having humans and Toons seem as if they're interacting with one another. It is clear from how well the imagery syncs that a lot of painstaking work went into this production—and clearly a lot of money." Duane Byrge (*The Hollywood Reporter*) termed the film a ". . . blazing, rollicking animation live action feature," and added, "Technically terrific and narratively engaging, this combination cartoon and live actioner is a wacky blend of old-style storytelling with state-of-the-art animation. Through this katzenjammer comedy, the animate characters look as three-dimensional as the actors." Peter Travers (*People* magazine) enthused, ". . . All ages will thrill to the pure enchantment of the visuals. There's Hoskins joyriding through L.A. in a cartoon cab, Daffy and Donald Duck uniting for a piano duet and a knockout finale featuring the starry likes of Mickey Mouse, Goofy, Porky Pig, Snow White, Bambi and Dumbo. Your eyeballs have no choice but to go boinnnnng." Richard Corliss (*Time* magazine) observed, "It is the film's nice conceit that Roger, Baby Herman and all the other characters from '40s Hollywood animation are creatures of a subhuman species known as Toons. They breathe, they emote, and sometimes they get cuckolded by their sultry wives." Yet, noted Corliss, ". . . not all the gags . . . have the limber wit of the cartoons that inspired them. Nor do the human actors add much. . . . Something got lost in the move from storyboard to screen, and in the stretch from seven minutes [the typical cartoon length] to 103."

As with most successful juvenile-oriented films, WHO FRAMED ROGER RABBIT resulted in all types of lucrative merchandising (toys, dolls, etc.) and several of the film's characters turned up in television commercials, not to mention a one-hour TV network special ("Toontown," CBS-TV, 9/13/88) which delved into the making of WHO FRAMED ROGER RABBIT, hosted by the film's co-star, Joanna Cassidy.

In its first twenty weeks at the box-office, WHO FRAMED ROGER RABBIT (which cost $35,000,000 + to produce) grossed $147,340,080.

WITHOUT A CLUE (Orion, 1988) Color 106 minutes.
Producer, Marc Stirdivant; associate producers, Diana Buckhantz,
Ben Moses; director, Thom Eberhardt; screenplay, Gary Murphy,
Larry Strawther; production designer, Brian Ackland-Snow; art
directors, Terry Ackland-Snow, Robin Tarsnane; set decorators,
Peter James, Ian Whittaker; costume designer, Judy Moorcroft;
music, Henry Mancini; assistant director, Don French; sound, David
Hildyard; camera, Alan Hume; editor, Peter Tanner.
Michael Caine (Sherlock Holmes [Reginald Kincaid]); Ben
Kingsley (Dr. John H. Watson); Jeffrey Jones (Inspector Lestrade);
Lysette Anthony (Fake Leslie); Paul Freeman (Professor Moriarty);
Nigel Davenport (Lord Smithwick); Pat Keen (Mrs. Hudson); Peter
Cook (Greenhough); Tim Killick (Sebastian); Matthew Savage
(Wiggins); and: Prince the Wonder Dog, Matthew Sim, John Warner.

Originally called SHERLOCK AND ME, this period comedy/
mystery satirizes the Sherlock Holmes legend by claiming it was
really Dr. Watson who solved the famous cases he wrote about, using
Holmes as a hero. (The film's subtitle is "The flip side of Sherlock
Holmes.") However, as the film explains, Holmes became so popular with readers that the good doctor was forced to find someone to
pretend to be the Baker Street sleuth, the job going to unemployed
actor Reginald Kincaid, whose ego expands with the size of his
growing fame.

Taking all he can from his self-created Frankenstein, Sherlock
Holmes alias bit actor Reginald Kincaid (Michael Caine), the brilliant Dr. John Watson (Ben Kingsley) tosses out the imposter after
he again takes credit for solving a big case. Watson then attempts to
go it alone, but his publisher rejects any stories without Holmes and
the doctor is forced to reconcile with the actor when the Chancellor
of the Exchequer announces he is coming to Baker Street to see
Holmes on an important matter. It seems that five-pound notes
from the Royal Mint have been stolen, and the government assigns
Holmes to the case. It turns out that Professor Moriarty (Paul
Freeman) is behind the elaborate scheme. Things get worse when
Watson is abducted and the pseudo-Holmes must go it alone against
his alleged arch-enemy to save the British Empire from financial
ruin.

"Die-hard Holmes fans may not particularly enjoy seeing their
idol cut down so thoroughly in size and stature, for the effect is that
of watching the infantilization of a genius," decided *Daily Variety*.
Still, Michael Caine as the bogus Holmes and Ben Kingsley as Dr.
Watson carry off their farcical roles with aplomb and the production
provides more than passable entertainment. Ironically, the ego-
bruising effect that the pseudo-Holmes has on Watson in this

motion picture is the same one the fictional Holmes had on his creator, Sir Arthur Conan Doyle.

THE WOMAN IN GREEN (Universal, 1945) 66 minutes. Producer/director, Roy William Neill; based on characters created by Sir Arthur Conan Doyle; screenplay, Bertram Millhauser; art directors, John B. Goodman, Martin Obzina; set decorators, Russell A. Gausman, Ted Von Hemert; costumes, Vera West; music director, Mark Levant; dialogue director, Raymond Kessler; sound, Bernard B. Brown, Glenn A. Anderson; special effects, John P. Fulton; camera, Virgil Miller; editor, Edward Curtis.

Basil Rathbone (Sherlock Holmes); Nigel Bruce (Dr. John H. Watson); Hillary Brooke (Lydia); Henry Daniell (Professor Moriarty); Paul Cavanagh (Fenwick); Matthew Boulton (Inspector Gregson); Eve Amber (Maude); Frederick Worlock (Onslow); Tom Bryson (Williams); Sally Shepherd (Crandon); Mary Gordon (Mrs. Hudson); Percival Vivian (Dr. Simnell); Olaf Hytten (Norris); Harold De Becker (Shabby Man); Tommy Hughes (Newsman); Billy Bevan (Street Peddler).

Scotland Yard is baffled by a quartet of murders in which attractive young women have been killed and one of their fingers severed; the press calls them the "finger murders." Meanwhile, Sir George Fenwick (Paul Cavanagh) attempts to romance attractive Lydia Marlowe (Hillary Brooke) and later wakes up in a cheap flat with a severed finger in his pocket. Sir George's daughter Maude (Eve Amber) sees her father bury the finger and goes to Sherlock Holmes (Basil Rathbone) for help, but her father is found murdered. Holmes believes a blackmail ring run by Professor Moriarty (Henry Daniell) is behind the killings and Moriarty comes to Baker Street to confront his old adversary. A later attempt to shoot Holmes from a house across the street fails and the sniper, who has been hypnotized, is soon found dead on Holmes' doorstep. Holmes and Watson attend a meeting of the Mesmer Club where hypnotists meet; Watson scoffs at the practice but is soon put under a hypnotic spell. There Holmes meets Lydia Marlowe, whom he had seen with Fenwick and romances her. She takes him to her apartment. There Moriarty and his men capture Holmes and Moriarty hypnotizes him and orders the famed detective to jump from a high ledge. Watson and Scotland Yard Inspector Gregson (Matthew Boulton) arrive and, as Moriarty attempts to elude them, it is he who falls off the ledge and plunges to his death below.

THE WOMAN IN GREEN is the ninth in Universal's Sherlock Holmes series and the fifth and last of the group to be scripted by Bertram Millhauser. It starts off well but eventually loses interest, although the programmer does give Holmes two mighty adversaries: Moriarty, excellently portrayed by Henry Daniell, and Hillary Brooke's sexually enticing Lydia Marlowe. Coming on the heels of the excellent HOUSE OF FEAR, *q.v.*, the same year, this feature pales by comparison, although it is on par with the film following it, PURSUIT TO ALGIERS, *q.v.* The *New York Herald Tribune* did feel it was "one of the better Sherlock Holmes mystery thrillers" and *Variety* judged it "a creditable addition" to the series.

X MARKS THE SPOT (Republic, 1942) 55 minutes.

Producer, Herbert J. Yates; associate producer/director, George Sherman; story, Mauri Grashin, Robert T. Shannon; screenplay, Stuart Palmer, Richard Murphy; art director, Russell Kimball; music director, Morton Scott; camera, Jack Marta; editor, Arthur Roberts.

Damian O'Flynn (Eddie Delaney); Helen Parrish (Linda Ward); Dick Purcell (Lieutenant Decker); Jack La Rue (Marty Clark); Neil Hamilton (John Underwood); Robert Homans (Sergeant Delaney); Anne Jeffreys (Lulu); Dick Wessel (Dizzy); Esther Muir (Bonnie); Joseph Kirk (Jerry); Edna Harris (Billie); Fred Kelsey (Riley); Vince Barnett (George).

Racketeering in commodities needed for the World War II effort provided perfect screen fodder, especially for B movies, and one of these areas was the theft of rubber required for the war effort. An offshoot of the plot premise was the substitution of shoddy tires which would soon wear out and cause accidents. Rubber racketeering was the plot idea behind several features like RUBBER RACKET-EERS (1942) and two detective yarns, NO PLACE FOR A LADY (1942), *q.v.*, and X MARKS THE SPOT. The latter was co-scripted by Stuart Palmer, the creator of one of fiction's most popular sleuths, Miss Hildegarde Withers.

Police Sergeant Delaney (Robert Homans) is on the trail of Prohibition era gangster Marty Clark (Jack La Rue), who is back in the rackets as the head of a rubber industry ring. When Delaney gets too close to them, Clark has him killed and the policeman's son, private detective Eddie Delaney (Damian O'Flynn), vows revenge. He gets on the track of the killers and, along the way, meets pretty Linda Ward (Helen Parrish), who aids him in his quest. Both get into several difficult situations before Delaney brings the gangster and his thugs to justice.

X MARKS THE SPOT was one of eight fast-clipped programmers George Sherman produced and directed for Republic in the early years of World War II. Another in the series was the detective film, MYSTERY BROADCAST (1943), *q.v.* Due to the success of these compact and entertaining quickies, George Sherman was promoted to "A" productions in 1944. *Variety* noted of X MARKS THE SPOT, "Producer-director George Sherman follows familiar routes in the unfolding and, although situations are trite, keeps things moving at a fast clip."

YOUNG SHERLOCK HOLMES (Paramount, 1985) Color 109 minutes.

Executive producers, Steven Spielberg, Frank Marshall, Kathleen Kennedy; producer, Mark Johnson; associate producer, Harry Benn; director, Barry Levinson; based on the characters created by Sir Arthur Conan Doyle; screenplay, Chris Columbus; production designer, Norman Reynolds; art directors, Fred Hole, Charles Bishop; set decorator, Michael Ford; costumes, Raymond Hughes; makeup, Peter Robb-King, Nick Dudman, Jane Royle; music, Bruce Broughton; stunt coordinator, Marc Boyle; assistant directors, Michael Murray Ian Hickinbotham; special effects, Kit West, Dennis Muren; sound, Paul Bruce Richardson; camera, Stephen Goldblatt; editor, Stu Linder.

Nicholas Rowe (Sherlock Holmes); Alan Cox (John H. Watson); Sophie Ward (Elizabeth); Anthony Higgins (Rathe); Susan Fleetwood (Mrs. Dribb); Freddie Jones (Cragwitch); Nigel Stock (Waxflatter); Roger Ashton-Griffiths (Lestrade); Earl Rhodes (Dudley); Brian Oulton (Master Snelgrove); Patrick Newell (Bobster); Donald Eccles (Reverend Nesbitt); Matthew Ryan, Matthew Blaksted, Jonathan Lacey (Dudley's Friends); Walter Sparrow (Ethan Engle); Nadim Sawalha (Egyptian Tavern Owner); Roger Brierley (Mr. Holmes); Vivienne Chandler (Mrs. Holmes); Lockwood West (Curio Shop Owner); John Scott Martin (Cemetery Caretaker); George Malpas (School Porter); Willoughby Goddard (School Reverend); Michael Cule (Policeman with Lestrade); Ralph Tabakin (Policeman in Shop Window); Nancy Nevinson (Hotel Receptionist); Michael Hordern (Voice of Older Watson).

In 1880s London a man (Patrick Newell) goes mad and commits suicide after having hallucinations. Other aging rich gentlemen die in the same fashion, one of whom is a professor (Nigel Stock) who was the mentor of brilliant young student Sherlock Holmes (Nicholas Rowe). The young man turns his attentions to these mysterious deaths and is aided by his school chum, John Watson (Alan Cox). Holmes' retired professor mentor had developed plans for a flying machine and Holmes feels that perhaps this was the reason for his murder, since he deduces that all the men were driven mad by the poison on darts fired from a blow gun. Holmes is further spurred on to solve the case since he is in love with the dead man's beautiful niece (Sophie Ward). Eventually, Holmes and Watson come to realize that devil worshippers, who want to sacrifice the girl, are behind the killings.

Stephen Spielberg served as co-executive producer of this fantasy outing, one which rather unsuccessfully attempts to combine the audiences of action pictures like RAIDERS OF THE LOST ARK (1981) and gentle science fiction items like E.T. THE EX-TRA-TERRESTRIAL (1982). In many ways, though, the film is appealing to Sherlock Holmes fans in that it tells a story which predates the Doyle novels and stories of the character as a consulting detective. It also shows how he met his life-long friend and comrade Watson, and the deep love for Elizabeth which led him to become loveless for the remainder of his life.

Vincent Canby (*New York Times*) wrote that the film is "a most winning speculation" and that it ". . . is full of references that attach it to other Spielberg films. . . . However, it also possesses an uncharacteristic, almost leisurely narrative pace and a spectacularly handsome period production that serve the memory of the Conan Doyle originals . . . one of the few really stylish entertaining American movies of 1985."

RADIO AND TELEVISION
DETECTIVE PROGRAMS*

(Compiled with the research cooperation of Vincent Terrace)

RADIO

ABBOTT MYSTERIES (Mutual, 1945-47) w. Charles Webster, Julie Stevens; later, Les Tremayne, Alice Reinhart.

THE ADVENTURES OF FATHER BROWN (1945) w. Karl Swenson.

THE ADVENTURES OF NERO WOLFE (1943-51, ABC) w. J. B. Williams; later, Santos Ortega, Sydney Greenstreet, Francis X. Bushman.

THE ADVENTURES OF PHILIP MARLOWE   *see*   PHILIP MARLOWE.

THE ADVENTURES OF SAM SPADE   *see*   SAM SPADE.

THE ADVENTURES OF SHERLOCK HOLMES   *see*   SHER-LOCK HOLMES.

THE ADVENTURES OF THE ABBOTTS (NBC, 1954-55) w. Claudia Morgan, Les Damon.

THE AFFAIRS OF PETER SALEM   *see*   PETER SALEM.

THE AMAZING MR. MALONE (ABC, 1951) w. Frank Lovejoy; later, George Petrie.

BARRIE CRAIG: CONFIDENTIAL INVESTIGATOR (NBC, 1951-55) w. William Gargan.

BILLY SWIFT, BOY DETECTIVE (Syndicated, 1938-39).

---

*Police and crime shows are *not* included.

BLACKSTONE, THE MAGIC DETECTIVE (Mutual, 1948-49, 1952) w. Ed Jerome.

BOSTON BLACKIE (NBC, 1944-50) w. Chester Morris; later Richard Kollmar.

BROADWAY IS MY BEAT (CBS, 1949-54) w. Larry Thor.

BULLDOG DRUMMOND (Mutual, 1941-47, 1953-54) w. George Coulouris; later, Santos Ortega, Ned Weaver.

CALLING ALL DETECTIVES (Syndicated, 1945-47) w. Vincent Pelletier; (Mutual, 1950) w. Frank Lovejoy.

CANDY MATSON, YUKON 28209 (NBC, 1949-51) w. Natalie Masters.

THE CASES OF MR. ACE (1947) w. George Raft, Jeanette Nolan.

CASEY, CRIME PHOTOGRAPHER (CBS, 1943-55) w. Staats Cotsworth, Jan Minor.

CBS MYSTERY THEATRE (CBS, 1974-82).

CHARLIE CHAN (NBC Blue, 1932-33; Mutual, 1937-38; NBC, 1944-45; ABC, 1945-46; Mutual, 1947-48) w. Walter Connolly; later, Ed Begley, Santos Ortega.

CHARLIE WILD, PRIVATE DETECTIVE (NBC, 1950-51; CBS, 1951) w. George Petrie.

CHICK CARTER, BOY DETECTIVE (Mutual, 1943-44) w. Billy Lipton; later, Leon Janney.

CRIME CLUB (Mutual, 1946-47).

THE CRIME DOCTOR (CBS, 1940-47) w. Ray Collins; later, House Jameson, Everett Sloane, John McIntire.

THE CRIME FILES OF FLAMMOND (Mutual, 1952-53, 1956-57) w. Everett Clarke.

DEADLINE MYSTERY (ABC, 1947) w. Steve Dunne.

DETECTIVE STORY (CBS, 1930).

DETECTIVES BLACK AND BLUE. (Syndicated, 1932-34).

DETECTIVE DALT AND ZUMBA (Syndicated, 1938).

DICK TRACY (Mutual, 1935-37; NBC, 1938-39; ABC, 1943-48) w. Ned Weaver; later, Matt Crowley, Barry Thomson.

DR. TIM, DETECTIVE.

DYKE EASTER, DETECTIVE (Syndicated, 1949).

ELLERY QUEEN (CBS, 1939-40; NBC, 1942-44; CBS, 1945-47; NBC, 1947-48) w. Hugh Marlowe; later, Lawrence Dobkin, Carleton Young, Sidney Smith.

ENO CRIME CLUB (CBS, 1931-32).

ENO CRIME CLUES (NBC, 1933-36).

THE FALCON (ABC, 1943; Mutual, 1945-50; NBC, 1950-52; Mutual, 1952-54) w. James Meighton; later, Les Damon, Berry Kroeger, Les Tremayne, George Petrie.

THE FAT MAN (ABC, 1945) w. J. Scott Smart; also separate Australian version.

FIVE MINUTE MYSTERIES (Mutual, 1947-48).

HERCULE POIROT (Mutual, 1945-47) w. Harold Huber.

I LOVE A MYSTERY (NBC, 1939-42; CBS, 1943-44; Mutual, 1949-51) w. Jim Bannon, Barton Yarborough, Michael Raffetto; later Russell Thorsen, Tony Randall.

I LOVE ADVENTURE (ABC, 1948) w. Jim Bannon, Barton Yarborough, Tom Collins.

INSPECTOR MAIGRET (Canadian Broadcasting Company).

INSPECTOR THORNE (BBC, 1951).

INSPECTOR WHITE OF SCOTLAND YARD (Mutual, 1936-37).

IT'S A CRIME, MR. COLLINS (Mutual, 1956-57) w. Mandel Kramer.

JEFF REGAN, INVESTIGATOR (CBS, 1948-50) w. Jack Webb; later Frank Graham.

JOHNNY MADERO, PIER 23 (Mutual, 1947) w. Jack Webb, Francis X. Bushman.

LEONIDAS WITHERALL (Mutual, 1944-45) w. Walter Hampden.

THE LONE WOLF (Mutual, 1948-49) w. Walter Coy.

McGARRY AND HIS MOUSE (NBC, 1946; Mutual, 1946-47) w. Wendell Corey, Peggy Conklin.

MARK SABRE *see* MYSTERY THEATRE.

MARTIN KANE, PRIVATE DETECTIVE (Mutual, 1949-52) w. William Gargan, Walter Kinsella.

MEET MISS SHERLOCK (CBS, 1946)

MICHAEL AND KITTY (NBC Blue, 1941) w. John Gibson, Elizabeth Reller.

MICHAEL SHAYNE, PRIVATE DETECTIVE (Mutual, 1944-47; ABC, 1950-53) w. Wally Maher; later, Jeff Chandler, Robert Sterling.

MICKEY SPILLANE MYSTERY (Mutual, 1953-54).

MISS MALLORY, PRIVATE EYE (ABC, 1953; CBS, 1956-57).

MISS PINKERTON (Syndicated, 1941) w. Joan Blondell, Dick Powell, Gale Gordon, Hanley Stafford.

MR. AND MRS. NORTH (NBC, 1942-47; CBS, 1947-54; Mutual, 1954-55) w. Peggy Conkin, Carl Eastman; later, Alice Frost, Joseph Curtin; Richard Denning, Barbara Britton.

MR. CHAMELEON (CBS, 1948-52) w. Karl Swenson.

MR. KEEN, TRACER OF LOST PERSONS (NBC Blue, 1937-42; CBS, 1942-55) w. Bennett Kilpack; later Phil Clarke, Arthur Hughes.

MR. MOTO (Syndicated, 1951) w. James Monks.

MURDER AND MR. MALONE (ABC, 1947-48) w. Eugene Raymond.

MURDER BY EXPERTS (Mutual, 1949-51) w. guest hosts John Dickson Carr, Brett Halliday, Alfred Hitchcock, et al.

MURDER CLINIC (Mutual, 1942-46).

MURDER IS MY HOBBY (Mutual, 1945-46) w. Glenn Langan.

MURDER WILL OUT (NBC Blue, 1945) w. Edmund MacDonald, Eddie Marr.

MYSTERY AWARD THEATRE (Syndicated, 1949).

MYSTERY IN THE AIR (NBC, 1945, 1947).

MYSTERY THEATRE (MARK SABRE) (ABC, 1951-54) w. Bill Johnstone.

THE NEW ADVENTURES OF THE THIN MAN see THE THIN MAN.

NICK CARTER, MASTER DETECTIVE (Mutual, 1943-44; ABC, 1944; Mutual, 1944-55) w. Lon Clark.

OFFICIAL DETECTIVE (Mutual, 1946-57) w. Craig McDonnell, Ed Begley.

PAT NOVAK FOR HIRE (ABC, 1946-47, 1949-50) w. Jack Webb.

PERRY MASON (CBS, 1943-55) w. Bartlett Robinson; later, Santos Ortega, Donald Briggs, John Larkin.

PETER SALEM (THE AFFAIRS OF PETER SALEM) (Mutual, 1949-53) w. Santos Ortega.

PHILCO MYSTERIES (Syndicated).

PHILIP MARLOWE (NBC, 1947; CBS, 1948-51)) w. Van Heflin; later, Gerald Mohr.

PHILO VANCE (NBC, 1945; Syndicated, 1948-50) w. Jackson Beck; later, Jose Ferrer.

PHYE COE MYSTERIES (Syndicated, 1937).

POCKET BOOK MYSTERY (Syndicated, 1946).

RAFFLES (Syndicated, 1943, 1945) w. Horace Brahan.

RAFFLES, THE AMATEUR CRACKSMAN (CBS, 1934).

RESULTS, INC. (Mutual, 1944-45) w. Lloyd Nolan, Claire Trevor.

RICHARD DIAMOND, PRIVATE DETECTIVE (NBC, 1949-51; ABC, 1951-52) w. Dick Powell, Ed Begley, Virginia Gregg.

ROCKY FORTUNE (NBC, 1953-54) w. Frank Sinatra.

ROGUE'S GALLERY (Mutual, 1945-46; NBC, 1946-47, ABC, 1950-52) w. Dick Powell.

ROSS DOLAN, DETECTIVE (Mutual, 1947-48).

THE SAINT (NBC, 1945; CBS, 1945-47; Mutual, 1949-50; ABC, 1950-51); w. Vincent Price; later, Edgar Barrier, Brian Aherne, Tom Conway, Barry Sullivan.

SAM SPADE (ABC, 1946; CBS, 1946-49; NBC, 1949-50; ABC, 1950-51) w. Howard Duff, Lurene Tuttle; later, Steve Dunne.

SCOTLAND YARD *see* SCOTLAND YARD'S INSPECTOR BURKE.

SCOTLAND YARD'S INSPECTOR BURKE (SCOTLAND YARD) (Mutual, 1947) w. Basil Rathbone, Alfred Shirley.

SEXTON BLAKE (BBC).

SHERLOCK HOLMES (THE ADVENTURES OF SHERLOCK HOLMES):
(NBC, 1930-34) w. William Gillette (first program); Richard Gordon, Leigh Lovell.
(NBC, 1934-35) w. Louis Hector, Leigh Lovell.
(NBC, 1936) w. Richard Gordon.
(NBC, 1939-43; Mutual, 1943-46) w. Basil Rathbone, Nigel Bruce, Mary Gordon.
(ABC, 1946-47) w. Tom Conway, Nigel Bruce.
(Mutual, 1947-48) w. John Stanley, Alfred Shirley.
(Mutual, 1948-49) w. Ben Wright, Eric Snowden.
(BBC, 1954; NBC, 1955) w. John Gielgud, Ralph Richardson.
(BBC, 1959-68) w. Carleton Hobbs, Norman Shelly.
(BBC, 1978) w. Barry Foster, David Buck.

TALES OF FATIMA (CBS, 1949) w. Basil Rathbone.

THAT HAMMER GUY (MIKE HAMMER) (Mutual, 1952-53) w. Ted de Corsia, Larry Haines.

THATCHER COLT (NBC, 1936-38) w. Hanley Stafford.

THE THIN MAN (NBC, 1941-42; CBS, 1943-47; NBC, 1947-49; Mutual, 1950) w. Les Damon, Claudia Morgan; later, David Gothard, Les Tremayne, Joseph Curtin.

TRUE DETECTIVE MYSTERIES (CBS, 1929-30; Mutual, 1936-39, 1944-59) w. John Shuttleworth.

TWO ON A CLUE (CBS, 1944-46) w. Ned Weaver, Louise Fitch.

THE WHISTLER (CBS, 1942-55) w. Bill Forman; later, Marvin Miller, Everett Clarke.

YOURS TRULY, JOHNNY DOLLAR (CBS, 1950-62) w. Charles Russell; later, Edmond O'Brien, John Lund, Bob Bailey, Bob Readrick, Mandel Kramer.

TELEVISION

ACE CRAWFORD, PRIVATE EYE (CBS, 3/15/83 to 4/19/83) w. Tim Conway, Joe Regalbuto.

THE ADVENTURES OF ELLERY QUEEN (DuMont, 10/19/50 to 12/6/51); (ABC, 12/16/51 to 11/26/52); (Syndicated 9/54-1955) w. Richard Hartz; later, Lee Bowman, Hugh Marlowe; Charlotte Keane, Florenz Ames.

THE AMAZING CHAN AND THE CHAN CLAN (CBS, 9/9/72 to 9/22/74) (cartoon) w. Keye Luke (voice).

AMY PRENTISS (NBC, 12/1/74 to 7/6/75) w. Jessica Walter, Helen Hunt, Art Metrano.

THE AQUANAUTS (CBS, 9/14/60 to 3/1/61) w. Keith Larsen, Jeremy Slate, Ron Ely.

ARCHER (NBC, 1/30/75 to 3/14/75) w. Brian Keith, John P. Ryan.

ARMCHAIR DETECTIVE (CBS, 7/6/49 to 9/28/49) w. John Milton Kennedy (host).

ASSIGNMENT DANGER see THE NEW ADVENTURES OF MARTIN KANE.

BANACEK (NBC, 9/13/72 to 11/21/73 and 1/15/74 to 9/3/74) w. George Peppard, Christine Belford.

BANYON (NBC, 9/15/72 to 1/12/73) w. Robert Forster, Richard Jaeckel, Joan Blondell.

BARETTA (ABC, 1/17/75 to 6/1/78) w. Robert Blake, Tom Ewell, Dana Elcar.

BARNABY JONES (CBS, 1/23/73 to 9/4/80) w. Buddy Ebsen, Lee Meriweather, Mark Shera.

BERGERAC (Entertainment Channel, 7/82 to 10/82) w. John Nettles.

BEVERLY HILLS BUNTZ (NBC, 11/5/87 to 3/25/88) w. Dennis Franz, Peter Jurasik.

BIG SHAMUS, LITTLE SHAMUS (CBS, 9/29/79 to 10/6/79) w. Brian Dennehy, Doug McKeon, Kathryn Leigh Scott, Dennis Cole.

BOSTON BLACKIE (Syndicated, 1951-53) w. Kent Taylor, Lois Collier, Frank Orth.

BOURBON STREET BEAT (ABC, 10/5/59 to 9/26/60) w. Andrew Duggan, Richard Long, Van Williams, Arlene Howell.

BRONK (CBS, 9/21/75 to 7/18/76) w. Jack Palance, Dina Ousley, Tony King.

THE BROTHERS BRANNAGAN (Syndicated, 1960) w. Steve Dunne, Mark Roberts.

CANNON (CBS, 9/14/71 to 9/19/76) w. William Conrad.

CARIBE (ABC, 2/17/75 to 8/11/75) w. Stacy Keach, Carl Franklin, Robert Mandan.

THE CASE OF THE DANGEROUS ROBIN (Syndicated, 1961) w. Rick Jason, Jean Blake.

THE CASEBOOK OF SHERLOCK HOLMES   *see*   SHERLOCK HOLMES.

THE CASES OF EDDIE DRAKE (CBS, 1949; Du Mont 3/6/52 to 5/24/52) w. Don Haggerty, Patricia Morison.

CASSIE AND COMPANY (NBC, 1/29/82 to 8/20/82) w. Angie Dickinson, John Ireland, Dori Brenner.

CHARLIE WILD, PRIVATE DETECTIVE (CBS, 12/22/50 to 6/27/51), (ABC, 9/11/51 to 3/4/52), (DuMont, 3/13/52 to 6/19/52) w. John McQuade; later, Kevin O'Morrison; Cloris Leachman.

CHARLIE'S ANGELS (ABC, 9/22/76 to 2/28/81, 6/3/81 to 8/19/81) w. Kate Jackson, Jaclyn Smith, Farrah Fawcett-Majors; later, Cheryl Ladd, Shelley Hack, Tanya Roberts; David Doyle, John Forsythe (voice).

THE CHEATERS (Syndicated, 1960) w. John Ireland, Robert Ayres.

CHECKMATE (CBS, 9/17/60 to 9/19/62) w. Anthony George, Doug McClure, Sebastian Cabot.

CHICAGOLAND MYSTERY THEATRE (WGN-TV Chicago, 1947-49), (DuMont, 9/18/49 to 7/30/50) w. Gordon Urquhart, Bob Smith.

CITY DETECTIVE (Syndicated, 1953) w. Rod Cameron.

COLONEL MARCH OF SCOTLAND YARD (ITV, 1954 - Syndicated, 1957) w. Boris Karloff.1

COLUMBO (NBC, 9/15/71 to 9/1/78) w. Peter Falk.

COOL AND LAM (Unaired Pilot—1957) w. Benay Venuta, Billy Pearson, Erle Stanley Gardner.

COOL MILLION (NBC, 10/25/72 to 7/11/73) w. James Farentino, Adele Mara.

CORONADO 9 (Syndicated, 1960) w. Rod Cameron.

THE COURT OF LAST RESORT (ABC, 10/4/57 to 4/11/58) w. Paul Birch, Lyle Bettger.

CRAIG KENNEDY, CRIMINOLOGIST (Syndicated, 1952) w. Donald Woods.

CRIME STORY (NBC, 9/18/86 to 5/17/88) w. Dennis Farina, Darlene Fluegel.

CRIME WITH FATHER (ABC, 8/31/51 to 1/25/52) w. Rusty Lane, Peggy Lobbin.

THE D.A. (NBC, 9/17/71 to 1/17/72) w. Robert Conrad, Harry Morgan, Julie Cobb, Ned Romero.

THE D.A.'s MAN (NBC, 1/3/59 to 9/29/59) w. John Compton, Ralph Manza.

DAN AUGUST (ABC, 9/23/70 to 9/9/71) w. Burt Reynolds, Norman Fell, Richard Anderson, Ned Romero.

DAN RAVEN (NBC, 9/23/60 to 1/6/61) w. Skip Homeier, Dan Barton, Quinn Redeker.

DEAR DETECTIVE (CBS, 3/28/79 to 4/18/79) w. Brenda Vaccaro, Jet Yardum, Jack Ging.

DELVECCHIO (CBS, 9/9/76 to 7/17/77) w. Judd Hirsch, Charles Haid, Michael Conrad, Mario Gallo.

DEPARTMENT S (Syndicated, 1971) w. Peter Wyngarde, Rosemary Nicols, William Gaunt.

DETECTIVE SCHOOL (ABC, 7/31/79 to 8/14/79 and 9/15/79 to 11/24/79) w. James Gregory, Randolph Mantooth, Douglas V. Fowley, LaWanda Page, Melinda Naud, Jo Ann Harris.

THE DETECTIVE'S WIFE (CBS, 7/7/50 to 10/6/50) w. Donald Curtis, Lynn Bari.

THE DEVLIN CONNECTION (CBS, 10/2/82 to 12/25/82) w. Rock Hudson, Jack Scalia, Leigh Taylor-Young.

DIAGNOSIS: UNKNOWN (CBS, 7/5/60 to 9/20/60) w. Patrick O'Neal, Phyllis Newman, Chester Morris.

DIAL 999 (Syndicated, 1959) w. Robert Beatty.

DIAMONDS (CBS, 9/22/87 to 9/13/88) w. Nicholas Campbell, Peggy Smithart.

DICK AND THE DUCHESS (CBS, 9/28/57 to 5/16/58) w. Patrick O'Neal, Hazel Court.

DICK TRACY (ABC, 9/11/50 to 2/12/51) w. Ralph Byrd, Joe Devlin, Angela Greene, Dick Elliott.

THE DUKE (NBC, 3/5/79 to 5/18/79) w. Robert Conrad, Larry Manetti.

THE EDDIE CAPRA MYSTERIES (NBC, 9/22/78 to 1/12/79) w. Vincent Baggetta, Wendy Phillips, Ken Swofford.

ELLERY QUEEN (NBC, 9/11/75 to 9/19/76) w. Jim Hutton, David Wayne, Tom Reese, Ken Swofford, John Hillerman.

ELLERY QUEEN *see* THE ADVENTURES OF ELLERY QUEEN; THE FURTHER ADVENTURES OF ELLERY QUEEN.

THE FALCON (STREETS OF DANGER) (Syndicated, 1955) w. Charles McGraw.

FARADAY AND COMPANY (NBC 9/26/73 to 8/30/74) w. Dan Dailey, James Naughton, Geraldine Brooks, Sharon Gless.

FATHER BROWN (PBS, 1982) w. Kenneth More, Dennis Burgess; (PBS, 1986-87) w. Bernard Cornwell.

FATHER DOWLING MYSTERIES (NBC, 1989 to date) w. Tom Bosley, Tracy Nelson, Mary Wickes.

THE FILES OF JEFFREY STONE (Syndicated, 1955) w. Don Haggerty, Gloria Henry.

FRONT PAGE DETECTIVE (DuMont, 7/6/51 to 11/3/53) (Syndicated, 1953) w. Edmund Lowe, Frank Jenks.

THE FURTHER ADVENTURES OF ELLERY QUEEN (NBC, 9/26/58 to 9/4/59) w. George Nader; later Lee Philips; Les Treymayne.

GIDEON, C.I.D. (GIDEON'S WAY) (Syndicated, 1966) w. John Gregson.

GIDEON'S WAY *see* GIDEON, C.I.D.

GRIFF (ABC, 9/29/73 to 1/4/74) w. Lorne Greene, Ben Murphy, Vic Tayback, Patricia Stich.

HAGEN (CBS, 3/1/80 to 4/24/80) w. Chad Everett, Arthur Hill.

HARDCASTLE AND McCORMICK (ABC, 9/18/83 to 7/23/86) w. Brian Keith, Daniel Hugh-Kelly.

THE HARDY BOYS (cartoon) (ABC, 9/6/69 to 9/4/71) w. Dallas McKennon, Jane Webb (voices).

THE HARDY BOYS MYSTERIES (ABC, 1/30/77 to 1/21/79 and 6/24/79 to 8/26/79) w. Shawn Cassidy, Parker Stevenson, Edmund Gilbert.

HARRY O (ABC, 9/12/74 to 8/12/76) w. David Janssen, Henry Darrow, Anthony Zerbe.

HAWAIIAN EYE (ABC, 10/7/59 to 9/10/63) w. Troy Donahue, Robert Conrad, Connie Stevens, Grant Williams, Anthony Eisley.

HAWAIIAN HEAT (ABC, 9/14/84 to 11/23/84; 12/21/84) w. Robert Ginty, Jeff McCracken, Tracy Scoggins.

HAWK (ABC, 9/15/66 to 12/29/66) w. Burt Reynolds, Leon Janney, John Marley, Bruce Glover.

HEC RAMSEY (NBC, 10/8/72 to 8/25/74) w. Richard Boone, Rick Lenz, Harry Morgan, Sharon Acker.

HOMICIDE SQUAD see THE MARK SABRE MYSTERY THEATRE.

HONEY WEST (ABC, 9/17/65 to 9/2/66) w. Anne Francis, John Ericson, Irene Hervey.

INCH HIGH PRIVATE EYE (cartoon) (NBC, 9/8/73 to 8/31/74) w. Lennie Weinrib, Ted Knight, Jamie Farr, Janet Waldo, Vic Perrin (voices).

INSPECTOR FABIAN OF SCOTLAND YARD (Syndicated, 1955) w. Bruce Seton.

INTERNATIONAL DETECTIVE (Syndicated, 1959) w. Arthur Fleming.

THE INVESTIGATORS (CBS, 9/21/61 to 12/28/61) w. James Philbrook, James Franciscus, Mary Murphy, June Kenney.

IT HAPPENED IN SPAIN (Syndicated, 1958) w. Scott McKay.

J. J. STARBUCK (NBC, 9/26/87 to 6/28/88) w. Dale Robertson, Shawn Weatherly, Ben Vereen.

JACK THE RIPPER (Syndicated, 1974) w. Sebastian Cabot (host), Alan Stratford-Johns, Frank Windsor.

JAKE AND THE FATMAN (CBS, 9/26/87 to date) w. William Conrad, Joe Penny, Lu Lennard.

JASON KING (Syndicated, 1972) w. Peter Wyngarde.

JOHNNY MIDNIGHT (Syndicated, 1960) w. Edmond O'Brien.

JOHNNY STACCATO (NBC, 9/10/59 to 3/24/60) w. John Cassavetes, Eduardo Ciannelli.

K-9 AND COMPANY (Syndicated, 1981) w. Elisabeth Sladen.

KATE LOVES A MYSTERY (NBC, 10/18/79 to 12/6/79) w. Kate Mulgrew, Lili Haydn, Henry Jones, Don Stroud.

KATE McSHANE (CBS, 9/10/75 to 11/12/75) w. Anne Meara, Sean McClory, Charles Haid.

KHAN! (CBS, 2/7/75 to 2/28/75) w. Khigh Dhiegh, Vic Tayback, Irene Yah-Ling Sun.

LANIGAN'S RABBI (NBC, 1/30/77 to 7/3/77) w. Art Carney, Janis Paige, Bruce Solomon.

LAS VEGAS BEAT (Unaired Pilot, 1963) w. Peter Graves, Jamie Farr, Diana Millay.

THE LAW AND HARRY McGRAW (CBS, 9/27/87 to 2/10/88) w. Jerry Orbach, Barbara Babcock.

THE LAWLESS YEARS (NBC, 4/16/59 to 9/3/59 and 5/12/61 to 9/22/61) w. James Gregory, Robert Karnes.

LEG WORK (CBS, 10/3/87 to 11/7/87) w. Margaret Colin, Patrick James Clarke.

LEGMEN (NBC, 1//20/84 to 4/6/84; 9/1/84) w. Bruce Greenwood, J. T. Terlesky, Don Calfa, Claude Akins.

LIME STREET (ABC, 9/28/85 to 10/26/85) w. Robert Wagner, John Standing, Lew Ayres, Samantha Smith, Maia Brewton, Patrick Macnee.

THE LONE WOLF (STREETS OF DANGER) (Syndicated, 1954) w. Louis Hayward.

LONGSTREET (ABC, 9/16/71 to 8/10/72) w. James Franciscus, Bradford Dillman, Martine Beswick.

McCOY (NBC, 9/15/75 to 9/12/76) w. Tony Curtis, Roscoe Lee Browne, Lucille Meredith.

McMILLAN (NBC, 12/5/76 to 8/21/77) w. Rock Hudson, Martha Raye, John Schuck.

McMILLAN AND WIFE (NBC, 9/29/71 to 9/12/76) w. Rock Hudson, Susan Saint James, Nancy Walker.

MAGNUM P.I. (CBS, 12/11/80 to 5/1/88) w. Tom Selleck, John Hillerman, Roger E. Mosley, Larry Manetti.

MAIGRET (BBC, 1958 to 1963) w. Rupert Davies.

MALIBU RUN (CBS, 3/1/61 to 9/27/61) w. Jeremy Slate, Ron Ely.

THE MAN AGAINST CRIME (CBS, 10/7/49 to 10/2/53), (DuMont, 10/11/53 to 4/4/54), (NBC 7/1/56 to 8/26/56) w. Ralph Bellamy; later, Frank Lovejoy; Robert Preston.

THE MAN FROM INTERPOL (NBC, 1/23/60 to 10/22/60) w. Richard Wyler, John Longden.

MAN IN A SUITCASE (ABC, 5/3/68 to 9/20/68) w. Richard Bradford.

MAN WITH A CAMERA (ABC, 10/10/58 to 1/29/60) w. Charles Bronson.

MANHUNTER (CBS, 9/11/74 to 4/10/75) w. Ken Howard, Hillary Thompson, Ford Rainey.

MANNIX (CBS, 9/9/67 to 8/27/75) w. Michael Connors, Gail Fisher, Joseph Campanella, Robert Reed.

THE MARK SABRE MYSTERY THEATRE (a.k.a. HOMICIDE SQUAD) (ABC, 10/5/51 to 6/30/54) w. Tom Conway, James Burke.

MARKHAM (CBS, 5/2/59 to 9/145/60) w. Ray Milland.

MARTIN KANE, PRIVATE EYE (NBC, 9/11/49 to 8/20/53) w. William Gargan; later Lloyd Nolan, Lee Tracy.

THE MASK (ABC, 1/10/54 to 5/16/54) w. Gary Merrill, William Prince.

MATLOCK (NBC, 9/23/86 to present) w. Andy Griffith, Linda Purl.

MATT HELM (ABC, 9/20/75 to 11/3/75) w. Tony Franciosa, Laraine Stephens, Gene Evans, Jeff Donnell.

MATT HOUSTON (ABC, 9/26/82 to 3/29/85) w. Lee Horsley, Buddy Ebsen, Pamela Hensley.

MEET McGRAW (NBC, 7/2/57 to 6/24/58) w. Frank Lovejoy.

THE MEN: JIGSAW (ABC, 10/12/72 to 8/11/73) w. James Wainwright.

MICHAEL SHAYNE, PRIVATE DETECTIVE (NBC, 9/30/60 to 9/22/61) w. Richard Denning, Patricia Donahue, Herbert Rudley.

MICKEY SPILLANE'S MIKE HAMMER (CBS, 1/26/84 to 4/14/84 and 8/30/84 to 1/12/85) w. Stacy Keach, Lindsay Bloom, Don Stroud.

MIKE HAMMER, DETECTIVE (Syndicated, 1958) w. Darren McGavin.

MR. AND MRS. MYSTERY (CBS, 1949-50) w. John Gay, Barbara Gay.

MR. AND MRS. NORTH (NBC, 7/4/49—pilot) w. Joseph Allen, Mary Lou Taylor; (CBS, 10/3/52 to 9/25/53) (NBC, 1/26/54 to 7/20/54) w. Richard Denning, Barbara Britton, Francis DeSales.

MRS. COLUMBO (NBC, 2/26/79 to 3/29/79) w. Kate Mulgrew, Lili Haydn, Henry Jones.

MOONLIGHTING (ABC 3/5/85 to) w. Cybill Shepherd, Bruce Wilis, Allyce Beasley.

MURDER, SHE WROTE (CBS, 9/30/84 to date) w. Angela Lansbury, Tom Bosley, William Windom.

MY FRIEND TONY (NBC, 1/5/69 to 8/31/69) w. James Whitmore.

MYSTERIES OF CHINATOWN (ABC, 12/4/49 to 10/23/50) w. Marvin Miller, Richard Crane, Bill Eythe, Gloria Saunders.

MYSTERY! (PBS 1981 to date) w. Vincent Price (host).

NBC MYSTERY MOVIES (NBC SUNDAY MYSTERY MOVIE (NBC, 1971-77) see AMY PRENTISS, COLUMBO, HEC RAMSEY, McMILLAN, McMILLAN AND WIFE.

NBC WEDNESDAY MYSTERY MOVIE (NBC, 1972-74) see BANACEK, COOL MILLION, FARADAY & COMPANY, THE SNOOP SISTERS, TENAFLY.

NANCY DREW MYSTERIES (ABC, 2/6/77 to 7/30/78) w. Pamela Sue Martin, Janet Louise Johnson, William Schallert.

NERO WOLFE (NBC, 1/16/81 to 8/25/81) w. William Conrad, Lee Horsley, George Wyner, George Voskovec, Robert Coote.

THE NEW ADVENTURES OF CHARLIE CHAN (Syndicated, 1957) w. J. Carrol Naish, James Hong.

THE NEW ADVENTURES OF MARTIN KANE (ASSIGNMENT: DANGER) (NBC, 8/27/53 to 6/17/54) w. Mark Stevens; later, William Gargan; Brian Reece.

THE NEW ADVENTURES OF SHERLOCK HOLMES *see* SHERLOCK HOLMES

THE NEW MIKE HAMMER (CBS, 9/27/86 to 9/9/87) w. Stacy Keach, Lindsay Bloom.

THE NEW PERRY MASON (CBS, 9/16/73 to 1/27/74) w. Monte Markham, Sharon Acker, Harry Guardino, Dane Clark.

NEW YORK CONFIDENTIAL (Syndicated, 1958) w. Lee Tracy.

OFFICIAL DETECTIVE (Syndicated, 1957) w. Everett Sloane.

THE OUTSIDER (NBC, 9/18/68 to 9/10/69) w. Darren McGavin.

PARTNERS IN CRIME (NBC, 9/22/84 to 12/29/84) w. Lynda Carter, Loni Anderson.

PERRY MASON (CBS, 9/21/57 to 9/4/66) w. Raymond Burr, Barbara Hale, William Hopper, Ray Collins, William Talman, Richard Anderson, Connie Cezon, Kenneth MacDonald, George E. Stone.

PETER GUNN (NBC, 9/2/58 to 9/27/60) (ABC, 10/3/60 to 9/21/61) w. Craig Stevens, Lola Albright, Herschel Bernardi, Hope Emerson, Minerva Urecal.

PHILIP MARLOWE (ABC, 10/6/59 to 3/29/60) w. Philip Carey.

PHILIP MARLOWE, PRIVATE EYE (HBO, 4/16/83 to 5/14/83) w. Powers Boothe.

PRIVATE EYE (NBC, 9/13/87 to 1/8/88) w. Michael Woods, Josh Brolin, Lisa Jane Persky.

REMINGTON STEELE (NBC, 10/1/82 to 8/2/86) w. Pierce Brosnan, Stephanie Zimbalist, Doris Roberts.

RETURN OF THE SAINT ((CBS, 12/21/79 to 8/15/80) w. Ian Ogilvy.

RICHARD DIAMOND, PRIVATE DETECTIVE (CBS, 7/1/57

to 9/23/57 and 12/25/59 to 1/25/60) (NBC 2/15/59 to 1/25/60) w. David Janssen, Mary Tyler Moore, Barbara Bain, Regis Toomey.

RICHIE BROCKELMAN, PRIVATE EYE (NBC, 3/17/78 to 4/14/78 and 8/10/78 to 8/24/78) w. Dennis Dugan, Barbara Bosson, Robert Hogan.

RIKER (CBS, 3/14/81 to 4/11/81) w. Josh Taylor.

THE ROARING 20s (ABC, 10/15/60 to 9/2/62) w. Dorothy Provine, Donald May, Rex Reason, Emile Meyer, Wally Brown.

THE ROCKFORD FILES ((NBC, 9/13/74 to 7/25/80) w. James Garner, Noah Beery Jr., Joe Santos.

ROCKY KING, INSIDE DETECTIVE (DuMont, 1/14/50 to 12/26/54) w. Roscoe Karns, Grace Carney, Todd Karns.

SABER OF LONDON (UNCOVERED) (NBC, 10/13/57 to 5/15/60) w. Donald Gray, Michael Balfour.

THE SAINT (Syndicated, 1963-66) (NBC, 1967-69) w. Roger Moore.

SCOTLAND YARD (Syndicated, 1955) w. Edgar Lustgarten.

77 SUNSET STRIP (ABC, 10/10/58 to 2/26/64) w. Efrem Zimbalist Jr., Roger Smith, Richard Long, Edd Byrnes, Jacqueline Beer, Robert Logan.

SHADOW OF THE CLOAK (DuMont, 6/6/51 to 3/20/52) w. Helmut Dantine.

SHAFT (CBS, 10/9/73 to 9/3/74) w. Richard Roundtree, Ed Barth.

SHANNON (Syndicated, 1961) w. George Nader, Regis Toomey.

SHERLOCK HOLMES (THE NEW ADVENTURES OF SHER-LOCK HOLMES)
(BBC, 1951) w. Alan Wheatley, Raymond Francis.
(Syndicated, 1954-55) w. Ronald Howard, H. Marion Crawford; a.k.a. THE CASEBOOK OF SHERLOCK HOLMES.
(BBC, 1964-65) w. Douglas Wilmer, Nigel Stock.
(BBC, 1968) w. Peter Cushing, Nigel Stock.
(Thames Television, 1984-85) w. Jeremy Brett, David Burke.
(Thames Television, 1986-88) w. Jeremy Brett, Edward Hardwicke.

SHOESTRING (Entertainment Channel, 9/4/82 to 12/30/82) w. Trevor Eve.

SLEDGE HAMMER (ABC, 9/23/86 to 2/12/88) w. David Rasche, Ann-Marie Martin, Harrison Page.

THE SNOOP SISTERS (NBC, 1/29/74 to 8/26/74) w. Helen Hayes, Mildred Natwick, Lou Antonio, Bert Convy.

SONNY SPOON (NBC, 2/12/88 to 11/88) w. Mario Van Peebles, Terry Donahoe, Joe Shea.

SPENSER FOR HIRE (ABC, 9/20/85 to date) w. Robert Urich, Barbara Stock, Richard Jaeckel.

STORIES OF THE CENTURY (Syndicated, 1956) w. Jim Davis, Mary Castle.

STREETS OF DANGER *see* THE FALCON.

STRYKER OF SCOTLAND YARD (Syndicated, 1957) w. Clifford Evans.

SURFSIDE SIX (ABC, 9/3/60 to 9/24/62) w. Troy Donahue, Van Williams, Lee Patterson, Diane McBain, Donald Barry, Richard Crane.

THE SWEENEY (Syndicated, 1976) w. John Thaw, Dennis Waterman, Garfield Morgan.

SWITCH (CBS, 9/9/75 to 1/16/78 and 6/25/78 to 9/3/78) w. Eddie Albert, Robert Wagner, Sharon Gless, Charlie Callas, Ken Swofford.

T AND T (Syndicated, 1/88 to date) w. Mr. T., Alex Amini.

TALLAHASSEE 7000 (Syndicated, 1961) w. Walter Matthau.

THE TELLTALE CLUE (CBS, 7/8/54 to 9/23/54) w. Anthony Ross.

TENAFLY (NBC, 10/2/73 to 1/2/74 and 4/30/74 to 8/26/74) w. James McEachin, Lilliam Lehman, David Huddleston, Ford Rainey.

TENSPEED AND BROWN SHOE (ABC, 1/27/80 to 3/30/80 and 5/30/80 to 7/11/80) w. Ben Vereen, Jeff Goldblum, James Beach.

THE THIN MAN (NBC, 9/20/57 to 6/26/59) w. Peter Lawford, Phyllis Kirk, Jack Albertson.

THE THIRD MAN (Syndicated, 1960) w. Michael Rennie.

TOMA (ABC, 10/4/73 to 9/6/74) w. Tony Musante, Susan Strasberg, Simon Oakland, David Toma.

21 BEACON STREET (NBC, 7/2/59 to 9/24/59 and 12/27/59 to 3/20/60) w. Dennis Morgan, Joanna Barnes, Brian Kelly.

VEGAS (ABC, 9/20/78 to 6/10/81) w. Robert Urich, Tony Curtis, Greg Morris, Phyllis Davis, Judy Landers.

WALTER WINCHELL FILE (ABC, 10/2/57 to 3/28/58) w. Walter Winchell (host/narrator).

WHODUNIT (GAME SHOW) (NBC, 4/12/79 to 5/17/79) w. Ed McMahon (host).

CHRONOLOGY OF FILMS

1905 ADVENTURES OF SHERLOCK HOLMES

1917 ARSENE LUPIN
      THE LONE WOLF

1920 TRENT'S LAST CASE

1921 THE WAKEFIELD CASE

1922 BULLDOG DRUMMOND
      SHERLOCK HOLMES

1923 THE SIGN OF FOUR

1924 THE LONE WOLF
      SHERLOCK JR.

1925 RAFFLES, THE AMATEUR CRACKSMAN

1926 THE BAT
      THE HOUSE WITHOUT A KEY
      THE LODGER
      THE LONE WOLF RETURNS

1927 ALIAS THE LONE WOLF
      THE CHINESE PARROT

1928 NUMBER SEVENTEEN
      THE TERROR

1929   THE "CANARY" MURDER CASE
      ALIBI
      BEHIND THAT CURTAIN
      BLACKMAIL
      BULLDOG DRUMMOND
      THE GHOST TALKS
      THE GREENE MURDER CASE
      THE HOUSE OF SECRETS
      DER HUND VON BASKERVILLE
      THE RETURN OF SHERLOCK HOLMES
      TRENT'S LAST CASE
      THE UNHOLY NIGHT
      UNMASKED

1930   THE BENSON MURDER CASE
      THE BISHOP MURDER CASE
      LAST OF THE LONE WOLF
      MURDER
      RAFFLES
      SCOTLAND YARD
      TEMPLE TOWER

1931   ALIBI
      THE BAT WHISPERS
      THE BLACK CAMEL
      BLACK COFFEE
      CHARLIE CHAN CARRIES ON
      CONVICTED
      EMIL UND DIE DETEKTIVE
      THE MALTESE FALCON
      MURDER AT MIDNIGHT

1931   SHERLOCK HOLMES' FATAL HOUR
       THE SPECKLED BAND

1932   ARSENE LUPIN
       CHEATERS AT PLAY
       THE CROOKED CIRCLE
       CROSS-EXAMINATION
       THE LODGER
       MISS PINKERTON
       THE MISSING REMBRANDT
       NIGHT CLUB LADY
       NUMBER SEVENTEEN
       THE PENGUIN POOL MURDER
       SHERLOCK HOLMES
       THE SIGN OF FOUR
       SINISTER HANDS
       STRANGE ADVENTURE
       STRANGERS OF THE EVENING
       THE THIRTEENTH GUEST

1933   THE CIRCUS QUEEN MURDER
       GIRL MISSING
       THE KENNEL MURDER CASE
       THE KEYHOLE
       THE MIDNIGHT WARNING
       PRIVATE DETECTIVE 62
       SECRET OF THE BLUE ROOM
       A STUDY IN SCARLET

1934   BOMBAY MAIL
       THE CASE OF THE HOWLING DOG

1934 CHARLIE CHAN IN LONDON
CHARLIE CHAN'S COURAGE
THE DRAGON MURDER CASE
LORD EDGWARE DIES
MURDER IN THE MUSEUM
MURDER IN TRINIDAD
MURDER ON THE BLACKBOARD
MURDER ON THE CAMPUS
THE THIN MAN

1935 THE CASE OF THE CURIOUS BRIDE
THE CASE OF THE LUCKY LEGS
THE CASINO MURDER CASE
CHARLIE CHAN IN EGYPT
CHARLIE CHAN IN PARIS
CHARLIE CHAN IN SHANGHAI
FATHER BROWN, DETECTIVE
THE GLASS KEY
THE GREAT HOTEL MURDER
THE MIDNIGHT PHANTOM
MR. DYNAMITE
MURDER ON A HONEYMOON
THE MYSTERY OF EDWIN DROOD
ONE FRIGHTENED NIGHT
REMEMBER LAST NIGHT?
SECRETS OF CHINATOWN
THE SPANISH CAPE MYSTERY
STAR OF MIDNIGHT
THE TRIUMPH OF SHERLOCK HOLMES
WHILE THE PATIENT SLEPT

1936   AFTER THE THIN MAN
THE CASE OF THE BLACK CAT
THE CASE OF THE VELVET CLAWS
CHARLIE CHAN AT THE CIRCUS
CHARLIE CHAN AT THE OPERA
CHARLIE CHAN AT THE RACE TRACK
CHARLIE CHAN'S SECRET
THE DARK HOUR
THE EX-MRS. BRADFORD
THE GARDEN MURDER CASE
THE HOUSE OF SECRETS
THE LONE WOLF RETURNS
MEET NERO WOLFE
MURDER BY AN ARISTOCRAT
THE MURDER OF DR. HARRIGAN
MURDER ON A BRIDLE PATH
THE PLOT THICKENS
THE ROGUES' TAVERN
SATAN MET A LADY
THE SCARAB MURDER CASE

1937   THE CASE OF THE STUTTERING BISHOP
CHARLIE CHAN AT MONTE CARLO
CHARLIE CHAN AT THE OLYMPICS
CHARLIE CHAN ON BROADWAY
THE CRIME NOBODY SAW
DICK TRACY
FORTY NAUGHTY GIRLS
INTERNATIONAL CRIME
THE LEAGUE OF FRIGHTENED MEN

1937 THE MANDARIN MYSTERY
MURDER ON DIAMOND ROW
A NIGHT OF MYSTERY
THE SHADOW STRIKES
SMART BLONDE
SUPER SLEUTH

1938 ARSENE LUPIN RETURNS
THE BLACK DOLL
BULLDOG DRUMMOND'S PERIL
CHARLIE CHAN IN HONOLULU
FAST COMPANY
LADY IN THE MORGUE
MR. WONG, DETECTIVE
MYSTERY HOUSE
NANCY DREW, DETECTIVE
THE PATIENT IN ROOM 18
THE SAINT IN NEW YORK
THE TERROR
THERE'S ALWAYS A WOMAN
TIME OUT FOR MURDER
WHILE NEW YORK SLEEPS

1939 THE ADVENTURE OF SHERLOCK HOLMES
THE ALIBI
ANOTHER THIN MAN
CHARLIE CHAN AT TREASURE ISLAND
CHARLIE CHAN IN RENO
CHARLIE CHAN IN THE CITY OF DARKNESS
CHARLIE McCARTHY, DETECTIVE
FAST AND FURIOUS

1939   FAST AND LOOSE
THE GRACIE ALLEN MURDER CASE
THE HOUSE OF FEAR
IT'S A WONDERFUL WORLD
THE LONE WOLF SPY HUNT
LYING LIPS
MIDNIGHT SHADOW
MIRACLES FOR SALE
MR. MOTO IN DANGER ISLAND
MR. MOTO'S LAST WARNING
PRIVATE DETECTIVE
RAFFLES
THE SAINT IN LONDON
TELL NO TALES
THERE'S THAT WOMAN AGAIN

1940   CHARLIE CHAN AT THE WAX MUSEUM
CHARLIE CHAN IN PANAMA
CHARLIE CHAN'S MURDER CRUISE
THE FATAL HOUR
HAUNTED HONEYMOON
THE LONE WOLF STRIKES
MICHAEL SHAYNE, PRIVATE DETECTIVE
MIDNIGHT LIMITED
THE MISSING PEOPLE
MURDER OVER NEW YORK
THE SHADOW

1941   BLUE, WHITE AND PERFECT
CHARLIE CHAN IN RIO
CONFESSIONS OF BOSTON BLACKIE

1941 DEAD MEN TELL
 DRESSED TO KILL
 THE GAY FALCON
 THE LONE WOLF TAKES A CHANCE
 THE MALTESE FALCON
 MR. AND MRS. NORTH
 NO HANDS ON THE CLOCK
 SCOTLAND YARD
 SHADOW OF THE THIN MAN
 WHISTLING IN THE DARK

1942 CASTLE IN THE DESERT
 ENEMY AGENTS MEET ELLERY QUEEN
 EYES IN THE NIGHT
 THE GLASS KEY
 GRAND CENTRAL MURDER
 THE LIVING GHOST
 THE MAN WHO WOULDN'T DIE
 THE PANTHER'S CLAW
 QUIET PLEASE, MURDER
 SHERLOCK HOLMES AND THE SECRET WEAPON
 SHERLOCK HOLMES AND THE VOICE OF TERROR
 TIME TO KILL
 X MARKS THE SPOT

1943 THE ALIBI
 CRIME DOCTOR
 THE FALCON AND THE CO-EDS
 FIND THE BLACKMAILER
 LADY OF BURLESQUE
 MYSTERY BROADCAST

1943 THE MYSTERY OF THE THIRTEENTH GUEST
A NIGHT TO REMEMBER
NO PLACE FOR A LADY
SHERLOCK HOLMES FACES DEATH
SHERLOCK HOLMES IN WASHINGTON

1944 BERMUDA MYSTERY
BLACK MAGIC
CHARLIE CHAN IN THE SECRET SERVICE
THE CHINESE CAT
CRIME BY NIGHT
DETECTIVE KITTY O'DAY
DOUBLE INDEMNITY
LEAVE IT TO THE IRISH
THE LODGER
MURDER, MY SWEET
THE PEARL OF DEATH
THE SCARLET CLAW
SHERLOCK HOLMES AND THE SPIDER WOMAN
THE SUSPECT
THE THIN MAN GOES HOME
THE WHISTLER

1945 AND THEN THERE WERE NONE
THE BIG SLEEP
FOLLOW THAT WOMAN
THE HIDDEN EYE
THE HOUSE OF FEAR
I LOVE A MYSTERY
THE JADE MASK
PURSUIT TO ALGIERS

1945   THE SCARLET CLUE
       SCOTLAND YARD INVESTIGATOR
       THE SHANGHAI COBRA
       THE SPIDER
       THE WOMAN IN GREEN

1946   ACCOMPLICE
       BEHIND THE MASK
       THE BLUE DAHLIA
       DANGEROUS MONEY
       DARK ALIBI
       THE DARK CORNER
       THE DEVIL'S MASK
       DRESSED TO KILL
       FEAR
       THE INNER CIRCLE
       LADY IN THE LAKE
       LARCENY IN HER HEART
       THE LAST CROOKED MILE
       MYSTERIOUS INTRUDER
       NOCTURNE
       THE RED DRAGON
       SHADOWS OVER CHINATOWN
       SO DARK THE NIGHT
       TERROR BY NIGHT
       THE UNDERCOVER WOMAN
       THE WALLS CAME TUMBLING DOWN

1947   BLACKMAIL
       BORN TO KILL
       THE BRASHER DOUBLOON

1947 THE CHINESE RING
THE CRIMSON KEY
DEAD RECKONING
DICK TRACY'S DILEMMA
EXPOSED
THE HATBOX MYSTERY
MY FAVORITE BRUNETTE
PHILO VANCE RETURNS
SONG OF THE THIN MAN
THE THIRTEENTH HOUR
THREE ON A TICKET
THE TRAP

1948 CAMPUS SLEUTH
THE DOCKS OF NEW ORLEANS
THE FEATHERED SERPEANT
THE GOLDEN EYE
PITFALL
THE SHANGHAI CHEST
SHED NO TEARS

1949 THE SKY DRAGON
STRANGE BARGAIN

1950 GUILTY BYSTANDER
MRS. O'MALLEY AND MR. MALONE
TRIAL WITHOUT JURY

1951 THE FAT MAN

1952 TRENT'S LAST CASE

1953 I, THE JURY

1953   PRIVATE EYES

1954   FATHER BROWN

1955   KISS ME DEADLY

1957   MY GUN IS QUICK

1959   THE BAT
      THE HOUND OF THE BASKERVILLES

1961   MURDER SHE SAID

1963   THE GIRL HUNTERS
      MURDER AT THE GALLOP

1964   EMIL AND THE DETECTIVES
      MURDER AHOY!
      MURDER MOST FOUL

1965   THE RETURN OF MR. MOTO
      A STUDY IN TERROR

1966   THE ALPHABET MURDERS
      HARPER
      TEN LITTLE INDIANS

1967   DEADLIER THAN THE MALE
      TONY ROME

1968   LADY IN CEMENT
      P.J.

1969   MARLOWE

1970   DARKER THAN AMBER
      THE PRIVATE LIFE OF SHERLOCK HOLMES

1971   CHANDLER

1971 ELLERY QUEEN: DON'T LOOK BEHIND YOU
GUMSHOE
SHAFT
THEY MIGHT BE GIANTS

1972 THE ADVENTURES OF NICK CARTER
THE HOUND OF THE BASKERVILLES
SHAFT'S BIG SCORE
A VERY MISSING PERSON

1973 DOUBLE INDEMNITY
I LOVE A MYSTERY
THE LONG GOODBYE
SHAFT IN AFRICA
SHAMUS

1974 CHINATOWN
MURDER ON THE ORIENT EXPRESS

1975 THE ADVENTURES OF SHERLOCK HOLMES'S
SMARTER BROTHER
THE BLACK BIRD
THE DROWNING POOL
ELLERY QUEEN: TOO MANY SUSPECTS
FAREWELL MY LOVELY
NIGHT MOVES
TEN LITTLE INDIANS

1976 LANIGAN'S RABBI
MURDER BY DEATH
THE RETURN OF THE WORLD'S GREATEST
DETECTIVE
THE SEVEN PER-CENT-SOLUTION
SHERLOCK HOLMES IN NEW YORK

1977 THE LATE SHOW

1978 THE BIG FIX
THE BIG SLEEP
THE CHEAP DETECTIVE
THE DAIN CURSE
DEATH ON THE NILE

1979 MURDER BY DECREE
NERO WOLFE

1980 THE HOUND OF THE BASKERVILLES
THE MIRROR CRACK'D
THE RETURN OF FRANK CANNON

1981 CHARLIE CHAN AND THE CURSE OF THE
DRAGON QUEEN
MICKEY SPILLANE'S MARGIN FOR MURDER

1982 AGATHA CHRISTIE'S MURDER IS EASY
DEAD MEN DON'T WEAR PLAID
EVIL UNDER THE SUN
HAMMETT
I, THE JURY

1983 AGATHA CHRISTIE'S A CARIBBEAN MYSTERY
AGATHA CHRISTIE'S SPARKLING CYANIDE
COCAINE AND BLUE EYES
THE HOUND OF THE BASKERVILLES
MICKEY SPILLANE'S MIKE HAMMER: MURDER ME,
MURDER YOU
THE SIGN OF FOUR
TRAVIS McGEE

1984 MASKS OF DEATH

1984 MICKEY SPILLANE'S MIKE HAMMER: MORE THAN MURDER

1985 AGATHA CHRISTIE'S THIRTEEN AT DINNER

FLETCH

PERRY MASON RETURNS

YOUNG SHERLOCK HOLMES

1986 AGATHA CHRISTIE'S MURDER IN THREE ACTS

MANHUNTER

A MASTERPIECE OF MURDER

PERRY MASON: THE CASE OF THE NOTORIOUS NUN

THE RETURN OF MICKEY SPILLANE'S MIKE HAMMER

1987 ANGEL HEART

DEADLY ILLUSION

MURDER BY THE BOOK

P.I. PRIVATE INVESTIGATIONS

PERRY MASON: THE CASE OF THE LOST LOVE

PERRY MASON: THE CASE OF THE MURDERED MADAM

PERRY MASON: THE CASE OF THE SCANDALOUS SCOUNDREL

PERRY MASON: THE CASE OF THE SINISTER SPIRIT

PRIVATE EYE

THE RETURN OF SHERLOCK HOLMES

THE ROSARY MURDERS

TOUGH GUYS DON'T DANCE

1988 APPOINTMENT WITH DEATH

PERRY MASON: THE CASE OF THE AVENGING ACE

PERRY MASON: THE CASE OF THE LADY IN THE LAKE

WHO FRAMED ROGER RABBIT

WITHOUT A CLUE

A BIBLIOGRAPHY OF
DETECTIVE FICTION SOURCES

by T. Allan Taylor

Among viewers and aficionados of the detective on film, there may be a desire to delve deeper into the possibilities of the written word in detective fiction. For this purpose, we are listing a few of the potential sources of further information about fictional detectives and sleuthing.

Some of the following books are bibliographic in nature, others are highly descriptive and annotative about individual authors and their fictional characters. It should be noted that many of these sources have within them further book lists indicating additional sources to which readers can turn.

Finally, while many of the following books may be found in major book stores or available on order from their publishers, most if not all of them will be found on the shelves of local public and private libraries.

A Catalogue of Crime; A Reader's Guide to the Literature of Mystery, Detection and Related Genres, by Jacques Barzun and Wendell Hertig Taylor. New York: Harper & Row, 1971.

Crime and Mystery: The 100 Best Books by H. R. F. Keating. New York: Carroll and Graf, 1987.

Crime Fiction, 1749-1980: A Comprehensive Bibliography, by Allen J. Hubin. New York & London: Garland Publishing, 1984.

Detectionary: A Biographical Dictionary of Leading Characters of Detective and Mystery Fiction, edited by Otto Penzler, Chris Steinbrunner and Marvin Lachman. Woodstock, N.Y.: Overlook Press, 1977.

Mystery Index: Subjects, Settings and Sleuths of 10,000 Titles, by Steven Olderr. Chicago: American Library Association, 1987.

Private Eyes: 1010 Knights (A Survey of American Detective Fiction, 1922-1984), by Robert A. Baker and Michael T. Nietzol. Bowling Green, Ohio: Bowling Green State University Popular Press, 1985.

The Subject Is Murder: A Selective Subject Guide to Mystery Fiction, by Albert J. Menendez. New York: Garland Publishing, 1986.

Twentieth-Century Crime and Mystery Writers. 2nd edition. Edited by John M. Reilly. New York: St. Martin's Press, 1985.
Note: This book has a valuable listing of other book sources. It is extensive and extremely useful.

What About Murder?: A Guide to Books About Mystery and Detective Fiction, by Jon L. Breen. Metuchen, N.J.: Scarecrow Press, 1981.

Whodunit: A Guide to Crime, Suspense and Spy Fiction, Edited by H. R. F. Keating. New York: Van Nostrand Reinhold, 1982.

ABOUT THE AUTHORS

JAMES ROBERT PARISH, Los Angeles-based direct marketing consultant and freelance writer, was born in Cambridge, Massachusetts. He attended the University of Pennsylvania and graduated Phi Beta Kappa with a degree in English. A graduate of the University of Pennsylvania Law School, he is a member of the New York Bar. As president of Entertainment Copyright Research Co., Inc. he headed a major researching facility for the film and television industries. Later he was a film reviewer-interviewer for *Motion Picture Daily* and *Variety* trade newspapers. He is the author of over 75 volumes, including *The Fox Girls, Good Dames, The Slapstick Queens, The RKO Gals, The Tough Guys, The Jeanette MacDonald Story, The Elvis Presley Scrapbook, The Hollywood Beauties* and *The Great Combat Pictures*. Among those he has co-written are *The MGM Stock Company, The Debonairs, Liza!, Hollywood Character Actors, The Hollywood Reliables, The Funsters, The Best of MGM, Black Action Pictures from Hollywood*, and his ongoing series, *Complete Actors Television Credits* with Vincent Terrace. With Michael R. Pitts, he has co-written such tomes as *Hollywood on Hollywood, The Great Western Pictures* (base and companion volumes), *The Great Gangster Pictures* (base and companion volumes), *The Great Spy Pictures* (base and companion volumes), *The Great Science Fiction Pictures* (base and companion volumes).

MICHAEL R. PITTS is a freelance writer who has written or co-authored numerous books on entertainment, including *Kate Smith: A BioBibliography, Western Movies, Hollywood and American History, Horror Film Stars, Famous Movie Detectives, Hollywood on Record, The Bible on Film*, and two editions of *Radio Soundtracks*. With Mr. Parish he has written *The Great . . . Pictures* series and its companion volumes. In addition, he has contributed to several other published books and his magazine articles have been published both here and abroad. With degrees in history and journalism, Mr. Pitts writes columns on record collecting for *The Big Reel* and *Classic Images*

615

magazines. He has written record album liner notes and lectures on film history and entertainment. Mr. Pitts resides in Indiana with his wife, Carolyn, and daughter, Angela.